WARFARE IN HISTORY

Alfred's Wars

Sources and Interpretations
of Anglo-Saxon Warfare
in the Viking Age

WARFARE IN HISTORY

ISSN 1358-779X

Series editors
Matthew Bennett, Royal Military Academy, Sandhurst
Anne Curry, University of Southampton
Stephen Morillo, Wabash College, Crawfordsville, USA

This series aims to provide a wide-ranging and scholarly approach to military history, offering both individual studies of topics or wars, and volumes giving a selection of contemporary and later accounts of particular battles; its scope ranges from the early medieval to the early modern period.

New proposals for the series are welcomed; they should be sent to the publisher at the address below.

Boydell and Brewer Limited, PO Box 9,
Woodbridge, Suffolk, IP12 3DF

*Previously published volumes in this series
are listed at the back of this volume*

Alfred's Wars

Sources and Interpretations of Anglo-Saxon Warfare in the Viking Age

Ryan Lavelle

THE BOYDELL PRESS

First published 2010
The Boydell Press, Woodbridge
Reprinted in paperback and transferred to digital printing 2012

ISBN 978-1-84383-569-1 hardback
ISBN 978-1-84383-739-8 paperback

The Boydell Press is an imprint of Boydell & Brewer Ltd
PO Box 9, Woodbridge, Suffolk IP12 3DF, UK
and of Boydell & Brewer Inc.
668 Mt Hope Avenue, Rochester, NY 14620, USA
website: www.boydellandbrewer.com

A CIP catalogue record for this book is available
from the British Library

MIX
Paper from
responsible sources
FSC
www.fsc.org   FSC® C013604

Typeset in Adobe Jenson Pro by
David Roberts, Pershore, Worcestershire

Printed in Great Britain by
CPI Group (UK) Ltd, Croydon CR0 4YY

Contents

List of Illustrations   vii

List of Tables   x

Source Acknowledgements   xi

Preface   xv

Abbreviations   xviii

1 Introduction: A Society at War: Mentalities of Warfare in Later Anglo-Saxon England   1

    Ealdorman Æthelweard: The writing of history and the experience of warfare in the tenth century   2

    The Study of later Anglo-Saxon warfare: Themes and their studies   6

    Ideologies of war   8

    Masculinity, youth and experience in Anglo-Saxon warfare   12

2 Friends and Foes   18

    Britons and the 'Kingdom of the English'   19

    The advent of the Vikings   32

    Their own worst enemy? Internal conflicts   44

3 Organization and Equipment: Land   47

    The nation at arms?   47

    'Five Hides and All That': aristocrats and military service   55

    A royal elite? The Housecarls   107

    Arms, armour, and status   111

    'A nobleman belongs on horseback': horses and equestrian equipment   129

    Summary   139

4 Organization and Equipment: Maritime   141

    Types of vessel   142

    Fleet logistics   145

    Æthelweard's Chronicon and records of nautical terminology   165

    The organization of coastal defence   171

    Summary   175

5   Campaigns and Strategies   177
       The movement of armies   177
       Amphibious warfare and combined operations: Ships in campaigns   200
       Summary   207

6   Fortifications   209
       The Burghal Hidage and the organization of fortifications   209
       Fortifications in action   226
       Fortifications in the Second Viking Age   235
       Summary and observations   262

7   Fields of Slaughter: Battles and Battlefields   264
       Courage, cowardice and motivation   266
       Medieval or classical sources?   269
       Fighting techniques and battlefield tactics   274
       Naval battles   286
       Locating and remembering battlefields   298
       Summary   314

8   After the Battle: Peacemaking and Peace Agreements   315
       Opportunities for negotiation   318
       Strategic peace: the use and abuse of peace?   322
       Truce, peace and peace treaties   324
       Summary   333

9   Conclusions   335

    Appendix: Chronology   339

    Bibliography   348
    Index   361

Illustrations

Fig. 2.1   (Map) Locations of English actions recorded in *Annales Cambriae* 27

Fig. 2.2   Grave marker from Lindisfarne, depicting Viking warriors armed with contemporary weapons (Illustration by Don Lavelle) 33

Fig. 2.3   Scutchamer Knob, East Hendred, Oxfordshire (formerly Berkshire): an Anglo-Saxon assembly site, from which a Viking force issued a challenge to battle in 1006 33

Fig. 2.4   (Map) Distribution of Viking Age rune-stones referring to expeditions in England 35

Fig. 2.5   Rune-stone (U 344) from Yttergärde, Uppsala, Sweden, recording gelds taken in England 39

Fig 3.1   Unarmoured English warriors in a probable temporary fortification at the Battle of Hastings depicted in the Bayeux Tapestry (Detail of the Bayeux Tapestry, 11th century, by special permission of the City of Bayeux) 52

Fig 3.2   Irish Defence Force extras drilling for the 1969 film, *Alfred the Great* (Courtesy of Captain Kevin McDonald, Irish Defence Force) 53

Fig. 3.3   (Diagram) Relative wealth and social standing of late Anglo-Saxon testators 123

Fig. 3.4   Pre-Conquest equestrian sculptures from (a) Gosforth (Cumberland), (b) Chester-le-Street (Co. Durham), (c) Neston (Cheshire), (d) Baldersby (Yorks.), (e) Sockburn (Co. Durham) (Illustrations by Don Lavelle; (d) redrawn by Don Lavelle after a sketch by Dawn Hadley) 132–3

Fig 3.5   Norman warriors on campaign in Brittany depicted in the Bayeux Tapestry (Detail of the Bayeux Tapestry, 11th century, by special permission of the City of Bayeux) 138

Fig 3.6   Norman cavalry at the Battle of Hastings depicted in the Bayeux Tapestry (Detail of the Bayeux Tapestry, 11th century, by special permission of the City of Bayeux) 139

Fig. 4.1   Different types of Viking-Age ship (Illustration by Don Lavelle) 143

Fig. 4.2   (Map) Coastal burhs during the reign of Alfred the Great posited by Edwin and Joyce Gifford 147

Fig. 4.3   (Map) Identifiable places referred to in a letter by Bishop Æthelric of Sherborne (S 1383) regarding the absence of 'ship scot' 165

Fig. 4.4   (Map) Ealdorman Æthelweard's references to different types of vessel *169*

Fig. 4.5   (Map) Coastal lands recorded in charters of King Æthelred II *173*

Fig. 4.6   (Map) Terrain of Æthelweard's Cornish estates recorded in the charter S 832 (Illustration by Don Lavelle) *175*

Fig. 5.1   (Diagram) Model of the relationship between supplies, cohesion and prestige in early medieval campaigns *179*

Fig. 5.2   (Map) The area of Wessex associated with the Edington campaign, 878 (Drawn by Don Lavelle) *181*

Fig. 5.3   Detail of a royal encampment, depicted in the eleventh-century *Old English Hexateuch* (London, British Library, MS Cotton Claudius B.IV, fol. 25r. Reproduced with permission.) *193*

Fig. 5.4   (Map) Terrain around Plumstead (Kent), an area discussed in the account of the recovery of the relics of St Ælfheah by the Archbishop of Canterbury's housecarls, 1023 (Illustration by Don Lavelle) *197*

Fig. 5.5   (Map) Royal and other actions outside England *201*

Fig. 5.6   (Map) Areas relating to the Godwine family and King Edward's actions, 1052 *207*

Fig. 6.1   (Map) Fortifications recorded in the Burghal Hidage and the areas pertaining to them *210*

Fig. 6.2   (Map) Armada beacons in Hampshire with known Saxon *weard* sites (Drawn by David Hill) *223*

Fig. 6.3   Twelfth-century depiction of a siege of a city from the Harley Psalter (London, British Library Harley MS 603, fol. 32v. Reproduced with permission) *227*

Fig. 6.4   (Map) Fortifications recorded during the reign of Edward the Elder *228*

Fig. 6.5   (Map) Lands held by housecarls in 1066 in shires around London *245*

Fig. 6.6   (Map) Attacks on English towns during the later tenth and eleventh centuries to 1066 *249*

Fig. 6.7   (Map) Locations of Viking activities around Exeter in 1001 *256*

Fig. 6.8   (Map) Urban assemblies and sites of surrender *257*

Fig. 7.1   An Anglo-Saxon 'shield-wall' depicted in the Bayeux Tapestry (Detail of the Bayeux Tapestry, 11th century, by special permission of the City of Bayeux) *275*

Fig. 7.2   Gyrth, brother of Harold, at the Battle of Hastings with his brother Leofwine depicted in the Bayeux Tapestry (Detail of the Bayeux Tapestry, 11th century, by special permission of the City of Bayeux) *279*

Fig. 7.3   Eleventh-century depiction of Abraham's army in pursuit of Lot's captors, followed by a battle on foot, illustrated in the *Old English Hexateuch* (London, British Library, MS Cotton Claudius B.IV, fol. 25r. Reproduced with permission.) *282*

Fig. 7.4   Mounted warriors depicted in the *Harley Psalter* (London, British Library, Harley MS 603, fol. 69r. Reproduced with permission.) *284*

Fig. 7.5   (Map) The possible course of actions recorded in the Anglo-Saxon Chronicle entry for 896 applied to Poole Harbour, on the English Channel coast *288*

Fig. 7.6   The end of the Battle of Hastings, depicted in the Bayeux Tapestry (Detail of the Bayeux Tapestry, 11th century, by special permission of the City of Bayeux) *305*

Fig. 7.7   (Map) The suggested locations for events in the *Ethandun* campaign, 878 *308*

Fig. 8.1   Norman vessels with shields raised, depicted in the Bayeux Tapestry (Detail of the Bayeux Tapestry, 11th century, by special permission of the City of Bayeux) *321*

Figs. 2.2, 3.4, 4.1, 4.6, and 5.4 courtesy of Don Lavelle.

Figs. 3.1, 3.5, 3.6, 7.1, 7.2, 7.6, and 8.1 by special permission of the City of Bayeux.

Fig. 3.2 courtesy of Captain Kevin McDonald, Irish Defence Force.

Figs. 5.3, 6.3, 7.3, and 7.4 reproduced with permission of the British Library, London.

Fig. 6.2 courtesy of David Hill.

All other images are by the author or from the author's collection. Maps were drawn with the aid of the *Online Map Creation* website, <http://www.aquarius. ifm-geomar.de/>.

Tables

Table 2.1 Scandinavian rune-stones referring to England from the late tenth and eleventh centuries 36

Table 3.1 Types of military service and their landed assessments 59

Table 3.2 Heriots and bequests of weapons in later Anglo-Saxon wills 124

Table 4.1 Terms for ships used in Æthelweard, *Chronicon*, and other narrative sources 167

Table 5.1 Names of witnesses in charters associated with King Athelstan's Scottish campaign, 934 184

Table 5.2 Suggested overland speeds of elements of an early medieval army 192

Table 5.3 Comparison of extracts from the Anglo-Saxon Chronicle manuscript entries CD and E for 1052, showing the Godwine family and King Edward's movements 203

Table 6.1 Factors concerning urban status and defensibility 238

Table 6.2 Attacks on English towns and their relative sizes 246

Table 6.3 Viking activities around Exeter 254

Table 7.1 Antiquarians' suggested locations for the events in the *Ethandun* campaign, 878 311

Source Acknowledgements

Extracts from primary and secondary sources are generally noted here if they are longer than a page of text from printed editions. Reprints of complete articles/chapters are marked with an asterisk.

The author and publishers are grateful to all the institutions and individuals listed for permission to reproduce the materials in which they hold copyright. Every effort has been made to trace the copyright holders; apologies are offered for any omission, and the publishers will be pleased to add any necessary acknowledgment in subsequent editions.

R. Poole, translation of *Lithsmannaflokkr*, from R. Poole, *Viking Poems on War and Peace: A Study in Skaldic Narrative*, Toronto Medieval Texts and Translations 8 (Toronto and London: University of Toronto Press, 1991), pp. 86–90 (courtesy of University of Toronto Press). Copyright © University of Toronto Press.

J. R. Green, *The Conquest of England* (London: Longmans, 1883), pp. 133–5.

F. M. Stenton, *Anglo-Saxon England*, Oxford History of England 2 (Oxford: Oxford University Press, 1943; 3rd edn, 1971), pp. 290–1 (courtesy of Oxford University Press). Copyright © Oxford University Press.

P. Vinogradoff, *English Society in the Eleventh Century: Essays in English Mediaeval History* (Oxford: Clarendon Press, 1908), pp. 28–30.

* C. W. Hollister, 'The Personnel of the Select Fyrd': chapter 4 of *Anglo-Saxon Military Institutions on the Eve of the Norman Conquest* (Oxford: Oxford University Press, 1962), pp. 59–84 (courtesy of Oxford University Press). Copyright © Oxford University Press.

R. P. Abels, *Lordship and Military Obligation in Anglo-Saxon England* (Berkeley and London: University of California Press, 1988), pp. 62–6 (courtesy of the author). Copyright © R. P. Abels.

R. P. Abels, *Lordship and Military Obligation in Anglo-Saxon England* (Berkeley and London: University of California Press, 1988), pp. 123–5 (courtesy of the author). Copyright © R. P. Abels.

* N. A. Hooper, 'Some Observations on the Navy', in *Studies in Medieval History presented to R. Allen Brown*, ed. C. Harper-Bill, C. Holdsworth, and J. L. Nelson (Woodbridge: Boydell Press, 1989), pp. 203–13 (courtesy of the author). Copyright © N. A. Hooper.

Extract from 'Textual Appendix: *Translatio Sancti Ælfegi Cantuariensis archiepiscopi et martiris (BHL* 2519): Osbern's account of the translation of St Ælfheah's relics from London to Canterbury, 8–11 June 1023', ed. and trans. A. R. Rumble and R. Morris, in *The Reign of Cnut: King of England, Denmark and Norway*, ed. A. R. Rumble, Studies in the Early History of Britain (London: Leicester University Press, 1994), pp. 283–15, at pp. 304–11 (courtesy of the editors). Copyright © A. R. Rumble and R. Morris.

* D. Hill and S. Sharp, 'An Anglo-Saxon Beacon System', in *Names, Places and People: An Onomastic Miscellany in Memory of John McNeal Dodgson*, ed. A. R. Rumble and A. D. Mills (Stamford: Shaun Tyas, 1997), pp. 157–65 (courtesy of the authors). Copyright © D. Hill and S. Sharp.

Fragmentary Annals of Ireland, ed. and trans. J. N. Radner (Dublin: Dublin Institute for Advanced Studies, 1978), pp. 169–73 (courtesy of the School of Celtic Studies, Dublin Institute for Advanced Studies). Copyright © The Dublin Institute for Advanced Studies (School of Celtic Studies).

B. P. C. Molloy and D. Grossman, 'Why Can't Johnny Kill? The Psychology and Physiology of Interpersonal Combat', in *The Cutting Edge: Studies in Ancient and Medieval Combat*, ed. B. Molloy (Stroud: Tempus, 2007), pp. 188–202, at p. 197. (courtesy of the authors). Copyright © B. P. C. Molloy and D. Grossman.

R. Abels and S. Morillo, 'A Lying Legacy? A Preliminary Discussion of Images of Antiquity and Altered Reality in Medieval Military History', *Journal of Medieval Military History* 3 (2005), pp. 1–13, at pp. 2–4 (courtesy of the authors). Copyright © R. Abels and S. Morillo.

* F. P. Magoun, 'King Alfred's Naval and Beach Battle with the Danes in 896', *Modern Language Review*, 37 (1942), pp. 409–14 (courtesy of the family of Francis Peabody Magoun Jr.). Copyright © the estate of Francis Peabody Magoun Jr.

W. C. Green, *The Story of Egil Skallagrimsson: Being an Icelandic Family History of the Ninth and Tenth Centuries* (London, 1893), ch. 52 (translation adapted from Green).

R. Lavelle, 'Towards a Political Contextualization of Peacemaking and Peace Agreements in Anglo-Saxon England', in *Peace and Negotiation: Strategies for Coexistence in the Middle Ages and the Renaissance*, ed. D. Wolfthal, Arizona Studies in the Middle Ages and the Renaissance 4 (Turnhout: Brepols, 2000), pp. 39–55 (used as the basis for chapter 8 courtesy of Brepols Publishers). Copyright © Brepols Publishers.

Note on sources

Unless otherwise indicated, translations of primary sources are mine, although I have endeavoured to provide references to standard editions where appropriate; for the reader's convenience references to editions translated into English are provided wherever possible. Where footnotes are linked to the text in reprinted secondary source extracts, they are from those of the original publications. In some cases references are adapted for clarity and/or to match the referencing conventions of this volume. I have endeavoured to include details of recent or standard editions of primary sources where possible, although references to the sources originally cited by the authors have generally been retained. This is most relevant to Domesday Book, where references can now be made to the Phillimore edition; it should be added that my own ability to ascertain specific entries in authorial intentions may be limited when the original reference is restricted to a folio. Further editorial additions are noted in square brackets, although these have been kept to a minimum in order to maintain the integrity of the original works as far as possible.

For Samuel,
whose arrival during the writing of this book
has made me appreciate the seriousness of its subject

Preface

ALTHOUGH this book provides a selection from sources and interpretations of warfare in Viking-Age England, and presents a consideration of them, it is more than a purely historiographical study. It investigates the current state of scholarship and the key points of its development, indicating areas for enquiry and pointing out some less familiar sources along the way. The intention is not to deal with the canon of historical works on the Anglo-Saxon army, for remarkably there is no 'canon' as such. Much, though by no means all, scholarship on the organization of military systems in the Anglo-Saxon state has been undertaken by historians and scholars from related disciplines for whom warfare is not a primary concern.

Many of the sources used will be familiar to students of early medieval England, but others are included because they are less often considered. Although I have provided my own interpretations of some of the documents, I have also attempted to give an indication of the wide range of interpretation applied to them. Following some of the volumes in the *Warfare in History* series 'Sources and Interpretations' titles, some chapters include extensive extracts (or even complete reprints) from important secondary sources.

I have not attempted to use a chronological structure, nor have I retold any particular narrative history of the English Kingdom during the Viking Age, although for the reader's convenience a chronology of events is included as an appendix. The focus is rather the exploration of the practice and politics of warfare. Observations can be made on the period from the ninth and eleventh centuries which show the similarities, differences and developments of practice during that time.

Although a defining factor of the period is the emergence of organized Viking attacks upon the English kingdoms in the mid ninth century and English defences against such attacks, the English experience of warfare against their Norman foes also has a bearing on my topic. The organization of the English army on the eve of the Norman Conquest is obviously relevant, as it relates directly to the developments of military organization during the ninth and tenth centuries. It should, though, be stated at the outset that it is not the aim of this volume to deal in detail with the campaigns of the Norman Conquest.[1]

As the first chapter shows, few pre-Conquest English sources were explicitly 'military' in their focus, but a great deal can be extrapolated from their mentions of warfare. Sources are addressed in terms of the information that they can convey for a particular aspect of late Anglo-Saxon warfare. A key example is the Anglo-Saxon Chronicle, which is examined in every chapter of this book for the

---

[1] A sister volume in this series, S. Morillo (ed.), *The Battle of Hastings: Sources and Interpretations* (Woodbridge, 1996), is recommended for detailed considerations of the 1066 campaigns.

evidence of the military interests of the Anglo-Saxon kingdoms and the West-Saxon-dominated English state.

In its terms of reference, this book reflects the terminology of studies of the early middle ages. Although the term 'Saxon' has largely been avoided, 'English' and 'Anglo-Saxon' are used interchangeably. With regard to the latter, Simon Keynes has made a cogent argument for the conscious creation of – or at least idea of – a 'kingdom of the Anglo-Saxons' in the late ninth and early tenth centuries;[2] for good or ill, the adjectival use of the term is a common historical currency, as reflected in many of the works cited here.[3] The term 'English' becomes more apparent in the historiography of the eleventh century, and this is reflected this volume.

Similarly, the term 'army' warrants comment. (The term 'navy' will be addressed in chapter 4.) While references to an 'army' may imply an organized and regular military system, the word is acceptable in discussion of military forces associated with the pre-Conquest English state. It is used more freely than some commentators on the subject might like, as it stretches a point when discussing the raiding activities undertaken by both Viking and Anglo-Saxon forces.[4] Comparisons of early medieval armies with modern ones are problematic, since modern ideas of 'army' imply professional service, clearly identifiable chains of command, logistics, and so on.[5] While aspects of these may apply in the early middle ages, direct comparison is impossible. However, alternative terms are laden with the values of modern historiography. 'Host', often used to refer to medieval forces, seems, justifiably or not, to conjure up visions of a disorganized rabble of warriors, while the Old English word 'fyrd' becomes inevitably tied up with notions inspired by Warren Hollister[6] of 'select' and 'general' fyrds, which are even more entrenched in non-specialist publications than they are in the academic field for which Hollister intended them;[7] in any case, a military force was not always a 'fyrd', as the word referred to participation in a military expedition.[8] Thus, while I may use terms

---

[2] S. D. Keynes, 'Edward, King of the Anglo-Saxons', in *Edward the Elder, 899–924*, ed. N. J. Higham and D. H. Hill (London, 2001), pp. 40–66.

[3] For reservations, see S. Reynolds, 'What Do We Mean by "Anglo-Saxon" and "Anglo-Saxons"?', *Journal of British Studies* 24 (1985), pp. 395–414.

[4] Following long-standing convention, I capitalize 'Viking', although it should be acknowledged, following the recent trend in using the term 'viking' (i.e. without a capital v), that the term can refer to people who were not from Scandinavia but followed 'viking' behaviour.

[5] See the comments on ninth-century organization in R. Abels, 'Alfred the Great, the *Micel Hæðen Here* and the Viking Threat', in *Alfred the Great: Papers from the Eleventh-Centenary Conferences*, ed. T. Reuter, Studies in Early Medieval Britain (Aldershot, 2003), pp. 265–79, at pp. 266–7.

[6] For comments on the use of the term 'fyrd', see C. W. Hollister, '1066: "The Feudal Revolution"', *American Historical Review* 73 (1968), pp. 708–23, at pp. 713–14. It is fair to say that much of the work inspired by Hollister does not reflect his original intentions.

[7] See e.g. V. Norman, *The Medieval Soldier*, Medieval Life (London, 1971), pp. 92–3. See also the brief but comparatively nuanced discussion on the subject as a topic for miniature wargames in S. Patten, *Shieldwall: Warfare in the Viking Age, 790–1085 AD* (Nottingham, 2002), p. 19.

[8] Bosworth-Toller, p. 351, §3.

such as 'commander' or 'strategy' or even 'tactics', they should not be taken to imply that the same values were held throughout the early middle ages.

The writing of this book has been a long process, during which its form has developed in many ways, and I have incurred many debts of gratitude. I am grateful to Matt Bennett for his editorship during the course of this process. His suggestions and advice in helping me to shape this book during this time have been much appreciated. I am also grateful to Caroline Palmer for her patience and support, especially during the final months of the completion of the manuscript.

Drafts of this book – in part or in total – have been read and commented on by Richard Abels, Chris Allen, Matt Bennett, Janine Lavelle, Vee Lavelle, Don Lavelle, Andrew Wareham, and Barbara Yorke; and work which led to the final chapter of this book was read and commented on by Katy Cubitt. Although I have not always been able to take into account every suggestion, all of my readers' comments and criticisms have proved very useful in helping me to frame discussions. I also wish to record my gratitude to Robin Bendrey, Carolin Esser, Guy Halsall, Charles Insley, Alex Langlands, Mary Murphy, Alan Williams, and Michael Wood, from whose knowledge and expertise, through often detailed discussion, I have also benefited.

Ideas which formed parts of this book have been presented in talks to Winchester audiences (as part of the Alfred the Great lecture series held at the Discovery Centre, Winchester, in February 2008, and to WARG: The Society for Winchester Archaeology and Local History in May 2009), and as a paper to the Wessex Centre for History and Archaeology conference, 'Castles, Crenallations and Defences', held in Salisbury in April 2008, and I am grateful to members of the audience at those events for posing useful questions. With any academic work there is a blurred line between teaching and research, and ideas and questions from students have often proved stimulating. I have endeavoured to credit specific suggestions or discussions where appropriate, though a few footnotes cannot do justice to all those students, from the University of Reading School of Continuing Education, New York University in London, and the University of Winchester, whom it has been my pleasure to teach and from whom I have learnt much during the time in which this book has been in progress.

The University of Winchester has provided a great deal of support during the writing of this book, for which I am grateful. Discussion with departmental colleagues has often proved fruitful, while the library staff have been most accommodating, quickly providing large numbers of often obscure articles and books. The University also provided Research and Knowledge Transfer funding, which has been very helpful in contributing towards reproduction costs of text and images. I also wish to record my gratitude for the support provided by my wife, Janine, and my parents, Don and Vee. Their understanding and encouragement was invaluable on many occasions while I was writing, and I wish them to know that I appreciate all that they have done to help me.

Abbreviations

AB	*Annales Bertiani*, ed. G. Waitz, MGH Scriptores Rerum Germanicarum 5 (Hannover, 1883); trans. J. L. Nelson, *The Annals of St Bertin*, Manchester Medieval Sources Ninth-Century Histories 1 (Manchester, 1991); cited by annal year
Æthelweard, *Chronicon*	*Chronicon Æthelweardi: The Chronicle of Æthelweard*, ed. and trans. A. Campbell, Medieval Texts (London, 1962)
AF	*Annales Fuldenses*, ed. F. Kurze, MGH Scriptores rerum Germanicarum 7 (Hanover, 1891); trans. T. Reuter, *The Annals of Fulda*, Ninth-Century Histories 2 (Manchester, 1992); cited by annal year
ANS	Various editors, *Proceedings of the Battle Conference on Anglo-Norman Studies* 1978 etc. (Woodbridge, 1979 etc.); cited by volume number, conference and publication years
ASC	Anglo-Saxon Chronicle: *The Anglo-Saxon Chronicle: A Collaborative Edition*, general eds D. N. Dumville and S. D. Keynes (Woodbridge, 9 vols published, 1983-present); cited by MS where versions differ substantially (MR = 'Mercian Register', in MSS B and C) and, unless otherwise noted, corrected annal year
ASE	*Anglo-Saxon England*; cited by volume and year
ASSAH	*Anglo-Saxon Studies in Archaeology and History*; cited by volume and year
Asser	Asser, *Vita Alfredi*: W. H. Stevenson (ed.), *Asser's Life of King Alfred, together with the Annals of Saint Neots erroneously ascribed to Asser* (Oxford, 1906); trans. S. D. Keynes and M. Lapidge (eds), *Alfred the Great: Asser's Life of King Alfred and Other Contemporary Sources* (Harmondsworth, 1983)
BAR	British Archaeological Reports
Bede, *HE*	Bede, *Historia ecclesiastica gentis Anglorum: Bede's Ecclesiastical History of the English People*, ed. and trans. B. Colgrave and R. A. B. Mynors, OMT (Oxford, 1969); cited by book, chapter and page
Bosworth-Toller	J. Bosworth and T. Toller, *An Anglo-Saxon Dictionary* (Oxford, 1898)
Carmen de Hastingae proelio	*The Carmen de Hastingae proelio of Guy, Bishop of Amiens*, ed. and trans. F. Barlow, OMT (Oxford, 1999)

DB	Domesday Book: reference to Greater Domesday (i.e. the 'Exchequer' manuscript) unless otherwise indicated ('LDB' denotes reference to the 'Little Domesday' manuscript); cited according to the relevant Phillimore county edition (J. Morris [general ed.], Chichester, 1975–86) and manuscript folio
EHD 1	*English Historical Documents vol. 1: c. 500–1042*, ed. D. Whitelock (London, 1955; 2nd edn, 1979)
EHD 2	*English Historical Documents vol. 2: 1042–1189*, ed. D. C. Douglas and G. W. Greenaway (London, 1953; 2nd edn, 1981)
EETS	Early English Text Society
EHR	*English Historical Review*
Encomium Emmae	*Encomium Emmae Reginae*, ed. A. Campbell, Camden 3rd series 72 (London, 1949)
EME	*Early Medieval Europe*
HH	Henry of Huntingdon, *Historia Anglorum: The History of the English People*, ed. and trans. Diana Greenway, OMT (Oxford, 1996); cited by book, chapter, and page
HSJ	*Haskins Society Journal*
JMMH	*Journal of Medieval Military History*
JW vol. 2	*The Chronicle of John of Worcester: Volume II: The Annals from 450–1066*, ed. and trans. R. R. Darlington and P. McGurk, OMT (Oxford, 1995); cited by annal and page
JW vol. 3	*The Chronicle of John of Worcester: Volume III: The Annals from 1067–1140 with the Gloucester Interpolations and the Continuation to 1141*, ed. and trans. P. McGurk, OMT (Oxford, 1998); cited by annal and page
Gesetze	*Die Gesetze der Angelsachsen*, ed. F. Liebermann (Halle, 3 vols, 1903–16)
MGH	Monumenta Germaniae Historica
ODNB	*Oxford Dictionary of National Biography* (Oxford, 2004)
OE Orosius	*The Old English Orosius*, ed. J. Bately, EETS supplementary series 6 (London, 1980); trans. B. Thorpe, 'Alfred's Anglo-Saxon Version of Orosius', in R. Pauli, *The Life of Alfred the Great*, trans. 'A. P.', ed. B. Thorpe (London, 1853), pp. 238–528; cited by book and chapter
OMT	Oxford Medieval Texts
Orosius, *Libri VII*	*Pauli Orosii Historiarum adversum Paganos libri VII*, ed. C. F. W. Zangemeister (Leipzig, 1889); trans. R. J. Deferrari, *Paulus Orosius: The Seven Books of Histories against the Pagans*, Fathers of the Church. A New Translation 50 (Washington DC, 1964); cited by book and chapter

O.S.   Ordnance Survey (used to denote National Grid References)

OV   *Orderici Vitalis Historia Æcclesiastica / The Ecclesiastical History of Orderic Vitalis*, ed. and trans. M. Chibnall, OMT (Oxford, 6 vols., 1968–80)

Plummer-Earle   C. Plummer and J. Earle, *Two of the Saxon Chronicles Parallel*, 2 vols (Oxford, 1892–9)

RS   Rolls Series

S   Citation of charter (with date or date range), catalogued in *Anglo-Saxon Charters: An Annotated List and Bibliography*, ed. P. H. Sawyer, Royal Historical Society Guides and Handbooks 8 (London, 1968); revised version ed. S. E. Kelly (forthcoming), edited by S. M. Miller for the British Academy–Royal Historical Society *Anglo-Saxon Charters* website <www.trin.cam.ac.uk/chartwww>

SEHB   Studies in the Early History of Britain

SEMA   Studies in the Early Middle Ages

TRHS   *Transactions of the Royal Historical Society*; cited by series, volume and year

VCH   *The Victoria History of the Counties of England*; cited by county volume

Wace   *Le Roman de Rou de Wace*, ed. A. J. Holden, Société des anciens textes français (Paris, 3 vols., 1970–3); trans. G. S. Burgess with E. M.C van Houts, *The History of the Norman People: Wace's Roman de Rou* (Woodbridge, 2004); cited by book and line numbers

WM, GP   William of Malmesbury, *Gesta Pontificum Anglorum, The History of the English Bishops: Volume 1*, ed. and trans. M. Winterbottom and R. M. Thomson, OMT (Oxford, 2007)

WM, GR   William of Malmesbury, *Gesta Regum Anglorum: The History of the English Kings, Volume 1*, ed. and trans. R. M. Thomson, M. Winterbottom and R. A. B. Mynors, OMT (Oxford, 1998); cited by book, chapter, and page number.

WP   *The Gesta Guillelmi of William of Poitiers*, ed. and trans. R. H. C. Davis and M. Chibnall, OMT (Oxford, 1998)

✦ 1 ✦

Introduction: A Society at War

Mentalities of Warfare in Later Anglo-Saxon England

T HE writing of a book on the sources and interpretations of Anglo-Saxon warfare is, in many ways, an exercise in extrapolation. Few extant sources from
the Anglo-Saxon period deal specifically with the art of war. There is no known
treatise equivalent to the work of the late Roman writer Vegetius, although it
is known that his manuscript was copied in eleventh-century England.[1] When
stripped down to its essence, even the bellicose language of such martial literature as the poem known as the *Battle of Maldon* tells us more about the ideals
with which a small, elite portion of late Anglo-Saxon society wished to see itself
than it does about issues in which military historians tend to be interested, such
as the ordering of an army for battle or such strategic concerns as their mustering for war.[2] Nonetheless, the major historical sources, narrative chronicles, saints'
lives, charters, wills, laws, and, of course, poetry all reflect the important part that
warfare played in the lives and preoccupations of later Anglo-Saxon society. To
refer to 'a society at war', as this chapter's title does, may overstate a point, but it is
nonetheless a pertinent overstatement, for which a case study will be useful.

---

[1] British Library MS Cleo. Di, fols. 83–128, cited by H. Gneuss, *Handlist of Anglo-Saxon
Manuscripts: A List of Manuscripts and Manuscript Fragments Written or Owned in England
up to 1100* (Tempe, 2001), no. 325.1. An edition of Vegetius' work is *Epitoma Rei Militaris*,
ed. M. D. Reeve, Scriptorum classicorum bibliotheca Oxoniensis (Oxford, 2004); trans.
N. P. Milner, *Vegetius: Epitome of Military Science*, Translated Texts for Historians vol. 16
(Liverpool, 1993). For a discussion of Vegetius' continental use, see B. S. Bachrach, 'The
Practical Use of Vegetius' *De Re Militari* During the Early Middle Ages', *The Historian* 47
(1985), pp. 239–45 (although Bachrach does not note the existence of an English example).
For a sceptical view of Vegetius' use in pre-Conquest England, see R. Abels and S. Morillo,
'A Lying Legacy? A Preliminary Discussion of Images of Antiquity and Altered Reality
in Medieval Military History', *JMMH* 3 (2005), pp. 1–13, at pp. 10–12. J. Kiff, 'Images of
War: Illustrations of Warfare in Early Eleventh-Century England', *ANS* 7 (1985 for 1984),
pp. 177–94 at p. 181, n. 22 (who also suggests that BL Harley MS 3859 [catalogued by the
British Library as twelfth-century] was an eleventh-century MS) argues that due to the
lack of Old English glosses in the manuscripts 'the texts were not in frequent use'.

[2] It may even be argued that what is said about battle is often a reflection of the writers'
views of records of warfare in Antiquity; see below, ch. 7.

I

Ealdorman Æthelweard:
The writing of history and the experience of warfare in the tenth century

While the following is not an unfamiliar case study,[3] it is no less illuminating for that. At some time in the 970s or 980s, the ealdorman Æthelweard wrote a Latin version of the Anglo-Saxon Chronicle. It was addressed to his cousin Matilda in the monastery of Essen in Germany, but in writing it he also created a monument to his own remarkable lay Latinity.[4] The manner in which the *Chronicon* records an account of English history as Æthelweard saw it provides some important insights to his own worldview and experience as an ealdorman (effectively a provincial governor) of the south-western provinces during the reigns of King Edgar 'the Peaceable' (957/9–75), Edward 'the Martyr' (975–8) and Æthelred 'the Unready' (978–1016).

Such ealdormen – especially Æthelweard – occupy a curious position in the historiographical imagination. On the one hand, their administrative responsibilities figure large: the manner in which they and their contemporaries are recorded in the witness lists of Anglo-Saxon charters reminds us of the crucial role that courtly politics, often related to the assembly of the great and the good of the kingdom for participation in a campaign, played in the wider political development of the later Anglo-Saxon state.[5] Moreover, ealdormanric taxational and gubernatorial responsibilities are evident in the legal records of the kingdom.[6]

---

[3] For an appraisal of Æthelweard's 'reflections on military leadership', see S. Baxter, *The Earls of Mercia: Lordship and Power in Late Anglo-Saxon England*, Oxford Historical Monographs (Oxford, 2007), pp. 79–85.

[4] For the quality of Latin in Æthelweard's account, see M. Winterbottom, 'The Style of Æthelweard', *Medium Ævum* 36 (1967), pp. 109–18. For Æthelweard's sense of connection with the Old Saxons, see K. Leyser, 'The Ottonians and Wessex', in his *Communications and Power in Medieval Europe: The Carolingian and Ottonian Centuries*, ed. T. Reuter (London, 1994), pp. 73–104, at p. 74.

[5] The key work here is S. D. Keynes, *The Diplomas of King Æthelred 'The Unready', 978–1016: A Study in Their Use as Historical Evidence*, Cambridge Studies in Medieval Life and Thought, 3rd series 13 (Cambridge, 1980). Recent studies have considered the court politics of the late Anglo-Saxon kingdom. A useful paper is C. Insley, 'Assemblies and Charters in Late Anglo-Saxon England', in *Political Assemblies in the Earlier Middle Ages*, ed. P. S. Barnwell and M. Mostert, SEMA 7 (Turnhout, 2003), pp. 47–59, but unpublished theses should also be highlighted: S. Jayakumar, 'The Politics of the English Kingdom, *c*. 955–*c*. 978' (DPhil thesis, Oxford University, 2001) and A. Trousdale, 'An Investigation of the Anglo-Saxon Political Situation during the Reign of King Edmund, 939–46 AD' (PhD thesis, Edinburgh University, 2007). For the relationship between warfare and assemblies in Carolingian and post-Carolingian Europe, see especially T. Reuter, 'Plunder and Tribute in the Carolingian Empire', *TRHS* 5th series 35 (1985), pp. 75–94; other relevant papers by Reuter are 'The Recruitment of Armies in the Early Middle Ages: What Can We Know?', in *Military Aspects of Scandinavian Society in a European Perspective, AD 1–1300*, ed. A. N. Jørgensen and B. L. Clausen, PNM Studies in Archaeology and History 2 (Copenhagen, 1997), pp. 32–7, at pp. 34–5; 'Assembly Politics in Western Europe from the Eighth Century to the Twelfth', in *The Medieval World*, ed. P. Lineham and J. L. Nelson (London, 2001), pp. 432–50.

[6] This is discussed by L. N. Banton, 'Ealdormen and Earls in England from the Reign of King Alfred to the Reign of King Æthelred II' (DPhil thesis, Oxford University, 1981),

On the other hand, the ealdorman had responsibilities for the defence of his allotted part of the kingdom.[7] Although such defensive responsibilities do not seem to have remained static throughout the Anglo-Saxon period, they were significant. We may wonder how Æthelweard was prepared to respond to attacks which could occur anywhere on nearly 500 miles of England's south-western coastline when he was elsewhere, writing his chronicle, reading Biblical exegesis, endowing a church,[8] or attending an assembly held in eastern Wessex or Mercia.[9] However, such defensive responsibilities were not incompatible with the interests of a lay intellectual in the early middle ages. The example of Nithard, a ninth-century Frankish nobleman in the retinue of Charles the Bald, shows that politics, warfare and the recording of history were not mutually exclusive.[10] There were also limits on what was possible. Defensive duties for Æthelweard and his contemporaries may provide an alternative explanation to the factional politics suggested by Simon Keynes for the ealdormanric absences from assemblies during the reign of Æthelred II.[11] After all, even if, as Stephen Baxter points out, there

pp. 24–39. Banton (p. 29) observes Archbishop Wulfstan of York's early eleventh-century comments on this matter in Die 'Institutes of Polity: Civil and Ecclesiastical': Ein Werk Erzbischof Wulfstans von York, ed. K. Jost, Schweizer Anglistische Arbeiten 47 (Bern, 1959), ch. 9, pp. 78–80. See also H. R. Loyn, The Governance of Anglo-Saxon England, 500–1087, The Governance of England 1 (London, 1984), pp. 131–3.

[7] Banton, 'Ealdormen and Earls', pp. 17–20. Banton cites Ælfric of Eynsham's defence of the policy suggested by W. Braekman, 'Wyrdwriteras: An Unpublished Ælfrician Text in Manuscript Hatton 115', Revue belge de philologie et d'histoire 44 (1966), pp. 959–70 (however, cf. the edition and comments in Homilies of Ælfric: A Supplementary Collection, ed. J. C. Pope, EETS 259–60, 2 vols [London, 1967–8], vol. 2, pp. 725–33). See Keynes, Diplomas of King Æthelred, pp. 206–8. For discussion of coastal guarding, see ch. 4, below.

[8] For a sensitive account of Æthelweard's connections with Ælfric of Cerne Abbas (later Abbot Ælfric of Eynsham), a quasi-Carolingian world in which 'cultures of scribe and warrior met', see P. Wormald, 'Æthelweard (d. 998?)', ODNB <http://www.oxforddnb.com/view/article/8918> (accessed 17 Sept. 2009). See also B. Yorke, 'Æthelmær, the Foundation of the Abbey of Cerne and the Politics of the Tenth Century', in The Cerne Abbas Millenary Lectures, ed. K. Barker (Cerne Abbas, 1988), pp. 15–26.

[9] The King's College London and University of Cambridge Prosopography of Anglo-Saxon England database <www.pase.ac.uk> provides details of two Æthelweards who are likely to have been the same ealdorman, as the dates seem to correspond and there are no cases of the same two appearing on the same witness list: 'Æthelweard 23' and 'Æthelweard 34'. The latter is associated with the witnessing of some 52 charters, under the Latin title dux (accessed 17 Sept. 2009). See also S. D. Keynes (ed.), An Atlas of Attestations in Anglo-Saxon Charters, c. 670–1066 (University of Cambridge, working edition, 1995), tables 58, and 62(1).

[10] Nithardi Historiarum Libri IIII, ed. G. H. Pertz, revised by E. Müller, MGH Scriptores rerum Germanicarum 44 (Hanover, 1907); trans. B. W. Scholz with B. Rogers, Carolingian Chronicles: Royal Frankish Annals and Nithard's Histories (Ann Arbor, 1970), pp. 129–74. For Nithard's motivation, see J. L. Nelson, 'Public Histories and Private History in the Work of Nithard', Speculum 60 (1985), pp. 251–93. See S. Ashley, 'The Lay Intellectual in Anglo-Saxon England: Ealdorman Æthelweard and the Politics of History', in Lay Intellectuals in the Carolingian World, ed. P. Wormald and J. L. Nelson (Cambridge, 2008), pp. 218–45.

[11] Loyn, Governance of Anglo-Saxon England, p. 132, highlights the low numbers of ealdormen recorded at assemblies during the reign of Æthelred; Keynes, Diplomas of King Æthelred, pp. 197–8, has attributed this to the factional politics of Æthelred's reign.

is no direct proof of his abilities as a war-leader,[12] Æthelweard still had the name 'noble-guardian' to live up to.[13]

It is perhaps no coincidence that Æthelweard's *Chronicon* is the one narrative account which names and gives details of the responsibilities of his fellow official, a reeve by the name of Beaduheard, in response to the first arrival of Viking ships in Wessex, in Portland (Dorset) around 789.[14] That record may be the result of Æthelweard's conscientious use of the version of the Anglo-Saxon Chronicle available to him,[15] but we should also note that a flotilla of three Viking ships attacked the same location in 982, during the resurgence of attacks in the early years of the reign of Æthelred II.[16] In itself, the Chronicle's historical record of that first raid on Wessex may be literary embellishment, but it is interesting to note that Æthelweard must have had to respond in the same manner as both Beaduheard and Ealdorman Æthelhelm, who, like Beaduheard, also died at Portland, fighting Vikings, in 840.[17] If the *c.* 789 attack had been viewed in hindsight as a momentous shock for the reeve Beaduheard and the West Saxon kingdom, then Æthelweard, likewise, found himself on the front line in the wars of the 'Second Viking Age'. Thus the ealdorman's experiences should be borne in mind when his account of the raids on Wessex is read. He states in his *Chronicon* that since the battle of *Brunanburh* (937) no fleets had come to England except under treaty, alluding to a bucolic paradise which had existed since then.[18] Given the state of grace portrayed by Æthelweard for the West Saxon kingdom before the arrival of the ships in

---

[12] Baxter, *Earls of Mercia*, pp. 84–5.

[13] For an alternative (though not mutually exclusive) translation of *eðelweardas*, in the context of the poem *Judith*, as 'guardians of the homeland', see J. E. Cross, 'The Ethic of War in Old English', in *England Before the Conquest: Studies in Primary Sources Presented to Dorothy Whitelock*, ed. P. Clemoes and K. Hughes (Cambridge, 1971), pp. 269–82, at p. 275.

[14] Æthelweard, *Chronicon*, pp. 26–7. For this record, see E. Barker, 'The Anglo-Saxon Chronicle used by Æthelweard', *Bulletin of the Institute of Historical Research* 40 (1967), pp. 74–91. For the observation on the impact of the first Viking raid in Wessex as recorded by Æthelweard, see B. Yorke, *Wessex in the Early Middle Ages*, SEHB (London, 1995), p. 107. The reference to three ships parallels the arrivals of Saxons in groups of three ships in ASC 477 and 514 and in *De Excidio Britanniae*, ch. 23, in Gildas, *The Ruin of Britain and Other Works*, ed. and trans. M. Winterbottom, History from the Sources (Chichester, 1978), pp. 26, 97 (for which see B. Yorke, 'Fact or Fiction? The Written Evidence for the Fifth and Sixth Centuries AD', *ASSAH* 6 (1993), pp. 45–50). *Alfred*, ch. 34 (*Gesetze*, vol. 1, pp. 68–9; trans. *EHD* 1, p. 413), which recorded the obligation for traders to establish their identity and intentions before the king's reeve, corroborates the likelihood that on this occasion Beaduheard had been required to fulfil administrative rather than defensive responsibilities.

[15] For discussion of this source, see Yorke, *Wessex in the Early Middle Ages*, pp. 106–7. See Barker, 'The Anglo-Saxon Chronicle used by Æthelweard'. R. I. Page, 'A Most Vile People': Early English Historians on the Vikings, Dorothea Coke Memorial Lecture in Northern Studies, 1986 (London, 1987), p. 23, notes that Æthelweard's reference to Beaduheard arriving *cum paucis* may have been translated from an Old English phrase [*wið*] *lytle werode* ('with a small band'), a phrase resonant with the sense of the heroic literary ideal.

[16] ASC C 982.

[17] For Æthelhelm's death, see ASC 840 (recorded in Æthelweard, *Chronicon*, p. 30).

[18] Compare the view of King Edgar in ASC D 975, in an epitaph which refers to the inability of hostile fleets to operate in England during Edgar's reign.

Portland around 789, one may wonder if he wrote with a creeping awareness of a new Viking threat.[19] As John Niles has observed, Æthelweard's *Chronicon* was written under different circumstances from those of many early medieval Latin writers.[20] Æthelweard is the only source known to refer to the punitive expedition to York of Æthelhelm, probably the ealdorman of Wiltshire, at the end of the ninth century.[21] He is also the only source to name Æthelnoth, the ealdorman of Somerset during Alfred's exile in the Somerset Levels[22] and, as Baxter points out, Æthelweard's record of Æthelnoth's aid 'rather spoils the story' painted by the Anglo-Saxon Chronicle and Asser, of the 'nadir of Alfred's fortunes'.[23] Æthelweard is also one of the few sources to record the Mercian ealdorman, Æthelred, as King of the Mercians (*rex Eðered Myrciorum*),[24] and also to record the burial of Æthelwulf, ealdorman of Berkshire.[25] All this suggests that Æthelweard had a historiographical affinity with earlier holders of his office, perhaps even an ealdormanric 'class consciousness', though the fact that the ealdormen he mentioned all shared the royal personal name element æthel- probably also helped to develop any affinity.[26] The *Chronicon* is a record which will continue to be referred to throughout this volume, but for the moment, with Ealdorman Æthelweard's

[19] Also note ASC 840, which reports the death of an ealdorman facing Viking opponents at Portland. See R. Lavelle, 'Geographies of Power in the Anglo-Saxon Chronicle: The Royal Estates of Wessex', in *Reading the Anglo-Saxon Chronicle: Language, Literature, History*, ed. A. D. Jorgensen, SEMA 23 (Turnhout, 2010), pp. 187–219, at p. 196. For a range of the period 978×88 and a preference for the latter years of that range for the dating of Æthelweard's *Chronicon* given the author's stated intention of writing a section about the 'deeds' of Æthelred, see Campbell's introduction, in Æthelweard, *Chronicon*, p. xiii, n. 2. For a discussion of the coastal responsibilities of Æthelweard, see ch. 4, below.

[20] J. D. Niles, *Old English Heroic Poems and the Social Life of Texts*, SEMA 20 (Turnhout, 2007), pp. 158–67. Although, it should be noted, that is the case as far as is known, and it is arguably only its semi-annalistic format, betraying its close link with its exemplar, the Anglo-Saxon Chronicle, which makes it different from the narrative account of the Frankish nobleman-historian, Nithard (for whom, see above, p. 3).

[21] Æthelweard, *Chronicon*, pp. 50–1 (he is identified as 'Æthelhelm 7' in the *Prosopography of Anglo-Saxon England* database <www.pase.ac.uk> [accessed 17 Sept. 2009]). The distinction between Æthelweard's information and that of the ASC ABCD 893 entry is also interesting in respect to Æthelweard's singling out of Æthelhelm's 'open preparation with a cavalry force' (*cum ... publice parauit equestri*) where the ASC refers to three ealdormen together. For discussion of horses in battle, see below, pp. 129–39 and 281–6.

[22] Æthelweard, *Chronicon*, p. 42.

[23] Baxter, *Earls of Mercia*, p. 82–3, citing ASC 878 and Asser, chs 52–6.

[24] Æthelweard, *Chronicon*, p. 50. Elsewhere in the *Chronicon*, he is referred to as ealdorman (*dux*) but Æthelred's control of a strengthened garrison in London (p. 46), not recorded in the Old English ASC 886, is another indication of his strength as perceived by Æthelweard. N. Cumberledge, 'Reading Between the Lines: The Place of Mercia in an Expanding Wessex', *Midland History* 27 (2002), pp. 1–15, at p. 3.

[25] Æthelweard, *Chronicon*, p. 37. This is not mentioned in ASC 871.

[26] For the recognition of the royal connection through Æthelweard's naming of his son, Æthelmær, and Odda of Deerhurst's cognomen Æthelwine, see A. Williams, *Land, Power and Politics: The Family and Career of Odda of Deerhurst*, Deerhurst Lecture 1996 (Deerhurst, 1997), p. 6. For further discussion of this, and Æthelweard's place in the royal line, see A. Williams, *The World Before Domesday: The English Aristocracy, 900–1066* (London, 2008), pp. 10–11.

existence and the impact of warfare upon his existence duly noted, we can move on to look more generally at warfare and to highlight the manner in which specific aspects of Anglo-Saxon warfare have been studied.

The study of later Anglo-Saxon warfare: Themes and their studies

The study of warfare in later Anglo-Saxon England is long-standing and contentious, associated with views of both pre- and post-Conquest English society and with the manner in which historians see their own society.[27] While it may be a truism that warfare is a condition under which both the best and the worst aspects of human behaviour manifest themselves, it is worthy of restatement that the study of warfare in the later Anglo-Saxon period is a lens through which both the successes and failures of the state's defensive operations may be viewed during an important period of English history. There were, of course, major failures. Both the Danes and the Normans ultimately triumphed over their Anglo-Saxon adversaries in 1016 and 1066 respectively, but there is still much to be said of the successes of the early English military systems, not least in terms of the manner in which those systems were adapted and survived in the face of the military threats which they faced.

Much study has been concerned with the development of military obligation and the equipment of the army (a topic for discussion in chapter 3) as this is an issue associated with both status and the control of land in a developing kingdom, as well as the relations between rulers and ecclesiastical authorities.[28] Perhaps unsurprisingly, given the lack of evidence, less has been written on the operations of the English 'navy' in this period. This topic is covered in chapter 4; as will be seen, much of what has been written on it is related, like discussion of land forces, to its organization rather than conduct at sea.[29] Similarly, little has been written on the movement of armies and their operations on the battlefield, topics discussed in chapters 5 and 7, but a tranche of publications from the later nineteenth and early twentieth centuries show the concerns of antiquarians in

---

[27] For discussion of views of pre- and post-Conquest English society in the historiography of the last nine centuries, see M. Chibnall, *The Debate on the Norman Conquest*, Issues in Historiography (Manchester, 1999). For discussion of the links between Victorian views of English society and military service, see ch. 3, below.

[28] The impact of this development in landscape terms is addressed by in K. Biddick, 'Field Edge, Forest Edge: Early Medieval Social Change and Resource Allocation', in *Archaeological Approaches to Medieval Europe*, ed. K. Biddick, Studies in Medieval Culture 18 (Kalamazoo, MI, 1984), pp. 105–18. From a diplomatic perspective, see P. Wormald, *Bede and the Conversion of England: The Charter Evidence*, Jarrow Lecture 1983 (Jarrow, 1984). For a possible shift of balance back in favour of early medieval states, see N. P. Brooks, 'The Development of Military Obligations in Eighth- and Ninth-Century England', in *England Before the Norman Conquest: Essays Presented to Dorothy Whitelock*, ed. P. Clemoes and K. Hughes (Cambridge, 1971), pp. 69–84.

[29] N. Hooper, 'Some Observations on the Navy in Late Anglo-Saxon England', in *Studies in Medieval History presented to R. Allen Brown*, ed. C. Harper-Bill, C. Holdsworth, and J. L. Nelson (Woodbridge, 1989), pp. 203–13 (reprinted below). For the applicability of the term 'navy' to the study of the middle ages, see below, p. 141.

locating battlefields and the movements of armies in the English landscape. Talk of 'military probability and reasonableness' by commentators, often of a military background, writing from a purely tactical and/or strategic perspective,[30] may be distinctly problematic in the light of nuanced 'cultural' readings of early medieval warfare,[31] but the knowledge of localities exhibited by a range of historians and antiquarians still deserves credit for laying some of the foundations of the study of pre-Conquest English history. Conduct on the battlefield itself in the period before the Battle of Hastings remains relatively neglected, except for discussion based on literal 'Germanic' readings of the poetic material, especially the *Battle of Maldon*.[32] The manner in which historians' interpretations of military systems influenced the discussion of the tactics of the battlefield is relevant in chapter 7. Although the significance of fortifications was recognized by a small number of scholars before the mid twentieth century, the operation of fortifications, discussed in chapter 6, is a topic which has developed in recent years as a result of the interdisciplinary collaboration of historians and archaeologists in conjunction with urban excavations.[33] Finally, discussion of the role of peacemaking in the transactions associated with Anglo-Saxon warfare is appropriate. My own work, adapted for inclusion here in chapter 8,[34] is a contribution to a relatively recent strand of Anglo-Saxon studies, arguably first addressed in its own terms in a paper by Richard Abels which showed the political construction of peace

---

[30] H. Burne, 'The Battle of Ashdown', *Transactions of the Newbury and District Field Club* 10 (1953), pp. 71–85, at p. 71. Although not considering Burne's work on early medieval warfare, see A. Curry, *The Battle of Agincourt: Sources and Interpretations*, Warfare in History (Woodbridge, 2000), pp. 400–1, which gives a balanced consideration of Burne's applications of 'Inherent Military Probability'.

[31] For criticism of military historians' approaches, see G. Halsall, *Warfare and Society in the Barbarian West, c. 450–900*, Warfare and History (London, 2003), p. 10, and N. Hooper, 'The Anglo-Saxons at War', in *Weapons and Warfare in Anglo-Saxon England*, ed. S. C. Hawkes, Oxford University Committee for Archaeology Monograph 21 (Oxford, 1989), pp. 191–202, at p. 191. See also R. P. Abels, 'Cultural Representation and the Practice of War in the Middle Ages', *JMMH* 6 (2008), pp. 1–31.

[32] R. Woolf, 'The Ideal of Men Dying with their Lord in the *Germania* and in *The Battle of Maldon*', *ASE* 5 (1976), pp. 63–81. Although, as will be seen in this study, S. Pollington, *The English Warrior from Earliest Times till 1066* (Hockwold-cum-Wilton, 1996; 2nd edn, 2001), is a valuable survey with some useful interpretations, it is very much based on readings of the poetic evidence.

[33] Important studies which built on the urban studies of the post-War years are J. Haslam (ed.), *Anglo-Saxon Towns in Southern England* (Chichester, 1984) and D. Hill and A. Rumble (eds), *The Defence of Wessex: The Burghal Hidage and Anglo-Saxon Fortifications* (Manchester, 1996). The administrative document known as the Burghal Hidage is limited to a single page in F. M. Stenton's magisterial *Anglo-Saxon England*, Oxford History of England 2 (Oxford, 1943; 3rd edn, 1971), p. 265; this is perhaps surprising, given Stenton's penchant for emphasizing the constitutional importance of 'little people' in Anglo-Saxon history, on whom the defences of burhs may have relied (see ch. 6).

[34] R. Lavelle, 'Towards a Political Contextualization of Peacemaking and Peace Agreements in Anglo-Saxon England', in *Peace and Negotiation: Strategies for Coexistence in the Middle Ages and the Renaissance*, ed. D. Wolfthal, Arizona Studies in the Middle Ages and the Renaissance 4 (Turnhout, 2000), pp. 39–55.

conducted according to established expectations in the same manner as 'ritual' warfare.[35]

In some ways this volume responds to the scholarship of the last half century, including that of Richard Abels, who has argued that the costly military system which had been developed during the reign of Alfred had declined by the later tenth century, to the extent that the English state was defeated twice in the space of fifty years.[36] Here it is argued that the military systems of the late Anglo-Saxon state were well organized. I concur with Abels that there is a direct link between lordship and military service, although some points of detail are debatable. However, further questions can be asked through the sources addressed here: was it an inevitable corollary of peacetime, witnessed in two generations in the Anglo-Saxon state, that the army should have been ineffective? What were the strengths and weaknesses of the Anglo-Saxon army? What was its flexibility in adapting to changes? While these questions may not be answered conclusively, it is important to pose them, as they allow us to address issues which are fundamental to the study of the development of the early English state.

Ideologies of war

With the structure of this volume established, two further issues will be discussed in this introductory chapter. One is the significance of warfare as the *raison d'être* of a section of male society. The other, addressed first, is its ideological significance.

Early medieval English society, not only the 'Germanic' but also 'Celtic' and Roman-centred elements, was focused on the pursuit of warfare as a means of achieving political goals and of developing social cohesion, at least within an elite part of society. With the advent of Christianity in the Anglo-Saxon kingdoms in the late sixth and seventh centuries, the pursuit of warfare developed an ideological agenda, associated with the conversion of pagan kingdoms by Christian over-kings. Although the extent to which Christianity was itself changed to adopt a 'Germanic' agenda is much debated,[37] the universal notion of peace in Christianity

---

[35] R. P. Abels, 'King Alfred's Peace-Making Strategies with the Vikings', *HSJ* 3 (1992), pp. 23–34; R. P. Abels, 'Paying the Danegeld: Anglo-Saxon Peacemaking with Vikings', in *War and Peace in Ancient and Medieval History*, ed. P. DeSouza and J. France (Cambridge, 2008), pp. 173–92. Other significant papers are N. Lund, 'Peace and Non-Peace in the Viking Age: Ottar in Biarmaland, the Rus in Byzantium, and Danes and Norwegians in England', in *Proceedings of the Tenth Viking Conference: Larkollen, Norway, 1985*, ed. J. E. Knirk (Oslo, 1987), pp. 255–69, and C. E. Fell, 'Unfrið: An Approach to a Definition', *Saga Book of the Viking Society* 21 (1982–3), pp. 85–100.

[36] R. P. Abels, 'From Alfred to Harold II: The Military Failure of the Late Anglo-Saxon State', in *The Normans and their Adversaries: Essays in Memory of C. Warren Hollister*, ed. R. P. Abels and B. S. Bachrach, Warfare in History (Woodbridge, 2001), pp. 15–30.

[37] See P. Wormald, 'Bede, Beowulf and the Conversion of the Anglo-Saxon Aristocracy', in *Bede and Anglo-Saxon England: Papers in Honour of the 1300th Anniversary of the Birth of Bede, given at Cornell University in 1973 and 1974*, ed. R. T. Farrell, BAR British Series 46 (Oxford, 1978), pp. 32–95, and P. Wormald, 'The Age of Bede and Aethelbald', in *The Anglo-Saxons*, ed. J. Campbell (London, 1982), pp. 70–100; J. C. Russell, *The Germanization of Early Medieval Christianity: A Sociohistorical Approach to Religious*

was adapted to suit the needs and interests of kings. By the eighth century, with predominantly Roman Christian kingdoms in lowland Britain, it may even be argued that the missionary agenda of muscular Anglo-Saxon Christianity had moved toward the Continent. An ideological backdrop to Frankish campaigns in and conquests of Frisia and Saxony in the late seventh and eighth centuries was provided by the missions of the Anglo-Saxons Willibrord and Boniface as well as the writing of Alcuin.[38] Therefore, in some ways, by virtue of the fact that the Frankish conquests were a stimulus to the economy of the North Sea region, the wars which the Anglo-Saxon kingdoms fought against Viking attacks in the ninth century were an indirect result of the aggressive actions taken by Western European Christians against their pagan neighbours in the seventh and eighth centuries.[39]

However, to take a broader view of the later Anglo-Saxon state, it is not always appreciated that this was also a society which was itself aggressive: as a state emerged in the tenth century which was West Saxon and (western) Mercian in character, these political characteristics and southern focus were shaped through attacks on Viking and Celtic territory in Britain.[40] A repeat performance of the Continental policy of the Carolingian Franks, paralleling the policies of the Ottonians, was inevitably circumscribed by the geography of mainland Britain.[41] Nonetheless, that aggressive intent should not be overlooked. Karl Leyser's early medieval take on Carl von Clausewitz's famous dictum on warfare as a 'continuation of policy by other means' – inverted to 'policy [as] a continuation of warfare by other means' – is applicable to Viking Age England.[42] Even in what are traditionally seen as the darkest days of Viking domination in the eleventh-century English kingdom, the English attacks on Normandy and the Isle of Man in 1000 and the participation of English warriors in Cnut's expeditions to Scandinavia in the 1020s may be argued to have been greater manifestations of English self-

---

Transformation (Oxford, 1996); B. Yorke, The Conversion of Britain: Religion, Politics and Society in Britain, 600–800, Religion, Politics and Society in Britain (London, 2006).

[38] I. Wood, The Missionary Life: Saints and the Evangelisation of Europe, 400–1050 (London, 2001), pp. 57–8.

[39] For discussions of the influence of the Frankish economy on a wider scale, see R. Hodges, Dark Age Economics: The Origins of Towns and Trade, 600–1000 (London, 1982) and K. Randsborg, The First Millennium AD in Europe and the Mediterranean: An Archaeological Essay (London, 1991). For the narrative of the Viking responses to a Frankish economic stimulus, see P. H. Sawyer, 'The Age of the Vikings and Before', in The Oxford Illustrated History of the Vikings, ed. P. H. Sawyer (Oxford, 1997). pp. 1–18, at pp. 3–8.

[40] For the narrative of this conquest, see, for example, P. Stafford, Unification and Conquest: A Political and Social History of England in the Tenth and Eleventh Centuries (London, 1989), pp. 31–4.

[41] T. Reuter, 'The Making of England and Germany, 850–1050: Points of Comparison and Difference', in Medieval Europeans: Studies in Ethnic Identity and National Perspectives in Medieval Europe, ed. A. P. Smyth (London, 1998), pp. 53–70.

[42] K. Leyser, 'Early Medieval Warfare', in The Battle of Maldon: Fiction and Fact, ed. J. Cooper (London, 1993), pp. 87–108, at p. 108. Clausewitz's phrase (in English) can be found in C. von Clausewitz, On War, ed. and trans. M. Howard and P. Paret (Princeton, NJ, 1976), p. 87.

confidence.[43] At the very least these missions give some continuity to the earlier tenth-century claims of domination outside the English kingdom.

The main title of this volume, *Alfred's Wars*, is thus intended to be more than the invocation of that famous king's name but recognizes the consequences of Alfredian policy from the later ninth century into the tenth and even eleventh centuries. One may even mischievously suggest *Edward's Wars* or even *Athelstan's Wars* as an alternative title, as the West Saxon king's son and grandson were arguably more aggressive and more successful in their achievements in establishing a tenth-century kingdom of the Anglo-Saxons.[44] Nonetheless, in considering *Alfred's Wars*, the Alfredian achievement is significant: the ninth-century shift from defence to offence is notable in terms of establishing a move from a pre-Viking 'heptarchy' to a state which was West Saxon in focus in terms of its institutions, while using a created notion of 'Englishness' to political advantage.[45]

In the ninth century a remarkable change in Anglo-Saxon society was not specifically military, although it had military consequences. A recent volume by David Pratt has emphasized the ideological significance of military reforms, demonstrating that the military agenda should not be divorced from its religious and social context.[46] Such issues as the renovation of Roman walls in defended towns had meanings which went beyond the practicalities of design and function: urban rebuilding projected a message of *Romanitas* associated with Christian Rome.[47] Alfredian reform thus had intrinsic military and Christian elements. Introducing a theme which was to be a familiar refrain throughout the Middle Ages,[48] Alfred wrote of the three orders of society, in his Old English translation of Boethius'

---

[43] However, for reservations on the attack on Normandy, see A. Williams, Æthelred the Unready: The Ill-Counselled King (London, 2003), p. 55. See below, pp. 200–2.

[44] For these legacies, see papers in N. J. Higham and D. H. Hill (eds), *Edward the Elder, 899–924* (London, 2001); P. Hill, *The Age of Athelstan: Britain's Forgotten History* (Stroud, 2004). J. Baker and S. Brookes, *Beyond the Burghal Hidage: Anglo-Saxon Civil Defence in the Viking Age* (Århus, forthcoming) make a case for the development of defences in tenth-century rather than ninth-century England (see ch. 6, below).

[45] P. Wormald, 'Engla Lond: The Making of an Allegiance', *Journal of Historical Sociology* 7 (1994), pp. 1–24; S. Foot, 'The Making of *Angelcynn*: English Identity before the Norman Conquest', *TRHS* 6th ser. 6 (1996), pp. 25–49. For the continuities of ninth-century ideologies in the tenth century, see S. Walker, 'A Context for "Brunanburh"?', in *Warriors and Churchmen in the High Middle Ages: Essays Presented to Karl Leyser*, ed. T. Reuter (London, 1992), pp. 21–39.

[46] D. Pratt, *The Political Thought of Alfred the Great*, Cambridge Studies in Medieval Life and Thought 4th series 67 (Cambridge, 2007), pp. 93–111.

[47] D. Hill, 'The Origin of Alfred's Urban Policies', in *Alfred the Great: Papers from the Eleventh-Centenary Conferences*, ed. T. Reuter, Studies in Early Medieval Britain (Aldershot, 2003), pp. 219–33. Cf. Abels and Morillo, 'A Lying Legacy?', pp. 7–10.

[48] As Richard Abels notes in *Lordship and Military Obligation in Anglo-Saxon England* (London, 1988), p. 66 (below, p.97), Adalbero of Laon uses this theme in his early eleventh-century poem, *Carmen ad Rodbertum regem*. For discussion of this, see J. Le Goff, 'Introduction: Medieval Man', in *The Medieval World*, ed. J. Le Goff and trans. L. G. Cochrane (London, 1990), pp. 1–35, at pp. 10–15, and G. Duby, *The Three Orders: Feudal Society Imagined*, trans. A. Goldhammer (Chicago, 1982). For a discussion of the English transmission of this theme, see T. Powell, 'The Three Orders of Society in Anglo-Saxon England', *ASE* 23 (1994), pp. 103–32.

Consolation of Philosophy. Placing an explicitly Old English Christian message in a work of Late Antique philosophy, Alfred showed that his conception of rulership saw fighting men as an essential tool for a king, part of society between those who prayed and those who worked.[49]

> When Wisdom had sung this song, he was then silent; and then answered Mind and spoke thus: 'Oh, Reason, behold, you know that greed and the greatness of this earthly power never pleased me very well, nor did I very much desire all this earthly kingdom, but nevertheless I desired tools and material for the deed which I was commanded to do, which was that I might honourably and fittingly steer and guide the authority which was entrusted to me. Behold, you know that no man may practice any craft nor steer or guide any authority without tools and resources. That is the resources of every craft without which no man may work the craft. Namely, that is the king's resources and his tools with which to rule are that he has his land fully manned: he ought to have praying men, fighting men, and working men [*gebedmen ond ferdmen ond weorcmen*]. Behold, you know that without these tools no king may make known his craft. It is also with his resources that he should have sustenance for the tools, the three societies [i.e. orders]. This is, then, their sustenance: land to inhabit, gifts, and weapons, and food, and ale, and clothes, and everything which the three societies have need of. Without these he may not possess those tools nor without those tools may he bring about any of the things which he was commanded to do.

Thus, for Alfred and his scholarly coterie, a warrior ethic was something which could be seen as intrinsically Christian, emphatically so in opposition to the threat of pagan Vikings.[50] Christianity could be closely linked to this society with a warrior class in a manner not dissimilar from the piety of Christian knighthood in the central middle ages.[51] Kent Hare has noted an increase in the appearance of 'martial' apparitions in later Anglo-Saxon and Anglo-Norman hagiography, contrasting them with the 'benign' or 'chastising' appearance of early Anglo-Saxon saints.[52] Although Hare's typology does not allow him to remark on the

---

[49] *King Alfred's Old English Version of Boethius De Consolatione Philosophiae*, ed. W. J. Sedgefield (Oxford, 1899), ch. 17, p. 40.

[50] However, for discussion of the shared values between Anglo-Saxon and Viking warriors, see below, p. 34.

[51] For 'classic' discussions of the religious development of knighthood and its role in the development of the central middle ages, see R. Southern, *The Making of the Middle Ages* (London, 1953), pp. 107–12, and Duby, *Three Orders*, pp. 293–307. Although saying little on Anglo-Saxon England, Christian ideologies of warfare in the eighth to eleventh centuries are discussed in D. S. Bachrach, *Religion and the Conduct of War, c. 300–1215*, Warfare in History (Woodbridge, 2003), pp. 32–107.

[52] K. G. Hare, 'Apparitions and War in Anglo-Saxon England', in *The Circle of War in the Middle Ages: Essays on Medieval Military and Naval History*, ed. D. J. Kagay and L. J. A. Villalon, Warfare in History (Woodbridge, 1999), pp. 75–86. For a relevant example, see L. Simpson, 'The King Alfred/ St Cuthbert Episode in the *Historia de sancto Cuthberto*: Its Significance for Mid-Tenth-Century English History', in *St Cuthbert, His Cult and His Community to AD 1200*, ed. G. Bonner, D. Rollason and C. Stancliffe (Woodbridge, 1989), pp. 397–411.

aristocratic lives led by early Anglo-Saxon saints[53] or to note the appearance of a 'spirit' (*spiritus*) to King Edwin of Northumbria who advised that acceptance of Christianity would bring military victory,[54] the broad point is a logical one. There was a significant link between religious beliefs and the military world of the aristocracy.[55] In an earlier paper, J. E. Cross provided a seminal consideration of the manner in which Anglo-Saxon society both adapted Christianity to the martial values of the warrior aristocracy and, conversely, also adapted the values of the warrior aristocracy to Christianity.[56] Alfred's writings are the most obvious example of how these ideas were adapted but he also noted other indications, such as in the work of Ælfric of Eynsham, who commented on what he saw as the rightful notions of the 'just war' (glossed from Isidore of Seville by Ælfric as 'rihtlic gefeoht') around the turn of the first millennium.[57] Although grounded in the disciplinary study of Old English literature, Cross had much to say about the social values of Anglo-Saxon warfare. Both a product of and a reaction to the social discourses on war and peace of the 1960s, Cross's paper was able to address Anglo-Saxon modes of violence in their own terms from ecclesiastical and social perspectives.

Masculinity, youth and experience in Anglo-Saxon warfare

Given the social significance of warfare, it may strike us today that Cross's arguments were unnecessary. But they were needed to restate a position which allowed what were at first sight different social positions to co-exist. A fundamental element of this is that warfare, with its inherent elements of social display and posturing, was evidently seen as something intrinsically masculine.[58] As Nick Stoodley has observed from the early Anglo-Saxon burial evidence, the 'spear' and 'spindle' sides of families could be (and often were) clearly delineated.[59]

Thus there are few records of female involvement in war, even though women

---

[53] For example, see the descriptions of St Wilfrid's followers in warlike terms in Stephen of Ripon, *Vita Wilfridi*, chs 13, 24, in *The Life of Bishop Wilfrid by Eddius Stephanus*, ed. and trans. B. Colgrave (Cambridge, 1927), pp. 26–9, 48–51. For discussion of such depictions, see Wormald, 'Bede, Beowulf and the Conversion of the Anglo-Saxon Aristocracy', pp. 54–6, and Wormald, 'Age of Bede and Aethelbald', pp. 89–91.

[54] Bede, *HE* II.12, pp. 180–1.

[55] For a wide-ranging survey of this subject, see C. Holdsworth, 'An Airier Aristocracy: The Saints at War', *TRHS* 6th series 6 (1996), pp. 103–22.

[56] Cross, 'Ethic of War in Old English'.

[57] Cross, 'Ethic of War in Old English', p. 272, citing *Aelfric's Lives of Saints, Being a Set of Sermons on Saints' Days Formerly Observed by the English Church*, ed. W. W. Skeat, EETS original series 76, 82, 2 vols (London, 1881, 1900), vol. 2, pp. 112–14.

[58] For the significance of display in war, see Leyser, 'Early Medieval Warfare', p. 93.

[59] N. Stoodley, *The Spindle and the Spear: A Critical Enquiry into the Construction and Meaning of Gender in the Early Anglo-Saxon Burial Rite*, BAR British Series 288 (Oxford, 1999). The delineation is made clear in written form in the will of King Alfred, S 1507 (AD 873×88 and ?896×99 for codicil).

were presumably amongst the camp followers of large armies.[60] Making observations on medieval warfare, Helen Nicholson points out that, while the language
and expectations of warrior culture were inherently masculine, there were exceptions.[61] Those exceptions show that this was a system of values rather than a representation of reality, and this should be borne in mind in considering the depictions of warfare in poetry and other forms of literature. Such literature may have
been borne out of and also reinforced social expectations as people attempted to
live by those codes of behaviour – but such codes were not so rigid as to place a
straitjacket upon social behaviour.[62]

How, then, were such characters as King Alfred's daughter Æthelflaed seen
by their contemporaries? Since the publication of a seminal paper by F. T. Wainwright, little work has been undertaken specifically on the 'Lady of the Mercians', although it could hardly be said that she has been forgotten in studies of
the tenth century.[63] It is interesting that *hlæfdige* (lady) the feminine version of
hlaford (lord), was used to refer to Æthelflaed, suggesting that while the West
Saxons could not allow her the consecrated title of 'Queen' (*cwen/regina*), her
status was nonetheless acknowledged. Given later references to the title 'Lady' in
the royal house (Ælfgifu-Emma, Edith) it was presumably a queenly one and,
of course, as Alfred's daughter and the daughter of a member of a branch of the
royal house of Mercia, Æthelflaed could hold such a title.[64] While there is no
evidence that Æthelflaed ever appeared on the battlefield, she is explicitly linked
with the military campaigns in the areas known as the Danelaw, including being

[60] ASC 893 notes the presence of women and children with the Vikings at Benfleet; the
matter-of-fact recording of their capture by the Anglo-Saxons and transit to London
(to be ransomed or sold as slaves?) suggests that although the record was exceptional,
their presence with an army was not. See J. Jesch, *Women in the Viking Age* (Woodbridge,
1991), pp. 96–8. The reference to the married status of the pseudo-peasant portrayed by
Bede's unfortunate thegn Imma may be indicative of women in the baggage train of the
Northumbrian army. Bede, *HE* IV.22, pp. 400–5.

[61] H. J. Nicholson, *Medieval Warfare: Theory and Practice of War in Europe, 300–1500*
(Basingstoke, 2004), pp. 59–65. For a brief survey of the exceptions in the burial evidence,
see Pollington, *English Warrior from Earliest Times till 1066*, pp. 75–7; cf. Stoodley, *Spindle
and the Spear*, pp. 29–30, 76–7, and C. Knüsel and K. Ripley, 'The *Berdache* or Man-
woman in Anglo-Saxon England and Early Medieval Europe', in *Social Identity in Early
Medieval Britain*, ed. W. O. Frazer and A. Tyrell, SEHB (London, 2000), pp. 159–91.

[62] See here C. J. Clover, 'Regardless of Sex: Men, Women, and Power in Early Northern
Europe', *Speculum* 68 (1993), pp. 363–87. I am grateful to Barbara Yorke for this reference.

[63] F. T. Wainwright, 'Æthelflæd, Lady of the Mercians', in *The Anglo-Saxons: Studies in
Some Aspects of their History and Culture Presented to Bruce Dickins*, ed. P. Clemoes
(London, 1959), pp. 53–69. An important exception to this is P. Stafford, '"The Annals
of Æthelflæd": Annals, History and Politics in Early Tenth-Century England', in *Myth,
Rulership, Church and Charters: Essays in Honour of Nicholas Brooks*, ed. J. Barrow and
A. Wareham (Aldershot, 2008), pp. 101–16. See also Stafford, *Unification and Conquest*,
pp. 31–2.

[64] For a discussion of Æthelflæd's background, see Wainwright, 'Æthelflæd, Lady of the
Mercians', pp. 53–4. The range of meanings of the word *hlæfdige* is addressed by P. Stafford,
Queen Emma and Queen Edith: Queenship and Women's Power in Eleventh-Century England
(Oxford, 1997), pp. 56–9.

remembered as the active agent in the building of fortifications.[65] It is nonetheless worth asking how the relationship between her and her warriors manifested itself if warrior relations were more usually expressed in terms of a man and his lord? How did the mental worldview of her warriors preparing themselves for battle differ from that of those who served a male lord? While these questions cannot be answered with certainty, they are worth reflecting upon with reference to the four thegns 'who were dear to her' (ðe hire besorge wæron) who were slain inside the gates of the borough of Derby in 917.[66] Given the echoes of the deaths of thegns inside the gates of a fortification with the Anglo-Saxon Chronicle's famous account of the death of Cynewulf in its entry for 757,[67] it may be suggested that the male-dominated theory of military lordship could have some flexibility in its application.[68]

Having laid out the social significance of warfare in Anglo-Saxon England, it is relevant to address how this was played out amongst different generations. It is a truth universally acknowledged in military history that, given a wish to learn from past lessons, generals refight their last war rather than the current one. If this can be applied to the Anglo-Saxon period, members of a generation of warriors who had experienced one major conflict would be alive and presumably able to influence the military policy of a later generation. A periodization of the major conflicts of the Viking Age can be posited, with the suggestion that during each of these periods of activities members of an elder generation who had participated in the conflicts of the previous generation were alive.

850s and 860s	Great Viking Army
870s	First phase of defence of Wessex
890s	Second phase of defence of Wessex (campaigns in eastern England)
900s/910s	First phase of 'reconquest' (campaigns in Midlands)
920s/930s	Second phase of 'reconquest' (campaigns in Midlands and North)
940s/950s	Punitive expeditions against Northumbria / Wales
960s/970s	Relative peace; some raids on Wales
980s/990s	Early Viking raids on English kingdom
1000s/1010s	Viking armies' conquest of English kingdom
1020s	Anglo-Danish expeditions in Scandinavia

---

[65] ASC MR 912, 913, 914, 915. The military depiction of Æthelflæd is discussed by Stafford, 'Annals of Æthelflæd', pp. 102–3.

[66] ASC MR 917.

[67] ASC s.a. 755 (r. 757). For this entry, see below, pp. 19–20.

[68] However, for a tentative gendered reading of 'woman's care and authority' implicit in the term besorge, see V. Thompson, Dying and Death in Later Anglo-Saxon England, Anglo-Saxon Studies 4 (Woodbridge, 2004), pp. 11–12. Bede, HE IV.22, pp. 404–5, refers to service as a reginae minister, in the household of Queen Æthelthryth. This is translated unambiguously into service in a military household in the Old English Bede to cwene ðegn. The Old English Version of Bede's Ecclesiastical History of the English People, ed. and trans. T. Miller, EETS 95, 96, 2 parts (Oxford, 1890–1), part 1, pp. 330.

1030s–50s	Civil wars and defensive preparations against Vikings
1050s/1060s	Punitive expeditions against Welsh
1060s/1070s	Battles against Vikings and Normans; English participation in Norman service
1080s	Renewed Danish threat

A parallel may be made here with an observation made by Guy Halsall in 1989 that in pre-Viking England there was, on average, a significant campaign by a kingdom upon its neighbours every generation (i.e. approximately every twenty years).[69] Although the Anglo-Saxon Chronicle's record of the deaths of 'many of the best king's thegns who were in the land' from the three years of murrain and plague in 893–6 suggests that the curtailment of the influence of a particular generation could be dramatic,[70] a steady attrition rate is indicated by the sporadic obits of the more prominent royal councillors recorded in the Chronicle's more detailed late ninth-century entries.[71]

While many of the military actions which took place in the two centuries before the Norman Conquest may not be referred to according to Halsall's classification of 'wars of conquest', their frequency nonetheless meant that each generation had a chance to participate in a significant campaign. If we assume that a male warrior's period of martial activity began in his early teens and (if he survived) lasted about two decades,[72] he would have been able bestow his experience or even leadership from those campaigns upon a younger generation. The exception – a very significant exception – was that of the reign of Edgar 'the Peaceable' (957/9–75), during which Viking threats had been kept at bay by a combination of employing Vikings in mercenary service and naval deterrence.[73]

Nonetheless each generation learnt from the previous one, even if they were sometimes the wrong lessons. As will be seen from some of the narratives of battles and campaigns, great store was placed upon the interactions of different generations at war, from the young warriors in the *Maldon* poem to the kings' sons and brothers in campaign, at Ashdown, Farnham and *Brunanburh*. This was hardly new. While the *geoguth* – the 'youth' – were a significant and indeed formally recognized element in the early Anglo-Saxon military household and on the battlefield,[74] one does not have to go as far as Philippe Contamine's move

[69] G. R. Halsall, 'Anthropology and the Study of Pre-Conquest Warfare and Society: The Ritual War in Anglo-Saxon England', in *Weapons and Warfare*, ed. Hawkes, pp. 155–77, at pp. 162, 173.

[70] ASC 896.

[71] ASC 888, 896, 897.

[72] This is a topic dealt with in Pollington, *English Warrior from Earliest Times till 1066*, p. 70. For a discussion of the development of young warriors (albeit not just in Anglo-Saxon England), see also H. E. Davidson, 'The Training of Warriors', in *Weapons and Warfare*, ed. Hawkes, pp. 11–24.

[73] S. Jayakumar, 'Some Reflections on the "Foreign Policies" of Edgar "the Peaceable"', *HSJ* 10 (2002 for 2001), pp. 17–37.

[74] Pollington, *English Warrior from Earliest Times till 1066*, pp. 30, 70–4; Abels, *Lordship and Military Obligation in Anglo-Saxon England*, p. 32; and R. P. Abels, 'Household Men,

'towards a history of courage' to accept the need for young warriors to prove themselves as a given in anthropological studies.[75]

Guy Halsall has argued for the development of 'ritual' warfare in Anglo-
Saxon society, related to the conduct of such young warriors. While distinctions
between what Halsall terms a 'ritual war' and a 'war of conquest' may have been
more blurred than such a bipartite model implies, a degree of generalization is
nonetheless necessary to draw conclusions from problematic evidence, and his
conclusions are significant.[76] Warfare could have a socially cohesive role, and the
low intensity of the 'ritual' warfare characterized by Halsall was important, indicating that the warfare of the Anglo-Saxons was conducted according to expected
'codes' of behaviour. Such behavioural expectations are significant when considering the impact of the Vikings.[77] 'Ritual' warfare is also noteworthy, because the
apparent lacunae in military activity implied by the absence of records of major
battles in the Anglo-Saxon Chronicle can be read as periods of 'small wars'. In the
two centuries on which this volume focuses, this is relevant to the records of the
Annales Cambriae, addressed in the next chapter.

Halsall draws observations on the application of anthropological parallels to
Anglo-Saxon society, noting that the social cohesion provided by 'ritual' warfare
in keeping warriors in Anglo-Saxon society active.[78] It was a logical conclusion,
but one which assumed a reductionist approach to the organization of early
Anglo-Saxon society. Such anthropological parallels were contended by Bernard

Mercenaries and Vikings in Anglo-Saxon England', in *Mercenaries and Paid Men: The Mercenary Identity in the Middle Ages: Proceedings of a Conference held at University of Wales, Swansea, 7th–9th July 2005*, ed. J. France, History of Warfare 47 (Leiden, 2008), pp. 143–66, at pp. 146–7.

[75] P. Contamine, *War in the Middle Ages*, trans. M. Jones (Oxford, 1984), pp. 250–9. See also J. Keegan, *A History of Warfare* (London, 1993), pp. 226–7, and, for a survey of anthropological approaches to warfare, pp. 79–94; M. Bennett, 'Military Masculinity in England and Northern France, *c.* 1050–1225', in *Masculinity in Medieval Europe*, ed. D. Hadley, Women and Men in History (Basingstoke, 1999), pp. 71–88, at pp. 76–9. For a consideration of what could be termed 'behaviourial archaeology', see B. P. C. Molloy and D. Grossman, 'Why Can't Johnny Kill? The Psychology and Physiology of Interpersonal Combat', in *The Cutting Edge: Studies in Ancient and Medieval Combat*, ed. B. Molloy (Stroud, 2007), pp. 188–202 (quoted below, p. 266).

[76] Halsall, 'Anthropology and the Study of Pre-Conquest Warfare and Society'. For a more recent reading by Halsall of varieties of campaigns, see his *Warfare and Society in the Barbarian West*, pp. 134–45.

[77] G. Halsall, 'Playing by Whose Rules? A Further Look at Viking Atrocity in the Ninth Century', *Medieval History* 2:2 (1992), pp. 2–12, and Halsall, *Warfare and Society in the Barbarian West*, pp. 142–3. See also J. Barrow, 'Demonstrative Behaviour and Political Communication in Later Anglo-Saxon England', *ASE* 34 (2007), pp. 127–50, at pp. 133–4. See below, pp. 42–3.

[78] Halsall, 'Anthropology and the Study of Pre-Conquest Warfare and Society'. The anthropological parallels cited by Halsall are with N. A. Chagnon, *Yanamanö: The Fierce People* (New York, 1963); K. Heider, *The Dugum Dani: A Papuan Culture in the Highlands of New Guinea* (Chicago, 1970); and P. Brown, *The Chimbu: A Study of Change in the New Guinea Highlands* (London, 1975). For a discussion of the cohesion of young warriors, see Davidson, 'Training of Warriors', who (p. 17) proposes an interpretation of the Old English poem *Wulf and Eadwacer* (in *A Choice of Anglo-Saxon Verse*, ed. and trans. R. Hamer [London, 1970], pp. 84–5) relating to a *Jomsviking*-style training encampment.

Bachrach in a paper which addresses points raised in Halsall's work (although making no explicit reference to Halsall). In his paper Bachrach does not explicitly critique anthropological parallels, but instead argues for the sophistication of post-Roman successor states.[79] This given, Bachrach appears to assume a primitivism in such warrior societies as those addressed by Halsall. Such an assumption can be questioned. Anthropological parallels are useful because they illuminate modes of behaviour which are explicitly organized according to inherent sets of customs or 'rules'. In this respect, whether early medieval commanders had a sense of 'grand strategy' is immaterial.[80] The important issue to be recognized here is that warfare fulfilled a fundamental social purpose.

One further observation is perhaps obvious but nonetheless needs to be made. Warfare in the later Anglo-Saxon period was very much influenced by conduct in the earlier pre-Viking period. Although the advent of organized Viking activities profoundly changed the political picture of late Anglo-Saxon England, not least the nature of warfare, many norms and expectations had been well established before the Vikings first arrived. While Anglo-Saxon society may not have been constantly at war, the elites within that society owed their position to warfare and were acutely aware of this. Although a discussion of the relations between Anglo-Saxon England and its neighbours is necessary in the following chapter, the ways in which such social and political impetus for military action manifested itself will be inherent in this and later chapters.

[79] B. S. Bachrach, 'Anthropologists and Early Medieval History: Some Problems', *Cithara* 34 (1994), pp. 3–10. A similar approach appears to have been taken by I. P. Stephenson, *The Late Anglo-Saxon Army* (Stroud, 2007), pp. 27–30, which draws attention to the parallels between classical and early medieval warfare. For an argument of continuity in the 'Western' way of war, see V. D. Hanson, *Carnage and Culture: Landmark Battles in the Rise of Western Power* (New York, 2001).

[80] Bachrach, 'Anthropologists and Early Medieval History'. For maximal statements of grand strategy, see Bachrach's studies, *Merovingian Military Organization, 481–751* (London, 1972) and *Early Carolingian Warfare: Prelude to Empire*, Middle Ages (Philadelphia, PA, 2001); C. R. Bowlus, 'Italia – Bavaria – Avaria: The Grand Strategy behind Charlemagne's *Renovatio Imperii* in the West', *JMMH* 1 (2003), pp. 43–60.

✦ 2 ✦

Friends and Foes

THIS chapter addresses the ways in which political and military relations between the Anglo-Saxon kingdoms and their neighbours were seen from the viewpoint of – for the most part – outside groups. The main focus is on Celts and Scandinavians, who are considered as adversaries and allies of Anglo-Saxons in the Viking period, showing their influences on the developing English kingdom and, in the case of the Celts, the importance of the continuity of their political relationships with the early Anglo-Saxon kingdoms. It is also appropriate to acknowledge the influences on Anglo-Saxon warfare of the Carolingian Franks and Ottonians. The significant exception of the Normans notwithstanding,[1] the Franks and Continental Saxons seem never to have encountered Anglo-Saxons in battle during the Viking Age either as an enemy or an ally. However, the two-way communication of military influences between England and the Continent is worthy of note in the assessment of late Anglo-Saxon warfare. The influences of Carolingian and Ottonian successes should never be ignored when considering the emergence of an English kingdom in the midst of warfare against neighbouring polities.[2]

---

[1] For a statement of the Duchy of Normandy as a Frankish successor state, see D. Bates, *Normandy Before 1066* (London, 1982).

[2] For the wider ninth-century perspective, see J. L. Nelson, "'A King Across the Sea": Alfred in Continental Perspective', *TRHS* 5th ser. 36 (1986), pp. 45–68; J. L. Nelson, 'England and the Continent in the Ninth Century: I, Ends and Beginnings', *TRHS* 6th ser. 12 (2002), pp. 1–21; J. L. Nelson, 'England and the Continent in the Ninth Century: II, the Vikings and Others', *TRHS* 6th ser. 13 (2003), pp. 1–28. The significant case here is that of fortification: M. Hassall and D. Hill, 'Pont de l'Arche: Frankish Influence on the West Saxon Burh?', *Archaeological Journal* 127 (1970), pp. 188–95; D. Tys, 'The Late Carolingian Ringforts in Coastal Flanders: Civil Defences against the Vikings or Comital Power Bases?', in *Landscapes of Defence in the Viking Age: Anglo-Saxon England and Comparative Perspectives*, ed. J. Baker, S. Brookes, D. Parsons, and A. Reynolds, SEMA 28 (Turnhout, forthcoming). For a consideration of the influence of the West Saxons on the Ottonian *burgen*, see E. J. Schoenfeld, 'Anglo-Saxon *Burhs* and Continental *Burgen*: Early Medieval Fortifications in Constitutional Perspective', *HSJ* 6 (1994), pp. 49–66. However, cf. Ian Howard's discussion of the English lack of horses, in comparison to a successful use of cavalry against Slavs and Scandinavians in Saxony: I. Howard, *Swein Forkbeard's Conquest of England, 991–1017*, Warfare in History (Woodbridge, 2003), pp. 24–6.

Britons and the 'Kingdom of the English'

The Anglo-Saxon Chronicle, compiled at or very close to the court of King Alfred during the 890s,[3] gives an impression of the inexorable advance of the kingdom of Wessex. The relationship between English and Celtic Britons, whether in the west or north of Britain, is portrayed as one of British subordination. Barbara Yorke, amongst others, has highlighted the manner in which English identity was ethnically defined according to such a subordinate relationship, in which Britons could have had economic and legal incentives to integrate with their Anglo-Saxon neighbours.[4] Although notions of early medieval ethnicity are multi-faceted and much debated, even in the ninth century the military conquest of neighbouring peoples was seen as something that defined Anglo-Saxon identity. From a West Saxon perspective this was evident in the Anglo-Saxon Chronicle's record of the heroic death of the West Saxon king Cynewulf at the hands of his usurping cousin, the ætheling (prince) Cyneheard: Cynewulf had been militarily successful against the Britons in a series of victories represented by control of a British hostage (*Bryttiscum gisle*) who had fought for Cynewulf during the fateful encounter. The Chronicle entry for 757, from which the following passage is taken, is often cited as representative of an ideal value in Anglo-Saxon society: the precedence of lordship over kinship.[5] The significance of lordship is evident, but in the narrative the British hostage fighting for his Anglo-Saxon lord represents the manner in which Cynewulf's conquests of the Britons were absolute, thus heightening the king's reputation.[6]

> In this year Cynewulf and the *witan* of the West Saxons deprived Sigeberht of his kingdom because of his unjust deeds; except for Hampshire; and he held that until he slew the ealdorman who remained with him longest; and then Cynewulf drove him into *Andredesweald*, and he remained there until a swineherd stabbed him to death at Privett's stream [Hants]; and he avenged Ealdorman Cumbra. And that Cynewulf often fought great battles against the Britons [*Bretwalum*]. And after thirty-one winters in which he had held the kingdom [i.e. in 786], he wished to expel an ætheling who was called Cyneheard, and that Cyneheard was the aforesaid Sigeberht's brother. And then he [i.e. Cyneheard] discovered that the king was with a small band meeting a woman at *Meretun*, and he overtook him

---

[3] J. Bateley, 'The Compilation of the Anglo-Saxon Chronicle, 60 BC to AD 890: Vocabulary as Evidence', *Proceedings of the British Academy* 64 (1978), pp. 93–129.

[4] Yorke, *Wessex in the Early Middle Ages*, p. 72. For recent discussion of this issue, see papers in N. J. Higham (ed.), *Britons in Anglo-Saxon England*, Publications of the Manchester Centre for Anglo-Saxon Studies 7 (Woodbridge, 2007), especially M. Grimmer, 'Britons in Early Wessex: The Evidence of the Law Code of Ine', pp. 102–14, and, for an alternative view, Woolf, 'Apartheid and Economics in Anglo-Saxon England', pp. 115–29.

[5] For discussion of this, see S. D. White, 'Kinship and Lordship in Early Medieval England: The Story of Sigeberht, Cynewulf, and Cyneheard', *Viator* 20 (1989), pp. 1–18, and J. M. Hill, *The Anglo-Saxon Warrior Ethic: Reconstructing Lordship in Early English Literature* (Gainesville, 2000), pp. 74–84.

[6] ASC 757 (*sub anno* 755). R. Lavelle, 'The Use and Abuse of Hostages in Later Anglo-Saxon England', *EME* 14 (2006), pp. 269–96, at p. 284.

there and surrounded the chamber from outside before the men who were with the king discovered him. And then the king realised this and he went to the door, and nobly defended himself until he looked upon the ætheling, and then he rushed out against him and greatly wounded him. And they all continued to fight against the king until they had slain him. Then by the woman's screams, the king's thegns discovered the disturbance and then they hurried there, whosoever was then ready and quickest. And the ætheling offered money and life to each of them and none of them would accept it. But they continued to fight until they all lay dead but for a British hostage, and he was severely wounded.

Two centuries later, the record of King Edgar's control of what was being briefly defined as the *imperium* of Britain may have been manifested in the remarkable ceremony in which Edgar was said to have been rowed down the River Dee at Chester in 973 by the different British 'under-kings' (*subreguli*). Edgar's use of a fleet, perhaps manned by Viking stipendiaries[7] and, famously, recorded in the 975 entry *Chronicon ex chronicis* of John of Worcester (formerly attributed to Florence of Worcester),[8] had implications for the idea of 'British' 'imperial' control. A ceremony on the River Dee, which followed Edgar's crowning at Bath in 973, was linked to such 'imperial' notions, at least in the eyes of later commentators.[9]

> Then, after a while, circumnavigating the north coast of Wales with a large fleet [*classis*], he came to the city of Chester, where eight of his subkings [*subreguli*], namely Kenneth, king of the Scots, Malcolm, king of the Cumbrians, Maccus, king of a great number of islands, and five others, Dufnal, Siferth, Hywel, and Iacob, met him as he had ordered; and they swore that they would be faithful and co-operative men to him [*sibi fideles … cooperatores*] on land and sea. With them, on a certain day, he boarded a skiff [*scapham ascendit*]; with them set to the oars, and having taken the handle of the rudder himself, he expertly piloted it through the course of the River Dee, and with a crowd of all the ealdormen [*duces*] and nobles following with a similar boat, sailed from the palace to the monastery of St John the Baptist. When he had prayed, he returned with the same pomp to the palace. While he was entering it he is asserted to have said to his *optimates* that at last each of his successors would be able to pride himself that he was king of the English, and with so many kings in submission to him would receive the pomp of such honour.

Julia Barrow has raised questions regarding the nature of this event, suggesting that it was a border peace-making ceremony rather than a ritual demonstration of superiority and that its triumphal gloss in the narratives of John of Worcester and William of Malmesbury was the result of Edgar's reputation as the force behind

---

[7] Jayakumar, 'Some Reflections on the "Foreign Policies" of Edgar "The Peaceable"', pp. 27–35. For the context of naval actions and defence, see below, ch. 4.

[8] JW vol. 2, s.a. 975, pp. 424–7.

[9] JW vol. 2, s.a. 973, pp. 422–4; Stenton, *Anglo-Saxon England*, 3rd edn, pp. 369–70.

the Benedictine reform movement of the later tenth century.[10] Nonetheless, the probably fictitious nature of the description of the events does not undermine the fact that such a story could develop, as Barrow acknowledges, around the start of the eleventh century.[11] Although the implications of Benedictine reform for the reputation of Edgar were understandably important, the story's use of expectations is also noteworthy. As with Otto the Great's reputation as an overlord served by his stem-rulers at an imperially ordained feast in 936,[12] Edgar's reputation could not have been undermined by 'imperial' relations, even if the realities of peacemaking had been more mundane.[13] A preoccupation with Vikings may be a manifestation of the tremulous fear of barbarism shared by modern historians and medieval chroniclers. However, for English kings, whose behaviour could stem from attitudes which followed their pre-Viking predecessors, defending against sea-raiders did not rate as highly as Celt-bashing and the extraction of tribute.[14] While tenth-century notions of *imperium* could be sophisticated in following Ottonian, Carolingian and Roman patterns, the idea of conquering territory and exacting tribute from neighbouring kingdoms was a means of establishing a reputation as a 'good king'.[15] We should therefore bear in mind the notion that, however 'strategically' misguided they may be perceived to be in hindsight, expeditions against Welsh, Scots and – to a lesser extent – Cornish could be goals in themselves for later Anglo-Saxon kings. This is an issue which is often overlooked in modern historiography. Thus when Æthelred II's kingdom was threatened by Viking armies, actions in the Irish Sea and Wales in 1000 and 1006 may have been logical from the point of view of a king concerned, even obsessed, with

[10] J. Barrow, 'Chester's Earliest Regatta? Edgar's Dee-Rowing Revisited', *EME* 10 (2001), pp. 81–93. For the significance of this event as an 'equality ritual', see Barrow, 'Demonstrative Behaviour and Political Communication in Later Anglo-Saxon England', p. 141 (for the context of negotiation and peace agreements, see also ch. 8, below). A. Williams, 'An Outing on the Dee: King Edgar at Chester, AD 973', *Mediaeval Scandinavia* 14 (2004), pp. 229–43, considers the political context of the event, stripping 'its twelfth-century accretions' (p. 242), giving a useful sense of the context of English-British relations. See also Jayakumar, 'Some Reflections on the "Foreign Policies" of Edgar "The Peaceable"', pp. 31–5. For other views of events from the perspectives of the British and Scandinavian rulers, see A. P. Smyth, *Warlords and Holy Men: Scotland, 80–1000*, The New History of Scotland 1 (London, 1984), p. 226–8, and D. E. Thornton, 'Edgar and the Eight Kings, AD 973: *textus et dramatis personae*', *EME* 10 (2001), pp. 49–79.

[11] Barrow, 'Chester's Earliest Regatta?', pp. 89–90.

[12] Widukind, *Rerum Gestarum Saxonicarum Libri Tres*, ed. P. Hirsch, MGH Scriptores Rerum Germanicarum 60 (Hanover, 1935), II.2, pp. 66–7. For the suggestion that Edgar's ceremony paralleled that of Otto, see T. Reuter, *Germany in the Early Middle Ages, c. 800–1056*, Longman History of Germany (London, 1991), p. 149.

[13] Although for the significance of the manner in which peacemaking could be used to enhance a ruler's reputation, see below ch. 8.

[14] See the discussion of 'ritual war', above, pp. 16–17. For the legacy of early Anglo-Saxon kingship in the Viking Age, see B. Yorke, *Kings and Kingdoms of Early Anglo-Saxon England* (London, 1989), pp. 157–78. For the devolution of defence, especially during the reign of Æthelred, see above, pp. 3–5, and below, pp. 171–5.

[15] The depiction of Scyld Scefing in *Beowulf*, lines 4–11, is pertinent here. R. Abels, *Alfred the Great: War, Kingship and Culture in Anglo-Saxon England*, The Medieval World (London, 1998), pp. 27–8.

the image of rule[16] – especially if stories of Edgar's imperial presence were by then in circulation.[17] What might be seen by a military strategist as a misguided sense of priorities may be better seen in terms of propaganda and image.

There were also less ambiguous examples of English dominance. The Anglo-Saxon Chronicle records Æthelflæd of Mercia's seizure of *Brecan Mere*, probably the *crannog* at Llangorse, Powys, showing a tenth-century English interest in mid-Welsh territory which complemented Æthelflæd and her brother Edward's campaigns in the midlands and north of England.[18] Edward's son, Athelstan, also made a reputation for himself by leading a large force into Scotland,[19] perhaps, as Michael Wood has argued, making use of Welsh auxiliaries.[20] Such actions by Anglo-Saxon rulers are reflected in the sense of injustice conveyed by the language of the tenth-century Welsh poem, *Armes Prydein* ('The Prophecy of Britain'), the author of which wrote of a day when the Celts of the island of Britain would rise up alongside Irish allies against the English invaders.[21] A century later, as Kelly DeVries has argued, Harold Godwineson's 'kingworthiness' was demonstrated by his actions in Wales against the rebellious Welsh king, Gruffudd ap Llywelyn, on behalf of Harold's own king, Edward the Confessor.[22] This was apparent in twelfth-century records of Anglo-Welsh relations in Gerald of Wales's *Description of Wales*, which alluded to comparison between Harold's military reputation and King David's Old Testament guerrilla campaigns (I Sam. 25), as well as a more direct comparison with earlier Anglo-Saxon conquerors of Wales:[23]

[16] R. Lavelle, *Aethelred II: King of the English* (Stroud, 2002; rev. edn, 2008), pp. 101–2, 119, 150–1. For a comparison of the northern expedition in 1000 with Athelstan's reputation, see Howard, *Swein Forkbeard's Invasions*, pp. 52–3. Howard, p. 61, makes the logical assumption that the 1000 campaign saw the mercenary employment of Vikings.

[17] Barrow, 'Chester's Earliest Regatta?', pp. 89–90.

[18] ASC MR 916. See M. Redknap and A. Lane, 'The Early Medieval Crannóg at Llangors, Powys: An Interim Statement on the 1989–1993 Seasons', *International Journal of Nautical Archaeology* 23 (1994), pp. 189–205, at pp. 200–1, 203.

[19] ASC 934; *Historia Regum*, s.a. 934, in *Symeonis Monachi Opera Omnia*, ed. T. Arnold, RS 75, 2 vols (London, 1882–5), vol. 2, p. 124; trans. *EHD* 1, p. 278.

[20] M. Wood, 'Brunanburh Revisited', *Saga Book of the Viking Society* 20 (1980), pp. 200–17, at p. 215, n. 36, citing the sizeable witness lists of charters S 425 (dated to 28 May 934 and purporting to be made in Winchester) and S 407 (7 June 934, Nottingham) as evidence for the campaigns recorded in the *Historia Regum* (*supra*). Wood also suggests Edmund's use of Welsh auxiliaries in Cumbria in 945, read from the 'support of King Hywel' (*adjutorio Loelini regis*) (*Rogeri de Wendover Chronica sive Flores Historiarum*, ed. H. G. Hewlett, RS 84, 3 vols [London, 1886–9] vol. 1, p. 500). I am grateful to Michael Wood for discussion on this subject. For discussion of forces in the 934 campaign, see ch. 5, below.

[21] I. Williams (ed.), *Armes Prydein: The Prophecy of Britain, from the Book of Taliesin*, trans. R. Bromwich, Mediaeval and Modern Welsh 6 (Dublin, 1972).

[22] K. DeVries, 'Harold Godwinson in Wales: Military Legitimacy in Late Anglo-Saxon England', in *The Normans and their Adversaries at War*, ed. R. P. Abels and B. S. Bachrach, Warfare in History (Woodbridge, 2001), pp. 65–85. For Harold's acquisition of hostages in this campaign, see Lavelle, 'Use and Abuse of Hostages', pp. 283–4.

[23] Gerald of Wales, *Itinerarium Kambriae et description Kambriae*, II.7, in *Giraldi Cambrensis Opera*, ed. J. F. Dimock, RS 21 (London, 1861–91), vol. 6, p. 217. For an alternative translation, see DeVries, 'Harold Godwinson in Wales', p. 83.

And thus by far fully the greatest Harold: who, himself on foot with infantry troop and light armour [*pedestri turba et levibus armis*], and strengthened by living off the land, entered and travelled around all of Wales so strongly that he 'left not one that pisseth against the wall' [I Sam. 25:22; I Kings 16:11].

In commemoration of his victory, and in perpetual memory, you will come across stones in Wales, erected by entitlement according to ancient tradition, in the many places in which he became the victor, most having letters inscribed: HERE WAS HAROLD THE VICTOR.

A modern editor of Gerald of Wales pointed out that 'no such stones have ever been found'.[24] This observation, while leading us to question the historicity of Gerald's account, is not surprising, considering that Gerald was recording the 'ancient tradition' (*more antiquo*) of triumphs whose memory is unlikely to have been maintained in subsequent centuries. Gerald's association of many of the inscribed stones with Harold's campaigns may have been prompted by a need to explain the early medieval monuments which Gerald encountered in Wales with a tangible triumph.[25]

Alongside the picture of English domination of the British Isles presented by contemporary sources (in the case of Gerald of Wales, not so contemporary), it should be borne in mind that some Anglo-Saxons and Celts could enjoy good relations. Charles Insley has shown that the degree of co-operation between the Cornish nobility and King Athelstan, evidenced in Athelstan's charters, stands in contrast to the image of the massacre and expulsion from Exeter of the Cornish Welsh depicted by William of Malmesbury.[26] Welsh kingdoms could provide useful military allies: the Anglo-Saxon Chronicle entry for 893, recording Alfred's pursuit of a Viking force on the River Severn, tells of the appearance of 'a certain division of the north Welsh race' (*sum dæl þæs Norð Weal cynnes*) alongside the West Saxon force.[27] Another annal records the Vikings' capture of the Welsh bishop of Archenfield, Cyfeiliog, for whom King Edward paid a £40 ransom, suggesting that he had a responsibility for or authority over the bishop.[28] There was evidently remarkable English interest in Wales, at least from a southern

[24] Gerald of Wales, *The Journey through Wales / The Description of Wales*, ed. and trans. L. Thorpe (Harmondsworth, 1978), p. 266, n. 615.

[25] The evidence of early medieval inscribed stones in Wales is discussed extensively in *A Corpus of Early Medieval Inscribed Stones and Stone Sculpture in Wales* (Cardiff, 2007), of which volumes 1 (by M. Redknap and J. M. Lewis) and 2 (by N. Edwards), covering south-eastern and south-western Wales respectively, have been published to date. However, for a discussion of the twelfth-century attitudes to 'barbarians' apparent in Gerald's writing, see R. Bartlett, *Gerald of Wales, 1146–1223*, Oxford Historical Monographs (Oxford, 1982), pp. 158–77.

[26] C. Insley, 'Athelstan, Charters and the English in Cornwall', in *Charters and Charter Scholarship in Britain and Ireland*, ed. J. Green and M. T. Flanagan (Basingstoke, 2005), pp. 15–31; WM, *GR*, II.134, pp. 216–17; WM, *GP*, II.94, pp. 314–15.

[27] ASC ABCD 893.

[28] ASC AD 914. See T. M. Charles-Edwards, 'Wales and Mercia, 613–918', in *Mercia: An Anglo-Saxon Kingdom in Europe*, ed. M. P. Brown and C. A. Farr, SEHB (London, 2001), pp. 89–105, at p. 104. Michael Swanton's reading is that Cyfeiliog was captured *in* Archenfield, which, as an inland place, would make sense in terms of the ASC's reference

and midland perspective, often rivalling interest in Anglo-Scandinavian affairs. Furthermore, Anglo-Welsh interests reveal continuities with the politics of the pre-Viking age, reflecting the fact that West Saxon and Mercian success depended on an understanding of the nuances of Welsh political geography, nurturing alliances and dealing with enemies in different kingdoms as appropriate.[29] Thus, famously, Asser's relationship with his patron, King Alfred, resulted in the record of a shifting range of Anglo-Welsh allegiances, an issue which warrants a quotation of the relevant passage in full:[30]

> Indeed, at that time, and long before, all the kingdoms [*regiones*] of the right-hand side of Britain belonged to King Alfred and still belong to him. Certainly, Hyfaidd, with all the inhabitants of the kingdom [*regio*] of Demetia [Dyfed], compelled by the strength of the six sons of Rhodri, had submitted himself to [Alfred's] royal overlordship [*imperium*]. Also Hywel son of Rhys, king of Glywysing, and Brochfael and Ffernfael, sons of Meurig, kings of Gwent, compelled by the strength and tyranny of Ealdorman [*comes*] Æthelred and of the Mercians, of their own accord sought the king, that they might have lordship [*dominium*] and protection [*defensio*] from him against their enemies. Also Elise, son of Tewdwr, king of Brycheiniog, compelled by the strength of the same sons of Rhodri, of his own accord asked for the lordship of the aforesaid king; also Anarawd, son of Rhodri, with his brothers, at last abandoning the friendship of the Northumbrians, from which he had had no good but harm, came into his presence eagerly seeking the friendship of the king; he was honourably received by the king, and by the hand of the bishop was accepted as a son in confirmation, and was enriched with magnificent gifts. He subjected himself with all his people to the lordship of the king [*regis dominio*], by the same condition, that in all things he thus would be obedient to the royal will, in the same way as Æthelred with the Mercians.

Asser may have been writing an account which followed contemporary models of Christian kingship, but it is also arguable that he wrote primarily for a Welsh audience, and therefore one of his aims was to portray Alfred as a benevolent protector.[31] Thus from a Welsh perspective Asser wrote of South Wales as 'right-hand' Wales. Asser's preoccupations here showed some slippage of the curtain of nascent English unity, revealing a degree of Mercian independence, in spite of Ealdorman Æthelred's marriage to Alfred's daughter, Æthelflæd, and Asser's

---

to Vikings taking him to their ships: M. J. Swanton (ed. and trans.), *The Anglo-Saxon Chronicles* (London, 1996), p. 98, n. 1.

[29] W. Davies, *Patterns of Power in Early Wales: O'Donnell Lectures, Delivered in the University of Oxford, 1983* (Oxford, 1990), p. 76.

[30] Asser, ch. 80.

[31] S. D. Keynes and M. Lapidge (ed. and trans.), *Alfred the Great: Asser's Life of King Alfred and Other Contemporary Sources* (Harmondsworth, 1983), p. 56. Although A. P. Smyth, *King Alfred the Great* (Oxford, 1996) argues that the 'Pseudo-Asser' was a skilful forger, Simon Keynes's review of his thesis effectively reinstates Asser into the pantheon of ninth-century sources, with Asser's Welsh perspective an important element of this: 'On the Authenticity of Asser's *Life of King Alfred*', *Journal of Ecclesiastical History* 47 (1996), pp. 529–51.

record of Mercia's subjection to Wessex under the same conditions as those of the Welsh kingdoms.[32] It is interesting that Asser's multiple agendas meant that he was willing to criticize the Mercians, showing that some English rulers could prove useful allies for Welsh rulers, just as renegade English nobles were useful to political interests in eleventh-century Wales.[33] The fact that Asser's account records southern Welsh alliances with the English may explain why the Anglo-Saxon Chronicle entry for 893 records a 'north Welsh' contingent on the Severn. Michael Swanton posits an explanation for this distinction: the southern Welsh were already Alfred's allies under an obligation to be present and were thus not recorded.[34] Swanton is perhaps supported here by the Chronicle's record of the death of a 'Welsh Reeve' in its entry for 896, a character with an English name who H. M. Chadwick suggested had responsibilities for the raising of both tribute and the levying of auxiliaries.[35] An alternative explanation may be seen from a West Saxon perspective in that the record of the 'north Welsh' may have been in contrast to the 'west Welsh' of Cornwall and thus may have been a general reference to Britons from Wales.[36] For the English rulers, the payoff was straightforward (Asser's account seems comparatively sanguine on this aspect): a traditional sense of overkingship and the enhancement of reputation and one-upmanship over their neighbours in a political game that was evidently multi-faceted.

Although *Armes Prydein* shows one poetic response to these Anglo-Celtic politics, such a sense of English overlordship can be seen quite clearly in the Welsh collection known as the *Annales Cambriae* ('Annals of Wales'), which contain a number of references to English affairs, highlighting the focus on events which affected the Welsh kingdoms. The entries of the *Annales Cambriae* relating to the politics and protagonists of Anglo-Saxon kingdoms from the arrival of the Great Viking Army in 865 are reproduced below, though for reasons of brevity annals relating only to Vikings in Wales are not included.[37] Although they do not reflect the complexities of politics relating to the disputes within and between Welsh kingdoms, they do hint at an aggressive side to English military activity during the reigns of Edgar and Æthelred II, a time when the English are traditionally considered to have been militarily dormant.[38] However, for the Welsh kingdoms

---

[32] See here Cumberledge, 'Reading Between the Lines: The Place of Mercia within an Expanding Wessex', pp. 2–7; cf. S. D. Keynes, 'Mercia and Wessex in the Ninth Century', in *Mercia*, ed. Brown and Farr, pp. 310–28, and Keynes, 'Edward, King of the Anglo-Saxons'.

[33] See here K. L. Maund, 'The Welsh Alliances of Earl Ælfgar of Mercia and his Family in the Mid-Eleventh Century', *ANS* 11 (1989 for 1988), pp. 181–90.

[34] Swanton, *Anglo-Saxon Chronicles*, p. 87, n. 12. See also K. Maund, *The Welsh Kings: The Medieval Rulers of Wales* (Stroud, 2002), pp. 43–4.

[35] ASC s.a. 896. H. M. Chadwick, *Studies on Anglo-Saxon Institutions* (Cambridge, 1905), p. 233.

[36] ASC 838 for *westwalas*; ASC 830, for a reference to *Norþwalas* as a likely synonym for the inhabitants of Wales. See also Æthelweard, *Chronicon*, p. 30, which renders them 'north Britons' (*Aquilonales Brittanos*).

[37] For these, see B. G. Charles, *Old Norse Relations with Wales* (Cardiff, 1934); W. Davies, *Wales in the Early Middle Ages*, SEHB (Leicester, 1982), pp. 116–20.

[38] For a recent reading of the limits of military organization in the second half of the tenth century, see Abels, 'From Alfred to Harold II', p. 22. An exception is Jayakumar, 'Some

the English were a pachydermous bedfellow, whose minor movements affected Welsh politics at every stage, and it seems that what the Anglo-Saxon Chronicle recorded was not necessarily what affected Mercia and/or Wales.[39]

Stephen Baxter's observation that the C Manuscript of the Anglo-Saxon Chronicle takes a Mercian perspective in its record of the events of the eleventh century may explain why its author takes an interest in Anglo-Welsh politics during the immediate pre-Conquest period.[40] By extension, that eleventh-century interest contrasts with the broad lack of consideration by the Chronicle's manuscripts of such issues at other points in the ninth, tenth and eleventh centuries. The *Annales Cambriae* show that English actions which are not recorded in surviving English sources were in 877, 880 (assuming that the 'vengeance' recorded for 880 was a net result of Anglo-Welsh conflict in 877), 894, 943, 950, 968, 983, 985, 993, 1012, and 1035. Most of these actions were attacks instigated by the English, although they may have been on a relatively small scale. They provide a sense of the comparative frequency of incessant raiding, similar to the frequent 'ritual' wars of the early Anglo-Saxon period addressed by Guy Halsall.[41]

866   The city of York was laid waste; that is the battle [*cat*] with the black gentiles.

877   Rhodri and his son Gwriad is murdered by the Saxons.

880   The battle [*gueit*] of Conwy. Vengeance for Rhodri by God. <The battle [*gueit*] of Cynan.>

894   Anarawd came with the Angles to lay waste Ceredigion and Ystrad Tywi.

898   <Athelstan king of the Saxons died.>

900   Albrit [i.e. Alfred] king of the Giuoys [i.e. Gewisse] is dead.

917   Queen Æthelflæd died.[42]

938   The battle [*bellum*] of Brune. [i.e. *Brunanburh*]

Reflections on the "Foreign Policies" of Edgar "The Peaceable"', p. 20, which illuminates the belligerence of Edgar's Welsh activities.

[39] For discussion of the treaty made with the Dunsæte, an agreement which does not seem to have been recorded in contemporary sources, see ch. 8, below.

[40] S. Baxter, 'MS C of the Anglo-Saxon Chronicle and the Politics of Mid-Eleventh Century England', *EHR* 122 (2007), pp. 1189–1227.

[41] Halsall, Anthropology and the Study of Pre-Conquest Warfare and Society, pp. 155–77. For discussion of this paper, see above, pp. 15–17. Extracts here are from *Annales Cambriae*, ed. J. Williams ab Ithel, RS 20 (London, 1860), pp. 14–25. Extracts up to 950 are from the tenth-century 'A' version; other extracts, including additions to the text from the 'A' version marked thus < > are from later MSS.

[42] A late source, the *Brut y Tywysogion* ('Chronicle of the Princes') s.a. 918 (*Brut y Tywysogion: The Gwentian Chronicle of Caradoc of Llancarvan*, ed. and trans. A. Owen, *Journal of the Cambrian Archæological Association* supplement (1863), pp. 20–1) conflates the death of Æthelflæd with the *Annales Cambriae* record of the battle of Dinas Newydd, s.a. 921, suggesting that Dinas Newydd was a battle against the prince of Glamorgan and Gwent. It is possible that this was a memory of Æthelflæd's campaign which included the attack on Llangorse (ASC MR 916) but this seems unlikely and we cannot be certain that *Dinas Newydd* was an Anglo-Welsh battle, and so it is not included here.

941 Athelstan <king of the Saxons> is dead.

943 Cadell son of Arthfael is dead by poison. And Idwal <son of Rhodri> and his son Elisedd are killed by the Saxons.

946 Cyngen son of Elisedd died by poison. And Eneuris bishop in Mynyw died. And Strathclyde was laid waste by the Saxons.

947 Edmund king of the Saxons was murdered.

950 … And Cadwgan ap Owain is murdered by the Saxons. And the battle [*bellum*] of Carno <between the sons of Hywel and the sons of Idwal>

[N.B. Following entries from later MSS]

968 [*approx.: entry not dated*]   The English laid waste the land of the sons of Idwal [i.e. Gwynedd]

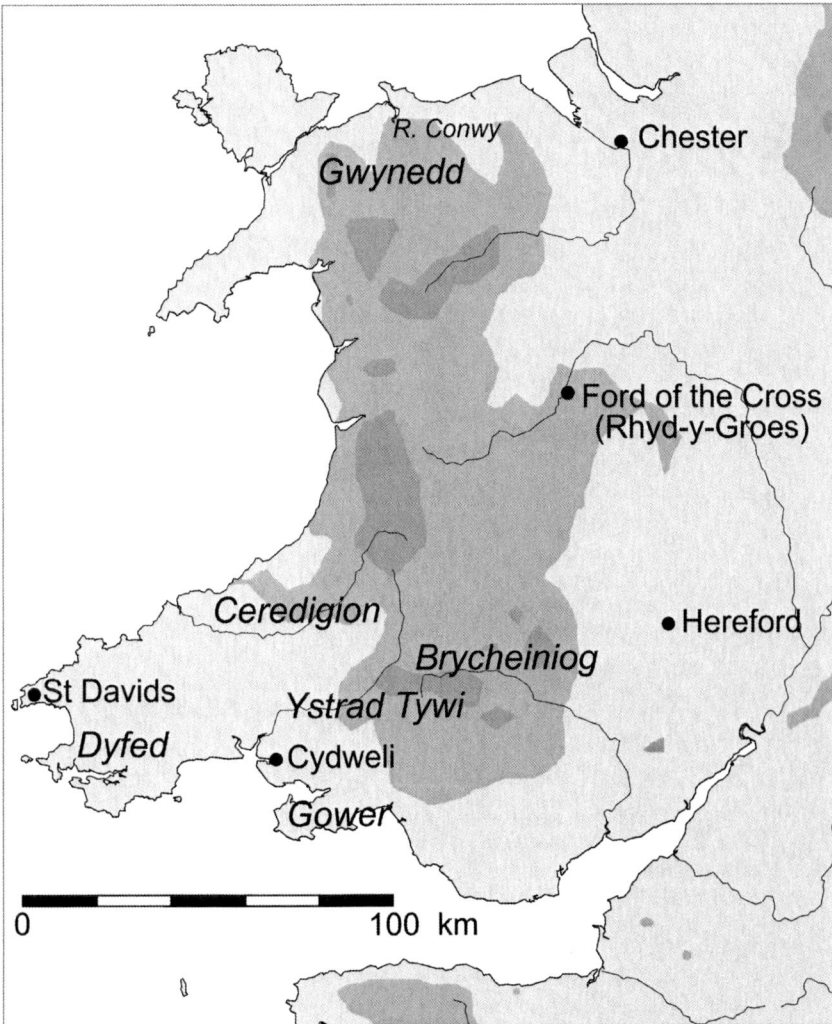

Fig. 2.1 Locations of English actions recorded in the *Annales Cambriae*

973   The meeting of the ships in the city of the Legions [i.e. Chester] by Edgar the King of the Saxons

975   Edgar King of the English died. Idwal ap Owain died.

983 [*approx.*]   Hywel ap Idwal and Alfre [Ælfhere or Ælfric, ealdorman of Mercia] *dux* of the English laid waste Brycheiniog and all of the lands of Einion ap Owain [i.e. Deheubarth][43] but Einion killed many of them.

985   Idwal was killed by the English.

993   Guyn ap Eynau, with the aid of the English *dux* Æthelsige[44] and the right side of Britain [South Wales?], devastated the lands of Maredudd, i.e. Demetia [Dyfed], Ceredigion, Gŵyr and Cydweli. A third of Menevia [St Davids] was laid waste.

1012   Menevia was laid waste by the Saxons, namely Edric and Ubi. The shipwreck of Swein father of Cnut.

1014   Swegn came to the land of the English. Æthelred son of Edgar was exiled from his kingdom because Swein invaded, but he himself [i.e. Swein] died.

1016   Cnut son of Swein seized the kingdom of the English.

1035   Maredudd ap Edwin was killed by the sons of Cynan; Caradog ap Rederch was killed by the English. Cnut son of Swein, king of the English, died.

1039   The Gentiles took Meurig ap Hywel. Iacob, King of the Venedotiae [Gwynedd] was killed. Gruffudd ap Llywelyn began to reign in North Wales; while he reigned, he was attacked by the English and Gentiles. He engaged in battle with them in the Ford of the Cross [i.e. Rhyd-y-Groes][45] on the River Severn and defeated them. In the same year he ruled the Britons on the right side and expelled Hywel ap Edwin from there.

1055   Gruffudd ap Llywelyn killed Gruffudd ap Rhydderch and laid waste Hereford.

1056[46]   Magnus son of Harold [Hardrada] laid waste the land of the English aided by Gruffudd King of Britain.

---

[43] For Einion ap Owain's kingship, see Maund, *Welsh Kings*, pp. 53–5.

[44] This *dux* cannot be corroborated with any other character by the name 'Æthelsige', suggesting that the term *dux* was probably not a reference to an ealdormanry. He is referred to as 'Æthelsige 22' in the *Prosopography of Anglo-Saxon England* database <www.pase.ac.uk> (accessed 18 Sept. 2009). For the land-appropriation in England of a noble or nobles by the name of Æthelsige around this time, see Keynes, *Diplomas of King Æthelred*, pp. 184–5.

[45] This is identified by R. Owen, 'Welsh Pool and Powys-land: A History of the Town and Borough of Welsh Pool, and the Surrounding District', *Montgomeryshire Collections* 29 (1896), pp. 161–288, at p. 219.

[46] Probably 1058 (ASC D *s.a.*).

1063   Gruffudd ap Llywelyn, most noble king of Britain, was killed by the deceit of his [men].

1066   Harold King of the Goths attempted to subject the English to himself, whom the other Harold son of Godwine caught and killed by sudden attack. He himself, however, William the Bastard, duke of the Normans, deprived of the English kingdom by possession of glorious victory.

Thus over two centuries, the 'Saxons' – a term which gradually gave way to 'English' (*Angli*) – were recorded in the *Annales Cambriae* as responsible for the deaths of seven members of Welsh royal dynasties. Given the number of kings and kingdoms in Wales during this period, this was hardly a relentless tide of regicides, but the impact was still substantial, especially when the English are seen as active participants in internecine Welsh warfare.[47] Welsh references to English events are also notable. Although, in the light of the implications of the Norman Conquest of England for Welsh rulers, it should hardly surprise us that the events of 1066 were recorded with such clarity,[48] the Scandinavian spellings of Viking names and the English spellings of English names are noteworthy. They may suggest a significant degree of English influence upon this Welsh source, although later scribal influences should be acknowledged in what are later manuscripts of earlier records.[49]

While it is pertinent, as Stephen Baxter has noted, that a number of tenth-century English actions in Wales are not recorded in Anglo-Saxon sources, Baxter considers the growth of the power of Gruffudd ap Llywelyn 'could not fail to register in English sources'.[50] It is perhaps for this reason, as well as because of the links with the positions of English earls, that eleventh-century Anglo-Welsh warfare often receives more historiographical attention than that of the ninth and tenth centuries.[51] However, the number of kings and rulers killed by the English between the ninth and eleventh centuries suggests some regularity, maybe even continuity, of border battles throughout the later Anglo-Saxon period. If such actions were not confined to the upheaval of the immediate pre-Conquest period, we may infer that raiding played an important part in Anglo-Welsh relations. For this reason, it is interesting, as Richard Abels has observed, that Chester seems to have had the most effective military system, which was still operating in the

---

[47] Maund, *Welsh Kings*, pp. 37–70, for a general survey of the mid ninth to eleventh centuries. For an indication of the politics of Welsh kingdoms in this period, see Davies, *Patterns of Power in Early Wales*, pp. 32–47.

[48] For the Continental significance of noting the significance of the Norman Conquest, see E. van Houts, 'The Norman Conquest Through European Eyes', *EHR* 110 (1995), pp. 832–53.

[49] K. Hughes, 'The Welsh Latin Chronicles: *Annales Cambriae* and related texts', *Proceedings of the British Academy* 59 (1973), pp. 233–58.

[50] Baxter, *Earls of Mercia*, p. 86.

[51] See, e.g., Baxter, *Earls of Mercia*, pp. 86–7; Maund, 'Welsh Alliances of Earl Ælfgar of Mercia'; DeVries, 'Harold Godwinson in Wales'; I. W. Walker, *Harold: The Last Anglo-Saxon King* (Stroud, 1997), pp. 77–90.

years preceding the Norman Conquest.[52] Anglo-Welsh wars in the tenth century should be considered in the light of the campaigns of the 1050s and 1060s. One further observation may also be made: if elements of the English army of 1066 can be thought of as battle-hardened by the Welsh campaigns,[53] then the lack of Viking wars in the reign of Edgar should not by themselves have diminished military effectiveness in the reign of Æthelred II. Mercian warriors and, indeed, Northumbrian warriors had been active in fighting border wars before the resurgence of Viking activities in England toward the end of the tenth century (see above, chapter 1, for a discussion of generations in military service). This may indicate why opposition from Mercia proved tough for the Viking attackers of the early eleventh century.[54]

'Anglo-Scottish' relations were somewhat different from 'Anglo-Welsh' ones in this period. Anglo-Saxon military expeditions into what is now Scotland encountered not only 'Scots' but Britons, Gaels, and Picts. Nonetheless, the developing unity of a kingdom of *Alba* is a characteristic of this period in Scottish history.[55] Perhaps this political unity may show why the nature of the military campaigns in Scotland was different from that of Wales. The campaigns of Athelstan and Edmund during the second quarter of the tenth century should be seen in the light of Anglo-Scottish relations, as they saw territorial aggrandizement in Scottish territory. In a sense, however, this was a relatively new phenomenon for the nascent English kingdom. While western Welsh were neighbours of the West Saxons in one form or other throughout the history of the West Saxon kingdom,[56] the northern neighbours of the expanding kingdom shifted during the period covered by this volume, from Mercians to Northumbrians, to the Britons of Strathclyde and, finally, to the kingdom of the Scots.

This volume focuses more on events towards the south of the English kingdom, as they are associated with the established interests of the West Saxon kingdom. Nonetheless, northern relations are significant to late Anglo-Saxon warfare. The record in *De Obsessione Dunelmi* ('On the siege of Durham') of the treatment of the heads of the Scottish dead after Uhtred of Bamburgh's relief of Durham in 1006 is worth noting here, as it may show the manner in which Scots could be treated as 'other'.[57]

[52] Abels, 'From Alfred to Harold II', p. 29. For a discussion of Chester, see below, pp. 215–16.

[53] F. Barlow, *Edward the Confessor*, English Monarchs (London, 1970), pp. 211–12, refers to the campaign of 1063 as marking 'the rebirth of England as a military power'.

[54] Viking activities in the 'Second Viking Age' were mostly in the south of England until very late in the Æthelred's reign (see e.g. ASC CDE 1016).

[55] A. Woolf, *From Pictland to Alba: 789–1070*, New Edinburgh History of Scotland 2 (Edinburgh, 2007).

[56] For the context of Wessex's western frontier in comparison with Northumbria, see J. R. Maddicott, 'Two Frontier States: Northumbria and Wessex, *c.* 650–750', in *The Medieval State: Essays Presented to James Campbell*, ed. J. R. Maddicott and D. Palliser (London, 2000), pp. 25–45.

[57] For this attitude in a later period, see J. Gillingham, 'Conquering the Barbarians: War and Chivalry in Twelfth-Century Britain', *HSJ* 4 (1993 for 1992), pp. 67–84, at pp. 79–80.

The aforesaid young man [Uhtred], seeing the land devastated by the enemy, and Durham surrounded by a siege and his father achieving nothing, assembled the army [*exercitus*] of the Northumbrians and of York, no little force [*manus*], and killed nearly all the horde of Scots, the king himself barely escaping through flight with a few men. The heads of the dead, with more elegant woven hair, as was then the custom in those times [*tunc temporibus*], he made to be transported to Durham; washed by four women, they were fixed on stakes all along the circuit of the walls. Moreover, they had given as payment to the women who had washed them a cow each.[58]

Of course, given Durham's northern location, the treatment of the heads of the dead may relate to Celtic practices,[59] and *De Obsessione's* sense of historicity in recording the custom 'in those times' of the wearing of the hair – conveniently braided for tying to stakes – is interesting in this respect.[60] The account details the treatment of the heads rather than the dead enemies' decapitations *per se*, suggesting that decapitation was not unusual. An English parallel for the displaying the heads of the dead Scots may be found in an Old English version of the *Seven Sleepers of Ephesus* legend, which indicates the manner in which the display of heads, perhaps as was the case in Durham, showed a ruler's imposition of authority. Adding to Gregory of Tours's version of the story, the Old English account tells of the heads of martyrs being displayed on head-stakes by a pagan ruler outside the walls of the town of Ephesus alongside those of executed thieves, hanging the headless bodies from the walls themselves.[61]

[58] *De Obsessione Dunhelmi*, in *Symeonis Monachi Opera Omnia*, ed. Arnold, vol. I, p. 216. An alternative translation is in C. J. Morris, *Marriage and Murder in Eleventh-Century Northumbria: A Study of 'De Obsessione Dunelmi'*, Borthwick Papers 82 (York, 1992), pp. 1–5. Morris (pp. 7–10) dates *De Obsessione* to either the 1070s or early twelfth century. See also B. Meehan, 'The Siege of Durham, the Battle of Carham and the Cession of Lothian', *Scottish Historical Review* 55 (1976), pp. 1–19.

[59] For a discussion of 'the cult of the severed head' in warfare in early Scotland, see N. Aitchison, *The Picts and the Scots at War* (Stroud, 2003), pp. 155–8. Thompson, *Dying and Death in Later Anglo-Saxon England*, pp. 193–4, argues, from a Northumbrian context, that the treatment of the Scots' bodies is undertaken out of respect.

[60] Cf. Morris, *Marriage and Murder*, p. 2, who reads 'perplexis' as a reference to Uhtred ordering the hair of the heads to be combed.

[61] *Aelfric's Lives of Saints*, ed. Skeat, vol. I, pp. 492–3. Cf. Gregory of Tours, *Glory of the Martyrs*, ed. and trans. R. Van Dam, Translated Texts for Historians, Latin Series 3 (Liverpool, 1988), pp. 116–17, which does not include these details. For a consideration of the meaning of such urban display, see below, ch. 6. For Ælfric's 'sense for sense' tradition of translation in the *Catholic Homilies*, see J. Hill, 'Translating the Tradition: Manuscripts, Models and Methodologies in the Composition of Ælfric's *Catholic Homilies*', in *Textual and Material Culture in Anglo-Saxon England: Thomas Northcote Toller and the Toller Memorial Lectures*, ed. D. Scragg, Publications of the Manchester Centre for Anglo-Saxon Studies I (Cambridge, 2003), pp. 241–59.

The advent of the Vikings

There is some debate regarding the impact and nature of the threat posed by the Vikings. Were they a major force which changed the nature of Anglo-Saxon society and politics because of the raids themselves or indeed because of their very existence? It may be argued that a concept of Vikings and Viking behaviour existed, certainly by the later tenth century. This had a major impact on the operation of English politics during the reign of Æthelred II, but arguably also as early as the early ninth century, when a grave marker from Lindisfarne was made (Fig. 2.2) depicting the agents of Apocalypse as Vikings, armed with weapons which were frighteningly realistic including what looked like contemporary swords. As such, it matters less whether the Vikings actually behaved as agents of Apocalpyse, wreaking bloody violence with an apparent lack of discrimination, or whether they were thought to behave as such by at least some sections of English society.[62] In terms of warrior expectations the behaviour of Vikings represented a shock to Anglo-Saxon military society, perhaps as much so in the late tenth century – with new ships – as in the early ninth.[63] Their mobility and the implications of that mobility have been addressed by, amongst others, Guy Halsall and Richard Abels.[64] The manner in which warfare operated on accepted social norms can thus be highlighted and the occasions where those norms were broken can be seen in context as deliberate infringements, not necessarily as evidence of Viking ferocity *per se*.[65] Halsall drew attention to the possible use of expected norms of warfare – in effect the pre-arranged arrival of groups of warriors – in such cases as the arrival of ships at Portland and the Vikings' activities at *Cwicelmshlaew*, a known meeting place in the landscape where a group of Vikings challenged the English warriors to battle (Cuckhamsley Barrow or Scutchamer Knob, Oxon.; see Fig. 2.3).[66] While it is less likely that Portland was seen by the West Saxons as a mutually understood location for battle, the inversion of expectations at *Cwicelmshlaew* in the Vikings' seizure of an symbolic point in the landscape is significant to note here, suggesting a 'Viking awareness' of Anglo-Saxon attitudes. As the Vikings were, in effect, summoning the local English warriors to an assembly, the

---

[62] M. Godden, 'Apocalypse and Invasion in Late Anglo-Saxon England', in *From Anglo-Saxon to Early Middle English: Essays Presented to E. G. Stanley*, ed. M. Godden, D. Gray, and T. Hoad (Oxford, 1994), pp. 130–62. For the context of responses, see also P. A. Stafford, 'Church and Society in the Age of Aelfric', in *The Old English Homily and its Backgrounds*, P. E. Szarmach and B. F. Huppé (Albany, NY, 1978), pp. 11–42, at pp. 30–2.

[63] For discussion of ships, see below, ch. 4.

[64] Halsall, 'Playing by Whose Rules?', pp. 2–12; see also Halsall, *Warfare and Society in the Barbarian West*, pp. 154–6; R. P. Abels, 'English Logistics and Military Administration, 871–1066: The Impact of the Viking Wars', in *Military Aspects of Scandinavian Society in a European Perspective, AD 1–1300*, ed. A. Nørgård Jørgensen and B. L. Clausen, PNM Studies in Archaeology and History 2 (Copenhagen, 1997), pp. 257–65.

[65] P. Griffith, *The Viking Art of War* (London, 1996), pp. 134–6. However, cf. M. P. Spiedel, 'Berserks: A History of Indo-European "Mad Warriors"', *Journal of World History* 13 (2002), pp. 253–90.

[66] Halsall, 'Anthropology and the Study of Pre-Conquest Warfare and Society', pp. 164–6.

Fig. 2.2 Grave marker from Lindisfarne, depicting Viking warriors armed with contemporary weapons

Fig. 2.3 Scutchamer Knob, East Hendred, Oxfordshire (formerly Berkshire): an Anglo-Saxon assembly site, from which a Viking force issued a challenge to battle in 1006

failure to respond to the challenge may be indicative less of cowardice on the part of the English than a refusal to respond to the Vikings' control of the landscape.[67]

However, the extracts dealt with here are sources which see England and the English from a Scandinavian perspective. The Viking warrior ethos stood in a similar milieu to that of the Anglo-Saxons depicted in their own war poetry. The memorial rune-stones of late Viking warriors who had fallen in battle while campaigning in England are testament to the manner in which the English campaigns were seen with a sense of glory and the Skaldic poetry (preserved from the tenth and eleventh centuries in later saga material) recorded English resilience against Viking attacks, presenting the English as worthy adversaries.[68] Although Anglo-Saxon warrior society was already infused with (or, at the least, veneered with) Christian values by the ninth century, to be followed by Scandinavian society in the tenth and eleventh century, it is remarkable that Anglo-Saxons and Vikings shared similar values and, to an extent, similar cultures.[69] In a characteristically acute observation, Patrick Wormald noted that the Anglo-Saxon warriors had more in common with their Viking adversaries, despite the religious differences, than they had with the less wealthy majority of their own countrymen.[70] This may help to explain why Anglo-Saxon kingdoms, like some Frankish provinces, were able to side with Vikings where the circumstances suited them: such actions were not the dramatic political shift that is sometimes portrayed by Christian sources.[71]

[67] Cf. Halsall, 'Anthropology and the Study of Pre-Conquest Warfare and Society', p. 166, and Halsall, *Warfare and Society in the Barbarian West*, p. 157. For discussion of the West Saxons' refusal to respond at *Cwicelmslæw*, see Lavelle, *Aethelred II*, pp. 117–18. The charter relating to the shire moot at *Cwicelmslæw* is S 1454 (AD 990×2). The barrow is discussed by H. Williams, *Death and Memory in Early Medieval Britain*, Cambridge Studies in Archaeology (Cambridge, 2006), pp. 207–10. See Page, 'A Most Vile People', p. 28, for discussion of the Vikings' heroic behaviour in boasting at Scutchamer Knob, a place which, James Campbell has argued, was in the safe 'heartland' of the English kingdom: 'England, c. 991', in *The Battle of Maldon: Fiction and Fact*, ed. J. Cooper (London, 1993), pp. 1–17, at p. 15.

[68] See R. G. Poole, 'Skaldic Verse and Anglo-Saxon History: Some Aspects of the Period 1009–1016', *Speculum* 62 (1987), pp. 265–98; R. G. Poole, *Viking Poems on War and Peace: A Study in Skaldic Narrative*, Toronto Medieval Texts and Translations 8 (London, 1991).

[69] See J. Jesch, 'Skaldic Verse in Scandinavian England', in *Vikings and the Danelaw: Select Papers of the Thirteenth Viking Congress*, ed. J. Graham-Campbell, R. Hall, J. Jesch, and D. N. Parsons (Oxford, 2001), pp. 313–25.

[70] P. Wormald, 'The Ninth Century', in *The Anglo-Saxons*, ed. J. Campbell (London, 1982), pp. 132–59, at p. 134. However, Wormald also notes the significance of the Vikings as pagans: 'Viking Studies: Whence and Whither?', in *The Vikings*, ed. R. T. Farrell (Chichester, 1982), pp. 128–53.

[71] R. Lavelle, 'The Politics of Rebellion: The Ætheling Æthelwold and West Saxon Royal Succession', in *Challenging the Boundaries of Medieval History: The Legacy of Timothy Reuter*, ed. P. Skinner, SEMA 22 (Turnhout, 2009), pp. 51–80; J. Campbell, 'What is not known about the Reign of Edward the Elder', in *Edward the Elder, 899–924*, ed. N. J. Higham and D. H. Hill (London, 2001), pp. 12–24. For a discussion of Pippin II's rebellious activities in Aquitaine, including the employment of Vikings, see J. Martindale, 'Charles the Bald and the Government of the Kingdom of Aquitaine', in *Charles the Bald: Court and Kingdom*, ed. M. Gibson and J. L. Nelson, BAR International Series 101 (Oxford, 1981), pp. 109–35.

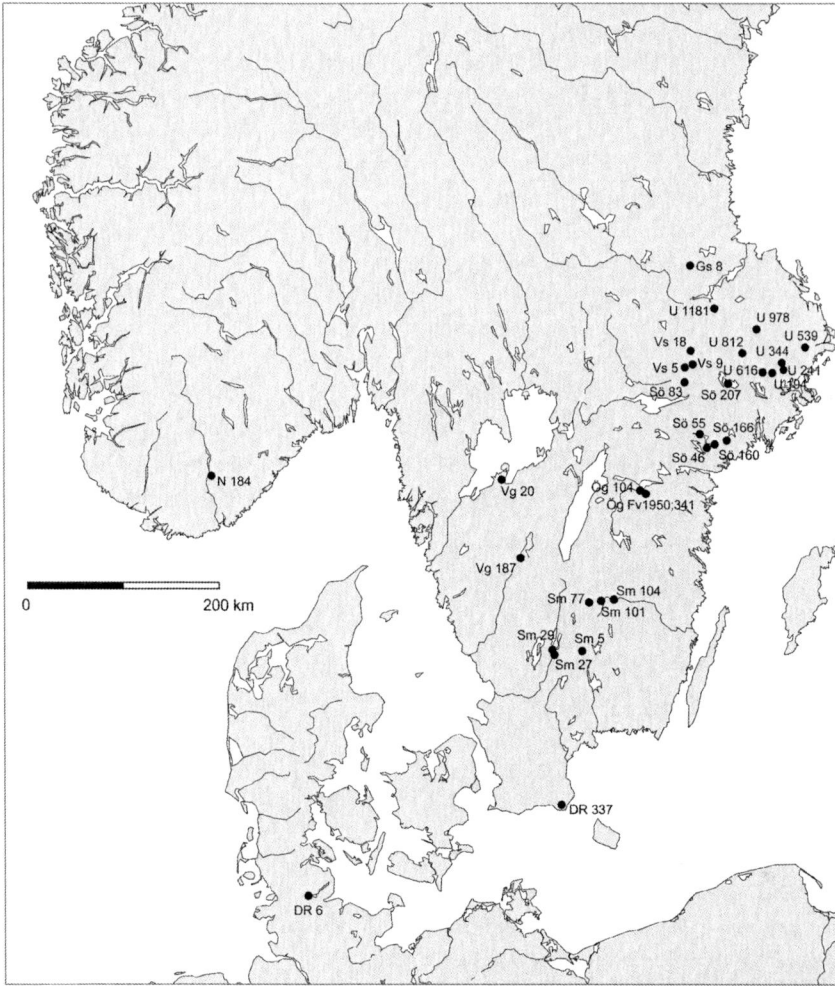

Fig. 2.4 Distribution of Viking Age rune-stones referring to expeditions in England

A small corpus of contemporary Scandinavian sources makes direct reference to Anglo-Saxon England. Of the most important are the memorial stones to Vikings who took part in expeditions to England in the late tenth and eleventh centuries,[72] many of whom were from Sweden (see Fig. 2.4 and Table 2.1), an area normally associated with Viking activities in Russia and the Baltic.[73] Some of these reveal England as a source of wealth, a place where geld could be won and thereafter,

---

[72] On the context of these stones, see B. Sawyer, *The Viking-Age Rune-Stones: Custom and Commemoration in Early Medieval Scandinavia* (Oxford, 2003), pp. 116–23, who notes (p. 123) that the record of travellers' commemoration is due to 'questions about their property and inheritance', not the travels *per se*.

[73] The evidence for the origins of Scandinavian *lithsmen* is discussed in N. Lund, 'The Danish Perspective', in *The Battle of Maldon, AD 991*, ed. D. Scragg (Oxford, 1991), pp. 114–42, at pp. 119–30.

Table 2.1 Scandinavian rune-stones referring to England
from the late tenth and eleventh centuries

Inscription code	Location of stone	Translation of transcription*
U 194	Väsby, Uppland, Sweden	Áli/Alli had this stone raised in memory of himself. He took Knútr's geld in England. May God help his spirit.
U 241	Lingsberg, Uppland, Sweden	And Danr and Húskarl and Sveinn had the stone erected in memory of Ulfríkr, their father's father. He had taken two geld in England. May God and God's mother help the souls of the father and son.
U 344	Yttergärde, Uppsala, Sweden; now in Orkesta, Sweden	And Ulfr has taken three gelds in England. That was the first that Tosti paid. Then Þorketill paid. Then Knútr paid.
U 539	Husby-Sjuhundra, Uppland, Sweden	Djarfr and Órœkja and Vígi and Jógeirr and Geirhjalmr, all of these brothers had / this stone raised in memory of Sveinn, their brother. He died in Jútland. He meant to / travel to England. May God and God's mother help his spirit and soul better than he deserved.
U 616	Tång, Uppland, Sweden	<fir–riui> had the monument erected in memory of his father Bósi(?)/Bausi(?) and (his) brother <kuru->. May God help <ul> <kuru> fell abroad in England.
U 812	Hjälsta, Uppland, Sweden	… his father. He died in England [N. B. complete transcription]
U 978	Gamla Uppsala, Uppland, Sweden	Sigviðr, traveller to England, raised this stone in memory of Védjarfr, (his) father … …
U 1181	Lilla Runhällen, Uppland, Sweden	… had (the stone) cut … (in memory of) himself, traveller to England, grandfather of <kunu-s>.
Sö 46	Hormesta, Södermanland, Sweden	Áskell and Gnauðimaðr(?) raised this stone in memory of their brother Sverri(?), who died in England. Ketill and Spakr(?) made this monument.
Sö 55	Bjudby, Södermanland, Sweden	Þorsteinn had this stone raised in memory of himself and his son Hefnir. The young valiant man travelled to England; then died grievously at home. May God help their souls. Brúni and Slóði, they carved this stone.
Sö 83	Tumbo, Södermanland, Sweden	He drowned in England's … [N. B. fragmentary, no longer extant]
Sö 160	Råby, Södermanland, Sweden	Eybjôrn raised this stone in memory of Skerðir. He died in the retinue [lið] in England

Table 2.1 *continued*

Inscription code	Location of stone	Translation of transcription*
Sö 166	Grinda, Södermanland, Sweden	Grjótgarðr (and) Einriði, the sons made [the stone] in memory of [their] able father. Guðvér was in the west; divided [up] payment in England; manfully attacked townships in Saxony.
Sö 207	Överselö, Södermanland, Sweden	Guð-... ... his father. He competently travelled to England. May God help his soul.
Vs 5	Vändle, Västmanland, Sweden	<kra-hni-> had the stone raised ... travelled to England, died in Spjallboði's ... May God help his soul ... Siggi cut the runes.
Vs 9	Saltängsbron, Västmanland, Sweden	Gísl had the bridge made in memory of Ásl/Ôsl, his son. He died in England. May God help his spirit and soul.
Vs 18	Berga, Västmanland, Sweden	Gunnvaldr had this stone raised in memory of Geirfastr, his son, a good valiant man. And (he) had travelled to England. May God help his soul.
Gs 8	Torsåker, Gästrikland, Sweden	Åsmundr ... ... He was abroad in the west in England ...
Ög 104	Gillberga, Östergötland, Sweden	Rauðr raised this stone in memory of Tóki, his brother, a very good valiant man, who was killed in England.
Ög Fv 1950;341	Kallerstad, Östergötland, Sweden; now in Linköping	...-björn and Ásbjôrn, they raised this stone in memory of Vígfastr, their father, Helga's son. He died in England.
Vg 20	Västanåker, Västergötland, Sweden	... raised the stone in memory of Guðmarr(?), his son, who was killed in England.
Vg 187	Vist, Västergötland, Sweden	Geiri placed this stone in memory of Guði, his brother, who forfeited his life in England.
Sm 5	Transjö, Småland, Sweden	Gautr placed this stone in memory of Ketill / his son. He was / the most unvillainous of men, who forfeited his life in England.
Sm 27	Berga, Småland, Sweden	Þórðr raised this/these(?) monument(s) ... met his end in England.
Sm 29	Ingelstad, Småland, Sweden	... raised the stone in memory of Þorgeirr, his father. He met his end in England.

Table 2.1 *continued*

Inscription code	Location of stone	Translation of transcription*
Sm 77	Sävsjö, Småland, Sweden	Vrái placed this stone in memory of Gunni, his brother. He died in England.
Sm 101	Nöbbelesholm, Småland, Sweden	Gunnkell placed this stone in memory of Gunnarr, his father, Hróði's son. Helgi laid him, his brother, in a stone coffin in Bath in England.
Sm 104	Vetlanda, Småland, Sweden	… in the west in England(?).
DR 337	Valleberga, Scania, now Sweden	Sveinn and Þorgautr/Þorgunn made this monument in memory of Manni and Sveini. / May God well help their souls. And they lie in London.
DR 6	Schleswig cathedral, now Germany	… had the stone raised in memory of / … … … dead … … and Guðmundr, they / carved the runes. [He] rests at Skía [Shoebury, Essex or Skidby, Yorks.]† in England. Christ … …
N 184	Galteland, Norway	Arnsteinn raised this stone in memory of Bjórr his son who died in the retinue [*i liði*] when Knútr attacked England. God is one.

* Translations from Rundata 2.5 for Windows, Uppsala Universitet, Samnordisk runtextdatabas (Scandinavian runic-text database), <http://www.nordiska.uu.se/forskn/samnord.htm> (accessed 12 Oct. 2009); translations of many of these stones are also in S. B. F. Jansson, The Runes of Sweden, trans. P. G. Foote (London, 1962), pp. 48–61.

† O. Pritsak, The Origin of Rus', vol. 1: Old Scandinavian Sources other than the Sagas (Cambridge, MA, 1981), p. 342.

as the Grinda rune-stone (Sö 166) records, divided – thus showing the fruits of military campaigning. None of these laconic sources explicitly reveal the English to have been worthy opponents, but observations can nonetheless be made. One is that England was an integral part of the North Sea world of the Vikings. This is not only because the rune-stones are from a time when Christianity was becoming widespread in Scandinavia, but may be seen in the easy familiarity with English places displayed by the stones. The other is that although it would be rash to assume that every one of these references is necessarily to Vikings who fought in battles, the military context of many of the references is notable.

In looking at the English as victims of Scandinavian *liths* and the mortality of those Scandinavian warriors who were wealthy enough to get Christian stones erected in their memory, three Uppland stones (U 194, U 241, and U 344) are most noteworthy in their references to England as a source of geld payments. As the three stones share a stylistic similarity, references to geld payments may have been the custom of one regional school of carving, as it could hardly be suggested that Upplanders were the only recipients of geld. Perhaps other warriors who had been in England did not see this as the most important issue to record, even if, as David Wilson has argued, there was an economic imperative in Denmark at least for the receipt of geld to pay for the massive state projects of the tenth century.[74]

The reference in the Grinda stone (Sö 166) to geld 'divided up' shows the real significance of geld – the one who divided the geld demonstrated his leadership.[75] It is relevant to note here that while we might expect those Scandinavian sources that survive to make reference to Viking depredations in England, the receipt of money seems to be of a high priority, thus indicating that mercenary service may have been an important component of the Viking view of the English kingdom.[76] Furthermore, given the eleventh-century context of the rune-stones, it is possible that they included references to Scandinavians who had taken service as housecarls in England. The Nöbbelesholm rune-stone's reference to 'a stone coffin in Bath' (Sm 101) suggests that such service could be related to settlement, perhaps like that of Urk (or Orc), a housecarl who founded Abbotsbury in Dorset,[77] or may even have stemmed from the sojourn of a Viking army in Bath recorded in the Anglo-Saxon Chronicle entry for 1013.[78] To this end, the rune-stone's record of the name of Bath in a form shared with the Old English *Bathum* (i.e. a plural form, as 'Baths') suggests a degree of continuing contact and influence.[79]

Fig. 2.5 Rune-stone (U 344) from Yttergärde, Uppsala, Sweden, recording gelds taken in England

---

[74] D. M. Wilson, 'Danish Kings and England in the Late Tenth and Early Eleventh Century: Economic Interpretations', *ANS* 3 (1981 for 1980), pp. 188–96.

[75] For an early example of the significance of the ruler's division of treasure (albeit recounted for didactic purposes), see *Gregorii episcopi turonensis historiarum libri X*, ed. B. Krusch, MGH Scriptores Rerum Merovingicarum 1.1 (Hanover, 1937), II.27, pp. 71–3; trans. L. Thorpe, *Gregory of Tours: The History of the Franks* (Harmondsworth, 1974), pp. 139–40. WM, *GR* II.28, p. 422, also refers to the problems arising from Harold's reluctance to share the spoils of the Battle of Stamford Bridge.

[76] See Abels 'Household Men, Mercenaries and Vikings', pp. 155–7, and below, pp. 107–10.

[77] For Urk's endowment, see S 1004 (AD 1044), 1063 (AD 1053×58), S 1064 (AD 1058×66); see S. Keynes, 'The Lost Cartulary of Abbotsbury', *ASE* 18 (1989), pp. 207–43.

[78] ASC CDE 1013; see below, pp. 256–7, for consideration of the context of this.

[79] See generally M. Townend, *Language and History in Viking Age England: Linguistic Relations between Speakers of Old Norse and Old English*, SEMA 6 (Turnhout, 2002).

The other significant written source is the corpus of Skaldic poetry recorded in many of the Norse sagas. Although sagas are much criticized for their unreliablity as historical records, their inclusion of stanzas of Skaldic verse, often composed in a formal fashion differing from those of the sagas, may reflect the survival of verses composed in a period prior to their inclusion in the sagas, perhaps even from the time to which they refer.[80] The intricacies of the poetry are not easily translated. As Roberta Frank has put it, 'skaldic poetry is a tantalizingly elusive source, resisting attempts at direct historical interrogation.'[81] However, Russell Poole's translation of *Liðsmannaflokkr*, which Poole has argued is a contemporary source, gives an indication of the worldview of eleventh-century Anglo-Viking expeditions.[82]

Let us go ashore, before warriors and large militias [*morðs ferðir*] learn that the English homelands are being traversed with shields: let us be brave in battle, brandish spears and hurl them; great numbers of the English flee before our swords.

Many an impetuous warrior puts on today the ugly old shirt, where we were born and bred: once more let us nourish the raven on the blood of Englishmen; the cautious poet will slip into that kind of shirt which the hammer sews.

That garrulous reveller who brings the girl up will be eager to make no undue haste to redden his sword at night: the warrior does not carry a shield ashore into English territory at this early hour, enraged, in quest of gold.

Þorkell's men [*liðar*] did not seem to me, as I saw [them], to lose time in joining battle – they did not fear the ringing of swords – before the Vikings fought a hard engagement on ?*hauðr*? heath; we encountered showers of weapons; the warband was in battle formation [*varð fylkt liði – harðða*].

This earl, who briskly broke the ravens' fast, seems to me outstanding – my clever girl asks if there was carnage – but the battle the king waged, on the banks of the Thames, seems a hard one to the bowmen.

Ulfcetel decided beforehand to await the Vikings, where spears made their din – the fighting grew fierce – and you saw from our appearance afterwards how that remorseless man could prevail against the bitter keeper of the stone [i.e. stronghold]; dissent arose.

Knútr decided, and commanded the Danes all to wait – the mighty warrior went bravely into battle – the army fought alongside the moat: lady, where we engaged the enemy forces, with helmets and mailcoats, it was almost as if a man held a maddened elk.

---

[80] For discussion of this, see Poole, *Viking Poems on War and Peace*, pp. 3–23.

[81] R. Frank, 'King Cnut in the Verse of his Skalds', in *The Reign of Cnut: King of England, Denmark and Norway*, ed. A. R. Rumble, SEHB (London, 1993), pp. 106–24, at p. 107.

[82] The extract is from Poole, *Viking Poems on War and Peace*, pp. 86–90. The dating of the poem ('composed almost contemporaneously with the events it describes') is discussed in Poole, 'Skaldic Verse and Anglo-Saxon History', pp. 284–6 (quotation at p. 286).

The pure widow who lives in stone[83] will look out – often weapons glitter in the air above the king in his helmet – [to see] how the Danish leader, eager for victory, valiantly assails the city's garrison; the sword rings against British mailcoats.[84]

Each morning, on the bank of the Thames, the lady sees swords stained with blood; the raven must not go hungry: the warrior who watches over Steinvor, north of Stad, does not redden his sword at this early hour.[85]

Every day the shield was stained with blood, [?lady?], where we were out [?early?] on our expedition with the king: now that these hard battles have been recently concluded, we can settle down, lady, in beautiful London.

Many of the allusions are, of course, stereotypical: the ravens and the visions of carnage portrayed in the poem are hardly surprising but the sense of the English kingdom as a theatre of war is apparent, as is the poet's sense of conquest. Poole has also noted the significance of the role attributed to Thorkell in the poem, which provides another perspective alongside the dominance of Cnut in the narratives of the English campaigns of 1014–16.[86] Although it takes a Russell Poole or Roberta Frank to bring out the political intrigue and the range of meanings from such stanzas, the references to war and siege cast light on other issues to be addressed in further chapters in this volume (chapters 6 and 7). The references to mailcoats highlight the importance of such equipment and the near-impregnability of London (or the perception thereof) but what we see here is the significance of the glimpses that the poem provides into the mentalities of professional, international warriors in the early eleventh century.

Studies of the Viking impact in England were much affected by the publication in 1962 of Peter Sawyer's *The Age of the Vikings*, which had tended to minimize the impact of Viking violence in early medieval Europe, both in terms of numbers and in terms of the expectations of violence perpetrated by Viking armies.[87] The best-known of these elements was a reassessment of the size of an army; Sawyer highlighted a chapter from the lawcode of King Ine (688–726), arguing that the pre-Viking expectations of a warband would have an influence on the interpretation of the size of 'armies':[88]

'Thieves' [*Ðeofas*] we call up to seven men, from seven to thirty-five a 'band' [*hloð*]; above that it is an 'army' [*here*].[89]

---

[83] Perhaps a reference to Queen Emma. For London's significance, see below, ch. 6.

[84] Given the context, 'English' is probably meant here, though encounters with Welsh are not impossible.

[85] Poole, *Viking Poems on War and Peace*, p. 95, suggests that the reference is to the parent or guardian of the lady to whom the poem is addressed, who was from north of Stad in Norway and evidently did not take part in the campaigns recorded in the poem.

[86] Poole, *Viking Poems on War and Peace*, pp. 99–107.

[87] P. H. Sawyer, *The Age of the Vikings* (London, 1962; 2nd edn, 1971). See also Sawyer, *Kings and Vikings: Scandinavia and Europe, AD 700–1100* (London, 1982).

[88] Sawyer, *Age of the Vikings*, p. 123.

[89] *Ine*, ch. 13.1: *Gesetze*, vol. I, pp. 94–5.

Of the works which were written in a climate of historiography affected by Sawyer's book, Nicholas Brooks's important 1979 article sought to reassess the size and impact of what he thought were substantial Viking armies.[90] The numbers of armies has been a consistent issue but Brooks's methodologies were hardly unsound, giving a consideration of the large fortified areas in which Vikings encamped, for example.[91] The size of fleets will be addressed in more detail in chapter 4, but the controversy of the size of fleets had implications for discussion of the size of armies, which had actually originated in Peter Sawyer's discussion of the extent of Viking settlement in 1958.[92] Sawyer pointed out the difficulties in estimating the sizes of fleets, given the presence of small boats with the large ships and many chroniclers' interests in exaggerating.[93] However, it may be observed that there is often some consistency of the numbers of vessels recorded. Sources from Al-Andalus, which had benefited from scientific methodological developments and an advanced naval system, recorded coastal destruction in 844 by a fleet numbering a hundred. Also, further large-scale raids were recorded in the ninth and tenth centuries, suggesting that while exaggeration was not impossible, the sense that sizeable Viking fleets were a significant problem was not an issue unique to Anglo-Saxon England and Francia.[94]

The question of numbers was not the only matter, however. Writing in the aftermath of the impact of Sawyer's studies, Brooks highlighted the sense of the violent impact of Viking activities[95] and this has been an element of the study of Viking-Age violence since the 1980s. R. I. Page made a defence of Viking heroics in the face of early and high medieval historians' opinions of the Vikings as 'a most vile people',[96] while Patrick Wormald made a strong case for the Vikings as a group who were significantly different, as pagans, from their early medieval contemporaries (even if Anglo-Saxon aristocrats shared some of the same martial values).[97] Although opinions of the Scandinavian impact on European history

[90] N. P. Brooks, 'England in the Ninth Century: The Crucible of Defeat', *TRHS* 5th ser. 29 (1979), pp. 1–20.

[91] Brooks, 'England in the Ninth Century', pp. 10–11.

[92] P. H. Sawyer, 'The Density of the Danish Settlement in England', *University of Birmingham Historical Journal* 6 (1958), pp. 1–17, at pp. 3–4.

[93] Sawyer, *Age of the Vikings*, pp. 123–7.

[94] L. V. Mott, 'Iberian Naval Power, 1000–1650', in *War at Sea in the Middle Ages and Renaissance*, ed. J. B. Hattendorf and R. W. Unger, Warfare in History (Woodbridge, 2003), pp. 105–18, at p. 105; J. Stefánsson, 'The Vikings in Spain. From Arabic (Moorish) and Spanish Sources', *Saga Book of the Viking Society* 6 (1909–10), pp. 31–46. A recent study is E. Morales Romero, *Historia de los Vikingos en España: Ataques e Incursiones contra los Reinos Cristianos y Musulmanes de la Península Ibérica en los siglos IX–XI* (Madrid, 2004); in English a basic introduction is provided by D. Nicolle, 'Moor against Majus: The Defence of Spain and Morocco against the Vikings, 844–972 AD', *Osprey Military Journal* 2:3 (2000), pp. 23–32. The issue of comparability of figures across England, Ireland, Francia and Spain is considered by Brooks, 'England in the Ninth Century', pp. 3–4.

[95] Brooks, 'England in the Ninth Century', pp. 12–13.

[96] Page, 'A Most Vile People'.

[97] Wormald, 'Viking Studies: Whence and Whither?'; see also Wormald, 'Ninth Century', p. 134. For a recent consideration of the shared interests of the Vikings and their European

have developed to the extent that Angelo Forte, Richard Oram and Frederik Pederson have written of *Viking Empires*,[98] the views of Viking violence expounded by Sawyer have remained influential. Writing in 1991, Sarah Foot sought to place the Vikings' activity in the context of their Christian victims, highlighting the fact that the Christian authors were concerned that the violence against the church and its property was *heathen* violence rather than the notion that it was violence perpetrated by another ethnic group.[99] Guy Halsall sought to provide a context to the language of violence in the early medieval sources; giving a further twist to his anthropologically focused notions of early medieval violence discussed in his 1989 article,[100] Halsall noted the manner in which Viking violence was something which was conducted according to a different set of 'rules' to those expected in England, Francia, or Ireland. As violence could be enacted according to a reasoned set of expectations and with counter-expectations, Halsall shows how, when those expectations were broken and subverted, deliberately or otherwise, the Vikings could have a real impact. The first occasion of 'rule'-breaking was the arrival of Viking raiders at Lindisfarne. Halsall drew attention to the fact that Alcuin's letter expressed surprise that *such* a route across the sea would be made.[101] For Halsall, as for many commentators on the Viking Age, the use of the ship was fundamental. This is reflected in the Scandinavian sources' references to ships. Ships were among the 'special circumstances' which made Peter Sawyer's 'extension of normal Dark Age activity' possible.[102] Following up on his article on anthropology and violence, Halsall pointed out that amphibious Viking raids could not be compensated for because the aggrieved party or their kindred would not know where they could gain revenge or restitution, as they would in the numerous 'small wars' of pre-Viking England.[103] Whether we treat the larger Viking armies of the mid ninth, late tenth and early eleventh centuries as agglomerations of raiding parties, as Richard Abels has suggested, or as larger organized groups of the sort envisaged by Nicholas Brooks,[104] it is reasonable to suggest that the Vikings were seen as 'different'.

contemporaries, see Nelson, 'England and the Continent in the Ninth Century: II, The Vikings and Others'.

[98] A. Forte, R. Oram and F. Pedersen, *Viking Empires* (Cambridge, 2005).

[99] S. Foot, 'Violence Against Christians? The Vikings and the Church in Ninth-Century England', *Medieval History* 1 (1991), pp. 3–16.

[100] Halsall, 'Anthropology and the Study of Pre-Conquest Warfare and Society'. For discussion of this, see above, pp. 16–17.

[101] *Epistolae Karolini Aevi*, vol. 2, ed. E. Dümmler, MGH Epistolae 4 (Berlin, 1895), no. 16, p. 42; trans. *EHD 1*, p. 842; Halsall, 'Playing by Whose Rules?', p. 5.

[102] Sawyer, *Age of the Vikings*, pp. 202–3.

[103] Halsall, 'Playing by Whose Rules?', pp. 6–7.

[104] Abels, 'Alfred the Great, the *Micel Hæðen Here* and the Viking Threat'; Brooks, 'England in the Ninth Century'.

Their own worst enemy? Internal conflicts

In assessing the relations of the Viking-Age English, it is important to acknowledge the potential problems of warfare within the state itself. The pre-Conquest English kingdom did not experience internecine civil wars, at least not in the manner suffered by the Carolingian Frankish realm, and the relative unity of the tenth- and eleventh-century state is remarkable, an issue which has been in historical currency since James Campbell's seminal 1975 article, 'Observations on English Government'.[105] Nonetheless, internally destructive disputes amongst the pre-Conquest English nobility should be acknowledged, such as those of 1051–2. The Anglo-Saxon Chronicle entries for 1052 provide much evidence of the conduct of a military campaign on land and sea, showing the potential dangers of privately endowed warriors in the retinue of Earl Godwine of Wessex and his family bringing the state to a point of civil war. The Chronicle is therefore considered at length in later chapters with regard to what it can tell us about that campaign and the battle which nearly resulted from it but the events of 1052 tell us about the checks and balances within society. This may have stemmed from the Old English aristocracy's allegiance to notions of a state or collective identity, which could prevent such a civil war from getting out of hand.[106]

> The king [Edward] likewise had a great land force [*landfyrde*] on his side besides his sailors [*scypmannum*], but it was hateful to almost all of them that they should fight with their own kinsmen, because there was little else which was anything great except English men on either side; and also they did not wish that this land through this were more open to foreign people because they destroyed each other themselves. Then it was determined that wise men be sent in the meantime, and they agreed a truce [*grið*] with each side; [*D MS ends; C continues*] and Godwine and his son Harold set off with as many of their fleet [*lið*] as they thought suited them. And there was the meeting of the *witan*. And Godwine was entirely restored to his earldom as fully as he first held it, and thus henceforth; and all his sons [were restored] to all that they formerly held, and his wife and his daughter just as fully as they formerly held, and thus henceforth. And they established full friendship [*freondscipe*] between themselves, and promised good law to all the

---

[105] J. Campbell, 'Observations on English Government from the Tenth Century to the Twelfth Century', *TRHS* 5th series 25 (1975), pp. 39–54, and, putting paid to notions of English *encellulement* and 'feudal anarchy', J. Campbell, 'Was it Infancy in England? Some Questions of Comparison', in *England and her Neighbours, 1066–1453: Essays in Honour of Pierre Chaplais*, ed. M. Jones and M. Vale (London, 1989), pp. 1–17. For discussions of the limits of state authority, see P. Stafford, 'The Reign of Æthelred II: A Study in the Limitations of Royal Policy and Action', in *Ethelred the Unready: Papers from the Millenary Conference*, ed. D. H. Hill, BAR British Series 59 (Oxford, 1978), pp. 15–46, and C. Insley, 'Politics and Kinship in Early Eleventh-Century Mercia', *Midland History* 25 (2000), pp. 203–13.

[106] ASC CD 1052. For discussion of collective identity, see Williams, *World Before Domesday*, pp. 39–61. See also Wormald, '*Engla Lond*: The Making of an Allegiance', pp. 1–24. This issue is addressed in S. Baxter, 'The Limits and the End of the Anglo-Saxon State', in *Staat und Staatlichkeit im Europäischen Frühmittelalter, 500–1050: Grundlagen, Grenzen, Entwicklungen*, ed. W. Pohl (Vienna, 2009), pp. 503–13. See also below, ch. 8.

people. And they outlawed all the French men who had previous promoted bad law [*unlage*] and ordained bad judgements and given bad counsel in this country, except as many as they decided that the king wanted to have with him who were true to him and all his people.

Given that Stephen Baxter observed a distinctly Mercian bias in the C manuscript of the Anglo-Saxon Chronicle,[107] it is interesting that a picture of confrontation leading to internal composition is presented in this account. Here we should observe both the tensions between the factions in the 1050s, which *could* have led to civil war, and the manner in which the interests of that aristocracy could collectively bring those tensions to an end or at least alleviate them.[108] However, those tensions are relevant, especially so during the upheavals of the reign of Æthelred II: the local and regional interests of the nobility could take precedence over defence against Viking attackers, even manifesting itself in campaigns against a rival's territory, as was seen with the actions of the ætheling Edmund ('Ironside') and Earl Uhtred against the lands of Eadric *Streona* in Staffordshire and Shropshire in 1015.[109] It is also worth noting at this stage that naval campaigns often seem to have been related to the independence of interests in the eleventh century, with particular magnates using their fleets to commit acts of rebellion.[110] This was apparent in Wulfnoth *Cild*'s actions in 1009, the Godwine family's actions in 1052, and in the case of Harold's brother Tostig's initial attempt to repeat his family's earlier successes on the south coast in 1066.[111]

Even in the ninth century it had been more usual for the Anglo-Saxon kingdoms to fight with each other than with external enemies.[112] The West Saxons had gained domination, albeit temporarily, of Mercia in the second quarter of the ninth century,[113] although two generations later, in the 860s, the West Saxons' appearance alongside Mercians in the siege of Nottingham may indicate a brief policy of co-operation against a common enemy.[114] Nonetheless, the 'pan-English'

[107] Baxter, 'MS C of the Anglo-Saxon Chronicle'.

[108] This may have been because of the relatively even distribution (with some exceptions) of the landed interests of the nobility around the kingdom, an issue noted by C. Wickham, *Problems in Doing Comparative History*, The Reuter Lecture 2004 (Southampton, 2005), pp. 25–7. See also P. A. Clarke, *The English Nobility under Edward the Confessor*, Oxford Historical Monographs (Oxford, 1994); Stafford, *Unification and Conquest*, pp. 137, 150–61, and Baxter, *Earls of Mercia*, pp. 118–24; cf. R. Fleming, *Kings and Lords in Conquest England*, Cambridge Studies in Medieval Life and Thought 4th series 15 (Cambridge, 1991), pp. 53–104.

[109] ASC CDE 1015. See A. Williams, 'Cockles Amongst the Wheat: Danes and English in the Western Midlands in the First Half of the Eleventh Century', *Midland History* 11 (1986), pp. 1–22, at p. 5.

[110] Links of magnates with fleets are observed by J. Pullen-Appleby, *English Sea Power, c. 871 to 1100* (Hockwold-cum-Wilton, 2005), pp. 34–9.

[111] ASC CDE 1009 (see below, ch. 4); ASC CD and E 1052 (see below, ch. 5); ASC CD 1066.

[112] See generally D. Kirby, *The Earliest English Kings* (London, 1991) and Yorke, *Kings and Kingdoms of Early Anglo-Saxon England* (p. 148 for discussion of early ninth-century Wessex).

[113] ASC 825, 829.

[114] Abels, *Alfred the Great*, pp. 119–20; S. D. Keynes, 'King Alfred and the Mercians', in *Kings*,

agenda professed by the West Saxon kingdom in the initial stages of conquest in the course of the tenth century may have meant that it had more opponents than allies within the ranks of the Anglo-Scandinavian nobility. Such opposition had less to do with inherently Scandinavian interests of these new strata of nobility than with the fact that these areas had traditionally held differing interests.[115] It is notable here that Edward the Elder gained allies amongst the Anglo-Scandinavian communities of parts of the Danelaw, who bought into the tenth-century English kingdom relatively easily, suggesting that interests were pragmatic on a political level.[116] To see the tenth century as an extension of the pre-Viking age of the 'Heptarchy' would be to stretch a point, as West Saxon rulers did develop their interests through co-operation and mutual interest as much as through naked aggression.[117] However, to ignore that facet of Anglo-Saxon history would be to impose an ahistorically unified straightjacket upon the study of the period. Royal control was important, and the discussion in the following chapter is relevant to its imposition, but it is important to acknowledge the limitations of royal power when considering the military policies of the later Anglo-Saxon period.[118]

Currency and Alliances: History and Coinage of Southern England in the Ninth Century, ed. M. A. S. Blackburn and D. N. Dumville, Studies in Anglo-Saxon History 9 (Woodbridge, 1998), pp. 1–46.

[115] M. Innes, 'Danelaw Identities: Ethnicity, Regionalism and Political Allegiance', in *Cultures in Contact: Scandinavians and Natives in the Danelaw*, ed. D. Hadley and J. Richards, SEMA 2 (Turnhout, 2001), pp. 65–88; D. Hadley, *The Northern Danelaw: Its Social Structure, c. 800–1100*, SEHB (London, 2000), esp. pp. 298–308.

[116] C. Hart, *The Danelaw* (London, 1992), pp. 15–16, citing *Liber Eliensis*, ed. E. O. Blake, Camden 3rd series 92 (London, 1962), p. xi. See *Liber Eliensis* I.42, pp. 56–7, and II.25, pp. 98–9; trans. J. Fairweather, *Liber Eliensis: A History of the Isle of Ely from the Seventh Century to the Twelfth* (Woodbridge, 2005), pp. 76, 121. See generally A. Wareham, *Lords and Communities in Early Medieval East Anglia* (Woodbridge, 2005) and Abels, *Lordship and Military Obligation in Anglo-Saxon England*, pp. 89–91. For this issue in the east Midlands, see ASC ABCD 914, A 917, as well as S 397 (AD 926) and 548 (AD 949), discussed in P. H. Sawyer (ed.), *Charters of Burton Abbey*, Anglo-Saxon Charters 2 (Oxford, 1979), pp. 6–7. I am grateful to Rutha Titterton for drawing these charters to my attention.

[117] See generally Stafford, *Unification and Conquest*.

[118] This is a theme dealt with in Stafford, 'Reign of Æthelred II'.

Organization and Equipment: Land

THE organization of military forces in pre-Conquest England is a key topic of
Anglo-Saxon military history and a significant aspect of the development of
the state and social relations. While the conduct of campaigns and battles naturally remains an abiding interest, the ways in which able-bodied men provided
service to their lord and/or the state could be said to be fundamental to relations
within English society. Understandably, these issues have been a historiographical
focus for at least two centuries, being relevant to the study of property, the legitimacy of lordship, and the state's relations with its subjects. It should be added that
a good deal of the historiography on this topic relates to the significance of landed
property but the historiography and evidence pertaining to landed property are
dealt with in this chapter insofar as they relate to the organization and/or the
arming of warriors.[1]

There is a degree of artificiality in the way in which this chapter and the next
are arranged. The recruitment of warriors was intrinsically related to the allocation of resources for their equipment, which is why the latter issue is included
here rather than dealt with later in the book. In turn, equipment pertained to the
warriors' status and, presumably, their ability to maintain land. Similarly, naval
service was related to the equipment of an army on land and the recruitment of
mariners (although this is treated separately in chapter 4). Although much of this
chapter is concerned with the relationship between lordship and military service,
it is appropriate to deal first with the national 'myths' of universal military service
as these are fundamental to the constitutional history of the English state.

The nation at arms?

For the nineteenth-century historians who dealt with the military organization
of the Anglo-Saxon kingdom, the constitutional relationship between the free
peasant landholder (*ceorl*) and the ruler was of primary importance. (It should
be noted that the use of 'peasant' here is not pejorative but rather should be taken
as equivalent to the French *paysan*.) The right to bear arms in defence of the
state was seen as part of the essentially libertarian, even egalitarian, nature of
the pre-Conquest state and was related to political thinking on both sides of the

---

[1] For a fuller consideration of the historiography of landed property, see R. Lavelle, *Royal
Estates in Anglo-Saxon Wessex: Land, Politics and Family Strategies*, BAR British Series 439
(Oxford, 2007), ch. 1.

Atlantic,[2] as well as to the wider influence of the development of military participation in nineteenth-century states. Although in the nineteenth century Great Britain was unique among major European states in eschewing conscription,[3] historical military participation was seen as lending validity to the state's legitimacy. The fact that Anglo-Saxon freemen participated in the defence of the kingdom was an endorsement of its constitutional continuity in the form of the very history which gave the state its legitimacy.[4] Thus for Reinold Pauli, writing in the mid nineteenth century, the survival of the West Saxon state, in part through the agency of those who served with Alfred during his period in the wilderness at Athelney, was seen as the essence of the English nation.[5] Richard Abels characterizes such interpretations as 'the military corollary of an assumption shared by most Victorian scholars about the nature of early Germanic society'.[6] It was hardly an unreasonable assumption by those scholars, as the source material could be, and has been, read in this fashion. References to the idea of universal military participation could be read, for example, in the Anglo-Saxon Chronicle's entry for 1016,[7] referring to the mustering of a force by the ætheling Edmund.

> Then they abandoned that army [fyrding] and each man took himself home. Then after that festival [i.e. Epiphany] the army [fyrd] was again ordered, according to the full penalty [fullum wite], that every man who was living should go forth; then the king was sent to in London, and they asked him that he return to the army [fyrd] with the help which he might gather. When they all came together, it achieved nothing more than it often did before.

[2] For views of pre-Conquest England, see generally J. W. Burrow, *A Liberal Descent: English Historians and the English Past* (Cambridge, 1981), pp. 155–228; Chibnall, *Debate on the Norman Conquest*, pp. 53–68; H. A. MacDougall, *Racial Myth in English History: Trojans, Teutons and Anglo-Saxons* (Hanover, NH, 1982). For a discussion of 'Teutonic' ideas in nineteenth-century America, see R. Fleming, 'Picturesque History and the Medieval in Nineteenth-Century America', *American Historical Review* 100 (1995), pp. 1061–4.

[3] See, for example, E. M. Spiers, *The Late Victorian Army 1868–1902*, Manchester History of the British Army (Manchester, 1992), pp. 224–5. I am grateful to Mark Allen for this reference.

[4] A good general introduction to the subject of military participation is found in Keegan, *History of Warfare*, pp. 221–34. For a detailed discussion of the relationship between the distribution of power and military participation, see S. Andreski, *Military Organization and Society* (London, 1954; 2nd edn, 1968), although it should be noted that Andreski used rather simplified historical interpretations in applying his models of participation, in which the (understandably, given when he wrote) 'free peasant' of Anglo-Saxon society figured large (pp. 64–5). W. Stubbs, *The Constitutional History of England in its Origin and Development*, vol. 1 (Oxford, 1854; 2nd edn, 1874), pp. 219–24, 34–5.

[5] R. Pauli, *The Life of Alfred the Great*, trans. 'A.P.', ed. B. Thorpe (London, 1853), pp. 99–100. See also the interpretation of archers on the English side at the Battle of Agincourt as Saxon yeomen alongside Henry V's Norman knights: F. Maurice, 'The Battle of Agincourt', *Cornhill* Magazine, 3rd series, 25 (1908), pp. 789–93, quoted in Curry, *Battle of Agincourt*, p. 398. For the notion of 'Saxons and Normans' in nineteenth-century historiography and society, see A. Briggs, *Saxons, Normans and Victorians*, 1066 Commemoration Series 5 (Bexhill, 1966).

[6] Abels, *Lordship and Military Obligation in Anglo-Saxon England*, p. 3.

[7] ASC CDE 1016.

It is easy to see how the implications of the idea of 'full penalty' could be interpreted as related to universal military service.[8] Such considerations of universal service have long been seen in military historiography. As early as the
twelfth century, Wace wrote of a proportion of the English force at Hastings as
peasants.[9]

Such interpretations are not just archaic, however. More recently, Stephen
Morillo has compared the participation of the fourteenth-century Flemish city
militias with the participation of warriors in the Anglo-Saxon state, arguing that
infantry service – admittedly a more organized infantry service than the rude
peasants of the fyrd – was a product of the organized state, while the the service
of cavalry was the work of the 'feudal' lords of a less centralized system.[10] However,
it is perhaps more appropriate to begin with the the nineteenth century's quint-
essential Anglo-Saxonist, John Richard Green. For such a Victorian historian as
Green, popular participation was seen as a key to the success of a national force.
Typifying these interpretations is his portrayal of what he saw as the the ragtag
force Alfred inherited almost 150 years before the events of Æthelred's reign cited
above:[11]

> Busy however as Ælfred was with the restoration of order and good government,
> his main efforts were directed to the military organization of his people. He had
> learned during the years of hard fighting with which his life began, how unsuited
> the military system of the country had become to the needs of war as the Danes
> practised it. The one national army was the fyrd, a force which had already received
> in the Karolingian legislation the name of 'landwehr' by which the German knows
> it still. The fyrd was in fact composed of the whole mass of free landowners who
> formed the folk: and to the last it could only be summoned by the voice of the
> folk-moot. In theory therefore such a host represented the whole available force
> of the country. But in actual warfare its attendance at the king's war-call was lim-
> ited by practical difficulties. Arms were costly; and the greater part of the fyrd
> came equipped with bludgeons and hedge-stakes, which could do little to meet
> the spear and battleaxe of the invader. The very growth of the kingdom too had
> broken down the old military system. A levy of every freeman was possible when
> one folk marched with another folk, when a single march took the warrior to the
> border, and a single fight settled the matter between the tiny peoples. But now that

---

[8] This may be related to the imposition of a death penalty and confiscation of property
   for those who deserted an army led by the king, in V Æthelred, ch. 28: *Gesetze*, vol. i,
   pp. 244–5; trans. *EHD* i, p. 445 (cf. VI Æthelred, ch. 35, in *Gesetze*, vol. i, p. 256, from
   1008, which has no reference to a death penalty but refers to confiscation of property).

[9] Wace, III.7669–7706. For the twelfth-century influences upon Wace's views of eleventh-
   and twelfth-century warfare, see M. Bennett, 'Poetry as History? The Roman de Rou of
   Wace as a Source for the Norman Conquest', *ANS* 5 (1983 for 1982), pp. 21–39, and M.
   Bennett, 'Wace and Warfare', *ANS* 11 (1989 for 1988), pp. 37–58.

[10] S. Morillo, 'The "Age of Cavalry" Revisited', in *The Circle of War in the Middle Ages: Essays
   on Medieval Military and Naval History*, ed. D. J. Kagay and L. J. A. Villalon, Warfare
   in History (Woodbridge, 1999), pp. 45–58. See also Morillo, 'Expecting Cowardice:
   Medieval Battle Tactics Reconsidered', *JMMH* 4 (2006), pp. 65–73, at p. 69.

[11] J. R. Green, *The Conquest of England* (London, 1883), pp. 133–5.

folk after folk had been absorbed in great kingdoms, now that the short march had lengthened into distant expeditions, the short fight into long campaigns, it was hard to reconcile the needs of labour and of daily bread with the needs of war. Ready as he might be to follow the king to a fight which ended the matter, the farmer who tilled his own farm could serve only as long as his home-needs would suffer him. Custom had fixed his service at a period of two months. But as the industrial condition of the country advanced such a service became more and more difficult to enforce; even in Ine's day it was needful to fix heavy fines by law for men who 'neglected the fyrd', and it broke down before the new conditions of warfare brought about by the strife with the Danes. However thoroughly they were beaten, the Danes had only to fall back behind their entrenchments, and wait in patience till the two months of the host's service were over, and the force which besieged them melted away. It was this which had again and again neutralized the successes of the West-Saxon kings.

It was the thinning of their own ranks in the hour of victory which forced Æthelred to conventions such as that of Nottingham, and Ælfred to conventions such as that of Exeter. The Dane in fact had changed the whole conditions of existing warfare. His forces were really standing armies, and a standing army of some sort was needed to meet them.

Green's commentary on the development of the English kingdom and society was an unashamedly populist account which tended towards the picturesque,[12] presumably using Wace's late twelfth-century imagining of a peasant army equipped with hedge-stakes and bludgeons.[13] Furthermore, the evidence Green uses for the two months of service is presumably that of Domesday Book, employed elsewhere to address Alfred's reforms. Green may have been focused on furnishing a general readership with mental pictures of the English landscape and its inhabitants, but he was influenced by and had an influence upon Victorian historiography.[14] To a Victorian historian raised on the Germanic idea of legitimacy as addressed by J. M. Kemble, expressed in what was seen as a proto-parliament of the *witanagemot*, the relation between their authority and the army was especially important.[15] If Green was drawing attention to the fact that English modes of organization could change in response to Viking actions, it is interesting that he showed the importance of military developments as a response to changes in conditions, as well as noting the need for reform.

Green's interpretations had been influenced by the publication a decade earlier, in 1867, of the first of the six volumes of Edward Augustus Freeman's *History of the Norman Conquest*. Freeman's influence upon Green is hardly surprising, as

---

[12] Burrow, *Liberal Descent*, pp. 200–4.

[13] Wace, III.7699–7706; see also below, p. 111.

[14] For the link between popular and academic histories of the early Anglo-Saxon period, see the discussion in B. Ward-Perkins, 'Why did the Anglo-Saxons not become more British?', *EHR* 115 (2000), pp. 513–33, at pp. 518–19.

[15] J. M. Kemble, *Saxons in England: A History of the English Commonwealth till the Period of the Norman Conquest* (London, 1849; 2nd edn, 2 vols, 1876), vol. 2, pp. 224–5. For discussion of the legitimacy of assemblies in campaigns, see below, ch. 5, pp. 179–85.

Freeman had referred to him as 'a rising scholar to whom I look for the continuation of my own work'.[16] The first volume of *The History of the Norman Conquest*
focused on setting the scene in England and Normandy. Although Freeman had
noted the difference between land held through lordship (emphatically not feudal,
he claimed, although many of the characteristics of what he defined as feudalism
were present in his interpretation)[17] and military service from the population in
general, this form of bipartite service was an interesting precursor of the views of
Warren Hollister, published a century later.[18] What captured Freeman's imagination was the idea of general military participation. For Freeman, the *ceorl* could
be equated with the Greek citizen and citizen soldier as a party who was fundamental in a system which he referred to as 'far more than Teutonic' but rather 'a
common Aryan possession'; the warriors, in turn, could be equated with those of
the Homeric Heroic Age.[19]

> All land in England was, by the earliest Common Law, subject to three burthens,
> to contributions to the three works most necessary for the defence of the coun-
> try. These were the famous *Trinoda Necessitas*, the obligation to service in the field
> (*fyrd*) and to a share in the repairs of fortresses and of bridges. But these are the
> duties of the citizen to the commonwealth, or of the subject to the Sovereign, not
> the duty of the personal Vassal to his personal Lord. His land, in an age when
> there was little property except in land, is simply taken as the measure of the con-
> tribution due from him to the common defence. From these burthens, as a rule, no
> land could be free; even church-lands were regularly subject to them, though in
> some cases their owners contrived to obtain exemptions. These ancient obligations
> pressed alike on the ancient allodial possession and on the land held by any more
> modern tenure. They were not feudal services, but a tax paid to the state. They
> were in fact the price paid to the commonwealth for its protection, or rather they
> were the share which each member of the commonwealth was bound to take in
> the protection of himself and his neighbours.

Here Freeman emphasized a social contract of sorts. The rustic, often poorly armed,
warrior was a staple of the images of the Battle of Hastings in the nineteenth century – an interpretation that remains influential, perhaps because it was given

---

[16] E. A. Freeman, *The History of the Norman Conquest of England, its Causes and its Results*,
6 vols (Oxford, 1867–79), vol. I, p. xii.

[17] Freeman, *History of the Norman Conquest*, vol. I, pp. 97–9.

[18] Below, pp. 68–91 (see also discussion of the work of P. Vinogradoff, below, pp. 65–8).

[19] Freeman, *History of the Norman Conquest*, vol. I, p. 86. The discussion is at pp. 86–100
and the passage quoted is from pp. 99–100. For Freeman's concepts of Aryanism, see
Burrow, *Liberal Descent*, pp. 188–92. The influence on western historiography of the
link between military service and state identity, whether as Greek citizen soldiers or
Macedonian subjects, is long-standing: see, e.g., J. F. C. Fuller, *The Decisive Battles of the
Western World, and their Influence Upon History*, 3 vols (London, 1954–6), abridged edn,
2 vols (London, 1970), vol. I, p. 84; R. Billows, *Kings and Colonists: Aspects of Military
Imperialism*, Columbia Studies in the Classical Tradition 22 (Leiden, 1995), pp. 15–18;
and Hanson, *Carnage and Culture*. This issue is raised in D. Karunanithy, 'Macedonian
Military Culture and World Impact: Perspectives and Impressions, Part 2', *Slingshot: The
Journal of the Society of Ancients* 258 (July 2008), pp. 3–13.

ANGLI : ET : FRA NCI : INPRELIO :·

Fig. 3.1 Unarmoured English warriors in a probable temporary fortification at the Battle of Hastings depicted in the Bayeux Tapestry

visual strength by the Bayeux Tapestry's depiction of a group of unarmoured warriors on the English side (Fig. 3.1). Green's portrayal of the English line at the Battle of Hastings is appropriate to highlight here.[20]

> On the fourteenth of October William led his men at dawn along the higher ground that leads from Hastings to the battle-field which Harold had chosen. From the mound of Telham the Normans saw the host of the English gathered thickly behind a rough trench and a stockade on the height of Senlac. Marshy ground covered their right; on the left, the most exposed part of the position, the hus-carls or bodyguard of Harold, men in full armour and wielding huge axes, were grouped round the Golden Dragon of Wessex and the Standard of the king. The rest of the ground was covered by thick masses of half-armed rustics who had flocked at Harold's summons to the fight with the stranger.

The significance of temporary fortifications on the battlefield will be considered in chapter 6, but here it is the appearance of hostile 'half-armed rustics' that is noteworthy, recalling as it does Green's interpretation of Alfred's army.[21] As Freeman also indicated, the participants of battles represented the constitutional notion of a popular rally to the defence of the kingdom. Even if a new historiography was beginning to emerge in the later twentieth century, such interpre-

---

[20] Green, *Conquest of England*, p. 570.

[21] M. K. Lawson, 'Observations on a Scene in the Bayeux Tapestry, the Battle of Hastings and the Military System of the Late Anglo-Saxon State', in *The Medieval State: Essays Presented to James Campbell*, ed. J. R. Maddicott and D. M. Palliser (London, 2000), pp. 73–91, at p. 79, sensibly suggests that they are not peasants but look like 'regular light infantry'.

Fig. 3.2 Irish Defence Force extras drilling for the 1969 film, *Alfred the Great* (Courtesy of Captain Kevin McDonald, Irish Defence Force)

tations remained influential; even the 1969 film *Alfred the Great* portrayed the West Saxon victory in 878 as a movement of the people to defend their kingdom and their king (see Fig. 3.2).[22] During the twentieth century Sir Frank Stenton had done much to promote the importance of the role of the Anglo-Saxon *ceorl*, indicating that military service came from those freemen who had five hides or more. Whether those freemen were thegns had no bearing on this military service, as thegnhood was, by definition, military service to a lord, and was only part of the picture of military organization. Thus to Stenton the association of the five-hide holding with military service was fundamental to the free status of the Anglo-Saxon *ceorl*, as it represented a military obligation of peasant proprietors, something which had been intrinsic to Anglo-Saxon society from its inception or at least from King Ine's day. Such a view as Stenton's assumes the stasis of *ceorls'* positions in comparison to those of kings.[23]

> Like other archaic forms of service, they were so familiar that few early documents ever attempt to define them. Nothing definite is known, for example, about the system by which the fyrd was recruited, and different scholars have come to very different opinions about the military value of the ceorl. The bare fact that men of this class served in the fyrd is proved by an explicit statement to that effect in Ine's laws.[24] Whatever the basis of their service may have been, it is only reasonable to

---

[22] For the training of extras, effectively replicating the idea of a citizen soldiery in Wessex, see M. J. Murphy, *Viking Summer: The Filming of MGM's 'Alfred the Great' in Galway in 1968* (Tuam, 2008), p. 76.

[23] Stenton, *Anglo-Saxon England*, 3rd edn, pp. 290–1.

[24] Ch. 51 (*Gesetze*, vol. i, p. 112).

assume that all able-bodied freemen would fight, or attempt to fight, when their country was invaded. The collapse of its defence meant slavery for the men and women who were worth the taking. The extent to which ceorls were called out in mass for distant expeditions is very uncertain. In the ninth century it was clearly unusual for the fyrd of a particular shire to serve beyond its borders. In all the recorded fighting of Anglo-Saxon history the typical warrior is the man of noble birth, fitted to be a king's companion, with far more than the equipment of an ordinary peasant, and dismounting only for battle. The peasant contingents in the host move very dimly behind this aristocratic foreground. But impressions derived from a few incidents, imperfectly recorded, can easily mislead, and there are facts which suggest that the ceorl may have been by no means negligible as a fighting man.[25] Even in the twelfth century the prosperous freeholder, who was his social representative, possessed an equipment for war comparable with that of the undistinguished knight. The numerous swords and shields found accompanying burials of the heathen period cannot all have belonged to kings' companions and their kin. The Kentish ceorl of Æthelberht's time was certainly rich enough to provide himself with an elaborate military equipment. Above all, the one text which illustrates the composition of the fyrd in the time before the Danish wars shows that kings were interesting themselves in its composition, and suggests that they were attempting to raise its quality by limiting its numbers. Between 799 and 802 Cenwulf of Mercia granted to one of his followers that an estate of thirty hides should furnish only five men when the fyrd was called out.[26]

In Stenton's model the limitations of service and the additional equipment which might be used to improve the military effectiveness of a *ceorlisc* warrior did not therefore mean the emergence of a new social stratum but a change in the perception of *ceorls*. Although Stenton recognized the importance of aristocratic warfare, what was notable in his model was the self-protection amongst *ceorls* to maintain a society of free peasant proprietors. Indeed, we may note, as Stenton and Green did, the significance of *ceorls* in Ine's lawcode from the later seventh century. The code associated military service – or rather fines for neglecting it – with such peasant proprietors, just as it did with the noble class of *gesiths*, who were of a rank which seems to have been synonymous with that of thegns:[27]

> If a *gesith*-born man owning land [*landagende*], neglects [*forsitte*] the *fyrd*, he shall give 120 shillings and forfeit his land; one owning no land, 60 shillings; [a] *ceorlisc* [man] 30 shillings, as fine for [neglect of] the *fyrd* [*fyrdwite*].

[25] Thus St Cuthbert, whose military service is mentioned by his first biographer, is known to have possessed at least a horse and a spear. There is no conclusive evidence as to his social status, but the well-recorded story which shows him tending his master's sheep *cum aliis pastoribus* ['with other shepherds'] makes it unlikely that he was of the class from which kings' companions were drawn. (*Two Lives of Saint Cuthbert: A Life by an Anonymous Monk of Lindisfarne; and Bede's Prose Life*, ed. B. Colgrave (Cambridge, 1940), pp. 68, 72, 172).

[26] W. de Gray Birch (ed.), *Cartularium Saxonicum*, 3 vols. (London 1885–9), no. 201 [S 106 (AD 764 for 767)].

[27] *Laws of King Ine*, ch. 51: *Gesetze*, vol. I, p. 112; trans. *EHD* I, p. 404.

The fact, as pointed out by W. G. Runciman,[28] that *ceorls* could be very rich helps us to consider that *ceorlisc* status was not necessarily the progenitor of a society of 'pot bellied equanimity' (to use Thomas Carlyle's inimitable phrase).[29] *Ceorls* were not necessarily peasants *per se*, but their potential for military service, as argued by Stenton, is notable. However as Abels has argued, such *ceorls* may have undertaken service through their link to a lord, perhaps in cases with a wish to gain wealth and fame through military means;[30] contrasted with Stenton's interpretation this did not mean that pre-Viking Anglo-Saxon armies were made up predominantly from the *ceorlisc* class.[31] By the tenth century the connection between the holding of land, military service and thegnly status seems to have been central; nonetheless, Dunnere, the *ceorl* recorded in the *Battle of Maldon* poem, could speak loudly and carry a big spear.[32]

However, Stenton's view of the military commitment of the *ceorl* differed somewhat from much historiography concerning post-Alfredian Anglo-Saxon armies, which mostly relates to the battlefield of 1066. In this respect much of the historiography of the last quarter of a century may even be said to have much in common with Green and his contemporaries, who placed the thegn in a quasi-feudal position, as a man with an obligation associated with a specific landholding, while Stenton stressed the military importance of *ceorlisc* participation on the battlefield. A fundamental difference between Green's approach, representing the establishment of nineteenth-century historiography, and that of Abels, Eric John and H. M. Chadwick, concerns the social status status of warriors. This school of historiography was, and indeed is, concerned with the social elevation intrinsic to thegnhood.

'Five Hides and All That': Aristocrats and military service

Like the idea of universal military service amongst the Anglo-Saxon free peasants, the relationship between aristocratic landholding and military service also had a long historiographical pedigree. This was with good reason. Eleventh-century tracts on social status, *Norðleoda laga* and *Geðyncðu*, referred to five-hide holdings

---

[28] W. G. Runciman, 'Accelerating Social Mobility: The Case of Anglo-Saxon England', *Past and Present* 104 (Aug. 1984), pp. 3–30. See also F. M. Stenton, 'The Thriving of the Anglo-Saxon Ceorl', in his *Preparatory to Anglo-Saxon. England*, ed. D. M. Stenton (Oxford, 1970), pp. 383–93.

[29] T. Carlyle, *History of Friedrich II of Prussia: Called Frederick the Great*, 4 vols (London, 1858–65), vol. I, p. 317.

[30] Abels, *Lordship and Military Obligation in Anglo-Saxon England*, p. 28.

[31] For tenth-century views of distinctions between warriors and *ceorls*, see Abels, *Lordship and Military Obligation in Anglo-Saxon England*, pp. 133–4.

[32] For a discussion of *ceorl's* position at Maldon, in comparison to the other warriors at the battle, see A. Williams, 'The Battle of Maldon and *The Battle of Maldon*: History, Poetry and Propaganda', *Medieval History* 2:2 (1992), pp. 35–44, at pp. 41–4. Cf. E. John, *Reassessing Anglo-Saxon England* (Manchester, 1996), p. 84, who argues that the term could mean 'a husband of whatever social class' and, earlier, in E. John, *Orbis Britanniae and Other Studies*, Studies in Early English History 4 (Leicester, 1966), p. 138, suggested that he was a *ceorl* 'who throve' and 'enjoyed thegnly status'.

as a mark of thegnhood,[33] while since at least the eighth century the ownership of land brought with it certain military obligations, sometimes referred to as the *trinoda necessitas*, the 'threefold obligations' of bridge-building, fortification-work, and army service.[34] Many historical studies have been interested in equal measure in the distinctions and continuities between pre-Conquest thegns and post-Conquest knights, with even the arch-Normanist R. A. Brown acknowledging the high status of the pre-Conquest thegn.[35] Although J. H. Round and F. W. Maitland, late nineteenth-century pioneers of methodologies for considering landholdings,[36] did not bring out the 'proto-feudal' consequences of their investigations, they paved the way for the study of the Anglo-Saxon army as an essentially aristocratic military force by addressing the issue of regularly sized land units. As well as some more obscure calculations, Domesday Book provides explicit statements on the nature of military service and their relationships with landholding. A significant source for their judgements, and for much historiography on the subject, is in the Domesday folios for Berkshire which records a 'TRE' (*Tempore Regis Edwardi*, 'At the time of King Edward') obligation:[37]

> When geld was paid TRE, commonly through all Berkshire, a hide gave 3½d before the [Feast of the] Nativity of the Lord and as much at Pentecost. If the king sent out an army somewhere from 5 hides only one *miles* went out. And for his supplies [*victus*] or pay [*stipendium*] from each hide was given to him 4s for 2 months. This money was not sent to the king but was given to the *milites*. If anyone was summoned on military service [*expeditio*] but did not go he forfeited all his land to the king. But if anyone staying behind promised to send another for himself, and yet he who should have been sent stayed behind his lord was quit for 50s. When a thegn [*tainus*] or a *miles* of the king's demesne was dying as relief [*releua* = ?heriot] he left all his weapons to the king, and a horse with a saddle and another without a saddle. But if he possessed hounds or hawks these were presented to the king, to accept if he wished.

As well as displaying an ambiguous attitude towards distinctions between *taini* and *milites*, the Domesday entry showed a direct connection between the holding of land and royal service, at least in Berkshire. However, although these folios contain the most explicit statement of the organization of military service, this

---

[33] *Gesetze*, vol. 1, pp. 456, 460; trans. *EHD* 1, pp. 468–9. For a discussion of five-hide holdings, see A. Williams, 'How Land Was Held Before and After the Norman Conquest', in *Domesday Book Studies*, ed. A. Williams and R. W. H. Erskine (London, 1986), pp. 37–8.

[34] W. H. Stevenson, 'Trinoda Necessitas', *EHR* 29 (1914), pp. 689–703. See also Brooks, 'Development of Military Obligations in Eighth- and Ninth-Century England'.

[35] R. A. Brown, 'The Status of the Norman Knight', in *War and Government in the Middle Ages: Essays in Honour of J. O. Prestwich*, ed. J. C. Holt and J. Gillingham (Woodbridge, 1984), pp. 18–32, at p. 18.

[36] F. W. Maitland, *Domesday Book and Beyond: Three Essays in the Early History of England* (Cambridge, 1897); J. H. Round, *Feudal England: Historical Studies on the Eleventh and Twelfth Centuries* (London, 1895; reset edn, 1964).

[37] DB Berks. B 10 (fol. 56c).

was not Domesday Book's only evidence. Another Domesday account of military service is recorded in the entry for Malmesbury (Wilts.):[38]

> When the king went on an expedition [*expeditio*], whether by land or by sea, he had from this borough [*burgus*] either 20s for the support [*ad pascendos*] of his butsecarls [*buzecarli*] or took with him one man for [each] honour [*pro honore*] of 5 hides.

Such variations in the records reflect the different methodologies taken in the organization of the Domesday survey in different areas of the English kingdom. It is pertinent to acknowledge the importance for historians of early England of Domesday Book for the understanding of military service and lordly obligation. For example, nineteenth-century historians had not benefited from the identification and detailed study of the different circuits used in the planning of the Domesday survey and which so characterize the terms used in the Domesday entries.[39] J. H. Round's series of tables and measurements in his 1895 *Feudal England*, work which had stemmed from his contribution to the 1886 volume *Domesday Studies*, was characteristic of the methodologically scientific work which was emerging on Domesday Book in the nineteenth century.[40] Round showed that in their fiscal assessments hundreds were organized into multiples of five hides.[41] Although his conclusions had far-reaching implications, he used these measurements to demonstrate that the hide bore no relationship to the monetary or mensural interpretations of land in Domesday Book. He remarked: 'With this I am only concerned here so far as it illustrates the presence of a five-hide unit.'[42] While the five-hide unit has attracted much attention from historians, Round also highlighted a variety of systems of assessment in Domesday England. Perhaps the most significant of these was what he logically referred to as the 'six carucate unit' in the Danelaw shires of Lincolnshire, Yorkshire, Derbyshire and Nottinghamshire,[43] drawing attention to the differences between the eastern and western areas of Mercia. Typical of these differences, he argued, was that between Warwick and Leicester:

> The military service of Warwick and Leicester was arranged on the same method, yet Leicester sent *twelve* 'burgesses' to the fyrd where Warwick sent *ten*.[44]

---

[38] DB Wilts B 5 (fol. 64c).

[39] C. Stephenson, 'Notes on the Composition and Interpretation of Domesday Book', *Speculum* 22 (1947), pp. 1–15. For a more recent discussion of the organization of the Domesday survey, see D. Roffe, *Decoding Domesday* (Woodbridge, 2007), pp. 64–97.

[40] J. H. Round, 'Danegeld and the Finance of Domesday', in *Domesday Studies: Being the Papers read at the Meetings of the Domesday Commemoration, 1886*, ed. P. E. Dove, 2 vols (London, 1888–91), vol. 1, pp. 79–142. For another example of the scientific approach of this period, see R. W. Eyton's imaginatively titled *A Key to Domesday, showing the Method and Exactitude of its Mensuration, and the … Meaning of its more Usual Formulæ. The Subject being … exemplified by an Analysis and Digest of the Dorset Survey* (London, 1878).

[41] Round, *Feudal England*, pp. 47–66.

[42] Round, *Feudal England*, p. 65.

[43] Round, *Feudal England*, pp. 66–76.

[44] Round, *Feudal England*, p. 68.

Round was emphatic in his insistence that the differences were not those of the variations between areas within and outside the Danelaw, for he noted that Cambridgeshire, a Danelaw county, was hidated in Domesday Book.[45] The other units of assessment, he noted, were the Leicestershire Hide, the Lancashire Hide, the 'Yorkshire Unit', East Anglian 'leets', and Kentish sulungs.[46]

The discrepancies within and between these assessments have continued to be a topic of debate,[47] which has had a subsequent impact upon the study of the military organization of Anglo-Saxon England. Even at the time of Round's observation of five-hide units, A. G. Little cast doubt on their existence as coherent units.[48] Almost a century later, Richard Abels emphasized that military service was based on a number of different types of arrangements, which could vary in their cadastral imposition. Abels argued for the significance of the five-hide unit at the end of the Anglo-Saxon period but, similarly, pointed out that the five-hide unit was not a universal military system.[49] This was an important reality check on historiographical interpretations of a state system which had tended toward increasing sophistication.[50] Nonetheless, the fact that the system *had* limitations highlighted that it was realistic, and it should be borne in mind that the limitations on the system were, as far as is known, not perceived as such in the pre-Conquest period. It was – in its own terms – an efficient and effective military system for its time.

However, while Maitland's approach of moving from Domesday Book to an Anglo-Saxon 'beyond' can be invaluable,[51] the variations in systems need to be addressed. We should note that the explicit statements of systems of military service before 1066 could be rather different from the 5 hide / 6 carucate assessments read from Domesday Book. To this end tabulation of the data is worthwhile (Table 3.1).

A study of the types of assessment shows that military service in different regions of the English kingdom could vary considerably. Therefore it is probable that in terms of its size, composition and equipment, the military force which was used by Alfred in the later ninth century was different from that of Harold Godwineson in the mid eleventh century.

That said, the continuity – *mutatis mutandis* – of Anglo-Saxon administrative systems should be acknowledged, and we may also be justified in noting that the eleventh-century Anglo-Saxon army owed a great deal to the organization of Alfred's Wessex. The appendix to the document recording the provision of

---

[45] Round, *Feudal England*, pp. 41–7. See Stephenson, 'Notes on the Composition and Interpretation of Domesday Book', who highlights Cambridgeshire's position in a different circuit from many other Danelaw counties.

[46] Round, *Feudal England*, pp. 76–82.

[47] See e.g. D. Roffe, *Domesday: The Inquest and the Book* (Oxford, 2000), pp. 10–16.

[48] A. G. Little, 'Gesiths and Thegns', *EHR* 4 (1889), pp. 723–9, at pp. 728–9.

[49] Abels, *Lordship and Military Obligation in Anglo-Saxon England*, pp. 108–15.

[50] This is most evident in Campbell, 'Observations on English Government from the Tenth Century to the Twelfth Century'. See above, p. 44, n. 105.

[51] Maitland, *Domesday Book and Beyond*, pp. 490–520.

Table 3.1 Types of military service and their landed assessments

Assessment type	Date range (approx.)	Source	Application	Related area	Length of service
1 man per hide	late 9th C/ early 10th C	Burghal hidage	fortification defence & maintenance	West Saxon kingdom & south Mercia	not recorded
'each man' to have 2 (well-) mounted men per plough	926×c. 930	Athelstan's Grately code	military service?	English kingdom, perhaps including Mercia/ parts of Danelaw[†]	not recorded
1 mailcoat & helmet per 8 hides; 1 ship per 310 hides	1008	Anglo-Saxon Chronicle CDE MSS	armour; ships	English kingdom	not recorded
5 hides	early 11th C	compilations on status	status of thegn	not indicated	not recorded
5 hides	1066×86	Domesday Book	Warrior maintenance	Berkshire & 23 towns[‡]	40 days

† For a consideration of the significance of the Grately lawcode in both a West Saxon and 'English' context, see R. Lavelle, 'Why Grateley? Reflections on Anglo-Saxon Kingship in a Hampshire Landscape', *Proceedings of the Hampshire Field Club and Archaeological Society* 60 (2005), pp. 154–69.

‡ C. W. Hollister, *Anglo-Saxon Military Institutions on the Eve of the Norman Conquest* (Oxford, 1962), p. 46.

fortifications known as the Burghal Hidage indicates a system of one man per hide; this did not necessarily imply that the military forces available to Alfred were five times larger than those available from Wessex on the eve of the Conquest. Such a suggestion contrasts with that of Nicholas Brooks, who maintained that the Burghal Hidage represented a force associated with the defence of fortifications (burhs) in addition to an army, using the Anglo-Saxon Chronicle's record of a burghal force alongside a field army which served in rotation.[52] It appears likely that, given its wide scale of intended application, the Burghal Hidage was calculated from a record which included provision of one or more mobile field forces, available to take part in campaigns, as indicated in the Anglo-Saxon Chronicle entry for 917, which makes reference to boroughs as assembly points.[53] If the Burghal Hidage provided for one man per hide or equivalent, it presumably

52 ASC ABCD 893. N. P. Brooks, 'The Administrative Background to the Burghal Hidage', in *Defence of Wessex*, ed. Hill and Rumble, pp. 128–59, at pp. 129–30. See also M. Powicke, *Military Obligation in Medieval England: A Study in Liberty and Duty* (Oxford, 1962), pp. 19–20.

53 ASC A 917. Cf. Banton, 'Ealdormen and Earls', p. 21, which contrasts borough armies with those which took part on campaign.

also included a workforce available to work on the maintenance of the fortifications, and those who were available to defend them.

The terms *waru* and *weal-stilling* in the Burghal Hidage refer to the building, maintenance and manning of fortification walls.[54] Alexander Rumble's consideration that *waru* refers to "'defence" in a military and/or fiscal sense' allows some flexibility in interpretation.[55] Thus, under Alfred, the burhs may have formed or were planned to form the basis of the entire military system. At a provision of one man per hide, a total of some 27,000 men for the West Saxon kingdom's estimated population of 450,000, would equate with a high ratio of military participation. As both Brooks and Abels have observed, this would have been comparable with those of early modern armies.[56] But there is a way of reconciling the high proportion inherent in the 'one man per hide' formula with that of later assessments if it included provision for the logistical support of ninth-century West Saxon armies. In an eleventh-century context it is difficult to conceive of each five-hide warrior stepping out on campaign with 20 shillings in his pouch for his two months' maintenance without any accompanying system of support,[57] although evidently that system was later twisted for fiscal reasons to allow the rapacious royal minister Ranulf Flambard to exact 10 shillings for 'maintenance' (*victum*) out of the pockets of each English warrior who answered King William II's summons in 1094.[58] If the figures of the Berkshire Domesday provision are extrapolated, with 4 shillings per hide equating with 20 shillings for a five-hide holding, the 20 shillings (240*d.*) to be given for two months' service could have provided one penny per day for four men over sixty days. As a penny could be said to have equated to a day's skilled wage,[59] the five-hide provision of the Berkshire Domesday customs perhaps had a link, even if only indirectly, with the one man per hide provision of the Burghal Hidage. Both documents probably related to provision for skilled warriors alongside their non-combatant retinue. These may be compared with the 50-shilling fine to be paid if a landholder failed to turn up for fyrd-service, recorded in the

---

[54] J. M. Dodgson, 'Appendix I: OE *Weal-stilling*' and A. R. Rumble, 'Appendix II: OE *waru*', in *Defence of Wessex*, ed. Hill and Rumble, pp. 176–7, 178–81.

[55] Rumble, 'Appendix II: OE *waru*', p. 179.

[56] Abels, 'English Logistics and Military Administration', p. 261; Brooks, 'England in the Ninth Century', pp. 18–19, does not estimate a ninth-century population but calculates a 1086 figure of 560,000, noting that this population would have been the result of having 'grown substantially' in the tenth and eleventh centuries (p. 19).

[57] For the suggestion that the money provided for warriors recorded in Domesday Book's Berkshire customs was intended for the purchase of supplies from accompanying merchants, see Abels, 'Household Men, Mercenaries and Vikings', p. 159. *AB* 876 records the shield-selling merchants in the baggage train of Charles the Bald at the Battle of Andernach. For discussion of such baggage trains, see Leyser, 'Early Medieval Warfare', pp. 103–5, and below, pp. 191–3.

[58] ASC 1094 and JW vol. 3, s.a. 1094, pp. 72–3. See J. O. Prestwich, *The Place of War in English History, 1066–1214*, ed. M. Prestwich [from the Ford Lectures, 1983], Warfare in History (Woodbridge, 2004), p. 126.

[59] I owe this suggestion to Gareth Williams. See D. M. Metcalf, *An Atlas of Anglo-Saxon and Norman Coin Finds, 973–1066*, Royal Numismatic Society Special Publications 32 (London, 1998), p. 14, who suggests it to be 'at least a day's earnings' in the eleventh century.

Berkshire Domesday customs, which presumably could be assigned to pay for a (mercenary) warrior and his support.

As we saw above, Sir Frank Stenton commented on the participation of peasant contingents who 'move very dimly' behind an 'aristocratic foreground',[60] but such people may not have served as warriors, as Stenton surmised, but rather as those who supported the warriors. While evidence on logistical support in pre-Conquest England does not compare with that to be found in Carolingian Francia, exemplified with the command on the construction of carts to support the army in *Capitulare 'de villis'*,[61] nuggets of information can nonetheless be found. Bede's *Historia ecclesiastica* famously records the fortunes of a Northumbrian thegn who pretended to be a 'poor peasant and married' (*rusticum ... et pauperem atque uxoreo*) in order to avoid execution by his Mercian captor following defeat in a seventh-century battle.[62] A version of the story is provided in the later Old English version of Bede's *Historia ecclesiastica*, dating from the eighth or ninth centuries:

> When he [i.e. his captor] asked him what he was, he feared to confess that he was a king's thegn [*cyninges þegn*], so he declared that he was a man of the people [*folclic man*], poor and married; and that he had come into the army [*in þa fyrd cwome*] in order to fetch supplies and food [*ondlifen ⁊ mete*] to the king's thegns and their companions [*cyninges þegnum ... mid heora heafodgemæccum*].[63]

The minor clarification of the reference to a *miles* in Bede's original Latin to 'king's thegn' (*cyninges þegn*) may indicate that the Old English translator had notions of service in mind when referring to Imma's pseudo-peasant going into the fyrd. While a reasonably faithful reading was being provided for Bede's account of Imma saying he had 'come to the expedition' (*in expeditionem ... uenisse* – which had presumably been a Latin rendering of a vernacular account in the first place), the Old English Bede could have avoided ambiguity and separated Imma's pseudo-peasant from the army by referring to him coming 'with' the fyrd, i.e. accompanying it. Evidently the translator chose not to do that, perhaps reflecting notions of service which were apparent to their own readers.

We should not necessarily infer from the account that a fighting force would always be tailed by poor married peasants, whether or not they were in carts

---

[60] Stenton, *Anglo-Saxon England*, 3rd edn, p. 290. See above, pp. 53–4.

[61] *Capitulare de villis*, §64, in *Capitularia regum francorum* 1, ed. A. Boretius, MGH Leges 2 (Hanover, 1883), pp. 82–91, at p. 89; trans. H. R. Loyn and J. Percival (eds), *The Reign of Charlemagne: Documents on Carolingian Government and Administration*, Documents of Medieval History 2 (London, 1975), pp. 64–79, at p. 72.

[62] Bede, *HE* IV.22, pp. 402–3. See Hooper, 'Anglo-Saxons at War', pp. 194–5, who raises the episode as an example of pre-Viking evidence, making comparison with Carolingian campaigns.

[63] *Old English Version of Bede's Ecclesiastical History of the English People*, trans. Miller, part 1, pp. 326–7 (translation adapted for clarity). I am grateful to Sharon Rowley for drawing my attention to the uncertainties of the dating of the Old English Bede, an issue which is highlighted in D. Whitelock, 'The Old English Bede', *Proceedings of the British Academy* 48 (1962), pp. 57–90.

or, indeed, accompanied by women. Nonetheless, eleventh-century records of 'carrying service' imposed on free men in such documents as the Tidenham (Glos.) estate survey[64] may be glimpses of how it could be achieved in a later context, with the obligations necessary for the everyday life of rural estates directed towards military ends. By extrapolation, Bede's account also allows us to address Abels's notion that warfare may have provided opportunities for social advancement for *unmarried* peasants who were brave enough to try their hand at fighting,[65] a notion distinct from the expectations of *ceorlisc* service addressed by Stenton.

A less often considered piece of evidence for military support is the provision recorded in Athelstan's lawcode promulgated at Grateley, Hampshire, *II Athelstan*, from between *c.* 926 and *c.* 930:

> Fifthly: that every man is to have two well-mounted men [*gehorsede men*] for every plough [*sylh*].[66]

Considering that ploughs, as recorded in Domesday Book, tend to be more numerous than hides, if this provision did relate to landholding, it would have been, as Dorothy Whitelock has noted, an onerous imposition of military service.[67] However, the 'sylh' in *II Athelstan* may be a term related to the Kentish *sulung* or the assessments of the tenth-century Danelaw, which were rough equivalents of two hides and a hide respectively.[68] By comparison with the five-hide warriors of the late Anglo-Saxon period, either interpretation of *sylh* would still have been onerous but may not be unrelated to the heriots recorded in surviving Anglo-Saxon wills and a Berkshire Domesday entry, which makes provision for pairs of horses, one harnessed and one without a harness.[69] One reading of this is that a mounted soldier with the harness necessary to carry him needed a squire or equivalent to accompany him and his equipment on campaign and to the battlefield.[70]

It is evident that Athelstan's lawcode was onerous: the imposition of royal expectation through the state is the tone of many of the laws, requiring the regular repair of boroughs (ch. 13) and high standards in the making of shields (ch. 15).[71] If we consider that the reference to the mounted men may be to the *support* of each warrior (the 'every man' of the lawcode) who could travel with the army at

---

[64] Williams, *World Before Domesday*, p. 80, citing S 1555 (probably eleventh-century).

[65] Abels, *Lordship and Military Obligation in Anglo-Saxon England*, p. 28.

[66] *II Athelstan*, ch. 16: *Gesetze*, vol. I, pp. 158–9; trans. *EHD* I, p. 420. The *wel* in reference to the mounting is from a later transcript of an eleventh-century manuscript of the code; *EHD* I, p. 420, n. 2.

[67] *EHD* I, p. 420, n. 3.

[68] See P. Grierson, 'Weights and Measures', in *Domesday Book Studies*, ed. A. Williams and R. W. H. Erskine (London, 1986), pp. 80–5, at p. 81. For a consideration of ploughlands as an early, pre-hide form of assessment recorded in Domesday Book for Northamptonshire, see C. Hart, *The Hidation of Northamptonshire*, Department of English Local History Occasional Papers 2nd series 3 (Leicester, 1970), pp. 24–32.

[69] DB Berks. B 10 (fol. 56c) (p. 56, above). For wills, see below, pp. 115–27.

[70] On such companions, see R. H. C. Davis, *The Medieval Warhorse: Origin, Development and Redevelopment* (London, 1989), pp. 74–5.

[71] *Gesetze*, vol. I, p. 156–8; trans. *EHD* I, pp. 419–20.

a fast pace rather than toddle along behind, the legal obligation moves closer to other late Anglo-Saxon systems of military provision.[72] If the *sylh* was the equivalent of two hides, the notion may be entertained that it was related to existing provisions of one man per hide addressed above, though this can only be speculation. Nonetheless, Athelstan's Grately code does indicate intentions of fielding a fast-moving army, which perhaps helps to explain the success of long-distance campaigns fought in hostile territory by Athelstan, who presumably learnt from the experiences of his father before him.[73] Of course, rulers before Edward the Elder had launched major campaigns in the territory of other kingdoms,[74] but in the earlier tenth century English rulers appear to have been consistently able to field armies capable of conquest as well as defence. Despite the variations in the system of military provision noted by Abels,[75] its relative integrity is remarkable, implying that a cohesive force was available to Alfred and his immediate successors. The areas subject to five-hide assessment first observed by Round are, for the most part,[76] focused on Wessex and western Mercia. They may be equated with the areas assessed by Alfred for the defences of the kingdom in the ninth century and by Æthelred, Æthelflæd and Edward the Elder in the English parts of Mercia.

It appears that there is more common ground between modern historians and Victorian historians than is normally acknowledged, even if J. R. Green read the social implications of military service through his interpretation of the pre-Alfredian period. As noted above, Green remarked on the social change from the force available to Alfred for the immediate defence of the kingdom in the 870s to the thegnly forces from which the later Alfredian and later English armies were composed, an issue which has continued to exercise historians.[77] The work of Abels and, before him, Eric John differs from earlier interpretations in highlighting that these distinctions were changes of assessment and organization rather than, as Green saw it, the emergence of a social class *per se*. Warfare in the pre-Viking period had been an occupation of a warrior class just as the aristocrats of the tenth and eleventh centuries were defined by their warrior status. Although social mobility was a long-standing concern for conservative churchmen,[78] a young man in the pre-Viking period might have been able to use the opportunities of service

---

[72] Cf. E. John, *Land Tenure in Early England: A Discussion of Some Problems*, Studies in Early English History 1 (Leicester, 1960), p. 123, who considers 'each man' to have been a warrior.

[73] For Athelstan's campaigns in context and the movement of armies, see below, ch. 5.

[74] For an assessment of early medieval overlordship achieved through war, see D. Tyler, 'Orchestrated Violence and the "Supremacy" of the Mercian Kings', in *Æthelbald and Offa: Two Eighth-Century Kings of Mercia*, ed. D. Hill and M. Worthington, BAR British Series 383 (Oxford, 2005), pp. 27–34.

[75] Above, p. 58.

[76] Round, *Feudal England*, p. 66; although Round notes the significance of five-hide units in Cambridgeshire.

[77] Green, *Conquest of England*, pp. 133–5. See above, pp. 49–50

[78] Wulfstan of York, *Sermo Lupi ad Anglos* (C version), in *The Homilies of Wulfstan*, ed. D. Bethurum (Oxford, 1957; corrected edn, 1971), pp. 263–4; trans. *EHD* 1, p. 932; *Geðyncðo: Gesetze*, vol. 1, pp. 456–7; trans. *EHD* 1, pp. 468–9; *Norðleoda Laga: Gesetze*, vol. 1, pp. 460–1; trans. *EHD* 1, p. 469. See Runciman, 'Accelerating Social Mobility'.

in a warband to gain aristocratic credibility and royal favour, as Abels observes.[79] One can only speculate that before and during the Viking Age, ambitious young men, unable to afford a large investment in arms and armour, provided the archery and light javelins which played a supplementary or supporting role before more distinguished groups of warriors clashed.[80]

It is important, however, to realize that the study of aristocratic participation in Anglo-Saxon warfare is often isolated from its European context. Anglophone scholarship has often been hampered by its interests in England's particularities just as Francophone scholarship has been interested in drawing wide conclusions from detailed case studies in assessing *la mutation feodale*.[81] The effects on Anglo-Saxon studies may be a result of the Germanist scholarship of the nineteenth century, in which J. M. Kemble argued that Continental Latin terminology should not be used in the study of Anglo-Saxon England and that 'we use no words but such as the Saxons themselves used'.[82] Nonetheless, there are some exceptions: it is instructive to see *un estudio comparativo* of Hampshire and Castile proposed by Ignacio Álvarez Borge, in which the 'feudal' social structures of tenth-century England fit well into a European context.[83] Such a study of localized change seen through a different lens is an appropriate counterpoint to the national scholarships commented on by Tim Reuter, which emerged largely during the nineteenth century and continue to affect the study of their respective national histories.[84]

A better-known example of scholarship informed by the wider European context is John Gillingham's 1995 observation that the late tenth and eleventh centuries saw the emergence of a socially distinct aristocratic class in England whose positions were based on military obligation – essentially similar to the knightly class that was emerging on the Continent.[85] While barriers were placed against

---

[79] Abels, *Lordship and Military Obligation in Anglo-Saxon England*, p. 11–37.

[80] J. M. Manley, 'The Archer and the Army in the Late Saxon Period', *ASSAH* 4 (1985), pp. 223–35. For the ritualized expectations of 'phases' in battle, see below, pp. 274–5.

[81] For criticism of the franco-centric approach, see T. Reuter, 'Debate: The "Feudal Revolution": III', *Past and Present* 155:1 (1997), pp. 177–95, at pp. 188–9. Significant examples of a paradigmatic approach are G. Duby, *La société aux xie et xiie siècles dans la région mâconnaise* (Paris, 1953; 2nd edn, 1971) and G. Bois, *The Transformation of the Year One Thousand: The Village of Lournand from Antiquity to Feudalism*, trans. J. Birrell (Manchester, 1992). Current French approaches are addressed in papers in D. Barthélemy and O. Bruand (eds), *Les Pouvoirs locaux dans la France du centre et de l'ouest (viiie–xie siècles): Implantation et moyens d'action* (Rennes, 2004).

[82] Kemble, *Saxons in England*, vol. 2, p. 196n.

[83] I. Álvarez Borge, *Communidades Locales y Transformaciones Sociales en la Alta Edad Media: Hampshire (Wessex) y el Sur de Castilla, un Estudio Comparativo*, Bibioteca de Investigación 25 (Logroño, 1999).

[84] Reuter, 'Debate: The "Feudal Revolution": III', p. 195.

[85] J. Gillingham, 'Thegns and Knights in Eleventh-Century England: Who was then the Gentleman?', *TRHS* 6th series 5 (1995), pp. 129–33. See also H. G. Richardson and G. O. Sayles, *The Governance of Mediaeval England from the Conquest to Magna Carta*, Edinburgh University Publications: History, Philosophy and Economics 16 (Edinburgh, 1963), pp. 55–61. For a less iconoclastic, though no less useful account, see also Williams, *World Before Domesday*, esp. pp. 63–104.

upward mobility into this particular class, this group was arguably larger than the warrior aristocratic class which existed in the ninth century, due to increasing economic prosperity and the wider availability of comparatively affordable arms and armour.[86] This was perhaps driven by or indeed helped to drive a long-term trend in metallurgical developments in the specialized production of weaponry. What may be identified as an improving and arguably increasingly methodical, albeit then still 'imperfectly understood', control of carbon in the production of swords using larger quantities of iron meant that the artisan process of pattern-welding was superseded in the production of more ductile blades.[87] Extrapolating from a population estimate of between 1.2 and 1.6 million in England south of the River Tees in 1086,[88] a social elite may have comprised 20,000 to 30,000 warriors (approximately 2 per cent of the population).[89] Such a size of force may seem lower than the manpower which could have been provided by the Burghal Hidage for Wessex. The difference may have been because the Burghal Hidage probably included calculation for provision of non-combatants supporting the 'front-line' warriors.

There was, however, a further issue related to both the 'nation-at-arms' and the warrior aristocracy. In 1908 Paul Vinogradoff highlighted a social distinction which Hollister was later to characterize as a distinction between the 'general fyrd' and the 'select fyrd'.[90] Writing of 'national levies', Vinogradoff discussed the landed obligations of late Anglo-Saxon military service. Although grounded in a consideration of the obligations of the *ceorl*, he highlighted a discrepancy which was

---

[86] Gillingham, 'Thegns and Knights' pp. 136–7. For an overview of the equipment of the eleventh century, see I. Peirce, 'Arms, Armour and Warfare in the Eleventh Century', *ANS* 10 (1988 for 1987), pp. 237–57.

[87] For the development of sword manufacture, see A. Williams, *The Knight and the Blast Furnace: A History of the Metallurgy of Armour in the Middle Ages & the Early Modern Period*, History of Warfare 12 (Leiden, 2003), pp. 12–16; A. Williams, 'Methods of Manufacture of Swords in Medieval Europe: Illustrated by the Metallurgy of Some Examples', *Gladius* 13 (1977), pp. 75–101 (quotation at p. 76); on the availability of carburized iron in the early middle ages, J. R. Finó, 'Notes sur la production du fer et la fabrication des armes en France eu moyen-age', *Gladius* 3 (1967), pp. 47–66, at pp. 54–7, and, for a consideration of the availability of Asian crucible steel in Europe, A. Williams, 'Crucible Steel in Medieval Swords', in *Metals and Mines: Studies in Archaeometallurgy*, ed. S. La Niece, D. Hook and P. Craddock (London, 2007), pp. 233–41, and A. Williams, 'Hypereutectoid Steel in Viking-Age Swords', paper presented at the *Archaeometallurgy in Europe Conference*, Aquileia, Italy, June 2007 (publication forthcoming; I am grateful to Dr Williams for a copy of this paper before its publication). Studies of the manufacture of armour tend to focus on the greater surviving quantities of later medieval plate armour; for the suggestion of the recycling of Roman armour in early medieval contexts, see A. Williams 'The Metallurgy of Medieval Arms and Armour', in *Companion to Medieval Arms and Armour*, ed. D. Nicolle (Woodbridge, 2002), pp. 45–54, at p. 49. However, caveats against technological determinism should also be noted: e.g. Abels, 'Cultural Representation and the Practice of War in the Middle Ages', and K. DeVries, 'Catapults Are Not Atomic Bombs: Towards a Redefinition of "Effectiveness" in Premodern Military Technology', *War in History* 4 (1997), pp. 454–70.

[88] H. C. Darby, *Domesday England* (Cambridge, 1977), p. 90.

[89] Cf. ASC E 1094, which refers to 'twenty-thousand Englishmen'.

[90] C. W. Hollister, *Anglo-Saxon Military Institutions on the Eve of the Norman Conquest* (Oxford, 1962); see below, pp. 70–91

beginning to be evident in terms of military effectiveness in the later Anglo-Saxon period. Vinogradoff had been among the first generation of historians to write of the *trinoda necessitas* recorded in Anglo-Saxon charters as a threefold obligation, generally of bridge-work, fortification work and army service, associated explictly with bookland rather than implicitly, as had previously been the case.[91] He developed this view in his *magnum opus* on eleventh-century English society.[92]

> As a matter of fact, however, the attendance at the *fyrd* became very early a burden of land-holding. If in the twelfth and thirteenth centuries it was not every person, but every independent householder, who could be assessed for service in the militia, because some independent property was necessary to carry out its injunctions, even so in the ruder conditions of the Old English age the duty of serving in the host necessarily fell chiefly to the lot of those who held land, and occupied a definite place in society. Landless men could not be sought out and looked after; in the natural order of things they had to range themselves behind the holders of land – the landowners or the men settled and rated under their authority.[93] And this administrative aspect of the situation was corroborated by the economic one; a man without a firm hold on a unit of husbandry, represented by a tenement, could not meet the expenses and requirements of the *fyrd* in regard to equipment, food, and necessary loss of time and labour. It was not merely as a fighting man that he had to appear on the scene, but as a self-supporting householder, and the *fyrd* had to be considered as much from the point of view of the drain on his resources as from that of personal prowess and possible bodily danger. In accordance with this, we find that the duty to serve in the *fyrd* is spoken of as one of the normal incidents of land-tenure.[94] The reservation as to the *trinoda necessitas* almost invariably accompanies any disposition in regard to landownership. And the original idea seems to have been that every hide should send one fully equipped soldier to the *fyrd*. The hundreds were taken to be equivalent to wapentakes, because they presented the common form of district organization for army purposes. All through the Germanic world the hundred appears as the group of 100 holdings, meant roughly to provide for the maintenance of a company of 100 soldiers.[95] But this standard could not be kept up. On the one hand, holdings were broken up in different ways, yardlands and oxgangs getting to be the regular allotment of many

---

[91] P. Vinogradoff, 'Folkland', *EHR* 8 (1893), pp. 1–17. See also Stevenson, 'Trinoda Necessitas'.

[92] P. Vinogradoff, *English Society in the Eleventh Century: Essays in English Mediaeval History* (Oxford, 1908), pp. 28–30.

[93] Hence the enactments about the settling of men by their mægths. II Æthelstan, ch. 2 [*Gesetze*, vol. 1, pp. 150–4].

[94] DB Worcs. 2:21 (fol. 173a): 'Quattuor liberi homines tenebant de episcopo TRE reddentes omnem socam et sacam et circset et sepultura et expeditione et nauigia et placita ad predictum hundredum: et nunc faciunt similiter qui tenent.' ['Four free men held it (Bishampton) from the bishop TRE, rendering all soke and sake and church-scot and military (service) and ship (service) and pleas to the said hundred: and now those who hold it do the same.']

[95] Ed. K. Von Amira, in H. Paul, *Grundriss der germanischen Philologie*, 2 vols (Strasbourg, 1889–93), vol. 2, p. 105; H. Brunner, *Deutsche Rechtsgeschichte*, 2 vols (Leipzig, 1887–92), vol. 1, pp. 133, 155.

households, while sometimes the free tenants were possessed of plots of irregular size and varying quantities. On the other hand, there arose many larger estates as combinations of several hides. And, what is even more important, it became impossible to perform the ordinary *fyrd* service, in frequent expeditions and in proper equipment, on the basis of a tenement of one hide, without help from outside. The coat of mail and the horse acquired more and more value from a military point of view – one as a means of defence in the hard struggles with the Danes, the other as a means of quick locomotion. Well-forged helmets and swords were scarce and very expensive.[96] Altogether, the difference between a well-armed warrior and a militiaman with indifferent equipment grew more and more important. This led ultimately to the formation of a professional force of knights and sergeants-at-arms, but it led also to changes in the scheme of the *fyrd* expeditions. The same reasons which produced the Lombard Assize of Arms of King Ahistulf, and the graduated service of Charlemagne's armies,[97] secured the transformation of the *fyrd* from a general force of free tribesmen into an array of specially selected warriors. Some of the customs followed in this respect to have been preserved by Domesday Book and one or two Saxon charters. The Berkshire arrangement is the clearest,[98] but there can be no doubt that it coincided in its main lines with similar arrangements in other counties. It was based on the priniciple that only one man per five hides is bound to go to war in case of a royal expedition, and that a sum of 4s. per hide has to be provided for him for two months' service. The Malmesbury and Exeter entries[99] confirm the statement by alluding to the normal service of one soldier per honour of five hides.

It is interesting that Vinogradoff did not use different terminology to distinguish between pre- and post-Conquest knights. For Vinogradoff, versed in the language of post-Conquest lordship, five hides could be an 'honour', and an elite warrior, financed with five hides of land, could be someone who was distinct from one seen as an Alfredian militiaman. Vinogradoff referred to horses as being for 'quick locomotion' rather than as weapons used in combat, but it is nonetheless interesting that he highlights the significance of riding – a factor which distinguished the military elites who emerged in late Carolingian and post-Carolingian Europe – noting that the five-hide units were thus assessed because of the

---

[96] Swords are the objects of bequests along with land and costly trinkets, e.g. Æðelstan Æðeling's will: J. Earle, *A Hand-Book of the Land-Charters and other Saxonic Documents* (Oxford, 1888), pp. 224 ff [S 1503 (AD 1014)]. The average prices of weapons in Austrasia about 800 are marked in Lex Rip[uaria], 36 §11 [ed. R. Sohm, in MGH Leges 5 (Hanover, 1875–89), pp. 231–2], and they are very high.

[97] Ahistulf, 2 [ed. G. H. Pertz, MGH Leges 4 (Hanover, 1868), p. 196]; A. Boretius (ed.), MGH Capitularia regum Francorum 1 (Hanover, 1883), no. 44, p. 123, ch. 6; no. 48, p. 134, ch. 2. [Quotations omitted here.]

[98] DB Berks. B 10 (fol. 56c) [for quotation, see above, p. 56].

[99] DB Wilts. B 5 (fol. 64c) [above, p. 57]; DB Devon C5 (fol. 100a).

provision of horses.[100] However, like his predecessors and indeed his contemporaries, Vinogradoff veered from seeing the system as distinctly feudal, despite using the term 'subinfeudation', because he saw the organization of the army as state- or community-based, noting, for example, the link with the hundredal unit.[101]

> The second point to be noticed is the fact that the array of picked men was turned out by the shire and its hundreds, and not as a mere consequence of feudal dependency. ... The great landowners holding estates rated at multiples of five hides might follow their own method in providing the contingent incumbent on them, and make subinfeudation the means of holding these contingents in readiness. But in the Old English *fyrd* system the apportionment of the service according to five-hide units was not feudal in itself. Small landowners would have to club together in order to fit out the representative of the unit, exactly as in the Lombard and Carolingian instances, and there are traces of such combinations of several participants for 'defending' estates from the *fyrd*, especially in the case of coheirs.

The idea that small landholders would 'club together' put a distinctly democratic (or at least participative) spin on the assessments of five-hide apportionments made by J. H. Round. Vinogradoff's use of the term 'picked', though unsupported by the source material, gives a further twist to the isssue of recruitment.

If Vinogradoff and, likewise, H. M. Chadwick were early commentators on the connections between aristocracy and warfare,[102] it was to be another half century before the issue was picked up again. Hollister's 1962 book represented a significant point in the historiography of military obligation, a logical move from the 'free peasant' interpretations of nineteenth- and early twentieth-century historians. Eric John's *Land Tenure in Early England*, published just two years earlier, and the culmination of work published in the 1950s, had responded to Stenton's work, and argued that military service had been the preserve of social elites in a pre-Conquest form of knight service.[103] Hollister, in an influential work, drew a path between the two extremes, arguing for what has since been interpreted as a dichotomous division between the elements of the Anglo-Saxon *Fyrd*. On the one hand, he coined the term 'Select Fyrd' to refer to the better-resourced warriors who had been organized through units of five hides of land. On the other, he wrote of the 'Great Fyrd' to refer to the mass of less-well-equipped warriors who

---

[100] Vinogradoff, *English Society in the Eleventh Century*, p. 34. For a useful emphasis upon the emergence of cavalry in medieval Europe, see J. F. Verbruggen, 'The Role of the Cavalry in Medieval Warfare', trans. K. DeVries, *JMMH* 3 (2005), pp. 46–71. For further discussion, see pp. 129–39 and pp. 281–6, below.

[101] Vinogradoff, *English Society in the Eleventh Century*, p. 33. For hundreds, see, pp. 99–101.

[102] Chadwick, *Studies on Anglo-Saxon Institutions*, pp. 79–85.

[103] John, *Land Tenure in Early England*; this was a development of his work from the 1950s, including E. John, 'The Imposition of the Common Burdens on the Lands of the English Church', *Bulletin of the Institute of Historical Research* 31 (1958), pp. 117–29, and E. John, 'An Alleged Worcester Charter of the Reign of Edgar', *Bulletin of the John Rylands Library, Manchester* 41 (1958), pp. 54–80. For a further development of John's discussion, see his *Orbis Britanniae*, pp. 128–53, 294–5.

were, he reasoned, called out from the general populace in periods of national emergency such as, most famously, the Viking and Norman threat of 1066.[104]

Hollister's terminology has entered common usage in much general work on Anglo-Saxon warfare,[105] even though, as may be seen from the extract of a significant chapter from his book, he merely intended the terms as convenient labels for what he saw as historical phenomena. Perhaps, as Abels has pointed out, Hollister's 'Great Fyrd' was strongly influenced by a historiographical tradition which kept its roots in Germanic democracy, reflecting the fact that as long ago as 1876, Freeman had argued for the parallel survival of a mostly English fyrd alongside the feudal host in post-Conquest England.[106] It was important for John to have shifted the historiographical focus on Anglo-Saxon society from the *ceorlisc* militia of Stenton and earlier historians, but John's work was problematic in placing much emphasis on tenth-century rights recorded in a group of dubious charters, now demonstrated to be later fabrications.[107] Hollister, on the other hand, was self-consciously balanced in his approach.[108] Richard Abels has pointed out how Hollister's work has come in for later criticism, notably from Nicholas Hooper, for its consideration of a *levée en masse* gleaned from post-Conquest and Continental sources, but Hollister wrote at a time when 'few seriously doubted that the Anglo-Saxons, like other early Germanic peoples, obliged all free men to defend their localities.'[109]

What is significant about Hollister's work is how revolutionary it was in its own terms.[110] Chadwick and John had noted the privatized nature of military holdings but Hollister put flesh on the bones of what he termed the 'Select Fyrd'. Writing in the 1960s, he stated that he was taking 'issue' with 'modern scholars';[111] amongst these was Stenton, who, even if he never reviewed Hollister's work, was

---

[104] For references to widescale participation, see above, pp. 48–9.

[105] See e.g. Norman, *The Medieval Soldier*, pp. 92–3, and M. Harrison, *Anglo-Saxon Thegn, AD 449–1066*, Warrior 5 (Oxford, 1993), pp. 8–10 (although it must be noted that Harrison acknowledges the neologisms, and points out that the distinctions between 'Select' and 'General' fyrds were 'probably blurred' [p. 9]).

[106] Abels, *Lordship and Military Obligation in Anglo-Saxon England*, p. 5. Freeman, *History of the Norman Conquest*, vol. 5, pp. 864–5; see Richardson and Sayles, *Governance of Mediaeval England*, p. 54.

[107] P. Wormald, 'Oswaldslow: An "Immunity"?', in *St. Oswald of Worcester: Life and Influence*, ed. N. P. Brooks and C. Cubitt, SEHB: The Makers of England 2 (London, 1996), pp. 117–28; P. Wormald, 'Lordship and Justice in the Early English Kingdom: Oswaldslow Revisited', in *Property and Power in the Early Middle Ages*, ed. W. Davies and P. Fouracre (Cambridge, 1995), pp. 114–36. However, such reservations were noted at the time of John's book: see F. M. Stenton's review of John, *Land Tenure in Early England*, EHR 77 (1962), pp. 551–2.

[108] See Abels, *Lordship and Military Obligation in Anglo-Saxon England*, pp. 4–5. Hollister refers to himself as a subscriber of a 'middle school' of historians in Hollister, '1066: The "Feudal Revolution"', p. 711.

[109] Abels, *Lordship and Military Obligation in Anglo-Saxon England*, p. 5, referring to N. Hooper, 'Anglo-Saxon Warfare on the Eve of the Conquest: A Brief Survey', ANS 1 (1979 for 1978), pp. 84–93, at pp. 87–8.

[110] Abels, *Lordship and Military Obligation in Anglo-Saxon England*, p. 5.

[111] Hollister, *Anglo-Saxon Military Institutions*, p. 64; see below, p. 74.

presumably considered by Hollister to be a member of his intended audience. Hollister's chapter is also included here because of its direct engagement with the work of Stenton, whose 1932 work on English Feudalism is quoted at length.[112]

· ·

The Personnel of the Select Fyrd

C. WARREN HOLLISTER

Again and again in the sources for the history of late-Saxon England, one encounters references to a three-fold obligation which rested upon the land. Almost without exception, tenants are said to owe military service, fortress work, and bridge repair. Even when a landholder is granted exemptions from almost every imaginable royal service, these three duties are reserved. They are mentioned in the laws of several pre-Conquest kings as obligations resting on everyone. Thus, according to 2 Cnut 65, 'If anybody neglects the repair of fortresses or bridges or military service, he shall pay 120s. as compensation to the king in districts under the English law, and the amount fixed by existing regulations in the Danelaw …'[113] These obligations have traditionally been called the *trinoda necessitas*, or, more correctly, *trimoda necessitas*, and although the legitimacy of this term has been questioned, I find it a convenient label for the threefold obligation and will henceforth use it accordingly.[114]

The *trimoda necessitas* appear with regularity in Anglo-Saxon land charters. The earliest reference to the obligations comes from Mercia in the late eighth century.[115] In Latin charters they are usually specified by such phrases as *expeditio et pontis arcisque restauratio*.[116] In Anglo-Saxon documents they appear under a variety of names. Military service might be expressed as *fyrd-faru, fyrd-foereld,*

---

[112] F. M. Stenton, *The First Century of English Feudalism, 1066–1166: Being the Ford Lectures Delivered in the University of Oxford in Hilary Term 1929* (Oxford, 1932). The chapter reproduced below is from Hollister, *Anglo-Saxon Military Institutions*, pp. 59–84.

[113] [*Gesteze*, vol. I, pp. 353–2]; cf. *II [recte V] Æthelred*, ch. 26.1 [*Gesetze*, vol. I, pp. 242–3]; *VI Æthelred*, ch. 32.3 [*Gesetze*, vol. I, pp. 254–5]; 2 Cnut, ch. 10 [*Gesetze*, vol. I, pp. 314–15].

[114] On the use and meaning of this term, see Stevenson, 'Trinoda Necessitas.'

[115] See Birch, *Cartularium Saxonicum*, no. 203 [S 59] (AD 770). Here fyrd duty itself is absent but fortress duty is expressed in military terms: '… praeter instructionibus pontium vel necessaris [*sic*] defensionibus arcium contra hostes.' ['except in the building of bridges or the necessary defences of fortifications against enemies.'] The more formal formula appears first in Birch, C.S., no. 274 [S 139] AD 793–6): '… preter expeditionalibus causis et pontium structionum et arcium munimentum quod omni populo necesse est …' ['except for the reason of expeditions and the construction of bridges and the building of fortresses which is necessary for all the people']. This passage suggests that the custom was by no means novel at the end of the eighth century. See Stevenson, 'Trinoda Necessitas', p. 696, and E. John, 'The Imposition of the Common Burdens on the Lands of the English Church', *Bulletin of the Institute of Historical Research* 31 (1958), pp. 117–29 [John, *Land Tenure in Early England*, pp. 64–79]. It should be emphasized that the three obligations probably did not arise simultaneously, and that there are early instances of one or two of the obligations appearing in charters without the third.

[116] Earle, *Hand-Book of the Land-Charters*, p. xxi.

fyrd-socne, or simply *fyrd*.[117] To pick at random an example of the *trimoda necessitas*
clause in an Old English charter, Ethelbert of Kent made an exchange of land
with his thegn Wulflaf in 858, with the stipulation that Wulflaf's land should be
free of all royal services and secular burdens except military service, the building
of bridges, and fortress work – *absque expeditione sola et pontium structura et
arcium munitionibus*.[118] Some variation of this reservation appears in most of the
charters of the age. In 957 King Edwig granted an estate to Oda, archbishop of
Canterbury, free from everything except for the three burdens which are common
to all people, i.e. *expeditionis et arcis pontisque constructione*.[119] Exemptions from
the *trimoda necessitas* are very rare in the Anglo-Saxon age, although they become
rather common in the era following the Norman Conquest.[120]

We must now determine the relationship between the military obligation of
the *trimoda necessitas* and the various sorts of fyrd service which have already been
examined. At first glance, the statement that the *trimoda necessitas* were burdens
common to all people might suggest an identification with service in the great
fyrd. But on the other hand, there is strong evidence that the military obligation
of the *trimoda necessitas* was based on hides and thus was identical to the select-
fyrd duty of producing warrior-representatives when the army was summoned. In
a document of AD 801, confirming an earlier grant of an estate of thirty hides in
Middlesex by Offa, king of Mercia, to Abbot Stithbert, we are told that the estate
owed the three public burdens, 'i.e. the construction of bridges and forts and also,
in the necessity of military service, only five men are to be sent'.[121] This is the only
charter known to stipulate the amount of military service owed in accordance

---

[117] Earle, *Land-Charters of the Land-Charters*, pp. xxi, 242; Stevenson, 'Trinoda Necessitas',
p. 689n.

[118] Earle, *Land Charters of the Land-Charters*, p. 126; J. M. Kemble (ed.), *Codex Diplomaticus
Ævi Saxonici Opera Johannis M. Kemble*, 6 vols (London, 1839–48) [hereafter 'Kemble,
C.D.'] no. 281; Birch, *Cartularium Saxonicum*, no. 496 [S 328 (AD 858)].

[119] Birch, *Cartularium Saxonicum*, no. 999 [S 646 (AD 957)]; A. S. Napier and W. H.
Stevenson (eds), *The Crawford Collection of Early Charters and Documents* (Oxford, 1895),
p. 10.

[120] Birch, *Cartularium Saxonicum*, no. 1343; Napier and Stevenson, *Crawford Collection*, p. 6;
Kemble, C.D., no. 240 [S 405 (AD 930)]. Some documents grant general exemptions
without mentioning the *trimoda necessitas*: e.g. C. G. O. Bridgeman (ed.), *Wulfric Spot's
Will*, in *Collections for a History of Staffordshire*, William Salt Archaeological Soc. (London,
1918), vol. 1916, pp. 1–66, at pp. 13–14 (S 1536 [AD 1002×4]) and Kemble, C.D., no. 805
(S 1408 [AD ?1051×6]). On the question of whether such general exemptions inluded
immunity from the threefold obligation, see Stevenson, 'Trinoda Necessitas', pp. 701ff., and
R. Stewart-Brown, '"Bridge-Work" at Chester', *EHR* 54 (1939), pp. 83–7, at p. 87. Professor
Stewart-Brown challenges Stevenson's statement that general exemption clauses did not
exempt lands from the *trimoda necessitas*. However, Stewart-Brown's evidence dates from
the thirteenth and fourteenth centuries, long after the age when the threefold burden was
regarded as sacrosanct.

[121] 'Trium tamen causarum puplicarum ratio reddatur hoc est instructio pontuum [*sic*] et
arcis verum etiam in expeditionis necessitatem vires [*sic*] v. tantum modo mittantur.' ['Yet
the due amount of the three public causes is to be paid, that is the construction of bridges
and forts, and also, in the necessity of military service, only five men are to be sent.' Trans.
EHD 1, p. 501] Birch, *Cartularium Saxonicum*, no. 201 [S 1186a (AD 799×801)].

with the *trimoda necessitas*. The estate owes five men from thirty hides or one man from every six hides. This has led more than one historian to speculate as to the existence of a widespread six-hide unit, competing, as it were, with the five-hide unit.[122] Miss Hollings, on the other hand, finds this charter perfectly compatible with the five-hide rule. She assumes that twenty-five of the thirty hides owed military service and that the remaining five hides, being inland, were exempt.[123] But there is nothing in the charter to indicate that the estate had an inland of five hides, nor, as we have seen, is it safe to assume that inland was exempt from military service. This charter is important to us neither as an illustration of the five-hide rule nor as an indication of an otherwise unknown six-hide rule. Its importance lies in the fact that it proves the relationship between the military service of the *trimoda necessitas* and the warrior-representative arrangements of the select fyrd. Five men serve from thirty hides and are therefore the warrior-representatives of the estate. The service is exceptional, to be sure, because it does not conform to the five-hide rule, but its connexion with select-fyrd duty is unmistakable. Nor should we be overly disturbed by the discovery of an exception to the five-hide recruitment system. On the contrary, we can be quite certain that if the Middlesex estate had followed the customary five-hide pattern, the number of warriors which it owed would never have been stipulated. We are told that the estate owed five warriors precisely because the assessment rate was exceptional. In no other grant is the amount of service specified. The normal charter states that the tenement contains a certain number of hides and that it owes military service. It was unnecessary to say more, since the service could always be calculated by dividing the total number of hides by five. We can perhaps appreciate more clearly the significance of King Offa's grant by comparing it with certain other unusual charters. In the mid eleventh century Bishop Ealdred of Worcester granted a lease of 1½ hides of land to Wulfgeat, who was to discharge the royal military obligations of this small estate at the rate of one hide.[124] In other words, Wulfgeat ought to have owed nearly one-third of a warrior to the select fyrd, but he owed instead only one-fifth. Or, to express the same thing in terms of the Berkshire support system, Wulfgeat was obliged to support the warrior-representative of his five-hide unit with 4s., the amount normally due from one hide, instead of 6s., the amount due from 1½ hides. Again, Abbot Ælfweard of Evesham leased to Æthelmar an estate which was assessed at three hides for home service (inware) and 1½ hides for national service (utware).[125] Utware, as we have seen, included

[122] E.g. H. M. Chadwick, *The Origin of the English Nation* (Cambridge, 1907; 2nd edn, 1924), p. 151.

[123] M. Hollings, 'The Survival of the Five-Hide Unit in the Western Midlands', *EHR* 63 (1948), pp. 453–87. On the five-hide unit in Middlesex, see J. H. Round, *Feudal England: Historical Studies on the Eleventh and Twelfth Centuries* (London, 1895), pp. 66–7. Round writes (p. 66): 'In Middlesex the five-hide unit is particularly prominent.'

[124] Kemble, *C.D.* no. 804 [S 1409 (AD 1051×5)].

[125] A. J. Robertson (ed.), *Anglo-Saxon Charters* (Cambridge, 1939; 2nd edn, 1956), p. 156 [S 1423 (AD 1016×23)].

royal military service, and would indicate here an obligation to pay 6s. toward the support of the warrior representative of the five-hide unit. Accordingly, we can say that King Offa's grant in Middlesex involved an estate of thirty hides which was to discharge the royal military obligation at the rate of twenty-five hides.

There is good evidence that bridge repair and fortress work, the two remaining burdens of the *trimoda necessitas*, were also assessed in terms of hides. According to the Domesday survey, the reeve of Chester had the right to summon one man from every hide in the county for the repair of the city wall and the bridge, and the burden of constructing and repairing Rochester bridge rested upon the neighbouring lands.[126] Thus, all three of the obligations were territorial rather than personal and were normally assessed in terms of hides. The military duty of the *trimoda necessitas* provides us with another avenue of approach to the structure of the select fyrd.

II

We have seen that service in the great fyrd was an obligation incumbent upon all freemen, but it may well he inquired what classes the select fyrd normally included. Stenton believes that the five-hide recruitment system described in the Berkshire passage of Domesday Book refers exclusively to peasants.[127] He maintains that there existed, apart from what I have termed the select-fyrd duty, an obligation incumbent upon all thegns to serve in the royal army as a consequence of their rank. The select-fyrd obligation was territorial rather than personal, whereas the military obligation of the thegn was personal rather than territorial.[128] We can certainly agree with Stenton that peasants served in the select fyrd, although it seems to me most doubtful that the select fyrd was limited to peasants. The Maldon poet describes the English force which Ealdorman Byrhtnoth led against the Danes in AD 991 as 'the flower of the East Saxons',[129] and if this is an accurate description rather than a mere rhetorical flourish we would assume that the personnel of Byrhtnoth's army included mercenaries and members of the select fyrd but excluded the great fyrd. If this assumption is valid, then we can be certain that the select fyrd included peasants, for a ceorl named Dunhere, armed with a lance, played an important role in the battle.[130] Indeed the very existence of a five-hide recruitment system implies the military service of peasants, for there were innumerable five-hide units throughout England which

---

[126] DB Cheshire C 21 (fol. 262d); Robertson, *Anglo-Saxon Charters*, p. 106 [S 1481d (? s. xiⁱ)]. The work for the seventh and eighth piers of the bridge, for example, is due 'from the Hoo people's *land*'. See E. Hasted, *The History and Topographical Survey of Kent*, 2nd edn (Canterbury, 1797–1801), vol. 2, pp. 15–22. For fortress work at Malmesbury, see A. Ballard, *The Domesday Boroughs* (Oxford, 1904), p. 34.

[127] Stenton, *First Century of English Feudalism*, pp. 116–17.

[128] Stenton, *First Century of English Feudalism*, pp. 118–19.

[129] Line 68 [D. Scragg (ed. and trans.), 'The Battle of Maldon', in *The Battle of Maldon, AD 991*, ed. D. Scragg (Oxford, 1991), p. 20; Scragg (p. 21) translates the term referred to by Hollister, *Eastseaxena ord*, as 'the Essex vanguard'].

[130] Lines 255–64 [Scragg, 'Battle of Maldon', pp. 28–9].

cannot possibly have been represented by thegns. For one thing, the unit might form only a part of a much larger estate held by a single thegn who had to find warrior-representatives for every five hides within his tenement. Again, the five-hide unit might not be part of any thegn's estate.

But on the other hand, the five-hide system disclosed by the Berkshire entry cannot have applied exclusively to peasants. For one thing, the Berkshire support system provided the warrior-representative with wages of 4d. per day, which seems unusually high for a peasant soldier. Fully armed mounted knights in the Anglo-Norman period were receiving wages of only 6d. per day,[131] and even in the late twelfth century the boatswains in the crusading fleet of King Richard the Lion-Hearted received 4d. per day and the sailors in the same fleet 2d. per day.[132] Moreover, the assumption that thegn duty was distinct from service in the select fyrd implies the existence of two mutually exclusive select armies. For that reason, as I have elsewhere observed,[133] the notion of a separate personal military obligation incumbent on all thegns is unreasonable on a priori grounds. The select peasant army would be if anything more exclusive than the military thegnhood. Numerous Domesday thegns held estates that were much smaller than five hides,[134] and might well have envied the prosperous peasant warrior with his 20s. for maintenance and wages. So I must take issue with Stenton and with the majority of modern scholars. The military obligation of the English thegns was not personal but territorial; it was founded on the duty of every five-hide unit to produce a competent warrior, and was therefore identical with the obligation of the select fyrd. Thegns served in the select fyrd as well as peasants and on exactly the same basis as peasants. Nor is this fact subversive to our conception of late-Saxon England as a strongly aristocratic society, for it should be remembered that the peasant warriors of the select fyrd constituted only a small fraction of the whole English peasantry. They doubtless represented the *élite* of their class

---

[131] C. W. Hollister, 'The Significance of Scutage Rates in Eleventh- and Twelfth-Century England', *EHR* 75 (1960), pp. 577–88, at pp. 580–1.

[132] Round, *Feudal England*, p. 273; Vinogradoff, *English Society in the Eleventh Century*, p. 18.

[133] C. W. Hollister, 'The Five-Hide Unit and the Old English Military Obligation', *Speculum* 36 (1961), pp. 61–74, at p. 71.

[134] E.g. DB Cheshire R 1:1–39 (fol. 269c), R 5:3, R 5:6 (fol. 270a), Lincs. 25:1(fol. 356b), 68:1–48 (fols. 370b–371c). See Little, 'Gesiths and Thegns', p. 729n, and Maitland, *Domesday Book and Beyond*, pp. 64 ff., 165, and the references there given. J. H. Beeler states that the military obligation of the thegn 'seems to have been purely personal, and was not due from the land': C. Oman, *The Art of War in the Middle Ages*, rev. and ed. J. H. Beeler (Ithaca, NY, 1953), p. 24. R. R. Darlington writes 'Thegn and peasant alike were under the obligation to serve in war when called upon by the king to do so, but the obligation of the thegn … was a personal one, the outcome of his rank …': 'The Last Phase of Anglo-Saxon History', *History* new series 22 (1937), pp. 1–13. G. O. Sayles states, 'It was because of the ancient traditions and duties connected with their social rank, and not because of the lands they held, that the thegns rendered service in war. The obligation was purely personal and not territorial': G. O. Sayles, *Medieval Foundations of England* (Philadelphia, 1950), p. 210. But modern scholars are not unanimous on this point; see J. E. A. Jolliffe, *The Constitutional History of Medieval England from the English Settlements to 1485* (New York and London, 1937), p. 96, and Hollings, 'Survival of the Five-Hide Unit', pp. 467 ff.

and were, to say the least, atypical. It would be grotesque to regard the select fyrd as an illustration of Old Saxon democracy or a microcosm of the classless society. But it would be equally wrong to insist that thegns and peasants cannot possibly have fought side by side, for we find them doing precisely that in every important battle from Maldon to Hastings.

But since the majority of historians now favour the notion that the thegn's military obligation was personal, we must explore the problem in detail. Modern historical opinion on the subject seems to be based on a passage in Stenton's distinguished book, *The First Century of English Feudalism*, and since the issue is so crucial to a correct understanding of the pre-Conquest military system, I will quote the passage in full:[135]

> The thegn's obligation was of no less ancient origin [than that of the peasants], but its basis was different. There is no doubt that in the eleventh century a king's thegn, when summoned to an expedition, must obey, under penalties which might amount to an entire forfeiture of his land. The same service was demanded from thegns who held of other lords than the king. In either case, so far as we can see, the obligation was purely personal. There is nowhere any suggestion that a thegn's military service was due in respect of an estate which the king or any other lord has given him. It is a duty which follows from his rank, the expression of the traditions of an order which, as a class, represented the military companions of a lord, the *gesithas*, of ancient times. These traditions were still strong in the century before the Norman Conquest. They are nowhere more clearly brought out than in the poem which relates the death of Byrhtnoth at Maldon in 991. The men who are most prominent in the poem are naturally the companions, the personal following of the earl, but they included landed Essex thegns and their close kinsmen. The ideas which moved these men must have been common to the whole class from which they sprung (*sic*). It is more than probable that many thegns of the eleventh century were country gentlemen, with no special aptitude for war. In most cases, the estates of a thegn of 1066 must have come to him by inheritance, and not by the gift of a king or any other lord. But his obligation to military service represented the ancient duty of attending a lord in battle.

In a later work, *Anglo-Saxon England*, Stenton summarizes his views as follows:[136]

> The military service of the thegn was a duty which fell on him as a consequence of his rank, and was inherent in the constitution of Old English

[135] Stenton, *First Century of English Feudalism*, pp. 118–19.

[136] F. M. Stenton, *Anglo-Saxon England*, Oxford History of England 2 (Oxford, 1943; 2nd edn, 1947), p. 275. But Stenton is not perfectly consistent. In an earlier work he states that thegnland 'denotes the holding of a thegn, land defended by military service' (*Types of Manorial Structure in the Northern Danelaw*, Oxford Studies in Social and Legal History 2 [Oxford, 1910], p. 13), and adds, 'Essentially, thegnland is a portion of an estate granted out to secure the performance of military service by the grantee' (p. 16, n. 2).

Society. There is evidence in Domesday Book suggesting that every thegn, or at least every thegn possessing rights of jurisdiction would receive a personal summons to the host, and that if he disobeyed it the king was entitled to confiscate his land.

The evidence which Stenton cites to support his position consists of three passages from Domesday Book. The first passage relates to Worcestershire:[137]

> When the king goes on a military expedition, if one who is summoned remains behind and if he is so free a man as to have his *soc* and *sac* [i.e. his rights of jurisdiction] and can go with his land to whomever he wishes, he is in the king's mercy for all his land. But if the freeman of another lord remains away from the army, and his lord leads another man to the host in his place, he pays 40s. to his lord who received the summons. But if nobody at all goes in his place, he shall pay his lord 40s. but his lord must pay the entire amount to the king.

The second passage pertains to Berkshire and runs as follows:[138]

> If anyone summoned on an expedition did not go, he forfeited all his land to the king. But if anyone for the sake of remaining behind promised to send another in his place, and yet he who was to have been sent remained behind, his lord was freed of obligation by the payment of 50s.

Finally, an Oxfordshire passage reports that 'whoever was to go on an expedition and did not do so owed 100s. to the king'.[139] Stenton then concludes:

> These passages leave innumerable points of detail unexplained, but they agree in suggesting that there lay on the landed thegn of the eleventh century a military duty which was essentially a personal obligation to obey a royal summons, and entirely distinct from his responsibility for seeing that the free men upon his estate served in accordance with local custom [i.e. in the select fyrd].

I have considerable difficulty in following Stenton's reasoning here, for I cannot discover in these Domesday passages the slightest suggestion that every landed thegn owed military service or that the thegn's military obligation was personal rather than territorial. Nor is there evidence that every thegn possessing

---

[137] These three passages are quoted in *First Century of English Feudalism*, p. 118n. For the first, see DB Worcs. C 5 (fol. 172a): 'Quando rex in hostem pergit si quis edictu eius vocatus remanserit, si ita liber homo est ut habeat socam suam et sacam et cum terra possit ire quo voluerit de omni terra sua est in misericordia regis. Cuiuscunque vero alterius domini liber homo, si de hoste remanserit, et dominus eius pro eo alium homiem duxerit, xl solidos domino suo xl solidos dabit; dominus autem eius totidem solidos regi emendabit.'

[138] DB Berks. B 10 (fol. 56c): 'Si quis in expeditionem summonitus non ibat, totam terram suam erga regem forisfaciebat. Quod si quis remanendi habens alium pro se mittere promitteret, et tamen qui mittendus erat remaneret, pro 1 solidis quietus erat dominus eius.' [For an alternative translation, see above, p. 56.]

[139] DB Oxon. 1:13 (fol. 154d): 'Qui monitus ire in expeditionem non vadit, c solidus regi dabat.'

jurisdictional rights was subject to the military summons. The Worcestershire passage, which is the only one that refers to jurisdictional rights, merely states that if the man who had been summoned to the fyrd and defaulted possessed rights of jurisdiction, he was to forfeit his land. But there were numerous landed thegns who lacked rights of jurisdiction. As Jolliffe has observed, 'it is clear that there was no common right of jurisdiction in the thegnage. Some king's thegns had their soke and some had not.'[140] More important still, the Worcestershire passage does not state that everyone with rights of jurisdiction received a summons. It merely reports that if the summoned defaulter happened to possess such rights he would be punished accordingly. Let us imagine for a moment that some assiduous scholar discovered a previously unknown Anglo-Saxon law stating that if anyone summoned to the fyrd was sick with the plague he would be excused from service. Would it be legitimate to conclude from this that every Englishman who was sick with the plague received a personal summons to the army? The truth of the matter is that the Worcestershire passage tells us nothing whatever about the military obligation of thegns. The summoned man might be a thegn or he might be a peasant. He might have *sac* and *soc* or he might not. He might possess an estate or he might be landless (he loses his land only if he has rights of jurisdiction). He might, in fact, be anyone at all.

The second passage is much shorter but is also a little more helpful, for it suggests that the man who was summoned was ordinarily a landholder. But peasants held land as well as thegns, and the passage is conspicuously silent on the matter of the summoned warrior's social status. The Oxfordshire passage, which is the third and last that Stenton quotes to support his view, says merely that if the man who was to serve in the fyrd defaulted, he owed 100s.; again we are unable to discover whether the defaulter was a peasant or a nobleman.

Perhaps Stenton means to imply that the military service of these men was personal rather than territorial because they received a personal summons. But the receiving of a summons is by no means incompatible with territorial service. If, for example, a thegn possessed an estate of five hides, he might very well be expected to perform the military service due from the five-hide unit and would doubtless receive a summons from the sheriff whenever the king wished to assemble his select fyrd. The summons would be personal, but the basis of the service would be territorial. Thus, the town of Warwick owed ten burghers to the select fyrd; if one of these ten was summoned but failed to go, he owed the king a *fyrdwite* of 100s.[141] Nobody could possibly suggest that the receipt of a military summons by a Warwick burgher proves that all townsmen owed personal service in the fyrd as a consequence of their social rank, for we are told in the same passage that aside from the ten burghers who served as warrior-representatives the remaining Warwick townsmen were exempt. Again, the reeve of Cheshire had the right to summon one man from every hide in the county to repair the city

---

[140] Jolliffe, *Constitutional History of Medieval England*, pp. 145–6.
[141] DB Warwicks. B 6 (fol. 238a).

walls and the bridge, on penalty of 40s. for default of service.[142] The summons was evidently personal but the service was clearly territorial.

We have already seen that the warrior-representative of the five-hide unit was not chosen by rotation, but was specially designated. The same man would normally serve on all campaigns, and it is to him that the military summons would go. Thus, Siwate and his three brothers inherited their father's estate in Lincolnshire, dividing it equally among them. In the event of a military expedition, Siwate normally served as the warrior-representative of the estate, his brothers giving him financial support on the pattern of the Berkshire system. Should Siwate be unable to go, one of his brothers served, and Siwate and the others aided him. But the passage concludes with the specific statement that Siwate was the king's man.[143] Was Siwate a thegn? So it would seem, but if he was, then the passage proves that all landed thegns did not serve in the army. For by the eleventh century thegnhood was hereditary and Siwate's brothers would be thegns as well as he.[144] In any event, Siwate was the specified warrior-representative of his estate, and therefore would receive the summons and, if necessary, pay the fyrdwite. Yet it is perfectly evident that Siwate's obligation was based on his land rather than his rank in society—it was territorial rather than personal.[145] Again, two brothers, Chetel and Turuer, divided their father's Lincolnshire estate in such a way that Chetel normally performed military service and Turuer supported him financially.[146] The service was territorial but the

[142] DB Cheshire C 21 (fol. 262d).

[143] DB Lincs. CS 38 (fol. 375d): 'Siuuate et Alnod et Fenchel et Anschil equaliter et pariliter diuiserunt inter se terram patris sui, TRE, et ita tenuerunt ut si opus fuit expeditione Regis et Siuuate potuit ire, alii fratres iuuerunt eum. Post istum, iuit alter, et Siuuate cum reliquis iuuit eum, et six de omnibus. Siuuate tamen fuit homo Regis.' ['Siwate (= Sighvatr), Alnoth, Fenkell and Eskil equally and jointly divided between themselves the land of their father TRE and held it in such a way that if work was necessary for a royal expedition and Siwate could go, the other brothers helped him. After him, another went and Siwate, with the rest, helped him; and so on with them all. However, Siwate was the King's man.']

[144] On the hereditary status of thegns, see Little, 'Gesiths and Thegns', p. 729, and Chadwick, *Studies on Anglo-Saxon Institutions*, pp. 79–80.

[145] There are many similar parage tenures recorded in Domesday Book: DB Kent 5:43 (fol. 7b); 5:198 (fol. 11b); Hants 1:12 (fol. 38b); 2:5 (fol. 40a); 23:18 (fol. 45b); 23:62 (fol. 46b); 69:44 (fol. 50c); Berks. 17:2 (fol. 60a); 64:1 (fol. 63c); 41:9 (fol. 72c); Dorset 52:1, 52:2 (fol. 83a); 55:1 (fol. 83c); 55:42 (fol. 84a); Som. 26:3 (fol. 96c); Devon 15:47 (fol. 105b); 39:14 (fol. 116a); Devon 44:1 (fol. 117a); Bucks. 5:10 (fols. 145b–c); 12:24 (fol. 146c); 43:4 (fol. 152a); Glos. 53:3 (fol. 168c); Beds. 23:53 (fol. 214a); Notts. 18:5 (fol. 291a); Lincs. 3:29 (fol. 341b); 22:22 (fol. 354a); 26:45 (fol. 357c); CS 21 (fol. 375a); Essex B 1 (LDB fol. 104r); Norfolk 20:29 (LDB fol. 229r) [N. B. samples are taken from the folios cited by Hollister, generally of the first example of parage tenure on a cited folio; some folios may have more than one example of what Hollister considered to have been parage]; Exon. Domesday [in *Liber Censualis qui vocatur Domesday Book, Additamenta*, ed. H. Ellis (London, 1816)], fols 202, 247, 329, 334, 354, 480. Cf. II Cnut, chs 70, 78 [*Gesetze*, vol. I, pp. 356, 364]. See also Vinogradoff, *English Society in the Eleventh Century*, pp. 245–50, and Maitland, *Domesday Book and Beyond*, p. 145.

[146] DB Lincs. 22:26 (fol. 354a).

summons was personal. If the personal summons which Chetel received meant that he performed his service as a consequence of his rank, then why was his brother exempt? These examples could be multiplied almost indefinitely, but it should by now be perfectly evident that the receiving of a military summons or the payment of fyrdwite is quite irrelevant to the question of whether the service has a personal or territorial basis. Stenton is probably correct in his statement that 'in the eleventh century a king's thegn, when summoned to an expedition, must obey, under penalties which might amount to an entire forfeiture of his land', but one cannot conclude from this fact that every thegn, or every landed thegn, or every thegn with jurisdictional rights owed personal military service. If any doubt remains on the matter, it should be dispelled by a passage from Ine's laws which alludes to common ceorls paying *fyrdwite* for failure to heed a military summons.[147]

Stenton goes on to state: 'There is nowhere any suggestion that a thegn's military service was due in respect of an estate which the king or any other lord has given him.' In connexion with this assertion, let us examine a passage from a well-known late-Saxon document, the *Rectitudines Singularum Personarum*: 'The law of the thegn is ... that he shall contribute three things in respect of his land: armed service and the repairing of fortressses and work on bridges.'[148] This passage is the only one I know of that lists military service as a normal obligation of thegns. It is perfectly clear on the point that the thegn's military service is territorial—that he owes armed service *in respect of his land*. It also connects the thegn's service with the *trimoda necessitas*, which we have already associated with the select-fyrd obligation and which we have found to have a territorial basis.

The passage from the *Rectitudines* is not conclusive, however, for Stenton and others would maintain that this obligation was essentially supervisorial—that the thegn was to make certain that the peasants on his estates performed the service due from the land. According to this interpretation, the passage in the *Rectitudines* does not actually refer to the thegn's military service at all, but rather to his obligation to supervise the recruitment of his ceorls.[149] But it seems clear that the passage refers to both. The thegn possessing a five-hide tenement served personally for his estate in the select fyrd, while the thegn with an estate of, say, fifteen hides, answered the summons personally and was also responsible for the appearance of two additional warrior-representatives. To deny that the passage

---

[147] Ine, ch. 51 [*Gesetze*, vol. I, pp. 112–13].

[148] 'Þæt he ðreo ðinc of his land do fyrd-færeld ⁊ burh-bote ⁊ bryc-geweorc.' 'et ut ita faciat pro terra sua, scilicet, expeditionem, burhbotam, et brigbotam.' The document is printed in *Gesetze*, vol. I, pp. 444–53. For a discussion of it, see F. Seebohm, *The English Village Community: Examined in its Relations to the Manorial and Trival Systems and to the Common or Open Field System of Husbandry: An Essay in Economic History* (Cambridge, 1883; 4th edn, London, 1890), pp. 129–47; Maitland, *Domesday Book and Beyond*, pp. 327–9; P. Vinogradoff, *Growth of the Manor* (London, 1905; 2nd edn, 1911), pp. 231–5.

[149] Stenton, *Anglo-Saxon England*, 2nd edn, p. 575; R. R. Reid, 'Baronage and Thanage', *EHR* 35 (1920), pp. 161–99, at p. 171.

has anything to do with the military service of thegns seems to me a hazardous assumption.

The thegn with five hides or more, or the thegn with a smaller estate who served as warrior-representative for a five-hide unit, was expected to contribute personally – to perform the duties encompassed by the *trimoda necessitas*. Accordingly, Bishop Denewulf of Winchester leased fifteen hides to a thegn named Beornwulf who was to contribute yearly to the repair of the church, to pay the church scots, and to perform (hewe) military service and bridge and fortress work 'as all others do'.[150] Around the middle of the eleventh century Bishop Ealdred of Worcester leased an estate of 1½ hides at Ditchford to his thegn, Wulfgeat, who, at the king's summons, was to redeem [*hredde*] it at the rate of one hide.[151] The same bishop granted to another of his thegns, Æthelstan the Fat, 'a certain piece of land, namely two hides along with what he had before and with the uninhabited land—and he shall discharge the obligations upon them at the rate of two hides. ... This estate shall be free of every burden except wall and bridge work and military service and church dues.'[152] At Peterborough a tenant named Ansford, who was the immediate tenurial successor of the well-known English warrior-hero, Hereward, performed military service for half a hide, and another Peterborough tenant, Robert de Guneges, served for three hides.[153] Bishop Oswald of Worcester stated explicitly that his leasehold tenants, most of whom were thegns, owed service to the king in proportion to the size of their holdings.[154]

It may perhaps be thought unlikely that a nobleman of the thegn class would

---

[150] Birch, *Cartularium Saxonicum*, no. 599 [S 1285 (AD 902)]: '7 fyrde 7 brycge 7 fester ge weorc hewe swa mon ofer eall dolc do.' On the meaning of *hewe* in this passage, see F. E. Harmer (ed.), *Select English Historical Documents of the Ninth and Tenth Centuries* (Cambridge, 1914), p. 113, and *Gesetze*, vol. 2, p. 331. Liebermann (editor of *Gesetze*) equates the term with *heawe* and suggests that it only applied to bridge and fortress work. But even if this is so, the passage provdes that thegns actually performed at least two items of the *trimoda necessitas*. Dr. Harmer believes that the term applies to all three obligations (*Select English Historical Documents of the Ninth and Tenth Centuries*, pp. 29, 60, 113).

[151] Robertson, *Anglo-Saxon Charters*, p. 208 [S 1409 (AD 1051×5)]. On the meaning of the verb *hreddan*, see Robertson, p. 459, and Hollings, 'Survival of the Five-Hide Unit', pp. 467–8.

[152] Robertson, *Anglo-Saxon Charters*, pp. 208–10 [S 1406 (AD 1046×53)]: '7 he hig eac werige for twa hida.' See Robertson, p. 460.

[153] *Chronicon Petroburgense*, ed. T. Stapleton, Camden Society 47 (London, 1849), p. 75. These holdings, however, are in Lincolnshire where gelds and military service were assessed by carucates. Why the obligations of the tenures were expressed in hides is unclear. On Ansford, see DB Lincs 8:34–5 (fol. 346b), CK4 (fol. 376d).

[154] Birch, *C.S.*, no. 1136 [S 1368 (c. AD 964)]: '... ad regale explendum semper illius archiductoris dominatui et voluntati qui episcopatui presidet propter beneficium quod illis prestitum est cum omni humilitate et subjectione subditi fiant secundum ipsius voluntatem *et terrarum quas quisque possidet quantitatem*.' ['... for the royal supplies for the power and will of that king who always guards the episcopate on account of the service which is discharged by him, furnishing all humility and subjection, let them be according to his will *and whatever quantity of lands he possesses*.'] Cf. Maitland, *Domesday Book and Beyond*, pp. 305ff.

be required to perform such menial services as bridge and fortress work. But in Domesday Book we find thegns who are obliged to do ploughing and to work at the harvest, and a twelfth-century charter of Bury St. Edmunds reports that knights customarily joined the free sokemen and burghers in repairing the ditch that surrounded the town.[155] A tenth-century Anglo-Saxon document, the Burghal Hidage, suggests that the obligation of fortress work was very closely associated with that of fortress defence, and that the same men performed both.[156] This view is strengthened by a passage from the Anglo-Saxon Chronicle reporting that King Edward the Elder went to Nottingham with his fyrd and had a fortress built on the south side of the river, exactly opposite an already-existing fort. He then had a bridge made over the Trent to connect the two strongholds.[157] here we find fyrd soldiers apparently doing both bridge and fortress work as a function of their military service, and we are shown that all three of the *trimoda neessitas* could be military in nature.

The second of the three Domesday entries which Stenton cites in support of the personal nature of the thegn's military obligation appears on closer examination to suggest precisely the opposite, and is itself a convincing indication of the territorial basis of thegn service. The passage comes from the Berkshire section of Domesday Book and is, in fact, immediately adjacent to the passage relating to the five-hide system which we have used to reconstruct the organization of the select fyrd. Let us look at the passage as a whole:[158]

> If the king sent an army anywhere, only one soldier went from five hides, and four shillings were given him from each hide as subsistence and wages for two months. This money, indeed, was not sent to the king but was given to the soldiers. If anyone summoned on an expedition did not go, he forfeited all his land to the king. But if anyone for the sake of remaining behind promised to send another in his place, and yet he who was to have been sent remained behind, his lord was freed of obligation by the payment of 50s.

According to Stenton's theory, the first half of this passage refers to the service of peasants in the select fyrd, whereas the last half refers to the personal obligation

---

[155] DB Cheshire R 1:40a (fol. 269d) [which refers to the thegns working on royal buildings 'as if they were [*sicut*] *villani*' and *sending* reapers to help with the king's harvest in August, but does not mention ploughing duties; this appears to have been the entry intended by Hollister in citing the folio]; cf. Jolliffe, *Constitutional History of Medieval England*, p. 94; A. Ballard (ed.), *British Borough Charters, 1042–1216* (Cambridge, 1913), p. 93.

[156] Robertson, *Anglo-Saxon Charters*, pp. 246–8, 494–6. See particularly p. 246: 'To anes æceres bræde on wealstillinge 7 to þære wære birigeað .XVI. hide ...' The editor translates the passage as follows: 'For the maintenance (?) and defence of an acre's breadth of wall 16 hides of land are required.' There is, however, considerable doubt as to the meaning of *wealstillinge*, translated above as 'maintenance'. See Robertson, p. 146. [See above, p. 60, and below, pp. 211–12.]

[157] ASC A 924 (923) [*recte* ASC A 920].

[158] DB Berks. B 10 (fol. 56c). For the Latin, see above [for part thereof, p. 76; alternative translation above, p. 56].

of thegns.[159] But again the peasant-thegn dichotomy can be sustained only by a forced and artificial interpretation of what otherwise would be a relatively clear statement. The section on default of service is illuminated by the examples of parage tenure which we have just discussed. Each five-hide unit had a more or less permanent warrior-representative who, like Siwate in Lincolnshire, was regarded as the king's man. It was upon him that the military obligation fell when the select fyrd was summoned. It was he who had to pay the *fyrdwite* or forfeit his land. As in the case of Siwate, the Berkshire warrior-representative might call upon a co-tenant in the five-hide unit to serve in his stead if he were unable to serve himself. But if the substitute failed to appear, the lord of the district paid a fine to the king and, presumably, collected a like sum from the defaulter. The entire Berkshire passage should be regarded as a self-consistent unit which refers neither to thegns exclusively nor to peasants exclusively but rather to the warrior-representatives of five-hide districts, whether thegn or peasant. This is surely the simplest and most reasonable interpretation of the passage and, when so interpreted, the passage makes perfectly good sense.

The next point which Stenton makes is that the alleged personal obligation of the thegn is 'the expression of the traditions of an order which, as a class, represented the military companions of a lord, the *gesithas*, of ancient times'. Here it is necessary to point out a certain ambiguity in Stenton's position. At one point he seems to be saying that every thegn with rights of jurisdiction served in the army,[160] and we have noted that a great many thegns lacked such rights. But elsewhere he seems to imply that every single thegn in England owed personal military service, although I do not believe that he attempts seriously to prove this notion. His observation regarding the ancient military traditions of the thegnhood as a class would be relevant only to the theory that every thegn owed military service. If there were numerous exceptions, then the military heritage would prove nothing. In other words, if the thegns actually inherited an all-inclusive personal military obligation from the *gesithas*, then every thegn without exception would be obliged to take up arms when summoned. This would hold true whether the thegn held half a county or half a virgate. But the parage tenures in Domesday prove quite conclusively, as we have seen, that every thegn did not serve. Anglo-Saxon records reveal a bewildering variety of thegns. There were Danish thegns as well as English thegns.[161] There were even Norman thegns.[162] The normal wergeld of a thegn was 1,200s., but we also encounter references to thegns with wergelds of only 200s.[163] The king's chamberlain was called a

---

[159] Stenton, *First Century of English Feudalism*, p. 116, n. 3.

[160] Stenton, *Anglo-Saxon England*, 2nd edn, p. 575.

[161] Robertson, *Anglo-Saxon Charters*, pp. 180 [S 1394 (AD 1042)], 208 [S 1409 (AD 1051×5)], 210 [S 1406 (AD 1046×53)].

[162] ASC E 1123. The *Chronicle* uses the term 'thegn' in an exceedingly broad sense: e.g. E 1086 (1087), 1123.

[163] Kemble, C.D., no. 731 (AD 1013–20) [S 985, dated by Sawyer as 1017×20].

• •

bur-thegn; the seneschal was a *disc-thegn* (dish-thegn); the steward was a
rail-thegn.[164] Larson observes that in late-Saxon times 'the term came to be applied
in Anglo-Saxon to almost every possible rank of men from serf to noble,'[165] and
Stenton himself declares, 'we are in virtually complete ignorance as to the social
position occupied by the smaller thegns of King Edward's day ...'[166]

Hence, the theory that every thegn in the eleventh century was obliged
to answer the military summons requires considerable documentation. It is
not sufficient to speculate as to the significance of ancient Germanic military
traditions unless it can be shown that these traditions actually applied to the late-
Saxon thegnhood. But the only evidence to which Stenton alludes is the poetic
account of the battle of Maldon:

> These traditions were still strong in the century before the Norman Conquest.
> They are nowhere more clearly brought out than in the poem which relates
> the death of Byrhtnoth at Maldon in 991. The men who are prominent in the
> poem are naturally the companions, the personal following of the earl, but
> they included landed Essex thegns and their close kinsmen. The ideas which
> moved these men must have been common to the whole class from which
> they sprung.[167]

We have already seen that the warriors *par excellence* of Byrhtnoth's force
were retainers – mercenaries – and this Stenton concedes. But he argues that
the remainder of the army also included men who were motivated by the Old
Germanic hero ideals. When Byrhtnoth fell dead, one of his warriors who was
not a retainer rallied the army with the following words: 'He who thinks to
avenge his lord, his chief in the press, may not waver or reckon for his life!' The
poet then tells how the English advanced bravely against the Danes, thinking
not of protecting their own lives but of avenging their lord's death.[168] All this is
markedly reminiscent of the barbarian *comitatus* which Tacitus describes. But the
warrior ethos cannot be said to apply exclusively to the thegns. Indeed, the man
who uttered these heroic words was not a thegn at all; he was, as the Maldon poet
expresses it, 'a simple ceorl'.[169] And he was used by the Maldon poet as a symbol of
the attitudes of his whole class.[170] There were many heroes among the English at
Maldon, but they were distributed among every class from the military retainers

---

[164] L. M. Larson, *The King's Household in England Before the Norman Conquest*, Bulletin of the
University of Wisconsin History Series 1.2 (Madison, WI, 1904), pp. 128ff.

[165] Larson, *King's Household in England*, p. 90. A tenant whom one Domesday passage calls
'Ketel teignus Stigandi' (DB Norfolk 32:2 [LDB fol. 254r]) is described in another passage
as 'Ketel liber homo Stigandi' (DB Norfolk 49:8 [LDB fol. 266r]).

[166] Stenton, *Types of Manorial Structure in the Northern Danelaw*, p. 22.

[167] Stenton, *First Century of English Feudalism*, p. 119.

[168] *Battle of Maldon*, lines 255–64 [Scragg, 'Battle of Maldon', pp. 28–9].

[169] *Battle of Maldon*, line 256 [Scragg, 'Battle of Maldon', pp. 28–9].

[170] See E. D. Laborde, *Byrhtnoth and Maldon* (London, 1936), pp. 115, 132.

to the peasants. Surely one finds no grounds in this poem for distinguishing between the military obligations of thegn and ceorl.[171]

Thus there is little support for the assumption that thegns owed a personal military service that was separate from the select-fyrd obligation. On the contrary, thegns and peasants coalesced into one force, which was recruited ordinarily on the basis of the five-hide unit. The obligation to serve in this force is identical with the military duty of the *trimoda necessitas* and is listed by the *Rectitudines Singularum Personarum* as a duty incumbent upon thegns in respect of their land. And it is possible to prove the point even more conclusively by demonstrating the existence of a direct relationship between the five-hide unit and the military thegnhood. This relationship is suggested in the Domesday passage relating to the military service of Malmesbury: 'When the king went on an expedition by land or sea, he had in this town either 20s. to feed his "buzecarles" or one man, as for an honour of five hides.'[172] Malmesbury conforms rigorously to the five-hide rule, but it should be noted that the town serves not only as five hides of land—it serves as an honour of five hides—as a five-hide estate such as is so frequently found to he possessed by Domesday thegns, and is, indeed, the typical thegn-holding of late-Saxon times.[173] A. G. Little believed that five hides was the normal and traditional holding of a Saxon king's thegn as far back as the seventh century.[174] We can perhaps never be sure whether originally the five-hide unit acquired its military significance because it was the normal thegn-holding, or whether the normal thegn owed military service because he held an estate of five hides. But the military obligation of the thegn and of the five-hide unit evidently have a common origin and, indeed, remain intimately related until the coming of the Normans.

The relationship is proven by an early-eleventh-century document known as the Promotion Law, which lists among the criteria that entitle a ceorl to the rights of thegnhood the possession of five hides of land.[175] A Law of Wergelds dating

---

[171] Another point to be considered is that the Maldon poet was writing in the old heroic tradition, and we cannot therefore be sure to what extent his own sentiments were actually shared by Byrhtnoth and his followers. See E. V. Gordon (ed.), *The Battle of Maldon*, Metheun's Old English Library (London, 1937; 2nd edn, 1949), p. 23: 'The aristocratic quality of *Maldon* is evident both in the glorification of the military ideals of the *comitatus* and in the close kinship in art and sentiment with other Old English court poetry.' See also Gordon, pp. 23–8, and B. S. Phillpotts, 'The Battle of Maldon: Some Danish Affinities', *Modern Language Review* 24 (1929), pp. 172–90.

[172] DB Wilts. B 5 (fol. 64c): 'Quando Rex ibat in expeditione vel terra vel mari, habebat de hoc burgo aut xx solidos ad pascendos suos buzecarlos, aut unum hominem ducebat secum, pro honore v hidarum.' [alternative translation above, p. 57]. See [Hollister, *Anglo-Saxon Military Institutions*,] pp. 23, 42.

[173] Birch, *Cartularium Saxonicum*, no. 246 [S 141 (AD 768×79)]; *Gesetze*, vol. 2, p. 419; R. H. Hodgkin, *A History of the Anglo-Saxons*, 2 vols (Oxford, 1935), vol. 2, p. 597; Maitland, *Domesday Book and Beyond*, p. 158; Vinogradoff, *Growth of the Manor*, pp. 127–8. Cf. Stenton, *Anglo-Saxon England*, 2nd edn, p. 480.

[174] Little, 'Gesiths and Thegns', pp. 728–9.

[175] *Gesetze*, vol. 1, pp. 456 ff.: Gethynctho, §2; cf. §3. This passage has been much discussed. See F. W. Maitland, 'Northumbrian Tenures', *EHR* 5 (1890), pp. 625–32; Chadwick,

from the same period reports that if a ceorl prospers to such an extent that he performs the king's *utware* on five hides of land, he is to be entitled to a thegn's wergeld.[176] The *utware* which the document refers to is, of course, primarily military. This fact is made clear by the next passage in the Law of Wergelds, stating that if a ceorl does not possess the five hides he cannot attain the thegn's wergeld even if he owns a helmet, a coat of mail, and a gold-plated sword.[177] It is not sufficient, in other words, merely to be a well-armed warrior-representative of a five-hide unit. The true thegn holds personally the five hides for which he serves. If a peasant becomes sole possessor of a five-hide unit, and if he meets certain other qualifications, he acquires the rights of a thegn,[178] and assumes the military role of the thegnhood. Moreover, if his son and grandson are also entitled to become thegns, then the status becomes hereditary. After a certain time, thegnhood becomes indelible, and thus we find numerous Domesday thegns with diminutive estates, much smaller than five hides. The Promotion Law is not also a demotion law. But it establishes the five-hide unit – the honour of five hides – as the crucial mark of the military thegnhood. Both the Promotion Law and the Law of Wergelds originated in northern England, but the customs to which they allude seem to have existed in the south long before the eleventh century. The Dooms of Ine, king of Wessex, stipulate that a Welshman possessing five hides of land is to have a wergeld of 600 s.[179] This law would not at first sight seem relevant to the thegn class, which was normally entitled to a wergeld of 1,200 s. But as H. M. Chadwick has pointed out, the Welsh peasant of that age had a wergeld which was about half the size of the English ceorl's wergeld. He concludes that in all likelihood the same ratio held good in the case of the landed proprietor, and consequently that even in the seventh century, when the Dooms of Ine were promulgated, the possession of five hides was a prerequisite to an Englishman's acquisition of a 1,200 s. wergeld.[180] Thus the connexion between the thegn and the five—hide unit emerges from a variety of Anglo-Saxon sources originating from diverse regions and dating from the seventh to the eleventh centuries.

It may be well at this point to anticipate a possible argument in favour of the thegn's personal military obligation. It might be pointed out that the heriot of

Studies on Anglo-Saxon Institutions, pp. 80ff.; Larson, *King's Household in England*, p. 101; Little, 'Gesiths and Thegns', pp. 723–9; Maitland, *Domesday Book and Beyond*, p. 164; W. H. Stevenson, 'Burh-geat-setl', *EHR* 12 (1897), pp. 489–92.

[176] *Gesetze*, vol. 1, pp. 456 ff.: *Norðleoda Laga*, §9. A thegn might, of course, hold an estate of less than five hides without forfeiting his inherited social and legal status.

[177] *Norðleoda Laga*, §10.

[178] There has been considerable dispute as to whether the ceorl who enjoys the rights of a thegn thereby actually *becomes* a thegn, but this controversy is not strictly relevant to our problem. Chadwick, *Studies on Anglo-Saxon Institutions*, p. 83, suggests that the Promotion Law refers to a king's thegn, whereas the Law of Wergelds applies to an ordinary thegn.

[179] Dooms of Ine, ch. 24.2 (AD 688–95) [*Gesetze*, vol. 1, pp. 100–1].

[180] Chadwick, *Studies on Anglo-Saxon Institutions*, pp. 91–3. Cf. Little, 'Gesiths and Thegns', pp. 728–9.

the thegn – the payment which his lord received in the event of his death – was usually military in nature, consisting of weapons, horses, or armour. If some thegns did not owe military service, why did they have a military heriot – why did they possess military equipment? It should be observed that many thegns did hold five hides or more, and many others with lesser estates doubtless served as warrior-representatives of five-hide units. As for those thegns who did not normally perform military service, it is important to note that the ordinary thegn was given an option as regards his heriot. According to 2 Cnut 71, his heriot was to consist of a horse and its trappings and his weapons, or his *healsfang*, the latter being a sum of money.[181] And it is by no means unusual to find thegns' heriots being rendered in money rather than arms.[182]

If any doubt remains as to the identity between the thegn's military obligation and the five-hide select-fyrd system described in the Berkshire Domesday, it should be dispelled by a careful analysis of a Wiltshire parage tenure which provides us with conclusive proof that the thegn's service is to be understood in the context of the Berkshire support system. Three Englishmen held a four-hide estate at Durnford, Wiltshire, which belonged to the church of Wilton. The conditions of the tenure were that two of the Englishmen rendered 5s. each and the third served as a thegn.[183] In itself, the passage leaves many points unclear, but it is possible to learn considerably more about this tenure by comparing it with other parage arrangements. First of all, we can be quite certain that the three Englishmen divided the four hides equally among themselves. Equal division is a characteristic of parage tenures, and, indeed, is required by law.[184] Hence, each of the three Englishmen held an estate of 1⅓ hides. The 5s. which two of them rendered might have been paid to the king or possibly to the church of Wilton. But again, a comparison with similar parage tenures reveals that the money was paid neither to the church nor to the king, but rather to the third tenant – the man who 'served as a thegn'.[185] It was his military support money. Now according

---

[181] See *The Laws of the Earliest English Kings*, ed. F. L. Attenborough (Cambridge, 1925), pp. 91–3 [*Gesetze*, vol. i, pp. 358–9].

[182] D. Whitelock (ed.), *Anglo-Saxon Wills* (Cambridge, 1930), pp. 74, 186 [S 1490 (AD 1042×3)], and 202–3; DB Notts. S 3 (fol. 67c); Yorks. C 40 (fol. 298d); F. E. Harmer (ed.), *Anglo-Saxon Writs* (Manchester, 1952), pp. 549–50. According to *II Cnut*, ch. 71 [*Gesetze*, vol. i, pp. 356–7], Mercian and East Anglian thegns had money heriots.

[183] DB Wilts. 13:3 (fol. 67d): 'Tres Angli tenuerunt TRE et non poterant ab aecclesia seperari. Duo ex eis reddebant v s. et tercius seruiebat sicut tainus.' ['Three Englishmen held it TRE and could not be separated from the church. Two of them rendered 5 s. and the third served as if he were a thegn.']

[184] E.g. DB Lincs. CS 21 (fol. 375b); CS 38 (fol. 375d): 'aequaliter et pariliter.' *II Cnut*, chs 70.1, 78. See also H. Ellis, *A General Introduction to Domesday Book*, 2 vols (London, 1833), vol. i, p. 141n.

[185] Cf. DB Lincs. 22:26 (fol. 354a): 'Chetel et Turuer fratres fuerunt et post mortem patris sui terram diuiserunt. Ita tamen ut Chetel faciens servitium regis haberet adiutorium Turuer fratris sui' ['Ketil and Thorfridh were brothers and after the death of their father divided the land. Yet accordingly as Ketil undertook royal service he should have the aid of Thorfridh his brother.']. See also DB Lincs. CS38 (fol. 375c–d).

to the Berkshire passage each hide of the five-hide unit contributed 4s. to the support of the military representative. A Berkshire tenant who held 1⅓ hides would therefore contribute 5s. 4d., or, in the round numbers which were usually preferred, 5s. And our Durnford passage shows that in Wiltshire also 1⅓ hides supported the warrior-representative to the extent of 5s. Doubtless the four hides which the three Englishmen held were combined with an adjacent hide to form a five-hide recruitment unit, for we know that the five-hide unit governed recruitment in Wiltshire.[186] The warrior-representative of this unit was the third Englishman mentioned in Domesday. When summoned to the fyrd, he was given 5s. by each of his companions and an additional 4s. by the holder of the adjacent hide. Here is a beautiful illustration of the Berkshire support system operating in an adjoining county. But the Durnford passage provides us with an even more valuable piece of information: it discloses that the warrior-representative *served as a thegn!* It proves our contention that warrior-representatives perform the military service which has been associated with the thegnhood, and, conversely, that the military obligation of thegns arises from the duty of five-hide units to produce warrior-representatives for the select fyrd.

III

The five-hide system was therefore the basis of both ceorl service and thegn service. Well-armed and well-supported members of both classes served in the select fyrd. In general, the military recruitment unit provided the fyrd with its best available warrior, and consequently the masses of the lower peasantry did not fight unless the great-fyrd obligation was invoked. The thegn was the typical select-fyrd warrior but there must have been numerous recruitment units which had no thegn to represent them. Pre-Conquest Berkshire, for example, contained 2,502 hides[187] and would therefore owe a total of about 500 men to the select fyrd at the rate of one man from five hides. The population of Berkshire in 1086, as compiled from Domesday Book, breaks down as follows: tenants-in-chief, 80; under-tenants, 185; *alodarii*, 5; *bordarii*, 1,827; *cotarii*, 750; miscellaneous, 53; *milites*, 4; priests, 5; *servi*, 792; *villani*, 2,623.[188] Out of a total population of 6,324, the bordars, cottagers, slaves, villains, and priests amount to 5,997, leaving 327 among the remaining classes including *alodarii* and miscellaneous. Admittedly these Domesday figures may not be precise, but we can expect them to be rather accurate with respect to the higher classes at least. It is also true that the population changed considerably in the two decades since 1066. Many thegns died at Hastings, and others went into exile or descended into the ranks of the peasantry. But on the other hand, the Domesday population figures include among the upper classes a substantial number of foreign newcomers. It seems

---

[186] DB Wilts B 5 (fol. 64c): Malmesbury. See [Hollister, *Anglo-Saxon Military Institutions*], pp. 23, 42, 76 [for latter, see above, p. 84].

[187] See F. H. Baring, *Domesday Tables* (London, 1909), pp. 50–1, and the references cited therein.

[188] Ellis, *General Introduction to Domesday Book*, vol. 2, p. 423.

most improbable that there were enough thegns in pre-Conquest Berkshire to meet its select-fyrd quota of 500 warriors.

In many instances the military representatives must have been chosen from one of the intermediate classes between the thegnhood and the ordinary peasantry. Certain sources allude to a class of people with wergelds of 600s. – sixhynde men – intermediate between the twihynde ceorls and the twelfhynde thegns. They are mentioned in Alfred 39, and again in several passages from the Leges Henrici Primi.[189] Chadwick shows that the men of this class were called radcnihts, and identifies them with the radchenistres and radmanni who are recorded in the Domesday sections relating to the western Midlands.[190] He believes that the sixhynde wergeld had virtually disappeared by the eleventh century and that sixhynde men became twelfhynde or twohynde.[191] But the old sixhynde classes continued, even though their wergeld may have changed. Vinogradoff observes that the radmanni of pre-Conquest times are frequently found to be the tenurial antecedents of Anglo-Norman military sergeants, and concludes that although there is no direct proof of military service being imposed upon them as a class, nevertheless they probably had a military function of some sort.[192] They served normally as mounted attendants of their lords, and therefore might well have been summoned, under certain circumstances, to the select fyrd. But like the thegns, the radmanni did not serve as a consequence of their rank but rather as warrior-representatives of territorial units of recruitment. If no thegn were available, a radmannus might very well be the best warrior that the five-hide unit could produce.

The obligation of riding for one's lord, either as an escort, a messenger, or a carrier, is ascribed to several classes, all of which were, for our purposes, nearly identical. Thus the cnihts, the radcnihts, the radmanni, the geneats,[193] and, in the north and west, the sokemen, may all be regarded as belonging to an intermediate group between the nobility and the common ceorls. In another sense, they can be considered members of the upper peasantry, for they often performed agricultural services of various kinds. But since they were good horsemen, many of them doubtless served as warrior-representatives. The military nature of the cniht is

[189] §§76.3, 82.9, 87.4; Gesetze, vol. 1, pp. 593, 599, 601. See also Dooms of Ine, ch. 70.

[190] Chadwick, Studies on Anglo-Saxon Institutions, pp. 88–9; Pseudoleges Canuti, ch. 6 [Instituta Cnuti, in Gesetze, vol. 1, p. 612].

[191] Chadwick, Studies on Anglo-Saxon Institutions, pp. 96–7. Stenton thinks that the sixhynde weregeld continued into post-Conquest times, although not in the Wessex shires south of the Thames. He agrees that the sixhynde man is probably to be identified with the radcniht of the west: Types of Manorial Structure in the Northern Danelaw, p. 18n.

[192] Vinogradoff, English Society in the Eleventh Century, pp. 70–1. See also Vinogradoff, Villainage in England: Essays in English Mediaeval History (Oxford, 1892), pp. 320, 323, 407; Maitland, Domesday Book and Beyond, pp. 57, 305.

[193] See Stenton, First Century of English Feudalism, pp. 132ff.; Vinogradoff, English Society in the Eleventh Century, p. 72; Harmer, Select English Historical Documents of the Ninth and Tenth Centuries, pp. 24, 108; Robertson, Anglo-Saxon Charters, p. 206; Rectitudines Singularum Personarum, ch. 2 [Gesetze, vol. 1, p. 445].

particularly striking, since the term was later used to describe the post-Conquest feudal cavalry. And, indeed, we find *cnihts* among the military lessees of the see of Worcester. A *cniht* named Æthelwold was granted an estate called Wolverton for three lives, free of all burdens except military service, bridge and wall work, and carrying service for the church. Another Worcester *cniht*, Osulf, was granted two manors for three lives, free of all burdens except *ferdfare*, *walgeweorc*, and *brygcgeweorc*.[194] As we have seen, the Worcester lessees were normally expected to perform personally the military service due from their lands.[195] Thus, the military obligations of *cnihts'* estates were ordinarily performed by the *cnihts* themselves.[196] The military nature of the *cniht* is further illustrated by the fact that the term is translated in Latin sources as *miles*.[197]

The military obligations of the pre-Conquest sokeman are somewhat less clear, although in at least one instance the same individual is referred to as a sokeman in one document and a *knihte* in another.[198] Indeed, there are a number of references to the military service of sokemen or of men living on their lord's sokeland. The Lincolnshire Domesday reports that one sokeland helped in the king's army on land and at sea.[199] The military obligation of certain sokemen on the estates of the abbey of Peterborough is mentioned in an intriguing twelfth-century document, the *Descriptio Militum de Abbatia de Burgo*. Here, all the sokemen

---

[194] Robertson, *Anglo-Saxon Charters*, p. 114 (AD 977) [S 1332]; p. 96 (AD 969) [S 1326].

[195] See above, p. 80. But there were exceptions: e.g. Robertson, *Anglo-Saxon Charters*, p. 86 [S 1309 (AD 966)], where a woman named Ælfhild holds three hides which owe the *trimoda necessitas*. Osulf's two manors (Robertson, p. 96 [S 1326 (AD 969)]) were to pass to his wife if she outlived his children, who were the immediate heirs.

[196] It should be remembered that the extent of the obligations of these Worcester estates is not specified. Here, too, the five-hide rule applied, and the leasehold tenements themselves were combined or divided into five-hide units for military-recruitment purposes. See [Hollister, *Anglo-Saxon Military Institutions*], ch. 3, and Round, *Feudal England*, pp. 60 ff.

[197] E.g. Robertson, *Anglo-Saxon Charters*, pp. 220, 472. D. C. Douglas writes of the term *cniht* as follows: 'And often in the later preconquest charters it is used in such a way that we are far from sure that we have not to deal with some sort of military tenure, however vaguely expressed': *Feudal Documents from the Abbey of Bury St. Edmunds*, Records of the Social and Economic History of England and Wales 8 (London, 1932), ci, n. 2, citing *Diplomatarium Anglicum Aevi Saxonici*, ed. B. Thorpe (London, 1865), pp. 571, 574, 583. See also ASC 1083, where a group of armed Normans are decribed as *cnihtas*. Cf. ASC 1088, 1094. Stenton regards the *cniht* as a retainer attached to the personal service of an ealdorman (*First Century of English Feudalism*, pp. 132–5), and in the will of an Anglo-Saxon ealdorman we find a reference to his *hired cnihtas*: Whitelock, *Anglo-Saxon Wills*, p. 24 [S 1498 (AD 971×83)].

[198] Whitelock, *Anglo-Saxon Wills*, p. 82 [S 1531 (AD 1043×5). Cf. DB Cambs. 14:75 (fol. 195d), and *Inquisitio Comitatus Cantabrigiensis … subjicitur Inquisitio Eliensis*, ed. N. E. S. A. Hamilton (London, 1876), fol. 90b. The matter is discussed in Whitelock, pp. 194–5.

[199] DB Lincs. 57:43 (fol. 368a): 'Haec soca talis fuit quod nichil reddebat, sed adiuabat in exercitu Regis in terra et in mari.' ['This *soke* was such that it rendered nothing, but it helped in the king's army on land and on sea.'] See Stenton, *Types of Manorial Structure in the Northern Danelaw*, pp. 28–9, where three other passages from the Lincolnshire Domesday are quoted. These passages relate to military service but their relevance to the problem of sokemen seems a little doubtful.

of six specified vills are required to serve along with the feudal knights – *cum militibus*.[200] It seems evident that the obligations of these sokemen originated in the Anglo-Saxon age, but it is difficult, at first sight, to identify them either with the great-fyrd or the select-fyrd obligation. There were numerous vills on the estates of Peterborough, in addition to the six mentioned in the *Descriptio Militum*, and most of them contained sokemen,[201] so we must conclude that only an isolated minority of the Peterborough sokemen were burdened with military service. Hence, the obligation of this specified group cannot have been connected with service in the great fyrd. On the other hand, the military sokemen cannot very well have been the direct military representatives of hide-units, since they are all clustered in six vills rather than being spread over the land. The problem which we face here is a very difficult one, and, since our information is based on a twelfth-century source, it is perhaps not entirely relevant to this study. I will therefore refrain from examining the problem in detail at this time, and will merely suggest what seems to me the proper avenue of approach. As we will see in the next chapter, an important territorial lord of Anglo-Saxon times would ordinarily be expected to lead the select fyrd which was recruited from his own lands, and would be held responsible for assembling it. Such were the obligations, for example, of the abbot of Peterborough. The select fyrd would be recruited, as elsewhere, on the basis of a specific ratio of men to hides or carucates, but it is entirely possible that the lord might choose to raise his army in some way other then demanding one man from every five hides. Thus, a lord with, say, 200 hides would owe forty men to the select fyrd. The king would not be concerned with how the men were recruited so long as they appeared properly armed and in proper numerical strength. The lord might demand two men from each of twenty hides and leave his remaining 180 hides exempt. He might maintain forty landless warriors in his own household. Or he might, as the abbots of Peterborough seem to have done, place the bulk of the military burden on six particular vills.

The personnel of the select fyrd was heterogeneous because the obligation was based upon units of land rather than social rank. Throughout much of England, each five-hide unit was obliged to produce a warrior-representative. The *miles* who was produced was normally a thegn, but if no thegns were available he might be a man of lower status. He might be a member of one of the intermediate groups – a *cniht*, a *radmannus*, a sokeman. And he might, if necessary, be a well-armed and well-supported member of the ordinary peasantry. The important thing was that he represented an appreciable territorial unit which was obliged to give him generous financial support. As such, he belonged to an exclusive military

---

[200] *Chronicon Petroburgense*, ed. Stapleton, pp. 172–3: Great Easton, Leicestershire; Walton, Wirrinton, Pilsgate, and Irthlingborough, all in Northamtonshire; and Elton, Huntingdonshire.

[201] This fact appears from an examination of the Domesday entries relating to the estates of Peterborough, and the *Liber Niger*, an early-twelfth-century Peterborough survey printed in *Chronicon Petroburgense*, ed. Stapleton, pp. 157–68.

group which can, in a sense, be considered a class in itself. And he may well have taken considerable pride in his connexion with the select territorial army of Saxon England.

The language of the warrior representative was still evident in Hollister's work; despite the title of the chapter, it was about how the army was paid for as much as who served with it. As Gareth Williams has pointed out, contemporary sources do not reflect the difference between 'general' and 'select' forms of military service discussed by Hollister.[202] It may be added that references to the 'whole folk' in the Anglo-Saxon Chronicle, while perhaps conjuring images of Freeman- and Green-inspired peasants armed with pitchforks, do not have to have been so democratically rooted in order to meet the Chronicle's interpretation. Considering how the later versions of the Anglo-Saxon Chronicle were written from distinctly regional viewpoints,[203] the 'whole folk' may have been, as Richard Abels has proposed, a phrase used to refer to the use of the fyrd from every shire in order to distinguish it from a locally raised force under the command of a local magnate.[204]

Williams usefully highlighted the significance of the roles of a range of social classes in the defence of Anglo-Saxon kingdoms. Using the case study of Mercia, albeit before the Viking Age, Williams addressed how offensive and defensive warfare could vary in scale. Offensive warfare, following Tim Reuter's well-known observations on Viking style campaigns undertaken by Carolingian Franks, could be essentially aristocratic in nature.[205] While we should note John France's reservations that it is difficult to draw precise distinctions between offensive and defensive warfare in the Carolingian period,[206] it is interesting that Williams pointed out that the use of subjects 'not inclined' to aid defence, presumably including both peasants and churchmen, could be involved in defensive organization.[207] While this may have precluded their role in battles themselves, the digging of ditches and

---

[202] G. Williams, 'Military Institutions and Royal Power', in *Mercia: An Anglo-Saxon Kingdom in Europe* ed. M. P. Brown and C. Farr, SEHB (London, 2001), pp. 295–309, at p. 296.

[203] For a straightforward introduction to the manuscripts of the ASC, see Whitelock's introduction in *EHD 1*, pp. 109–17. For the London perspective of the C Chronicler during the reign of Æthelred II, see S. D. Keynes, 'The Declining Reputation of King Æthelred the Unready', in *Ethelred the Unready: Papers from the Millenary Conference*, ed. D. H. Hill, BAR British Series 59 (Oxford, 1978), pp. 227–53, at pp. 229–32.

[204] Abels, *Lordship and Military Obligation in Anglo-Saxon England*, pp. 175–8.

[205] Williams, 'Military Institutions and Royal Power', pp. 299–300, citing Reuter, 'Plunder and Tribute in the Carolingian Empire'. See also Tyler, 'Orchestrated Violence and the "Supremacy" of the Mercian Kings'.

[206] J. France, 'The Composition and Raising of the Armies of Charlemagne', *JMMH* 1 (2002), pp. 61–82, at p. 66.

[207] Williams, 'Military Institutions and Royal Power', p. 300. For the compulsion of monks in the building of public works, see Brooks, 'Development of Military Obligations in Eighth- and Ninth-Century England', pp. 77–8, which cites Boniface's letter of 747 to Cuthbert, Archbishop of Canterbury: *S. Bonifatii et Lulli epistolae*, ed. M. Tangl, MGH Epistolae Selectae in usum scholarum separatim editae 1 (Berlin, 1916), no. 78, pp. 161–70.

building of fortifications was also part of a military system. Therefore, like the role of peasants and an artisan class in the building of castles in the central and later middle ages[208] the military systems of Anglo-Saxon England would involve large parts of the whole population, while the fighting itself would have been an activity of the military class. This is indicated by the Anglo-Saxon Chronicle's scornful reference to a construction team of *ceorls* who were unable to defend a half-built fortification against an unexpected Viking attack during the reign of Alfred the Great.[209]

It is pertinent here to return to the work of Richard Abels. His monograph, published in 1988 but drawing on earlier work,[210] highlighted the fact that the possession of bookland precipitated a military revolution which had emerged in the eighth and ninth centuries in Mercia and Wessex before the widescale Viking invasions. Abels's work was a response to redefinitions of ideas proposed by Eric John in the 1960s, Nicholas Brooks in 1971 and, to an extent, Hollister, which had all directed the study of bookland away from the common burdens associated with the Anglo-Saxon peasantry (or citizenry, if we recall the definitions of Edward Freeman).[211] For Abels, the use of bookland saw 'stirrings toward a redefinition of kingship'.[212] Bookland meant, as Abels saw it, a select military force which was aristocratic in nature, consisting of lords and their followers. Such a force was unable to match either the mobility or, arguably, the ferocity of Viking attacks, showing the limitations of the system from which it stemmed.[213]

With an eye to a narrative of historical development, Abels highlighted an important moment in West Saxon history under Alfred, drawing attention to the crucial 893 entry of the Anglo-Saxon Chronicle, which recorded the division of the West Saxons' military force:

> The king had divided his army [*his fierd*] into two, such that they were always half at home, half out, apart from the men who were to guard the *burhs* [*butan þæm mannum þe þa burga healdan scolden*].

This was a reference which, as Michael Swanton and others have noted, recalled the Anglo-Saxons' interpretation of the divisions of the Amazonian army (*here*) in the *Old English Orosius*.[214] Guy Halsall suggested that it equated with the tripartite division indicated in the *Trinoda Necessitas* of the charter formulae and

---

[208] For a discussion of forced labour in early castle building in eleventh- and twelfth-century England, see N. J. G. Pounds, *The Medieval Castle in England and Wales: A Social and Political History* (Cambridge, 1990), pp. 18–19.

[209] ASC ABCD 893; for the citation of this, see below, pp. 213–14.

[210] Abels, *Lordship and Military Obligation in Anglo-Saxon England*. His key paper, published in 1985, was 'Bookland and Fyrd Service in Late Saxon England', *ANS* 7 (1985 for 1984), pp. 1–25.

[211] Freeman, *History of the Norman Conquest*, vol. 1, p. 86–100. For discussion of and a citation from this, see above, p. 51.

[212] Abels, *Lordship and Military Obligation in Anglo-Saxon England*, p. 60.

[213] Abels, *Lordship and Military Obligation in Anglo-Saxon England*, p. 62.

[214] OE *Orosius* I.10. The Old English version removes the Latin original's reference (Orosius, *Libri VII*, I.15) to the drawing of lots for the responsibilities of defence and attack.

was related to the organization of an army whose members would spend half their service time in the fortifications (also providing bridge-work, as fortifications were often associated with river crossings) and the other half on campaign.[215] Brooks, in a review of Halsall's work, objected to this, arguing that the reference to burghal service was an indication of a wider scale of military service in addition to that of the warriors of the mobile army.[216] However, it should also be observed that although the entry is important, the context of the Vikings' campaign in 893 may not be coincidental; as will be seen in chapter 5, at this point Alfred was especially concerned with Viking mobility,[217] and it may be that the 893 entry simply recorded arrangements specific to the circumstances of the time.

Whatever the precise meaning of the 893 entry of the Anglo-Saxon Chronicle and, despite the contentions about the dates of the beginning of a modified military system for the West Saxon kingdom,[218] it is clear that in the late ninth century a modified system of military organization was at work. We shall see that Abels's interpretation of the force related in the 893 Chronicle entry is closer to that of Halsall than to Brooks. Abels's discussion of this is worth citing in full:[219]

> Alfred had won a respite with his victory at Edington in the spring of 878, but this did not wipe out the memory of his desperate flight into the Somerset marshes. He could not rely upon the existing military system to counter the continuing threat offered by the Danes. If he were to survive and consolidate his hold upon Wessex, he would have to innovate.
>
> And innovate he did. The king's adoption of Danish tactics in the winter of 878, such as his use of strongholds and small mobile raiding parties to harry the lands of his enemies, was forced upon him by the immediate circumstances.[220] Over the next twenty years of his reign, however, he was to revolutionize Anglo-Saxon military practice. Just as King Offa had responded a century earlier to the proliferation of bookland and to the pressures of the first Norse raids by imposing the 'common burdens' upon bookland tenure, Alfred answered the Danish challenge by creating an impressive system of fortified boroughs throughout his realm and by reforming the West Saxon fyrd, changing it from a sporadic levy of king's men and their retinues into a standing force. The defensive system that Alfred sponsored, and its extension to Mercia under the ealdorman Æthelred and the lady Æthelflæd,

---

[215] Halsall, *Warfare and Society in the Barbarian West*, pp. 104–5. A threefold interpretation of the division of the army is also made by N. Hooper and M. Bennett, *The Cambridge Illustrated Atlas of Warfare: The Middle Ages, 768–1487* (Cambridge, 1996), p. 25, although Hooper and Bennett do not make the connection with the *Trinoda Necessitas* made by Halsall.

[216] N. P. Brooks, review of Halsall, *Warfare and Society in the Barbarian West*, EHR 120 (2005), pp. 424–6, at p. 425. For a discussion of the scale of burghal service, see Brooks, 'Administrative Background to the Burghal Hidage'.

[217] See below, p. 188.

[218] See here J. Haslam, 'King Alfred and the Vikings: Strategies and Tactics, 876–886 AD', ASSAH 13 (2006), pp. 122–54, esp. pp. 129–33.

[219] Abels, *Lordship and Military Obligation in Anglo-Saxon England*, pp. 62–6.

[220] Asser, chs 53, 55. See also Æthelweard, *Chronicon*, p. 42.

enabled his kingdom to survive and formed the basis for the reconquest of the Danelaw by his son Edward and his grandson Æthelstan.[221]

The Chronicle entry under 891 [for 893], a long and involved annal that supplies invaluable information about the character of military operations during the last years of Alfred's reign, allows us to glimpse the emergent military system:

> The king had divided his army [*his fierd*] into two, so that always half of its men were at home, half on service, apart from the men who guarded the boroughs [*butan thaem mannum the tha burga healdan scolden*].[222]

Passing over for the moment the reference to the burghal system, let us consider Alfred's reform of the fyrd. The division of the fyrd into two rotatating contingents was designed to give some continuity to West Saxon military actions. Rather than respond to Viking incursions with ad hoc levies which were disbanded when the crisis had passed, the West Saxons would now always have a force in the field. Moreover, Alfred's fyrd, like the Danish *heres*, was to be composed of mounted warriors possessing the necessary mobility to pursue an enemy known for its elusiveness.[223]

The fyrdmen who waited their turn 'at home' also filled a necessary defensive function. It was essential that some king's thegns and their retainers remain behind to guard their lands and those of their neighbors on campaign against sudden raids, if for no other reason than the obvious one that landholders would have been reluctant to leave their estates and families totally undefended.[224] The West Frankish king Charles the Bald learned this lesson in dramatic fashion in the summer of 856 when he summoned a general assembly to deal with a viking invasion of the Seine basin and his magnates refused to attend, fearing to leave their own lands undefended.[225] King Alfred was wise enough not to present his noblemen with that dilemma.

---

[221] R. H. C. Davis, 'Alfred the Great: Propaganda and Truth', *History* 56 (1971), pp. 169–82, at pp. 177–80.

[222] ASC 893. Edward the Elder preserved his father's arrangements. See ASC A 917.

[223] ASC 871, 895, 900. See J. H. Clapham, 'The Horsing of the Danes', *EHR* 25 (1910), pp. 287–93.

[224] Plummer-Earle, vol. 2, p. 109, notes the remarkable similarity between Alfred's fyrd system and Amazon military practice as described in the Old English translation of Orosius sponsored by the king: 'Hie [the Amazons' two queens, Marsepia and Lampida] heora here on to todældon, other æt ham beon [?sceolde] heora lond to healdanne, other ut faran to winanne' ('They divided their army into two parts, one of which remained at home to guard their land, the other of which went out on campaign to wage war'). Cf. ASC 893 (note especially the similar phraseology). If, as Plummer believed, the idea for Alfred's reform came from his reading of Orosius, then the purpose behind leaving one half of the fighting force beomces clear. Cf. *OE Orosius* I.10.

[225] C. M. Gillmor, 'The Mobilization of a Work Force on the Fortified Bridges of the Seine, 862–888', Paper presented at the Third Annual Meeting of the Haskins Society, Houston, Texas, 10 November 1984, p. 5 [see now 'The Logistics of Fortified Bridge Building on the Seine Under Charles the Bald', *ANS* 11 (1989 for 1988), pp. 87–106, and 'The Fortified Bridges of Charles the Bald', *Journal of Medieval History* 17 (1991), pp. 1–12]. Cf. F. Lot, 'La grande invasion normande de 856–862', in *Recueil des travaux historiques de Ferdinand Lot,*

The charter evidence even suggests that a general summons of a shire fyrd in the early tenth century did not require every local landed thegn to serve in the host. Goda, a prominent Kentish thegn, did not join the shire fyrd when King Edward called 'all the men of Kent to battle' in 902.[226] He seems to have been excused from serving, for if he had been derelict in his duty to the king, his adversary in a law-suit over the Kentish estate of Cooling, Queen Eadgifu, would have certainly mentioned it, and she does not.[227] Goda may well have been one of the landowners permitted to remain behind with their warrior-retainers to guard the shire against sudden incursions and to preserve the king's peace.

The warriors who remained home or who had completed their tour of duty appear to have been obliged to join the garrisons of the nearby boroughs on local forays. When Ealdorman Æthelred of Mercia, Æthelhelm of Wiltshire, and Æthelnoth of Somerset raised the forces of the western shires against a viking army that had made a stronghold on the Severn at Buttington in the autumn of 893, they assembled an army from the nearby borough garrisons which included 'the king's thegns who were at home [æt ham] near the fortifications'.[228] The duty of these thegns to defend their localities, rather than the survival of an ancient obligation of all free men to military service, explains the appearance of the *other folc* fighting alongside the London *burwaran* in 895 and identifies the *land leod* who routed the *here* of Northampton in 916.[229]

Alfred also had compelling administrative reasons for his division between the fyrd. The Anglo-Saxons did not draw a rigorous distinction between 'military' and 'police' actions. The same men who led the king's hosts, his thegns, reeves, and ealdormen, also did justice, a point driven home by Ælfric of Eynsham's choice of the term *gemotman* to gloss the Latin *decurio*.[230] Similarly, the mounted men who were responsible according to Æthelstan's laws for the capture of lawbreakers were the same men who defended the boroughs in war.[231] The thin line between a posse and a fyrd was driven home by Edward the Elder's 'expedition' against his

Centre de Recherches d'Histoire et de Philologie de la vɪᵉ section de l'École pratique des hautes études 5, 3 vols (Geneva, 1968–73), vol. 2, pp. 714–15.

[226] ASC ABCD 903; ASC MR 903. Harmer, *Select English Historical Documents of the Ninth and Tenth Centuries*, pp. 37–8 = Birch, *Cartularium Saxonicum*, no. 1064 (S 1211 [c. AD 959]), no. 1065 (S 1212 [AD 961]). Goda possessed bookland at Osterland in Kent and attested a grant by the Archbishop of Canterbury, c. 905. Birch, CS 638 (S 1288).

[227] Harmer, *Select English Historical Documents of the Ninth and Tenth Centuries*, pp. 37–8.

[228] ASC 893.

[229] ASC 895, 919. See Hollister, *Anglo-Saxon Military Institutions*, pp. 29–30; Powicke, *Military Obligation in Medieval England*, pp. 8–14.

[230] *Ælfrics Grammatik und Glossar*, ed. J. Zupitz, Sammlung englischer Denkmäler 1 (Berlin, 1880; reprinted Berlin, 1966), p. 34, line 14 ('Grammatik'). Cf. 'Glossar', ch. 2, line 75: *gemotman* 'contionator' (i.e. speaker at a popular assembly). For the judicial authority of ealdormen, reeves, and thegns, see Asser, ch. 91, 106. One should also note that Alfred rotated his household. His *bellatores* and *nobiles ministri* spent one month at court and two at home, looking after their own affairs. Asser, ch. 100; cf. *IV Athelstan*, chs 7, 5, §4 [*Gesetze*, vol. 1, p. 170].

[231] *II Athelstan*, chs 16, 20, §1–4 [*Gesetze*, vol. 1, pp. 158, 160]; *VI Athelstan*, chs 4, 5, 8, §§2–4 [*Gesetze*, vol. 1, pp. 175–6, 178–9]. (All these laws concern the administration of boroughs.)

cousin Æthelwold's retinue in the winter of 899.[232] In a sense, one could conceive of the fyrd as a posse led by the king himself.[233] It is little wonder, then, that Alfred should require part of his thegnage to serve his interests by remaining 'at home'. After all, the Danish invasions did not end ordinary criminal activity; on the contrary, from Alfred's treaty with Guthrum it would appear that English lawbreakers could find men among the vikings who were willing to buy their stolen goods and even find refuge from West Saxon law.[234] The threat that an invasion of this sort could pose to social discipline is eloquently illustrated by Wulfstan's 'Sermon of the Wolf', written under analogous circumstances a century later.[235]

Alfred's innovations did not affect the basic makeup of the fyrd, which remained composed of nobles and their lesser-born followers.[236] Certainly, tenth- and eleventh-century glosses studiously avoid terms connoting social rank when defining words such as *bellator*, *belliger*, or even *miles*.[237] And the single exception, *miles ordinarius: anlang cempa vel heanra cempa, idem gregarius*,[238] at least suggests that some *miles* were of humble origin. The Chronicle annals for 895 and 1010 even imply that king's thegns formed a minority of the king's fighting forces.[239] However, it is equally certain that Alfred's fyrds were not thought of as peasant levies. For one thing, Alfred's forces were mounted. The Chronicle consistently has them 'riding after the Danes' and at one point reports that the English fyrd besieging a Viking army in Chester used the crops in the field to feed their horses.[240] The 'great horse' of the Middle Ages was unknown to the Anglo-Saxons, and even in the eleventh century the heriot of thegns called for 'palfreys' (in the Domesday Book scribes' terminology) rather than destriers.[241] Horses, nevertheless, were valuable animals in ninth- and tenth-century England, and their use by the warriors of the fyrd argues strongly for a select rather than a mass levy.[242] Furthermore,

---

[232] ASC 900.

[233] Powicke, *Military Obligations in Medieval England*, p. 13.

[234] *Alfred–Guthrum*, ch. 4, 5 [*Gesetze*, vol. 1, pp. 128–9]. Cf. II *Æthelred*, ch. 6, §2 [*Gesetze*, vol. 1, p. 224].

[235] D. Bethurum (ed.), *The Homilies of Wulfstan* (Oxford, 1957; reprinted, 1971), pp. 255–75; trans. *EHD* 1, pp. 929–34. Note especially the archbishop's concern about slaves fleeing their masters only to return as viking raiders.

[236] Cf. John, *Orbis Britanniae and Other Studies*, p. 139.

[237] T. Wright and R. P. Wülcker, *Anglo-Saxon and Old English Vocabularies*, 2nd edn, 2 vols (London, 1884), vol. 1, pp. 193, 194, 304, 309, 429, 442; A. S. Napier (ed.), *Old English Glosses: Chiefly Unpublished* (Oxford, 1900), §1, lines 387, 741, 893; §2, line 330.

[238] Wright and Wülcker, *Anglo-Saxon and Old English Vocabularies*, vol. 1, p. 450 (eleventh-century).

[239] ASC 1010: 'And many other good thegns [were killed at *Ringmere*] and a countless number of people.' Cf. ASC 895, where only four king's thegns are said to have fallen in a rout of a London fyrd.

[240] ASC 893.

[241] DB Cambs. B 13 (fol. 189a) (Cambridge).

[242] *Dunsæte*, ch. 7 [*Gesetze*, vol. 1, pp. 378–9] establishes the value of a horse at 30 shillings, as compared to 30 *d.* (= 6 *s.*) for an ox. Cf. VI *Athelstan*, ch. 6, §§1–2 [*Gesetze*, vol. 1, pp. 176–7] (one half-pound for an average horse; 30 *d.* for an ox). II *Athelstan*, ch. 18 [*Gesetze*, vol. 1, p. 158–9] forbids selling horses overseas, a clear sign of their importance. Horses also appear in the bequests of nobles in the tenth and eleventh centuries, where

the summoning of a fyrd appears to have left ordinary agricultural activities, such as the harvest, largely unaffected. In the autumn of 895 King Alfred encamped the fyrd in the vicinity of London in order to protect the peasants of the area while they harvested their crops. The Danes had established a stronghold on the Lea about twenty miles north of London, and Alfred feared that they would steal or burn the crops. The distinction between those who guarded the fields and those who harvested the crops is quite clear in the Chronicle's account.[243]

Alfred's limitation of military service to a half year could not have been predicated upon agricultural concerns, as some have suggested.[244] If the fyrd had been composed of peasant levies taken from the fields, one would expect to find exemptions for sowing, harvest, and the like, rather than a limitation on the length of service. A more plausible explanation for the limitation to a half-year period would be the difficulty of keeping an army provisioned for a more extended period. Indeed, the Chronicle entry for 893 specifically links logistics with the fyrdmen's term of service. The English fyrd led by Prince Edward had cornered a fleeing viking army on the islet of Thorney, where they besieged them 'for as long as their provisions lasted; but they had completed their term of service and used up their provisions.'[245] Despite certain victory, Edward's contingent disbanded and returned to their homes, passing King Alfred and their relief on the way.

The king himself drew a clear distinction between those who labored and those who fought. Alfred the Great is the first medieval writer to divide society into the three orders that were later to be popularized by Adalbéron of Laon.[246] In the midst of his rather loose translation of Boethius's *Consolation of Philosophy*, Alfred added a personal observation of statecraft: [*for which, see above, p. 11*] ...

they are often associated with swords and armour. See e.g. Whitlock, *Anglo-Saxon Wills*, no. 3, pp. 12, 14 (S 1539 [*c.* AD 950]); no. 20, pp. 58–60 (S 1503 [AD 1014]). Magnates maintained their own stud farms: H. P. R. Finberg, *The Agrarian History of England and Wales*, vol. I, book 2: AD 43–1042 (Cambridge, 1972), p. 498.

[243] Cf. ASC 1006, where Æthelred II called out the 'whole nation' from Wessex and Mercia, which 'cost the people of the country every sort of harm, so that they profited neither from the native army nor the foreign army.' Again, there seems to be an implicit distinction here between those who fight – and ravage – and those who till the soil.

[244] Wormald, 'Ninth Century', pp. 150, 154. Cf. John, *Orbis Britanniae and Other Studies*, pp. 137–8.

[245] *EHD* 1, p. 202.

[246] On the history of this concept, see G. Duby, 'The Origins of a System of Social Classifications', in *The Chivalrous Society* (Berkeley, 1977), pp. 88–93. Nicholas Brooks assumes that Alfred was merely echoing 'the ideas of the contemporary Carolingian monastic schools': N. Brooks, 'Arms, Status and Warfare in Late-Saxon England', in *Ethelred the Unready: Papers from the Millenary Conference*, ed. D. Hill, BAR British Series 59 (1978), pp. 81–103, at p. 81. This argument, however, may be reversed, and the tripartite classification may have reached the Continent through English writers. Certainly, Adalbéron's statement far more resembles Alfred's and those made by Ælfric and Wulfstan at the beginning of the eleventh century than the vague formulations that appear in Carolingian texts. Cf. J. M. Wallace-Hadrill, 'War and Peace in the Earlier Middle Ages', *TRHS* 5th series 25 (1975), pp. 157–74, at pp. 172–4. For the possibility of Irish influence upon Alfred's system, see D. Dubuison, 'L'Irlande et la théorie médiévale des "trois ordres"', *Revue de l'histoire des religions* 188 (1975), pp. 35–61, esp. pp. 58–63.

For Alfred, beadsmen (*gebedmen*) prayed, warriors (*fyrdmen* fought, and workers (*weorcmen*) labored, each a necessary, distinct class. This tripartite classification of society according to function, which was to be repeated with greater elaboration by Abbot Ælfric of Eynsham and Archbishop Wulfstan II of York a century later,[247] tells against the notion of peasant levies and farmer warriors.

This is not to argue that the Alfredian fyrd was composed exclusively of noble landowners and their lesser-born retainers. The law code that Alfred issued sometime around 890 stipulates a double penalty for breaking into the fortified dwelling of a noble (*burhbryce*) or through a ceorl's fence (*ceorles edorbryce*) 'while the fyrd is out [in the field]',[248] which implies that some peasant landowners answered the summons to the host. It is questionable, however, whether such landholding commoners, whose fields were probably worked by slaves and geburs, should be characterized as 'peasants'. On the whole, the evidence leads one to believe that the Alfredian fyrd was made up of landed lords and their military retainers, rather than peasants who exchanged the plough for the sword every half year.

It is perhaps significant that Abels saw the West Saxon fyrd before the Alfredian reforms as a 'sporadic levy'. The verbal echoes of Green and the 'traditional' historiography are notable, and it is remarkable that the same term, 'levy', was used to refer to something so different from that envisaged by his predecessors. For Green and, indeed, for Freeman, it signified a ragtag force of poorly armed peasants, whereas for Abels it was a reference to an unreliably periodic force of aristocratic warriors. Although other authors, since at least the nineteenth century, had noted the importance of Alfredian reforms, Abels's interpretation of the Alfredian fyrd was the crux of his study. Abels's pre-Alfredian fyrd may have been a 'sporadic levy' but, like the later fyrd characterized by Eric John, it was essentially aristocratic in character.[249] Thus Alfred's armies were focused on the specialized military aspect of warriors' status.

The temporal limitations of military service may be addressed in the light of Abels's work. The impatient warriors at Thorney that Abels refers to hardly compared to the worst excesses of later medieval 'feudal' service, exemplified by the case of Hugh fitz Heyr, who turned up on campaign for Edward I and loosed a single arrow before departing homewards.[250] Nonetheless, the restrictions of pre-Conquest service have exercised many historians, who have long focused on its 'part-time' nature. The contrasts amongst the range of opinions here is notable in two different contributions in the classic 1982 survey of early England, *The Anglo-Saxons*: one by Patrick Wormald, who noted a military force which was summoned from the peasantry, and another by Eric John, who stopped just shy

---

[247] *EHD* 1, p. 928; *Die Hirtenbriefe Ælfrics in Altenglischer und Lateinischer Fassung*, ed. B. Fehr, Bibliothek der Angelsächsischen Prosa 9 (Hamburg, 1914; reprinted Darmstadt, 1966), p. 225; *Die 'Institutes of Polity: Civil and Ecclesiastical'*, ed. Jost, ch. 4, pp. 55–6. See discussion [in Abels, *Lordship and Military Obligation in Anglo-Saxon England*, pp. 132–4].

[248] *Alfred*, ch. 40, §1 [*Gesetze*, vol. 1, pp. 74–5].

[249] John, *Orbis Britanniae and Other Studies*, pp. 128–53.

[250] Nicholson, *Medieval Warfare*, p. 47, citing P. Coss, *The Knight in Medieval England, 1000–1400* (Stroud, 1993), p. 102. For the Thorney campaign, see below, ch. 5.

of arguing for pre-Conquest English knighthood.[251] If there were a two-month period of service, as indicated in the Berkshire Domesday customs (rather than the half-year service suggested by Abels, in the extract above),[252] this placed restrictions on what the force was capable of achieving if travelling outside its own territory. But we should also note the permeability of distinctions between what was expected of a warrior and what a warrior might undertake on campaign if he wished to gain the attention of his lord and/or king, and thus win a share of the riches from that campaign. The warriors who left for home at Thorney may have fulfilled their obligations, but we do not know the circumstances under which they made their decisions to leave the campaign. As we shall see in chapter 5, campaigns, such as those under Edward the Elder and Athelstan, could range across long distances, and last over two months. Presumably by then a successful ruler no longer relied on what he could expect from the military obligations of his warriors but instead on how he could reward them or promise to do so.[253]

Abels's focus on the aristocratic nature of the reorganized force of Alfred's kingdom allowed a new perspective, highlighting the significance of logistics in military organization, an issue on which Abels has continued to reflect.[254] It may be added that it was important to eat and drink *well*,[255] so the reciprocity of a ruler's act of feeding his followers could enhance his status, and thus reinforce his followers' obligations to him. In this respect, the institutions of the Anglo-Saxon state and the credentials of Alfred the Great were inherently personal,[256] bearing great similarity to the manner in which Carolingian authority rested on the military significance of assembly politics.[257] It is therefore worthwhile to give some attention to the suggestion made by Abels and by John that the hundredal

---

[251] Wormald, 'Ninth Century'; E. John, 'The Age of Edgar', and 'The End of Anglo-Saxon England', in *The Anglo-Saxons*, ed. J. Campbell (London, 1982), pp. 132–59, at p. 150; pp. 160–89, at pp. 168–9; and pp. 214–39, at pp. 236–7. See also here John, *Reassessing Anglo-Saxon England*, p. 84, who noted that the *ceorlisc* nature of the fyrd was based on 'constant repetition by historians' rather than on any particular evidence.

[252] Cf. later work by Abels, *Alfred the Great*, pp. 194–207, and 'English Logistics and Military Administration', pp. 258–60, where a two-month period of service is proposed.

[253] I am grateful to an anonymous student at the University of Reading's School of Continuing Education for raising this issue and making me think more about the nature of the evidence here, an issue related to notions of royally convened plundering expeditions of the manner addressed in Reuter, 'Plunder and Tribute in the Carolingian Empire'.

[254] Abels, *Alfred the Great*, pp. 194–207; Abels, 'English Logistics and Military Administration', pp. 258–60.

[255] See here Lavelle, *Royal Estates in Anglo-Saxon Wessex*, esp. pp. 74–6. Cf. A. Gautier, *Le Festin dans l'Angleterre anglo-saxonne (v^e–xie siècle)*, Collection "Histoire" (Rennes, 2006), pp. 27–9.

[256] The relationship between royal renders (*feorm*) and military campaigns as a reinforcement of royal authority is addressed in Lavelle, 'Geographies of Power in the Anglo-Saxon Chronicle'.

[257] Reuter, 'Assembly Politics in Western Europe from the Eighth Century to the Twelfth'; S. Airlie, 'Talking Heads: Assemblies in Early Medieval Germany', in *Political Assemblies in the Earlier Middle Ages*, ed. P. S. Barnwell and M. Mostert, SEMA 7 (Turnhout, 2003), pp. 29–46.

organization of the late Anglo-Saxon army may have had more significance than it is normally credited with.[258] From a practical point of view, given that there was no clear distinction between what we might now call 'police' and 'military' actions,[259] the attention given in the tenth-century *Hundred Ordinance* to the obligations of the men of the hundred to take part in the pursuit of criminals is noteworthy.[260]

> 1. First, that they assemble every four weeks, and each man do justice to another.

> 2. [Marginal Rubric: 'That men go quickly after thieves.'] If the need is at hand [i.e. urgent], one shall say this to the head of the hundred [*hundredesman*], and he, afterwards to the heads of the tithings [*teoðingmen*], and all go forth, as God may guide them, that they might come to [the criminal]; justice shall be done to the thief, just as it was previously Edmund's decree.

> …

> 5. Moreover, we decreed, if a hundred drives him [a thief] to a trail in another hundred, that one declare to the head of the hundred, and he then go there with them.

> 5.1. If he neglect this, he shall pay the king thirty shillings.

Geld was collected through the hundred; this relationship was a key mechanism by which the late Anglo-Saxon state manifested itself in the lives of its subjects[261] and it is hardly surprising that, as Abels notes, the Latin military term *decurio* was glossed as *gemotman* by Ælfric of Eynsham (an issue which is all the more pertinent given Ælfric's close connections with Ealdorman Æthelweard, who was presumably knowledgeable about local government representatives).[262] Given that the areas of the 'reconquered' Danelaw of the tenth century are likely to have been reorganized into West Saxon-style hundreds,[263] the defensive obligations of the hundred may have had particular significance in ensuring that order was imposed in areas which may have been subject to the dangers of raids from

---

[258] Abels, *Lordship and Military Obligation in Anglo-Saxon England*, pp. 67, 182–4; John, 'Age of Edgar', pp. 172–3. It is pertinent to note here Alex Woolf's arguments for the operation of multiple identities in social and political organization: A. Woolf, 'Community, Identity and Kingship in Early England', in *Social Identity in Early Medieval Britain*, ed. W. O. Frazer and A. Tyrrell, Studies in Early Britain (London, 2000), pp. 91–109.

[259] In addition to Abels's observations, note Powicke, *Military Obligation in Medieval England*, p. 13.

[260] *Hundred Ordinance: Gesetze*, vol. 1, p. 192. See also *IV Athelstan* ('Ordinance of the Bishops and Reeves of London'), chs 3–5, *Gesetze*, vol. 1, pp. 175–6; trans. *EHD 1*, p. 424, and the implicit connection between wapentake assemblies and weapons in the twelfth-century *Leges Edwardi Confessoris*, ch. 30; *Gesetze*, vol. 1, pp. 652–3.

[261] See Loyn, *Governance of Anglo-Saxon England*, pp. 140–8.

[262] Abels, *Lordship and Military Obligation in Anglo-Saxon England*, p. 64 (above, p. 95). As John observed ('Age of Edgar', p. 172), Æthelweard used 'hundreds' (*centurias*, translated by Campbell as 'troops') as a synonym for a military force in a reference to events in the early ninth century: Æthelweard, *Chronicon*, p. 28. For references to discussion of Ælfric and Æthelweard, see above, p. 3, n. 8).

[263] Hart proposes a model in *Hidation of Northamptonshire*, pp. 39–42.

the Viking kingdom of York. Perhaps some credence can be given to William of Malmesbury's reference to the organization of Alfred's kingdom through hundredal and tithing organization, if it is considered to refer to tenth-century reorganization beyond Wessex:[264]

> And because, with the opportunity of the barbarians, even the natives had lusted after booty, to such a degree that there was no safe communication without the protection of arms, he instituted centuries [*centurias*] which they call hundreds [*hundrez*] and tenths [*decimas*] which they call tithings [*tithingas*], so that every Englishman, living within the law, should have a century and a tenth.

William of Malmesbury's account of a state of near anarchy is probably exaggerated, and William's account is concerned with law and order rather than specifically with military organization, but there is a further, cultural, factor, linked with aspects of lordship, in the use of the hundred: the antiquity of some hundredal units should also be noted because of their links with assemblies.[265] Such territorial units had been important in the early kingdoms of southern England, where the evidence of continuity is strongest. If many hundreds had grown from royal *regiones*, the territorial units of early Anglo-Saxon kingship through which kings could entertain their closest followers in the warband,[266] then the later obligations of hundreds could be said to descend from these personal bonds of lordship. The connection may not have been explicitly felt by, say, the tenth century, but it gives further weight to Abels's thesis of the significance of the bonds of lordship in the organization of the late Anglo-Saxon military system.

Abels's work is also significant in consideration of the five-hide provision, showing that the organization of the army did not necessarily have to distinguish directly between elite warriors and peasants. The army could have had an element whose responsibility was directly associated with the raising of warriors from commended men. This represented a distinction from much of the earlier scholarship,[267] noting that bookland referred to two distinct groups. While Abels did not employ Hollister's terminology of 'select' and 'general' fyrds to refer to these groups, it would not have been unreasonable for him to have chosen to do so. Avoiding confusion with the terminology of Hollister's study, Abels chose to refer to them as groups A and B, referring to king's men and those sub-contracted (my term) to provide military service. Abels's citation of the Worcester customs, recorded in Domesday Book is significant, relating to issues raised by Hollister:

---

[264] WM, GR I.122, p. 188.

[265] For the importance of the gathering of the nobility in the Edington campaign, see below, ch. 5. Banton, 'Ealdormen and Earls', p. 28, highlights the significance of the twice-yearly assembly of the shire for military purposes.

[266] Note here the attention paid to maintaining many of these units through the obligations of royal estates providing *feorm*: Lavelle, *Royal Estates in Anglo-Saxon Wessex*, pp. 26–47.

[267] Chadwick's recognition of a distinction between kings' thegns and 'inferior' thegns is a rare exception here, although this idea does not seem to have been followed in much of the twentieth-century scholarship before Abels: Chadwick, *Studies on Anglo-Saxon Institutions*, pp. 79–85.

The Church of St Mary of Worcester has one hundred called Oswaldslow, in which lie 300 hides. From these the bishop of the same church has by a constitution of ancient times [*a constitutione antiquorum temporum*] all the profits of jurisdiction [*redditiones socharum*] and all customary dues pertaining therein to the demesne support and to the king's service [*regis servitium*] and his own, so that no sheriff can have claim there for any plea or any other cause. Thus the whole county witnesses.

Noting the clarification provided by Hemming to Domesday Book's reference to a sheriff, as Hemming adds 'or *exactor* of royal service' to his description, Abels comments on the implications of the Domesday passage.[268]

The landholders of Oswaldslow thus 'defended' their land to the bishop rather than to the king or to one of his agents. The exclusion of the sheriff meant that the bishop himself would have been responsible for bringing his complement of fyrd-warriors into the field, and indeed, in 1066 we find that the bishop had a tenant named Eadric, whom Hemming describes as 'the pilot of the bishop's ship and the leader of the same bishop's military forces owed to the king's service [*ductor exercitus eiusdem episcopi ad servitium regis*]'.[269] Undoubtedly, the bishop of Worcester should be numbered among the lords of the fyrdmen of group B.

Although the bishop of Worcester's position in the shire was exceptional, there were others 'so free that they had their soke and sake and could go with their land to whomsoever they wished'. Three other churches, Evesham, Pershore, and Westminster, held between them the lordship of four hundreds.[270] St. Peter's of Westminster possessed its lands 'as quit and free of all claims as King Edward held

---

[268] *Hemingi Chartularium Ecclesiae Wigornensis*, ed. T. Hearne, 2 vols (Oxford, 1723), vol. I, p. 287. The extract is from Abels, *Lordship and Military Obligation in Anglo-Saxon England*, pp. 123–5.

[269] *Hemingi Chartularium*, ed. Hearne, vol. I, p. 81: 'Edricus, qui fuit, tempore Regis Edwardi, stermannus navis episcopi et ductor exercitus eiusdem episcopi ad servitium regis.' ['Eadric, who was, at the time of King Edward, steersman of a ship of the bishop and the same bishop's army leader for royal service.'] Cf. DB Worcs. 2:52 (fol. 173c) (Hindlip and Offerton): 'Edricus stirman (in suprascript) tenuit et deserviebat cum aliis servitiis ad regem et episcopum pertinientibus.' ['Eadric the steersman held [it] and gave service, with other services belonging to the king and bishop.'] Also *Hemingi Chartularium*, ed. Hearne, vol. I, p. 77: 'Et (episcopus) deracionavit socam et sacam de Hamtona ad suum hundred de Oswaldes law, quod ibi debent placitare et geldum ad expeditionem … persolvere', ['And [the bishop] established *soke* and *sake* concerning Hampton to his hundred of Oswaldslaw; in which manner they must make pleas and render payment for campaigns there.'] cited by Maitland, *Domesday Book and Beyond*, p. 308. See also John, *Land Tenure in Early England*, pp. 115–26; John, *Orbis Britanniae and Other Studies*, pp. 149–51. Stenton's interpretation, given in *First Century of English Feudalism*, p. 128, is based upon the notion that fyrd service was an obligation of peasants, and does not take into account Hemming's description of the Crowle lease.

[270] DB Worcs. C 1–5 (fol. 172a) (the county customs); 2:1 (fol. 172c) (lands of Worcester); 8:1 (fol. 174c) (lands of Westminster); 9:1–7 (fols. 175b–c) (lands of Pershore); 10:1–17 (fols. 175c–d) (lands of Evesham). See also Harmer, *Anglo-Saxon Writs*, nos. 73–106, pp. 286–372 (referring to the church of Westminster); nos. 115–16, pp. 407–11 (referring to the church of Worcester).

in his demesne',[271] and all enjoyed the pleas of their free men and most forfeitures that they might make.[272] As Domesday Book put it in its description of Pershore, the abbot 'has the forfeitures from his 100 hides as he ought to have from his own land … and all others enjoy the same from their lands.'[273] The implication seems to be that in Worcestershire book-right ordinarily carried with it sake and soke over the inhabitants of the estate. If this is correct, then a king's thegn such as Beorhtwine who, in Hemming's words, had his land 'freely by inheritance, having, that is, the power of giving it to whomsoever he wished since it was his paternal inheritance, for which he owed service to no man but the king' would also have had jurisdictional rights and, consequently, would have been responsible for the fyrd service arising from the lands of his tenants.[274] These pre-Conquest grants of liberty had in fact alienated so much of the profits of royal justice that the sheriff was provoked to complain in the shire return: 'In this county there are twelve hundreds; seven are so quit, the shire says, that the sheriff has nothing in them and therefore he [the sheriff] says that he loses much in farm [*in firma*].'[275] And if we can generalize from the triple hundred of Oswaldslow, the sheriff had also been deprived of his military command in these seven hundreds. The Worcestershire military customs, concerned as they are with the money fines arising from neglect of the fyrd, can only be fully appreciated if read in light of this county's jurisdictional arrangements.

An analysis of the Worcestershire customs thus suggests that there were two distinct grades of fyrdmen in this shire. On the one hand, there were the great landowners, the king's prelates, agents and thegns, all of whom held privileged tenures and seigniorial rights over the lands of other free men. These were the men to whom the king addressed his summonses and writs.[276] On the other hand,

---

[271] DB Worcs. C 1–5 (fol. 172a) (the county customs), Worcs. 8:1–28 (fols. 174c–175b) (Pershore, Worcs.). Cf. Harmer, *Anglo-Saxon Writs*, nos. 99–100, pp. 363–5 [S 1143 and S 1144 (AD 1042×66))].

[272] The county customs state that the king usually reserved the forfeitures arising from breach of the peace (*frithbryce*), obstruction of justice (*forsteall*), forcible entry into a home (*heimfare*, elsewhere termed *hamsocn*), and rape (for which their was no monetary compensation, the only amends being *de corpore justicia*). The Church of Worcester was unique in possessing these forfeitures in its lands. See Harmer, *Anglo-Saxon Writs*, p. 319. One should note the absence of *fyrdwite* from this list.

[273] DB Worcs. 9:7 (fol. 175c) (*terra Sanctae Mariae de Persore*, Worcs.).

[274] *Hemingi Chartularium*, ed. Hearne, vol. 1, p. 263, cited by J. H. Round in *VCH Worcs.*, vol. 1, ed. H. A. Doubleday (London, 1901), p. 267.

[275] DB Worcs. C 3 (fol. 172a). Cf. Harmer, *Anglo-Saxon Writs*, no. 100, pp. 364–5 [S 1144 (AD 1042×66)]: 'And I command and enjoin that all the thegns of the lands be henceforth subject to the minster, to the abbot and to the monks, and pay to Christ and St. Peter and the brethren all the rights (or dues) and the recognition (of lordship) which belong to me, for I will not permit that anyone have any authority there (Deerhurst and Pershore) except the abbot and the brethren.' Also Harmer, *Anglo-Saxon Writs*, no. 85, pp. 351–2 [S 1129 (AD 1053×66)].

[276] Harmer, *Anglo-Saxon Writs*, pp. 14, 52–4. Cf. DB Cheshire C 21 (fol. 262d) (Chester), on the lord's receipt of a summons from the royal reeve ordering him to supply men for the repair of the city's walls.

there were lesser fyrdmen drawn from the lower rungs of free society, 200-shilling men who were commended to and sometimes held their land under the jurisdiction of the local magnates.[277] (In practice, of course, these two groups were not so distinct as the shire customs suggests, since thegns in this county and others occasionally held land not only by book-right but also as tenants of the great churches or of greater lords. The Domesday Book custumals, one must remember, present only a simplified paradigm of how royal administration *was supposed* to operate. They were not concerned with anomalies, which must have been dealt with on an ad hoc basis.)

The gulf between the social and legal status of the two groups of warriors in Worcestershire helps explain the discrepancy in the penalties they faced for neglect of military service. The fyrdmen of group A stood in an especially close relationship to the king. They held their land by book-right, which made them the king's justiciables; they themselves possessed by royal favour rights of jurisdiction; and they were the king's own men. This threefold tie to the king aggravated their offense. Although the law codes regard simple neglect of the 'common burdens' as emendable by the payment of *wite*,[278] the fyrdmen of group A were guilty of more than mere neglect. They had received a personal summons to attend their royal lord in battle, and their failure to respond was wilful disobedience.[279] Loss of their property was appropriate punishment. As king's thegns they were entitled to their bookland, to use the language of the *Rectitudines*, but their rank also obliged them to 'do three things in regard to their land', one of which was the performance of fyrd service.[280] Both the refusal to acquit his land as he ought and his despite of the king's just command called into question a thegn's 'worthiness' to hold the

---

[277] There is a good deal of evidence for commoners bearing arms and attending the fyrd in eleventh-century England. See, e.g., *Northleoda Laga*, ch. 10 [*Gesetze*, vol. 1, pp. 460–1]; *EHD* 1, p. 469: 'Even if a *ceorl* prospers, so that he possesses a helmet and a coat of mail and a gold-plated sword, if he has not the land, he is a *ceorl* all the same.' Not also the implication of ASC C 1052: 'Earl Harold came from Ireland … and the inhabitants, both from Somerset and from Devonshire, gathered to oppose him, and he put them to flight and slew there more than thirty good thegns *besides other men*' [emphasis added]. Plummer-Earle, vol. 1, p. 179. Cf. DB Hants 69:16 (fol. 50a); Norfolk 66:41 (LDB fol. 275v); Suffolk 31:50 (LDB fol. 409v); Suffolk 76:20 (LDB fol. 449r), for notices of liberi homines who fell in the Battle of Hastings. See discussion in [Abels, *Lordship and Military Obligation in Anglo-Saxon England*], ch. 7 at n. 94.

[278] *II Cnut*, ch. 65 [*Gesetze*, vol. 1, pp. 352–3]. Cf. *VI Æthelred*, ch. 35 [*Gesetze*, vol. 1, pp. 256–7], which associates the desertion of a fyrd personally led by the king with the forfeiture of a property, and *V Æthelred*, ch. 28, §1 [*Gesetze*, vol. 1, p. 244], which states that he who deserts a fyrd led by someone other than the king must compensate the king with a payment of 120 shillings (= the *fyrdwite* of *II Cnut*, ch. 65). It is possible that the punishment for neglect of fyrd service was increased between the reigns of Cnut and Edward the Confessor.

[279] *Leges Henrici Primi*, ed. and trans. L. J. Downer (Oxford, 1972), ch. 13, §1, p. 116: 'Hec mittunt hominem in misercordia regis … contemptus breuim suorum et quicquid ad propriam eius personam uel mandatorum suorum contumeliatur inuriam.' ['The following place a man in the king's mercy … contempt of his writs and anything which slanders injuriously his own person or his commands'; trans. Downer, p. 117.]

[280] *Rectitudines*, ch. 1 [*Gesetze*, vol. 1, p. 444].

book.[281] It is not surprising that the king should have regarded it as having been forfeited into his hands.[282]

The situation of the fyrdmen of group B was entirely different. They held their tenures either by loan from a lord other than the king, from whom they 'could not recede' (that is, whose permission was needed if they wished to place this land under the protection of another lord),[283] or under his seignory. A fyrdman of this sort was obligated to serive his lord, not the king, and his lord was the one responsible for the *cinges utwaru* arising from the tenement. Simply put, the king demanded a certain number of fyrd warriors from a certain number of hides. Whoever held an estate 'freely' or possessed jurisdiction over it was a matter of little consequence to the king. A lord was thus quit with the king if he brought his full quota of provisioned warriors on campaign. If one of the fyrdmen whom the magnate expected to go remained behind, the lord was expected to find a suitable replacement. The absentee, for his part, was amerced forty shillings, payable to the man he had wronged, his lord. The king, having received the required complement of warriors from the magnate's lands, stood outside this transaction. But if the lord for some reason was unable to secure a substitute, and the king received less than his due, the lord owed the king compensation for his dereliction. Hence the forty shillings that the nobleman exacted from the absent fyrdman were turned over by him in full to the king, which meant, in practice, to the sheriff. The failure of the lesser fyrdman to accompany his landhlaford was viewed simultaneously as the fault of the lord, for which *wite* had to be paid to the king, and an injury to the lord, for which he was compensated by the wrongdoer.[284]

Although Abels is careful to couch his discussion in terms of military obligation in Worcestershire and avoids drawing too many generalizations, he notes the similarity with the system of royal obligation recorded for eleventh-century Berkshire (cited above).[285] However, some issues can be drawn from Abels's conclusions. One is that if the service of the B-class of thegn could be replaced by paid mercenary service, this may help us understand why the state became so reliant upon such paid service during the Viking wars of Æthelred II.[286] The second issue is that a bipartite army, of lords summoned directly by the king alongside warriors summoned directly by *their* lords has implications for our views on

---

[281] Cf. *III Edgar*, ch. 3 and *II Cnut*, ch. 15, §1, both of which stipulate that a thegn who possesses jurisdictional rights is to forfeit his rank and privileges if found guilty of malfeasance. A. J. Robertson (ed.), *The Laws of Kings of England from Edmund to Henry I* (Cambridge, 1925), pp. 24–5, 180–1 [*Gesetze*, vol. I, pp. 200–3, 318–19]. Cf. also *VI Æthelred*, ch. 5, §3 [*Gesetze*, vol. I, pp. 248–9], which states that a cleric is to be entitled (*wyrthe*) to the rights of a thegn (*thegenrihtes*), and 5, §4, which adds: 'And he who will not do what befits his order shall impair his status before God and man.'

[282] Cf. *Ine*, ch. 51 [*Gesetze*, vol. I, pp. 112–13].

[283] C. Stephenson, 'Commendation and Related Problems in Domesday Book', in *Medieval Institutions: Selected Essays*, ed. B. Lyons (Ithaca, NY, 1954), pp. 159–65.

[284] Cf. Maitland, *Domesday Book and Beyond*, p. 159.

[285] Abels, *Lordship and Military Obligation in Anglo-Saxon England*, pp. 125–6.

[286] Abels refers to this as a response to the 'inadequacy' of military resources recognized by Æthelred, in 'Household Men, Mercenaries and Vikings', p. 155.

Anglo-Saxon warfare. We cannot really countenance the idea of a king fighting on the battlefield surrounded by his closest lieutenants (notwithstanding, of course, such warriors in his household as those discussed below) if those lieutenants were themselves lords of other contingents of men.[287] Such an issue has implications for the consideration of armies on the battlefield, related as it is to the notion that battles could take place across a relatively wide area, with different divisions of an army fighting in different parts of the battlefield.[288] Armies could be organized according to geographical regions, perhaps reflecting the organization of the kingdoms of pre-Viking England and the regional interests of Anglo-Saxon lords.[289] Two post-Conquest writers, Wace and John of Salisbury, highlight the organization of the English army in this fashion, both relating the prime position held by the men of Kent. Wace records that 'wherever the king might go in the battle [of Hastings], the first blow should be theirs' (*ou que li reis auge en estor, li premier colp deit estre lor*),[290] as well as the protection of the king by the men of London (perhaps, as we shall see, the housecarls).[291] John of Salisbury records a right which had, he said, been in place in the days of Cnut, that the men of Kent were in the first cohort of the army with the right to 'the first contest with the enemy in all battles' (*primos congressus hostium ... in omnibus praeliis*), followed in battle by the men of Wiltshire, Devon and Cornwall.[292] Campbell has noted the possible continuity of such pre-Conquest organization, drawing attention to the Anglo-Saxon Chronicle's record of the deaths of Kentish nobles in the Battle of the Holme (902) because they 'lingered behind there against his [the king's] command [*ofer his bebod*]'.[293] Campbell, noting John of Salisbury's reference, argued that this may have been because they had formed the vanguard of Edward the Elder's advance into East Anglia.[294] These issues are significant in an early medieval force, concerned with individual and group prestige. The ruler's noblemen may not have fought alongside him in battle, but to be seen to fight at the front was evidently a matter of prestige which paralleled the jostling for position at court. The notion of elite warriors forming a household cadre of support is at the heart of this matter.

---

[287] See the reference to the 'companions who ride with me' in the will of Ælfhelm, S 1487 (AD 975×1016), below, p. 118.

[288] See below, pp. 277–8.

[289] Hollister, *Anglo-Saxon Military Institutions*, pp. 91–5; Abels, *Lordship and Military Obligation in Anglo-Saxon England*, pp. 67, 179–82.

[290] Wace, III.7819–24.

[291] Wace, III.7825–30.

[292] *Ioannis Saresberiensis episcopi Carnotensis policratici*, ed. Webb, vol. 2, pp. 47–8; trans. C. J. Nederman, *Policratus: Of the Frivolities of Courtiers and the Footprints of Philosophers*, Cambridge Texts in the History of Political Thought (Cambridge, 1990), p. 118.

[293] ASC ABCD 903.

[294] Campbell, 'What is not known about the Reign of Edward the Elder', p. 17. For speculation on the later reputation of the battle, see Lavelle, 'Politics of Rebellion', pp. 78–9.

A royal elite? The housecarls

Much has been written by historians on the significance of the housecarls, who appear in post-1016 administrative and narrative records. Housecarls appear to fulfil the notion of an elite royal guard who died alongside their lord at the Battle of Hastings, and in this lends credibility to the suggestion that a lord might be surrounded by his brightest and best warriors on the battlefield, a Praetorian Guard of sorts. However, the role of the housecarls (literally 'household servants') had wider implications. The unwavering loyalty of a group of warriors meant that the ruler could impose his will as he saw fit, as Harthacnut did with the ravaging of Worcestershire in 1042[295] and, arguably, Cnut with the seizure of the relics of St Ælfheah in 1023.[296]

Although as we have seen from Green's account of the Battle of Hastings, housecarls can attract the lion's share of attention in popular histories as an elite force fighting for King Harold,[297] the structures of organization and payment have been a topic of much debate. For example, it was proposed by L. M. Larson in 1904 and Hollister in 1962 that the housecarls were a Scandinavian elite force related to the Vikings of Jomsburg, imported wholesale by the new Danish dynasty;[298] James Campbell argued that they were a significant part of the Old English state as essentially a standing army;[299] and, in the concluding paragraph to his 1985 study, Nicholas Hooper contended that historians have been seduced by the source material and that the idea of the existence of housecarls before and during 1066 has been much exaggerated:[300]

> The housecarls did not form a distinctive element in Old English military organisation, a standing army and a law-bound guild. Those who held land must have been indistinguishable from their neighbours, and together with their tenants the thegns and housecarls formed the shire hosts. Those who lived at their lord's side are also unlikely to have differed from English thegns, although together they may have possessed an edge over the countrydwellers. As retainers they may have had greater *esprit de corps* and superior arms and training. They most likely received a stipend for their services. This does not make a standing army. The status and

---

[295] ASC CD 1041.

[296] A. R. Rumble and R. Morris (ed. and trans.), 'Textual Appendix: *Translatio Sancti Ælfegi Cantuariensis archiepiscopi et martiris* (BHL 2519): Osbern's account of the translation of St Ælfheah's relics from London to Canterbury, 8–11 June 1023', in *The Reign of Cnut: King of England, Denmark and Norway*, ed. A. R. Rumble, SEHB (London, 1994), pp. 283–15, at pp. 308–11 (below, pp. 194–6).

[297] See above, p. 52. For a more recent example, see P. Poyntz Wright, *Hastings*, Great Battles (Moreton-in-Marsh, 1996), pp. 67–72.

[298] Larson, *King's Household in England*, pp. 151–71. See also Hollister, *Anglo-Saxon Military Institutions*, pp. 12–19. For Jomsvikings, see also 'The Saga of the Vikings of Jom', in *English and Norse Documents Relating to the Reign of Ethelred the Unready*, ed. M. Ashdown (Cambridge, 1930), pp. 184–9, and for comments, p. 235.

[299] J. Campbell, 'Some Agents and Agencies of the Late Anglo-Saxon State', in *Domesday Studies*, ed. J. C. Holt (Woodbridge, 1986), pp. 201–18.

[300] N. Hooper, 'The Housecarls in England in the Eleventh Century', *ANS* 7 (1985 for 1984), pp. 161–76, at pp. 175–6.

function of the housecarls and thegns were identical – Hardecnut's use of his own housecarls to collect tax in 1041 was abnormal, for he had only just entered England as an invader.[301] All were expected to possess the arms appropriate to their station, to exercise their military prowess and to fight for the king when summoned. In rejecting the traditional view of the housecarls we make the English defeat at Hastings more understandable, and in some measure increase the reputation of the men who did fight alongside Harold in 1066.

If housecarls were an identifiable group in any form, they were probably the direct result of the imposition of Danish royal control on the English state as a result of the conquest of 1016 and they may have developed an identity as an elite warrior formation in order to maintain that position in English society. Domesday Book may have referred to a 'housecarl' simply as a synonym for a royal thegn in places, although a distinction is made between a royal thegn, royal housecarl and an earlish thegn in three consecutive Gloucestershire entries,[302] and the preponderance of Scandinavian names amongst those southern and midland landholders recorded as 'housecarls' in Domesday Book is noteworthy, showing that 'Viking' identities remained important even if they were not first-generation settlers.[303] Later Scandinavian historical traditions, recorded in the twelfth and thirteenth centuries, have been used to argue the context of elite communities of warriors with distinct communal identities.[304] The significance of Scandinavian warrior rituals amongst housecarls in England, such as the expulsion of Swein Godwinsson as a *nithing* in 1049, has been used to suggest that Scandinavian traditions played a part in maintaining the group identity of housecarls in England,[305] and, indeed, many of the later Scandinavian rune-stones recorded in chapter 2

---

[301] ASC CD 1041.

[302] DB Glos. 1:58–60 (fol. 164a).

[303] Of the eighteen estates in counties around London held by housecarls addressed in p. 244, n. 139, below, sixteen were recorded as being in the hands of predominantly royal housecarls with what could be considered Scandinavian names: Ulf (DB Midx. 7:2 [fol. 129a]), Toki (7:8 [fol. 129b]), Gøti (a housecarl of Earl Harold) (8:3 [fol. 129b]), Azur son of Toti (11:1 [fol. 130a]; Bucks. 49:1 [fol. 152c]), Aki (Midx. 17:1 [fol. 130c]), Saxi (DB Herts. 15:2 [fol. 136c]), Brand (27:1 [fol. 138d]), Anund (34:15 [fol. 140c]), Goldnir (Bucks. 12:36 [fol. 146d]), Burghard of Shenley (13:2 [fol. 146d]), Thori (for Thorir) (14:35, 43:11 [fols 147d and 152a-b]), Ulf Fenman (18:1 [fol. 149b]), Healfdene (an Old English form of a Scandinavian name) (46:1 [fol. 152b]), Alli of Lavendon (53:4 [fol. 152d]). See O. von Feilitzen, *The Pre-Conquest Personal Names of Domesday Book*, Arkiv för Germansk Namnforskning Utgivet AV Jöran Sahlgren 3 (Uppsala, 1937), s.vv.

[304] Sven Aggesen, 'Lex Castrensis', in *Scriptores minores historiæ Danicæ medii ævi ex codicibus denuo recensuit M. Cl. Gertz: Udg. af Selskabet for Udgivelse af Kilder til dansk Historie*, ed. M. C. Gertz, 2 vols (Copenhagen, 1917–22), vol. I, pp. 64–93, discussed in N. Lund, 'The Armies of Swein Forkbeard and Cnut: Leding or Lið?', ASE 15 (1986), pp. 105–18, at p. 110; Saxo Grammaticus, *Saxonis Gesta Danorum*, vol. I, ed. J. Olrik and H. Ræder (Copenhagen, 1931), p. 133; trans. P. Fisher and H. E. Davidson, *The History of the Danes, Books I–IX*, 2 vols (Cambridge, 1979), vol. I, p. 148. See also I. McDougall, 'Serious Entertainments: An Examination of a Peculiar Type of Viking Atrocity', ASE 22 (1993), pp. 201–25.

[305] ASC C 1049. The observation is made in Hollister, *Anglo-Saxon Military Institutions*, p. 15; here the building and arming of high-status vessels by Godwine may be noted (below, p. 145, n. 19). The service of English warriors in Byzantium after 1066 may be argued to

may have commemorated the deaths of warriors who took service *for* the English kingdom.

However, in a wider context the work of Robin Fleming and Kathryn Mack provides a good case for the revolutionary aspects of the Danish conquest of English society in 1016,[306] but that should not necessarily mean that housecarls filled a *de novo* position in their organization. Cnut and his sons were not unique in being part of a non-native dynasty who needed to impose their will against territory not wholly enthusiastic in giving its loyalty. Given that before 1016 kings from the West Saxon dynasty needed to impose their control in less-than-perfect circumstances, sometimes in areas outside their 'core' territory,[307] such as in Æthelred's attack on Rochester,[308] Eadred's attack on Thetford[309] or even the more dramatic actions in the Benedictine Reform, which essentially resulted in the state-approved confiscation of property,[310] it is worth noting that there was a need for an equivalent to the housecarls even if they were not known as such. By analogy, as I have noted elsewhere, the Norman Conquest saw the imposition of a new class of royal sergeants, *seruienti regis*, who supplemented the existing royal thegns (*taini regis*), in the administration of the royal estates.[311]

Thus an alternative can be proposed to Larson's Scandinavian view of the fraternal appearance of housecarls by way of a modification to Hooper's reductive interpretation quoted above.[312] Housecarls may not have represented a major change, but rather signify the existence of an elite military force in pre-Conquest England who were intimately associated with the king and, where appropriate, the royal family.[313] The composition of the royal household changed dramatically after 1016, so differences in terminology should not have been surprising. Given that forms of service could supplement each other, that Cnut had been efficient in the elimination of opposition and potential opposition, and considering that 'housecarl' could be a Scandinavianization of an Old English term meaning 'royal thegn/ servant', it seems reasonable to assume that the pre-1016 English had their own hired warriors in service with the royal household. As Abels suggests, the

have been part of this continuing group identity: J. Godfrey, 'The Defeated Anglo-Saxons Take Service with the Byzantine Emperor', *ANS* 1 (1979 for 1978), pp. 63–74 .

[306] K. Mack, 'Changing Thegns: Cnut's Conquest and the English Aristocracy', *Albion* 16 (1984), pp. 375–87; Fleming, *Kings and Lords in Conquest England*, pp. 21–52.

[307] Here note the acute observation by Tim Reuter on the limits of royal authority shown up in the use of harrying – 'state-directed Bissonic violence' – in late Anglo-Saxon England: Reuter, 'Debate: The "Feudal Revolution": III', p. 191. Reuter is referring to Thomas Bisson's work, best exemplified in his recent book, *The Crisis of the Twelfth Century: Power, Lordship, and the Origins of European Government* (Princeton, 2008).

[308] ASC CDE 986.

[309] ASC D 952.

[310] ASC A 962.

[311] Lavelle, *Royal Estates in Anglo-Saxon Wessex*, pp. 114–16.

[312] See also N. Hooper, 'Military Developments in the Reign of Cnut', in *Reign of Cnut*, ed. Rumble, pp. 89–100.

[313] ASC E 1035 refers to the protection of Queen Emma by the housecarls of 'her son the king'. For discussion of the relationship between the queen and housecarls, see Stafford, *Queen Emma and Queen Edith*, p. 114.

post-1016 developments (he referred to *liðsmen* and housecarls) were less innovations than 'variations on existing themes'.[314] Furthermore, it is likely that at least some in pre-1016 service were Scandinavians, a group of people whose presence at Edgar's court has been noted by Shashi Jayakumar.[315]

Abels has suggested that Alfred's achievements may have been based on the service of men attracted to the West Saxon court from elsewhere, although, as indicated by Asser's record of *faselli* (for *vassali* – vassals) at Athelney and his reference to those from outside Wessex who attended Alfred's court, including Scandinavians (*pagani*), 'Asser may well have recast Alfred's hired soldiers and sailors as loyal *hiredmen*'. Alfred's lordly relationships were portrayed in the traditional language of lordship through gift-giving rather than shown as a strictly commercial mercenary transaction.[316] Æthelweard is similarly oblique, recording that at Athelney Alfred 'had then no other reinforcements except servants who had royal maintenance [i.e. *feorm*]' (*nec aliæ tunc ei adiutrices excepto his qui regio pastu utebantur famulis*).[317] One might assume that he wrote of a loyal West Saxon following but we should note that Æthelweard wrote of this in the light of contemporary practice, with both Edgar and Æthelred II employing Scandinavians in (or associated with) the royal household.[318] Such service was important for the royal house's support, perhaps reflecting the nature of the enlarged English kingdom during the tenth and eleventh centuries. Rulers needed warriors on whom they could rely and who were removed from the tensions and rivalries of the wider kingdom. This need appears to have been fulfilled both before and after 1016 by elite troops associated with the royal household, whether or not they are described in our sources as 'housecarls'.

---

[314] Abels, 'Household Men, Mercenaries and Vikings', p. 157. Abels's point was in response to Hooper, 'Military Developments in the Reign of Cnut'. For *liðsmen*, see below, pp. 144–5.

[315] Jayakumar, 'Some Reflections on the "Foreign Policies" of Edgar "The Peaceable"', pp. 17–37.

[316] Abels, 'Household Men, Mercenaries and Vikings', pp. 147–53 (the quotation is at p. 153). Abels draws attention to the Frankish tradition which Asser drew on with the term *vassali* (p. 149). I am grateful to Barbara Yorke for her comments on this matter. For a de-'Othering' of the reading of Asser's use of *pagani*, see Nelson, 'England and the Continent in the Ninth Century: II, The Vikings and Others', p. 6. For the question of the purchase of naval service, see Hooper, 'Some Observations on the Navy in Late Anglo-Saxon England' (below, pp. 152–63). During Æthelred's reign, the ASC CDE 1012 record that the king would feed and clothe (*scyrdan*) the Vikings has similar implications of lordship when we take into account the high-quality silk of late Anglo-Saxon England (for which, see R. Fleming, 'Acquiring, Flaunting and Destroying Silk in Late Anglo-Saxon England', *EME* 15 [2007], pp. 127–58).

[317] Æthelweard, *Chronicon*, p. 42.

[318] For a balanced discussion of the Vikings employed by Æthelred, see Abels, 'Household Men, Mercenaries and Vikings', pp. 154–7. Ann Williams, *Æthelred the Unready: The Ill-Counselled King* (London, 2003), p. 53, suggests that the St Brice's Day massacre of 13 November 1002 may have been aimed against Scandinavians in garrison service. For a more conventional interpretation, see R. Lavelle, 'Ethnic Cleansing in Anglo-Saxon England', *BBC History Magazine* 3:11 (November 2002), pp. 42–4.

Arms, armour, and status

The equipment of an army is related to the provision of its personnel but has implications of both 'state' and 'private' provision. This section will focus on the written evidence for both the weapons themselves and for the significance of the status of weapons in a warrior society. The wide definition of social status through the carrying of weapons is apparent in late Anglo-Saxon society, for example in the imprisonment of an oathbreaker referred to in Alfred's lawcode, who would 'give his weapons and his possessions into his friends' keeping' to go into imprisonment for forty days or, if forced, 'he is to forfeit his weapons and his possessions'.[319] The enforced loss of weapons was therefore a statement on a lack of legal freedom; this was different from the discussion of the military participation in the Anglo-Saxon state, though it was not entirely unrelated. Indeed, a comparison may be made with the right to bear arms as a mark of legal freedom in the USA (a freedom denied to convicted felons), linked with the participation in the legitimacy of the state but ultimately functioning in the self-definition and, of course, self-defence of the individual.

Although we can move away from interpreting the English as armies of pitchfork-armed yokels, 'racial' readings of English modes of warfare have a long historiographical legacy. Wace's twelfth-century account of English peasants at Hastings carrying 'cudgels and great pikes, iron forks and clubs' and a certain English warrior wearing 'a helmet made entirely out of wood [fust], such that a blow to the head would not harm him',[320] are perhaps intended to distinguish what Wace presumably saw, from his twelfth-century perspective, as a non-chivalric mode of warfare of the Normans' English opponents.[321] This is hardly surprising in view of the twelfth-century writers' developments of ethnic identity, and the drawing out of what Wace may have seen as modes of warfare may have been an aspect.[322] Likewise, given the obsession of many Victorian writers with 'race', it unsurprising that attribution of martial characteristics took place in the nineteenth century. Charles Oman identified the use of the bow with the racial attributes of the Scandinavian Vikings, though not the Anglo-Saxons.[323] By contrast, Martin Biddle's more recent interpretation of a crossbow bolt found in a ninth- to tenth-century level in the Winchester excavations, which Biddle has suggested owes its presence to Frankish influence, might lead to more flexibility in our views of Anglo-Saxon warfare.[324] The consideration of modes of behaviour should be based on more

[319] Alfred, chs 1.2, 1.4: Gesetze, vol. 1, p. 48; trans. EHD 1, p. 409.

[320] Wace, III.7669–7706, III.8371–8378.

[321] This aspect of warfare is discussed in Bennett, 'Wace and Warfare', p. 49, although Bennett points out that Wace is aware of the importance of 'non-noble' warriors.

[322] For ethnic identities in the post-Conquest period, see H. Thomas, The English and the Normans: Ethnic Hostility, Assimilation and Identity, 1066–c. 1220 (Oxford, 2003), esp. pp. 297–306.

[323] C. Oman, A History of the Art of War: The Middle Ages from the Fourth to the Fourteenth Century (Oxford, 1898), pp. 129–30.

[324] B. Yorke, Alfred the Great: Warfare, Wealth and Wisdom: A Book to Accompany the Exhibition at Winchester Discovery Centre, February-April 2008 (Winchester, 2008),

than the cultural expectations of those texts which focused on pitched battles, as these were just one aspect of the broad range of violent activities that constituted Anglo-Saxon warfare.

A key account in the Anglo-Saxon Chronicle was an account of 'national' organization, recorded in the entry for 1008:

> Here [i.e. in this year] the king ordered that there should be resolutely built [wyrcan] ships all over England: that is, from three hundred and ten hides, one warship [scegð] and from 8 hides a helmet and a mailcoat.

The problems of interpreting the assessment of the provision of warships will be addressed in the next chapter, but some of its implications for armouring individual warriors, in its reference to helmets and mailcoats, can be addressed here. The meaning of this assessment, like so many others in pre-Conquest England, is ambiguous. While the figure associated with the provision of a ship presumably included its crew, it may be questioned whether the provision of ships was an imposition *in addition* to the provision of warriors. Or did some areas – perhaps coastal areas – provide ships while other areas provided warriors?[325]

Richard Abels calculated that if every eight hides provided a mailcoat and helmet, then, using Domesday Book's figures of some 70,000 hides for the whole kingdom south of the River Tees provided in Domesday Book (figures which show some continuity throughout the pre-Conquest period),[326] around 9,000 warriors could have been so equipped.[327] This would have been expensive in terms of quantities of metal required and the timescale expected, even if, as Alan Williams has

p. 7, draws attention to the three crossbow boltheads recorded in M. Biddle, *Object and Economy in Medieval Winchester: Artefacts from Medieval Winchester*, Winchester Studies 7.2.2 (Oxford, 1990), p. 1078, which come from early ninth-century and mid–late tenth-century contexts. A catch for a crossbow mechanism was found in a grave at Burbage (Wilts.) and was identified as Romano-British (Sites and Monuments Record SU25NWU04) but, given the fact that it was assigned to this period on the basis of Roman and post-Conquest usage of crossbows, the early Anglo-Saxon style decoration of the accompanying bone-work (perhaps from a comb) may equally assign this find to an early Anglo-Saxon context: E. H. Goddard, 'Notes on a Roman Cross-Bow, &c., found at Southgrove Farm, Burbage', *Wiltshire Archaeological and Natural History Magazine* 28 (1895), pp. 87–90. Cf. the account of the Battle of Hastings by Baudri of Bourgueil, *Adelae Comitissae*, in *Baldricus Burgulianus: Carmina*, ed. K. Hilbert, Editiones Heidelbergenses 19 (Heidelberg, 1979), no. 134, lines 409–16, p. 160, who writes that the English had not encountered crossbows before. This is discussed in M. K. Lawson, *The Battle of Hastings, 1066*, Battles and Campaigns (Stroud, 2002; reset edn, 2007), pp. 211–12, and Biddle, *Object and Economy in Medieval Winchester*, p. 1077.

[325] A reading of this is by Howard, *Swein Forkbeard's Invasions*, pp. 163–7. See below, pp. 148–51.

[326] This is indicated, at least in southern England, by the hideage assessments associated with the shires for the boroughs recorded in Domesday Book, which match closely with those recorded in the Burghal Hidage: P. H. Sawyer, *From Roman Britain to Norman England* (London, 1978), pp. 227–8. For discussion of this, see Brooks, 'Administrative Background to the Burghal Hidage', and D. A. Hinton, 'The Fortifications and their Shires', in *Defence of Wessex*, ed. Hill and Rumble, pp. 128–50, at pp. 136–7, 151–9. See also Yorke, *Wessex in the Early Middle Ages*, pp. 89–90.

[327] Abels, 'English Logistics and Military Administration', p. 262.

posited, Roman mail armour may have been available in larger quantities than is normally acknowledged.[328] As Abels pointed out, Thietmar of Merseberg referred to what he had heard was an 'incredible number' of 24,000 mailcoats stored by Æthelred in London in 1016;[329] even allowing for the inevitable exaggeration of hearsay, the notion that the English kingdom had undertaken a vast rearmaments programme was evidently widely understood. Michael Swanton suggested an alternative possibility that the helmets and mailcoats were intended for the crews of the ships.[330] Assuming this with a 64-oar *scægð*,[331] each of these vessels and associated equipment would have required 822 hides (310 hides for the ship and 512 hides for the equipment). Notwithstanding the non-decimal or even non-duodecimal nature of this figure, then, from the 70,000 hides for the kingdom addressed above, a theoretical total of some 85 ships could have been provisioned and 5,440 warriors could have been equipped.

The eight-hide unit for armour provision is not recorded anywhere apart from the Anglo-Saxon Chronicle. It is probable that its imposition was an isolated event.[332] Abels has commented on the impossibility of knowing how King Æthelred intended to distribute this equipment to his warriors,[333] but it is relevant to note Nicholas Brooks's suggestion that the Anglo-Saxon Chronicle's 1008 entry can be compared with other evidence. Brooks observed that, in the corpus of wills that survive from the late Anglo-Saxon period, a number that can be dated to after 1008 record bequests of armour, whereas those from before that date rarely do so.[334] He also noted a distinct lack of references to English armour in the *Battle of Maldon* poem, which he suggested reflected the situation before 1008.[335] Carla Morini has emphasized the significance of such absence, noting that references to mail in Old English sources tend to indicate the wearer's foreignness,[336] while Brooks, interpreting a lack of armour on English warriors in the Battle of Maldon, drew attention to the 'moral bankruptcy of a state which sought by such

[328] Williams, 'Metallurgy of Medieval Arms and Armour', p. 49. For discussion of the logistics of metalworking, see above, p. 65, n. 87.

[329] *Thietmari Merseburgensis episcopi Chronicon*, ed. R. Holtzmann, MGH Scriptores Rerum Germanicarum Nova Series 9 (Berlin, 1935; 2nd edn, 1955), VII.40, pp. 446–7; trans. EHD 1, p. 348. This is cited by Abels, 'English Logistics and Military Administration', p. 262. For Thietmar's informant, see Leyser, 'The Ottonians and Wessex', p. 95.

[330] Swanton, *Anglo-Saxon Chronicles*, p. 138, n. 6.

[331] As recorded in S 1492 (below, p. 119).

[332] However, A. R. Rumble, 'The Structure and Reliability of the "Codex Wintoniensis" (British Museum Additional MS 15350; The Cartulary of Winchester Cathedral Priory)' (PhD thesis, Univ. of London, 1980), p. 92, notes the preponderance of both five-hide and three-hide measurements amongst the estates in the Winchester archive. Although without wider investigation it can only be a hypothesis, it is not inconceivable that such figures were used to reach the eight-hide unit recorded in the ASC.

[333] Abels, 'English Logistics and Military Administration', p. 262.

[334] Brooks, 'Arms, Status and Warfare in Late-Saxon England', pp. 85–90.

[335] N. P. Brooks, 'Weapons and Armour', in *The Battle of Maldon*, AD 991, ed. D. Scragg (Oxford, 1991), pp. 208–19, at pp. 215–17.

[336] C. Morini, 'OE *Hring*: Anglo-Saxon or Viking Armour?', ASSAH 13 (2005), pp. 155–72, at pp. 160–1.

propaganda [as the poem] to encourage its troops to resist the invading enemy without giving them the equipment to make such resistance effective.'[337] Guy Halsall has commented on Brooks's thesis, suggesting that if late tenth-century warriors were unarmoured as they went into battle against Vikings, they may have been thus equipped for cultural reasons, perhaps in part the result of a generation's fast-moving campaigns against very mobile Welsh and Scottish enemies: 'uncomfortable armour may have become unpopular or even unfashionable and been discarded.'[338] Halsall points out that we should not read from this that the campaigns of the West Saxon state in the ninth and early tenth centuries had necessarily been undertaken by poorly protected warriors.[339]

Abels makes a plea for caution, that we should not draw too many conclusions about the apparently unarmoured Anglo-Saxon warriors from a small corpus of evidence.[340] The wills are a case in point. Many wills recorded the payment of heriot to kings by the testator, which was often provided in the form of weapons and armour ('heriot', from the Old English *here-geat*, literally meant 'army/ war-gear'). These payments represented the return of arms to a lord who had bestowed them for the man's service during his lifetime. Heriots were payments, probably made in public,[341] which affirmed the thegnly status, showing their implicit connection with landholding, and providing them with a right to bequeath the rest of their wealth.[342] Such heriots did not exclude female landholders, suggesting that

---

[337] Brooks, 'Weapons and Armour', p. 217.

[338] Halsall, *Warfare and Society in the Barbarian West*, pp. 172–3. For the eleventh-century use of light armour in a discussion of mobility, see P. Hill and J. Wileman, *Landscapes of War: The Archaeology of Aggression and Defence* (Stroud, 2002), p. 139, who discuss (though do not cite) references to light (?leather) armour in the twelfth-century writings of Gerald of Wales and John of Salisbury: Gerald of Wales, *Itinerarium Kambriae et descriptio Kambriae*, ed. Dimock, book 2, ch. 7, p. 217 (see above, pp. 22–3) and *Ioannis Saresberiensis ... policratici*, ed. Webb, vol. 2, VI.6, p. 19; trans. Nederman, *Policratus: Of the Frivolities of Courtiers and the Footprints of Philosophers*, p. 113–14. The mobility of heavy infantry in light armour was commented on by Freeman, *History of the Norman Conquest*, vol. 2, pp. 473–4, who (p. 473n) also interpreted the *Vita Ædwardi Regis's* account of when 'the English hastening under Harold joined / fast columns and platoons of Tostig's men' (*cum uolocres Angli sub Haroldo preside iuncti / Tostini cuneis agminibusque citis*) in Wales (*Vita Ædwardi Regis: The Life of King Edward who Rests at Westminster*, ed. F. Barlow, OMT, 2nd edn [Oxford, 1992], pp. 86–7) as a 'distinct allusion to the change of tactics'.

[339] Halsall, *Warfare and Society in the Barbarian West*, p. 173. For a reference to a mailcoat in the late seventh/ early eighth century, see *Ine*, ch. 54.1: *Gesetze*, vol. 1, p. 114; trans. *EHD* 1, p. 405.

[340] Abels, 'From Alfred to Harold II', p. 25, n. 43.

[341] See King Æthelred's confirmation of Æthelric's will, S 1501 (AD 961×95). For a discussion of the witnessing of wills in public, see M. M. Sheehan, *The Will in Medieval England: From the Conversion of the Anglo-Saxons to the End of the Thirteenth Century*, Studies and Texts 6 (Toronto, 1963), pp. 47–54. For the legal significance of wills as a record of an oral disposition made before witnesses, see H. D. Hazeltine, 'Comments on the Writings Known as Anglo-Saxon Wills', in Whitelock, *Anglo-Saxon Wills*, pp. vii–xl.

[342] For the significance of heriot as a means of buying a lord's support, see Maitland, *Domesday Book and Beyond*, pp. 289–90, and Sheehan, *Will in Medieval England*, pp. 81–2. See also L. Tollerton Hall, 'Wills and Will-making in Late Anglo-Saxon England' (DPhil thesis, Univ. of York, 2005), pp. 86–97. Wills and bequests which do not include references to heriots in the surviving manuscripts are: S 1493 (AD 978×1016), S 1500 (AD 805×32),

the link with status could also be symbolic rather than reflecting military service *per se*, though women's heriots were not always recorded as payments of weapons. As far as we can see, too, the records refer to heriots made to kings, but presumably, as Nicholas Banton observed, there were also bequests of weapons by thegns to non-royal lords (in effect, Abels's 'B-thegns'). The evidence of heriot payments by men who were commended to anyone but rulers is sparse, limited to the will of a man commended to Archbishop Stigand (S 1519), while some wills do not refer to lords as 'royal lords', the context of most suggests that the king was still meant (an exception here may be S 1534, where the testator requested their lord to act as an advocate for his widow and daughter). However, payments by commended men to their lords may be reflected in the wealth of ealdormanric heriots[343] and the reference in Cnut's lawcode to a 'lawful heriot' (*rihtan heregeata*) to which a lord was entitled to from a man who died intestate. As might be expected, the value of a heriot could vary. Ostensibly this was based on a man's rank. The laws of Cnut explicitly link the provision of heriot with social ranks.[344]

> 70. And if one depart from this life without a will, be it through his carelessness, be it through sudden death, then the lord shall take no more from his property than his lawful heriot [*rihtan heregeata*].
>
> 70.1. Moreover, according to his disposition, the property shall be distributed very lawfully to the wife and children and near-kinsmen; to each by their status as appropriate to him.
>
> 71. And heriots shall be established just as is fitting [*mæðlic*]:
>
> 71a. An earl's as appropriate thereto, that is 8 horses, 4 saddled and 4 unsaddled, and 4 helmets and 4 mail-coats and 8 spears and likewise as many shields and 4 swords and two hundred mancuses of gold.
>
> 71.1. And next, the king's thegns, who are nearest to him: 4 horses, 2 saddled and 2 unsaddled, and 2 swords and 4 spears and as many shields, and a helmet and mail-coat and 50 mancuses of gold.
>
> 71.2. And of the ordinary thegns [*medemra þegna*]: a horse and its trappings [*gerædna*], and his weapons or his *healsfang* in Wessex; and in Mercia 2 pounds and in East Anglia 2 pounds.
>
> 71.3. And the heriot of the king's thegn among the Danes, who has his *soke*: 4 pounds.

S 1502 (AD 1048×50), S 1503a (? AD 986), S 1506 (AD 941×58, perhaps 958), S 1508 (AD 871×88), S 1509 (AD 932×9), S 1510 (AD 845×53), S 1513 (*c.* AD 900), S 1514 (*c.* AD 855), S 1518 (*c.* AD 1013), S 1522 (AD 998), S 1532 (*c.* AD 1050), S 1533 (AD 931×9, probably 933×9). A lack of references to heriot in a surviving manuscript (which may date from a later century) does not necessarily mean that a heriot would not be paid, but it should lead us to note that a heriot was significant in the cases where it was recorded.

343 Banton, 'Ealdormen and Earls', pp. 157, 269.

344 *II Cnut*; *Gesetze*, vol. 1, pp. 356–8.

71.4. And if he have further relation to the king: 2 horses, 1 saddled and the other unsaddled, and a sword and 2 spears and 2 shields and 50 mancuses of gold.

71.5. And he who be of lesser means: 2 pounds.

As Brooks observed, the appearance of mailcoats in the expectation of heriot payments is particularly striking in this period, which post-dated the Anglo-Saxon Chronicle's record of the armouring of English warriors cited above.[345] Perhaps the heriot of a mailcoat may even have been an innovation of the reign of Cnut, associated with what Morini has suggested was a distinction of the mailcoat's 'foreign' perception.[346]

Nonetheless, the evidence of heriots raises the wider question of the links between weaponry and social status. More can be gleaned from the corpus of wills. The following extracts, while not an exhaustive collection, are intended to set out the evidence for references to war-gear, and the context of such war-gear in the payment of heriots.[347]

> ℂ Theodred, Bishop of London, S 1526 (AD 942×51)
>
> First, he grants his lord his heriot, that is, two hundred marks of red gold and two silver cups, and four horses, as I have best, and two swords, as I have best, and four shields and four spears. And the estate which I have at Duxford [Cambs.], and the estate which I have at Illington [prob. Norfolk], and the estate which I have at Arrington [Cambs.].

> ℂ Ælfgar, S 1483 (AD 946×51)
>
> First that I grant to my lord two ?sheathed swords [*suerde fetelsade*],[348] and two armlets, each of fifty mancuses of gold; and three steeds; and three shields; and three spears. And Bishop Theodred and the Ealdorman Eadric said to me, when I gave to my lord the sword which King Edmund gave to me, worth a hundred and twenty mancuses of gold and [with] four pounds of silver on the sheath [*fetelse*], that I might be worthy of my will [i.e. might make it]; and I have never done wrong, on God's witness, against my lord that I may not [have this right].

---

[345] Brooks, 'Arms, Status and Warfare in Late-Saxon England', p. 90.

[346] Morini, 'OE *Hring*', pp. 160–1.

[347] With the exceptions of S 1492 (*Councils and Synods with Other Documents relating to the English Church, I: AD 871–1204*, ed. D. Whitelock, M. Brett and C. N. L. Brooke, 2 parts (Oxford, 1981), part 1, pp. 383–6) and S 1497 (D. Whitelock, N. Ker, and R. Rennell, *The Will of Æthelgifu*, Roxburghe Club [Oxford, 1968]), S 1517 (S. D. Keynes, 'A Lost Cartulary of St Albans Abbey', *ASE* 22 [1993], pp. 253–79), and S 1532 (S. D. Keynes, 'The Will of Wulf', *Old English Newsletter* 26.3 [Spring, 1993], pp. 16–21), the extracts presented here are translated from Whitelock, *Anglo-Saxon Wills*, and mostly follow Whitelock's chronological order.

[348] Whitelock, *Anglo-Saxon Wills*, p. 27, has 'swords with sheaths', but as Old English *fetel* (Bosworth-Toller, p. 284) refers to a belt, this term may refer to more than just the sheath but the belt trappings associated with the sword.

⟨ Ælfgifu, S 1484 (AD 966×75)

And I grant to my royal lord the estates at Wing, and at Linslade, and at Haver-sham [all Bucks.], and at Hatfield [prob. Herts.], and at Masworth [Bucks.] and at Gussage [Dorset]; and two armlets, each is [worth] a hundred and twenty man-cuses, and a drinking cup and six horses and as many shields and spears.

⟨ Ælfheah, Ealdorman of Central Wessex, S 1485 (*c.* AD 968×71)

And he grants to his royal lord the one hundred and twenty hides at Worth and the estates at Cookham, and at Thatcham [Berks.], and at Chelworth [Wilts], and at *Incgenæsham* [Inglesham, Wilts.?], and at Aylesbury, and at Wendover [Bucks.]; and three hundred mancuses of gold and a dish of three pounds and a drinking-cup of three pounds and a short sword [*handsex*]; and on the *lecg* [i.e. hilt?][349] are eighty mancuses of gold; and six swords and six horses with trappings [*geredan*], and as many spears and shields. And he grants to Ælfthryth the King's wife, his godmother [*gefædere*], the estate at *Scyræburnan* just as it stands; and to the elder ætheling, the king's son and her's [i.e. Edmund ætheling], thirty mancuses of gold and a sword; and to the younger [i.e. Æthelred ætheling] the estate at Walkhamp-stead [Surrey].

⟨ Æthelmær, Ealdorman of Hampshire, S 1498 (AD 971×83)

And I bequeathe to my royal lord as my heriot 4 armlets of three hundred man-cuses of gold, and 4 swords and 8 horses, four with trappings [*gerædode*] and 4 without trappings [*ungerædode*], and 4 helmets and 4 mailcoats [*byrnan*] and 8 spears and 8 shields.

⟨ Brihtric and Ælfswith, his wife, S 1511 (AD 973×87, ?980×7)

First to his royal lord an armlet of eighty mancuses of gold, and a short sword [*handsecs*] of the same value, and four horses, two with trappings [*twa geræd-ede*], and two ?sheathed swords [*sweord gefetelsode*], and two hawks and all his staghounds. And to the [royal] lady an armlet of thirty mancuses of gold and a steed for her advocacy that the will might stand.

⟨ Æthelwold, S 1505 (after AD 987)

And he bequeathed to his royal lord as his heriot an armlet of 30 mancuses, and two *lecga* [?hilts] and 2 horses and 2 swords and 2 shields and two spears. … And I grant to my son one hide of land at Upton [Scudamore, Wilts.?], and one *lecg* [?hilt]

---

[349] Whitelock, *Anglo-Saxon Wills*, p. 31, suggests a scabbard but, given the significance of the separation of parts of weapons (most obviously apparent in items in the recently discovered Staffordshire Hoard) and that a hilt could be fashioned as part of a sword while a scabbard was presumably specific to a particular blade, the definition of 'some part of a weapon, the cross bar in the hilt[?]', given in Bosworth-Toller, p. 627, seems more plausible; OE *lecgan* signifies lying down, which would be appropriate to the hilt or part thereof. One may even speculate as to whether the term was a synecdoche for the whole sword.

❦ Ælfhelm, S 1487 (AD 975×1016)

First to his lord a hundred mancuses of gold; and two swords and four shields; and four spears; and four horses, two with trappings, two without trappings.

... And I grant my ship [scæðe] for my soul's sake to Ramsey, half for the abbot and half for the community. And I grant to my wife half of the stud at Troston [Suffolk], and half to my companions [gefaran] who ride with me.

❦ Æthelflæd, second wife of King Edmund, S 1494 (AD 962×91, prob. after 975)

First I grant to my lord the estate at Lambourn and those at Cholsey and at Reading [all in Berks.], and four armlets of two hundred mancuses of gold, and 4 robes and 4 cups and 4 bowls and 4 horses.

❦ Æthelric [of Bocking], S 1501 (AD 961×95)

First of all, to my lord sixty mancuses of gold, and my sword with the belt, and two horses as well, two targan [i.e. small shields] and two javelins [francan]. ...

❦ From Æthelred's confirmation of Æthelric's will, S 939 (AD 995×99, prob. 995×6)

It was many years before Æthelric died that the King was told that he [i.e. Æthelric] was in the bad plan [unræde] that Swein should be received in Essex when first he came thither with a fleet. And the king before many witnesses, told Archbishop Sigeric of it, who was then his advocate for the sake of the estate at Bocking [Essex] which he had bequeathed to Christchurch. Then he was uncleared of this charge as well as unatoned, both during his life and after, until his widow brought his heriot to the King at Cookham [Berks.], where he had gathered his witan from far and wide.

❦ Æthelgifu, S 1497 (AD 990×1001)

... that is to her lord the king 30 mancuses of gold, and two steeds which are commanded by him, and my headerhundas [?best dogs], and to my lady 30 mancuses of gold and the estate at Westwick [in St Albans, Herts.] just as [she] defended [it].

❦ Wulfgeat of Donington, S 1534 (c. AD 1000)

And he gives to his lord 2 horses and 2 swords and 4 shields and 4 spears and 10 mares with 10 colts. And he asks his lord, for God's love, that he be a friend [i.e. advocate] of his wife and daughter.

... And all those who receive my property are to pay to Brun 20 mancuses of gold, and I give to thank him 6 mares with 6 colts. And the horses which are left are to be for my wife and my daughters, to each likewise as many.

❦ Wulfric [Spot], S 1536 (AD 1002×4)

That is [my will] that I grant to my lord two hundred mancuses of gold, and two silver-hilted swords [seolforhilted sweord] and four horses, two saddled [gesadelode] and two unsaddled, and the weapons which pertain thereto [ꝼ þa wæpna þe þærto gebyriað].

... And to the minster at Burton [Staffs.] a hundred wild horses, and sixteen tame geldings [*hencgestas*] and as well all that I posess in livestock and that remaining except that which I have bequeathed.

❦ Archbishop Ælfric of Canterbury, S 1488 (AD 1003×4)

And he bequeathed to his lord his best ship [*scip*] and the sailing tackle [*segelgeræda*] thereto, and 60 helmets [*healma*] and 60 mailcoats [*beornena*].

... And he bequeathed that with what money remained it should be taken and first every debt paid, and afterwards it [i.e. what is left] should be provided for his heriot as it should be had [i.e. his due heriot]. And he gave a ship [*scip*] to the people of Kent and another to Wiltshire.

❦ Bishop Ælfwold of Crediton, S 1492 (AD 1008×12)

And he grants to his lord four horses, two saddled and two unsaddled, and four shields and 4 spears, and two helmets, and two mailcoats, and 50 mancuses of gold which Ælfnoth owes him from Woodleigh [Devon], and a 64-oar ship [*scegð*] which is all ready except the *hanon* [rowing stations?].[350] He would get it fully ready for his lord, for honour, if God had allowed him.

... And to the ætheling 40 mancuses of gold and the wild horses on the land at Ashburton [Devon], and to his three kinsmen Eadwold and Æthelnoth and Grimketil, to them each 20 mancuses of gold and to them each a horse, and to Wulfgar his kinsman two tapestries and two seat-coverings and three mailcoats; and to Godric his brother-in-law, two mailcoats, ... and to Cenwold a helmet and a mailcoat, and to Boia a horse; ... and to Leofwine 'Polga' and Mælpatrick and Byrhtsige, to each of the three of them a horse; and to each of his household men [*hiredmen*] his mount which he had loaned [*alæned*] them; and to all his *hiredcnihtas* 5 pounds to divide, each by his right.

❦ Ætheling Athelstan, S 1503 (AD 1014)

...and the sword with the silver hilt [*mid þam sylfrenan hiltan*] which Wulfric made, and the gold belt and the armlet which Wulfric made, and the drinking-horn which I previously bought from the household [*hirede*] at the Old Minster. [to the Old Minster, Winchester] ...

[N. B. perhaps not as heriot] And I grant to my father, King Æthelred, the land at Chalton [Hants], except the eight hides which I have granted to my *cniht* Ælfmær; and the estate at *Northtune*, and the estate at Mollington [Oxon.]; and the silver-hilted [*seolferhiltan*] sword which Ulfketel possessed; and the mailcoat [*byrnan*] which is with Morcar; and the horse which Thurbrand gave to me; and the white horse which Leofwine gave to me.

And to Edmund my brother I grant the sword which King Offa possessed; and the sword with 'pitted' hilt; and a blade and a silver-coated blowing-horn [*blædhorn*] ... And I grant to Eadwig my brother a silver-hilted sword. And I grant to Bishop Ælfsige the golden cross which is with Eadric, Wynflæd's son; and a black steed. ...

---

[350] See N. A. M. Rodger, 'Cnut's Geld and the Size of Danish Ships' *EHR* 110 (1995), pp. 392–403, which (pp. 392–3) points out the problems with Whitelock's translation of the term as 'rowlocks' (*EHD* 1, p. 581).

... the inlaid sword which Withar possessed [*malswurdes þe Wiðer ahte*], and my horse with my trappings [*mid minon gerædon*] [to Ælfwine, mass-priest]...

... a pied stallion and the ?notched [*sceardan*] sword and my *targe* [i.e. small shield] [to Ælfmær, *discþegn*]...

... and a sword and a horse and my *bohscyld* [?curved shield][351] [to Siferth]...

... And I grant to Eadric, Wynflæd's son, the sword on which the hand is marked [*þe sea hand is on gemearcod*]. And I grant to my *cniht* Æthelwine the sword which he previously gave to me. And I grant to Ælfnoth my sword-polisher the ?notched inlaid sword ['*þæs sceardan malswurdes*'], and to my staghuntsman the stud which is on *Colungahrycg*.

❧ Wulfsige, S 1537 (AD 1022×43)

And I grant to my royal lord 2 horses and a helmet and a mailcoat [*brinie*], and a sword and a gold-worked spear [i.e. inlaid with gold]. ... and my brother's children their own land, and 2 horses with harness [*mid sadelgarun*], and one coat of mail and one cloak.

❧ Thurstan, S 1531 (AD 1043×45)

And I grant to my royal lord as heriot two marks of gold and two horses and trappings [*sadelfate*], and a helmet and a coat of mail and a sword and two shields and two spears. And I desire that the estate at *Bidicheseye* shall be sold, and that two marks of gold shall be taken from that estate for the King's heriot.

❧ Eadwine of Caddington (Beds.), S 1517 (c. AD 1050)

And then to his lord, as heriot to him, 4 horses, 2 saddled and 2 unsaddled, and 2 swords.

❧ Ulf (or Wulf), S 1532 (c. AD 1050)

And I grant to Othin 2 marks of weighed silver, and to Earl Sihtric half a mark of gold, to Osgod 6 ores of gold and 4 marks of silver, and to his brother 4 marks of silver; and to Dagfinn a mark of gold, more if he merit more, and to Æfin 2 [marks] of weighed silver, and a horse, and to Æthelric Swegn 2 marks, and to Edward a horse; and otherwise to each of my household *cnihts* [*hiredcnihta*] who have no land, a horse, and to Thorod the Little 2 [marks] of weighed [silver], and Saxa is to maintain the child and the money, or entrust him to a certain minster with the money. And if there remain anything, in gold or in silver or in vestments, they shall have the most who best merit [it] from me and will do the most for my soul. And 30 men are to be freed for my soul.

❧ Ketel, S 1519 (AD 1062×66)

And I grant to Archbishop Stigand, my lord, the estate at Harling [Norfolk] as it stands, except that the men shall all be free and that I grant ten acres to the church. And if I do not come [back] again, I grant to him as my heriot a helmet, and a mailcoat, and horse, and harness [*gereade*], and sword and spear.

---

[351] An alternative is 'shoulder shield': Bosworth-Toller, p. 115.

It can be seen that the wills not only recorded bequests of wealth to royal lords but also to household men and women. The significance of household warriors and the importance of post-mortem rewards is indicated by the distribution of horses to landless household servants (*hiredcnihtas*)[352] in the mid eleventh-century will of a certain Ulf (or Wulf) (S 1532), by Ælfhelm's late tenth- or early eleventh-century bequest of half his stud at Troston (Suffolk) to his 'companions [*gefaran*] who ride with me' (S 1487), by Bishop Ælfwold's granting of weapons as well as the horses 'loaned' (*alæned*) to his household men (S 1492), and by the ætheling Athelstan's distribution of weapons to his followers in 1014 (S 1503). If, in addition to a will's public enactment after the testator's death, a will was also a document of a statement made in front of witnesses,[353] then the promise of wealth made therein presumably helped to bind the lord's followers to him.

There does appear to be some relationship between the value of heriots and the wealth and social standing of those making the bequest.[354] In 1978 Nicholas Brooks tabulated some of the data from the corpus of wills in order to use the weapons sets to distinguish between the ranks of the late Anglo-Saxon nobility.[355] Table 3.2 differs from that of Brooks by including a wider range of data from wills which refer to heriots. Along with the details of the heriots, the table includes dates, details of bequests of weapons and relevant movable goods which were not heriots (marked in italics), evidence of the archives in which the wills were deposited, as well as an assessment of the social status of the testator and the number of estates which they bequeathed. The survival of wills is associated with that of particular archives, suggesting the use of such archives as repositories associated with donor families linked to particular religious houses.[356] This issue should be borne in mind to address Brooks's question, raised above, of whether mail armour was commonly worn before 1008. It is true that the only evidence of laymen of thegnly rank bequeathing a helmet and mailcoat in heriots survives from the eleventh century after 1008; but we should note that

---

[352] For Hollister's discussion of *cnihtas*, see above, pp. 88–9.

[353] See above, n. 341.

[354] For discussions of personal wealth in the late tenth and eleventh centuries, including the evidence in wills, see D. A. Hinton, *Gold and Gilt, Pots and Pins: Possessions and People in Medieval Britain*, Medieval History and Archaeology (Oxford, 2005), pp. 141–70, and Williams, *World Before Domesday*, pp. 105–21. Although Hinton stresses the increasing importance of the bullion value of precious metal items over their decorative significance, a picture of the link between status and display expressed through portable wealth is hard to ignore, as Williams's account indicates.

[355] Brooks, 'Arms, Status and Warfare in Late-Saxon England', pp. 86, 88.

[356] The fact that so many later wills and so few early wills survive probably reflects the interest of those houses in preserving those documents in post-Conquest cartularies, while the fact that most wills survive from the later tenth century onwards presumably reflects these archival interests. To this end it is perhaps significant that S 1510 (AD 845×53), a comparatively early will, makes specific reference to the need for the community of Christchurch to 'keep one [copy] with their charters'. A discussion of the maintenance of the archive of Old Minster, Winchester, as a repository for documents (including, but not solely, wills) from the local and regional communities is in Rumble, 'Structure and Reliability of the "Codex Wintoniensis"', pp. 120–66.

the evidence for this is limited to two wills from Bury St Edmunds – one relating to a king's thegn and the other to a thegn of Archbishop Stigand.[357] It may also be observed that much of that house's evidence is from the eleventh century, from which period there are two, possibly three, thegns' wills that, likewise, do *not* include reference to armour in the heriots.[358] The few eleventh-century wills of thegns from archives other than that of Bury St Edmunds do not record it, either.[359]

In all, the evidence is limited, and while it does not disprove Brooks's suggestions, neither does it prove them. If Cnut's lawcode is significant for the increase in the provision of armour for eleventh-century English warriors, it is important for what it says about the provision of a lawful heriot (*rihtan heregeata*). Although, as Brooks noted, the heriots in wills often corresponded with the status assigned to those heriots recorded by Cnut, and showing that they 'had already been in force under his predecessor',[360] the variations in what was provided suggest that these heriots also reflected the give and take of relations between lords and their commended men. Presumably if a man wished to ensure his lord's favour in making a will, it was better to err on the side of post-mortem generosity,[361] or at least to ensure that it was recognized, when some eleventh-century testators echoed the words of Cnut's lawcode, that they were providing their 'lawful heriot'.

Using the evidence of the wills, an attempt can be made to address the economic wealth and social status of the Anglo-Saxon nobility in relation to military equipment, as shown in Fig. 3.3. This chart shows the relative landed wealth of the great and good of later Anglo-Saxon England alongside the value of their military equipment paid as heriot, measured in terms of how many warriors they would have been able to equip.[362] The sizes of the 'bubbles' are proportionate to assessments of the social standing of individuals, assigned from 1 (minor thegn) through to 5 (archbishop or ætheling), with ealdormen ranked in the middle.[363] Rankings are also determined by connections to royal figures and significant religious houses as well as land in more than one shire.[364] Of course, there is room

---

[357] These are S 1537 (AD 1022×43) and S 1519 (AD 1062×6) respectively. Williams, *World Before Domesday*, p. 66, 116–17, notes the significance of the Bury St Edmunds archive.

[358] S 1490 (AD 1042×3); S 1528 (AD 1020).

[359] S 1517 (*c.* AD 1050); S 1535 (AD 1042×53). S 1487, which is only dated to between 975×1016, may be added to these. Ealdormanric and episcopal wills have been excluded from this discussion, as S 1488 (AD 1003×4) and S 1498 (AD 971×83) include mailcoats and helmets.

[360] Brooks, 'Arms, Status and Warfare in Late-Saxon England', pp. 87–90 (quotation at p. 89).

[361] See S 1487, which rings a strong note of uncertainty as to whether their lord (the king?) would allow the will to be fulfilled.

[362] N. B. the assignment of four warriors here for the heriot of Bishop Ælfwold (S 1492) does not take account of the sixty-four-oar ship bequeathed to the king, as it does not appear to have included provision for the warriors therein.

[363] For a discussion of the changes to the offices of ealdormen in 1006, see Keynes, *Diplomas of King Æthelred*, pp. 209–14. There are, however, no wills of any of the higher post-1006 status ealdormen.

[364] Assuming a level of nobility for the ability to make a will, distinctions here have been made between those ranked 1 or 2, perhaps the most contentious of these classifications, on the basis of bequests outside one's own kin group or to more than one regionally significant

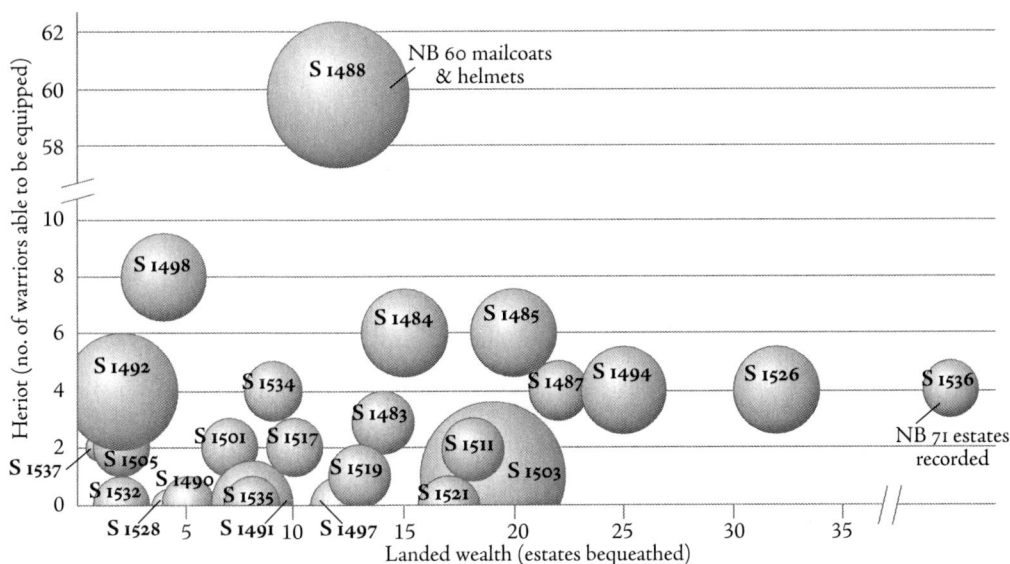

Fig. 3.3 Relative wealth and social standing (indicated by size of bubble) of Anglo-Saxon testators

for debate in addressing the social standing of such figures, especially as their social and political standing could change[365] (though it is likely that the wills represented the final versions as executed after the testators' deaths).[366] However, it is not appropriate to undertake extensive prosopographical assessments in this study. What is presented here is a working model for the purposes of considering the significance of the heriots.

The landed wealth measurements used in Table 3.2 and applied to Fig. 3.3 are somewhat less arbitrary. Laying aside the question of the variations in value of

church (i.e. to more than a proprietary church; for example, it has been assumed that the otherwise unknown church of Holme was only a minor institution). Thegnly rank is normally noted through ownership of land and/or display of material wealth (for more detailed discussions of thegnly ranks, see C. Senecal, 'Keeping up with the Godwinesons: In Pursuit of Aristocratic Status in Late Anglo-Saxon England', *ANS* 23 [2001 for 2000], pp. 251–66, and Williams, *World Before Domesday*, pp. 1–24) and in an assessment of social ranking on the basis of social networks outside the kindred or immediate household it will be noted that Anglo-Saxon women are rarely seen as able to do this (for which issue, see A. L. Klinck, 'Anglo-Saxon Women and the Law', *Journal of Medieval Studies* 8 [1982], pp. 107–21; J. Crick, 'Women, Posthumous Benefaction, and Family Strategy in Pre-Conquest England', *Journal of British Studies* 38 [1999], pp. 399–422).

[365] The classic study of the changes in status at court is Keynes, *Diplomas of King Æthelred*. However, for the eleventh century see also Baxter, *Earls of Mercia*.

[366] A reference is made by King Alfred in his will (S 1507 [AD 873×88 and ?896×99 for codicil]) to the fact that an earlier version of the will had been written but that copies of an earlier will or wills had been burnt, and that '[s]hould any one of them be found, it stands for nothing'. This hints at the fact that even a king could have difficulty imposing his will upon an archive and the possibility that he knew of an earlier version of the will that survived. As Alfred's will was in part the expression of the familial interests of the ruler, it does not seem unlikely that less well resourced aristocrats could face similar problems. S. M. Miller (ed.), *Charters of New Minster, Winchester*, Anglo-Saxon Charters 9 (Oxford, 2001), p. 6; trans. Keynes and Lapidge, *Alfred the Great*, p. 177.

Table 3.2 Heriots and bequests of weapons in Anglo-Saxon wills

Ref. no.	Date	Archive*	Noble	Probable lord	Landed wealth	Rank of weapons heriot	Social standing	Weapons	Armour	Animals	Other
S 1483	946× c. 951	Bury	Ælfgar	Eadwig	14	3	2	2 ?sheathed swords, 3 spears; 1 sword from K. Edmund worth 120 mancuses with 4 lb silver on sheath	3 shields	3 stallions	
S 1494	962×91	OMW	Æthelflæd	Edgar, Edward or prob. Æthelred	25	4	3	–	–	4 horses	3 estates, 4 armlets of 200 mancuses gold, 4 robes, 4 cups, 4 bowls
S 1485	968×71	OMW	Ealdorman Ælfheah of Central Wessex	Edgar	20	6	3	short sword with ?hilt, 80 mancuses gold, 6 swords, 6 spears (+ sword to *ætheling*)	6 shields	6 horses with trappings	6 estates, 300 mancuses gold, 3 lb dish, 3 lb drinking-cup
S 1487	975×1016	Wmnstr	Ælfhelm	Æthelred	22	4	2	2 swords, 4 spears	4 shields	4 horses (2 with trappings) (*stud to wife*)	100 mancuses gold (*ship to Ramsey*)
S 1488	1003×4	Abdon	Archbishop Ælfric	Æthelred	12	60	5	–	60 helmets, 60 mailcoats	–	Best ship with sailing tackle (*ship each to Kent & Wilts.*)
S 1490	1042×3	Bury	Ælfric Modercope	Edward	5	0	2	–	–	–	1 mark of gold, to be paid by brother

Table 3.2 continued

Ref. no.	Date	Archive* Noble	Probable lord	Landed wealth	Rank of weapons heriot	Social standing	Weapons	Armour	Animals	Other
S 1491	955×8	NMW Bishop Ælfsige of Winchester	Eadwig or Edgar	8	0	3	–			
S 1492	1008×12	Exeter, ex. Crediton Bishop Ælfwold of Crediton	Æthelred	2	4	4	4 spears	4 shields, 2 helmets, 2 mailcoats (+ helmet & 3 mailcoats bequeathed)	4 horses (2 saddled) (+ various horses bequeathed)	50 mancuses (claim thereto); 1 nearly complete 64-oar ship
S 1484	966×75	Bury Ælfgifu	Edgar	15	6	3	6 spears	6 shields	6 horses	6 estates, 2 armlets each of 120 mancuses; drinking cup
S 1497	990×1001	St Albans Æthelgifu	Æthelred	12	?	2	–	–	2 steeds, dogs	30 mancuses (30 mancuses & Herts. land to lady [Ælfthyrth?] for advocacy)
S 1498	971×83	NMW Ealdorman Æthelmær of Hants	Edgar, Edward or Æthelred	4	8	3	4 swords, 8 spears	8 shields, 4 helmets, 4 mailcoats	8 horses (4 with trappings)	4 armlets of 300 mancuses gold
S 1501	961×95	CCC & Bury Æthelric of Bocking	Æthelred	7	2	2	1 sword with belt; 2 javelins	2 targes	2 horses	60 mancuses
S 1503	1015	CCC & NMW Ætheling Athelstan	Æthelred	19	1	5	Silver-hilted sword (as heriot?) (swords as gifts)	mailcoat (2 shields as gifts)	2 horses (horse & stud as gifts)	3 estates

Table 3.2 continued

Ref. no.	Date	Archive*	Noble	Probable lord	Landed wealth	Rank of weapons heriot	Social standing	Weapons	Armour	Animals	Other
S 1505	c. 987	NMW	Æthelwold	Æthelred	2	2	2	2 ?hilts, 2 swords, 2 spears	2 shields	2 horses	1 armlet of 30 mancuses
S 1511	973×87	Roch'r	Brihtric & Ælfswith, his wife	Edward or Æthelred	18	2	2	1 short sword, 2 ?sheathed swords		2 hawks with staghounds (+ stallion to queen)	1 armlet of 80 mancuses gold; (+1 armlet of 30 mancuses to queen)
S 1517	c. 1050	St Albans	Eadwine of Caddington	Edward	10	2	2	2 swords	–	4 horses (2 saddled)	–
S 1519	1062×66	Bury	Ketel	A'bishop Stigand	13	1	2	1 sword, 1 spear	1 helmet, 1 mailcoat	1 horse with harness	Norfolk estate (prob. Not as heriot)
S 1521	1035×44	Bury	Leofgifu	Harald, Hcnut or Edward & Emma?	17	0	2	–	–	–	2 marks of gold to king; Essex estate to 'lady' (prob. queen)
S 1526	942×51	Bury	Bishop Theodred of London	Edmund, Eadred or Eadwig	32	4	3	2 swords ('the best'), 4 spears	4 shields	4 horses ('the best')	200 marks red gold, 2 silver cups, 3 estates
S 1528	1020	Bury	Thurketel Heyng	Cnut (or anon. noble?)	4	?	1	'due heriot' (rihte heregete)			
S 1532	c. 1050	St Albans	Ulf/Wulf	Edward	2	0	2			(2 horses to named persons, + horses to landless hiredcnihtas)	

Table 3.2 continued

Ref. no.	Date	Archive*	Noble	Probable lord	Landed wealth	Rank of weapons heriot	Social standing	Weapons	Armour	Animals	Other
S 1534	c. 1000	Worc'r	Wulfgeat	Æthelred	7	4	2	2 swords, 4 spears	4 shields	2 horses, 10 mares, 10 colts (6 mares & colts to Brun; remainder to wife & daughter)	–
S 1535	1042×53	CCC	Wulfgyth	Edward	8	?	2	'due heriot' (ryte heriet)			
S 1536	1002×4	Burton	Wulfric Spot	Æthelred	71	4	2	2 silver-hilted swords; weapons pertaining to horses	–	4 horses (2 saddled) (100 wild horses, 16 geldings to Burton, & remaining livestock)	200 mancuses
S 1537	1022×43	Bury	Wulfsige	Cnut, Harald, Harthacnut or Edward	1	2	1	1 sword, 1 spear inlaid with gold	1 helmet, 1 mailcoat (1 mailcoat to brother's children)	(2 saddled horses to brother's children)	– (cloak to brother's children)

* Abdon = Abingdon, Bury = Bury St Edmunds, CCC = Christ Church Canterbury, NMW = New Minster Winchester, OMW = Old Minster Winchester, Wmnstr = Westminster

estates, wealth here is measured in terms of the number of estates bequeathed.[367] No direct correlation is apparent between the known landed wealth of Anglo-Saxon aristocrats to the heriots that they paid. Of course, indirect links presumably existed, as a degree of social standing depended upon rank, which had, as we have seen, particular heriot obligations, but it should not be assumed that an increase in wealth automatically meant an increase in social standing and thus a promotion to office. The link between heriot and status was evidently not a matter of wealth but of rank (presumably defined, *strictu sensu*, by royal service), highlighted by the necessity to bequeath weapons to the king. Just as we should not use early Anglo-Saxon grave goods to draw comparisons with the organization of pre-Viking armies,[368] so we should note that the heriot was symbolic, and therefore should not necessarily read modes of warfare from such evidence, even if heriots and grave goods were rooted in social and military realities. The symbolic importance of the heriot is marked by the fact that, compared with many other items recorded amongst the movable wealth in Anglo-Saxon wills and the quality of swords, a spear could be a relatively inexpensive item, defined by its function rather than its form. However, judging by the gold-inlaid spear bequeathed by a certain Wulfsige to his lord, it did not have to be.[369] Similarly, the provision of a shield can be seen as a mark of status rather than an item which was simply functional and expendable.[370] Perhaps given the evident value of the shields bequeathed we may expect at least some shields to have been comparable with the object buried at Sutton Hoo, symbolic of the warrior's status as well as of the heriot itself.[371]

One final point may be made about the study of weapons. In the age before chemically propelled weapons, and indeed before the fully armoured knight, there appears to be a tacit complicity in assuming the general similarity of weapons. Few, beyond specialists, recognize that a Geibig 'type 2' sword blade is likely to have been different from, for example, a Geibig 'type 3' blade. Most of those who are interested in such differences are aware of the differences primarily for reasons

---

[367] The approximation here is not entirely unfounded. Rumble, 'Structure and Reliability of the "Codex Wintoniensis"', p. 92, comments on the rarity of the receipt by individual laypeople of estates larger than twenty hides at a time.

[368] Cf. S. S. Evans, *Lords of Battle: Image and Reality of the Comitatus in Dark-Age Britain* (Woodbridge, 1997), pp. 38–40.

[369] S 1537 (AD 1022×43). Many Viking-Age spearheads were pattern-welded, which could help the item to appear impressive to the onlooker: for example, a 'winged' spearhead in the Reading Museum collection (accession number REDMG: 1958.250.1), and another found in Lappland, Helsinki 3631:2; the latter can be seen in I. G. Peirce, *Swords of the Viking Age* (Woodbridge, 2002), p. 151. I am grateful to Jillian Greenaway for the Reading reference.

[370] I. P. Stephenson, *The Anglo-Saxon Shield* (Stroud, 2002), pp. 118–21. For the social value of a shield, see T. Dickinson and H. Härke, *Early Anglo-Saxon Shields*, Society of Antiquaries Archaeologia 110 (London, 1992), pp. 61–2, and Pollington, *English Warrior from Earliest Times till 1066*, pp. 140–50.

[371] R. L. S. Bruce-Mitford, *The Sutton Hoo Ship-Burial*, vol. 2: *Arms, Armour and Regalia* (London, 1978), pp. 1–137.

of stylistic identification.[372] Thus the features of equipment which drove a whole section of society are often overlooked, and the importance of the medieval smith, in providing weaponry which was ever lighter, stronger, and less liable to fracture, often underestimated.[373] In a textually focused analysis of the sources for Anglo-Saxon warfare, this can hardly be helped, but it should be said that references in wills or other documents to weapons – especially swords – were signifiers, often referring to a specific weapon.[374] This does not necessarily mean references to what may have been seen as an important weapon signified that it was the most effective weapon available,[375] but bearing a weapon in battle and in actions associated with warfare was a social act, showing that the bearer was *capable* of fighting, whether or not that weapon was actually used in combat.[376] Thus the weapon itself could operate as an indicator of social status. If warfare was about status and posture, status and posture were themselves elements of battle, and the equipment carried into battle was no less a part of this.

'A nobleman belongs on horseback': horses and equestrian equipment

Such posturing and status is also relevant to the use of horses, equally apparent in wills. While considering the weaponry of the warriors who fought in pre-Conquest forces, it is useful to address the extent to which the Anglo-Saxons considered horses to be weapons. Although the use of horses in campaigns and battles is dealt with in chapters 5 and 7, horses warrant attention here for their significance as war-gear. Guy Halsall, who takes a revisionist view on this topic, has pointed out the contentiousness of the question of horses on the pre-Conquest English

---

[372] See L. A. Jones, 'Overview of Hilt and Blade Classifications', in Peirce, *Swords of the Viking Age*, pp. 15–24, at pp. 21–4, citing A. Geibig, *Beiträge zur morphologischen Entwicklung des Schwertes im Mittelalter: Eine Analyse des Fundmaterials vom ausgehenden 8. bis zum 12. Jahrhundert aus Sammlungen der Bundesrepublik Deutschland* (Neumünster, 1991).

[373] For a useful, wide-ranging review of the evidence for Anglo-Saxon smithing, see D. A. Hinton, 'Anglo-Saxon Smiths and Myths', in *Textual and Material Culture in Anglo-Saxon England: Thomas Northcote Toller and the Toller Memorial Lectures*, ed. D. Scragg, Publications of the Manchester Centre for Anglo-Saxon Studies 1 (Cambridge, 2003), pp. 261–82.

[374] Dorothy Whitelock, *Beginnings of English Society*, Pelican History of England 2 (Harmondsworth, 1952; rev. edn, 1965), p. 95, aptly commented that 'men speak with loving precision of such things in their wills'. See the pithy but still precise references to swords in the will of the ætheling Athelstan, S 1503 (AD 1014), quoted above, pp. 119–20; Banton, 'Ealdormen and Earls', p. 16 (building on a suggestion made in A. J. Robertson [ed.], *Anglo-Saxon Charters* [Cambridge, 1939], p. 338, in reference to S 1447 [*c.* AD 950–68]) suggests that special arms were granted by rulers to denote ealdormanric office. A useful survey of the significance of Anglo-Saxon swords using mostly literary sources is provided by H. E. Davidson, *The Sword in Anglo-Saxon England: Its Archaeology and Literature* (Oxford, 1962).

[375] For reservations on technological determinism, see DeVries, 'Catapults are not Atomic Bombs'.

[376] Williams, 'Hypereutectoid Steel in Viking-Age Swords', discusses a number of early medieval swords with the inscription VLFBERHT, amongst which the quality of the metal could vary quite dramatically, presumably with the potential to affect reliability in combat.

battlefield.[377] His assertion of 2003 that they were used in battle remains valid, despite Ann Williams's recent pronouncement of the resolution of the debate.[378] One could compromise and suggest that it is immaterial whether Anglo-Saxon warriors rode to battle and proceeded to fight on foot, as such a position would not undermine the fact that horses were amongst the most important possessions of Anglo-Saxon nobles. However, the issue gets to the heart of the ways in which Anglo-Saxon warfare was seen. If horses were part of the military equipment of the warrior, it has implications for the relative wealth of those warriors and the social status of participation in warfare.

Halsall noted that the historians' interests in English cavalry as something intrinsically post-Conquest is a historiographical legacy of the nineteenth-century distinctions between cavalry and infantry.[379] It may also be argued that this view is a legacy from the twelfth or even late eleventh century. Descendants of surviving pre-Conquest English families may have been intermixing with the descendants of Continental families by the twelfth century,[380] but by then historical perceptions of the English and Normans, especially those of Orderic Vitalis, emphasize or even construct apparent ethnic differences between English and Normans, in which the Normans' use of horses is an important ethnic identifier.[381] However, the horse was not the *sine qua non* of identity in war. As Halsall pointed out with regard to sixth-century Ostrogoths and ninth-century Franks,[382] and John Gillingham, with regard to twelfth-century Norman rebels,[383] fighting on foot meant that, without horses, warriors could not escape quickly. In effect, they made a statement that they would stand and fight using mutually understood cultural norms of early medieval warfare.

---

[377] Halsall, *Warfare and Society in the Barbarian West*, pp. 180–8. See Brooks's review of Halsall's book, pp. 425–6.

[378] Williams, *World Before Domesday*, p. 111.

[379] Halsall, *Warfare and Society in the Barbarian West*, pp. 180–1.

[380] See here A. Williams, *The English and the Norman Conquest* (Woodbridge, 1995), esp. pp. 187–219; Thomas, *English and the Normans*, pp. 105–37.

[381] A recent consideration of this is D. Barthélemy, 'The Chivalric Transformation and the Origins of Tournament as seen through Norman Chroniclers', trans. G. R. Edwards, *HSJ* 20 (2009 for 2008), pp. 141–60, which develops Barthélemy's views of the emergence of chivalry in the late eleventh and twelfth centuries discussed in *La Chevalerie: de la Germanie antique à la France du XIIᵉ siècle* (Paris, 2007). For the emergence of the Normans' interests and abilities in horse-breeding for warfare in the eleventh century, see R. H. C. Davis, 'The Warhorses of the Normans', *ANS* 10 (1987 for 1986), pp. 67–82, and Davis, *Medieval Warhorse*, pp. 55–8. For a recent consideration of Orderic Vitalis's sense of Norman ethnogenesis, see E. Albu, *The Normans in their Histories: Propaganda, Myth and Subversion* (Woodbridge, 2001), pp. 180–213.

[382] Halsall, *Warfare and Society in the Barbarian West*, pp. 183, 188, citing Procopius, *History of the Wars*, 8.35.19, in Procopius vol. 5, ed. and trans. H. B. Dewing, Loeb Classical Library (London, 1928), pp. 412–13, and the *Chronicon* of Regino of Prüm s.a. 891, in *Reginonis abbatis Prumiensis Chronicon cum continuatione Treverensi*, ed. F. Kurze, MGH Scriptores rerum Germanicarum 50 (Hanover, 1890), pp. 137–8; trans. S. Maclean (ed.), *History and Politics in Late Carolingian and Ottonian Europe: The Chronicle of Regino of Prüm and Adalbert of Magdeburg*, Manchester Medieval Texts (Manchester, 2009), pp. 211–12.

[383] Gillingham, 'Thegns and Knights', pp. 146–7, discussing OV, vol. 6, pp. 348–51.

Similarly, it would be appropriate to note at this stage that if comments about the use of foot are symbolic of the refusal to retreat, the record of use of horses *at an appropriate time* may have been synonymous with victory in the source material. As will be seen in the discussion of conduct in battle, this did not preclude their use by Anglo-Saxon warriors.[384] James Graham-Campbell has drawn attention to the significance of eleventh-century 'Anglo-Scandinavian' equestrian equipment found largely as decorative metalwork,[385] while sculptural evidence indicates a long-standing equestrian culture in pre-Conquest England. Viking-Age sculptures of mounted figures survive from northern English regions, such as those at Gosforth (Cumberland), Chester-le-Street, Gainford, Hart, Sockburn (Co. Durham), Baldersby, Brompton (Yorks.), Neston (Cheshire), and Crowle (Lincs.), showing the connection of horses with warrior status.[386] As can be seen from Fig. 3.4, many of these figures are shown actively brandishing their weapons and, indeed, the figure on the Neston stone has been interpreted as jousting.[387] Such mounted figures were not the only form of warrior sculpture, and were part of a corpus of Anglo-Scandinavian sculpture which included warriors on foot and legendary figures. This, however, serves to highlight the range of ways warriors could be depicted, meeting what Dawn Hadley has noted as 'a new demand to depict the attributes of aristocratic masculinity on sculpture' in an area at the edge of royal authority in the tenth century.[388]

Warriors on horseback could and did invoke status, and the sculptors of the tenth-century Danelaw were evidently aware of this. An *eorl* (i.e. a warrior, as poetically distinct from a *ceorl*), as an Old English proverb recorded in the tenth-century Exeter Book had it, 'shall be on horseback'.[389] Given that noble status was

---

[384] See below, pp. 281–6.

[385] J. Graham-Campbell, 'Anglo-Scandinavian Equestrian Equipment in Eleventh-Century England', *ANS* 14 (1992 for 1991), pp. 77–89. For the context of the early use of horses, see C. Fern, 'Early Anglo-Saxon Horse Burial of the Fifth to Seventh Centuries AD', *ASSAH* 14 (Oxford, 2007), pp. 92–109. Fern observes that the corpus of evidence for equestrian burials has increased substantially since the publication of H. Vierck's survey, 'Pferdegräber im angelsächsischen England', in *Pferdegrab und Pferdeopfer im frühen Mittelalter*, ed. M. Müller-Wille, Berichten van de Rijksdienst voor het Oudheidkundig Bodemonderzoek Jaargang 20/21 (1970/1), pp. 189–99. It may be wondered how different our picture of Anglo-Saxon warrior traditions might have been had the extent of early equestrian burial been appreciated by scholars before Fern.

[386] For many of these sculptures, see D. H. Hadley, 'Warriors, Heroes and Companions: Negotiating Masculinity in Viking-Age England', *ASSAH* 15 (2008), pp. 270–84, at pp. 275–8.

[387] R. H. White, 'Viking-period Sculpture at Neston, Cheshire'. *Journal of the Chester Archaeological Society* 69 (1988 for 1986), pp. 45–58.

[388] Hadley, 'Warriors, Heroes and Companions', pp. 277–8 (quotation at p. 278). For discussion of aristocratic authority in the Danelaw, see also her '"Hamlet and the Princes of Denmark": Lordship in the Danelaw, *c.* 860–954', in *Cultures in Contact: Scandinavian Settlement in England in the Ninth and Tenth Centuries*, ed. D. M. Hadley and J. D. Richards, SEMA 2 (Turnhout, 2000), pp. 107–32.

[389] 'Maxims I', Line 62, in *The Anglo-Saxon Poetic Records: A Collective Edition, No. 3: The Exeter Book*, ed. G. Krapp and E. Dobbie (New York, 1936), p. 159. An alternative translation is in S. A. J. Bradley, *Anglo-Saxon Poetry: An Anthology of Old English Poems*, Everyman's Library (London, 1982), p. 347.

(a)

(b)

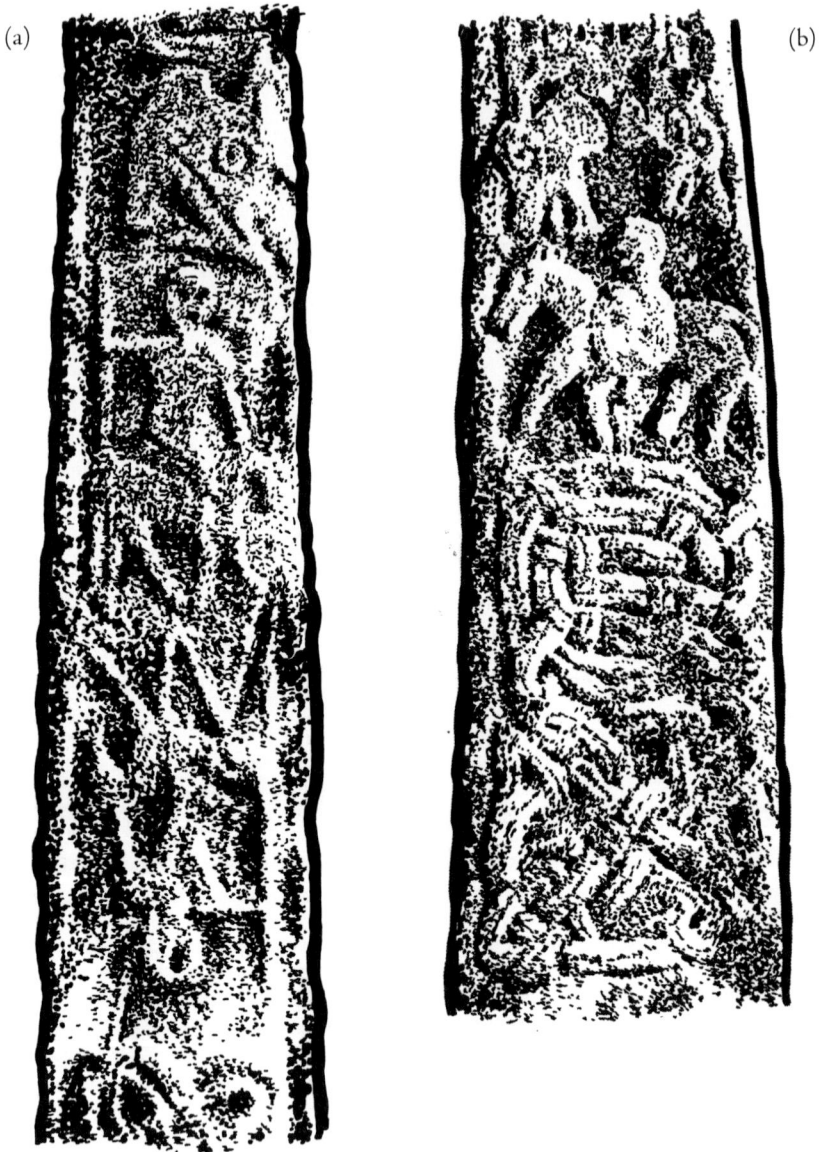

Fig. 3.4 Pre-Conquest equestrian sculptures from (a) Gosforth (Cumberland), (b) Chester-le-Street (Co. Durham), (c) Neston (Cheshire), (d) Baldersby (Yorks.), (e) Sockburn (Co. Durham)

(c)

(d)

(e)

invoked through warfare, and *Maxims I*, from which the utterance comes, tends to use truisms regarding Anglo-Saxon society, this should not be dismissed lightly. The early seventh-century Sutton Hoo helmet's depiction of a warrior riding down his enemy was a motif echoed on the eighth-century Repton Stone.[390] These were images of triumph and successful war-leadership which echoed a Roman image of triumph, such as that depicted on funery sculptures portraying auxiliary cavalry-men.[391] Furthermore, such triumphs do not seem to have been manifested solely in displays of individual prowess, as collective horsemanship was also seen to have brought success on the battlefield. The Anglo-Saxon Chronicle's poem on the Battle of *Brunanburh* has 'troops' (*eorodcistum*) of West Saxons riding down their defeated foes.[392] Such a 'troop' (*eorod*), the Exeter Book proverb said, 'shall ride closely together'.

As Halsall has pointed out, the historiography on this subject has been shaped by the experiences of modern warfare.[393] Many nineteenth-century historians were interested in distinctions between dedicated cavalry forces and mounted infantry (dragoons) and thus, with an eye to the racial determinism of 'modes' of warfare, the Anglo-Saxons have been seen in this light. Such issues as the English interpretations of the victory over French knights at the Battle of Agincourt may have affected popular views of the English at war.[394] In terms of academic inter-pretations this was established to the extent that Vinogradoff, above, referred to the horse for 'quick locomotion',[395] while in a recent reading of the evidence, Ian Stephenson, defines the operation of 'cavalry' in a collective body in order to state

---

[390] Bruce-Mitford, *The Sutton Hoo Ship-Burial*, vol. 2, pp. 138–231; M. Biddle and B. Kjølbye-Biddle, 'The Repton Stone', *ASE* 14 (1985), pp. 233–92.

[391] For Roman funery sculptures, see G. de la Bédoyère, *Eagles over Britannia: The Roman Army in Britain* (Stroud, 2001), pp. 156–8. The fact that the images tended to be of auxiliaries may show that this was an image of *Romanitas* which had been transmitted to the provinces. Cf. Stephenson, *Late Anglo-Saxon Army*, p. 46, who suggests that the Sutton Hoo helmet design reflects contemporary Swedish warfare, rather than Anglo-Saxon. (Stephenson's source for early Vendel warfare is J. Engström, 'The Vendel Chieftains: A Study of Military Tactics', in *Military Aspects of Scandinavian Society*, ed. Jørgensen and Clausen, pp. 248–55.) Biddle and Biddle, 'Repton Stone', pp. 271, propose that the exemplar is a specifically imperial image from an 'easily portable object such as a cameo, an ivory diptych or a silver dish'.

[392] ASC ABCD 937.

[393] Halsall, *Warfare and Society in the Barbarian West*, pp. 181–2; cf. Stephenson, *Late Anglo-Saxon Army*, pp. 40–1.

[394] For the range of interpretations from the eighteenth to early twentieth centuries, see Curry, *Battle of Agincourt*, pp. 370–401. Curry cites (p. 384), an article by Sir Herbert Maxwell which makes a link between the infantry of the First World War and the English infantry of 1415, at the time of the five-hundredth anniversary of the battle in 1915: 'The Campaign of Agincourt', *Cornhill Magazine*, 3rd series 39 (1915), pp. 524–41. For an important commentary on the medieval debate, see M. Bennett, 'The Myth of the Military Supremacy of Knightly Cavalry', in *Armies, Chivalry and Warfare in Medieval Britain and France*, ed. M. Strickland, Harlaxton Medieval Studies new series 7 (Stamford, 1998), pp. 304–16.

[395] Vinogradoff, *English Society in the Eleventh Century*, p. 30 (above, p. 67).

that 'in this context ... the Anglo-Saxons did not possess cavalry'.[396] However, the suggestion that rigid distinctions between foot and cavalry is a false dichotomy, as championed by Guy Halsall,[397] is a new perspective on a long-standing debate. In the early twentieth century H. M. Chadwick emphasized the mounted nature of the Anglo-Saxon fyrd,[398] and, shortly afterwards, in 1910, J. H. Clapham developed the theme.[399] Although ostensibly focusing on the question of whether the Viking armies used horses to travel overland in Anglo-Saxon England, Clapham noted the extensive use of horses by English armies in attempting to counter them, commenting along the way on the nature of the Anglo-Saxon fyrd and on the battle scenes presented in Old English literature, Cynewulf's *Elene* and the *Old English Exodus*.[400]

H. G. Richardson and G. O. Sayles addressed the Anglo-Saxons in terms of their 'knighthood' and thus saw no distinction between the horses of the Normans and those of the English depicted on the Bayeux Tapestry.[401] The other significant piece of work was that of Richard Glover, who, in a paper published in 1952, addressed Snorri Sturluson's early thirteenth-century account of the Battle of Stamford Bridge, which recorded the English as fighting their Norwegian opponents from horseback.[402] There were implicit problems with the historicization of an account as late as that of Snorri, but Glover opened a line of enquiry which was taken up with aplomb by historians of the Norman world.[403]

In an important article and book, both published in 1989, R. H. C. Davis took a middle path between the arguments for and against the Anglo-Saxons fighting

---

[396] Stephenson, *Late Anglo-Saxon Army*, p. 41. In fairness to Stephenson, his assessment of the evidence (pp. 40–52) remains open-minded, and some of his conclusions are not dissimilar from my own.

[397] Halsall, *Warfare and Society in the Barbarian West*, pp. 180–8.

[398] Chadwick, *The Origin of the English Nation*, p. 150.

[399] Clapham, 'Horsing of the Danes'.

[400] Clapham, 'Horsing of the Danes', p. 289, n. 11 for a brief discussion of the literature and pp. 292–3 for discussion of the nature of the fyrd. There is ambiguity regarding the depiction of horses before a battle, in one of the texts mentioned by Clapham, Cynewulf's *Elene*, lines 46–55, as it is not stated whether the horses were used *in* the battle (a point made in Halsall, *Warfare and Society in the Barbarian West*, pp. 183–4): Cynewulf's *Elene*, ed. P. O. E. Gradon, Methuen's Old English Library (London, 1958), p. 28; trans. Bradley, *Anglo-Saxon Poetry*, p. 166; *The Old English Exodus: Text, Translation and Commentary*, ed. and trans. J. R. R. Tolkien and J. Turville-Petre (Oxford, 1981), esp. lines 142–79, pp. 5–6, trans. pp. 23–4.

[401] Richardson and Sayles, *Governance of Mediaeval England*, p. 61, n. 3.

[402] R. Glover, 'English Warfare in 1066', EHR 67 (1952), pp. 1–18. Snorri Sturluson, *Harald's Saga Sigurðarsonar*, ch. 92 in *Heimskringla*, ed. B. S. Kristjánsdóttir (Reykjavík, 1991), p. 684; trans. *Heimskringla: History of the Kings of Norway*, ed. L. M. Hollander (Austin, TX, 1964), p. 655.

[403] R. A. Brown, *The Origins of English Feudalism*, Historical Problems, Studies and Documents 19 (London, 1973), pp. 34–43; see the discussion of this in M. Strickland, 'Introduction', in *Anglo-Norman Warfare: Studies in Late Anglo-Saxon and Anglo-Norman Military Organization and Warfare*, ed. M. Strickland (Woodbridge, 1992), pp. ix–xxiii, at p. xxi, and M. Strickland, 'Military Technology and Conquest: The Anomaly of Anglo-Saxon England', ANS 19 (1997 for 1996), pp. 353–82.

from horseback.[404] Like Richardson and Sayles, he pointed out that the arguments for the idea of uniquely specialized breeding of Norman warhorses fall away if the evidence for similarly specialized breeding of Anglo-Saxon horses is considered. 'The English probably did not have as many warhorses as the Normans, and it may well be that their quality was not as good either', he posited, 'but what evidence there is all points to the fact that they existed.'[405] Davis pointed out that there was evidence for stud farms,[406] and that the Anglo-Saxons were just as capable of riding into battle as the Normans. As a horse-breeder, Ann Hyland took a similar stance. She contended that if so much effort was put into breeding horses, with specific references to mares, and given the influence of the use of warhorses on the Continent, 'the people of England would have been totally blinkered not to have noted Frankish military customs and, where suitable, adapted them to their own situations'.[407] While an important theme in the present volume's discussion is the significance of the rituals and the collective behaviour of warfare; thus it might be said that even if the English had the horses they did not necessarily *have* to use them. Nonetheless, coming from such a practical perspective, Hyland's argument is persuasive. One of the most recent surveys of the use of the horse in Anglo-Saxon England, that of Sarah Larratt Keefer, is surprisingly circumspect in consideration of the use of the horse in battle, considering that the balance of evidence is with the suggestion that Anglo-Saxon warriors rode into battle but dismounted to fight. As we have seen, Keefer's interpretation is supported by much historiographical opinion, but it seems a pity that in her detailed consideration of bloodstock and improvements to breeding programmes during the later Anglo-Saxon period she did not bring in the implications of the developments in breeding for the use of the horse on the battlefield, beyond a review of earlier discussions.[408] If the later tenth-century warriors did not customarily wear armour, as has been suggested by Halsall from the evidence of fast-moving campaigns in Wales,[409] it may provide an alternative perspective on the use of horses in battle in Anglo-Saxon England. Although of course the evidence from 1066 is invaluable, reflection on the events of the period in the two centuries before

---

[404] R. H. C. Davis, 'Did the Anglo-Saxons have Warhorses?', in *Weapons and Warfare*, ed. Hawkes, pp. 141–4, and Davis, *Medieval Warhorse*, pp. 70–8.

[405] Davis, *Medieval Warhorse*, p. 76.

[406] S 1487 and S 1503. Wills and studs are discussed in Davis, 'Did the Anglo-Saxons have Warhorses?', pp. 141–2, and A. Hyland, *The Medieval Warhorse: From Byzantium to the Crusades* (Stroud, 1994), pp. 77–9 (although Hyland does seem to base her reading of selective horsebreeding on a Hollister-inspired reading of the division between 'Select' and 'General' Fyrds).

[407] Hyland, *Medieval Warhorse*, pp. 76–9 (quotation at p. 79). Hyland cites the reference to mares in the will of Wulfgeat (S 1534 [*c.* AD 1000]).

[408] S. L. Keefer, 'Hwær Cwom Mearh? The Horse in Anglo-Saxon England', *Journal of Medieval History* 23 (1996), pp. 115–34, at pp. 121–2, 134. For the wider context of the early Anglo-Saxon use of horses, see N. J. Higham, 'Cavalry in Early Bernicia?' *Northern History* 27 (1991), pp. 236–41; C. Cessford, 'Cavalry in Early Bernicia: A Reply', *Northern History* 27 (1991), pp. 236–41; and N. Hooper, 'The Aberlemno Stone and Cavalry in Anglo-Saxon England', *Northern History* 29 (1993), pp. 188–96.

[409] Halsall, *Warfare and Society in the Barbarian West*, pp. 172–3.

Hastings is worthwhile in its own right rather than as a prelude to a defeat of English 'infantry' by Norman 'cavalry'.

Athelstan's laws are emphatic on the value of horses. As with the later references to horses in heriots in late tenth and early eleventh centuries, they are perceived as having a military value. We have seen that Athelstan's Grately lawcode include the provision of mounted men from 'every plough' (ch. 16); the lawcode also decreed that 'no-one is to sell a horse across the sea, unless he wishes to give it' (ch. 18).[410] The similarity to Charles the Bald's edict of Pîtres, which prohibited the sale of weapons and horses across the sea (i.e. to the Franks' Viking foes), and, likewise to the prohibitions of the fifth-century Theodosian Code, is significant here, but it reflects practical needs of a kingdom which evidently took its horses seriously, as part of its military equipment.[411]

A similar practical issue can be seen during the reign of Cnut. No other Anglo-Saxon ruler repeats Athelstan and Charles the Bald's Theodosian prohibition, but horses appear to have been significant in Cnut's codification of 'legal' heriots.[412] On one level Cnut was attempting to be seen as fair, but a commensurate benefit was the king's receipt of horses from his nobility. A reason for this may have been the continuing threat of Viking in the eleventh century, which was only checked by Cnut's activities in Scandinavia.[413] Perhaps, given the emergence of the staller during the reign of Cnut, it is significant to note Davis's suggestion that the office was associated, at least in terms of prestige, with the control of horses.[414] Few executors would have chanced passing an old nag to the king's agent. After all, the maintenance of bloodstock in the horse population of the kingdom could have been beneficial for the development of an important military force – the housecarls.

Once we accept that the Anglo-Saxons were not the 'nation-at-arms' that they were formerly seen to be, and the effects of that historiographical legacy are recognized,[415] it follows that horse-riding was one of the necessary skills of the English warriors *before* 1066. The Bayeux Tapestry shows very little differ-

---

[410] *II Athelstan*, ch. 18; *Gesetze*, vol. I, p. 158; trans. *EHD* I, p. 420.

[411] *Edictum Pistense*, ed. A. Boretius, MGH Capitularia regum Francorum II (Hanover, 1911), no. 273, pp. 310–28, discussed by J. L. Nelson, 'Translating Images of Authority: The Christian Roman Emperors in the Carolingian World', in Nelson, *The Frankish World, 750–900* (London, 1993), pp. 89–98, at pp. 94–5.

[412] *II Cnut*, ch. 70 (above, p. 115).

[413] For these activities, see P. Sawyer, 'Cnut's Scandinavian Empire', in *The Reign of Cnut*, ed. Rumble, pp. 10–22, and M. K. Lawson, *Cnut: The Danes in England in the Early Eleventh Century*, The Medieval World (London, 1991), pp. 95–102.

[414] See Davis, 'Did the Anglo-Saxons have Warhorses?', pp. 143–4, developing work on the significance of stallers in K. Mack, 'The Stallers: Administrative Innovation in the Reign of Edward the Confessor', *Journal of Medieval History* 12 (1986), pp. 123–34, and P. Nightingale, 'The Origin of the Court of Husting and Danish Influence on London's Development into a Capital City', *EHR* 102 (1987), pp. 564–6. *II Cnut*, ch. 69.1, in *Gesetze*, vol. I, pp. 356–7; *EHD* I, p. 465, suggests that Cnut was reorganizing systems of royal provision, indicating administrative innovation during his reign (see Lavelle, *Royal Estates in Anglo-Saxon Wessex*, p. 47).

[415] See Abels, *Lordship and Military Obligation in Anglo-Saxon England*, pp. 178–9.

Fig. 3.5   Norman warriors on campaign in Brittany depicted in the Bayeux Tapestry

ence between English and Norman horses, but Harold and those accompanying him – presumably his household men – seem to have taken part in the campaign in Brittany alongside Normans (Fig. 3.5). A comparison with ducal Normandy is instructive. If we lacked the evidence of the Bayeux Tapestry, which uses the image of mounted warriors to identify the Norman aristocracy (Fig. 3.6), our picture of the eleventh-century Norman use of horses in battle might well be different, perhaps more circumspect, conforming to the picture presented in the aftermath of the Battle of Hastings by the *Carmen de Hastingae proelio*.[416] The young Duke William would still be seen as performing feats of chivalry in William of Poitiers' panegyric,[417] and large groups of knights would still pursue one another,[418] but for consistent affirmations of Norman *chevalerie* we would have to turn to the twelfth-century accounts of the Normans' identity, such as that of

---

[416] *Carmen de Hastingae proelio*, a source which its most recent editor, Frank Barlow, realistically dated to the years immediately after 1066 (pp. xxiv–xlii). References are made to the use of horses by the Normans, which can be seen as nascent chivalry, including in the famous account of the challenge to single combat by Taillefer (lines 395–404, pp. 24–5) and an explanation of an apparent English preference for fighting on foot (lines 369–70, pp. 22–3) but the author makes considerable specific reference to Normans fighting on foot (lines 379–88, pp. 22–5; lines 409–22, pp. 24–7; line 445). For discussion of the significance of Norman and French foot soldiers at Hastings, see Lawson, *Battle of Hastings*, pp. 209–15. Dudo of St-Quentin refers to Normans (presumably as infantry) 'with shields overlapping and locked together' (*conjunctis complicatisque ad invicem clypeis*) during a dawn raid on the lands of Theobald I of Blois-Chartres in the reign of Duke Richard I: *De moribus et actis primorum Normanniae Ducum*, ed. J. Lair (Caen, 1865), IV.112; trans. E. Christiansen in *Dudo of St Quentin: History of the Normans* (Woodbridge, 1998), p. 149.

[417] WP I.12, pp. 14–17.

[418] Note, e.g. the *ruse de guerre* following the siege of Arques *c.* 1051, recorded in *The Gesta Normannorum Ducum of William of Jumièges, Orderic Vitalis and Robert of Torigni*, ed. and trans. E. M. C. van Houts, OMT, 2 vols (Oxford, 1992–5), vol. 2, pp. 104–5.

Fig. 3.6 Norman cavalry at the Battle of Hastings depicted in the Bayeux Tapestry

Wace.[419] If this hypothetical picture were the case, it might be said that twelfth-century accounts of the Normans and English at war highlighted perceived ethnic differences and the eventual chivalric assimilation of the English and the Normans. An example can be found in the Anglo-Saxon Chronicle and John of Worcester's accounts of the summons of English warriors of 1094 (probably including Franco-Norman settlers considered as 'English' by virtue of their English holdings). John of Worcester, writing in the 1120s, renders the 'Englishmen' recorded by the Anglo-Saxon Chronicle as 'foot soldiers' (*pedones*), whereas, as Eric John noted, there was little distinction made between French and English *fyrds* in the Anglo-Saxon Chronicle's entries written in the generation after 1066.[420]

Summary

This chapter has discussed an issue that was fundamental to the organization of the later Anglo-Saxon state and the way it has been seen since 1066. The issue of military organization gives insights into the state's responses to the conditions of war and peace. Although the picture may be complicated, one issue of continuity does emerge: Alfredian organization was an important aspect of military reforms, and the relevance of the Domesday evidence in the eleventh century to the system recorded in the Burghal Hidage in the early tenth century was important, suggesting some integrity of the system. These documents give some indication of the extensive organization of the state for wars fought on a defensive

---

[419] See Bennett, 'Wace and Warfare'. For the development of chivalry in the twelfth century, see Barthélemy, *La Chevalerie*, who sees a later move toward chivalric ideals than that suggested by M. Strickland, *War and Chivalry: The Conduct and Perception of War in England and Normandy, 1066–1217* (Cambridge, 1996).

[420] JW vol. 3, s.a. 1094, pp. 72–3; ASC E 1094; John, 'End of Anglo-Saxon England', p. 237, and John, *Land Tenure in Early England*, p. 157n.

footing, with a high level of participation expected even if many of those related to armies did not necessarily fight. There was nonetheless a 'warrior elite' in later Anglo-Saxon England, indicating some continuity with the warrior aristocrats of the pre-Viking period. There is evidence for elite warriors, including house-carls, suggesting that even if many of the English did not have battle experience in the generation before 1066, Hollister's admiration for English organization is well justified. The relationship between royal lordship – and private lordship – is evidenced in associated military equipment. Finally, horses and equestrian equip-ment may be identified as related to military service, an issue which is of relevance to the discussion in chapter 7.

❖ 4 ❖

Organization and Equipment: Maritime

ALTHOUGH much more can be said about land-based than ship-based military forces in the early middle ages and (notwithstanding Nicholas Hooper's comments on the subject, reproduced in this chapter) to refer to it as a 'navy' suggests a level of permanent organization not supported by the sources,[1] maritime organization nonetheless deserves consideration in its own right. The limitations of the evidence mean that this is a shorter discussion and, as with land warfare, what can be deduced of maritime operations will be considered in chapters 5 and 7. The historiography of this subject is limited, too. Although a great deal was written by Victorian and Edwardian historians on a putative association between King Alfred and some embryonic 'Royal Navy',[2] the modern literature of early medieval nautical technology is dominated by the study of Scandinavian vessels. Rare exceptions to this are the early chapters of N. A. M. Rodger's lengthy study of British sea power, *Safeguard of the Sea*,[3] an important article by Nicholas Hooper,[4] and a book by John Pullen-Appleby,[5] although, naturally, links between Scandinavian maritime customs and those of the British Isles are hardly inconsequential to the study of Viking Age England.

After discussing the influence of the development of ship technology around the North Sea in the Viking Age, this chapter will address the logistics of ship provision, followed by a case study of the written source material and – pertinent to the link between land and maritime warfare – a discussion of the evidence for coastal guard duties.[6]

---

[1] For a discussion of the problems and implications of discussing 'naval power' in the context of medieval history, see R. W. Unger, 'Conclusion: Toward a History of Medieval Sea Power', in *War at Sea in the Middle Ages and the Renaissance*, ed. J. B. Hattendorf and R. W. Unger, Warfare in History (Woodbridge, 2003), pp. 249–61.

[2] For an indication of the link here, see the record of the launch of *HMS King Alfred* in A. Bowker, *The King Alfred Millenary: A Record of the Proceedings of the National Commemoration* (London, 1902), pp. 146–52. See generally B. Yorke, 'Alfredism: The Use and Abuse of Alfred's Reputation in Later Centuries', in *Alfred the Great*, ed. Reuter, pp. 361–80.

[3] N. A. M. Rodger, *Safeguard of the Sea: A Naval History of Britain*, vol. 1: *660–1649* (London, 1997), pp. 1–49.

[4] Hooper, 'Some Observations on the Navy in Late Anglo-Saxon England'.

[5] Pullen-Appleby, *English Sea Power, c. 871 to 1100*.

[6] This is relevant to fortifications. See below, pp. 217–25.

Types of vessel

As with the consideration of land-based military organization before and during the Viking Age, changes and developments are relevant. Organized naval forces seem to have existed in England before the ninth century. John Haywood provides a case for the strength of early Anglo-Saxon naval power, though he notes that there is little evidence for this in the period immediately preceding the advent of the Vikings.[7] Providing a maximal view of seventh-century Northumbria, James Campbell highlighted the fact that campaigns would not have been possible without 'maritime power' at the command of kings, while Barbara Yorke has pointed out how the ability to strike rapidly at kingdoms a long distance away was an integral part of Anglo-Saxon overlordship.[8] The maritime significance of early vessels, represented by the seventh-century ship discovered at Sutton Hoo, may be linked to the early tenth-century vessel found at Graveney (Kent).[9] Such developments were related to those of Viking ship design, which are crucial to an understanding of early medieval maritime technology. Major steps in ship design can be identified in the North Sea region in the early middle ages. These developments are likely to have had an effect on the organization of naval forces, in what could be seen as an arms race of sorts, arguably with English responses to Viking threats. Four significant types of vessels can be identified from the evidence of the ninth, tenth and eleventh centuries:

(i) Perhaps most significant type is the ninth-century 'classic' Viking ship type, from Scandinavia, best represented by the vessel excavated at Gokstad in the Oslo Fjord during the nineteenth century. As Alan Binns has suggested, this may have been exceptional, as a particularly high status royal vessel[10] but it is still noteworthy in its seagoing capabilities, representing a design which permitted the success of a generation of Viking raiders.

(ii) A Frisian type is mentioned in passing by the Anglo-Saxon Chronicle in the late ninth century.[11] Little is known about such vessels, although it does highlight the possibility of the English recruitment of foreign sailors, and draws our attention to the range of cross-Channel and North Sea vessels seen in English waters during the Viking Age.

---

[7] J. Haywood, *Dark Age Naval Power: A Reassessment of Frankish and Anglo-Saxon Seafaring Activity* (London, 1991), p. 75.

[8] J. Campbell, 'The First Christian Kings', in *The Anglo-Saxons*, ed. Campbell, pp. 45–69, at p. 64; Yorke, *Kings and Kingdoms of Early Anglo-Saxon England*, pp. 158–9.

[9] E. Gifford and J. Gifford, 'Alfred's New Longships', in *Alfred the Great*, ed. Reuter, pp. 281–9 at pp. 282–3. For the vessel at Sutton Hoo, see A. C. Evans and R. L. S. Bruce-Mitford, 'The Ship', in Bruce-Mitford, *The Sutton Hoo Ship-Burial*, vol. 1: *Excavations, Background, the Ship, Dating and Inventory* (London, 1975), pp. 345–435.

[10] A. Binns, 'The Ships of the Vikings, Were they "Viking Ships"?', *Proceedings of the Eighth Viking Congress, Århus, 24–31 August 1977*, ed. H. Bekker-Nielsen, P. G. Foote and O. Olsen, Mediaeval Scandinavia Supplements 2 (Odense, 1981), pp. 287–94; Rodger, *Safeguard of the Sea*, pp. 12–13.

[11] ASC 896.

Graveney

Gokstad

Sutton Hoo

Skuldelev 2/4

Alfred

0   5 m

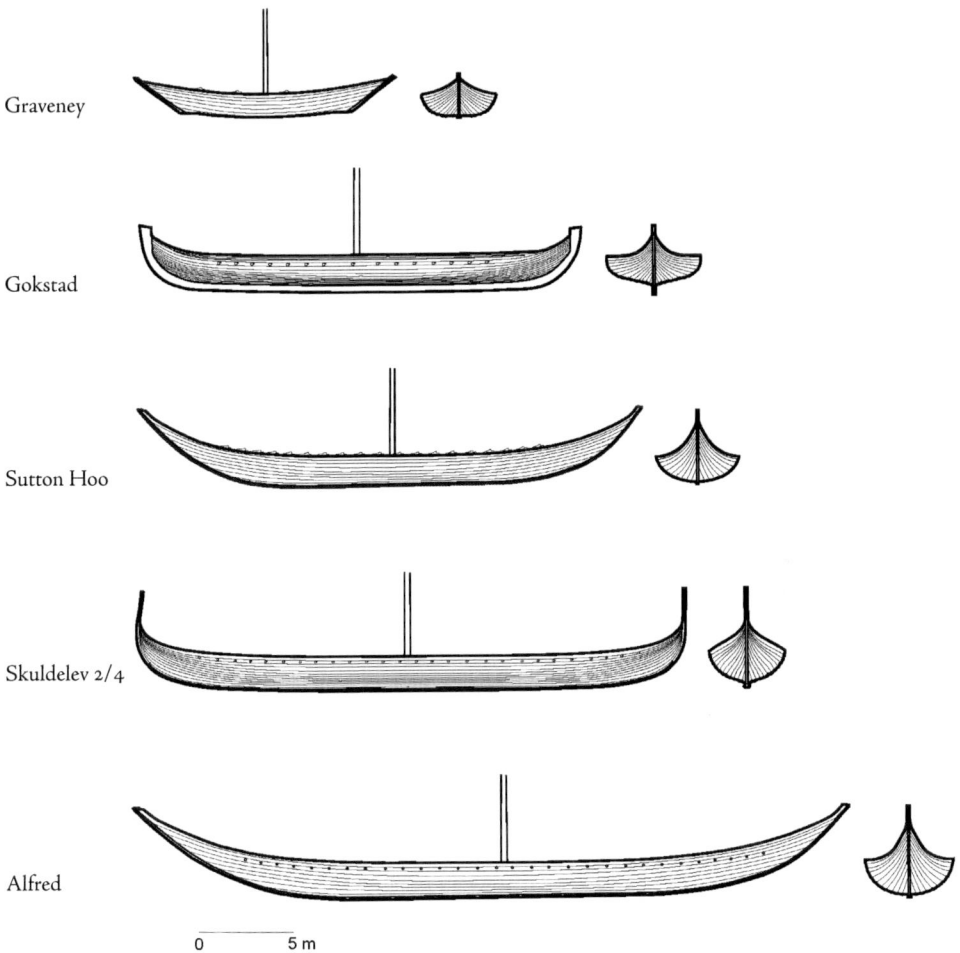

Fig. 4.1 Different types of Viking-Age ship
(The Alfredian design is postulated, redrawn after a reconstruction by Edwin and Joyce Gifford.)

(iii) What could be termed an 'Alfredian' type is referred to by the Anglo-Saxon Chronicle as being 'nearly twice as long' as other vessels and built 'neither on the Frisian nor the Danish pattern'. It is remarkable in representing the recognition of the importance of technological developments. Perhaps, as Edwin and Joyce Gifford argued, this type was related to maritime shipbuilding traditions in East Anglia and Kent, represented by the seventh-century Sutton Hoo and tenth-century Graveney vessels.[12]

(iv) The later tenth- and early eleventh-century development of the long dragon ship in Scandinavia is evidenced by finds at Hedeby and in Roskilde Fjord,

[12] Gifford and Gifford, 'Alfred's New Longships', pp. 282–3. See also M. J. Swanton, 'King Alfred's Ships: Text and Context', *ASE* 28 (1999), pp. 1–22.

Denmark.[13] These are relevant to the English kingdom not only because the English were victims of such vessels. Rodger has discussed how post-1016 finances were organized to pay for such vessels and their crews in the Anglo-Danish realm.[14]

Attention was evidently paid to developments in maritime technology in Anglo-Saxon England. If the English were not at the forefront of technological developments, there was certainly a close interest in the effective use of ships.

However, lest we focus all our attention upon the function of vessels, it should also be noted that a ship could also demonstrate the authority of a lord, in no small part through an ostentatious display of wealth. Just as the burials at Sutton Hoo and in the Oslo Fjord showed the posthumous importance of those buried in the vessels,[15] a ship could also make an impact in a social context. Literary, often classicizing, descriptions of the decorations of vessels, as provided by the *Encomium Emmae Reginae*, show the personal importance ascribed to ships. If, as we have seen, display and posture was an integral element of warfare, the ability to command highly decorated ships must be seen in a similar vein.[16]

> Then the king [Cnut], saying farewell to his mother and brother, returned to the area of the winding coast, where he had already assembled the splendid spectacle of two hundred ships. For here were such a great number of arms [*armae*] that one of the ships would have most abundantly furnished weapons [*tela*], if they had been deficient for all those remaining. Moreover there were so many types of shields that you would have believed that a host [*agmina*] of all peoples was present. So great, also, was the ornamentation pertaining to the ships, that the eyes of the beholders were dazzled, and to those looking from afar they seemed more of flame than wood. If indeed, when the sun cast the brightness of its rays among them here the flashing of arms shone, there, truly, the flame of hanging shields. Gold blazed in the prows, silver also flashed in the varied shapes of ships. So great, indeed, was the magnificence of the fleet, that if its lord wished to conquer any people, merely the ships would have terrified the enemies before their warriors engaged in any battle. For who could gaze upon the lions of the foes, terrible with the brightness of gold, who upon the metal men, menacing with golden face, who upon the dragons burning with pure gold, who upon the bulls on the

---

[13] O. Crumlin-Pedersen, *Viking-Age Ships and Shipbuilding in Hedeby/Haithabu and Schleswig*, Ships and Boats of the North 2 (Schleswig, 1997), pp. 81–95; O. Crumlin-Pedersen, *The Skuldelev Ships I: Topography, Archaeology, History, Conservation and Display*, Ships and Boats of the North 4.1 (Roskilde, 2002), pp. 141–94.

[14] Rodger, 'Cnut's Geld and the Size of Danish Ships', pp. 392–403. See the debate on the accuracy of the figures related in the Anglo-Saxon Chronicle addressed in J. Gillingham, '"The Most Precious Jewel in the English Crown": Levels of Danegeld and Heregeld in the Early Eleventh Century', *EHR* 104 (1989), pp. 373–84, and M. K. Lawson, 'Danegeld and Heregeld Once More', *EHR* 105 (1990), pp. 951–61.

[15] See papers in O. Crumlin-Pedersen and B. Munch Tye (ed.), *The Ship as Symbol in Prehistoric and Medieval Scandinavia: Papers from an International Research Seminar at the National Museum, Copenhagen, 5th–7th May, 1994*, PNM Publications of the National Museum Studies in Archaeology and History 1 (Copenhagen, 1995).

[16] *Encomium Emmae*, II.2, pp. 18–21. A similarly ebullient account of Swein's ship is in I.4, pp. 12–13.

ships threatening death, with horns gleaming with gold, without fearing any dread of the king of such a force? Furthermore, in so great an expedition there was found no slave, no-one freed from slavery, no-one of low birth, no-one debilitated by old age; indeed all were noble, all strong in the vigour of maturity, all suitably skilled in any type of warfare, all of such speed that the swiftness of riding would be contemptible to them.

R. I. Page questioned the wisdom of taking the description of this vessel at face value, as C. R. Dodwell had done,[17] and indeed the Encomiast's comment on the speed of the warriors surpassing that of riding indicates the level of rhetoric in the account.[18] However, the fact that it was used to demonstrate a leader's riches and, associated with this, his power, reflects the connection between such inherently portable wealth and personal authority.[19]

Fleet logistics

In his magisterial survey of British naval history, Rodger reads from the absence of evidence that there were no fleets at crucial moments for West Saxon or English defence. His juxtaposition of the famous 896 entry of the Anglo-Saxon Chronicle, which records the building and deployment of Alfred's new longships, with events in the previous year is logical.[20] Rodger argues that in 895 'the fact that the Danes were able to sail up the Thames, that they were willing to sail up the Lea without fear for their retreat, and that in the end Alfred sent no ships to intercept their escape, indicates that there was no substantial English fleet to oppose them.'[21] Rodger's reading of the context of these events make sense in terms of the capacities of a state which had prioritized land defence in the generation after the victory at Edington. Rodger also applied his point to the payments of geld to Vikings after the Battle of Maldon, arguing that they were not only 'the most effective possible advertisement of England's wealth and vulnerability' but also an

---

[17] Page,'A Most Vile People', pp. 29–30; C. R. Dodwell, Anglo-Saxon Art: A New Perspective, Manchester Studies in the History of Art 3 (Manchester, 1982), pp. 190–2.

[18] On the nuances and allusions of the Encomiast, see E. M. Tyler, '"The Eyes of the Beholders Were Dazzled": Treasure and Artifice in Encomium Emmae Reginae', EME 8 (1999), pp. 247–70.

[19] For similar accounts of ornamented ships, given as gifts see: (i) WM, GR, II.135, pp. 216–17, for an account of a gift from Harold, a Norwegian king, to Athelstan; (ii) JW vol. 2, s.a. 1040, pp. 530–1, and WM, GR II.188, pp. 338–9, for a gift from Godwine to Harthacnut; (iii) Vita Ædwardi Regis: The Life of King Edward who Rests at Westminster, ed. and trans. F. Barlow, OMT (Oxford, 2nd edn, 1992), I.1, pp. 20 for an account of a gift by Earl Godwine to Edward the Confessor. Tyler, 'The Eyes of the Beholders were Dazzled', pp. 264–5, notes the possible Scandinavian influences on these descriptions, although points out (p. 265) that that the Encomium's descriptions 'are of a different order all together'. For a textual reading of Godwine's gift of a ship to Edward, see Tyler, '"When Wings Incarnadine with Gold are Spread": The Vita Ædwardi Regis and the Display of Treasure at the Court of Edward the Confessor', in Treasure in the Medieval West, ed. E. M. Tyler (York, 2000), pp. 83–107, at pp. 90–9.

[20] For reference to this, see below, pp. 287–97

[21] Rodger, Safeguard of the Sea, p. 11.

indication of 'naval weakness'. Byrhtnoth's acceptance of battle in the face of what Rodger suggested were superior Viking numbers was taken 'lest a mobile enemy take to their ships and strike somewhere else where there was no army prepared to meet them'.[22]

From an ideological point of view, too (see chapter 1), it may be relevant that there are fewer Biblical models of the importance of a fleet than there are of mighty land armies. However, if a ruler needed inspiration, examples were available: there is a reference to Solomon's fleet in I Kings 10.22. The fleet's provision of wealth to the king on a triennial basis could hardly have been unappealing. Neither, indeed, could the example from a more recent past of Charlemagne's fleet, related as it was to a system of fortifications which guarded river estuaries from Viking attacks. This was recorded in Einhard's *Vita Karoli*, a text which was well known in ninth-century Wessex.[23]

However, fleets were expensive. Rodger argues that the organization of a fleet would have been a major drain on the resources of the English state during times of relative peace. The suggestion that years of peace had led to the disrepair of vessels is supported by Ann Williams's observation that the Anglo-Saxon Chronicle entry for 992 specifically refers to the summoning of 'all the ships that were any use', indicating 'a fall in military preparedness since the time of Edgar'.[24] For Rodger, a naval historian, a coherently organized fleet was the essential criterion; this was distinct from small flotillas of two or three ships deployed where necessary. Nonetheless, the evidence suggests that the English kingdom was able to develop fleets in such a fashion that it was considered as a coherent entity, even if only at particular times. A pertinent question is whether Alfred's long-ships represented part of that development or a short-term expedient. Patrick Wormald remarked on the possible continuity of the ships recorded in the Anglo-Saxon Chronicle, as sixty oars (i.e. thirty 'rooms'), as they represented a link with later pre-Conquest English ships,[25] while Rodger and Alfred Smyth, for different reasons, suggest that these ships represented an experiment in design which was not pursued further.[26] Although the verb *faran*, related to Old English *fyrd*

---

[22] Rodger, *Safeguard of the Sea*, p. 21.

[23] Einhard, *Vita Karoli Magni*, ed. George Waitz, MGH Scriptores Rerum Germanicarum 25 (Hanover, 1911), ch. 17, p. 21; trans. P. E. Dutton, *Charlemagne's Courtier: The Complete Einhard*, Readings in Medieval Civilizations and Cultures 3 (Peterborough, Ontario, 1998), p. 27. Dutton points out (p. xx) that the account seems to relate to the preoccupations of Louis the Pious's reign (i.e. 814–40). The dissemination of Einhard is considered in M. Tischler, *Einharts Vita Karoli: Studien zur Entstehung, Überlieferung und Rezeption*, MGH Schriften 48 (Hanover, 2002) (reference from R. McKitterick, *Charlemagne: The Formation of a European Identity* [Cambridge, 2008], p. 7). The c. 893 date of the composition of Asser's *Life of King Alfred* is perhaps an explanation for why the text did not include reference to an Alfredian navy (which is ascribed by the ASC to 896). In any case, Anton Scharer shows that Einhard was not Asser's only inspiration for this portrait of kingship: A. Scharer, 'The Writing of History at King Alfred's Court', *EME* 5 (1996), pp. 177–206, at p. 204.

[24] ASC CDE 992; Williams, *Æthelred the Unready*, p. 46.

[25] Wormald, 'Ninth Century', p. 150.

[26] Rodger, *Safeguard of the Sea*, p. 17; Smyth, *King Alfred the Great*, pp. 112–13.

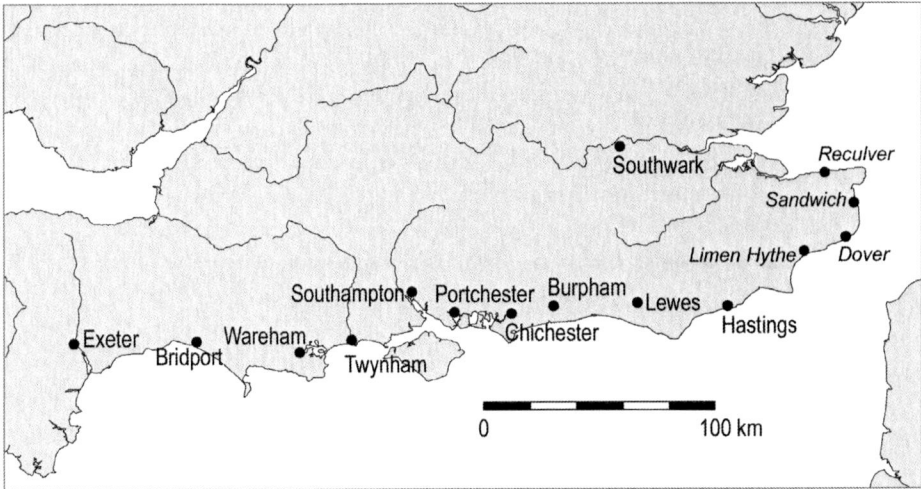

Fig. 4.2 Coastal burhs during the reign of Alfred the Great posited by Edwin and Joyce Gifford (Locations in italics indicate a suggestion for *Eorpeburnan* ['*Limen Hythe*'] and places not recorded in the Burghal Hidage.)

('army', 'force') is used to refer to Alfred's command despatching them, it is note-worthy that the nine Anglo-Saxon vessels recorded in the 896 entry of the Anglo-Saxon Chronicle are never referred to collectively as a *scipfyrd* ('ship-force'), a term which is used in later Anglo-Saxon Chronicle entries to refer to much larger fleets.[27]

Edwin and Joyce Gifford, writing in 2003, made the sensible suggestion that the naval forces of the West Saxon kingdom were linked with burghal organiza-tion, noting that coastal burhs were rarely more than 25 miles (40.2 km) from one another (see Fig. 4.2).[28] The Giffords' readings of the distances between the burhs may be underestimated in places, and from their interpretation one may also wonder why, if naval capacity was such an important factor, the Burghal Hidage did not name a fortification on the Isle of Wight. Small numbers of ships stationed at a few coastal burhs hardly constituted a fleet as such, and there are only two references to steersmen amongst the holders of urban estates in Domes-day Book, two centuries later,[29] but nonetheless, the link between naval forces and burghal centres is worth noting. If drawing a line of descent from Alfred to the

[27] The fleet recorded in ASC CDE 1009 is clearly a large one. The reference to Godwine's fleet in ASC CD 1052 as a *scipfyrd* presumably indicates that it is substantial. For discussion of the naval actions of 896 and 1052, see below, ch. 7.

[28] Gifford and Gifford, 'Alfred's New Longships', p. 283. Fig. 4.2 has been drawn using the Giffords' interpretation of the Channel coast burhs. Burpham and Lewes are not right on the coast but they are arguably chosen as suitable places for harbours. For the geology of the Channel coast in the early middle ages, see D. Meier, *Seafarers, Merchants and Pirates in the Middle Ages*, trans. A. McGeogh (Woodbridge, 2006), p. 54.

[29] These are in Southampton (DB Hants S 3 [fol. 52a]) and the distinctly landlocked town of Warwick (DB Warwicks. B 2 [fol. 238a]). Domesday Book provides references to other non-urban estates held by steersmen (see the discussion of this in Hooper's 'Some Observations on the Navy in Late Anglo-Saxon England', pp. 210–11 [below, p. 160]).

Royal Navy is no longer realistic, evidently he should not yet be discarded from naval studies.

It is likely that there were tenth-century fleets, however: Athelstan appeared to have employed fleets in combined land-sea operations in the north of England and Scotland in 934[30] as well as in a cross-Channel operation in 939 in support of Louis d'Outremer, the exiled king of France. Athelstan's successor, Edmund, may have invoked the threat of such operations when he sent messengers to the *Dux Francorum*, Hugh the Great, to demand the restoration of Louis in 946.[31]

The area in Worcestershire recorded in Domesday Book as *Oswaldslow* has been considered for its maritime significance, as a 300-hide area providing a ship, perhaps the equivalent of what is later called a 'ship-soke'.[32] While, as has been observed in chapter 2, the evidence for the 'liberty' of that area is problematic, the links between major landholders and maritime provision are significant. Archbishop Ælfric of Canterbury bequeathed two ships, one to the people of Wiltshire and another to the people of Kent; the fact that the people of the landlocked shire of Wiltshire needed a ship suggests that this was in order to meet an obligation for public provision.[33] Another prelate, Bishop Ælfwold of Crediton, willed a vessel to the king, probably as heriot,[34] while two charters record lands of the bishoprics of Sherborne and London which were intended to provide ships.[35] Perhaps like an army on land, with so many high status vessels arrayed to represent the interests of the magnates of the kingdom, a *scipfyrd* could be more than the sum of its parts.

In the context of the second Viking Age of the tenth and eleventh centuries, from which the late Anglo-Saxon wills recording ships survive, it is appropriate to return to the Anglo-Saxon Chronicle's entry for 1008, as the discrepancy between manuscripts of the Chronicle for this account should be addressed.[36] In his translation of the Anglo-Saxon Chronicle, G. N. Garmonsway assumes, from a conflation of the manuscripts, that a 310-hide unit was intended to provide 'one large warship' from 300 hides and 'a cutter' from every ten hides.[37] The D manuscript

[30] ASC 934.

[31] Flodoard, *Annals* s.a. 939 and 946: P. Lauer, *Les Annales de Flodoard* (Paris, 1905), pp. 73, 101; trans. B. Bachrach and S. Fanning, *The 'Annals' of Flodoard of Reims, 919–966*, Readings in Medieval Civilizations and Cultures 9 (Peterborough, Ontario, 2004), pp 31–2, 44. Richer of Reims's later tenth-century account of the 939 episode is discussed by D. Hill and S. Sharp, 'An Anglo-Saxon Beacon System', in *Names, Places and People: An Onomastic Miscellany in Memory of John McNeal Dodgson*, ed. A. R. Rumble and A. D. Mills (Stamford, 1997), pp. 157–65, at p. 160 (reprinted below, p. 220).

[32] DB Worcs. 2:1 (fol. 172c). John, *Land Tenure in Early England*, pp. 113–26, discussing S 731 ('AD 964'). See discussion in Hooper, 'Some Observations on the Navy in Late Anglo-Saxon England', pp. 209–10 (below, p. 159).

[33] S 1488 (AD 1003×4) (above, p. 119).

[34] S 1492 (AD 1008×12) (above, p. 119).

[35] S 1383 (AD 1001×12); S 1458a (c. AD 1000).

[36] For this account, see above, pp. 112–13.

[37] *The Anglo-Saxon Chronicle*, ed. G. N. Garmonsway, Everyman's Library (London, 1953; 2nd edn, 1972), p. 138. A similar conclusion is reached by Hollister, *Anglo-Saxon Military Institutions*, p. 41.

records 'of þrym hund scipum ⁊ .x. be tynum anne scægð', which can be translated as 'from three hundred [hides] a ship and from ten a *scægð*'. The E manuscript's 'of þrym hund hidum. ⁊ of .x. hidon ænne scegð' (literally 'from three hundred hides and from ten hides a *scægð*') is probably a more realistic assessment, suggesting that the D manuscript had mistranscribed the first *hidum* as *scypum*. Considering that Bishop Ælfwold of Crediton had bequeathed a sixty-four-oar *scegð* to the king in his will (S 1492) we can be reasonably sure that the D manuscript was a corrupt text and that a *scegð* was a comparatively large warship, and indeed the number of oars of that vessel from a 310-hide provision *almost* equates to five hides per oar – a seductively close approximation to other five-hide provisions in pre-Conquest systems.[38]

Given that some 300 hides were to build a ship or – more likely – the resources to acquire one and that the English kingdom had approximately 70,000 hides of land south of the River Tees, this potentially allowed some 200 ships.[39] This English fleet represented a significant moment – a point at which it was realized that a naval defence would have been the best means of countering the threatened invasion of Thorkell the Tall and probably also that of Swein Forkbeard. Thus the kingdom had to prepare for the building and use of a fleet. The deployment of the fleet in 1009, recorded in the Anglo-Saxon Chronicle C manuscript, can be related to this, suggesting that a fleet had been ordered, constructed and assembled.

> Here in this year the ships which we earlier spoke about were prepared, and there was never as many of them before, as books tell us, in England in any king's day. And all were then brought together to Sandwich, and should lie there and guard [*healden*] this country against every foreign force [*ælcne uthere*].

The entry highlights Sandwich's developing importance during the eleventh century, perhaps indicating that its historical importance should be placed in a *longue durée* of the middle ages.[40] The fact that a naval force could 'lie' (*licgan*) in a place and 'guard' (*healden*) the kingdom suggests that, as the Chronicler saw it, the ships and crews had been in readiness.[41] It is open to debate what a naval force numbering hundreds would actually impose on a community, at a time when ships could not wait for long offshore at anchor,[42] but the implications for the logistics should

---

[38] 320 hides divide precisely into 64 multiples of five hides: I am grateful to Matt Bennett for noting this point. Howard, *Swein Forkbeard's Invasions*, pp. 163–7, provides a detailed textual analysis of the accounts in the different manuscripts of the ASC, suggesting that a 'taxation schedule' was used as its source.

[39] For other permutations, see above, p. 113.

[40] The strategic significance of Sandwich is observed in Pullen-Appleby, *English Sea Power, c. 871 to 1100*, p. 75 (see also below, n. 84).

[41] For the sense of resistance inherent in the Old English term *healdan*, see Bosworth-Toller, p. 517, §VI, which cites, amongst other documents, the account of resistance against the Danes in ASC CDE 1013.

[42] On the difficulties of waiting at anchor, see C. Grainge and G. Grainge, 'The Pevensey Expedition: Brilliantly Executed Plan or Near Disaster?', in *The Battle of Hastings: Sources and Interpretations*, ed. Morillo, pp. 130–44, at p. 140. I am grateful to Matt Bennett for drawing this issue to my attention.

not pass without comment. The sea-frontage required for ships with beams of some 4 metres (see Fig. 4.1) to beach alongside each other could have been considerable. The crews of the ships could presumably only remain in the area for a short time because of the logistical difficulties in feeding them while ashore.

The entry's reference to 'books' may also be relevant here. Although an understanding of the Chronicler's perspective is now well established as one written from hindsight,[43] given that Edgar's reign was known for its naval organization, the fact that the Chronicler relates the size of the fleet to past precedent suggests that this was a deliberate point of comparison. While we may ponder whether he was alluding to otherwise unknown historical records – narrative or administrative[44] or simply referring to earlier entries in the manuscripts of the Anglo-Saxon Chronicle,[45] there was good precedent for the build-up of fleets during the reigns of Alfred, Athelstan, and Edgar, as well as during Æthelred's early reign. Bede's *Historia ecclesiastica*, a manuscript which was widely copied in the early middle ages, also referred to coastal expeditions by rulers, which may have had an impact on the Chronicler's sense of historical achievement.[46]

Unfortunately for the Anglo-Saxon state, it was in vain:

> Then it happened at this same time, or a little before, that Brihtric, Ealdorman Eadric's brother, accused Wulfnoth *Cild* [DE: 'the South Saxon'] to the king, and he then went away and persuaded [people] to him until he had 20 ships. And he then harried everywhere along the south coast, and wrought every evil. Then it was said to the *scipfyrd* that that they [Wulfnoth's party] might be surrounded with ease, if people wished to go about [it]. Then the aforesaid Brihtric took 80 ships for himself, and thought that he should make great words [i.e. a great name] for himself and seize Wulfnoth alive or dead. But when they were going thither there arose against them a wind such that no man remembered before, and it beat and thrashed all the ships, and cast them ashore. And at once the aforesaid Wulfnoth came and burned the ships. When it was known to those other ships where the king was how the others had fared, it was then as if it were all in confusion, and the king took himself home, and the ealdormen, and the high-*witan*, and abandoned the ships thus lightly. And the people who were on the ships brought them back to London, and thus lightly let the toil of all the nation perish. And the victory in which all the English people had held hope was no better.

The Chronicler refers to the accusation of Wulfnoth as perhaps having taken place 'a little before' the general levy of the ships. We may consider whether one

---

[43] Keynes, 'Declining Reputation of King Æthelred the Unready', pp. 227–53.

[44] I am grateful once more to Matt Bennett for the latter suggestion, a point which would be commensurate with the observation in Howard, *Swein Forkbeard's Invasions*, p. 163, that a 'taxation schedule' was used as a source for the hidages quoted by the Chronicler. See generally Keynes, 'Declining Reputation of King Æthelred the Unready', pp. 233–4.

[45] The comparative point is ASC CDE 992 (discussed above, p. 146).

[46] Bede, *HE* IV.16; 26 (see above, p. 142). Bede's accounts of Roman fleets (I.2; 12) are also relevant, reflected in ASC DE for 60 BC. For the dissemination of Bede, see R. H. C. Davis, 'Bede After Bede', in *Studies in Medieval History presented to R. Allen Brown*, ed. C. Harper-Bill, C. Holdsworth, and J. L. Nelson (Woodbridge, 1989), pp. 103–16.

of the purposes of the levy of the ships was to defend the southern coasts against general disorder, of which Wulfnoth's actions were only an element. It is nonetheless interesting that the Chronicler subsequently prefaces his record of the attack of Thorkell's army upon Sandwich and Canterbury with the comment '[w]hen this *scypfyrd* had ended thus', implying that, although its dramatic termination was hardly desirable, the calling out of a naval force was an event specific to a period of time. Although the 'ships' could be referred to individually as vessels, it was only the levy of the ships which could be referred to collectively as a 'shipfyrd'.

Nicholas Higham has commented on the fact that the dead recorded in the Anglo-Saxon Chronicle for 1009 can be related to men from two different parts of the kingdom. One group was from an area which would not have been the natural choice for a seafaring community.[47] This may suggest that systems of assemblies were associated with naval forces as with those on land. We should not necessarily see the events of 1009 as a failure of military systems, however. Rather, Wulfnoth's actions, insofar as they are recorded in the Chronicle, were a consequence of the weaknesses of the kingdom itself.[48] In this context it perhaps matters less that the fleet of 1009 was destroyed in an internal conflict than that the state was able to gather a large fleet in one place, using the supplies and infrastructure necessary for its successful operation.[49]

Although the Anglo-Saxon state could presumably rely on pressing 'civilian' vessels into service when required for the transport of warriors, the building of specialist vessels for war was still important for a naval fleet. The Anglo-Saxon Chronicle records that it took more than a year to gather the fleet, and mentions the building of ships. In contrast to Carol Gillmor's assessment of the limitations of materials and labour in ducal Normandy before the invasion of 1066,[50] the construction of a fleet in 1008–9 was within the capabilities of the English kingdom on a 300-hide basis.

Nicholas Hooper's work, 'Some Observations on the Navy' (1989), is included below, as it considers the key pieces of evidence for the late Anglo-Saxon period and the context of naval organization, including in post-1016 England. Drawing distinctions between the study of *butsecarls* and other ship crews, Hooper highlights the importance of Domesday Book for identifying the links between naval service and landholding in coastal regions, especially in Kent and London.

---

[47] N. J. Higham, *The Death of Anglo-Saxon England* (Stroud, 1997), p. 51.

[48] Lavelle, *Aethelred II*, pp. 155–6. For the wider issue of weaknesses in the kingdom, see Stafford, 'Reign of Æthelred II'.

[49] An important issue for vessels, if their crews were to use the oar propulsion available, is the ready availability of supplies of drinking water or mild ale. Water intake per crew member during a sustained period of rowing on a hot day could have been high, which would have limited the capacity of vessels if they were to be at sea for long. For discussion of an intake of 7 litres per man per day (although with the reservation that the climates are not comparable), see J. Coates, 'The Naval Architecture and Oar Systems of Ancient Galleys', in *The Age of the Galley: Mediterranean Oared Vessels Since Pre-Classical Times*, ed. R. Gardiner, Conway's History of the Ship (London, 1995), pp. 127–41, at p. 130.

[50] C. M. Gillmor, 'Naval Logistics of the Cross-Channel Operation, 1066', *ANS* 7 (1985 for 1984), pp. 105–31.

· ·

Some Observations on the Navy in Late Anglo-Saxon England*

NICHOLAS HOOPER

[*Author's note appended at foot of page: I wish to take this opportunity to register
my thanks to Allen for the way in which he inspired me to study medieval history
in my first weeks at King's. The evidence for the eleventh century has been discussed
by C. Warren Hollister, *Anglo-Saxon Military Institutions on the Eve of the Norman
Conquest* (Oxford 1962), chapters 1 and 6. This paper is intended in part as a
modification of some of his conclusions.]

'Lo, it is nearly 350 years that we and our fathers have inhabited this most lovely
land, and never before has such terror appeared in Britain as we have suffered
from a pagan race, nor was it thought that such an inroad from the sea could be
made.'[51] Thus wrote Alcuin to Æthelred, king of Northumbria, following the
Viking raid on the monastery of Lindisfarne in 793. At first sight his shock seems
misplaced. The English had come to Britain as seaborne raiders before they began
to settle and conquer. It would appear unlikely that they were unaware other races
could use the sea in the same way. And yet in Northumbria and Kent at least,
important monasteries occupied exposed coastal sites, as if the sea was truly a
highway for traders and travellers alone. Subsequent generations learned the need
to take precautions against attack from the sea. Allen Brown has always expressed
surprise at the way in which late Anglo-Saxon kings were able to raise fleets at
'the drop of a hat'. It is the intention of this paper to re-examine some aspects of
naval organisation in the late Anglo-Saxon state.

  Every schoolboy used to know that the founder of the Royal Navy was Alfred.
The *Anglo-Saxon Chronicle* does not make this claim for him when it describes
his new model ships under the year 896,[52] but it has not always been noticed
that there are references to English naval activity before this. Some versions of
the *Chronicle* note that the West Saxons opposed the Vikings by sea as early as
851, and Alfred's first recorded voyage, in the summer of 875, ended in victory
over a small flotilla. Two further successes are recorded for Alfred in 882 and 885,
although in the latter year a West Saxon defeat at sea is mentioned too.[53] The vital
information missing is how Alfred and his predecessors raised and manned the
ships mentioned in the annals. The tone of the passage describing the 'new vessels'
suggests they were the king's ships, for among the casualties were a king's reeve
and *geneat*, perhaps a member of Alfred's household. The annals for 875 and 882
point in the same direction. The presence of Frisians among the West Saxon dead
in 896 also suggests these were Alfred's ships and that he had bought in naval

---

[51] *EHD* 1, p. 842.

[52] ASC 896; Plummer-Earle, vol. 1, pp. 90–1. Quotations from ASC are taken from *EHD*
with some changes.

[53] ASC 851 (A and Asser omit the information that King Athelstan and Ealdorman
Ealhhere were in ships), 875, 882, 885: Plummer-Earle, vol. 1, pp. 64–5, 74–5, 76–9.

expertise. A late source hints that he might also have employed Danes to man his ships.[54] The 885 fleet was from Kent, however, and so may have been raised from the people of the region.

Whatever method Alfred used to provide these vessels they appear to have been few us number and of only limited value. The *Chronicle* references show them making coastal patrols and dealing with small Viking flotillas, on one occasion carrying war into Danish East Anglia, although significantly this was followed by defeat. It was only during the tenth century that the West Saxon fleet became larger and more effective in projecting the authority of its kings into Scotland, the Irish Sea and across the Channel. In the time of Edgar, it was noted, 'nor was there fleet so proud nor host so strong that got itself prey in England'.[55] In the eleventh century too English ships exerted power on the seas as Æthelred employed them in the Irish Sea again and against Normandy, Cnut used them in Sweden and Norway and their services were requested by the Emperor Henry III and Swein of Denmark[56] — these in addition to the defence of England from seaborne invasion, a task which was performed with mixed success. In the eleventh century England was successfully invaded on several occasions. From this time we are fortunate to possess a considerable amount of information on the ways in which these naval forces were raised. In examining this evidence it is proposed to consider the stipendiary element first and then the ships provided by the nation.[57]

We have already come across Frisians in Alfred's employment, and it seems likely that some of the 'foreigners ... and harmful people' attracted to England by Edgar were employed by him in keeping the seas.[58] There is more substantial evidence from the eleventh century. In 1001 Æthelred already had Scandinavians in his employment, for Pallig, who is said to have been the brother-in-law of Swein of Denmark, deserted with 'the ships he could collect', despite his

---

[54] What W. H. Stevenson, *Asser's Life of King Alfred* (Oxford 1904) printed as chapter 50c of his reconstruction of the *Life* was taken from a thirteenth-century St Alban's chronicle. It puts Alfred's decision to build 'longships' under 877 and refers to the crews as *piratis*. Plummer-Earle, vol. 2, pp. 111–12, assumed them to have been Frisians. That Alfred might have employed Scandinavians is suggested by the presence of 'Vikings' in his household, and of' someone of Viking parentage' in his monastery at Athelney (Asser chs 71, 94 in Keynes and Lapidge, *Alfred the Great*, pp. 91, 103.

[55] ASC DE 975; Plummer-Earle, vol. 2, p. 121.

[56] ASC 911 (*recte* 910), 931, 1000, E 1025 (*recte* 1021). CDEF 1028, D 1048 (*recte* 1047), CD 1049, CD 1054, DE 1063; Plummer-Earle, vol. 1, pp. 96, 106, 133. 157, 166–7, 181–5, 190–1; Flodoard's *Annals* s.a. 939, printed in *EHD* 1, pp. 344–5; *Gesta Normannorum Ducum of William of Jumièges*, ed. Van Houts, OMT, 2 vols (Oxford, 1992–5), vol. 2, pp. 10–15.

[57] For earlier accounts of the stipendiary forces, see Hollister, *Anglo-Saxon Military Institutions*, ch. 1.

[58] ASC DEF 959; Plummer-Earle, vol. 1, pp. 114–15; see also Sawyer, *From Roman Britain to Norman England*, p. 127.

pledges to the king and the gifts of lands and gold and silver he had received.[59]
Subsequently the Danish chieftain Thorkell the Tall joined Æthelred with forty-
five ships of the immense raiding army' which had already been ravaging England
since August 1009, and which reportedly received the huge payment of £48,000
before dispersing in 1012. The terms of their service were that Æthelred was to
feed and clothe them, in return for which they would defend England.[60] This
agreement did not prevent them from taking their own measures in the following
year. In their entries for 1051 MS D of the *Chronicle* and 'Florence' of Worcester's
chronicle refer to the abolition of the tax known as the *heregeld* in. respectively,
the thirty-ninth and thirty-eighth year since Æthelred established it to pay
the 'Danish soldiers' (*solidarii*). Since this refers to 1012 or 1013 it is clear that
Thorkell's fleet, which was waiting for payment and supplies at Greenwich in
1013, is meant.[61] It may have been the same force which received £21,000 at
Greenwich in 1014. However, when Æthelred returned from his refuge in
Normandy in 1014 he seems to have had a new Scandinavian ally, the Norwegian
Olaf Haraldsson.[62]

When Cnut became king he employed his own ships: in 1018 forty ships
of the fleet which conquered England, falling to sixteen vessels by the end of
the reign. This figure was maintained by his successor Harold Harefoot, but
Harthecnut brought some sixty ships with him in 1040 and still had thirty-two
of them in service the following year. The last references to the hired fleet concern
its end. Edward paid off nine out of fourteen crews in 1049 and the remainder
in 1050. It was after this that the *heregeld* was abolished, demonstrating the
close relationship between the hired fleet and this tax. The rate of pay was eight
marks a rowlock, probably with the higher sum of twelve marks to a steersman.
The rates of pay make it possible to calculate that there were some eighty men
to each of these ships,[63] a figure which receives confirmation from 'Florence'
of Worcester's description of a ship and eighty very heavily armed warriors
presented to Harthecnut by Godwine in 1040.[64] The fact that the men paid off
in 1050 took the ships with them suggests that the vessels were their own. The
lithsmen do not reappear in English history, although it is by no means certain
that the *heregeld* was not reinstituted before 1066. The advantages of possessing

[59] ASC A 1001; Plummer-Earle, vol. 1, p. 132.

[60] ASC CDE 1012; Plummer-Earle, vol. 1, p. 143.

[61] ASC D 1052 (*recte* 1051); Plummer-Earle, vol. 1, p. 173, and JW vol. 2, s.a. 1051, pp. 556–9;
ASC CDE 1013; Plummer-Earle, vol. 1, p. 144.

[62] ASC CDE 1014; Plummer-Earle, vol. 1, p. 145. Olaf's support is implied by the skaldic
verse of Otar the Black in *EHD* 1, p. 333. The identity of the forty ships Ealdorman Eadric
defected with in 1014 is unknown.

[63] ASC CDE 1018, CD 1040, E 1039 (*recte* 1040) (62 ships). E 1040 (*recte* 1041), C 1049.
E 1047 (*recte* 1050), C 1050; Plummer-Earle, vol. 1, pp. 154, 160–3, 171–2; M. K. Lawson,
'The Collection of Danegeld and Heregeld in the Reigns of Aethelred II and Cnut',
EHR 99 (1984), pp. 721–38, at pp. 721–2, 737–8.

[64] JW vol. 2, s.a. 1040, pp. 530–1.

such a force may not, in Edward's opinion, have outweighed the potential threat they represented to his own freedom of action.[65]

This fleet represented a permanent military force in a way that the housecarls did not. The distinction is an important one. The fleet is referred to in the *chronicle* by the name *lithsmen* (or the variants *litsmen* and *litsmanna*) which seems to mean men of the fleet or army (the difference may not have been important in the eleventh century). They are presumably the royal vessels referred to in 1049 when Earl Godwine commanded a squadron of two of the king's ships, captained by his sons Harold and Tostig, and forty-two of the people's ships. In peacetime too they could be an influential body. During the limbo which followed the death of Cnut in 1035 the *lithsmen* in London were among those who chose Harold Harefoot to rule. Queen Emma held Winchester with Earl Godwine and Harthecnut's housecarls, but this was not sufficient to prevent Harold becoming full king.[66] It may be that he did not trust the *lithsmen* which led Harthecnut to entrust his housecarls with the collection of tax in 1041. Elsewhere I have argued that the housecarls should not be seen as a standing army but as the sort of household following which princes commonly maintained.[67] It is in comparison with the *lithsmen* that this distinction becomes important, for we know that they were paid wages and possibly based at London as a body. There is no evidence that they received grants of land, as housecarls certainly did, and it is suggestive that the *lithsmen* could be paid off *en masse* where housecarls as landowners are found in England beyond 1066. This is not to deny that housecarls did have 'some of the functions of a standing army',[68] but if we are looking for such a force in eleventh-century England then the evidence makes it necessary to see it in the *lithsmen*. It is interesting, moreover, to note the relationship of some earls to the *lithsmen*. When Beorn was murdered by Swein Godwineson in 1049 it was his 'friends and *lithsmen* from London' who retrieved the body. As Harold, Tostig Godwineson and Beorn himself had captained royal ships that year, it is possible that they had official duties with the *lithsmen*, even that they were reckoned members of the fleet.[69]

In addition to *lithsmen*, the *butsecarls* ('boatmen') have been identified as

---

[65] For the possibility that *heregeld* was levied after 1051, see Barlow, *Edward the Confessor*, p. 106, n. 5, and p. 102 for the political potential of the *lithsmen*. The belief than they were taken on again 1051 (Hollister, *Anglo-Saxon Military Institutions*, pp. 17–18) rests on a mistaken interpretation of *lið* in ASC C 1066 (Plummer-Earle, vol. 1, p. 197) where it means no more than 'troops' or 'force'. It is used in this sense several times in the accounts of 1052 and 1066.

[66] ASC E 1046 (*recte* 1049), E 1036 (*recte* 1035); Plummer-Earle, vol. 1, pp. 168, 159.

[67] Hooper, 'Housecarls in England in the Eleventh Century'.

[68] Campbell, 'Some Agents and Agencies of the Late Anglo-Saxon State', pp. 203–4. Cf. Mr Campbell's suggestion that 'housecarl' meant *domesticus miles* with my own that housecarls 'differed little from the *milites* of other princely households, whether they were described as thegns, *chevaliers* or housecarls' (Hooper, 'Housecarls in England in the Eleventh Century', p. 171).

[69] ASC E 1046 (*recte* 1049); Plummer-Earle, vol. 1, p. 168. Barlow, *Edward the Confessor*, p. 100, suggests that Beorn commanded them.

another mercenary force on the strength of a passage in Domesday Book. This notes that when the king went on an expedition he had from Malmesbury 'either twenty shillings to feed his boatmen (*ad pascendos suos buzecarlis*) or he took one man from each honour of five hides'.[70] Against this must be set the significant link between Hastings, Romney, Hythe, Dover and Sandwich, which were later the 'head ports' of the Cinque Ports, and the use of the term in the *Chronicle*. The link is clear in the account of 1052. On his return from exile in Flanders Earl Godwine 'enticed all the men of Kent and all the *butsecarls* from the district of Hastings' and many more besides. Later Godwine and Harold 'went towards Sandwich and kept on collecting all the *butsecarls* they met, and so they came to Sandwich with an overwhelming force.' The 'E' manuscript does not refer to *butsecarls* but lists the ports from which they took ships, and presumably their crews, as Pevensey, Dungeness, Romney, Hythe, Folkestone and Sandwich.[71] In 1066 Tostig also took *butsecarls* from Sandwich, 'some willingly and some unwillingly', before proceeding northwards. After his defeat by Earls Edwin and Morcar they deserted, leaving him with twelve small ships (*snaccum*) of his original force of sixty vessels.[72] Domesday Book gives added significance to these references as it records that Dover, Sandwich and Romney had received privileges in return for naval services. At Dover the duty owed was twenty ships, each with twenty-one men, for fifteen days, *ad custodiendum mare*.[73]

The interpretation that these *butsecarls* were mercenary garrisons appears to strain the evidence. A more natural reading of the *Chronicle* and Domesday Book than Hollister's leads to the conclusion that *butsecarls* were the inhabitants of the maritime towns of Kent and Sussex, some of whom owed naval service to the king and whose obligations would later lead to the Cinque Ports organisation. But others among them were doubtless ready to join in ventures for personal gain. Whether Edward made a bargain with these towns when he paid off the *lithsmen* in 1051, as Murray suggested, or the service is older, cannot be answered. Hollister's objection to this explanation, on the grounds that not all naval mercenaries were paid off in 1051, has already been shown to be based

[70] DB Wilts. B 5 (fol. 64c). Hollister, *Anglo-Saxon Military Institutions*, pp. 12–19.

[71] ASC CE 1052; Plummer-Earle, vol. I, pp. 178–9.

[72] ASC CD 1066; Plummer-Earle, vol. I, pp. 196–7.

[73] Dover, DB Kent D 2 (fol. 1r); Sandwich, DB Kent 2:2 (fol. 3a), 'renders to the king the same service as Dover'; Romney, DB Kent 2:43 (fol. 4c); 5:178 (fol. 10d), 'service at sea'; Hythe had the same exemption from payment of customary dues as Romney, although there is no reference to naval duties: A. Ballard, *An Eleventh-Century Inquisition of St Augustine's, Canterbury*, British Academy Records of Social and Economic History 4 (1920), p. 20. From the Sussex borough of Lewes the king could send his men *ad mare custodiendum*, although if he did not join them 20s were collected 'from all the men ... and this money had those who were in charge of the arms in the ships' (DB Sussex 12:1 [fol. 26a]). This is an obscure reference – does it mean the king's ships or those of Lewes? Hastings is practically ignored in Domesday Book but its ships captured two of Swein Godwineson's vessels in 1050 (ASC D 1051 (*recte* 1050); Plummer-Earle, vol. I, p. 170). Maldon, in Essex, also owed one ship to the king (DB Essex 24:63 [LDB fol. 48r]). See in general Hollister, *Anglo-Saxon Military Institutions*, pp. 115–23.

on a mistaken reading of the *Chronicle*.[74] What is clear is that by the time of Edward the Confessor the crown was taking advantage of the ships of its subjects for naval service. If this interpretation of the *butsecarls* is to be accepted it is necessary to explain the identity of those at London late in 1066 who wished to raise Edgar the Ætheling to the throne. They were perhaps part of the fleet Harold is reputed to have sent to blockade Hastings after the Norman landing and which did not return to their ports because of William's harrying.[75] This is also the only element of Old English naval forces which can be traced after the Conquest. William I used *butsecarls* against Ely in 1071 and his son Henry set them to guard the sea when he heard of Duke Robert's intended invasion, although they deserted him.[76]

Butsecarls and *lithsmen* represented only a fraction of English naval resources in the eleventh century. Much more impressive is the organisation which raised a fleet from the English kingdom. This is sometimes called *scipfyrd*, although in Old English this meant any naval force. The earliest reference to it may be in 992 when it was 'decreed that all the ships that were any use should be assembled in London'.[77] The decision of 1008 to build a new fleet was probably taken because the existing vessels were decayed beyond repair. The work was done all over the country, 'a warship (*scegth*) from three hundred hides and ten, and a helmet and mailcoat from eight'.[78] An indication of the number of ships collected at Sandwich the following year is that Brihtric's squadron contained eighty vessels.[79] No more is heard of the ship-levy until the reign of Edward the Confessor. The great fleet (*scyphere*) Edward stationed at Sandwich in 1049 included a Mercian contingent which was soon stood down. The ship service of Wessex must have been Earl Godwine's squadron of forty-two of the people's vessels (*landes manna scipa*).[80] Another fleet at Sandwich in 1052 consisted of forty small vessels (*snacca*), according to the 'C' and 'D' versions of the *Chronicle*. This might indicate that it

---

[74] See above, n. 65. K. M. E. Murray, *The Constitutional History of the Cinque Ports* (Manchester, 1935), pp. 25–6. In his discussion of butsecarls and the Cinque Ports (*Anglo-Saxon Military Institutions*, pp. 18 and 116–22) Hollister does not notice the close link between them.

[75] JW vol. 2, s.a. 1066, pp. 604–7; WP II.14, pp. 124–5. Vengeance was taken at Romney, and Dover burned by the Normans (WP II.27, pp. 142–5).

[76] JW vol. 3, s.a. 1071, pp. 20–1; 1101, pp. 96–9 (Simeon of Durham [*Historia Regum*, s.a. 1071 and 1101, in *Symeonis Monachi Opera Omnia*, ed. Arnold, vol. 2, pp. 195, 233] and Roger of Howden [*Chronica magistri Rogeri de Houedene*, ed. W. Stubbs, RS 51, 4 vols (London, 1868–71), vol. 1, pp. 125, 158], follow him in this usage).

[77] Another fleet was assembled in 999, ASC CDE 992, 999; Plummer-Earle, vol. 1, pp. 127, 133.

[78] ASC CDE 1008; Plummer-Earle, vol. 1, p. 138. The law-code V Æthelred, from the same year, exhorts the supplying of ships so that they may be ready after Easter, and the associated VI Æthelred adds that the penalty for damaging a 'warship of the people' was reparation and a fine (*EHD* 1, p. 415, §27 and n. 8). The ASC's figure is usually emended to 300 hides.

[79] ASC CDE 1009; Plummer-Earle, vol. 1, pp. 166–9.

[80] ASC CD 1049, E 1046 (*recte* 1049); Plummer-Earle, vol. 1, pp. 166–9.

was raised in a different way, perhaps from the ports of the south-east. The 'E' version, however, records that the ships returned to London for relief crews and earls to command them. This suggests that the ships were indeed the national ship-levy. Shortly after this the king and his loyal earls had fifty ships at London.[81] The last recorded muster of the ship-levy was in 1066 when Harold summoned a fleet which slowly assembled at Sandwich, but appears to have been positioned at the Isle of Wight as the threat was from Normandy rather than the north. It held station for up to four months throughout summer and harvest until, on 8 September, 'the provisions … were gone' and the fleet was sent home.[82]

This narrative raises many questions, some of which it is possible to answer. The gathering of ships in 992 suggests that the organisation already existed, indeed that the ships had been built long enough before then for decay to be a problem. The working life of medieval vessels is not known. The *Chronicle* describes the Danes in 896 using the ships they had built 'many years before'. The tenth-century ship found in Kent is thought to have had a life of some twenty years. This may suggest that Edgar established these arrangements, and in later years there was a tradition than he had maintained a powerful fleet. It is no more than a tradition and the details are apocryphal, yet there is no evidence to refute the suggestion that the fleet as it existed in the eleventh century owed its organisation to Edgar.[83] The importance of Sandwich (on several occasions) and the Isle of Wight (in 1066, but possibly also in 1022) as mustering points has been seen.[84] The several references to fleets assembling at London, or returning there at the end of a campaign, make it possible to suggest tentatively that London was a naval base of some sort, perhaps where ships could be beached above the bridge.

The way in which these ships were provided by the people of England appears at first straightforward. In 1008 the *Chronicle* says that districts of uniform size were responsible for building ships. As Bishop Æthelric declared to Ealdorman Æthelmær that his bishopric (Sherborne) had lost thirty-three hides of 'the three hundred that other bishops had for their shire' and so was not receiving the full amount of 'ship-scot', it is likely the *Chronicle's* figure of three hundred and ten

[81] ASC CDE 1052; Plummer-Earle, vol. 1, pp. 177–81.

[82] ASC C 1066; Plummer-Earle, vol. 1, p. 196. The length of time the fleet was out suggests it returned to London for relief crews half-way through its service (see below).

[83] ASC 896; Plummer-Earle, vol. 1, p. 90; *The Graveney Boat: A Tenth-Century Find from Kent*, ed. V. Fenwick, BAR British 53 (Oxford, 1978), p. xix. For Edgar's fleet, see WM, GR II.157, pp. 256–7, and JW vol. 2, s.a. 975, pp. 424–7. The naval element of Edgar's coronation ceremony (ASC DE 972 (*recte* 973); JW vol. 2, s.a. 973, pp. 422–5) must be seen in this context.

[84] Cnut took his ships to the Isle of Wight in 1022 for no recorded reason (ASC CDE 1022: Plummer-Earle, vol. 1, pp. 154–5). For Sandwich, see Hollister, *Anglo-Saxon Military Institutions*, p. 125. In the eleventh century it occupied a strategic site: its now silted-up bay formed a safe anchorage in the sheltered lee of Thanet from which ships could move north, along the channel of the Stour into the Thames estuary; move south and west along the coast of Wessex; or stay put to intercept fleets from Scandinavia.

hides is corrupt.[85] The most famous example of an ecclesiastical endowment of three hundred hides is Worcester. It seems impossible to maintain that the charter by which Edgar established a triple hundred for Bishop Oswald is genuine.[86] Not all the privileges claimed in this charter were spurious, however. According to Domesday Book Worcester did have three hundred hides at Oswaldslow where 'no sheriff can have any claim ... and if any portion of them was leased to any man, for the service to be done to the bishop for it, he who held that land on lease could not ... retain the land beyond the completion of the term agreed between them, or betake himself anywhere with that land'. There is no reference here to a ship. but one of the estates of Oswaldslow was held by four *liberi homines* rendering sake and soke, churchscot and burial dues, military service and *nauigia* ('ship-service').[87] That the bishop did supply a ship to the royal host is confirmed by a reference in Hemming's cartulary to 'Eadric, who was in the time of King Edward, the steersman of the bishop's ship, and the leader of the same bishop's army in the king's service'.[88]

The *Chronicle* entry for 1008 and the twelfth-century *Leges Henrici Primi* imply that the organisation to supply ships covered the whole kingdom. According to the latter every county was divided into these areas, which it calls 'ship-sokes' (*sipessocna*).[89] Although these arrangements can have been little more than a century old by the time Domesday Book was made, and were still in use up to the Conquest itself, they have left remarkably little trace. This may indicate that they were a lot less regular than has been assumed or that they were rapidly modified as a result of bargains between subjects and kings during the eleventh century. Moreover, none of the examples which have been collected refer to ship-service north of the Humber. It is possible that the organisation was never extended into the kingdom of York.

Most evidence for naval service is ecclesiastical. Despite the evidence of Bishop Æthelric's declaration, no other episcopal endowments are as distinctive as Worcester's. The Sherborne ship-soke is probably to be seen in the head manors of three hundreds held in 1086 by the bishop of Salisbury, whence the bishopric had been moved, although only 228 hides were to be found there.[90] The bishop

[85] S 1383; printed in F. E. Harmer, *Anglo-Saxon Wills* (Cambridge, 1930), no. 63. The date is 1001×1012 (Whitelock, *Anglo-Saxon Wills*, pp. 141, 144f., prefers 1002). The MS reads *scypegesceote*, for which Harmer suggested 'contribution to supply a ship'.

[86] E. John's attempts to produce a genuine version of this charter, S 731 (*Land Tenure in Early England*, pp. 113–20, 162–7) have been widely rejected, N. P. Brooks, 'Anglo-Saxon Charters: The Work of the Last Twenty Years', *ASE* 3 (1971), p. 229, notes that 'beyond all reasonable doubt ... this charter is a compilation of the twelfth century and ... no part of it can reasonably be used as evidence for the tenth'. It is worth adding that the terms *naucupletio* and *scypfylleth* seem to be unique to this document while *scipsocn* occurs only in twelfth-century contexts.

[87] DB Worcs. 2:1 (fol. 172c); 2:21 (fol. 173a) ('Bisantune').

[88] DB Worcs. 2:52 (fol. 173c); *Hemingi Chartularium*, ed Hearne, vol. I, p. 80.

[89] *Leges Henrici Primi*, ed. Downer, p. 97.

[90] *VCH Dorset*, vol. 3, ed. R. B. Pugh (London, 1968), pp. 124, 132, 145. The bishop later held all three hundreds.

of Dorchester also possessed three hundreds which have been seen as strongly reminiscent of a ship-soke.[91] Pershore abbey held three hundreds until Edward gave two to Westminster.[92] The bishop of Winchester did not hold the whole of Taunton hundred, but the men of it were under his jurisdiction and had to go 'on military service with the bishop's men', which may represent a trace of a composite ship-soke.[93] Lastly, there is the list of men for a ship from St Paul's. While the memorandum does not account for sufficient men to crew a vessel of sixty or so oars (see below) it is presumably to the bishop's warship that it refers.[94]

Another indication of a ship-soke, or at least of ship-service, is reference to a steersman. We have seen that the Worcester ship and contingent were commanded by Eadric the steersman. In the same county another steersman, Thorkell, held in 1066 an estate which King Edward had given to Westminster. It is likely he commanded a warship owed by Westminster from the two hundreds it had received from Edward. As these two had been held by Pershore, with a third which the house still had, this probably represents the Pershore ship-soke. In Norfolk Eadric, rector navis regis Edwardi, was the tenant of St Benet of Holme for Horning. After the Conquest he was outlawed to Denmark.[95] A context is provided for this story by the fourteenth-century chronicle of St Benet attributed to John of Oxenedes, according to which the abbot was entrusted with the defence of the coast by Harold and was forced to seek refuge in Denmark by William. The story is late but not implausible. Eadric also appears as a benefactor in a spurious charter in the St Benet cartulary, where he is described as sciresman, surely a misreading for steersman.[96] The only other steersman I have been able to trace is 'Ulfech' (Wulfheah), King Edward's steersman, who is not recorded holding of an ecclesiastical institution. As his land was held by Countess Judith in 1086 he may have been a tenant of Tostig and captain of the earl's vessel.[97]

Among the laity there are fewer references to the organisation for levying ships. The eighteen Domesday hundreds of Buckinghamshire were arranged in six groups of three, perhaps as early as 1086, and so may reflect lay ship-sokes. Pipe Rolls refer to ship-sokes in Warwickshire in the twelfth century. However,

[91] VCH Oxon., vol. 7, ed. R. B. Pugh (London, 1962), p. 2.

[92] DB Worcs. 8:1 (fol. 174c) and VCH Worcs., vol. 1, pp. 175, 259, 299, 304–5.

[93] DB Som. 2:2 (fol. 87c) and VCH Somerset, vol. 1, ed. W. Page (London, 1906), p. 442.

[94] Robertson, Anglo-Saxon Charters, 2nd edn, pp. 144–5, 389–92. The list accounts for forty-five men. It may be incomplete, or the remaining men may have been found in some other way. It is even possible, although unlikely, that the bishop of London's ship was smaller than others which are known.

[95] DB Norfolk 10:76;77 (LDB fol. 200r) and VCH Norfolk, vol. 2, ed. W. Page (London, 1906), p. 122.

[96] Chronica Johannis de Oxenedes, ed. H. Ellis, RS 13 (London, 1859), pp. 291, 293; F. M. Stenton, 'St Benet of Holme and the Norman Conquest', EHR 37 (1922), pp. 225–35 at pp. 227, 233. I have not consulted the manuscript, only J. R. West (ed.), The Eleventh- and Twelfth-Century Sections of Cott. MS. Galba E.ii. The Register of the Abbey St Benet of Holme, Norfolk Record Society 2–3, 2 vols (Fakenham and London, 1932), pp. 2–5 (= S 1055).

[97] DB Beds. 53:15 (fol. 217c) and VCH Beds., vol. 1, ed. H. A. Doubleday and W. Page (London, 1904), p. 258.

here the association between three hundred hides and ship-sokes breaks down. Of the three Warwickshire ship-sokes identified in Pipe Rolls only Knightlow consisted of three hundreds, but it cannot be established how many hides were there. Kineton contained four hundreds and Hemlingford one. Few hundreds did in fact consist of a round one hundred hides. Some were very much smaller and others a great deal larger. In the case of Buckinghamshire each of the groups of hundreds contained more than three hundred hides, and the Aylesbury group consisted of four hundred.[98] This must have complicated the organisation of ship service and made it impossible to spread the burden evenly. A further complication were towns, which did not fit in consistently. Some served with the surrounding land, for example Stamford as twelve-and-a-half hundreds *in navigio*, Bedford as half a hundred 'by land and sea' and Exeter as five hides.[99] Others had made special arrangements: Leicester provided four horses for carrying service to London if service was by sea, Warwick furnished four sailors (*bat suein*), Colchester 6d from each house annually and Maldon provided a ship.[100]

There are, moreover, references to a tax for ships rather than the actual provision of vessels. Thus Bishop Æthelric's memorandum complains that it is the contributions to the ship-scot that he has lost, and a writ of William I refers to the day when 'most recently in the time of King Edward a tax was taken to build ships'.[101] Hollister's suggestion is that some ship-sokes commuted 'their obligation of providing a ship by paying a sum of money instead. Ship-scot may have replaced the actual ship-building obligation over large areas of inland England'.[102] The effort of constructing a national fleet was a great one, as calculation of the resources required to raise a fleet in Normandy in 1066 has shown, and the necessary ship-wrights can only have been found in coastal districts.[103]

The bequests of ships to religious and lay communities in the reign of Æthelred II suggests that the rich shouldered some of this burden. At some time

---

[98] *Great Roll of the Pipe for the Sixteenth Year of the Reign of King Henry II*, AD 1169–70, Pipe Roll Society 15 (London, 1892), p. 90, 'sipe socha de Cnichtelawa, sipe socha de Chinton'; *The Great Roll of the Pipe for the Twenty-First Year of the Reign of King Henry II*, AD 1174–5, Pipe Roll Society 22 (London, 1897), p. 94, 'sipe socha de Humeliford' (H. M. Cam, 'Early Groups of Hundreds', in *Liberties and Communities in Medieval England* [Cambridge, 1944], pp. 91–6). This suggests that a complete level of organization of resources could exist leaving practically no trace in eleventh-century documents. For Buckinghamshire, see *VCH Bucks.*, vol. 1, ed. W. Page (London, 1905), pp. 225–6. I am grateful to Jim Bradbury for his figures.

[99] Stamford, DB Lincs. S 1 (fol. 336d); Bedford, DB Beds. B 1 (fol. 209a); Exeter, DB Devon C 5 (fol. 100a).

[100] Leicester, DB Leics. C 2 (fol. 230a); Warwick, DB Warwicks. B 6 (fol. 238a); Colchester, DB Essex B 6 (LDB fol. 107r); Maldon, DB Essex 24:63 (LDB fol. 48r). Hollister (*Anglo-Saxon Military Organization*, p. 115, n. 2) notes that the Maldon ship served for forty days in the twelfth century.

[101] *Hemingi Chartularium*, ed. Hearne, vol. 1, p. 78.

[102] Hollister, *Anglo-Saxon Military Institutions*, pp. 114–15.

[103] Gillmor, 'Naval Logistics of the Cross-Channel Operation, 1066'.

in the reign the thegn Ælfhelm bequeathed a *scegth* to the Ramsey community. Archbishop Ælfric of Canterbury left three ships, the best with sixty helmets and mailcoats to the king, another to the people of his diocese and a third to Wiltshire where he had formerly been bishop. Bishop Ælfwold of Crediton also left Æthelred a *scegth* of sixty-four oars, 'all ready except for the rowlocks'.[104] Perhaps the most significant of these examples is Æthelhelm's ownership of a ship of which he could dispose in his will. It implies that while the kingdom was organised to pay for ships and to provide their crews, the actual ownership of vessels could be vested in individuals. This opens a further possibility, that part of the cost could be offset by employing the vessels for personal gain when they were not required for war.

The necessity of providing crews remained, however. Hollister has demonstrated that the obligation to serve in the host covered service by both land and sea and that the same men performed both services. At the rate of service given in the Domesday survey of Berkshire, that is one man from five hides, a crew of sixty men would be provided from three hundred hides. The Domesday passage also sets the term of service at two months. This explains why Edward's fleet returned to London for relief crews in 1051, and how Harold was able to keep a fleet on the south coast until early September in 1066.[105] The size of the crew is confirmed by the equipment Archbishop Æhelhelm included in the vessel he bequeathed to the king, although the sixty-four oars of the Crediton ship warns against imposing uniformity where it is not to be expected. If the ships provided by the ship-sokes were likely to have been of different sizes, we should not press too closely the link between sixty men and three hundred hides. Reality is untidy whereas historians sometimes look too hard for patterns. What exactly a *scegth* was is not clear. The term is of Scandinavian origin and meant 'longship'. The gloss, *scapha, vel trieris, litel scip tel sceigth* is contradictory and the explanation that 'evidently it was the shape, not the size, which was the distinguishing feature of the *scegþ*' appears wide of the mark.[106] Nevertheless, the evidence that the normal English warship of the late tenth and eleventh century had some sixty oars takes us back to Alfred's ships at the end of the ninth century.

The naval resources of men and money available to the rulers of England in the eleventh century were several and considerable. They are powerful testimony to the control these kings had over their subjects, and to the co-operation they had from them. Yet in defence they were inadequate. There were three successful takeovers of England in the first seventy years of the century by Cnut, Harthecnut and William.[107] Moreover, on a lesser scale the returns from exile

---

[104] S 1487, Whitelock, *Anglo-Saxon Wills*, no. 13, dated 975–1016; S 1488, Whitelock, *Anglo-Saxon Wills*, no. 18, dated 1003×1004; S 1492, Napier and Stevenson, *Crawford Collection*, no. 10, *EHD 1*, no. 122 [above, pp. 118–19].

[105] Hollister, *Anglo-Saxon Military Institutions*, pp. 104–8; DB Berks. B 10 (fol. 56b).

[106] Whitelock, *Anglo-Saxon Wills*, p. 137.

[107] A fourth was attempted in 1058 by Magnus of Norway, although it is dismissed by the chronicler [ASC D 1058]; cf. Stenton, *Anglo-Saxon England*, 3rd edn, p. 560.

of Godwine in 1052 and Ælfgar in 1055 could not be prevented, although Tostig was eventually driven off in 1066. Nor was it possible to prevent Viking raids.[108] William did not employ Old English methods against the Scandinavian invasions. real or projected, of 1069–70 and 1085 due partly to the destruction of the indigenous military resources during the Conquest. But as a successful invader. poacher turned gamekeeper, he may have understood the problems of defending an island, problems which were to recur to English kings for four more centuries. The fleets which Æthelred and Edward mustered at Sandwich were essentially a deterrent to invasion. The chance that they would actually intercept an enemy fleet at sea and fight was remote. The available resources were most successfully employed in projecting English power abroad. Within the British Isles the last success of the Old English fleet came in 1063 when Harold led ships from Bristol (presumably the ship-service of the shires around the Severn) to north Wales.[109] When it came to preventing invasions, raids on the coasts of England or landings by invaders with support within the kingdom, medieval naval technology had no answer in the eleventh century as in the fifteenth.[110]

Some issues may be explored which suggest maintenance of a phenomenon which, while not *strictu sensu*, a 'navy', was a significant naval force. Other interpretations have focused on the 'foreign' service of naval organization. Shashi Jayakumar highlighted the significance of the establishment of a new system of organization under Edgar. For Jayakumar, the contentious systems of ship-sokes were not so much an issue as the use of mercenaries who played an important role in maintaining English defence during the middle years of the tenth century.[111]

An original perspective was taken by Hirokazu Tsurushima, who noted the difference between salmon and herring fleets in English waters in the eleventh century. Salmon fishermen were prevalant in western England while, Tsurushima wrote, the organization of ship fyrds in south-eastern England could be related to the organization of herring fleets in the eleventh century.[112] While, notwithstanding the olfactory implications, one may question whether the different types of fishing vessels were necessarily prime movers for naval strategy or whether their crews were part-time fishermen, Tsurushima's paper highlights the likelihood that there was no clear distinction between 'naval' and 'civilian' vessels. One does

[108] ASC C 1048; Plummer-Earle, vol. I, p. 166, when the fleet was called out after the attack.

[109] ASC D 1063; Plummer-Earle, vol. I, p. 191.

[110] I am thinking of C. F. Richmond, 'English Naval Power in the Fifteenth Century', *History* 52 (1967), pp. 1–15.

[111] Jayakumar, 'Some Reflections on the "Foreign Policies" of Edgar "The Peaceable"', pp. 17–37. A useful – though more conventional – summary of Edgar's naval systems is in P. Rex, *Edgar: King of the English, 959–75* (Stroud, 2007), pp. 74–83.

[112] H. Tsurushima, 'The Eleventh Century in England Through Fish-Eyes: Salmon, Herring, Oysters, and 1066', *ANS* 29 (2007 for 2006), pp. 193–213.

not have to be an exponent of the part-time 'general fyrd' to see the benefits of the naval service of fishing fleets and the fact that specialized vessels may also have been employed for other duties.

Hooper makes useful observations on the connections between naval service and the endowment of ecclesiastics.[113] Amongst the evidence which he highlights is a document relating to the bishopric of London, which seems to be a memorandum referring to the lands providing the crew members, presumably for a ship provided by the bishopric.[114] S 1383, a letter dating from between 1001 and 1012 from Bishop Æthelric of Sherborne to Æthelmær, the official (perhaps acting ealdorman)[115] of the South-Western Provinces, indicates Æthelmær's responsibilities in the oversight of the receipt of a ship-scot.[116]

> Bishop Æthelric cordially greets Æthelmær. And I declare that there is an absence of ship-scot of the amount which many of my predecessors [had] by the witness of the whole people, at New[ton?]: One [hide] at *Bubbancumbe*, and two at Alton, seven at Up Cerne, five at Clifton, at Hewish […], at Trill two, at *Wyllon* one, at *Buchæmatune* five, at Dibberworth three,[117] at *Peder*[…], of the abbess, one. This is, in all, an absence of thirty-three hides from three-hundred hides which other bishops previously had in their *scyr*. And if it were your will, you might readily do that so I had it all thus [i.e. in the same manner]. Yet it is said to us that we may not be allowed the estate at Holcombe which we previously had in times past. Therefore, I shall suffer [the loss] of all the amount [i.e. at Holcombe] and all that which my predecessors had. That is [in total] forty-two hides.

Although Katherine Barker considers the date of the charter to after 1008, on the basis that it is a response to the provision of ships recorded in the Anglo-Saxon Chronicle,[118] Æthelric's letter may relate to a different system from that of

---

[113] Hooper, 'Some Observations on the Navy in Late Anglo-Saxon England', pp. 210–11 (pp. 158–60, above).

[114] S 1458a (*c.* AD 1000). See P. Taylor, 'The Endowment and Military Obligations of the See of London: A Reassessment of Three Sources', *ANS* 14 (1992 for 1991), pp. 287–312, and, for the Essex estates related in the document, Hart, *The Danelaw*, pp. 205–20. I am grateful to Matt Bennett for the suggestion that the order of these estates is an indication of a mnemonic for the transmission of an oral record, but I am not convinced that there is sufficient alliteration in the name forms to sustain this suggestion.

[115] See Keynes, *Diplomas of King Æthelred*, p. 197, n. 163.

[116] M. A. O'Donovan (ed.), *Charters of Sherborne*, Anglo-Saxon Charters 3 (London, 1988), pp. 46–7. An alternative translation and edition is provided by Harmer, *Anglo-Saxon Writs*, pp. 269–70.

[117] Harmer, *Anglo-Saxon Writs*, p. 270, reads 'Dibberwurðe' as 'Dibberford'. However, Dibberworth, alias Dibberwood, was a discrete messuage near Broadwindsor in the eighteenth century: Somerset Archive and Record Service, DD\DNL/149, Bailward of Horsington Manuscripts, accessed via The National Archives 'Access to Archives' site, <http://www.nationalarchives.gov.uk/A2A/> (accessed 20 Jan. 2010).

[118] K. Barker, 'Sherborne in AD 998: The Benedictine Abbey and its Estate', in *St. Wulfsige and Sherborne: Essays to Celebrate the Millenium of the Benedictine Abbey, 998–1998*, ed. K. Barker, D. A. Hinton, and A. Hunt, Bournemouth University School of Conservation Sciences Occasional Paper 8 (Oxford, 2005), pp. 149–63, at p. 159 (citing ASC CDE 1008). However, see also O'Donovan, *Charters of Sherborne*, p. 50, who dates it to 1001×12.

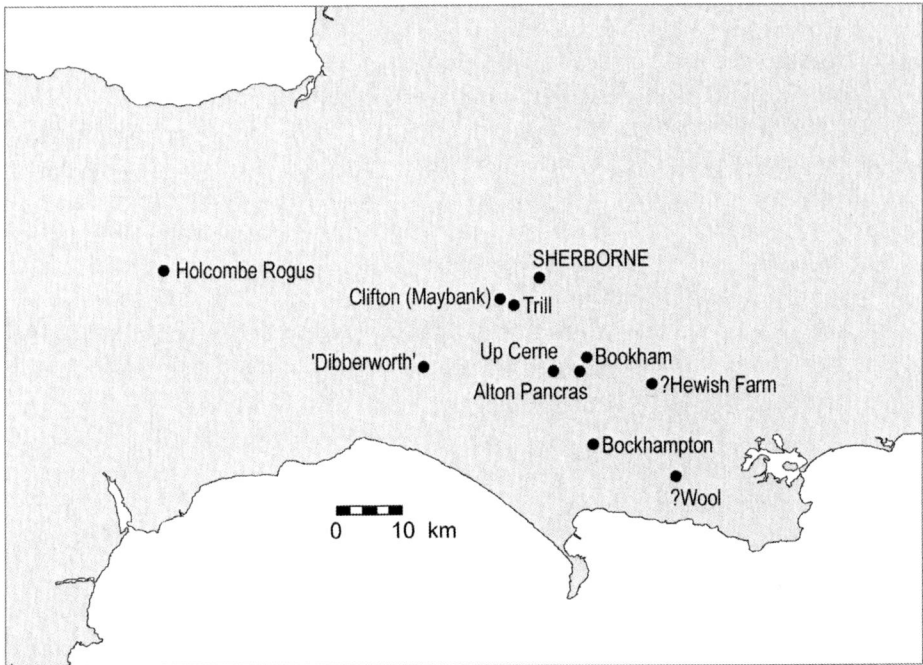

Fig. 4.3 Identifiable places referred to in a letter by Bishop Æthelric of Sherborne (S 1383) regarding the absence of 'ship scot'. (Bookham and Bockhampton are possible candidates for *Buchæmatune*.)

1008, namely that a *scir* (presumably in its original meaning of a 'share' [of land] rather than a shire) would provide a ship: not a diocese *per se*, nor every 300 hides in the kingdom. The document allows a glimpse of how the maintenance of obligations was a process, arguably an ongoing process, of claims and negotiations.[119] In this process the bishop presumably felt it appropriate to labour his point by providing a summary of the loss of lands and income at the end of the document. Mary O'Donovan, the most recent editor of the charter, suggests that it points 'to a substratum of administrative documents that must have existed in the late pre-Conquest period, letters exchanged between officials concerning administrative affairs, which may have borrowed the format of more weighty documents, but had no particular testatory powers in themselves.'[120] Finally, the notion that the ealdorman (or someone acting in that capacity) had such responsibilities sheds light on Æthelmær's predecessor, his father Æthelweard.

Æthelweard's Chronicon and records of nautical terminology

References to ships in Æthelweard's *Chronicon* deserve consideration in their own right. Æthelweard wrote at an important point in maritime development,

[119] For a Norman comparison, see E. M. C. van Houts, 'The Ship List of William the Conqueror', *ANS* 10 (1988 for 1987), pp. 159–83.
[120] O'Donovan, *Charters of Sherborne*, p. 48.

at the beginning of the Second Viking Age. The Viking Wars of Alfred were remembered using evidence from Æthelweard's own time. Æthelweard's elaborate Latin vocabulary and limitations in syntax are well known,[121] but the ealdorman's experience should not be dismissed lightly when considering his nautical references. Similar arguments have been proposed by William Sayers regarding Geffrei Gaimar's use, two centuries after Æthelweard, of Norse-derived nautical vocabulary in relation to the Viking attacks on England – so it should hardly be surprising that vocabulary reflected experience.[122] Publishing his edition of the *Chronicon* in 1962, Æthelweard's editor, Alistair Campbell, was not aware of the developments in maritime technology which were were better understood from that same year onwards following the raising of a variety of eleventh-century vessels wrecked in Roskilde Fjord, and so did not infer substantive differences between the types of vessels in the terminology used by Æthelweard, which Campbell attributed to access to glosses.[123]

As Table 4.1 shows, Æthelweard seems to have sought suitable Latin terms to describe specific vessels. This is indicated most clearly by his use of the term *lembus* to refer to what the Anglo-Saxon Chronicle recorded as a 'boat without oars' (*bate butan ælcum gereþrum*) from Ireland (i.e. a sewn-hide boat). Amongst the more obviously warlike vessels, the most common Latin term is *dromon*, which refers to a specific type of longship.[124] The general words *carinae*, *puppes* and *naves*, as well as the term for a fleet, *classus*, are used for Æthelweard's collective descriptions of larger fleets. Given that he says that no 'fleet' ('classicus' – *sic*) had come to England since Athelstan's day, this may cast light on Æthelweard's early Æthelredian context:[125] a fleet was different from the sporadic activities of Viking pirates, which seem to have been characteristic of the Viking activities of the early part of Æthelred's reign.[126]

Of the words available to Æthelweard, *dromon* presumably met the need to describe a warship when referring to single appearances or small flotillas of Viking ships. The term *dromon* was rare in a tenth-century English context, suggesting that, although a deliberate Grecism (as the term for a type of Byzantine vessel),

---

[121] Winterbottom, 'The Style of Æthelweard'. See above, pp. 2–3, and Campbell's introduction in Æthelweard, *Chronicon*, p. ix and, on Æthelweard's glossal interests, pp. xlvi–xlvii.

[122] W. Sayers, 'Ships and Sailors in Geiffrei Gaimar's *Estoire des Engleis*', *Modern Language Review* 98 (2003), pp. 299–310. See also W. Sayers, 'Twelfth-Century Norman and Irish Literary Evidence for Ship-Building and Sea-Faring Techniques of Norse Origin', *The Heroic Age: A Journal of Early Medieval Northwestern Europe* 8 (2005) <http://www.heroicage.org/issues/8/sayers.html> (accessed 24 Sept. 2009).

[123] Crumlin-Pedersen, *The Skuldelev Ships I*, pp. 23–41, and, for 'Skuldelev 2' (originally thought to have been the remains of more than one vessel), pp. 142–5 (above, p. 166). Campbell, 'Introduction', p. xlvi.

[124] R. E. Latham and D. R. Howlett (eds), *Dictionary of Medieval Latin from British Sources*, vol. I, 5 fascicules (Oxford, 1975–97), fasc. 4, p. 728. Æthelweard's use appears to be the earliest medieval Insular use before the twelfth century.

[125] Æthelweard, *Chronicon*, p. 54. See ch. 1.

[126] See Lavelle, *Aethelred II*, pp. 52–7.

Table 4.1 Terms for ships used in *Æthelweard*, *Chronicon*, and other narrative sources

Term used	ASC term	Others	Location	Year	Notes (*Æthelweard; other sources if appropriate*)
dromones	scipu	iii naves normannorum (Annals of St Neots s.a. 789)†	Dorchester (Dorset)	c. 789 (p. 26)	
carinae	sciphlaesta		Carhampton (Som.)	836 (given as 833, p. 30)	sciphlæsta (also recorded at Carhampton in ASC 843 but Æthelweard places that action on land)
dromones	scipu	ex navibus eorum novem naves (Asser, ch. 6)	Kent	851 (p. 31)	ships captured by Anglo-Saxons (Asser: lit. 'from their ships nine ships')
classis ... paganorum / carinae	scipu	magnus paganorum exercitus / naves (Asser, ch. 4)	Thames	851 (p. 31)	large fleet ('350 ships')
dromon	n/a (no reference)		arrival of Sceaf in Skaney	855 (p. 33)	reference to Anglo-Saxons' ancestry
naves	n/a		n/a	n/a (p. 38)	metaphor of port
dromon	sciphere / sciplæsta	sex naves paganorum (Asser, ch. 48)	off Wessex coast	875 (p. 41)	captured by Alfred (ship captured referred to as 'one' in ASC)
carinae (supremae)	sciphere		Exeter (Devon) & Swanage (Dorset)	877 (p. 42)	
moneres	mid xiii scipum		Devon	878 (p. 43)	
artemon	n/a (no ships mentioned)		Gaul	880 (p. 43)	Gaul 'sought by ship'

Table 4.1 continued

Term used	ASC term	Others	Location	Year	Notes (Æthelweard; other sources if appropriate)
exiuit nauigio / dromones quatuor	mid scipum ut on sæ / feower sciphlæstas Deniscra monna / scipa tu genam / scipheras	navali proelio contra paganicas naves in mare congressus est (Asser, ch. 64)	Off Wessex coast?	882 (p. 44)	Alfred 'went out by ship' and met vessels (ASC: 'four ship-crews of Danish men'; seized two ships'; Asser: Alfred 'fought a naval battle against the pagan ships at sea')
proprias sedes	scipu		Kentish coast?	885 (p. 44)	'their own stations' (proprias sedes) used to refer to ships
karinæ	xvi scipu wicenga	Naves (Asser, ch. 67)	Stour mouth	885 (p. 45)	16 ships met King Alfred's fleet
cetera classis piratica / deponunt scarmos	micelne sciphere wicenga	Naves / navali proelio (Asser, ch. 67)	Kentish coast	885 (p. 45)	'the rest of the pirate fleet' met; reference to rowing gear being laid aside by Vikings for sea battle (ASC: 'great ship army of Vikings'; Asser refers to a 'naval battle')
lembus	anum bate butan ælcum gerebrum		Ireland to Cornwall	891 (p. 48)	Details provided of a small boat sewn from hides; Æthelweard provides more details on the actions of the pilgrims than ASC (perhaps due to the pilgrims' arrival in Cornwall?)
construunt classem	wurdon gescipode		Boulogne	892 (p. 48)	fleet 'built' in Æthelweard & ASC
rostra / puppes	Crossing related in general terms / mid .ccl. (hunde) scipa		Lympne harbour / Appledore (Kent)	892 (p. 48)	ASC relates the number; Æthelweard does not
naues	n/a (ASC does not refer directly to Lympne fleet)		Mersea (Essex)	893 (p. 50)	Fleet from Appledore 'made a good voyage.' Mersea is referred to as Kent but actually off Essex, as ASC acknowledges (perhaps Æthelweard saw it as part of Kentish province from his south-western perspective?)

† The Annals of St Neots with Vita Prima Sancti Neoti, ed. D. N. Dumville and M. Lapidge, Anglo-Saxon Chronicle: A Collaborative Edition 17 (Cambridge, 1985), p. 39.

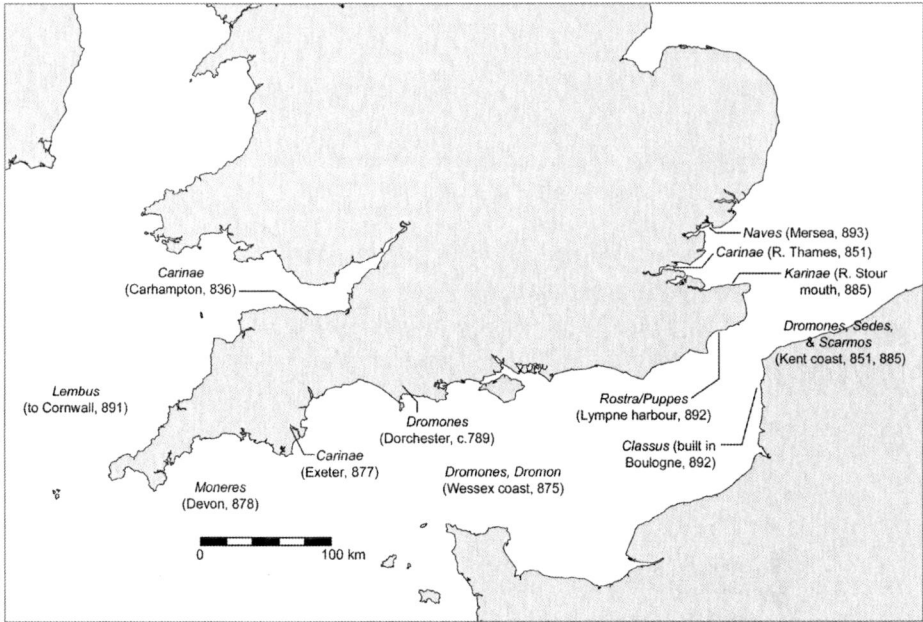

Fig. 4.4 Ealdorman Æthelweard's references to different types of vessel

it met a specific need.[127] This usage was in contrast to the Anglo-Saxon Chronicle's mostly consistent use of *scipu* and *scipherigas*, as well as Asser's descriptions of Viking fleets, which are often just referred to as *naves*,[128] and it may reflect knowledge of a development of specialist warships, forerunners of the Hedeby and Skuldelev types.

Such differences in terminology are not illogical for Æthelweard, whose area of jurisdiction was almost entirely coastal. Æthelweard's consistent distinctions between *dromones* and *carinae* (keels) are noteworthy.[129] As may be seen in Fig. 4.4, *carinae* appear in references to ships drawn up on the coast or, more often, on river estuaries; *dromones* tend to be referred to as individual ships (in the case of those landing at Portland, Dorset, *c.* 789, three ships) or small numbers of ships at sea. This is unlikely to mean that Æthelweard thought that they were actually different types of vessel but perhaps shows a perception that a ship at sea would function as a warship, a type of vessel which was becoming distinct in the naval architecture of the later tenth century and which would be an obvious threat

[127] J. H. Pryor, 'From Drōmon to Galea: Mediterranean Bireme Galleys, AD 500–1300', in *Age of the Galley*, ed. Gardiner, pp. 101–16.

[128] ASC and Asser references are indicated in Table 4.1. References to *naves* and variant forms thereof can also be found in ninth-century Frankish sources, e.g. AB 862, 863, and 865.

[129] The term *cyuli* translated by Michael Winterbottom as 'keels', is used to refer 'in [the Saxons'] own language' to *longis navibus* in Gildas' references to the arrival of ships in Britain in *De Excidio Britanniae*, ch. 23, in Gildas, *The Ruin of Britain and Other Works*, trans. Winterbottom, pp. 26 (trans.) and 97 (text).

if seen from the coast.[130] On the other hand, once on the coast their function as carriers – 'keels' – was most apparent. This may be revealing of an author who was conversant with naval defence and the historiographical expectations of what constituted an attacking force.

The lack of exaggeration for the number of ships recorded in the *Chronicon*'s 892 entry, in comparison with the Anglo-Saxon Chronicle's large number, is also noteworthy. Quantifying fleets is a long-standing controversy in the study of medieval armies. As we have seen, the issue of the size of armies and their associated fleets was raised in Peter Sawyer's *Age of the Vikings*,[131] but we should also bear in mind a comment made by J. O. Prestwich on counting vessels at anchor from an advantageous viewpoint. Prestwich highlighted the fact that under such circumstances fleets could be gauged 'with tolerable accuracy'.[132] Æthelweard may have had a vested interest in understanding the number of ships in a fleet, although the large figure of 350 vessels in 851, recorded by Æthelweard, Asser and the Anglo-Saxon Chronicle alike, suggests that we should probably not place too much store on the 892 record.

It is perhaps revealing that, in common with Asser (who wrote around 893), Æthelweard did not provide an equivalent passage to the Anglo-Saxon Chronicle's record of the building of ships and their use in 896.[133] This may suggest that the building of the longships was an experiment of the late ninth century which did not have a direct impact upon Æthelweard's own experience in the tenth century.[134] The most contemporary, detailed entries of the Anglo-Saxon Chronicle, those of the 890s, also refer to the Danish ships as *æscas*. This was an Anglicization of a specific Old Norse term, *askr*, noting that they were a particular threat.[135] At this point there was a particular interest in naval building, perhaps at a time in the ninth century when it mattered most.[136] Æthelweard seems to have shown an equivalent interest in what he saw as significant events from a late tenth-century perspective. It is interesting that an early eleventh-century Anglo-Saxon Chronicle entry provided a direct reference to a type of warship in Old English, a *sceið*.[137] One can only wonder what Latin terms Æthelweard would have used if he had occasion to record English vessels from his own time rather than the range of threats of Viking ships from an earlier age.

---

[130] See below, pp. 174–5.

[131] Sawyer, *The Age of the Vikings*, pp. 120–31. See also J. L. Nelson, 'The Vikings in Francia', in *The Oxford Illustrated History of the Vikings*, ed. P. Sawyer (Oxford, 1997), pp. 19–47, at p. 39. See above, pp. 41–2.

[132] Prestwich, *Place of War in English History*, p. 33, referring to the Second Crusade fleet at Dartmouth (Devon) in 1147.

[133] Above, p. 143. For a discussion of their operation, see below, pp. 287–97.

[134] Rodger, *Safeguard of the Sea*, p. 17.

[135] ASC 896. See Swanton, *Anglo-Saxon Chronicles*, p. 98, n. 1.

[136] For the context of the annals for 893–6, see S. D. Keynes, 'A Tale of Two Kings: Alfred the Great and Æthelred the Unready', *TRHS* 5th ser. 36 (1986), pp. 195–217, at pp. 200–1.

[137] ASC CDE 1008; see above, p. 157.

The organization of coastal defence

Having established the knowledge of naval architecture indicated by Æthel-weard's *Chronicon*, it is pertinent to address the organization of the maritime system related to this knowledge.[138] A charter from the time of Edward 'the Martyr' referred to the responsibilities of Æthelweard's office. It is the only charter grant-ing land to Æthelweard which survives, and is interesting that coastal watch was one of the responsibilities associated with that land. It was 'to be free from all royal dues, except fyrd-service, construction of fortresses and maritime watch' (*libere ab omni regali censu excepta expeditione arcisue munimine et uigiliis marinis*).[139] More normally, as Dorothy Whitelock noted, bridge-building would be the expected third service reserved from the general immunity that a charter bestowed. So, presumably, the maritime guard reservation was related to the coastal position of the land in the charter.[140] This appears to be the only charter referring to land, coastal or otherwise, which makes this explicit reservation, although as some later charters are not as explicit,[141] it cannot be assumed that other lands held as bookland did not include maritime guard. The eleventh-century *Rectitudines Singularum Personarum* makes it clear that this was an expected service of a thegn in return for the right of landholding.[142] However, the record of maritime service is rare in the surviving corpus of evidence. While it may not have been a unique reservation, it was not typical of coastal lands either, though it may be indicative of Æthelweard's service. There is no indication that 'vigiliis marinis' referred to in the charter (a synonym for the Old English *sæ-weard*, 'sea watch') included the obligation to intercept ships at sea as well as looking out for them from land. The *Rectitudines Singularum Personarum* also refers to a thegn's obligation to provide for a 'guard ship' (*scorp to friðscipe*) so it may well have been associated with such obligations, as indeed may any fleet which had operated during the reign of Edgar, if it were still extant in 977. Although we cannot expect Æthelweard to have undertaken any such naval duties himself, one might expect the responsibility for coastal watch to have been of a high status. This is apparent in view of Æthel-weard's record of the name of the unfortunate Beaduheard, who met Viking raid-ers around 789 at Portland, where there is a coastal promontory not unlike those of Cornwall.[143] Such high status is also indicated in the appearance in *Beowulf* of a coastguard who hailed Beowulf upon his arrival in the land of the Danes.[144]

---

[138] See also the discussion of beacons in ch. 6, below.

[139] S 832 (AD 977). Reservations on the charter's authenticity, made by P. Chaplais, 'The Authenticity of the Royal Anglo-Saxon Diplomas of Exeter', *Bulletin of the Institute of Historical Research* 39 (1966), pp. 1–34, at p. 16, should be noted but cf. the later observations in n. 148, below.

[140] *EHD* 1, p. 566.

[141] Another south-western charter, S 951 (AD 1018), although of problematic provenance, does not describe the reservation of services.

[142] *Gesetze*, vol. 1, p. 444; trans. *EHD* 2, p. 875.

[143] Æthelweard, *Chronicon*, p. 26; *Annals of St Neots*, ed. Dumville and Lapidge, p. 39.

[144] *Beowulf*, lines 229–57, in *The Anglo-Saxon Poetic Records: A Collective Edition, No. 4: Beowulf and Judith*, ed. E. van K. Dobbie (New York, 1953), pp. 9–10.

While I do not propose to make a case for south-western England in the origin of the *Beowulf* poem, it may be noted that there are echoes in the cliff-top vigil of the unnamed watchman of the poem for the cliff-tops of southern Cornwall, for which Æthelweard had responsibility.[145] In view of the poem's eleventh-century transmission (regardless of whether it was written in the eleventh century),[146] the coastguard's remarks in the poem about protecting the land of the Danes from a ship-army (*scip-herge*)[147] must have been supremely ironic to a contemporary English audience.

With this in mind, it seems unusual that charters relating to coastal land were not more explicit in recording the duties of maritime watch. Until there is a full assessment of the rights and duties associated with Anglo-Saxon charter formulae in the context of the landscape, we can only speculate as to whether the reference to *vigiliis marinis* in S 832 was a new duty associated with a new grant of land. Alternatively, as Charles Insley has suggested, citing the appearance of *vigiliis marinis* in another charter from Plympton Priory, Devon, this may have been a peculiarly south-western element in charter records for a maritime region subject to piracy,[148] an area which did not have fortifications west of Lydford.

A number of lands on the south coast of England are associated with grants from Edward's successor, Æthelred II (Fig. 4.5).[149] At least one of these grants indicates the possibility of ministerial landholding associated with defence, even if an explicit reference to maritime watch is not included in the formulae. Mary O'Donovan suggests that the recipient of Seaton (*Fleet*), in Devon may have been the reeve mentioned in the Anglo-Saxon Chronicle A MS entry from four years earlier, associated with the Devon battle of Pinhoe in 1001.[150] Although the viewshed provided by the land was not as good as that at Beer, to the west,[151] the presence of a *herepath* – an 'army road' – in the bounds of the charter, reflected in the modern 'Harepath Hill', may indicate that the land was associated with

---

[145] This observation is made in Hill and Sharp, 'Anglo-Saxon Beacon System', p. 158 (reprinted below, p. 219).

[146] C. Chase (ed.), *The Dating of Beowulf*, Toronto Old English 6 (Toronto, 1981).

[147] *Beowulf*, line 243. For the Danish landscape of *Beowulf*, including a discussion of Danish cliffs (although seen from the perspective of Beowulf rather than from that of the coastguard), see G. R. Overing and M. Osborn, *Landscape of Desire: Partial Stories of the Medieval Scandinavian World* (Minneapolis, 1994), pp. 1–37. See also M. Gelling, 'The Landscape of Beowulf', *ASE* 31 (2002), pp. 7–11.

[148] Insley, 'Athelstan, Charters and the English in Cornwall', pp. 21–3, citing O. J. Padel, 'Two New Pre-Conquest Charters for Cornwall', *Cornish Studies* 6 (1978), pp. 20–7.

[149] Calshot, Hants (S 836 [AD 980]) (although a grant for a fishery), Havant, Hants (S 837 [AD 980]), Bathingbourne and Fratton, Hants (confirmed in S 842 [AD 982]), South Heighton, Sussex (S 869 [AD 988]), Colworth, Sussex (S 872 [AD 988]), Chalk, Kent (S 877 [AD 996]), Lyme, Dorset (S 895 [AD 998], confirmation), Seaton, Devon (S 910 [AD 1005]), Lawling in Latchingdon, Essex (S 911 [AD 1005], a confirmation), Graveney, Cooling and Thanet, Kent, and Lawling, Essex (S 914 [AD 1006 for 1002], confirmation), Wyke Regis, Dorset (S 938 [undated]), Weston in South Stoneham, Hants (S 944 [AD 990]).

[150] O'Donovan, *Charters of Sherborne*, p. 67.

[151] See J. B. Davidson, 'Seaton Before the Conquest', *Transactions of the Devonshire Association* 17 (1885), pp. 193–8.

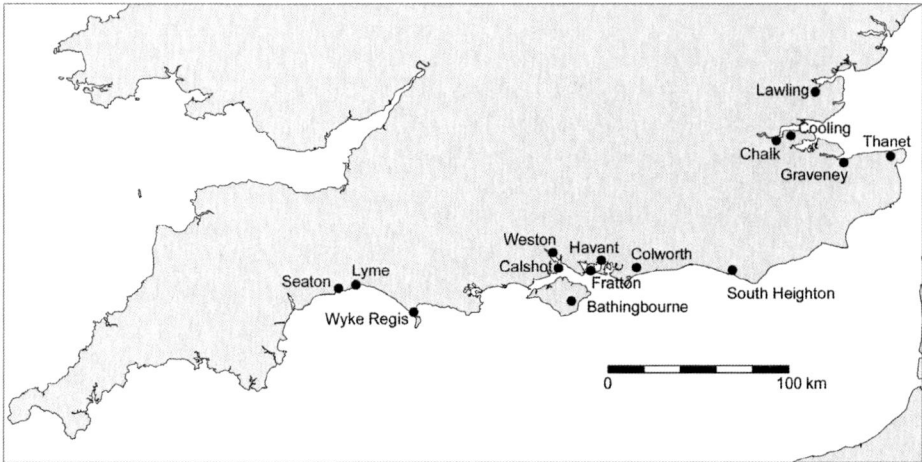

Fig. 4.5 Coastal lands referred to in charters of King Æthelred II

defence, even if the charter did not specify that fact.[152] The charter may be evidence, albeit on a smaller scale, of the sort of policies suggested by Robin Fleming of the reallocation of defensive responsibilities into private hands,[153] though the receipt of the *mancuses* described in the charter in exchange for the land may have been Æthelred's primary motivation for agreeing to it.

The record of the grant by Æthelred of another coastal land, at Wyke Regis, by the strategic site of Portland, Dorset, to a certain Atsere, is more problematic.[154] The witness list of the charter recording the grant may have been altered when later copied by a Winchester scribe, to invoke the names of Saints Dunstan, Æthelwold and Oswald, who were presumably seen as adding gravitas to those who were present to witness the original transaction. The name of the recipient, Atsere, is associated with the witnessing of an early Old Minster charter of Cnut, S 956, dating from 1019, but the other witnesses in the Wyke Regis charter, S 938, appear together on the witness lists of other Æthelredian southern English charters. Therefore, once the saintly presences of Dunstan, Æthelwold and Oswald have been dismissed, the composition of the witness list of S 938 may date the charter to the later part of the reign of King Æthelred.[155]

---

[152] O.S. SY238917. For a discussion of the strategic significance of roads, see below, p. 187.

[153] Fleming, *Kings and Lords in Conquest England*, pp. 91–103, for the eleventh century; for ninth- and tenth-century royal acquisition of 'strategic' land, R. Fleming, 'Monastic Lands and England's Defence in the Viking Age', *EHR* 100 (1985), pp. 247–65. Reservations regarding the details of Fleming's arguments are made by D. N. Dumville, *Wessex and England from Alfred to Edgar: Six Essays on Political, Cultural and Ecclesiastical Revival*, Studies in Anglo-Saxon History 3 (Woodbridge, 1992), pp. 29–54.

[154] S 938 (undated).

[155] Witnesses from S 938 can be seen in S 910 (AD 1005), 911 (AD 1005), 912 (AD 1005), 915 (AD 1007), 918 (AD 1008). See Keynes, *Atlas of Attestations in Anglo-Saxon Charters*, tables lx–lxiv. Lyfing and Ulfcetel's presence in the witness list may date S 938's witness list to between 1002 and 1012: Keynes, *Diplomas of King Æthelred*, p. 268. Keynes (p. 84), notes

To return to Æthelweard's Cornish estates, as can be seen from Fig. 4.6, lands on the Lizard Peninsula would have been well placed for coastal sighting and signalling. Although, as Della Hooke noted, the lands circumscribed in S 832 were inland, this was comparatively high ground, parts of which offered views far out to sea to the west, south and east.[156] Considering that any ships travelling around the Lizard Peninsula would have had to give a wide berth to the coastline immediately below the cliff tops, any viewsheds were advantageous so long as a defensive system was well maintained; thus, the territory of the English kingdom was effectively extended.[157] Perhaps, given that other areas, such as Land's End, offered similar viewsheds of strategically important coastlines, S 832 might be indicative of a number of charters now lost to us. David Hill and Sheila Sharp, in a paper reproduced in chapter 6, have highlighted the references to beacons in Anglo-Saxon charters relating to estates further inland but we should note that charter boundary clauses generally only recorded points which marked the boundaries of estates rather than features inside the boundaries. Of course, the guard duty could have been fulfilled in a different place from where the estate was held, but the estate itself was well placed for such a vigil; the excellent location of a coastal estate and the record of the duty of coastal guard can hardly be a coincidence. At this location it is likely that any potentially hostile vessel travelling east along the English Channel would have been heading to the southern coast and this may explain why the estate recorded such a crucial duty.

If the estate had maritime responsibilities, this chapter may be concluded by taking into account the significance of the reeve's responsibilities for escorting Vikings to the royal tun c. 789. This did not necessarily mean that the reeve was in Portland on coastal guard duties, but that he had connections with the man or men assigned the responsibilities. The evidence of a charter of the late ninth century, relating to land at Sutton Poyntz, on the coast of Dorset near to Portland, may indicate that attention was given to the importance of the duties associated with coastal lands.[158] King Alfred received Sutton Poyntz in exchange for estates

---

that S 938, amongst other charters, uses formulations from Edgar and early Æthelred charters, although for S 938 his argument is partly based on the style of attestation for Archbishop Dunstan and the immunity clause, a type which can also be found in S 896 (AD 999), an authentic Abingdon charter.

[156] Useful points are Keverne Beacon, at O.S. SW 773198, and further east at O.S. SW 795203. The boundaries are described in D. Hooke, *Pre-Conquest Charter-Bounds of Devon and Cornwall* (Woodbridge, 1994), pp. 46–52, and the identification of Keverne Beacon on the southern boundary is at p. 49, citing C. Henderson, 'The Topography of the Parish of St Keverne', *Annual Rep R Cornwall Polytechnic Soc*, new ser. 7:1 (1931), pp. 49–75, at p. 61 (notes related to this article are available online as C. Henderson, *The Topography of the Parish of St Keverne Cornwall from the Original Documents and Personal Investigations*, at <www.st-keverne.com/History/Book/hendersons.html> [accessed 2 Sept. 2009]). Although there is no beacon described in the bounds of S 832, this should not preclude the pre-Conquest establishment of one.

[157] It is pertinent to note here the 'mutability' of boundaries noted in K. M. Wickham-Crowley, 'Living on the *Ecg*: The Mutable Boundaries of Land and Water in Anglo-Saxon Contexts', in *A Place to Believe In: Locating Medieval Landscapes*, ed. C. A. Lees and G. R. Overing (University Park, PA, 2006), pp. 85–110.

[158] S 347 (AD 891).

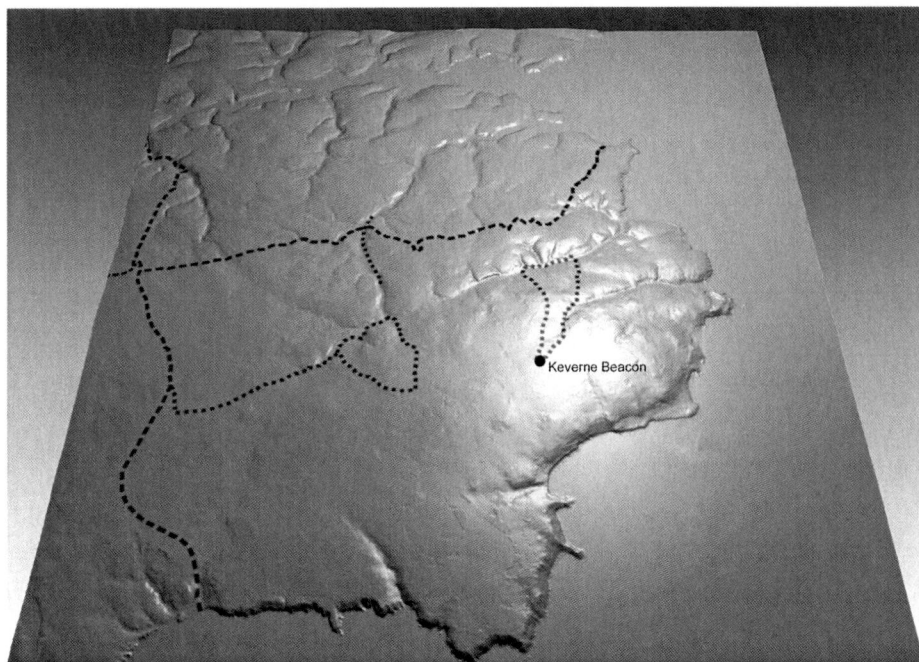

Fig. 4.6 Terrain of Æthelweard's Cornish estates recorded in the charter S 832. Dashed lines indicate parish boundaries; dotted lines follow the approximate course of those bounds in the charter which have been identified by Della Hooke. The view is from the south; the peninsula is approx. 3.4 miles/ 5.4 km at its widest point.

further inland in Somerset and Dorset, from a certain Beorhtwulf, *comes*, perhaps the same man as the ealdorman of Essex recorded by the Anglo-Saxon Chronicle as having died 'of the mortality of cattle and men' in 896. Such lands were not necessarily officially linked to the duties of an ealdorman[159] but it would not seem illogical for lands associated with rewards for duties to have been strategically located, while rulers and their nobles negotiated and renegotiated their landed interests as best they saw fit.[160]

Summary

The relationship between naval service and the defence of the land is notable, as is the evident attention paid to the creation of fleets at least three times during the Viking Age: during the reigns of Alfred, Edgar and Æthelred. If we add to this picture the triumphalist records of Athelstan's naval campaigns, along with the strength of the fleet after the Danish conquests of 1016, the generational significance of naval service is apparent. The need to rebuild a fleet often seems to have emerged in response to the need for defence or offence in almost equal measure.

[159] Lavelle, *Royal Estates in Anglo-Saxon Wessex*, p. 95.
[160] See Fleming, 'Monastic Lands and England's Defence'.

Given the evident connection between private lordship and the possession of ships, it is hardly surprising that a large functioning fleet was not always the first priority. That said, a naval system is evident in the second half of the tenth century. Even if this was no proto-Royal Navy and could not be relied upon to defend the shores against a possible invasion, our glimpses of the attention given to a system suggest that the reasoning behind it was sound. A large, ornately decorated vessel may have been the pride of the posturing super-magnates of the late Anglo-Saxon period, but such vessels, the men willing and able to crew them, and the sentries shivering on cliff-tops provided some stability in times of great threats.

◆ 5 ◆

Campaigns and Strategies

[M]ost recent historians have been so busy getting their armies into the field that they have left themselves little room in which to consider what they did once they were there.

John Gillingham, 'Richard I and the Science of War'[1]

JOHN Gillingham made this incisive comment with regard to the battlefields of the Third Crusade rather than to Anglo-Saxon England, but his point is important: medieval armies were not recruited just for posturing and social cohesion. Nonetheless, the scene he commented on is no longer so limited, and a better understanding of campaign strategies is arguably easier to obtain than it once was. Writing on tenth-century 'grand strategy', Richard Abels commented that, while we know little about Anglo-Saxon tactics on the battlefield, the strategic movements of armies are more discernible in the sources.[2] The logistical arrangements of Anglo-Saxon and Viking forces are, of course, related to how they were paid for, raised and armed. This was discussed in chapters 3 and 4. However, the importance of victualing armies in the field and moving them, whether across land or sea, is addressed in this chapter. 'Universal military principles' raised by military strategists in addressing the strategies of pre-modern armies have their greatest value here, but the balance of different factors may be debatable. For example, such modern strategic concepts as 'Command, Control, Communication, and Intelligence' (C³I) may not translate directly into an early medieval context.[3]

The movement of armies

Campaign strategies may be better understood by considering the problems faced by an army moving across a landscape. This is a process relevant to Viking campaigns in England, and indeed the tenth-century West Saxon and Mercian campaigns. The main factors to be considered are:

[1] J. Gillingham, 'Richard I and the Science of War in the Middle Ages', in *War and Government in the Middle Ages*, ed. J. Gillingham and J. C. Holt (Woodbridge, 1984), pp. 78–91, at p. 78.

[2] R. Abels, 'English Tactics, Strategy and Military Organization in the Late Tenth Century', in *The Battle of Maldon, AD 991*, ed. Scragg, pp. 143–55, at pp. 143–5.

[3] See Gareth Williams's review of Griffith, *The Viking Art of War*, in *EME* 6 (1997), p. 106. Definitions of C³ and C³I are from K. Macksey and W. Woodhouse, *The Penguin Encyclopedia of Modern Warfare from the Crimean War to the Present Day* (Harmondsworth, 1991), p. 60.

Food and supplies – a force needed to be close to centres of power where food was collected and/ or be able to gain supplies by foraging/ ravaging and/ or purchasing food.

Cohesion and co-ordination – a force needed to be kept together where possible, to maintain momentum, to minimize the vulnerability of small groups or individual warriors, while safeguarding against the possibility of disease (the latter issue being affected by the size of an army).

Prestige – a force needed to be seen to be victorious, to seize or hold significant estates and/or towns (or, in the case of defenders, defend them) and win victories where battles took place.

One might note here the influence of A. H. Maslow's famous 'hierarchy of needs', in which the individual human requires basic physiological needs, a sense of group belonging, and ultimately strives for 'self-actualization'.[4] Although necessarily simplistic, the supplies–cohesion–prestige model (see Fig. 5.1) can be applied to most medieval campaigns, as well as many ancient and modern campaigns, indicating a campaigning force's 'hierarchy of needs'. While the art of pre-modern logistics is now a well-established area of study,[5] the balance of the practicality of logistics, a concern of some modern commentators,[6] should be considered with other factors. Keeping such a balance may not have been consciously considered by medieval commanders but it seems to have had a bearing on the decisions taken. Although the principle of feeding an army arguably took precedence over that of keeping it together and, likewise, the latter would have been of more immediate concern to a commander than retaining and enhancing prestige, each of these factors is nonetheless significant and presumably played a part in decision-making; ultimately, to enhance prestige was the 'self-actualization' that a commander needed.

As with Maslow's view of human motivation, too much attention to one factor would have been detrimental to others. In gaining food and supplies (*feorm* or *fostre* in Old English),[7] while ravaging enemy territory could be a strategic aim in itself, an army engaged in foraging (pillaging) lacked cohesion. Thus, as Gillingham noted, its constituent parts were vulnerable to attacks if an enemy force was

---

[4] A. H. Maslow, 'A Theory of Human Motivation', *Psychological Review* 50 (1943), pp. 370–96. I am grateful to Matt Bennett for discussion on this point.

[5] D. W. Engels, *Alexander the Great and the Logistics of the Macedonian Army* (Berkeley, 1978); J. H. Pryor (ed.), *Logistics of Warfare in the Age of the Crusades: Proceedings of a Workshop Held at the Centre for Medieval Studies, University of Sydney, 30 September to 4 October 2002* (Aldershot, 2005); S. McLeod, 'Feeding the *Micel Here* in England *c.* 865–878', *Journal of the Australian Early Medieval Association* 2 (2006), pp. 141–56, available online at <http://home.vicnet.net.au/~medieval/jaema2/mcleod.html> (accessed 24 June 2009). See also B. S. Bachrach, 'Logistics in Pre-Crusade Europe', in *Feeding Mars: Logistics in Western Warfare from the Middle Ages to the Present*, ed. J. A. Lynn, History and Warfare (Boulder, CO, 1993), pp. 57–78.

[6] E.g. Bachrach, 'Logistics in Pre-Crusade Europe'.

[7] Lavelle, 'Geographies of Power in the Anglo-Saxon Chronicle'.

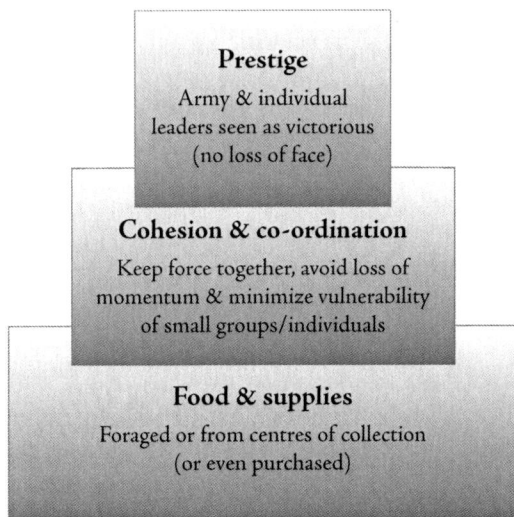

Fig. 5.1 Model of the relationship between supplies, cohesion and prestige in early medieval campaigns

nearby.[8] If an army had to rely on foraging because of inadequate supplies, inertia would have been a problem as the army concentrated on taking supplies rather than on any wider strategic aims.

However, the very collection of renders from estates had a positive return by way of the prestige it conferred upon the recipient. For a Viking force, the seizure of royal, ecclesiastical and aristocratic estates was a statement of the Vikings' dominance of an area, an issue which was not missed by the author of the Anglo-Saxon Chronicle for the years of Æthelred's reign.[9] For a force led by a king or member of the royal family, the use of royal estates was a means of asserting – or reasserting – legitimate power. This is especially apparent in Alfred's campaigns leading up to the Battle of Edington in 878. The former controversies over the location of the battle are discussed in chapter 7,[10] but it is worth setting out the relevant extract from the Anglo-Saxon Chronicle.[11]

> And after, at Easter King Alfred with a small band constructed a fortification [geweorc] at Athelney, and from that fortification he fought the here with the part [dǽl] of the Somerset people who were nearest to it. Then in the seventh week after Easter he rode to Egbert's Stone, to the east of Selwood, and all the people of Somerset and Wiltshire and the part of Hampshire which was on this side of the sea came there to meet him, and were joyful [to see] him. And he set out after one night from those camps [wicum] to Iley [Oak], and afterwards one [night]

[8] J. Gillingham, 'William the Bastard at War', in *Studies in Medieval History Presented to R. Allen Brown*, ed. C. Harper-Bill, C. Holdsworth and J. Nelson (Woodbridge, 1989), pp. 141–58; 'Richard I and the Science of War', p. 85.

[9] Lavelle, 'Geographies of Power in the Anglo-Saxon Chronicle', pp. 208–10

[10] See below, pp. 308–14.

[11] ASC 878.

later to Edington; and there he fought against all the *here*, and put it to flight, and rode after it up to the fortification [*geweorc*], and there laid siege for a fortnight; and then the *here* gave preliminary hostages [*foregislas*] to him, and great oaths that they would [go] from his kingdom, and likewise promised him that their king would accept baptism; and this they performed thus … [the making of peace is discussed in chapter 8, below]

The campaign leading up to the battle of Edington was a conscious statement of royal leadership. As I have argued elsewhere, Alfred's control of Athelney meant control of a region associated with a royal territory.[12] This may be reinforced by Æthelweard's record of Alfred's close followers' receipt of *pastum*, a term which Campbell translates as 'royal maintenance' but may have been a Latin synonym for *feorm*.[13] Furthermore, Alfred's movement across the Somerset and Wiltshire landscape, using the render from significant West Saxon royal estates as he travelled, was a summons of his people; in effect a statement of kingship, highlighting his legitimacy. These were the only royal nightly sojourns recorded in the Anglo-Saxon Chronicle before the eleventh century.[14] Such actions fulfilled the threefold requirements of a supplies-cohesion-prestige model: the king was able to exert control over the landscape with the use of central places maintaining control over a disparate West Saxon force, elevating the king through the link between assemblies and warfare.[15]

Although from a much later source, the account of the assembly of the West Saxon forces before the battle of Edington recorded in Geffrei Gaimar's twelfth-century verse history, *L'Estoire des Engleis*, is notable here. It indicates the link between warfare and assembly politics for the Anglo-Saxons in a manner that suggests access to sources now lost.[16]

> Ceolmer came to him [Alfred] and Chude
> With the nobles [*baruns*] of Somerset,
> Of Wiltshire and of Dorset;
> From Hampshire came Chilman,
> Who had summoned the nobles by *ban*.

[12] Lavelle, 'Geographies of Power in the Anglo-Saxon Chronicle', pp. 202–4

[13] Æthelweard, *Chronicon*, p. 42. See above, p. 110.

[14] The significance of this is discussed in Lavelle, 'Geographies of Power in the Anglo-Saxon Chronicle', pp. 204–10. The eleventh-century accounts, in ASC CDE 1004 and 1006 are recorded during the reign of Æthelred and may be used to criticize a lack of royal power. The royal estates associated with places recorded in the Chronicle render 'farms of one night' an important element in the corpus of royal lands: For Gillingham, close to Penselwood (and presumably Egbert's Stone), see DB Dorset 1:4 (fol. 75b); for Warminster, the hundred of which was close to Iley Oak, see DB Wilts 1:4 (fol. 64d) and, for the hundred, *VCH Wilts.*, vol. 8, ed. E. Critall (London, 1965), pp. 1–5. For the relationship between hundredal organization and the organization of the 'farm of one night', see Lavelle, *Royal Estates in Anglo-Saxon Wessex*, pp. 26–47. For an alternative hypothesis based on reading Alfredian strategic thinking from events, see J. Peddie, *Alfred the Good Soldier: His Life and Campaigns* (Bath, 1989), pp. 106–7.

[15] For this see above, pp. 99–100.

[16] Geiffrei Gaimar, *L'Estoire des Engleis*, ed. A. Bell, Anglo-Norman Texts 14–16 (Oxford, 1960), lines 3162–6, p. 101.

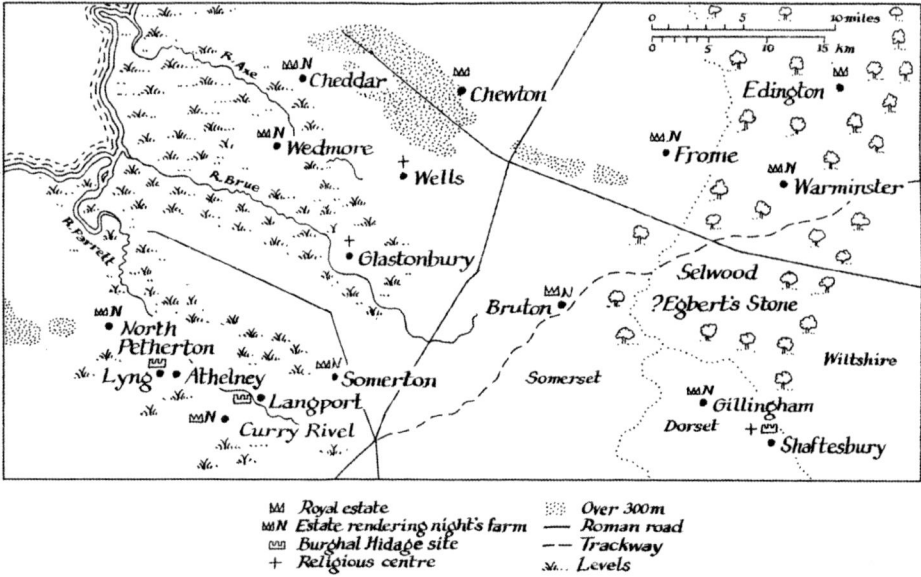

Fig. 5.2 The area of Wessex associated with the Edington campaign, 878

These names are not mentioned in other sources recording the 878 campaign; the significance of this has hitherto not really been explored beyond Reinhold Pauli's suggestion that Gaimar confused Asser's account's reference to Selwood as *Coit Maur*.[17] It seems unlikely that the names were products of Gaimar's imagination, even if he added to the account the Continental notion of the summons by *ban*.[18] They were recorded in twelfth-century French forms, but they were contemporary Old English names. Ninth-century charters record names with a *Ceol-* name element, including a number called Ceolmund.[19] Furthermore, a Ceolmund was an ealdorman of Kent in Alfred's reign[20] and there is a Ceude recorded amongst the Anglo-Saxon pilgrims who scratched their names in the catacombs of Rome.[21] While we cannot say that any of these was at Edington,

---

[17] Pauli, *Life of Alfred the Great*, p. 107n. Asser, ch. 55.

[18] For the significance of *bannum* as a military summons in Francia (as *heribannum*), see F. L. Ganshof, *Frankish Institutions under Charlemagne*, trans. B. Lyon and M. Lyon (Providence, 1968), pp. 11–12, 42.

[19] 'Ceolmunds' can be found in the witness lists of S 206 (AD 855), S 208 (c. AD 857), S 211 (AD 866), S 212 (AD 866), S 214 (AD 869), S 291 (AD 842), S 294 (AD 844), S 294b (AD 844), S 315 (AD 855), S 316 (AD 853), S 327 (AD 860), S 344 (AD 873), S 1196 (AD 859), S 1202 (AD 870×89), S 1203 (AD 875), S 1508 (AD 871×99). These are referred to as 'Ceolmund 5', 'Ceolmund 6', 'Ceolmund 8', and 'Ceolmund 10' in the *Prosopography of Anglo-Saxon England* database <www.pase.ac.uk> (accessed 25 June 2009).

[20] His death is recorded in ASC 896.

[21] The reference is in the *Prosopography of Anglo-Saxon England* database under 'Ceude 1' (dated to the seventh to ninth centuries), citing C. Carletti, 'I graffiti sull'affresco di S. Luca nel cimitero di Commodilla: addenda et corrigenda', *Rendiconti della Pontificia Accademia Romana di Archeologia* 57 (1986), pp. 129–43.

alliterating name patterns were common within pre-Conquest Anglo-Saxon families[22] and Gaimar's account should taken seriously as a record of those associated with the support of Alfred. As James Campbell pointed out, Gaimar implies that he had knowledge of an official version of the Anglo-Saxon Chronicle, and his access to local West Saxon traditions is remarkable.[23] In the context of the events of 878, Gaimar shows how a successful campaign had to demonstrate the support enjoyed by a ruler and, by extension, leads us to recognize the manner in which Viking campaigns exacerbated or even stemmed from tensions within royal families and amongst the nobility.[24]

In the two generations of rule following Alfred, the importance of prestige in campaigns of conquest was demonstrated upon a larger stage than Wessex. The campaigns of Alfred's daughter, Æthelflæd – ruling in place of her dead husband Æthelred but using her links to the West Saxon and Mercian houses[25] – and her brother Edward in the midlands and north-west of England, and in Wales show an assertion of royal control over new and reconquered territory through successful campaigns.[26] In the next generation, King Athelstan's campaigns can be seen as a Carolingian-style demonstration of royal or even quasi-imperial legitimacy. Michael Wood has highlighted the utility of witness lists of two charters, S 425 and S 407, associated with assemblies in Winchester and Nottingham for the information that they provide on the participants in Athelstan's 934 campaign into Scotland with a land and naval force.[27] The witness list of S 425 is associated with an assembly convened in Winchester on 28 May 934, and S 407 is associated with an assembly in Nottingham on 7 June. The witness lists of the charters are juxtaposed in Table 5.1, which shows the relative positions of names in those lists. These witness lists give a sense of the large numbers of the English nobles who attended royally convened assemblies associated with warfare. The study of assembly politics is involved and much debated, especially when the study of Anglo-Saxon charters comes into

[22] M. A. Redin, *Studies on Uncompounded Personal Names in Old English*, Uppsala Universitets Årsskrift Filosofi, språkvetenskap och historiska vetenskaper 2 (Uppsala, 1919), pp. xxxvii–xxxviii.

[23] Campbell, 'What is not known about the Reign of Edward the Elder', pp. 15–16, citing Bell's introduction in Gaimar, *Estoire des Engleis*, pp. liii–liv. For discussion of Gaimar's knowledge of Hampshire, see Bell, pp. ix–x. See also A. Gransden, *Historical Writing in England, c. 550–c. 1307* (London, 1974), pp. 209–12, although Gransden is not convinced that Gaimar provides much additional information from the version of the ASC available to him.

[24] For discussion of the desertion of Wulfhere, ealdorman of Wiltshire, see Yorke, *Wessex in the Early Middle Ages*, p. 111. See also Lavelle, 'Politics of Rebellion'.

[25] See discussion in ch. 1, above, pp. 13–14

[26] ASC ABCD 910, 911, 912, 913, 914; DE 910; A 915, 916, 917, 918, 919, 920; MR 912, 913, 914, 915, 916, 917, 918. D. Hill, *Atlas of Anglo-Saxon England* (Oxford, 1984), pp. 54–9, and Fig. 6.3, below. See Wainwright, 'Æthelflæd, Lady of the Mercians', pp. 57–62, who treats the strategy as that of Edward, but highlights Æthelflæd's importance in it.

[27] ASC 934. The charters are discussed in M. Wood, 'Brunanburh Revisited', p. 206, and M. Wood, *Domesday: In Search of the Roots of England* (London, 1986), pp. 104–112. I am grateful to Michael Wood for discussion on this issue.

play.[28] It is notable that the charters indicate an identifiable group of aristocrats and magnates, since many of the thegns and *duces* (ealdormen) are recorded as witnesses to both.[29] They evidently made progress together as a coherent group – an army – with aristocrats on horseback and perhaps ox-carts bringing up the rear. There were presumably limits to the provision of horses referred to in the Grately lawcode as the rates of progress indicated in the charters were limited by those who travelled in support (see below) but by the time that they reached Nottingham, the assembly was a military force. The description of many of those who were present when the assembly recorded in S 407 was held is telling. They are described as the 'many other warriors [*milites*], whose names are recorded in the charter.'[30]

Assuming that none of the thegns had been promoted between 28 May and 7 June, the record of thegns shows the patterns of groups at the Winchester assembly repeated in Nottingham. Nineteen thegns were present in both witness lists. Perhaps more had joined in the midlands, as some recorded in S 407 were not in the much longer witness list of S 425. This confirms that S 407 had an original exemplar which was drawn up independently of S 425. Some bishops, those of Cornwall and Chester-le-Street, are more prominent at Nottingham, whereas those of Winchester and Worcester had dropped in prominence, presumably because the party had moved away from Winchester. The list of ealdormen is again comparatively conservative, though some with Danish names rose in the Nottingham witness list, perhaps reflecting their local jurisdiction. It is noteworthy that the abbots recorded in the Winchester assembly were not recorded as present at Nottingham, so perhaps did not travel north to participate in Athelstan's campaign. Given the disruption to monastic life which had been suffered in the midlands in earlier generations,[31] it is perhaps unsurprising that no local abbots were present in Nottingham to take the place of those who had been at Winchester. Their absence serves to enhance the prominence of those bishops who assembled in Nottingham and, presumably, also participated on the campaign.

Athelstan's progress from Winchester to Nottingham was across land he controlled, presumably, because it was a war of conquest rather than defence, under conditions which were more favourable than when Harold led his army up to

---

[28] See above, p. 2, n. 5. Athelstan's charters and their attestations are dealt with in R. Drögereit, 'Gab es eine Angelsächsische Königskanzlei?', *Archiv für Urkundenforschung* 13 (1935), pp. 335–436.

[29] A similar sense of royal progress on campaign during the reign of King Egbert can be seen in S 272 and S 273 (AD 825), which relate to battles in *Creodantreow* (Corn. or Devon) and *Ellendun* (Wroughton, Wilts.), although there are more problems with the reliability of those charters. See Lavelle, *Royal Estates in Anglo-Saxon Wessex*, p. 55.

[30] Evidently making such a statement was a way of abbreviating a long list when copying it into a later manuscript (surviving copies are from the fourteenth century), but by reference to 'the charter' the copyist drew attention to the fact that in his own day an original copy survived and was intended to survive, thus giving an indication of the charter's likely authenticity.

[31] This issue has been discussed in S. Foot, *Monastic Life in Anglo-Saxon England, c. 600–900* (Cambridge, 2006), pp. 341–5.

Table. 5.1 Names of witnesses in charters associated with King Athelstan's Scottish campaign, 934

S 425 (Winchester, 28 May)	S 407 (Nottingham, 7 June)
King Athelstan	King Athelstan
Archbishop Wulfhelm of Canterbury	Archbishop Wulfhelm of Canterbury
Archbishop Wulfstan of York	Archbishop Wulfstan of York
Hywel, *subregulus*	Howæl, *subregulus*
Idwal, *subregulus*	Morgan, *subregulus*
Morgan, *subregulus*	Idwal, *subregulus*
Tewdwr, *subregulus*	Bishop Ælfwine of Lichfield
Bishop Ælfwine of Lichfield	Bishop Theodred of London
Bishop Eadwulf of Crediton	Bishop Wulfhun of Selsey
Bishop Cenwald of Worcester	Bishop Ælfheah
Bishop Beornstan of Winchester	Bishop Oda of Ramsbury
Bishop Theodred of London	Bishop Alfred ?of Sherborne
Bishop Wulfhun of Selsey	Bishop Conan of Cornwall
Bishop Wynsige of Dorchester	Bishop Cynesige
Bishop Alfred (1 = ?of Sherborne)	Bishop Wulfhelm of Wells
Bishop Tidhelm of Hereford	Bishop Wigred of Chester-le-Street
Bishop Burgric of Rochester	Bishop Eadwulf of Crediton
Bishop Alfred (2)	Bishop Cenwald of Worcester
Bishop Conan of Cornwall	Bishop Beornstan of Winchester
Bishop Wulfhelm of Wells	Ealdorman Ælfwald
Bishop Cynesige	Ealdorman Osferth
Bishop Wigred of Chester-le-Street	Ealdorman Æthelstan of East Anglia
Bishop Sæxhelm	Ealdorman Oswulf
Bishop Æscbyrht	Ealdorman Uhtred (1)
Abbot Ælfric	Ealdorman Ælfstan of (part) Mercia
Abbot Eadwine	Ealdorman Uhtred (2)
Abbot Æthelnoth	Ealdorman Regenwald
Abbot Beorhtsige	Ealdorman Inhwær
Ealdorman Ælfwald	Ealdorman Hadd
Ealdorman Osferth	Ealdorman Scule
Ealdorman Æthelstan of East Anglia	Ealdorman Thurferth
Ealdorman Urm (Thurum)	Ealdorman Healfdene
Ealdorman Inhwær	
Ealdorman Healfdene	
Ealdorman Oswulf	
Ealdorman Uhtred	
Ealdorman Æscberht	
Ealdorman Ælfstan of (part) Mercia	
Ealdorman Scule	
Ealdorman Hadd	

Wulfheah, *minister*
Wulflaf, *minister*
Wulfgar, *minister* (1)
Wulfmær, *minister*
Wulfnath, *minister*
Ordheah, *minister*
Ælfgar, *minister*
Æthelhelm, *minister*
Æthelwold, *minister*
Eadstan, *minister*
Æthelred, *minister*
Odda, *minister*
Wulfgar, *minister* (2)
Æthelstan, *minister*
Ælfheah, *minister*
Wulfsige, *minister*
Wihtgar, *minister*
Ælfhere, *minister*
Eadric, *minister*
Æthelwold, *minister*
Eadwald, *minister*
Ælfric, *minister*
Edmund, *minister*
Wulfric, *minister*
Hun, *minister*
Æthelberht, *minister*
Wynsige, *minister*
Æthelferth, *minister*
Ælfstan, *minister*
Æthelmund, *minister*
Æthelnoth, *minister*
Eadnoth, *minister*
Æthelwulf, *minister*
Hæðred, *minister*
Sigered, *minister*
Æthelred, *minister*
Eadwald, *minister*
Sigeferth, *minister*
Edward, *minister*
Æthelsige, *minister*
Ælfstan, *minister*
Wulfric, *minister*
Ælfsige, *minister* (1)
Beorhstan, *minister*
Ælfsige, *minister* (2)
Beorhthelm, *minister*
Eadsige, *minister*
Tiobcon, *minister*
Wulfsige, *minister*
Ealhelm, *minister*
Wulstan, *minister*
Beorhtric, *minister*

Odda, *minister*
Wulfgar, *minister*
Ælfheah, *minister*
Æthelstan, *minister*
Æthelmund, *minister*
Æthelnoth, *minister*
Ælfsige, *minister*
Wulfmær, *minister*
Helmstan, *minister*
Wulflaf, *minister*
Wulfhelm, *minister*
Wulfnoth, *minister*
Wulfbold
Ælfhere
Æthelwold
Eadric (1)
Wynsige
Sigered
Ælfweard
Ælfhere
Eadric (2)
Æthelsige
Ælfric
Æthelferth

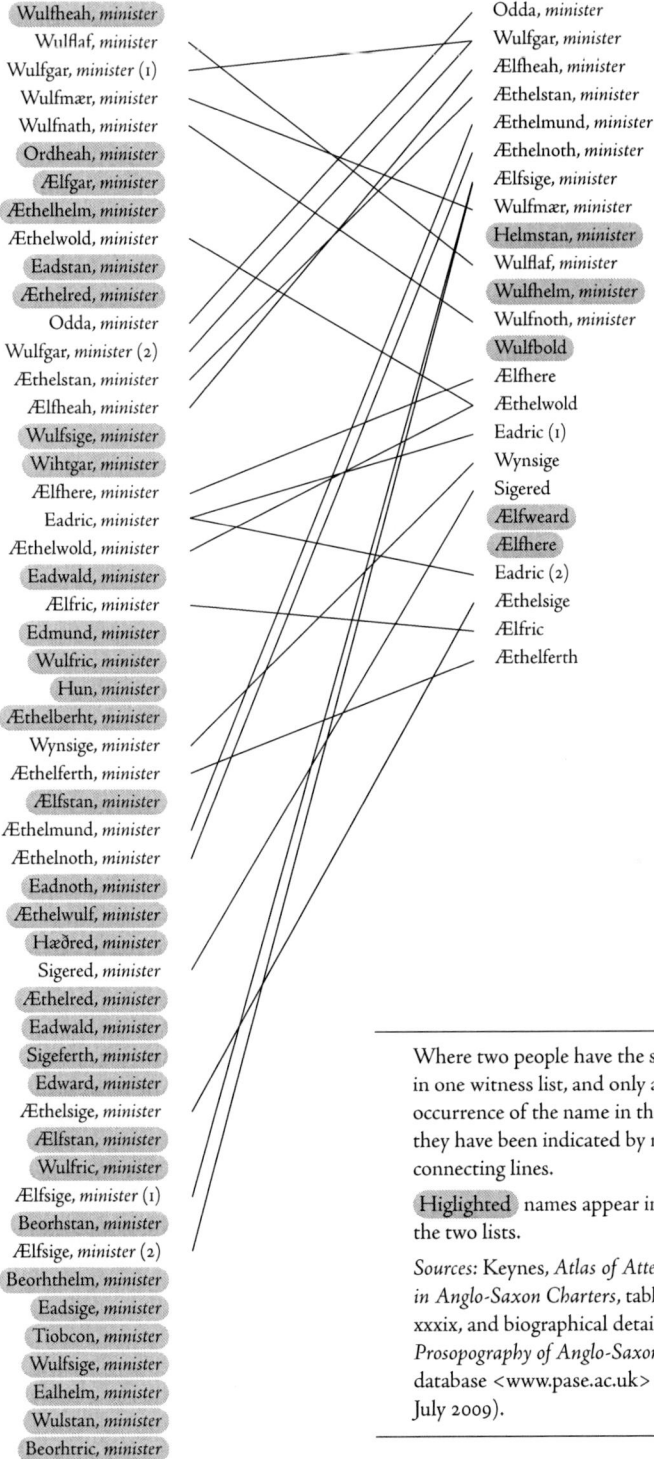

Where two people have the same name in one witness list, and only a single occurrence of the name in the other, they have been indicated by multiple connecting lines.

Higlighted names appear in only one of the two lists.

Sources: Keynes, *Atlas of Attestations in Anglo-Saxon Charters*, tables xxxvi–xxxix, and biographical details from the *Prosopography of Anglo-Saxon England* database <www.pase.ac.uk> (accessed 1 July 2009).

York and back again in 1066.[32] An army such as Athelstan's would needed to have been of an optimum size to avoid losing cohesion when ravaging enemy territory. A small army would have been ineffective, whereas a large force would have had problems in maintaining cohesion and being supplied, something Athelstan presumably had to take into consideration when he moved his army north from Nottingham in 934.[33] Furthermore, the maintenance of cohesion while remaining mobile presented a major problem in whatever territory an army travelled, not to mention the dangers of attrition from disease which could arise.[34] Terrain, weather and lines of communication were vital, just as they are for modern armies. Both English and Viking forces used ships for transport around the coast[35] but, for the most part, riverine communication seems to have been more difficult than in West Francia, the Anglo-Saxons' nearest Continental neighbour, where long, wide estuarine rivers allowed large fleets to travel far inland.[36] Therefore, even if ships were also employed, an army needed to move overland if they wished to make a political impact in controlling territory. (Indeed, the Anglo-Saxon Chronicle used the verb *ridan* to evoke control of a kingdom by rulers or invaders.)[37] Armies had to take account of the lie of the land. Hills, mountainous terrain (in Wales and parts of northern England), forests, woods, where to cross marshes and rivers and, where appropriate, use roads were all factors which needed to be considered. Presumably, no matter what size an army was, it could always go astray, and elements could lose communication with each other. Therefore knowledge

---

[32] On the progress of the English army in 1066, see K. DeVries, *The Norwegian Invasion of England in 1066*, Warfare in History (Woodbridge, 1999), pp. 262–9, 297–9.

[33] See Hill, *Atlas of Anglo-Saxon England*, p. 60.

[34] Plagues are recorded in ASC 896 and A 962, although not explicitly associated with military campaigns. WP II.27, pp. 144–5, records the contracting of dysentery by Norman troops at Dover. This topic has not been dealt with in regard to late Anglo-Saxon England, but see generally J. Maddicott, 'Plague in Seventh-Century England', *Past and Present* 156 (1997), pp. 7–54, and for diseases in Continental campaigns, Leyser, 'Early Medieval Warfare', pp. 102–3.

[35] See below, pp. 200–7.

[36] J. L. Nelson, 'The Frankish Empire', in *The Oxford Illustrated History of the Vikings*, ed. P. H. Sawyer (Oxford, 1997), pp. 19–47, at pp. 30–4. For a discussion of riverine strategies and counter-strategies in Francia, see C. M. Gillmor, 'War on the Rivers: Viking Numbers and Mobility on the Seine and Loire, 841–886', *Viator* 19 (1988), pp. 79–109. For a discussion concentrating on the economic and social significance of the use of waterways in early medieval England (albeit with little discussion of the use of waterways by Vikings), see generally J. Blair (ed.) *Waterways and Canal-Building in Medieval England*, Medieval History and Archaeology (Oxford, 2007). Wessex waterways (in a different period) are also considered in A. Sherratt, 'Why Wessex? The Avon River Route and River Transport in Later British Prehistory', *Oxford Journal of Archaeology* 15 (1996), pp. 211–234.

[37] This is especially apparent in ASC 878: Davis, 'Alfred the Great: Propaganda and Truth', pp. 171–2; D. Whitelock, 'The Importance of the Battle of Edington', in D. Whitelock, *From Bede to Alfred: Studies in Early Anglo-Saxon Literature and History* (London, 1980), no. XIII, pp. 9–10; in Lavelle, 'Geographies of Power in the Anglo-Saxon Chronicle', p. 207, I note the verb's reappearance in recording Alfred's reclamation of his kingdom, as a counterpoint to the Vikings' seizure of it. The notion is used again in ASC CDE 999 and DE 1010.

of the terrain was paramount.[38] It is perhaps no coincidence that at one of the most significant moments of campaigning, in 892, the Anglo-Saxon Chronicler records in some detail the geography of the strategically significant region of the *Andredesweald*. Similarly, from a Viking perspective, the fact that a battle took place in 871 at Wilton, which was near the junction of a Roman road running to Wimborne, where King Alfred could be found at his brother Æthelred's funeral, may indicate knowledge of arterial routes and, indeed, of events in the kingdom.[39]

Although the knowledge of local people was important, this might be supplemented by scouts. A passage from the *Old English Orosius* shows the advantages of knowledge of scouting activity:

After that the Carthaginians proceeded against Scipio [i.e. Publius Cornelius Scipio Africanus Major] with all their force, and made camp [*wicstowe namon*] in two places, near the city that is called Utica; in the one were the Carthaginians, in the other the Numidians, who were in the force with them, and had thought they should have winter-quarters [*wintersetl*] there. But after Scipio learned that the forward guards [*foreweardas*] were set far from the fortress [*fæsten*] and also that there were no others near, he then secretly led his army [*fyrd*] between the guards [*weardas*], and sent a few men to one of their fortresses, that they might set fire to one end of it, so that then almost all who were within might go toward the fire,

---

[38] For a discussion of movement through the landscape, see generally D. Hooke, *The Landscape of Anglo-Saxon England* (London, 1998), pp. 84–102, which discusses the significance of perambulations in Anglo-Saxon charters. The uses of place-names in journeys are discussed in A. Cole, 'The Anglo-Saxon Traveller', *Nomina* 17 (1994), pp. 7–18, and M. Gelling and A. Cole, *The Landscape of Place-Names* (Stamford, 1994), esp. pp. 65–96. I am grateful to Barbara Yorke for the suggestion that Archbishop Wulfstan's millennial complaint regarding slaves turning against their former masters may indicate the Viking use of slaves for local topographical knowledge: Wulfstan of York, *Sermo Lupi ad Anglos* (C version), in *Homilies of Wulfstan*, ed. Bethurum, pp. 263–4; trans. *EHD* 1, p. 932.

[39] ASC 871; Æthelweard, *Chronicon*, p. 39, indicates Alfred's absence from the battle because of the funeral. Roads in Wessex are considered by D. A. E. Pelteret, 'The Roads of Anglo-Saxon England', *Wiltshire Archaeological and Natural History Magazine* 79 (1985 for 1984), pp. 155–63, and G. B. Grundy, 'The Ancient Highways and Tracks of Wiltshire, Berkshire and Hampshire, and the Saxon Battlefields of Wiltshire', *Archaeological Journal* 75 (1918), pp. 69–194. See Hill, *Atlas of Anglo-Saxon England*, pp. 155–16, and, for a wider medieval context, F. M. Stenton, 'The Road System of Medieval England', *Economic History Review* 7 (1936), pp. 1–21, and B. P. Hindle, 'The Road Network of Medieval England', *Journal of Historical Geography* 2 (1976), pp. 207–21. D. Harrison, *The Bridges of Medieval England: Transport and Society 400–1800*, Oxford Historical Monographs (Oxford, 2004), pp. 47–54, provides a survey of the limits of the Roman road system in the middle ages, though indicates the continuity of some sections of Roman roads. Alex Langlands's doctoral study at the University of Winchester, currently in progress, is focused on the use of road networks in later Anglo-Saxon Wessex. Although there are obvious difficulties in getting to know the details of the speed of news and rumours in the early middle ages, C. A. J. Armstrong, 'Some Examples of the Distribution and Speed of News in England at the Time of the Wars of the Roses', in *Studies in Medieval History Presented to Frederick Maurice Powicke*, ed. R. W. Hunt, W. A. Pantin and R. W. Southern (Oxford, 1948), pp. 429–54, details some surprisingly quick movements of information in fifteenth-century England (a reference for which I am gratefully indebted to Richard Brown).

supposing that they would quench it. He then, Scipio, among them, slew almost all of them.⁴⁰

Orosius's original text does not include reference to warriors in front of the fortifications, suggesting that the Old English author added this detail as a logical reading of events.⁴¹ It is significant that here Scipio is recorded as learning where his enemy had posted his guards. Such knowledge came from one's own use of scouts. It is remarkable that an Old English author could acknowledge that an army could pass between elements of the opposing army, indicating that armies did not necessarily move *en masse*. However, the reference to *fore-warders* in the Old English Orosius is a rare reference to scouting, especially interesting given that it is referred to as undertaken by a defensive force. Evidently scouting was not always recorded in the heroic military traditions of Old English literature. As with the use of archery on the battlefield,⁴² actions which could give strategic or tactical advantages did not always warrant explicit mention in written records. For example, it is reasonable to expect the confrontation of the two contenders for the West Saxon crown in 899–900 (recorded in an entry in the Anglo-Saxon Chronicle which John Hill has raised into the canon of Old English literature)⁴³ to have been one such case. Given that Edward the Elder counteracted his cousin's strategies at Wimborne by moving his forces to the nearby hillfort of Badbury Rings, the use of scouts does not seem unlikely.⁴⁴ A clearer case is evident in 893, for which the Anglo-Saxon Chronicle records Alfred's strategies in the land between Milton Regis and Appledore (Kent) to ensure that the Viking army ranged against him was unable to coalesce. Alfred may have gathered his army, as the Chronicle's account has it, but in order to find a convenient point to deploy, he or his scouts had to reconnoitre actively.⁴⁵ The annal entry, as is seen elsewhere in this volume, famously includes the account of the division of Alfred's army, but the use of fortifications for small bands of warriors to ensure that Vikings remained divided is important. There are also echoes of the passage from Orosius in the Chronicle's references to the movement of forces between fortifications.⁴⁶

> And then King Alfred gathered his army [*fierd*], and set out so that he encamped [*gewicode*] between the two *heres* where he had the nearest space concerning the wood-fortress [*wudufæstenne*] and the water-fortress [*wæterfæstenne*], so that he might reach either [of the *heres*], if they chose to seek any field. Then they [i.e. the *heres*] went out afterwards about the Weald as bands and mounted troops [*hlopum ⁊ flocradum*] along whichever side was then defenceless; and they were also sought by other bands [MS A: *floccum*] nearly every day, either by day or by night, both by the army [*fierde*] and also from the *burhs*.

⁴⁰ *OE Orosius*, IV.10.

⁴¹ Orosius, *Libri VII*, IV.18. See below, pp. 250–1

⁴² For the use of missiles, see below, pp. 274–5.

⁴³ Hill, *The Anglo-Saxon Warrior Ethic*, pp. 88–92.

⁴⁴ Lavelle, 'Politics of Rebellion', pp. 77–8.

⁴⁵ Abels, *Alfred the Great*, pp. 292–3.

⁴⁶ For another Orosian echo in the same Chronicle annal, see above, p. 92.

We need not rely on drawing conclusions from the 'military probability' of circumstances, however. As well as William of Malmesbury's well-known account of the capture of Harold's scouts before the Battle of Hastings,[47] there is direct reference to scouting activities in Anglo-Saxon sources. Referring to Edmund Ironside's embassy to Cnut in 1016, the *Encomium Emmae* shows knowledge of scouts, indicated by the fact that the Danes were recorded as mistaking the embassy:[48]

> When those men coming were first looked upon by the Danes they were suspected by them to be scouts [*exploratores*]. But after they saw them approaching nearer, having been summoned to them, they began to ask what they sought.

Although an army can only move as fast as its slowest elements, the entire force does not need to move simultaneously for it to be perceived as advancing. We have already seen how the Anglo-Saxon Chronicle associated 'riding' with the notion of the control of a kingdom[49] but it would have been difficult to transport large numbers of horses across the English Channel or North Sea.[50] While there are records of the seizure or submission of horses to Vikings from English estates,[51] it seems doubtful that the Vikings could have depended upon this, so entire Viking armies are unlikely to have been able to travel on horseback while campaigning in England.[52] These issues can be reconciled if mounted warriors formed advance parties, scouts in all but name, an issue which was perhaps alluded to when Æthelweard referred to the Vikings moving across Wessex in 871 'as swift ... as scouts [*explorationis*]'.[53] In the eleventh century scouting was well entrenched in Norman military strategies, though as with Anglo-Saxon sources they were recorded only when the circumstances were exceptional, as John Gillingham points out.[54] While Viking forces are not normally noted for organizational discipline,[55] their use of scouting parties moving at a steady pace from a main army and returning regular

[47] WM, GR III.239, pp. 450–1.

[48] *Encomium Emmae*, II.13, p. 29.

[49] ASC 878. See above, p. 186.

[50] ASC 892. See the reservations of Howard, *Swein Forkbeard's Invasions*, p. 27. The subject of transporting horses is addressed in Sawyer, *Age of the Vikings*, pp. 77, 127. An average vessel would not have been able to transport many horses.

[51] ASC 866, CDE 994, 999, DE 1010, CDE 1013, 1014, 1015.

[52] The division of the Viking force in ASC CDE 1010 suggests this. Cf. Sawyer, 'Density of the Danish Settlement in England', p. 5, who highlights the problems of obtaining and feeding horses, drawing the conclusion that entire armies were mounted and must therefore have been small.

[53] Æthelweard, *Chronicon*, p. 37. See also the reference to forward parties issued by the Egyptian army prior to battle in *Old English Exodus*, trans. Tolkien and Turville-Petre, lines 154–5, p. 5; trans. p. 23.

[54] Gillingham. 'William the Bastard at War', pp. 154–5, discussing Duke William's actions after landing in England (WP II.9, pp. 114–17) and reconnaissance outside Exeter (OV, vol. 2, pp. 212–3 [below, pp. 258–9]). Other examples of ducal reconnaissance prior to 1066 are WP I.17, pp. 24–7, and (probably) I.12, pp. 14–17. The former is discussed by Gillingham (pp. 149–50), and I owe the suggestion of the latter to Professor Gillingham, *pers. comm.*

[55] For discussion of Vikings as 'armies' and 'bands', see Abels, 'Alfred the Great, the *Micel Hæðen Here* and the Viking Threat'.

reports seems likely, as it would explain the rapid progress which Viking armies were able to maintain.[56] We might expect such scouts to have been less surreptitious in their actions than a modern army's reconnaissance unit, whose standing orders tend to be to avoid contact with the enemy.[57] Smoke from burning buildings and crops would announce the presence of any army, with commensurate effects on morale for all concerned. The Anglo-Saxon Chronicle's ironic reference to the Vikings of 1006 'lighting their beacons as they went' suggests that the activities of advance parties marked out the line of advance for the main body of the Viking army.[58]

Whether such actions were intended as deliberate 'battle-seeking' strategies is open to debate. A recent line of discussion has been opened between Stephen Morillo, Clifford Rogers and John Gillingham about the 'orthodoxy' of battle avoidance – what Gillingham has considered the 'Vegetian' mode of warfare (i.e. after Vegetius), a notion that battle is to be turned to only as a last resort.[59] It is difficult to determine strategic motivations at different times: while the English army needed to meet their enemies in order to deal a decisive blow in 1066 and on other occasions,[60] Viking forces often did not need to engage with their enemy in order to gain their objective of taking wealth. However, the Anglo-Saxon Chronicle entry for 893 relates that Alfred seems to have employed a strategy of denying the enemy mobility and cohesion, an issue of evident interest to the Chronicler. It was important to have the upper hand when meeting the enemy. For example, it would be rash to attack a town unless there was a prospect that the inhabitants would surrender; although the formalities of sieges do not seem to have been established in pre-Conquest England, arriving prematurely at the walls of a city might result in a hail of stones[61] or a counter-attack from its defenders. The inherent danger of attempting to attack quickly was that the enemy might be encountered on unfavourable terms. Poor scouting could result in an unexpected engagement, especially if the enemy knew the territory better. If a commander were to influence the course of a battle, it was important

---

[56] I am grateful to Ben Salter for this suggestion.

[57] D. Grossman, *On Killing: The Psychological Cost of Learning to Kill in War and Society* (Boston, MA, 1995), p. 60. For a later twelfth-century 'object lesson' in surreptitious reconnaissance, see J. Gillingham, 'War and Chivalry in the History of William the Marshall', in *Thirteenth Century England, Volume 2: Proceedings of the Newcastle upon Tyne Conference 1987*, ed. P. R. Coss and S. D. Lloyd (Woodbridge, 1988), pp. 1–13, at p. 9.

[58] ASC CDE 1006. For this account, see Lavelle, *Aethelred II*, pp. 117–18. The significance of this is discussed by Hill and Sharp, 'Anglo-Saxon Beacon System', p. 157 (reprinted below, p. 218).

[59] S. Morillo, 'Battle Seeking: The Contexts and Limits of Vegetian Strategy', *JMMH* 1 (2002), pp. 21–41, and Gillingham's response, '"Up with Orthodoxy": In Defense of Vegetian Warfare', *JMMH* 2 (2003), pp. 148–59. The papers which established the 'orthodoxy' are Gillingham, 'William the Bastard at War' and 'Richard I and the Science of War'. For some realistic observations on Vegetius, see Halsall, *Warfare and Society in the Barbarian West*, p. 145. For discussion of Vegetius in Anglo-Saxon England, see above, p. 1, n. 1.

[60] See e.g. ASC CDE 1010.

[61] See Fig. 6.3 and discussion below, p. 226.

to choose a battlefield well, even if it was not the only factor in assuring victory. Such a problem was effectively addressed by choice of the hill on which to deploy by the English commander Harold II at Hastings, albeit ultimately without success.[62]

Consideration of medieval travel must take into account a number of factors. If 20 miles (31.2 km) was a long day's march, 10 miles (16.1 km) may be reckoned to be the maximum distance after which a force could still be expected to be in condition to fight after travelling. Such mobility must have been problematic for defenders, especially if an enemy could make a rapid march to launch a surprise attack.[63] Estimates may be made (see Table 5.2), although the limitations of these estimates must be acknowledged as travel conditions would presumably have varied according to a range of factors, such as weather and terrain, as well as levels of fatigue and morale.[64]

As shown in chapter 3, while we do not have direct evidence of the logistical tail of early medieval armies in Britain, there is indirect evidence.[65] For one thing, kings and their nobles had to sleep and eat in a manner appropriate to their status. Although ravaging in hostile territory or collecting renders from estates in 'friendly' territories were strategies employed to provide sustenance on campaigns, armies also needed to bring with them such baggage as tents and the paraphernalia of office. Karl Leyser has drawn attention to the need for nobles as much as rulers to show their their wealth while on campaign and 'to reward good service there and then'. Such activity was not mere froth; it was essential to a demonstration of status.[66] Thus on a prestigious war of conquest, Anglo-Saxon rulers would not travel light, as the *Old English Hexateuch*'s illustration of Abraham's campaign encampment shows what was evidently a high-quality tent.[67] (See Fig. 5.3.) Packhorses capable of carrying 187 lb (85 kg) loads were rather insubstantial for the

---

[62] For an assessment of the battlefield site, see Lawson, *Battle of Hastings*, pp. 47–58, 199–209.

[63] The issue of marching a distance into battle is addressed in Engels, *Alexander the Great*, p. 52. For marginally faster daily rates (of 30–40 miles per day for a 'mounted core') and discussion of the significance of fast marches, see S. Morillo, *Warfare under the Anglo-Norman Kings, 1066–1135* (Woodbridge, 1996), pp. 113–17. For a discussion of rapid movements for the purposes of surprise, see Gillingham, 'War and Chivalry in the History of William the Marshall', pp. 8–9.

[64] For discussion of some of these factors, see B. P. Hindle, 'Seasonal Variations in Travel in Medieval England', *Journal of Transport History*, new ser. 4 (1977–8), pp. 170–8, and J. Nesbitt, 'The Rate of March of Crusading Armies in Europe: A Study and Computation', *Traditio* 19 (1963), pp. 167–82.

[65] See above, pp. 58–63.

[66] Leyser, 'Early Medieval Warfare', pp. 92–4 (quotation at p. 94). Leyser cites Ottonian and later examples, but for the ninth century the *Life* of George, Archbishop of Ravenna, in Agnellus, *Liber Pontificalis Ecclesiae Ravennatis*, ch. 174, trans. D. M. Deliyannis, *The Book of the Pontiffs of the Church of Ravenna* (Washington, DC, 2004), pp. 301–4, describes the loss and destruction of the church's treasures and documents after the capture of Archbishop George at the battle of Fontenoy. Presumably these were a demonstration of the archbishop's status while on campaign (although George protested that he had other intentions), in the manner described by Leyser.

[67] BL Cotton MS Claudius B.IV, fol. 24r. Tents are evidently valuable items in the wills of Wynflæd (S 1539 [AD 950]) and Archbishop Ælfric (S 1488 [AD 1003×4]).

Table 5.2 Suggested overland speeds of elements of an early medieval army

Type	Average speed	Approx. daily distance moved (assuming spring/summer)
mounted scouts	4 mph / 6.4 kph +	30 miles/ 48 km +[a]
foot	2.5 mph / 4 kph (perhaps 3–4 mph / 5–6.4 kph for short period)	15–20 miles/ 24–31 km[b]
mounted warriors	4 mph / 6.4 kph	max. 30 miles/ 48 km[c]
supply train (assuming oxen), camp followers etc.	2 mph / 3.2 kph	10 miles/ 16 km[d]

a Assuming eight hours' riding. This would have necessitated resting horses and shoeing on a regular (perhaps even daily) basis: see Hyland, *Medieval Warhorse*, p. 74.

b Engels, *Alexander the Great*, pp. 16, 153–4, calculates an average fifteen-mile daily march rate for Alexander the Great's army, though presumably this could vary under different conditions and a very different climate from Alexander's campaigns.

c Assuming eight hours' travel per day at 4 mph.: Engels, *Alexander the Great*, p. 15. For a lower estimate of twenty miles, see Stenton, 'Road System of Medieval England', p. 16.

d Assuming a limit of five hours' travel per day at 2 mph: Engels, *Alexander the Great*, pp. 15–16.

requirements of a large army[68] in comparison to the 1,102 lb (500 kg) loads that could be transported by two-wheeled carts.[69] The use of somewhat more mobile horse-drawn carts was not widespread until some years after the Norman Conquest; ox-drawn carts were likely to have accompanied or followed an army that was travelling much more than a day's march from friendly territory, and thus may have circumscribed its strategic mobility.[70] The two charters of Athelstan

[68] The calculation is from J. Haldon, 'Roads and Communications in the Byzantine Empire: Wagons, Horses, and Supplies', in *Logistics of Warfare*, ed. Pryor, pp. 131–58, at p. 146. Though cf. II *Æthelstan*, discussed above, pp. 62–3).

[69] B. S. Bachrach, 'Animals and Warfare in Early Medieval Europe', *Settimane di Studio del Centro Italiano di Studi sull'alto Medioevo* 31 (1985), vol. 1, pp. 707–64, cited by Haldon, 'Roads and Communications', p. 146. Bachrach has four-wheel carts carrying 1443 lb (650 kg) but argues that they could travel 15 or 19–24 km per day. See also J. P. Roth, *The Logistics of Roman Army at War: 264 BC – AD 235*, Columbia Studies in the Classical Tradition 23 (Leiden, 1999), pp. 198–214.

[70] On the development of the horse harness, see J. Langdon, 'Horse Hauling: A Revolution in Vehicle Transport in Twelfth-and Thirteenth-Century England', *Past and Present* 103 (1984), pp. 37–66, and, for a wider context, J. Langdon, *Horses, Oxen and Technological Innovation: The Use of Draught Animals in English Farming from 1066 to 1500*, Past and Present Publications (Cambridge, 1986). Longer-term developments are discussed in S. Piggott, *Wagon, Chariot and Carriage: Symbol and Status in the History of Transport* (London, 1992). For a discussion of Anglo-Saxon ox-drawn carts, such as that depicted in the *Old English Hexateuch* (BL MS Cotton B.IV), fol. 67r, see D. Hill, 'Anglo-Saxon Technology: 1. The Oxcart', *Medieval Life* 10 (1998), pp. 13–18.

Fig. 5.3 Detail of a royal encampment, depicted in the eleventh-century *Old English Hexateuch*

discussed above may show the northward progress of his army, covering the 130 miles (178 km) between Winchester and Nottingham at an average of 13 miles (17.8 km) or – presumably – more per day between 28 May and 7 June.[71] We may assume that the army decamped soon after the feast with which S 425 was associated, and any feasts provided *en route* were for one night only. If associated ox-carts in train could cover only ten miles a day, this particular army did not have to travel as a single unit while in friendly territory and presumably at least some of the supplies which entertained Athelstan's army at Nottingham must have been locally obtained.

Perhaps the encumbrance of campaigning casts a different light on Asser's famous account of the candle-clock recorded in the *Life of King Alfred*. The story of how Alfred ordered the use of thinned ox-horn to construct a translucent container for a candle, marked in hours to divide his time spiritual devotion and earthly tasks, recalls a picture of the king as a diligent scholar in draughty buildings,[72] but the story warrants mention here as it reveals Asser's experience in the entourage of the king. Asser refers to the vignette applying to churches *or* tents (*tentoria*) a minor detail which, when seen in relation to the correspondence of the date of composition of the *Life of King Alfred* with a period of campaigning, suggests that the experience of life under canvas was not far from Asser's mind when writing this famous passage. Although not associated with a campaign, it is pertinent, too, to mention the Durham Ritual's inclusion of a colophon by Aldred, provost of Chester-le-Street, written at Oakley, south of Woodyates (Dorset) 'in

---

[71] For the purposes of this study, the distance of 130 miles is a figure taken directly from point to point, a figure which does not take account of variations of possible routes. However, see Hill, *Atlas of Anglo-Saxon England*, p. 60, who reconstructs Athelstan's movements in context.

[72] Asser, chs 103–4. A recent consideration of this (although without explicit consideration of the locations of Alfred's studies) is Pratt, *Political Thought of Alfred the Great*, pp. 186–7.

his tent' on 10 August 970.[73] Although the ability to add to manuscripts may seem a minor issue in the context of military campaigns, as we have seen, it was presumably usual for churchmen to accompany campaigning kings. It would not be too facetious to speculate on whether Aldred and his contemporaries had benefited from Alfred's invention, and on how many Anglo-Saxon manuscripts were written or amended while on campaign.

A somewhat unusual, though no less prestigious, campaign is indicated in Osbern's account of the seizure of relics of St Ælfheah from St Paul's, London. Osbern indicates the distance travelled by an army; his description of the view of the dust raised by people on the move highlights the preoccupations of an early medieval commander. The account begins with an apparently quick decision by Cnut[74] to support Æthelnoth of Canterbury's attempt to claim the martyr's body with a classic diversionary tactic for what could be read as an early medieval 'special operation':[75]

> He told all the soldiers of his household ['familię sųe militibus'], who are called 'housecarls' in the language of the Danes, that some of them should incite strife at the outer gates of the city, and others, fully armed, should take possession of the bridge and the banks of the river, so that the people of London would not be able to stand in the way of those leaving with the saint's body.

The account highlights the communal authority of the people of London as a group (an issue discussed below, in chapter 6) as well as the importance of the use of the king's housecarls as a relatively substantial group on whom the king could rely in the face of potential opposition (given that nobles could have retinues, it is not impossible that Osbern later also referred to the archbishop's household troops). After relating the *topos* of miracles demonstrating Ælfheah's body's willingness to travel to Canterbury,[76] the account goes on to relate the translation:[77]

> God's high priest came nearer so that he could move and lift the revered corpse with his own hands, but he sorrowed in his soul, for he could see no bier on which the body could be placed to be taken to a ship. As he stood doubting, in great desperation, he noticed that there was a wooden board lying under the body, so that at any time, with no difficulty the saint could be lifted, with his body intact,

---

[73] *The Durham Ritual*, ed. T.J. Brown, Early English Manuscripts in Facsimile 16 (Copenhagen, 1969), pp. 23–4, fol. 84r, cited in P. Wormald, *The Making of English Law: King Alfred to the Twelfth Century*, vol. 1: *Legislation and its Limits* (Oxford, 1999), p. 437.

[74] The archbishop of Canterbury arrived in London on 1 June. The seizure of the relics was on 8 June.

[75] Rumble and Morris, 'Textual Appendix: *Translatio Sancti Ælfegi Cantuariensis archiepiscopi et martiris*', pp. 302–3 (translation on p. 303) [references to the text given as *Translatio Sancti Ælfegi* and the commentary as 'Textual Appendix'; minor amendment of Rumble and Morris's translation is indicated by footnotes]. Y. N. Harari, *Special Operations in the Age of Chivalry 1100–1550*, Warfare in History (Woodbridge, 2007) is a rare attempt to discuss the high and later medieval context of 'special operations' but, by definition, does not include much discussion of the early middle ages.

[76] *Translatio Sancti Ælfegi*, ed. and trans. Rumble and Morris, pp. 304–7.

[77] *Translatio Sancti Ælfegi*, ed. and trans. Rumble and Morris, pp. 306–11.

from that place. So, rejoicing, and made more happy than they could have hoped, they took up the shroud which his servant Godric had brought with him for the service of the pontiff, and they wound it round the holy body together with the plank lying under it. But, since a part of the body remained uncovered, the aforesaid monk ran to the altar of St Paul the Apostle, snatched the altar cloth lying upon it and, leaving half a pound of gold to pay for the altar cloth, hurrying back, he returned to wrap it around the rest of the body. Then, having raised the precious treasure of the precious body on their shoulders, the monks descended the narrow street which led to the river Thames, followed by the king and the archbishop, both of them devoting their attention to God. When they approached the river, Lo! they met a royal longship [*regia nauis*] with golden dragon prows, full of armed men [*armigeris replete militibus*], come to meet the martyr. Quick as a flash the king jumped in and, with open arms, received the martyr. Then, offering his right hand, he helped the pontiff aboard.

Soon the ship had sailed from the shore with the king at the helm, steering it to the opposite bank of the river [i.e. Southwark]. Thus you would have seen that the great power of God showed favour to the martyr's service, as you would have seen the bridge and the entire banks of the river lined with armoured men [*loricatis … militibus*];[78] over there you would have heard the pretended strife incited at the outer gates of the city; you would have espied the king steering the ship, the noble oarsmen pulling on the oars, the archbishop praying and the holy monks performed obsequies.

Dry land was quickly reached, and the king, disembarking first from the ship, received the body and laid it on a waggon. After this, he despatched it with a strong band of soldiers [*ualida … manu militum*]. He himself waited with the archbishop at the far end of the bridge, until those who had gone before were considered to be far enough from the city, for he feared the attacks of the citizens. Then he rose and, with great good humour, jested with the archbishop and said:

By my help you have been freed from the threat of death, from which you must have thought you could not be delivered. Now go in safety to the saint, and humbly beg him to bless us with more favourable times. I would also go with you, if I were not, as you know, occupied with great affairs of state. The Queen dwells in Kent with my son Harthacnut. I will order her to come and meet you with all the nobility.

Leaving the king therefore, the archbishop set off after the advance party [*pręcedentes*] with a strong force of houscarls [*cum ingenti huscarlium turba*]. As they approached, a cloud of dust rising in the sky could be seen by those who had gone ahead and who continually looked behind them. These were afraid that the citizens had come out of the city, so that they quickly sent the attendant monks and the martyr on ahead with a few men. They themselves, coming to the village of Plumstead, deployed in a narrow place [*obsident angusta loca*],[79] and setting up

[78] Rumble and Morris translate this as 'armed men'.
[79] Rumble and Morris translate this as 'fortified'.

three ranks [*tribus turmis tria pręlia instituentes*], prepared to die for the love of the blessed martyr. But seeing near at hand the banner of the Cross [*crucis vexillum*], they recognized as friends those who they had feared to be enemies, and rejoiced more than they could have thought possible. So they made their way onwards and were met, as they rested that same night in the estate called *Earhetha* [?'Eard' = Crayford] by a large crowd of Kentish folk, on horseback and on foot, men and women, old and young, each leading choirs through their ranks, striking harps, as though escorting with song the Ark of the Lord's Covenant. ...

Alexander Rumble urges caution in reading the text, noting similarities with other hagiographical narratives of the period, and suggesting that the Anglo-Saxon Chronicle D manuscript's more celebratory annal for 1023 contains 'significant differences' in its account.[80] One might even also argue that the *Translatio* is a freely modified version of the Chronicle's account, which mentions ferrying across the river. If conditions were as dangerous as Osbern suggests, why risk travel over land when Cnut had command of a ship? However, one can hardly have expected the bishop of London to be entirely willing to part with the saint's body, a theme familiar in the theft of saints' relics in early and high medieval Europe; if anything, the Chronicle's account of an unproblematic translation seems to be understated.[81] Given that by the end of the summer's day the 'advance party' (*precedentes*) with the body on a cart seem to have made it to Crayford, a day's travel (some 14 miles/ 22.5 km) from Southwark, it is possible that the body had been taken early in the morning in order to minimize opposition to its seizure. Millennial crowds were not always compliant, after all.[82] While this may be stretching a point, the appearance of the housecarls in the account, specifically referred to as such by Osbern, is an indication of a sense of historicity, especially given that the Anglo-Saxon Chronicle accounts for Cnut's reign do not refer to housecarls.[83] Of course, Osbern probably exaggerated the potential opposition that Londoners offered to armoured troops, and this hardly reads as a standard campaign, but the reference to the visible cloud of dust and the necessity of well-trained troops to hold firm in a narrow place are noteworthy. Osbern had not just chosen to refer to Plumstead because, as Rumble points out, Plumstead had been a land-holding of St Augustine's, Canterbury.[84] Had land-holding been the important issue for Osbern, it would have been appropriate to refer to a Christ Church Canterbury estate rather

---

[80] Rumble and Morris, 'Textual Appendix', pp. 285–8 (the quotation is at p. 285). Similar accounts cited by Rumble are the account of the translation of St Mildred, in Harmer, *Anglo-Saxon Writs*, p. 193, and of St Felix, by Cnut, in *Chronicon Abbatiæ Ramesiensis*, ed. W. D. Macray, RS 83 (London, 1886), pp. 127–8.

[81] See generally P. Geary, *Furta Sacra: Thefts of Relics in the Central Middle Ages* (Princeton, 1978; rev. edn, 1990), esp. pp. 87–107.

[82] Although under different circumstances, an indication of this is provided by R. Landes, 'Between Aristocracy and Heresy: Popular Participation in the Limousin Peace of God, 994–1033', in *The Peace of God: Social Violence and Religious Response in France around the Year 1000*, ed. T. Head and R. Landes (Ithaca, NY, 1992), pp. 184–218.

[83] The first record is ASC E 1035.

[84] Rumble and Morris, 'Textual Appendix', p. 286, citing S 809 (961×71), an admittedly problematic charter.

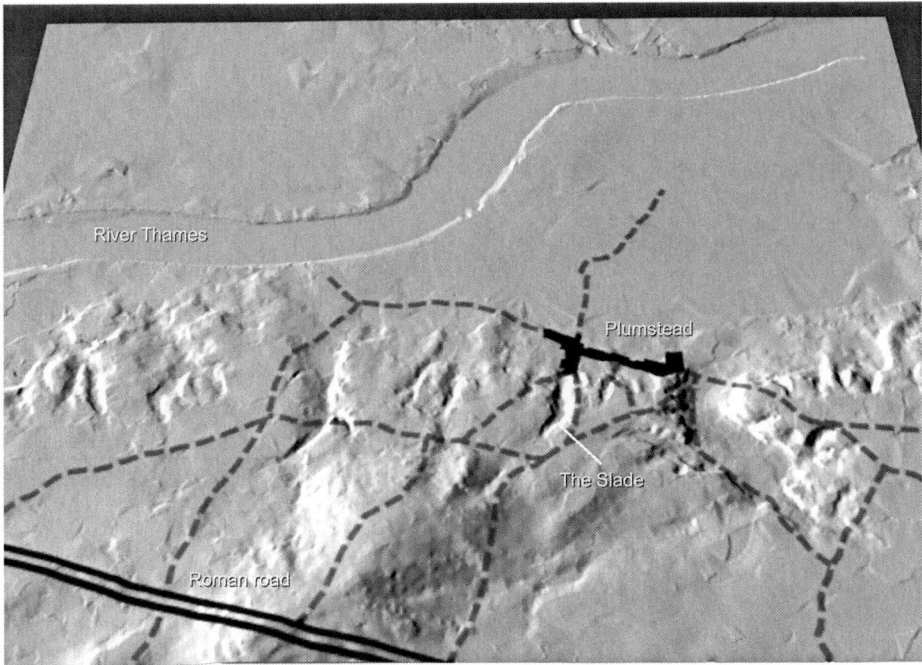

Fig. 5.4 Terrain around Plumstead (Kent), an area discussed in the account of the recovery of the relics of St Ælfheah by the Archbishop of Canterbury's housecarls, 1023. Details of roads and tracks and the village of Plumstead are taken from early edition Ordnance Survey maps. The view is from the south; distance from north to south is approx. 3 miles / 4.7 km

than one held by the rival neighbouring monastery of St Augustine's. Plumstead may have been mentioned because the road across Plumstead Common, about a mile north of the Roman road from London to Rochester, is particularly narrow, passing eastwards up a hill, with the north side of the hill dropping steeply into a ravine known as The Slade. This is an ideal candidate for the 'narrow place' referred to in the account, where a small group of disciplined warriors could make a defence.[85] (See Fig. 5.4.) While this does not in itself determine the account's historicity, it does at least show that the area's topography was related to the event described, and that Osbern certainly knew how far one could travel from London in a day. If the events did not happen quite as Osbern relates them, then we should at least appreciate that an eleventh-century author with his head in ecclesiastical concerns of sanctity knew to write about them.[86]

Although the *Translatio* is debatable as an account of a 'military' campaign, it draws attention to the fact that armies did not necessarily travel across the landscape as a homogenous group. Scouts, if they were able to travel at twice the speed of the main body of the army, presumably needed to be some 5–10 miles

[85] O.S. TQ 450777. I am grateful to Jack Curry for his helpful discussion on the topography of this area.

[86] See J. C. Rubenstein, 'Osbern (d. 1094?)', *ODNB* <www.oxforddnb.com/view/article/20865> (accessed 16 June 2009).

(8–16 km) from the main army in order to be effective. It would have been wise for them to remain a similar distance from a fortification (i.e. outside visibility range). Any closer would force a direct engagement of the scouts by a stronger enemy.

We should also note that mobility in enemy territory could be compromised by the success of an army. Success would have made an army more vulnerable, as its baggage train became ever more encumbered. This is famously apparent in the ambush of Charlemagne's force at Roncesvalles as it withdrew through the Pyrenees after capturing Pamploma in 783,[87] and it was also noted by Karl Leyser that the mobility of the Magyars could be compromised by their success.[88] Although there are no cases of a 'classic' ambush upon a baggage train known from late Viking Age England, Michael Wood has suggested that the vulnerability of a Hiberno-Norse-Scots-British-Northumbrian force which had penetrated deep into Athelstan's territory played a role in the success of a well-timed counter-attack made by the West Saxon and Mercian forces in the Battle of *Brunanburh*.[89] A similar case can be made for the West Saxon and Mercian victory against a Viking force at Tettenhall (Shropshire). This force had, according to Æthelweard, been laden with 'great spoils' in 'western [districts]' (i.e. in western Mercia) and was caught 'suddenly' (*repente*) while crossing a bridge at *Cantbricg* (=?*Cuatbricg*, i.e. Bridgnorth).[90] Vulnerability may also explain the absence of a siege when a Viking force passed by the gates of Winchester in 1006 on their way back to their ships after successful campaigning. Even if the Vikings' collective sense of prestige and general morale had been enhanced by their activities, the risks of further activities for such a force laden with booty were presumably seen as outweighing any benefits.

The mobility and effectiveness of an army was equally related to its retreat following a defeat. The fact that the army of Æthelred I and Alfred was able to run from its defeat at Reading in 871 and – significantly – managed to escape successfully shows the importance of ensuring that lines of retreat were clear, something which their Frankish contemporary, Charles the Bald, was unable to achieve after the battle of Andernach in 876.[91] Evidently, as with the British Expeditionary Force's departure from Dunkirk in 1940, a retreat could be remembered as a victory if it so suited the audience.[92] Geffrei Gaimar's account of the 871 retreat from Reading is suggestive of a local tradition.[93]

> The fourth day after came Æthelred
> The king, and his brother Alfred,
> To Reading, with a great host,

[87] P. Sénac, *Les Carolingiens et al-Andalus* (viii*e*–ix*e* siècles) (Paris, 2002), pp. 53–6.

[88] K. Leyser, 'Battle of the Lech', *History* 50 (1965), pp. 1–25, at p. 8.

[89] Wood, 'Brunanburh Revisited', pp. 203–6. This interpretation does depend somewhat on the reading of the location of the battle. See below, pp. 298–301.

[90] Æthelweard, *Chronicon*, p. 53. See also ASC CD 910.

[91] AB 876. This is discussed by Leyser, 'Early Medieval Warfare', p. 105.

[92] For the presentation of Alfred's situation as 'not as bad as it actually was' by the ASC entries for the 870s, see Keynes, 'Tale of Two Kings', p. 198.

[93] Gaimar, *Estoire des Engleis*, lines 2953–67, pp. 94–5. See above, n. 23.

And the Danes came out quickly.
In an open field they offered battle
Which did not cease in all the day.
There was [Ealdorman] Æthelwulf slain,
The splendid man (of whom I told you earlier),
And Æthelred and Alfred
were driven to *Wiceled*.
There one host came in pursuit,
And did not know the ford across the river.
By the name of Twyford the ford has always been called,
Where the Danes turned back,
And the English escaped.
But many were killed and wounded there,
Thus the Danes held the victory ...

While the escape of Æthelred and Alfred may have been no more than a local legend, inspired by the Old Testament account of the Israelites' flight from Egypt (Exodus 14:15–30), it is interesting that a ford on a river should have been the means of escape rather than, as traditionally seen, the slaughter of the defeated side,[94] reflecting the importance of maintaining lines of communication. It is perhaps telling that the Vikings were not able to find the ford or to pursue their West Saxon foes, indicating that the Vikings may have been on foot. If one force could not follow the trail of another, it may also indicate that the forces involved were small. Whistley, to the east of Reading, seems to correspond with the *Wiceled* of Gaimar's account,[95] and the Twyford mentioned by Gaimar is an area which remains subject to flooding from the nearby River Lodden.[96] Though we can only speculate as to where Alfred and his brother intended to make their ultimate escape, the account of the significance of an escape itself is important.

Fighting retreats by Viking forces are recorded, suggesting that this was not uncommon. Sir Frank Stenton discusses the Vikings in 893 using a similar technique to that of Alfred and his brother, taking refuge on the islet of Thorney (probably near Iver, Bucks.).[97] The Vikings escaping from the defeat at Edington in 878 also managed to remain coherent enough to withstand a two-week siege at their fortification (*geweorc*: probably Chippenham). The fact that the Anglo-Saxon Chronicler records the loss of men and horses outside the fortification indicates that their escape had been a close-run thing.[98]

---

[94] See e.g. the account of Ecgfrith's victory over the Picts *c.* 673, which describes the filling of two rivers with the dead: *Life of Bishop Wilfrid by Eddius Stephanus*, trans. Colgrave, ch. 19, pp. 40–3. Grossman, *On Killing*, pp. 127–9, comments on the perils of turning one's back on a pursuing enemy.

[95] For forms of the place-name, see E. Ekwall, *The Concise Oxford Dictionary of English Place-Names*, 4th edn (Oxford, 1960), p. 513.

[96] Flood information from Environment Agency site, < http://www.environment-agency. gov.uk/homeandleisure/floods/default.aspx> (accessed 7 Feb. 2010).

[97] F. M. Stenton, 'The Danes at Thorney Island in 893', *EHR* 27 (1912), pp. 512–13.

[98] ASC 878.

The significance of the maintenance of roads and bridges should be borne in mind when considering Viking Age campaigns. Mobility was obviously imperative, and building and maintaining bridges played an important role in this.[99] In the later years of Æthelred's reign and during the crisis of 1051–2, London appears to have had the only bridge known to have fulfilled a defensive function in a manner to match the now well-known fortified bridges of Charles the Bald in Francia.[100] It would, though, be surprising if London were the only case.[101] As Abels has pointed out, there were blurred lines between 'military' and 'police' actions.[102] The right to collect tolls was presumably exercised on river traffic in addition to road traffic, and it was only a short step from an unauthorized trading vessel being a dangerous raiding vessel.

Amphibious warfare and combined operations: Ships in campaigns

Although naval battles were rare in Anglo-Saxon England, ships formed an element in what could be referred to as early medieval 'combined operations', in which a naval force plays an 'offensive-defensive' role in supporting forces on land.[103] N. A. M. Rodger has drawn attention to how the ships of the late Anglo-Saxon state were used as extensions of royal power, whether in Wales, Scotland, the Irish Sea, or on the coast of northern France, depositing bands of warriors as and when necessary or simply using the threat of force.[104] Such actions may be seen as more fitting to the context of the early Anglo-Saxon kings, as providing rapid means of transport, allowing Anglo-Saxon kings and nobles to 'go viking'. By such means, the ships of the late Anglo-Saxon state may be seen, as Rodger has suggested, as the equivalents of horses for land transport (as they are normally seen in the historiography), carrying warriors to the battle but avoiding use *in* battle.[105]

[99] Harrison, *Bridges of Medieval England*, pp. 38–54; A. Cooper, *Bridges, Law and Power in Medieval England, 700–1400* (Woodbridge, 2006), pp. 39–65. The seminal paper on the maintainence of bridges in military obligations is Brooks, 'Development of Military Obligations in Eighth- and Ninth-Century England'. For roads, see n. 39, above.

[100] J. R. Hagland and B. Watson, 'Fact or Folklore: The Viking Attack on London Bridge', *London Archaeologist* 10 (2005), pp. 328–32, discusses the evidence for an attack on the bridge in 1014. ASC CD 1052 (for which see below, p. 297). For Francia, see AB 864, 865. S. Coupland, 'The Fortified Bridges of Charles the Bald', *Journal of Medieval History* 17 (1991), pp. 1–12.

[101] Cf. Cooper, *Bridges, Law and Power*, pp. 44–6, who argues against the use of bridges as fortifications. David Hill has recently suggested to me, *pers. comm.*, that the fortification at Wallingford was one such fortified bridge, similar to the Frankish type on the Seine at Pont de l'Arche.

[102] Abels, *Lordship and Military Obligation in Anglo-Saxon England*, p. 64 (above, p. 95).

[103] For discussion of the principles of these, see J. B. Hattendorf, 'Introduction: Theories of Naval Power: A. T. Mahan and the Naval History of Medieval and Renaissance Europe', in *War at Sea*, ed. Hattendorf and Unger, pp. 1–22, at pp. 11–12, citing A. T. Mahan, *Naval Strategy*, ch. 9, in *Mahan on Naval Strategy*, ed. J. B. Hattendorf, Classics of Sea Power (Annapolis, 1991), pp. 219–20.

[104] Rodger, *Safeguard of the Sea*, pp. 18–20. See also Pullen-Appleby, *English Sea Power, c. 871 to 1100*, pp. 55–69, 129. Pullen-Appleby makes a good case for Edgarian hegemony in the Irish Sea region on pp. 58–9.

[105] Rodger, *Safeguard of the Sea*, p. 4.

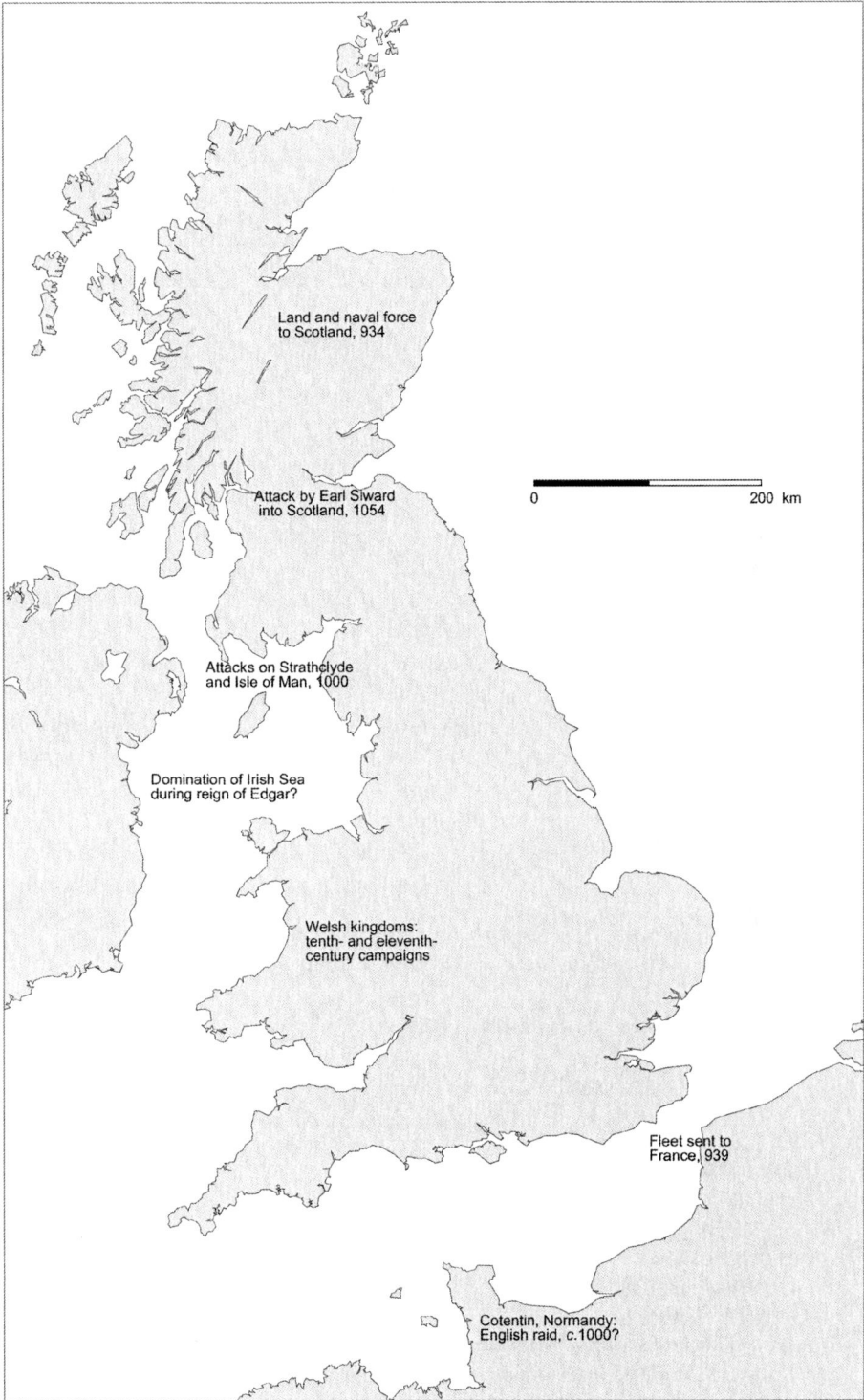

Land and naval force
to Scotland, 934

Attack by Earl Siward
into Scotland, 1054

0   200 km

Attacks on Strathclyde
and Isle of Man, 1000

Domination of Irish Sea
during reign of Edgar?

Welsh kingdoms:
tenth- and eleventh-
century campaigns

Fleet sent to
France, 939

Cotentin, Normandy:
English raid, c.1000?

Fig 5.5 Royal and other actions outside England

While there are some fleeting ninth-century references to battles at sea (see chapter 7), the use of ships to project power is striking. Examples of the use of ships in campaigns can be seen in Scotland and on the coast of France during the reign of Athelstan[106] and, during the reign of Æthelred, in Normandy[107] and the Isle of Man,[108] and during the reign of Edward the Confessor by Earls Harold and Tostig in Gwynedd, Wales,[109] and by Earl Siward in Scotland.[110] Amphibious 'combined operations' campaigns saw land forces supported by ship. While we may not know the details of how such forces communicated with one another or kept their actions cohesive,[111] the important fact to note is that such actions did happen and were recorded, presumably because, as Pullen-Appleby points out, they could be associated with successful kingship[112] – an assertion of power to complement the conquest of territory.

The account of Earl Godwine's family's actions in the summer of 1052 shows an amphibious campaign which was essentially 'Viking' in nature. The different manuscripts of the Anglo-Saxon Chronicle are a good indication of the elements of such a campaign. The E manuscript, while generally sympathetic to the Godwine family, obviously indicates the places of local interest to Canterbury which were attacked and affected by the family's actions (not just Canterbury lands), perhaps even distinguishing between references to the landing of ships and the movement of raiders further inland. The C manuscript, written from a Mercian perspective,[113] takes a different geographical view, recording mostly the 'major' places which were targeted in the campaign.[114] The primary sources have been tabulated (Table 5.3) so that the geographical interests of the different accounts can be compared where they refer to the different actions of the protagonists. Although the two accounts mainly follow the same narrative structure, it may be reasoned that they do not simply represent variations on an exemplar source as the CD manuscript begins with Harold's return from Ireland – something which would be more apparent to a Mercian-informed source – while the E manuscript refers to Harold's return from Ireland further on in the account.

The extracts show the importance for Godwine's family of ravaging places along the coast. At points the detail of locations recorded shows that journeys

---

[106] For the Scottish campaign, see ASC 934; for France, see Flodoard, *Annals* s.a. 939 and 946: Lauer, *Annales de Flodoard*, pp. 73, 101; trans. Bachrach and Fanning, 'Annals' of *Flodoard of Reims*, pp. 31–2, 44.

[107] *Gesta Normannorum Ducum*, ed. Van Houts, OMT, 2 vols (Oxford, 1992–5), vol. 2, pp. 10–15. For reservations on the historicity of this account, see Williams, *Æthelred the Unready*, p. 55.

[108] ASC CDE 1000.

[109] ASC DE 1063.

[110] ASC CD 1054.

[111] See discussion of the use of a lighthouse in 939, by Hill and Sharp, 'Anglo-Saxon Beacon System', p. 160 (p. 220, below).

[112] Pullen-Appleby, *English Sea Power, c. 871 to 1100*, p. 129.

[113] Baxter, 'MS C of the Anglo-Saxon Chronicle'.

[114] This is relevant in consideration of the CDE and A manuscripts of the chronicle with regard to the attacks on the area around Exeter in 1003. See below, pp. 253–5.

Table 5.3 Comparison of extracts from the Anglo-Saxon Chronicle manuscript entries CD and E for 1052, showing the Godwine family and King Edward's movements, with places shown in **bold**

ASC CD	ASC E
In this year Earl Harold came from **Ireland** with ships	*for Harold's arrival from Ireland, see below, marked (*)*
to the **mouth of the Severn**	
near the boundary of **Somerset and Devon**, and there harried greatly, and the local people gathered against him both from Somerset and Devon, and he caused them to flee and there slew more than thirty good thegns, apart from other people,	
and soon after that he went about **Land's End.**	
Then King Edward had forty small boats [*snacca*] equipped [*scypian*] which lay at **Sandwich** [C: 'for many weeks'] so that they should lie in wait for	And in the same year the king and his council determined that ships would be sent out to **Sandwich**, and Earl Ralph and Earl Odda appointed thereto as *heafodmannum* [i.e. commanders]
Earl Godwine who was in **Bruges** that winter.	Then Earl Godwine went out from **Bruges** with his ships
	to the [**River**] **Yser**
Yet he arrived in **this land** first, as they did not know it.	And put out [to sea] a day before the eve of the midsummer feast, so that he came to **Dungeness** which is south of Romney
And while he was here in this country he persuaded all the **men of Kent** to him	
and all the *butsecarls* of the **Hastings district**	
and **everywhere there by the sea-coast** [part of Sussex?],	
and **all Essex** [C has *eastend* = Essex?]	
[C only: 'and **Sussex**']	
and **Surrey** and a great deal else beside. Then they all declared that with him they would live and die.	
When the fleet [*lið*] that lay at **Sandwich** learned about Godwine's expedition [*fare*], they set out after him;	Then it came to the knowledge of the earls out at **Sandwich**, and then they then went out after the other ships, and a land force [*landfyrd*] was ordered out against the ships.

Table 5.3 *continued*

ASC CD	ASC E
	Then meanwhile Earl Godwine was warned; and then he went to **Pevensey**, and the weather became so violent that the earls could not find out what had happened to Earl Godwine.
and he escaped them [C: 'and protected himself where he then might'],	And then Earl Godwine set out again so that he came back to **Bruges**,
And the fleet returned again to **Sandwich**,	and the other ships went back again to **Sandwich**.
and thus homeward to **London**.	Then it was determined that the ships should go back again to **London**, and that other earls and other oarsmen should be assigned to the ships.
	Then it was delayed so long that the *scipfyrd* all left and all took themselves home.
When Godwine learned that the fleet that had been lying at Sandwich was returning home, he then went back again to the **Isle of Wight**,	Earl Godwine found out about this and brought up his sail and fleet and they went west straight to the **Isle of Wight**
	and went inland there [*eodon þær up*], and harried so long there that the people paid them as much as they imposed on them,
	and then they went westward until they came to **Portland** went inland there, and did what damage they could.
	(*) Then Harold had gone from **Ireland** with nine ships,
	and he landed [*com þa up*] at **Porlock**, and there were many people gathered there against him, but he did not flinch from obtaining provisions for himself, and he went inland and killed a great part of the people, and seized for himself what came his way in cattle, men, and property;
and there lay by the coast as long as it took for his son Earl Harold and he to come together.	and then he went eastward to his father,
	and they both went eastward until they came to the **Isle of Wight**, and there took what was earlier [left] behind them.

Table 5.3 *continued*

ASC CD	ASC E
And they did no great harm after they came together except that they took provisions. But they enticed all the local people to them, along the sea-coast and also inland.	Then they went on to **Pevensey** and took with them as many ships as were able to go
	and so onward until they came to **Dungeness**.
	And he took all the ships that that were at **Romney**
	and **Hythe**
	and **Folkestone**,
	and they went east then to **Dover** and went there inland and seized ships there for themselves and hostages, as many as they wished,
And they went towards **Sandwich** and always collected all the *butsecarls* that they met, and they came then to Sandwich with an overwhelming force [*here*].	and so they travelled to **Sandwich** and there they did exactly the same, and everywhere they were given hostages and provisions wherever they desired.
When Edward learned this, he sent inland for more help, but it came very late, and Godwine kept on towards London with his fleet [*lið*], until he came to **Southwark**, where he waited a while until the tide came up. In that time he treated with the citizens so that they wanted almost all what he wanted. [*for the rest of this entry, see p. 297 and p. 44*]	They went then to the **North mouth** [of the River Stour] and thus toward London,
	and some of the ships went into **Sheppey** and did there much damage,
	And they went to the King's Middle-tun [i.e. **King's Milton**] and burnt it all.
	And they were going toward London after the earls. When they came to **London**, there lay against them there the king and earls with fifty ships ready. Then the earls sent to the king and asked him that they might be worthy of all of the things that were unjustly taken from them [i.e. that seized possessions would be returned]. Then the king objected for some while, nevertheless – for so long that the men who were with the earl were very agitated against the king and against his men, so much that the earl himself calmed those men [only] with difficulty. Then Bishop Stigand went with the help of God, and the wise men both inside the *burh* and without, and they decided that hostages should be confirmed on both sides.

Table 5.3 *continued*

ASC CD	ASC E
	And it was thus done. Then Archbishop Robert and the Frenchmen found out about this, so that they took their horses and left,
	some west to **Pentecost's castle** [*perhaps Ewyas Harold, Herefords.ᵃ or Hereford*][b]
	And some north to **Robert's castle.** [*perhaps Canfield Castle, Essex*][c]
	And Archbishop Robert and Bishop Ulf and their companions went out at the **east gate** [of London] and slew or otherwise murdered many young men,
	and went straight to **Eadulf's ness** [the Naze, Essex], and there he got on a wretched ship, and went straight on overseas ....
	Then there was declared a great council **outside London**, and all the earls and the chief men who were in this land were at the council.

[a] A. Pettifer, *English Castles: A Guide by Counties* (Woodbridge, 1995), p. 95.

[b] Williams, *World Before Domesday*, p. 143.

[c] Pettifer, *English Castles*, p. 70.

covered comparatively short distances, such as that between the Isle of Wight and Portland (some 50 nautical miles). This may indicate that legs of voyages by flotillas or single ships were recorded by the different versions of the Chronicle.

It is remarkable that right at the end of the Viking period, there is an account of 'Viking' actions perpetrated by a noble family and their followers who were Scandinavian in their connections and – arguably – their outlook.[115] We might note that these lessons were learnt in the twilight years of the Anglo-Saxon kingdom: Harold's actions in Wales included an amphibious element[116] and Tostig attempted to replicate his family's 1052 success on the south coast of England in 1066, though he failed to win the level of support that his family had earlier gained.[117]

[115] Wulfnoth's seizure of twenty ships in 1009, an episode addressed above (pp. 149–51) has been referred to by Eric John as an act of going 'into the Viking business of his own account': John, *Reassessing Anglo-Saxon England*, p. 146. Given Godwine's use of ships to pursue a private agenda in 1051–2, it is noteworthy that Godwine was a follower of Wulfnoth during the 1009 escapade.

[116] ASC DE 1063. Note that the D MS records Harold's destruction of ships and equipment 'which belonged to' Gruffudd's residence at Rhuddlan (also burnt) and that Harold was brought the figurehead of his enemy's ship, symbolizing the importance of the naval element of the campaign.

[117] DeVries, *Norwegian Invasion of England*, pp. 242–8, notes this possibility amongst other possible motivations for Tostig's actions.

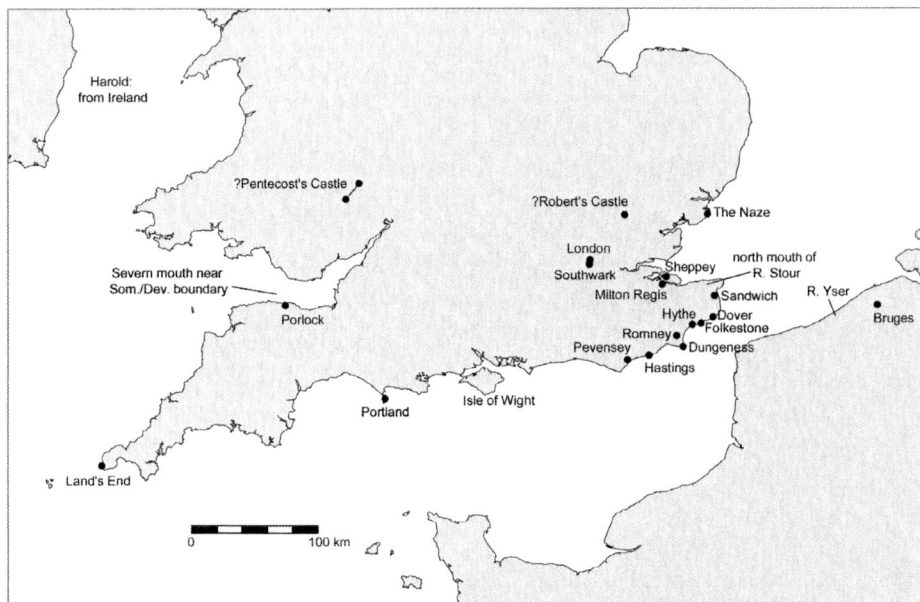

Fig. 5.6 Areas relating to the Godwine family and King Edward's actions, 1052

If nothing else, the Godwine family's campaign of 1051–2 should serve to remind us that not all post-Edgar actions were defensive and organized under the auspices of a centralizing state. Perhaps this was a foretaste of Harold's actions in Wales, but from his point of view such warfare undertaken in the interests of family and patronage was perfectly legitimate. The same, indeed, may be said about the actions of the ætheling Æthelwold, and I have suggested elsewhere that Æthelwold's attack on his cousin also used ships when he arrived at Christchurch in 899 or 900.[118]

Summary

The strategies of campaigns in the Viking period were evidently significant. Although the organization of Viking forces is often dismissed, they were capable of well ordered military campaigns into territory held by Anglo-Saxon rulers, just as Anglo-Saxon rulers were capable of launching campaigns into hostile territory. The movement of forces was a problem which exercised early medieval commanders, reflecting the importance of knowledge of landscapes for both attacking and defending forces.

We should also note the significance of prestige to an early medieval commander. Warfare might be an end in itself, but it was a successful war that gave prestige. If battle was an action that could be devastatingly unpredictable and *could* be something to avoid where possible, then the posturing inherent in a campaign, either in enemy territory or even, in the case of Alfred's recovery of

---

[118] Lavelle, 'Politics of Rebellion', pp. 67–8.

his kingdom in 878, could help to achieve success. Such posturing was especially important in those campaigns associated with conquest, where demonstrations of status appear to have been paramount.

The organization of men and material has been noted, and in the distances involved in campaigns we can see the significance of the use of horses (and, arguably, ox-carts) for transport. Given the flexibility of the prosecution of warfare and the fact that early medieval commanders could also utilize ships, the early medieval development of 'combined operations', was not an unnecessary luxury. We should not necessarily marvel that all this was possible in an age before the availability of topographical maps, but we should note the importance of campaigning as fundamental to the making of war in the early middle ages.

✦ 6 ✦

Fortifications

THE Anglo-Saxon use of fortifications is a particularly controversial and much-debated topic, related as it is to the organization of the state and the role of people within it. The study of fortifications from early medieval England has also played an important role in the development of medieval archaeology in British towns and cities. The work of archaeologists during periods of post-war urban development led directly to a better understanding of the organization of early towns, giving impetus to interdisciplinary study of the early middle ages.[1] The document known as the Burghal Hidage (discussed in chapter 3), dating from the early tenth century in its extant form but probably related to a system from the reign of King Alfred,[2] is often considered as central to the study of fortifications in early medieval Wessex, and this will be addressed in the first section of this chapter. However, for the Burghal Hidage to be addressed effectively, it should be considered in the context of other evidence for fortifications.[3] Therefore this chapter will also address the role of fortifications in sieges, and will conclude with observations on the wider significance of fortifications in the wars of the Second Viking Age during the reign of Æthelred II.

The Burghal Hidage and the organization of fortifications

Archaeologists have often focused on the building of fortifications and their remains in relation to the modern streets of English towns.[4] But even more important than the layout of late Anglo-Saxon fortifications is their organization.

---

[1] Important articles in the development of this study are N. P. Brooks, 'The Unidentified Forts of the Burghal Hidage', *Medieval Archaeology* 8 (1964), pp. 74–90, and D. H. Hill, 'The Burghal Hidage: The Establishment of a Text', *Medieval Archaeology* 13 (1969), pp. 84–92.

[2] See Brooks, 'Administrative Background to the Burghal Hidage', which takes a long view of the Burghal Hidage in West Saxon administration, including consideration of fortifications in Wessex before Alfred. For a focus on an early tenth-century context on the document (though not necessarily all elements of the system), see D. Hill, 'The Calculation and Purpose of the Burghal Hidage', in *Defence of Wessex*, ed. Hill and Rumble, pp. 92–7. For other discussions of the Burghal Hidage, see above, pp. 58–61.

[3] This is an issue noted by J. Baker and S. Brookes, *Beyond the Burghal Hidage: Anglo-Saxon Civil Defence in the Viking Age* (Århus, forthcoming).

[4] A good summary of investigations is provided by D. Hill, 'Gazetteer of Burghal Hidage Sites', in *Defence of Wessex*, ed. Hill and Rumble, pp. 189–231. A recent example of detailed work focusing on urban development is A. Dodd (ed.), *Oxford Before the University: The Late Saxon and Norman Archaeology of the Thames Crossing, the Defences and the Town*, Thames Valley Landscapes Monograph 17 (Oxford, 2003).

Fig. 6.1 Fortifications recorded in the Burghal Hidage and the areas pertaining to them

A system of fortifications was organized according to a theory of 'defence in depth', as Bernard Bachrach and Rutherford Aris refer to it.[5] From a modern military perspective, informed by such works as Edward Luttwak's strategic study of the control of the Roman Empire,[6] a 'defence in depth' allowed fortifications to be mutually supportive, to control strategic points in the countryside which were often related to the income from royal estates. The use of the fortifications could deny the Vikings mobility, even though they could not prevent them from gaining access to the heartland of the West Saxon kingdom.[7]

It is worth beginning with a record of the Burghal Hidage, which contains references to the land allocated to fortifications in Wessex and southern Mercia, and a formula associated with those allocations.[8]

[5] B. S. Bachrach and R. Aris, 'Military Technology and Garrison Organization: Some Observations on Anglo-Saxon Military Thinking in Light of the Burghal Hidage', *Technology and Culture* 31 (1990), pp. 1–17.

[6] E. N. Luttwak, *Grand Strategy of the Roman Empire: From the First Century AD to the Third* (Baltimore, 1976), pp. 125–90.

[7] Abels, 'English Logistics and Military Administration', p. 260.

[8] A critical edition of the Burghal Hidage is in *Defence of Wessex*, ed. Hill and Rumble, pp. 24–31, with Rumble's translation at pp. 32–3.

324 hides belong to *Eorpeburnan*; to Hastings belong 500 hides; and to Lewes belong 1,300 hides; and to Burpham belong 720 hides; to Chichester belong 1,500 hides. Then to Portchester belong 500 hides; and 150 hides belong to Southampton; and to Winchester belong 2,400 hides; and to Wilton belong 1,400 hides; and to Chisbury belong 700 [or 500?] hides, and to Shaftesbury likewise; and to Twynham [Christchurch] belong 500 hides less 30 hides; and to Wareham belong 1,600 hides; and to Bridport belong 800 hides less 40 hides; and to Exeter belong 734 hides; and to Halwell belong 400 hides; and to Lydford belong 150 hides less 10 hides; and to Pilton belong 400 hides less 40 hides; and to Watchet belong 513 hides; and to Axbridge belong 400 hides; and to Lyng belong 100 hides; and to Langport belong 600 hides; and to Bath belong 1,000 hides; and 1,200 hides belong to Malmesbury; and to Cricklade belong 1,400 hides; and 1,500 hides to Oxford; and to Wallingford belong 2,400 hides; and 1,600 hides belong to Buckingham; and to Sashes belong 1,000 hides; and 600 hides belong to Eashing; and to Southwark belong 1,800 hides.

As David Hill noted, the clockwise circuit of the towns recorded in the Burghal Hidage corresponds to the way in which other Anglo-Saxon circuits, such as those of charter bounds, were organized.[9] Furthermore, the differences in the formulae used to record the allocation of hidages reflect different areas which may preserve differences in administrative practices. The '*x* hides less *y*' formula used for some south-western burhs is different from the 'to *a* belong *x* hides' and '*x* hides belong to *a*' formulae, while the hidages are also recorded in notably different sets of multiples.[10] Of no less importance is what appears to be a working formula in the A recension of the Burghal Hidage:[11]

> For an acre's breadth *on wealstillinge* 7 *to þære wære* [i.e. the maintenance and defence of wall], are required 16 hides: if each hide be manned by one man, then may each pole [of wall] be set with four men; then are required for 20 poles *on wealstillinge*, eighty hides; and for a furlong are required 160 hides, by the same reckoning that I stated here above. For two furlongs, are required 320 hides; for three furlongs, 480 hides. Then are required for 4 furlongs, 640 hides; for five furlongs of circuit [*ymbgang*] are required eight hundred hides *on wealstillinge*; for six furlongs are required 960 hides; for seven furlongs, 1,120 hides; for eight furlongs of circuit *wealstillinge* 1,280 hides; for nine furlongs, 1,440 hides; for 10 furlongs are required 1,600 hides; for eleven furlongs are required 1,760 hides; for 12 furlongs of circuit *wealstillinge* are required 1,920 hides. If the circuit be more, then the additional amount can be deduced from this account, for always for one furlong are required 160 men then each pole is set with four men.

Both Nicholas Brooks and David Hinton have suggested that this version of

[9] Hill, 'Burghal Hidage: Establishment of a Text', pp. 88–9.

[10] On the recording of the figures, see Hill, 'Burghal Hidage: Establishment of a Text'; Hill's ideas are refined in 'The Nature of the Figures', in *Defence of Wessex*, ed. Hill and Rumble, pp. 74–87, at pp. 80–1.

[11] *Defence of Wessex*, ed. Hill and Rumble, p. 30.

the document, which includes a formula with a set of pre-calculated figures as an aid to working, indicates that the sizes of the fortifications and the resources of the kingdom were known.[12] This may suggest that the Burghal Hidage as we know it was a manifestation of a functioning system rather than *the* manifestation of a system, and was perhaps only a 'paper exercise'. It was probably the product of an energetic and enquiring administrator, rather than the setting out of an unchangeable system; such potential for change was raised when F. W. Maitland first addressed the implications of the Burghal Hidage in 1897.[13]

The system of West Saxon fortifications is usually attributed to the reign of Alfred the Great, after the victory at the Battle of Edington in 878.[14] However, recent works have ascribed the significance of organization, especially that of fortifications in Mercian territory, to the pre-Viking kingdom of Mercia[15] and to the organization of the 'Anglo-Saxon' kingdom of Edward the Elder during the period of the so-called 'Re-Conquest' of the Danelaw.[16] None of these periods of development are necessarily mutually exclusive, as we need not assume that there was a single point of reorganization. Nor should the development of fortifications in Francia necessarily be a pre-requisite for the organization of fortifications in the West Saxon kingdom.[17] Conversely, the existence of Charles the Bald's statement (via Hincmar of Reims) in the Edict of Pîtres (864) that the Franks should follow a custom (*consuetudo*) that is 'ancient and of [i.e. followed by] other peoples' (*antiquam et aliarum gentium*) in organizing their defensive obligations could be an indication that a Mercian or earlier West Saxon system was the inspiration for Frankish organization under Charles the Bald. But Mercia or Wessex did not have to have been the inspiration for Charles. After all, his priority was to refer to the fifth-century Theodosian Code.[18] Independent parallel developments are not

---

[12] Brooks, 'Administrative Background to the Burghal Hidage'; Hinton, 'Fortifications and their Shires,'; N. P. Brooks, 'Alfredian Government: The West Saxon Inheritance', in *Alfred the Great: Papers from the Eleventh-Centenary Conferences*, ed. T. Reuter, Studies in Early Medieval Britain (Aldershot, 2003), pp. 153–73. For earlier discussion of the figures of the Burghal Hidage, see Maitland, *Domesday Book and Beyond*, pp. 187–8, 502–6; see also Chadwick, *Studies on Anglo-Saxon Institutions*, pp. 204–27.

[13] Maitland, *Domesday Book and Beyond*, p. 186. For a sceptical review of a system based on Winchester as a model of town-planning, see S. Joly, 'Alfred le Grand et les burhs planifies anglo-saxons: conception et adoption d'un modèle', in *Village et ville au moyen age: les dynamiques morphologiques*, ed. B. Gauthiez, E. Zadora-Rio and H. Galinié, Collection perspectives 'villes et territoires' 5, 2 vols (Tours, 2003), vol. 1, pp. 353–72 (text) and vol. 2, pp. 363–7 (illustrations).

[14] For an extreme interpretation of this, see Haslam, 'King Alfred and the Vikings'.

[15] S. R. Bassett, 'Divide and Rule? The Military Infrastructure of Eighth- and Ninth-Century Mercia', *EME* 15 (2007), pp. 53–85; 'The Middle and Late Anglo-Saxon Defences of Western Mercian Towns', *ASSAH* 15 (2008), pp. 180–239.

[16] Baker and Brookes, *Beyond the Burghal Hidage*. I am grateful to Keith Richardson for discussion on this subject. For the emergence of a 'kingdom of the Anglo-Saxons', see above, pp. xvi, 10.

[17] Hassall and Hill, 'Pont de l'Arche: Frankish Influence on the West Saxon *Burh*?'.

[18] *Edictum Pistense*, ed. A. Boretius, MGH Capitularia regum Francorum 2 (Hanover, 1911), no. 273, pp. 310–28, at pp. 321–2. This is highlighted by Nelson, 'Translating Images of Authority', p. 95 (a reference for which I am grateful to Barbara Yorke).

unknown in the history of the organization of military systems. To hazard a comparison, tanks were developed simultaneously in both Great Britain and France during the First World War in response to the conditions of trench warfare. The stimulus of a demonstration of a track-laying vehicle may have been the same for both parties, but the fact that broadly the same type of vehicle was created from that stimulus is a rejoinder against becoming too complacent in attributing influence.[19] It follows that the West Saxons and Franks should have developed systems of fortification in response to similar conditions, and we need not necessarily focus on who inspired whom – more on what conditions led to what solutions.

An important aspect of the manifestation of influence was the perceived link between kingship and Roman authority. *Romanitas* emphasized status. Hill usefully pointed out that burhs evoked an idea of Rome, an issue which may not have been unconnected with Alfred's childhood visits to the Eternal City.[20] Although the Anglo-Saxon Chronicle does not make much of the urban legacy of the Romans in Britain, Æthelweard makes one of the most explicit late Anglo-Saxon statements on this subject: 'They made cities, forts [*castella*], bridges and streets with skill, and these are to be seen to this day.'[21] While we cannot know precisely what Æthelweard had seen at the time of the composition of the *Chronicon*, this was an impressive endorsement of the Roman legacy.

A connection between the organization and building of fortifications and the imposition of kingship by Alfred – indeed through what are referred to at one point as 'imperial decrees' – can be seen in Asser's *Life of Alfred*:[22]

> But if, between these royal exhortations [*regalia exhortamenta*], through the slothfulness of the people these commands were not fulfilled or, having been begun late at a time of necessity, they could not be produced in time for the use of those working [on them]. For I should speak of the fortifications [*castella*] ordered by him which are not yet begun or by being begun too late, have not been conducted to completion, and many enemies rushed in by land and by sea – or, as often happens, by both places – then those who opposed the imperial decrees [*imperiales diffinitiones*] were put to shame in empty penitence by near destruction. That is to say, I refer to 'empty penitence' by the testimony of scripture, in which numerous men who had perpetrated insidious deeds often suffered by being struck down by severe calamity.

The reference to the organization of the forces of Alfred's army in the 890s suggests that a system of fortifications became an important element of military organization. The Anglo-Saxon Chronicle entry for 893 has already been cited in chapter 3,[23] but it is worth noting that its reference to a tripartite organization, with a force stationied in the fortifications, is juxtaposed with a consideration of

---

[19] K. Macksey and J. H. Batchelor, *Tank: A History of the Armoured Fighting Vehicle* (London, 1970; rev. edn, 1973), pp. 20–6.

[20] D. Hill, 'The Origins of Alfred's Urban Policies', in *Alfred the Great*, ed. Reuter, pp. 219–33.

[21] Æthelweard, *Chronicon*, p. 5. He also includes a description of Hadrian's Wall.

[22] Asser, ch. 91.

[23] Above, pp. 92–3.

a near-disaster with an unfinished fortification in 892. As Simon Keynes has suggested, this event may have led to Asser's record of Alfred's chastisement.[24]

> Here in this year the great *here* which we formerly spoke about [went] again from the east kingdom westward to Boulogne, and there were provided with ships such that they came over in one voyage, with horses and everything, and then came up into the Lympne mouth with 250 ships. That river-mouth is in east Kent, at the east end of the great forest [*wudu*] which we call Andred [*Andredesweald*]. This forest along the east and along the is a hundred and twenty miles long or longer, and thirty miles broad; the river avout which we spoke earlier flows out from the *weald*; they rowed their ships up the river to the *weald*, four miles from the outward part of the river-mouth, and there stormed a fort ['abræcon an geweorc']; within the fortification[25] were set a few *ceorlisc* men, and it was partly built.

However, if Asser was particularly censorious in reporting Alfred's chastisement, recognizing potential limitations in a system of fortifications, it is notable that the event recorded by the Chronicle took place in Kent, which does not seem to have been represented in the Burghal Hidage. It has been suggested that the otherwise unidentified Burghal Hidage fortress of *Eorpeburnan* was the fortification recorded in the Chronicle entry for 892 but this does not have to have been the case.[26] We need not assume that the Viking attack upon the *Andredesweald* fortification in 892 resulted in its exclusion from the system recorded in the Burghal Hidage. At this point in the 890s, Alfred's son Edward seems to have held a sub-kingship in Kent,[27] so perhaps any system of Kentish fortifications, building on a Mercian legacy from the early ninth century, had a separate status; Kentish land, after all, was assessed in sulungs and the Burghal Hidage was concerned with assessment in hides.[28]

There are other indications of reorganization of the fortifications in territory under Alfred's influence. In recording the donation of rights at Worcester, a late-ninth century Old English charter provides evidence of the establishment of the burh there:[29]

> To the Almighty God, the True Unity and the Holy Trinity in heaven, let there be praise and glory and thankful deeds for all the goodness which he has given to us. For whose love at first, and for St Peter and of the church at Worcester, and also at

---

[24] Keynes and Lapidge, *Alfred the Great*, p. 271.

[25] Reading *fæstenne* from ASC B 892 rather than *fenne* (perhaps an abbreviated version of *fæstenne?*), as in other MSS. On this issue, see *EHD* 1, p. 201, n. 11.

[26] This issue is discussed by F. Kitchen, 'The Burghal Hidage: Towards the Identification of *Eorpeburnan*', *Medieval Archaeology* 28 (1984), pp. 175–8, who posits Rye as a possible site. See also Brooks, 'Unidentified Forts of the Burghal Hidage'.

[27] S. D. Keynes, 'The Control of Kent in the Ninth Century', *EME* 2 (1993), pp. 111–32, citing S 350 (AD 898); also B. Yorke, 'Edward as Ætheling', in *Edward the Elder, 899–924*, ed. D. Hill and N. J. Higham (London, 2001), pp. 25–39, at pp. 31–2; Æthelweard, *Chronicon*, pp. 49–50.

[28] See Grierson, 'Weights and Measures', p. 81.

[29] S 223 (AD 884×901); Harmer, *Select English Historical Documents of the Ninth and Tenth Centuries*, pp. 22–3.

the request of Bishop Wærferth their friend, Ealdorman Æthelred and Æthelflæd ordered to be built [hehtan bewyrcean] the burh at Worcester for the defence [to gebeorge] of all the people, and also therein to exalt the praise of God. And they now declare in this charter with God's witness that they wish, from each of their rights which belong to their lordship – either in the marketplace or in the street, within the byrg as outside – to grant half to God and St Peter and to the lord of that church. So that therefore they [the rights] may be more honourable in that place, and also that they may more easily help that community by some measure, and that their memory be observed the more firmly in that place for eternity, while God's lordship be at that minster.

And Bishop Wærferth and the community have set these divine services before that which is done daily, both during their life as well as after their life; that is at each matins and at each evensong and at every tierce, the psalm De profundis, while they live, and after their life Laudate Dominum; and each Saturday in St Peter's church thirty psalms and their mass, both for them living and also passed away.

And moreover Æthelred and Æthelflæd declare with devoted spirit that they wish to grant this to God and St Peter in the witness of King Alfred and of all the witan who are in the land of the Mercians; except that the wagon-shilling and the load-penny go to the king's hand just as they always did at Droitwich. But other-wise, whether land-rent, the fine for fighting, theft, dishonest trading, or damaging the burh wall [burhwealles sceatinge], or any the offences which require compensa-tion, are to belong half to the lord of the church, for the pleasure of God and St Peter, just as it has been set for the market-place and the streets. And outside the market-place, the bishop is to be worthy of his land and all his rights, just as our predecessors earlier set and freed [i.e. privileged] it.

And Æthelred and Æthelflæd did this in witness of King Alfred and of all the witan of the Mercians whose names hereafter stand written. And in the name of God Almighty they beseech all their successors that no man may diminish this alms-gift which they have given to that church for the love of God and St Peter.

As can be seen from the Worcester charter, a system of fortifications seems to have been imposed beyond the kingdom of Wessex, perhaps again building on the legacy of the Mercian kingdom.[30] Further north in the territory subject to the former Mercian kingdom,[31] the Domesday entry for Chester indicates attention to the maintenance of the city walls on a basis which was not dissimilar from the one man per hide formula continued in the B recension of the Burghal Hidage:[32]

---

[30] Bassett, 'Divide and Rule?'; Brooks, 'Development of Military Obligations in Eighth- and Ninth-Century England', pp. 80–1, highlights early ninth-century Mercian charters which record the obligation of obligations of burdens of service against 'pagans' (i.e. Vikings). See also Bassett's paper, 'The Middle and Late Anglo-Saxon Defences of Western Mercian Towns', ASSAH 15 (2008), pp. 180–239, although he notes (pp. 226–30) the limited archaeological evidence for early Worcester defences.

[31] On Cheshire's place in the Mercian kingdom, see N. J. Higham, The Origins of Cheshire, Origins of the Shire (Manchester, 1993), pp. 102–14.

[32] DB Cheshire C 21 (fol. 262d).

For the city wall and bridge to be repaired [*reedificandum*] the reeve used to call out [*educere*] one man to come from each hide in the county. The lord of any man who did not come paid a fine of 40s to the king and the earl. This forfeiture [*foris-factura*] was outside the farm [i.e. customary payment].

Richard Abels has suggested that the continuity of Chester's burghal system until 1066, in contrast to its absence in the rest of the English counties, highlights a gradual abandonment of the system elsewhere during the course of the tenth century. The borders with Wales were, he argued, a special case which warranted special attention to their defence,[33] although, as will be seen below, the continuity of urban fortifications also warrants consideration.

Several suggestions have been made for other stages in urban development. David Hill tentatively suggested that Athelstan's reign saw a planned system of towns developing in the wake of the campaigns undertaken by his father and aunt,[34] while F. T. Wainwright had earlier highlighted the importance of a system of fortifications used by Æthelflæd and Edward the Elder to protect their conquests in the Danelaw region.[35]

On the basis of the peak in numismatic evidence attributed to some towns, another network of fortifications has been proposed by Gareth Williams for late tenth-century Lincolnshire. He suggests that this was an abortive attempt to develop a system of fortifications under Æthelred. Williams likens this to an endeavour to develop a system organized along the lines of that of the Burghal Hidage in eastern England.[36] Such a system may have been supplemented by other better-known so-called 'emergency' boroughs newly built at South Cadbury (Somerset), Cissbury (Sussex), and Old Sarum (Wilts.), as well by as the rebuilding of such fortifications as those at Watchet (Somerset) and Wareham (Dorset).[37]

Towns fulfilled defensive and economic functions, but in relation to how burhs

---

[33] Abels, 'From Alfred to Harold II', p. 29.

[34] D. Hill, 'Athelstan's Urban Reforms', *ASSAH* 11 (2000), pp. 173–86.

[35] Wainwright, 'Æthelflæd, Lady of the Mercians', pp. 57–62. For a fortification built by Edward the Elder in Rhuddlan, north Wales, see J. Manley, 'Cledemutha: A Late Saxon Burh in North Wales', *Medieval Archaeology* 31 (1987), pp. 13–46. See below, pp. 228–30.

[36] G. Williams, 'Civil Defence or Royal Powerbase? Military and Non-Military Functions of the Late Anglo-Saxon Burh', in *Landscapes of Defence in the Viking Age: Anglo-Saxon England and Comparative Perspectives*, ed. J. Baker, S. Brookes, D. Parsons, and A. Reynolds, SEMA 28 (Turnhout, forthcoming).

[37] Abels, 'From Alfred to Harold II', p. 25, citing G. Astill, 'The Towns of Berkshire', J. Haslam, 'The Towns of Wiltshire', D. A. Hinton, 'The Towns of Hampshire', M. Aston, 'The Towns of Somerset', J. Haslam, 'The Towns of Devon', in *Anglo-Saxon Towns in Southern England*, ed. J. Haslam (Chichester, 1984), pp. 53–86, at p. 76; pp. 87–147, at pp. 109, 128, 137; pp. 149–65, at p. 153; pp. 167–201, at pp. 188, 193; pp. 249–84, at p. 258. For 'emergency burhs', see also D. Hill, 'Trends in the Development of Towns During the Reign of Ethelred II', in *Ethelred the Unready: Papers from the Millenary Conference*, ed. D. Hill, BAR British Series 59 (Oxford, 1978), pp. 213–26, and L. Alcock, *Cadbury Castle, Somerset: The Early Medieval Archaeology* (Cardiff, 1995), pp. 44–59, 154–70. I also grateful to Jeremy Haslam for sending me a copy of his forthcoming paper, 'The Late Saxon Burhs at Daws Castle near Watchet, Somerset'.

reflect a creation and imposition of royal authority,[38] it is worth commenting on the picture presented by *De Obsessione Dunelmi* of the heads of Scottish corpses displayed on poles from the walls of Durham in 1006, as well as the dismembered corpses of martyrs in the Old English version of the *Seven Sleepers of Ephesus*.[39] Given the authoritarian impulse behind the display of bodies in the landscape,[40] guard duty on the ramparts of a burh or life within a town may have constituted a regular interaction with – and, crucially, a continuous reminder of – royal authority.[41] To that end, an external threat represented an opportunity for the furtherment of the English project.

If that royal authority operated with regard to the organization of fortifications, it needed to operate with a network of roads and signalling systems to ensure that connections between the fortifications were maintained. The relationship between fortifications, roads and bridges may be noted, even if it is difficult to discern the precise operation of road connections in that network.[42] Forthcoming work from a research team at University College London considers the network of signalling sites and smaller fortifications,[43] but here it is relevant to reprint an important but little-known article by David Hill and Sheila Sharp. Originally published in a collection of papers on place-names, it is a preliminary study of the places associated with what the authors propose was a network of beacons in Anglo-Saxon England.[44] The implications of this with regard to coastal defences have already been raised in chapter 4 but the article is reprinted in full below, as it provides a useful exploration of the evidence for an integrated network of defences in Anglo-Saxon England. The exploration is not comprehensive but it collects a great deal of evidence on the subject, and deserves further recognition for that.

[38] D. van Dommelen, 'Social and Political Reconstruction in Late Anglo-Saxon England', in *Landscapes of Defence*, ed. Baker *et al.*

[39] *De Obsessione Dunhelmi*, in *Symeonis Monachi Opera Omnia*, ed. Arnold, vol. 1, p. 216; *Aelfric's Lives of Saints*, ed. Skeat, vol. 1, pp. 492–3. See above, p. 31.

[40] See generally A. J. Reynolds, *Anglo-Saxon Deviant Burial Customs*, Medieval History and Archaeology (Oxford, 2009).

[41] This issue, and the wider issue of the relationship between royal authority and urban life, has been discussed in C. Cubitt, 'As the Lawbook Teaches': Reeves, Lawbooks and Urban Life in the Anonymous Old English Legend of the Seven Sleepers', *EHR* 124 (2009), pp. 1021–49.

[42] Loyn, *Governance of Anglo-Saxon England*, p. 155; Harrison, *Bridges of Medieval England*, pp. 38–54. Cf. Cooper, *Bridges, Law and Power*, pp. 40–6, which associates bridge-work with governance rather than with military interests, whereas Brooks, 'Development of Military Obligations in Eighth- and Ninth-Century England', pp. 71–2, notes bridge and fortress as a 'single military unit'.

[43] Baker and Brookes, *Beyond the Burghal Hidage*. Other works are G. Pepper, 'Tothill Street Westminster, and Anglo-Saxon Civil Defence', *London Archaeologist* 7:16 (1996), pp. 432–4; G. Gower, 'A Suggested Anglo-Saxon Signalling System Between Chichester and London', *London Archaeologist* 10:3 (2002), pp. 59–63.

[44] Hill and Sharp, 'Anglo-Saxon Beacon System'. The idea of a network of beacons was raised in Hill, *Atlas of Anglo-Saxon England*, p. 92, relating to an early modern system recorded in H. T. White, 'The Beacon System in Hampshire', *Proceedings of the Hampshire Field Club and Archaeological Society* 10 (1926–30), pp. 252–78.

An Anglo-Saxon Beacon System

DAVID HILL AND SHEILA SHARP

This article is intended to draw together the slim, and, in some cases, suspect, evidence for Anglo-Saxon beacons. It is an important aspect of warfare which, taken as an integrated system including coastguards, beacons, *fyrd* and fortifications, had an influence on the wars with the Danes, and even on the Hastings campaign. It has been a commonplace, when discussing the Anglo-Saxon defences against the Vikings in the ninth and tenth centuries, to assume that some sort of beacon system was in use by the West Saxons. The meagre information has never been brought together, although writers on beacons have always accepted an earlier date for the English system than the thirteenth century at which date records are explicit. The necessity for a discussion is underlined by the footnote in Stenton who, when considering the timing of the Hastings campaign of 1066, remarks 'without the aid of beacons, for which there is no tradition …'[45]

That beacons existed is demonstrated by the ironic remark in the Anglo-Saxon Chronicle, s.a. 1006:

> They [the Vikings] betook themselves to the entertainment waiting them, out through Hampshire into Berkshire to Reading; and always they observed their ancient custom, lighting their beacons [*hiora here-beacen*] as they went.[46]

The imagery of the beacon appears twice in *Beowulf* and in many other contexts both literary and poetic, and in the Chronicle the visual imagery of the burning farms and houses in the wake of the Vikings could be summoned up by referring to the beacons, demonstrating that the concept was widely understood; it is worthwhile to note that the term *here-beacen* meant 'army-beacon'. Unfortunately, any further enquiry tends to be halted by the fact that there appears to be no pre-Conquest place-name containing the element 'beacon', unless, that is, we can accept OE *weard* as an approximate alternative. Helge Kökeritz lists two on the Isle of Wight — *la Wyrde* and *la Wirdde*.[47] Yet beacon-systems were a commonplace at the time all over Europe; as may be seen in a reference from the 'History of the Sons of Louis the Pious', written in the first half of the ninth century:

> October, 841. So Charles (the Bald) ordered some men to guard Paris and Meulan, and others to take up positions wherever he knew there were fords and ferries. He himself pitched camp in a central position across from St Cloud so he could, if necessary, prevent Lothair from crossing, or help his men if Lothair should plan to attack them anywhere. To make it easy to learn

---

[45] Stenton, *Anglo-Saxon England*, 3rd edn, p. 592.

[46] D. Whitelock (ed.), *The Anglo-Saxon Chronicle* (London, 1965), p. 88.

[47] H. Kökeritz, *The Place-Names of the Isle of Wight*, Arkiv for germansk Namnforskning 6 (Uppsala, 1940), p. 66.

where help was needed, he arranged signs and guards at critical points, as is usually done on the coast.[48]

Other sources for the events of 841 tell us that these signs were piles of wood to be lit at the appropriate moment. This might seem to be a continuation of the system originally started by Caligula, when he built a lighthouse at Boulogne, *c.* AD 40, followed by a similar one at Dover. A similar system was used by Charlemagne when setting up strongpoints and coast-guard stations on the shores threatened by the Danes,[49] in the course of which, *c.* AD 800, he restored the *Tour de l'Ordre* at Boulogne (quite possibly Caligula's construction).[50] There is also a tradition that Louis the Pious built the first light-tower on the Isle of Cordouan.

In England there is no comparable clear statement of a system, although it can be inferred from such charters as Sawyer 832 that there was some organization of coast-watch. This charter, dated to 977, is a grant by Edward the Martyr to Æthelweard, *comes*, of estates in St Keverne in Cornwall 'free from all royal dues except military service and the fortification of fortresses and maritime guard [*vigiliis marinis*]'. This substitution of maritime guard for the more normal duties regarding bridges suggests an organized coast-watch, such as appears to have been known to the author of *Beowulf* (lines 229 ff.):

> Then the watchman of the Scyldings, whose duty it was to guard the sea-cliffs, saw from the height bright shields and battle equipment ready for use borne over the gangway. A desire to know who the men were pressed on his thoughts. The thane of Hrothgar went to the shore riding his steed; mightily he brandished his spear in his hands, spoke forth a question: 'What warriors are ye, clad in corselets, who have come thus bringing the high ship over the way of waters, hither over the floods? Lo! for a time I have been guardian of our coasts, I have kept watch by the sea lest any enemies should make ravage with their sea raiders on the land of the Danes ...'[51]

However, there is an implied reference to an early beacon system in Lambarde's use of 'ancient records', and the remarks of Sir Roger Twysden, Captain of the Defences under Elizabeth I, that Lambarde had told him that great stacks of wood had been used for burning in ancient times.[52] Furthermore, Leland, in describing Dover, says:

> On the toppe of the hye dive betwene the towne and the peere remayneth yet, about a flyte shot up ynto the land fro the very biymme of the se clyffe,

---

[48] Nithard, 'Histories', in *Carolingian Chronicles*, trans. Scholz and Rogers, p. 159.

[49] Loyn and Percival, *Reign of Charlemagne*, p. 16.

[50] B. de Montfaucon, *Supplement to Antiquity Explained* (London, 1725), IV.6, p. 464.

[51] R. K. Gordon (ed. and trans.), *Beowulf* (London, 1954).

[52] R. M. Warnicke, *William Lambarde* (London/Chichester, 1973), *passim*.

a mine of a towr, the which hath bene as a pharos or a mark to shyppes on the se...[53]

More prosaically there are the following references in the document known as the 'Rights and Ranks of People', *Rectitudines Singularum Personarum*, a record of the duties assignable to the various grades of society in the England of the first half of the eleventh century:

> *Thegn's Law* ... also in respect of many states, further service arises on the king's order such as ... equipping a guard ship and guarding the coast ...

> *Cottar's-right* ... let him also perform services on his lord's demesne land if he is ordered, keeping watch on the sea-coast ...[54]

Furthermore, there are two references in continental sources which show, by implication, that coastal beacons were in use in tenth-century England. The first is found in Richer's 'L'histoire de France', where the author, in describing the return of Louis d'Outremer, tells how King Æthelstan made arrangements for the proper reception of his nephew at Boulogne:

> ... and so the duke [Hugh the Great] with the princes of the Gauls, came to Boulogne to receive the lord king and, gathered together on the sand of the nearby shores, announced their presence to those who were on the other shore by burning some hovels. For King Æthelstan had gone there with his royal cavalry ready to send his nephew to the waiting Gauls. By his command several houses were burned, demonstrating to those opposite that he himself had arrived.[55]

Richer was a monk, whose father had been a soldier in service with Louis d'Outremer and who could thereby have received some personal information on the firing of these signals. From this, it may easily be understood how the remains of Charlemagne's wooden lighthouse could have been thought of as 'hovels' and, although Latouche, the editor, doubts whether a fire in Dover could have been seen from Boulogne, a beacon on a lighthouse would have been perfectly visible.

Finally, the Saga of Hakon the Good tells us that part of this King of Norway's most abiding work was as an organizer of military forces. Amongst other reforms, he instituted a system of war-signals *(Varder)* 'whereby beacons were lighted on the mountain tops when danger was at hand. By these means, it was said, the whole of Norway could be called to arms within a week'.[56] This all might seem very far away from Anglo-Saxon England, but it should not be forgotten that Hakon had been fostered by Æthelstan. Coast-watch can therefore

---

[53] L. Toulmin Smith (ed.), *Leland's Itinerary in England and Wales* (London, 1909), vol. 5, part VIII, p. 50.

[54] *EHD* 2, p. 813.

[55] *Richer: Histoire de France (888–995)*, Tom. 1: 888–954, ed. R. Latouche, Les Classiques de l'histoire de France au moyen âge 12 (Paris, 1930), pp. 128–30.

[56] K. Gjerset, *History of the Norwegian People*, vol. 1 (New York, 1927), pp. 164–6.

be shown on quite sound evidence to have been widespread and organized, but the passage of the information and warning(s) gathered by that watch to the countryside at large by means of beacons is nowhere specifically mentioned. That there was a link is self-evident, but to prove that link and to demonstrate that that link was by means of beacons is extremely difficult.

There are sources of documentary evidence which might be used to redress the deficit in chronicles and histories. Many Anglo-Saxon charters have a set of bounds describing the physical points which delimited the periphery of the estate. The distribution of the evidence is therefore random. Among the bounds there are some that contain reference to such features as *weard-setl*, translated by Bosworth and Toller as a 'place where guard is kept, those who keep watch, a guard'.[57] Also listed are *weardan hyll*, translated as 'beacon hill', *weard-dūn* 'beacon hill', and *weard-steall* 'guard house'. There is obviously some connection between the house, the place and the beacon, if the *Dictionary* is to be trusted. The charters in which these terms appear and which seem to be relevant are as follows:

S 258 (dated 749): King Cuthred donates Highclere, Hants, to the church of Winchester; the OE bounds mention *Þeardsetle* (BCS [i.e. W. de Gray Birch (ed.), *Cartularium Saxonicum*, 3 vols. (London, 1885–9)] 179).

S 383 (undated): King Edward the Elder confirms Highclere; *Þeard feld* is in error for *Þeard setle* (BCS 628).

S 400 (dated 928): King Æthelstan to Byrhtferth, grant of Odstock, Wilts.; OE bounds contain *Þeardan hylle* (BCS 663).

S 405 (dated 930): King Æthelstan to the bishop and *familia* at Crediton, a grant of land at Sandford, Devon; OE bounds contain *Þeard setl* (BCS 1343).

S 487 (dated 943): King Edmund to Ælfswith, grant of land at Burghclere, Hants; OE bounds contain *Þeardsetle* (BCS 787).

S 491 (dated 943): King Edmund to Eadric, a grant of land at Leckhamstead, Berks.; OE bounds contain *Þeardan dune* (BCS 789).

S 565 (dated 955): King Eadred to the bishop of Winchester, a grant of land at Highclere, Hants; OE bounds contain *Þeard setle* (BCS 905).

S 671 (dated 955 for ?973): King Edgar to Rochester Cathedral, a grant of land at Bromley, Kent; OE bounds contain *Þeard setlan* (BCS 1295).

S 680 (dated 959): King Edgar to Ælfwine, a grant of land at Highclere, Hants; OE bounds contain *Þearð seð* (BCS 1051).

S 738 (dated 966): King Edgar to Ælfgifu, a grant of land at Newnham Murren, Oxon.; OE bounds contain *up on Þearddune þær þæt cristel mæl stod* (BCS 1176).

---

[57] Bosworth-Toller, s.vv.

S 864 (dated 987): King Æthelred II to Æthelsige, a grant of land at Bromley, Kent; OE bounds contain *weardsetle* (KCD [i.e. J. M. Kemble (ed.), *Codex Diplomaticus Ævi Saxonici Opera Johannis M. Kemble* (London, 6 vols, 1839–48)] 657).

S 1591 (undated): bounds of Crowle, Worcs., contain *weard setl* (BCS vol. 2, 2, attached to BCS 428).

Five of these twelve charters mentioned deal with the Cleres in northern Hants. These Þ*eard setl*/Þ*eard feld* boundary-points appear in both Highclere and Burghclere charters. It is therefore obvious, no matter what the arguments concerning the solving of these several bounds, that the *weard* complex existed on the boundary between the adjoining estates, and it is common ground that these features are associated with Beacon Hill (at SU 458574), and close to the present parish boundaries between Highclere and Burghclere. Whoever sat in that guardhouse was not looking out for Danes and Vikings coming up the lanes from Crux Easton or some other hamlet in the nearby valleys, he was looking to the distant horizons for signs from afar. Beacon Hill, Burghclere, was a beacon site in Anglo-Saxon days: it was also a beacon site at the time of the Spanish Armada. The views from this hill have not changed from the pre-Conquest period, except in detail. In fact, our surest document for the period we are discussing is not to be found in the library, it is the landscape itself.

Fortunately, one of the counties in which the sixteenth-century evidence for beacon-systems has been investigated is Hampshire, and we have a map of these beacons, together with their lines of intervisibility (see [Fig. 6.2]). These are fully documented.[58] We are told that Highclere was receiving warnings from Farley Mount to the south, a few miles from the royal city of Winchester. To the north, Camden records that the warning was passed on from Highclere to the major beacon of Berkshire, Cuckhamsley Barrow on Ashdown. The choice of these sites would appear to be unchangeable, for the whole system is interlocking. If one removes the beacon from the site at Highclere, one finds that other beacons have to be moved as well. The beacons were not simply fires on the highest hills, they were sited to look down valleys, or round the mass of a higher hill, since the choice of an unnecessarily higher hill increased the risk of that site being more frequently blanketed by low cloud.

The continuity of the site at Highclere, itself a low hill in the valley between the Downs and lower than the hills to either side, argues for the continuity of the system of which it is part, for it must be repeated that no beacon stood alone, if this is true, and referring to [Fig. 6.2], the Hampshire system would be postulated as working in the following manner:

> On the coast of the Isle of Wight the cottar, *cot-setla*, was keeping his watch on the sea coast, *sæ-weard*, under the guidance of the thegn whose duty it was to organize the watch. A foreign fleet, seen off the west of the island, would

---

[58] White, 'Beacon System in Hampshire', pp. 252–78.

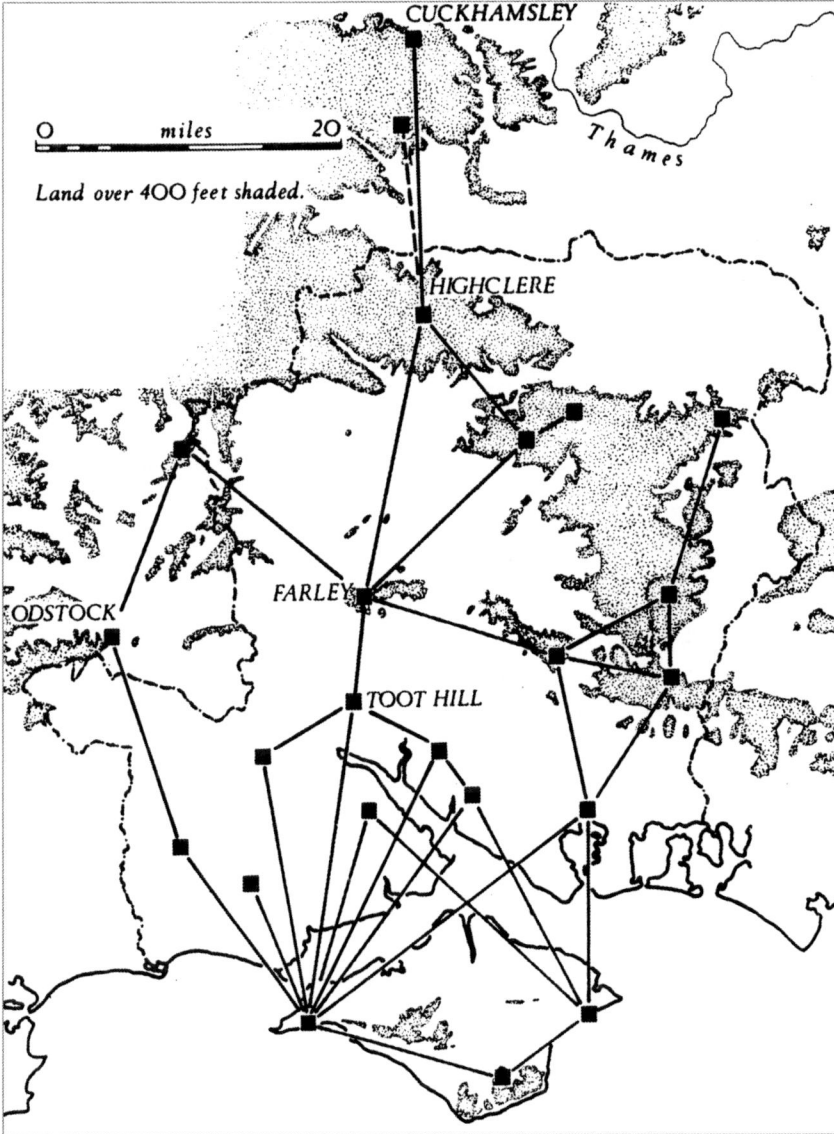

Fig. 6.2 Armada beacons in Hampshire with known Saxon weard sites

cause the lighting of the beacon of the Freshwater area; this would lead to the triggering off of up to nine beacons in Armada times. [Fig. 6.2] makes this clear. The purpose of the concentration of beacons in this area would appear to be to ensure that the message was carried across the Solent, where coastal conditions might make the visibility patchy. On the mainland side, the chain of beacons could pass the warning to Toot Hill, and then north to Farley Mount. The message had also been passed across the Isle of Wight via Smerdown to Bembridge, which set off the Portsdown beacon and this easterly chain not only confirmed the message to Farley Mount, but also sent the warning via Butser, Barnet and Crondall into Surrey. The westernmost series is more interesting to us, because the Burley beacon warned Wiltshire by way of the *weardan hyll* of Odstock, in Sawyer 400.

At Farley Mount, near Winchester, the message could have arrived from either south or east, and the lighting of this beacon would be seen by the first of the Wiltshire beacons. To the north, the key beacon of Highclere, eighteen miles away, would have yet another *cot-setla* sitting in the *weard-setl*. The *cot-setla* would see the fire at Farley Mount, far down the valley, twinkle across the silent landscape. (Perhaps he would have carefully set up a pair of whitened posts aligned on Farley Mount, so that he could check that it surely was the beacon, and not some accidental firing of barn or rick.) The watcher would light his beacon and run off to rouse the neighbourhood. The next major beacon at Cuckhamsley would alert the whole of the shire of Berkshire and the visible parts of Oxfordshire across the Thames. The bounds of Sawyer 738 for Newnham Murren are still unclear, but the whole of the eastern part of the parish can clearly see Cuckhamsley and, wherever this Oxfordshire beacon stood on its *weard dūn*, it was dependent on the Berkshire beacon nine miles away at Cuckhamsley. The chain of lights then passed on into the Midlands.

It is clear that, apart from the key beacons, there were local beacons to warn valleys that were shielded from the main beacon chain. Leckhamstead might be such a beacon. The *weardan dūn* is in clear sight of Highclere, and would warn the Kennet Valley.

Presumably, the same type of argument can be applied to Crowle in Worcestershire, to Bromley in Kent, and to Sandford in Devon; in other words that they could be associated with either the major or minor chains of beacons. However, the best evidence is to be found in the interrelated beacons of Hampshire and its adjoining counties. Among the later place-names there is, for example, *Wareberg* 'Wardy Gate' in Nottinghamshire which, taken along with such names as Old Warden, Chipping Warden, etc. (from *weard-dūn*), show us that the system was found over much of England. Unfortunately, the names are too general for us to identify exact locations, or to be sure what form of watch and ward is being referred to.

Of the means and methods of operating the beacon system, we only know the general duties laid on estates, but there is one suspect piece of evidence that might be of interest. In H. P. R. Finberg, *The Early Charters of Wessex* (Leicester, 1964) there appears a charter (no. 614 = S 895, *KCD* 701 *ex* Hearne [*The Itinerary of John Leland*, ed. T. Hearne (Oxford, 3rd edn, 1769–70), vol. 2, pp. 80–1], dated 998, whereby Æthelred, king of all Albion, gives permission to reorganize the church of Sherborne as a Benedictine Abbey. The charter is marked ** (Charter available in later copy, or copies, thought to embody the substance of the original, but having some material probably spurious or interpolated) but Finberg summarizes a section as follows:

> The lands are to be held free of all but the three common dues, and are not liable to anyone for the building of castle-mounds ('*in rogi constructione*'), for the abbey itself needs this service.

Such an addition might be seen as an obvious anachronism and destroy any trust in the charter; it does seem, however, that another interpretation is possible. The most recent translation of *rogus* is 'pile of wood, beacon, c. 550, 1136, c. 1325; fire, 8th. century'.[59] In the period of the great Danish wars, with Æthelred II making efforts to organize the defences of the kingdom, the liability to build beacons from piles of wood is in no way an anachronism for 998. (As also may be seen in the quotation from Richer, above.) If this charter, or the passage referred to above, has a sound basis, then we have a glimpse of the tenants of the abbey building beacons.

There is, therefore, more than enough evidence to argue for the organization of an Anglo-Saxon beacon system. The idea is a commonplace and the landscape links in the chain can be demonstrated. The difference between the basic landscape of the early medieval period and that of Tudor days was small, and so must any needful changes in the beacon system have been. The beacons formed an essential part of the defences of the Saxon kingdoms as organized by Alfred the Great, with the sea-watch firing the beacons and the whole countryside fleeing to the fortifications. There they were safer, the valuables of the countryside were brought together, and the available manpower concentrated ready to strike out in any direction that the king decided, by sending messages only to the relevant fortifications.[60]

---

[59] R. E. Latham, *Revised Medieval Latin Word-List from British and Irish Sources* (London, 1965), p. 411.

[60] Additional bibliography provided for the original article: Abels, *Lordship and Military Obligation in Anglo-Saxon England*; D. B. Hague and R. Christie, *Lighthouses: Their Architecture, History and Archaeology* (Llandysul, 1975); Hollister, *Anglo-Saxon Military Institutions*; G. Turville-Petre, *The Heroic Age of Scandinavia* (London, 1951), pp. 121–2.

Fortifications in action

As a fundamental principle, from a military perspective, a wall could act as a 'force multiplier' for the defenders. To be aware of this one does not have to go as far as Bernard Bachrach and Rutherford Aris's extensive calculations of the areas of 'killing ground' seen from the ramparts of a fortification.[61] As the author of the *Old English Orosius* noted in reference to Republican Rome, a townsperson, male or female, could become a warrior when standing behind well-constructed walls.[62] A post-Conquest copy of a Carolingian illustration of a siege, in the *Harley Psalter* (BL Harley MS 603), shows the practical aspect of this: quite simply, stones could be lobbed from a rampart onto an attacking enemy below (see Fig. 6.3). In this respect, the notion outlined in the Burghal Hidage that a pole's length of wall could be defended by four men relates to a practical notion of administration as well as an administrative mind (if read literally, of course).[63] Bachrach and Aris's account is useful as a consideration of the military efficacy of a rampart manned by archers against an advancing enemy before they reached a point where they were within a thrown rock's distance. Martin Biddle's observation on the possibility of pre-Conquest crossbow bolts having been found in Winchester is also interesting, related to the practical utility of fortifications and, with the additional power available from a crossbow, extending the potential 'killing ground' from its ramparts.[64] However, if this were indeed a crossbow, its potential never seems to have been exploited in pre-Conquest England, perhaps because such specialist equipment, highly adaptable to the static siege warfare of the high middle ages, was simply unnecessary in the defence of cities in the early middle ages.[65]

Nonetheless, Old English sources show that sieges were known of during the Anglo-Saxon period. They are specifically referred to in five Anglo-Saxon Chronicle entries for the ninth and tenth centuries,[66] but as we will see, they were also alluded to in other sources. Therefore it is hardly surprising that, as Stephen Pollington notes, one of the Old English riddles probably refers to a battering ram:[67]

---

[61] Bachrach and Aris, 'Military Technology and Garrison Organization'.

[62] *OE Orosius*, IV.10; Orosius, *Libri VII*, IV.17.

[63] Vegetius' calculation of the three-foot frontage taken by armed men is perhaps relevant here, although it will be apparent from the notes in p. 1, n. 1 above that I do not consider there to have been a direct transmission, and, it should be noted, Vegetius' advice here was on deployment in the field rather than behind fortifications. Vegetius, *Epitoma Rei Militaris*, ed. Reeve, III.15, p. 97; trans. Milner, *Vegetius: Epitome of Military Science*, p. 91.

[64] Biddle, *Object and Economy in Medieval Winchester*, p. 1078. See discussion on p. 111, n. 324, above.

[65] For a useful, though dated, discussion of the uses of crossbows, see R. Payne-Gallwey, *The Crossbow: Medieval and Modern, Military and Sporting: Its History, Construction and Management, with a Treatise on the Ballista and Catapult of the Ancients* (London, 1903).

[66] ASC 868 (cf. Asser, ch. 30, who, perhaps making a logical deduction, refers to an agreement of peace as a result of the stalemate at the walls), 885, 893, A 917, CDE 994.

[67] Pollington, *English Warrior from Earliest Times till 1066*, pp. 233–4; Riddle 53, in *Anglo-Saxon Poetic Records*, No. 3. *The Exeter Book*, ed. Krapp and Dobbie, p. 207.

&refugium meum ·in | adiutor meuf tibi | una uidf fufceptor mfcf
dic tribulationif mee | pfallam | df mf mifericordia mea

INFINE HIS QUINMU | SCRIPTIOSE DAUID INDOC | ET CONUERTIT IOABET PCUSSIT
TABUNTUR INITIULI IN | TRIHA CU SUCCENDIT SYRIA | IN UALLE SALINARU ·XII·MILIA·

Fig. 6.3 Twelfth-century depiction of a siege of a city from the *Harley Psalter*

> I saw in a grove a tree towering up, bright with branches;
> That tree was joyous, growing wood;
> Water and earth sweetly fed it,
> Until it, old in other days, became wretched, deeply damaged,
> Dumb in bonds, wound round wounds,
> Furnished in front with stained trappings [*hyrste*];
> Now, deceitfully, by the strength of its head,
> It clears a way for for another war-guest;
> Often in a storm they, united, plundered a hoard;
> Alert and swift was the follower,
> If the leader was able to dare to make an attack in a narrow place.

As with so many of our sources of warfare in the early middle ages, classical accounts of siege warfare may have influenced the author's view. We may entertain the possibility that the author of this riddle had first-hand knowledge of the construction and use of a battering ram or even, considering the author's critical language, had been on the receiving end of one. Alternatively, the riddle reflected a classical notion of such an object. In defence of the former suggestion, the Old English riddles tend to record objects that were in everyday use rather than 'exotica'.[68] Although as Pollington suggests, the riddle implies that work was undertaken to turn a tree trunk into a ram,[69] the notion of cutting down a tree to attack a fortification is hardly the height of sophistication (notwithstanding the manner in which the riddle subverts the theme of the use of a tree apparent in the more famous *Dream of the Rood*).[70] This is especially

---

[68] J. Wilcox, 'Riddles, Old English', in *The Blackwell Encyclopaedia of Anglo-Saxon England*, ed. M. Lapidge, J. Blair, S. D. Keynes and D. Scragg (Oxford, 1999), pp. 393–4.

[69] Pollington, *English Warrior from Earliest Times till 1066*, p. 234.

[70] *A Choice of Anglo-Saxon Verse*, trans. Hamer, pp. 160–71.

Fig. 6.4 Fortifications recorded during the reign of Edward the Elder (899–924)

apparent when comparison is made with the enormous wheeled battering rams constructed by Vikings recorded in Abbo's account of the 885–6 siege of Paris.[71]

That long siege of Paris, known in Anglo-Saxon sources, appears to have been exceptional, perhaps bearing comparison only with the defence of London by the English during the last years of Æthelred's reign.[72] Otherwise, for the most part, the Anglo-Saxons' Viking opponents seem to have fulfilled the notion of 'barbarian' modes of warfare in their apparent unwillingness to besiege their enemies.[73] Although fortifications were used extensively in campaigns, long

[71] The Viking Attacks on Paris: The 'Bella parisiacae urbis' of Abbo of Saint-Germain-des Prés, ed. and trans. N. Dass, Dallas Medieval Texts and Translations 7 (Leuven, 2007), pp. 38–9.

[72] ASC 887 refers to Vikings as going 'up beyond the bridge' at Paris, a result of the aftermath of the siege. There is no equivalent reference for Æthelred's reign but a similar reference appears regarding the movement of ships ('through the bridge') under different circumstances at London in 1052 (below, p. 297).

[73] For the observation of this in the late antique period, see G. Halsall, 'Funny Foreigners: Laughing with the Barbarians in Late Antiquity', in Humour, History and Politics in Late Antiquity and the Early Middle Ages, ed. G. Halsall (Cambridge, 2002), pp. 89–113, at p. 93.

sieges appear to have been rare in Viking-Age England. Where the Anglo-Saxon Chronicle includes details there are references to the West Saxons' two-week siege of a fortification to which the Vikings had retreated (probably Chippenham) in 878 and two days spent by the West Saxons and Mercians outside Chester in 893 (it is doubtful as to whether the Vikings' attempt to storm Towcester, fighting 'all day against the burh' in 917, can be thought of as a siege).[74] The Anglo-Saxons' Viking opponents appear to have been aware of the value of fortifications in warfare, and reference to the fortnight spent by the West Saxons encamped outside the Viking fortress (geweorc) in 878 is conspicuous by the detail of the time spent there.[75]

Perhaps the use of fortifications by Vikings in England may have been an indicator of their value, acting as a stimulus for increased fortification-building on the part of the Anglo-Saxons.[76] The unfortunate Franks who became trapped in a Viking fortress at Asselt highlight contemporary interest in Viking fortifications.[77] While there is no comparable episode from Anglo-Saxon England, the construction of new fortifications appears to have been used as a deliberate counter-strategy against existing Danish fortifications in the early tenth century in Æthelflæd and Edward the Elder's campaigns in the Danelaw regions of the midlands. An example is that built at Stamford, which was directly over the river

---

[74] ASC 878, 893; A 917. It is possible that the Viking retreat in 878 was to the nearby hillfort at Bratton Camp, but Chippenham seems more likely, given the length of the siege; this issue which was addressed in the nineteenth century by J. Thurnham, 'On the Barrow at Lanhill near Chippenham, with Remarks on the Site of, and on the Events Connected with the Battles of Cynuit and Ethandun, AD 878', Wiltshire Archaeological and Natural History Magazine 3 (1857), pp. 67–86, at pp. 76–7, and Pauli, Life of King Alfred the Great, p. 107.

[75] See also the reference to the Vikings at Buttington resorting to eating horses during a siege recorded in ASC, something which presumably emphasized their pagan nature to an Anglo-Saxon readership (for a papal prohibition of eating horseflesh, see the legatine report of 786 in Epistolae Karolini Aevi, vol. 2, ed. Dümmler, no. 3, p. 27; trans. EHD 1, p. 838).

[76] Viking fortifications are discussed in Brooks, 'England in the Ninth Century', pp. 9–11, and generally by E. Christiansen, The Norsemen in the Viking Age, The Peoples of Europe (Oxford, 2002), pp. 177–8. Brooks discusses references to fortresses built by 'pagans' recorded in S 1264 (AD 811) and S 186 (AD 822) in 'Development of Military Obligations in Eighth- and Ninth-Century England', p. 80. For detailed discussion of a specific example, see M. Biddle and B. Kjølbye-Biddle, 'Repton and the Great Heathen Army, 873–4', in Vikings and the Danelaw, ed. Graham-Campbell et al., pp. 45–96. Although a probable Iron-Age site and assumed by F. C. J. Spurell, its nineteenth-century surveyor, to have been an irregularly shaped ringwork prior to coastal erosion, the D-shaped fortification that he recorded, protected on the landward side, at the coast at Shoeburyness (Essex), bears a remarkable similarity to the enclosure at Repton (Derbys.) and longphoirt constructed in Ireland, and is a possible (though unproven) candidate for a late ninth-century Viking fortress: F. C. J. Spurell, 'Hæsten's Camps at Shoebury and Benfleet, Essex', Essex Naturalist 4 (1890), pp. 150–3, and VCH Essex, vol. 1, ed. H. A. Doubleday and W. Page (London, 1903), pp. 286–7. Shane Mcleod, pers. comm., has also tentatively suggested that position of St Martin's church on the defensive perimeter of Wareham (Dorset) may be related to the design of Viking fortified encampments.

[77] AF 882. See below, p. 320.

from the Danish fortresses.[78] It is possible that Edward the Elder realized the effectiveness of such a strategy in 899 or 900, when he used the Iron Age hillfort of Badbury Rings as a siege fortress against his cousin Æthelwold, a pretender for the throne, who had seized the nearby *tun* of Wimborne (Dorset) and had 'closed the gates' (*ða gatu forworhte*) against Edward in what was perceived by the Anglo-Saxon Chronicle as an act of rebellion.[79]

A rare narrative account survives of the defence of a fortification during a siege. The *Fragmentary Annals of Ireland* record the defence of the city of Chester under Æthelflæd during the early tenth century. Parts of the narrative are somewhat fantastical but, as what is probably an eleventh-century account of tenth-century events, it is nonetheless useful to reproduce it here.[80]

> Now the Norwegians left Ireland, as we said, and their leader was Ingimund, and they went then to the island of Britain. The son of Cadell son of Rhodri was king of the Britons at that time. The Britons assembled against them, and gave them hard and strong battle, and they were driven by force out of British territory.
>
> After that Ingimund with his troops came to Aethelflaed, Queen of the Saxons; for her husband, Aethelred, was sick at that time. (Let no one reproach me, though I have related the death of Aethelred above, because this was prior to Aethelred's death and it was of this very sickness that Aethelred died, but I did not wish to leave unwritten what the Norwegians did after leaving Ireland.) Now Ingimund was asking the Queen for lands in which he would settle, and on which he would build barns and dwellings, for he was tired of war at that time. Aethelflaed gave him lands near Chester, and he stayed there for a time.
>
> What resulted was that when he saw the wealthy city, and the choice lands around it, he yearned to possess them. Ingimund came then to the chieftains of the Norwegians and Danes; he was complaining bitterly before them, and said that they were not well off unless they had good lands, and that they all ought to go and seize Chester and possess it with its wealth and lands. From that there resulted many great battles and wars. What he said was, 'Let us entreat and implore them ourselves first, and if we do not get them good lands willingly like that, let us fight for them by force.' All the chieftains of the Norwegians and Danes consented to that.
>
> Ingimund returned home after that, having arranged for a hosting to follow him. Although they held that council secretly, the Queen learned of it. The Queen then gathered a large army about her from the adjoining regions, and filled the city of Chester with her troops.[81]
>
>   ...
>
> The armies of the Danes and the Norwegians mustered to attack Chester, and since they did not get their terms accepted through request or entreaty, they

---

[78] Wainwright, 'Æthelflæd, Lady of the Mercians', p. 62. Others were Hertford (CD 912), Buckingham (ASC ABCD 914), and Bedford (ASC A 915).

[79] Lavelle, 'Politics of Rebellion', p. 78. I am grateful to Ann Williams for discussing this.

[80] *Fragmentary Annals of Ireland*, ed. and trans. J. N. Radner (Dublin 1978), pp. 169–73.

[81] A record of a battle between Norwegians and Scots, *c.* 918, is cut here for clarity.

proclaimed battle on a certain day. They came to attack the city on that day, and there was a great army with many freemen in the city to meet them. When the troops who were in the city saw, from the city wall, the many hosts of the Danes and Norwegians coming to attack them, they sent messengers to the King of the Saxons, who was sick and on the verge of death at that time, to ask his advice and the advice of the Queen. What he advised was that they do battle outside, near the city, with the gate of the city open, and that they choose a troop of horsemen to be concealed on the inside; and those of the people of the city who would be strongest in battle should flee back into the city as if defeated, and when most of the army of the Norwegians had come in through the gate of the city, the troop that was in hiding beyond should close the gate after that horde, and without pretending any more they should attack the throng that had come into the city and kill them all.

Everything was done accordingly, and the Danes and Norwegians were frightfully slaughtered in that way. Great as that massacre was, however, the Norwegians did not abandon the city, for they were hard and savage; but they all said that they would make many hurdles, and place props under them, and that they would make a hole in the wall underneath them. This was not delayed; the hurdles were made, and the hosts were under them making a hole in the wall, because they wanted to take the city, and avenge their people.

It was then that the King (who was on the verge of death) and the Queen sent messengers to the Irish who were among the pagans (for the pagans had many Irish fosterlings), to say to the Irishmen, 'Life and health to you from the King of the Saxons, who is ill, and from the Queen, who holds all authority over the Saxons, and they are certain that you are true and trustworthy friends to them. Therefore you should take their side: for they have given no greater honour to any Saxon warrior or cleric than they have given to each warrior or cleric who has come to them from Ireland, for this inimical race of pagans is equally hostile to you also. You must, then, since you are faithful friends, help them on this occasion.' This was the same as saying to them, 'Since we have come from faithful friends of yours to converse with you, you should ask the Danes what gifts in lands and property they would give to the people who would betray the city to them. If they will make terms for that, bring them to swear an oath in a place where it would be convenient to kill them, and when they are taking the oath on their swords and their shields, as is their custom, they will put aside all their good shooting weapons.'

All was done accordingly, and they set aside their arms. And the reason why those Irish acted against the Danes was because they were less friends to them than the Norwegians. Then many of them were killed in that way, for huge rocks and beams were hurled onto their heads. Another great number were killed by spears and by arrows, and by every means of killing men.

However, the other army, the Norwegians, was under the hurdles, making a hole in the wall. What the Saxons and the Irish who were among them did was to hurl down huge boulders, so that they crushed the hurdles on their heads. What they did to prevent that was to put great columns under the hurdles. What the Saxons did was to put the ale and water they found in the town into the town's cauldrons, and to boil it and throw it over the people who were under the hurdles, so that their skin peeled off them. The Norwegians response to that was to spread hides on top of the hurdles. The Saxons then scattered all the beehives there were in the town on top of the besiegers, which prevented them from moving their feet and hands because of the number of bees stinging them. After that they gave up the city, and left it.

The account is problematic but its most recent editor, Joan Radner, has made a case for the dating of the composition of the annals' entries to the eleventh century.[82] Although Radner does not discuss the siege itself, it may be reasonable to suppose that these events have more to say about the reception of a view of events in eleventh-century Ireland than the reality of events in tenth-century Chester. Nonetheless, aspects of the source have a ring of authenticity, not least because of corroboration of Ingimund's arrival from Ireland in the *Annales Cambriae*.[83] The focus on the different groups of Vikings, who may be equated with Danes and Norwegians, is a preoccupation of Irish sources[84] although the poem on the seizure of the Five Boroughs, recorded in the Anglo-Saxon Chronicle's 942 entry, also refers to the relations between the two perceived Viking groups, suggesting that such rivalries were not just an Irish concern.[85] The reference to Æthelflæd as queen and to Æthelred as king may have more in common with the notion of the Mercian view of kingship in the early tenth-century than it did with the West Saxon view of Mercia, giving a glimpse behind the picture of West Saxon domination presented by partisan sources.[86] Although some of the details may be faintly farcical (albeit tragically so for the attackers), one could speculate as to whether such tactics as the *ruse de guerre* described by the *Fragmentary Annals* could work under the stresses of a siege. The contents of a large cauldron of boiling water or

[82] J. N. Radner, 'Writing History: Early Irish Historiography and the Significance of Form', *Celtica* 23 (1999), pp. 312–25.

[83] *Annales Cambriae*, ed. Williams ab Ithel, RS 20 (London, 1860), s.a. 902, p. 16; F. T. Wainwright, 'Ingimund's Invasion', *EHR* 63 (1948), pp. 145–69. See also N. J. Higham, 'Northumbria, Mercia and the Irish Sea Norse, 893–926', in *Viking Treasure from the North-West: The Cuerdale Hoard in its Context*, ed. J. A. Graham-Campbell, National Museums and Galleries on Merseyside Occasional Papers 5 (Liverpool, 1992), pp. 21–30, at p. 24. I grateful to Chris Lewis for discussion of this issue.

[84] For a reading of the different 'sequences' of Viking-age groups in Ireland, see D. N. Dumville, 'Old Dubliners and New Dubliners in Ireland and Britain: A Viking-Age Story', in *Medieval Dublin IV: Proceedings of the Friends of Medieval Dublin Symposium 2004*, ed. S. Duffy (Dublin, 2005), pp. 78–93. See also Higham, 'Northumbria, Mercia and the Irish Sea Norse', p. 24. For background of the rivalries, see D. Ó Cróinín, *Early Medieval Ireland 400–1200*, Longman History of Ireland 1 (London, 1995), pp. 250–6.

[85] ASC 942. For the heterogeneity of Scandinavian and Viking groups, see Innes, 'Danelaw Identities', and, in a wider context, S. McLeod, 'Know Thine Enemy: Scandinavian Identity in the Viking Age', in *Vikings and Their Enemies: Proceedings of a Symposium held in Melbourne, 24 November 2007*, ed. K. Burge (Melbourne, 2008), pp. 3–14.

[86] *Annales Cambriae*, ed. Williams ab Ithel, s.a. 917, p. 17 (above, p. 26) also refers to her as *regina* in the record of her death. See Cumberledge, 'Reading Between the Lines: The Place of Mercia in an Expanding Wessex', p. 6. Wainwright, 'Ingimund's Invasion', p. 153, reads the royal titles as errors on the part of an Irish author, arguing that the information could not be gleaned from an English source.

ale, when poured quickly from high ramparts can indeed remain hot enough to inflict injuries upon reaching ground level.[87] It is possible that the author of the *Fragmentary Annals* was making a classical allusion to the use of beehives against attackers, and, furthermore, references to bees and bee-keeping are prevalent in early Irish texts,[88] but in a study of the use of insects in warfare, Jeffrey Lockwood has argued that there is extensive evidence of the use of hives full of bees as weapons in the middle ages.[89] Unfortunately, the question of whether bees were kept in the city is difficult to answer through archaeological investigation, and the normally detailed customs of Chester recorded in Domesday Book are not particularly forthcoming on apiculture.[90] Nonetheless, the source is useful for showing the exigencies of a siege, such as the need for defenders to respond to multiple breaches of a wall.

The source highlights the balance necessary in defence: notwithstanding well-sited castles, a large fortification is intrinsically more effective than a small one if only because a large town allowed a greater number of people to be marshalled to its defence under extreme circumstances (a reason why the account of the inhabitants boiling water and ale should not be lightly dismissed). Balanced against optimizing the size of fortifications was the need to ensure that they were not sited too far apart from one another, not to mention the fact that the greater the population therein, the more difficult it would have been to ensure food supplies during times of war. Given the attention to the issue of the size of fortifications in the Burghal Hidage, we can say that at the very least one person in the kingdom of the Anglo-Saxons considered these issues. It would not be unreasonable to suggest that such consideration was ongoing throughout the Viking Age.

Fortifications also fulfilled an important role on the battlefield at a 'tactical' level. Although, as Philip Sabin has observed in his study of ancient warfare, fighting from a field fortification could have a detrimental effect on the initiative of a competent army in a battle,[91] the presence of fortifications could also be beneficial. Barbara Yorke observes that the Anglo-Saxon Chronicle says little about the places recorded in the Burghal Hidage, and records many other places as fortifications, using the terms *fæsten*, *geweorc*, and, occasionally, *byrig* rather than

---

[87] Boiling oil is the classic defensive weapon, but the walls of a burh were lower than those of a high medieval castle. I am grateful to Don Lavelle for discussing the issue of the rate of loss of temperature of boiling water under such circumstances.

[88] For an introduction to this, see Ó Cróinín, *Early Medieval Ireland*, pp. 106–7, although Ó Cróinín points out (p. 107) that 'bees and bee-keeping were probably no more important in Ireland than elsewhere'.

[89] J. A. Lockwood, *Six-Legged Soldiers* (New York, 2009), pp. 21–3 (Chester is considered, albeit with errors of interpretation, on p. 21). Lockwood does not entertain the possibility of the *Fragmentary Annals* providing a classical allusion but he cites the record of the tactic of releasing bees against tunnellers by Aeneias the Tactician (fourth century BC) (p. 18). For general consideration of the siege of Chester, see also J. Bradbury, *The Medieval Siege* (Woodbridge, 1992), pp. 41–2.

[90] DB Cheshire C 3–25 (fol. 262c–d).

[91] P. Sabin, *Lost Battles: Reconstructing the Great Clashes of the Ancient World* (London, 2007), p. 55.

burh, often interchangeably.[92] It is thus likely, as Yorke points out, that there was a grey area between temporary battlefield fortifications and those which were integrated into a formal system (if indeed there was a 'formal' system as such).[93] Thus some of the smaller fortifications in the Burghal Hidage may have represented strategic interests at the time of the composition of the document rather than a master-plan intended for the long-term future of the kingdom. Many of the fortifications cited by Yorke are those in campaigns recorded in the ninth-century narrative sources,[94] but the Battle of Hastings also saw the use of a temporary fortification. Ken Lawson has recently resurrected a notion that the Bayeux Tapestry showed the English army's occupation of a field fortification on the battlefield of Hastings, perhaps lined with defensive spikes,[95] but William of Poitiers' account of a 'broken rampart and multitude of ditches ['praerupti ualli et frequentium fossarum']', called the 'Evil Ditch' (*Malfosse*) by Orderic Vitalis, is also relevant. William of Poitiers, followed by Orderic, refers to a stand made by some English warriors after the main battle, using a fortification away from the main battlefield on Senlac Hill.[96] The fortification portrayed in the Tapestry (see Fig. 3.1), perhaps related to the *Malfosse*, may represent such a retreat to a secure place.[97] Holding a fortification could give the defenders the opportunity to negotiate, as the Vikings

[92] B. Yorke, 'Fortifications in the Anglo-Saxon Chronicle', in *Landscapes of Defence in the Viking Age: Anglo-Saxon England and Comparative Perspectives*, ed. J. Baker, S. Brookes, D. Parsons, and A. Reynolds, SEMA 28 (Turnhout, forthcoming). Among the ninth-century entries, see ASC 868 for a reference to a *geweorc* at Nottingham in 868; 878 for a West Saxon *geweorc* at Athelney and Viking *geweorc* at (probably) Chippenham; 885 for a *fæsten* (also referred to as a *geweorc*) built by Vikings during their siege of Rochester; 892 for an Anglo-Saxon *geweorc* at *Andredesweald*; 892 and 893 for a *geweorc*, *wudufæsten* and *wæterfæsten*, built by Vikings in Kent, a West Saxon *geweorc* in Devon, a Viking *fæsten* at Buttington on the River Severn, a Viking *geweorc* in Essex, and a reference to the deserted city of Chester used by Vikings as a *geweorc*, as well as *geweorcum* to refer generally to the West Saxon kingdom's fortresses; 895 for Viking *geweorcum* on the River Lea (also referred to as a *byrig*) and Bridgenorth on the Severn. *Byrig* is used as a place-name element in ASC 872 (London), 893 (London and Shoebury, Essex), 895 (London), and 899/900 (Badbury Rings, Dorset), as well as to refer to 'every *byrig* east of the Parrett' in ASC ABCD 893, and to refer to the Viking fortification on the Lea in ASC 895.

[93] Maitland's interpretation, in *Domesday Book and Beyond*, pp. 172–219, is hierarchical, referring to '"county boroughs"' (p. 186) and 'the old national boroughs' (p. 203).

[94] Yorke, 'Fortifications in the Anglo-Saxon Chronicle', highlights the use of the fortification recorded at *Cynuit*, in Asser, ch. 54, and the use of Wimborne by Æthelwold, in ASC s.a. 899/900.

[95] Lawson, 'Observations upon a Scene in the Bayeux Tapestry', pp. 73–92. This was originally posited as an 'outpost' in Freeman, *History of the Norman Conquest*, vol. 3, pp. 444–5, 490–1. See D. M. Wilson, *The Bayeux Tapestry* (London, 1985), pp. 192–3, for the comments on the 'stakes', and discussed by Lawson, 'Observations upon a Scene in the Bayeux Tapestry', pp. 79–80 (though they may simply be depictions of plants).

[96] WP II.24, pp. 138–9; OV, vol. 2, pp. 176–7. See also WM, GR III.242, pp. 454–5. However, as Wilson, *Bayeux Tapestry*, pp. 192–3, points out, William of Malmesbury may have based his account of the episode on seeing the Tapestry.

[97] A similar context may be posited for the role of Maldon in the aftermath of the Battle of Maldon. See below, pp. 249–51.

did from Chippenham after their defeat at Edington in 878,[98] but those who held the fortification had to be sure of their own value. There was a tangible risk for the defenders, for, had Duke William followed Count Eustace of Boulogne's advice to retreat, the surviving English could have been by-passed and cut off.[99] Nonetheless, William of Poitiers' record that, following Eustace's receipt of a debilitating blow from the surviving English, Duke William 'charged his enemies and laid them low', paying a high price with his own troops, is an indication that the use of a field fortification had the potential to be very effective.

Fortifications in the Second Viking Age

Applying the standards of the ninth century to the second Viking Age of the later tenth and early eleventh century is a valuable exercise. While historians and archaeologists are generally in agreement on the efficacy of the fortifications of ninth-century Wessex and the tenth-century 'Reconquest' (albeit without consensus on their attribution to a particular ruler), the wider significance of the development of the military function of early medieval urban fortifications, as opposed to their economic and social development, receives less attention.[100] A standard narrative is one of the steady abandonment of intense policies of the system recorded in the Burghal Hidage, presumably due in part to the sheer expense of maintaining the system and to the increase in urban growth in the tenth century. As Martin Biddle put it in 1976, providing a synthesis of the urban archaeology which had taken place in post-war Britain, later Anglo-Saxon towns 'were usually undefended and seem rarely to exhibit any degree of deliberate planning, as might indeed be expected given their essentially uncontrolled genesis.'[101] If Alfredian policies had been designed to encourage economic growth through the formation of towns in the ninth century and to allow kings to benefit from the control of that growth, they were achieving their aims in the tenth century.[102] Economic growth was perhaps given extra impetus by landless peasants who now had urban opportunities as an alternative to enslavement.[103] But the commensurate result of

---

[98] ASC 878. Note that, by contrast, Æthelwold ran from Wimborne (ASC 899/900), suggesting that the size of one's following made a difference.

[99] Although note Gillingham, 'William the Bastard at War', pp. 155–6, which observes the occasions on which William himself retreated after a campaign. Perhaps Eustace was suggesting what the duke was expected to do.

[100] For an exception, which considers the continuity of Roman models of defence in depth, see B. S. Bachrach, 'Imperial Walled Cities in the West: An Examination of their Early Medieval *Nachleben*', in *City Walls: The Urban Enceinte in Global Perspective*, ed. J. D. Tracy (Cambridge, 2000), pp. 192–218. Although mostly focused on the later middle ages, comparative consideration of cities in medieval warfare is provided by papers in I. A. Corfis and M. Wolfe (eds), *The Medieval City Under Siege* (Woodbridge, 1999).

[101] M. Biddle, 'Towns', in *The Archaeology of Anglo-Saxon England*, ed. D. M. Wilson (London, 1976), pp. 99–150, at pp. 137–8. For an example of suburban development, see Dodd, *Oxford Before the University*, pp. 41–2.

[102] See Hill, 'Athelstan's Urban Reforms'.

[103] I am grateful to Elaine Ball for drawing my attention to this. Cf. D. A. E. Pelteret, *Slavery in Mediaeval England from the Reign of Alfred Until the Twelfth Century*, Studies in

this was that, as can be seen from the archaeological evidence, suburban development undermined the effectiveness of defences. The maintenance of fortifications
– especially smaller fortifications with 'non-urban' characteristics – would have
been an undesirable expense during times of peace.

This following discussion provides a reflection on two issues. The first of these
was, as we have seen, raised by Richard Abels as 'the military failure' of the late
Anglo-Saxon state. For Abels, as for many historians, after the mid tenth century
towns provided sanctuary for the local population rather than defence in depth
in anything approximating the ninth-century system. This situation, it may be
argued, led to the failures of Æthelred II's kingdom in the face of Viking attacks,
and was in clear contrast to the cripplingly expensive Alfredian strategy of the
ninth and early tenth centuries.[104] There may be room for debate. Yorke, for one,
has highlighted the likelihood of some continuity of the defensive function of
towns in southern England in the reign of Æthelred.[105]

The second issue concerns the effectiveness of defences provided by city walls.
In his study of siege warfare, Jim Bradbury refers to the apparent contrast between
Anglo-Saxon England and its Continental neighbours in the late tenth and eleventh centuries. Bradbury characterizes England as having 'retained a pre-castle
form of warfare' in the eleventh century, whereas the Continent was characterized
by the building of private fortifications.[106] While his suggestion that there were
no private fortifications in pre-Conquest England is questionable,[107] his observations on the siege of an urban site are valuable for highlighting the weaknesses of
urban defences:

> It might be thought that smaller fortifications would be easier to surround and to
> take, but they were also easier to defend in depth. It would normally be possible
> to find a vulnerable point in a long stretch of town walls, easier to find one traitor
> among a mass of citizens, easier to implant spies among the hundreds of ordinary

Anglo-Saxon History 7 (Woodbridge, 1995), pp. 251–4, who attributes the the decline of
slavery to agrarian developments in the later Anglo-Saxon period (issues which are not,
admittedly, entirely removed from urban developments).

[104] Abels, 'From Alfred to Harold II'; Abels, *Lordship and Miltary Obligation in Anglo-Saxon
England*, pp. 91–3.

[105] Yorke, *Wessex in the Early Middle Ages*, pp. 139–40.

[106] Bradbury, *Medieval Siege*, p. 56.

[107] Indeed, elsewhere Bradbury discusses the manner in which the laws of Alfred the Great
refer to conventions of sieges in pursuing private warfare: *Medieval Siege*, p. 42; the relevant
law is *Alfred*, ch. 42.1: *Gesetze*, vol. 1, pp. 74–5; trans. *EHD* 1, p. 415. For discussion of
private fortifications in pre-Conquest England, see A. Williams, 'A Bell-house and a Burh-
geat: Lordly Residences in England before the Norman Conquest', in *Medieval Knighthood,
4: Papers From the Fifth Strawberry Hill Conference, 1990*, ed. C. Harper-Bill and R. Harvey
(Woodbridge, 1992), pp. 221–40, and D. Renn, 'Burhgeat and Gonfanon: Two Sidelights
from the Bayeux Tapestry', *ANS* 16 (1994 for 1993), pp. 177–98. An early discussion of
this subject, though rather maximal in its reading of the evidence is H. Davies-Price, 'The
Alleged "Norman" Origin of Castles in England', *EHR* 20 (1905), pp. 703–11, responding
to E. S. Armitage, 'Early Norman Castles in England', *EHR* 19 (1904), pp. 209–45, 417–55.

folk, than to get into a highly fortified castle, well sited and with a committed garrison.[108]

This is reasonable analysis, which can be applied to the Anglo-Saxon period in varying degrees. But had urban fortifications had their day by the end of the tenth century?

Table 6.1 sets out the evidence for a number of English towns. The factors used in the table differ from archaeological assessments of early medieval urban settlements,[109] as they are concerned with urban status and therefore the defensibility of a site:

(i) Recorded in the Burghal Hidage
(ii) Known mint at the site
(iii) Domesday Book record of 'urban' status
(iv) Episcopal seat
(v) Royally convened assembly
(vi) 'Other': evidence of gilds, defensive responsibilities, or housecarls

The first three of these categories can be considered together as signs of urban status. Of these, the issue of whether a place is one of the thirty-three sites mentioned in the Burghal Hidage as being associated with an area of land, signifies that the named site was considered for defence around the end of the ninth and/or the beginning of the tenth centuries, as discussed above. The second of the categories, whether a mint is known to have been at the site, provides another indication of the town's role at various points in the tenth and eleventh centuries.[110] While the table does not assess scale, such as how many moneyers were active or how many coins have been found from those mints, it is relevant to include consideration of chronology. The evidence for the production of coins is the name of the moneyer and the place at which coin was struck on its obverse, recorded as a matter of policy from the tenth century onwards.[111] In the late 920s, King Athelstan promulgated a lawcode at Grateley in Hampshire which stated that money had to be

---

[108] Bradbury, *Medieval Siege*, p. 57.

[109] The criteria, as laid out in C. M. Heighway, *The Erosion of History, Archaeology and Planning in Towns: A Study of Historic Towns Affected by Modern Development in England, Wales and Scotland* (London, 1972), pp. 8–10, and cited by Biddle in reference to early medieval towns, in 'Towns', p. 100, are: '[D]efences, a planned street-system, a market(s), a mint, legal autonomy, a role as a central place, a relatively large and diverse population, a diversified economic base, plots and houses of "urban" type, social differentiation, complex religious organization, a judicial centre' (N. B. Biddle's numbering is removed from the quotation for clarity of citation).

[110] This has been compiled from mints recorded in Hill, *Atlas of Anglo-Saxon England*, pp. 126–32; Metcalf, *Atlas of Anglo-Saxon and Norman Coin Finds*, pp. 192–248; and the Fitzwilliam Museum Department of Coins and Medals's *Corpus of Early Medieval Coin Finds* <www-cm.fitzmuseum.cam.ac.uk/emc/> (accessed 7 April 2008).

[111] An accessible introduction to this subject is due to be published by G. Williams, *Late Anglo-Saxon and Viking Coins*, Shire Archaeology (Oxford, forthcoming).

Table 6.1 Factors concerning urban status and defensibility

Town	Shire	Burghal Hidage	Mint	DB	Bishop	Other
Arundel	Sussex			✓		
Ashwell	Herts.			✓		
Axbridge	Som.	✓	Ætd.	✓		
Barnstaple	Devon	? (as Pilton?)	Ætd., Ed.	✓		
Bath	Som.	✓	Ath., Ætd., Ed.	✓		
Beccles	Suffolk			✓		
Bedford	Beds.		Ætd., Ed.	✓		
Bedwyn / Chisbury	Wilts.		Ed.	✓		gild
Berkhampstead	Herts.			✓		
Bodmin	Cornwall			✓		
Bradford on Avon	Wilts.			✓		
Bridlington	Yorks.			✓		
Bridport	Dorset	✓	Ath., Ætd., Ed.	✓		housecarls
Bristol	Glos.		Ætd., Ed.	✓		
Bruton	Som.		Ætd.	✓		
Buckingham	Bucks	✓	Ætd., Ed.	✓		
Burpham	Sussex	✓				
Bury St Edmunds	Suffolk		Ed.	✓		
Calne	Wilts.			✓		
Cambridge	Cambs.		Ætd., Ed.	✓		gild
Canterbury	Kent		Ath., Ætd., Ed.	✓	✓	royal guard, gild
Chester	Cheshire		Ath., Ætd., Ed.	✓		
Chichester (& Cissbury)	Sussex	✓	Ath., Ætd., Ed.	✓		
Clare	Suffolk			✓		
Clifford	Herefords.			✓		
Colchester	Essex		Ætd., Ed.	✓		
Cricklade	Wilts.	✓	Ætd., Ed.	✓		
Dadsley	Yorks.			✓		
Derby	Derbys.		Ath., Ætd., Ed.	✓		
Dorchester	Dorset		Ath., Ætd., Ed.	✓		housecarls
Dover	Kent		Ath., Ætd., Ed.	✓		
Droitwich	Worcs.		(Harold II)	✓		
Dunwich	Suffolk		Ed. (recorded in Blythborough in DB)	✓	✓	
Durham	Durham				✓	
Eashing	Surrey	✓				
Eorpeburnan		✓				
Ewias Harold	Herefords.			✓		
Exeter	Devon	✓	Ath., Ætd., Ed.	✓ (fr/1050)	✓	gild
Eye	Suffolk			✓		

Table 6.1 *continued*

Town	Shire	Burghal Hidage	Mint	DB	Bishop	Other
Fordwich	Kent			✓		
Frome	Som.		Ed.	✓		
Gloucester	Glos.		Ath., Ætd., Ed.	✓		
Grantham	Lincs.			✓		
Guildford	Surrey		Ætd., Ed.	✓		
Halwell	Devon	✓				
Hastings	Sussex	✓	Ath., Ætd., Ed.	✓		
Hereford	Herefords.		Ath., Ætd., Ed.	✓	✓	
Hertford	Herts.		Ath., Ætd., Ed.	✓		
Huntingdon	Hunts.		Ætd., Ed.	✓		
Hythe	Kent		Ed.	✓		
Ilchester (& South Cadbury)	Som.		Ætd., Ed.	✓		
Ipswich	Suffolk		Ætd., Ed.	✓		
Langport	Som.	✓	Ath., Ed.	✓		
Leicester	Leics.		Ath., Ætd., Ed.	✓	✓ (to 9th c.)	
Lewes	Sussex	✓	Ath., Ætd., Ed.	✓		
Lincoln	Lincs.		(Edmund), Ætd., Ed.	✓		
London	Middx.		Ath., Ætd., Ed.	✓	✓	
Louth	Lincs.			✓		
Lydford	Devon	✓	Ætd., Ed.	✓		
Lyng	Som.	✓				
Maldon	Essex		Ath., Ætd., Ed.	✓		
Malmesbury	Wilts.	✓	Ætd., Ed.	✓		
Marlborough	Wilts.			✓		
Milborne Port	Som.		Ætd.	✓		
Milverton	Som.			✓		
Newark	Notts.		Ætd.	✓		
Newport Pagnell	Bucks.		Ætd., Ed.	✓		
Northampton	Northants		Ætd., Ed.	✓		
Norwich	Norfolk		Ath., Ætd., Ed.	✓		
Nottingham	Notts.		Ath., Ætd., Ed.	✓		
Okehampton	Devon			✓		
Oxford	Oxon	✓	Ath., Ætd., Ed	✓		
Penwortham	Lancs.			✓		
Pershore	Worcs.			✓		
Pevensey	Sussex			✓		
Pocklington	Yorks.			✓		
Portchester	Hants	✓				
Quatford	Salop.			✓		
Reading	Berks.		Ed.	✓		
Rhuddlann	Cheshire			✓		

Table 6.1 *continued*

Town	Shire	Burghal Hidage	Mint	DB	Bishop	Other
Rochester	Kent		Ath., Ætd., Ed.	✓	✓	
Romney	Kent		Ætd.	✓		
Rye	Sussex			✓		
St Albans	Herts.			✓		
Salisbury	Wilts.		Ætd.	✓	✓ (fr/1062)	
Sandwich	Kent		Ed.	✓		royal guard
Sashes/Cookham	Berks.	✓				
Seasalter	Kent			✓		
Shaftesbury	Dorset	✓	Ath., Ætd., Ed.	✓		housecarls
Shrewsbury	Salop.		Ath., Ætd., Ed.	✓		
Southampton	Hants	✓	Ath., Ætd.	✓		
Southwark	Surrey	✓	Ætd., Ed.	✓		
Stafford	Staffs.		Ath., Ætd., Ed.	✓		
Stamford	Lincs.		Ætd., Ed.	✓		
Stanstead Abbots	Herts.			✓		
Steyning	Sussex		Ed.	✓		
Sudbury	Suffolk		Ætd., Ed.	✓		
Tamworth	Staffs.		Ath., Ætd., Ed.	✓		
Tanshelf	Yorks.			✓		
Taunton	Som.		Ætd., Ed.	✓		
Tewkesbury	Glos.			✓		
Thetford	Norfolk		Ætd., Ed.	✓		
Tilshead	Wilts.			✓		
Torksey	Lincs.		Ætd.	✓		
Totnes	Devon		Ætd.	✓		
Tutbury	Staffs.			✓		
Twynham (Christchurch)	Hants	✓		✓		
Wallingford	Berks.	✓	Ath., Ætd., Ed.	✓		housecarls
Wareham	Dorset	✓	Ath., Ætd., Ed.	✓		housecarls
Warminster	Wilts.		Ætd., Ed.	✓		
Warwick	Warwicks.	✓	Ath., Ætd., Ed.	✓		
Watchet	Som.	✓	Ætd., Ed.			
Wigmore	Herefords.			✓		
Wilton	Wilts.	✓	Ætd., Ed.	✓	✓ (w/Ramsbury)	
Wimborne Minster	Dorset			✓		
Winchcombe	Glos.		Ætd., Ed.	✓		
Winchester	Hants	✓	Ath., Ætd., Ed.	✓	✓	gild
Windsor	Berks			✓		mail-clad guard
Worcester	Worcs.	✓	Ætd., Ed.	✓	✓	
Yarmouth	Norfolk			✓		
York	Yorks.		Ath., Ætd., Ed.	✓	✓	

struck in towns, in effect providing the conditions for licences to a royal mint.[112] These towns associated with mints during the reign of Athelstan are marked on the table as appropriate. As far as we know, some of the mints were only striking coins in the reign of King Edward the Confessor, although many of them were producing at least as early as the reign of King Æthelred. These are marked in the table as 'Ath.', 'Ætd.', and 'Ed.', as appropriate.[113] The third category, relating to whether there is an indication of urban status in Domesday Book, provides a useful *terminus ante quem* using H. C. Darby's handlist of Domesday towns.[114] As previously discussed, these varied widely in scale from a few burgesses in a settlement to a city, and not all places named as towns in Domesday Book were urban in the early eleventh century. Nonetheless, that very urban status is what warrants attention.

The fourth category, whether the town had an episcopal seat, is hardly unsurprising, as many cities, as post-Roman urban centres, were associated with *Romanitas* in the early Anglo-Saxon period, and therefore it made sense that a bishop – effectively a representative of *Romanitas* – should be based in a city. A bishop had administrative responsibilities, which should be considered in an assessment of later Anglo-Saxon defences.[115] The Cambridge thegns' gild refers to the obligations upon gild members to behave themselves: they could not eat with a man who slew a gild-brother unless it was in the presence of the king, ealdorman or the bishop of the diocese, highlighting the role of such figures.[116] The term 'prince bishop' is rarely applied in a pre-Conquest English perspective, but it is part of the currency of lordship discussed in a Continental context.[117] Although we may not be too ready to assign 'feudal' rights to lords in later Anglo-Saxon England,

[112] *II Athelstan*, ch. 14.2: *Gesetze*, vol. I, pp. 158–9; trans. *EHD* I, p. 420. See M. A. S. Blackburn, 'Mints, Burhs, and the Grately Code, Cap. 14.2', in *Defence of Wessex*, ed. Hill and Rumble, pp. 160–75.

[113] A number of the places which are recorded in Domesday Book as towns in 1066, for which there is no evidence of a pre-Conquest mint, were mint locations by the later eleventh or twelfth centuries, indicating the close links between pre- and post-Conquest urban growth. These are not marked on the table but are: Christchurch (Anglo-Saxon *Twynham*), Durham, Eye, Marlborough, Pevensey, Rhuddlan, and Rye.

[114] Darby, *Domesday England*, pp. 296–7. For the grey areas between town and countryside, see C. Dyer, 'Towns and Cottages in Eleventh-Century England', in *Studies in Medieval History Presented to R. H. C. Davis*, ed. H. Mayr-Harting and R. I. Moore (London, 1985), pp. 91–106.

[115] Benedict Coffin, *pers. comm.* For the naval responsibilities of the bishop of London, see Taylor, 'Endowment and Military Obligations of the See of London', pp. 287–312 (discussed with Sherborne above, p. 164). Note, however, that bishops were not the only parties with responsibilities, as perhaps indicated by the implication of the 'French Reeve' in the fall of Exeter in ASC CDE 1003; see *II Æthelred* in ch. 8, below, for the significance of ealdorman in the administration of towns. Note also Æthelred of Mercia's control of London, recorded in ASC 886.

[116] *Diplomatarium Anglicum Aevi Saxonici*, ed. Thorpe, pp. 610–13; trans. *EHD* I, p. 604.

[117] For the context of the defences of tenth-century Liège, see A. Verhulst, *The Rise of Cities in North-Western Europe*, Themes in International Urban History (Cambridge, 1999), pp. 70–2. See generally T. Reuter, 'Episcopi cum sua militia: The Prelate as Warrior in the Early Staufer Era', in *Warriors and Churchmen in the High Middle Ages: Essays Presented to Karl Leyser*, ed. T. Reuter (London, 1992), pp. 79–94.

ecclesiastical defensive responsibilities are significant in the study of this period. Perhaps Swithun, the mid-ninth-century bishop of Winchester, as Martin Biddle's candidate for the progenitor of Winchester's defences, may not have been so different from his later successor, Henry de Blois.[118] For a mid-eleventh-century example we may take Leofric of Exeter, who has been suggested as playing a role in the city's rebellion of 1067–8 and was instrumental in negotiating a favourable outcome following William's siege.[119] The independence of bishops is interesting, especially in view of Æthelred's attack on Rochester in the late tenth century,[120] and, indeed, Rochester's survival of a Viking siege in 999.[121] It may also be pertinent to note here that on on one occasion during the reign of Athelstan, an assembly was called outside Winchester, at nearby Kings Worthy rather than in the city itself, perhaps in order to mitigate the influence of the bishop of Winchester.[122] The account of the translation of the relics of St Ælfheah from London to Canterbury during the reign of Cnut is also an indication of the power of the Bishop of London, despite Cnut's control of a palace in London.[123] In an interesting twist on the expectations of Viking behaviour, a strong show of force was used in order to relocate these relics. Presumably this was the only way in which royal power could be brought to bear against the interests of a powerful episcopal figure.[124]

The fifth of the categories refers to whether a town was the location of a royally attended assembly. These were recorded in chronicles, lawcodes, saints' *lives* and, most often, in Anglo-Saxon charters.[125] We we do not know where every assembly took place, as many charters do not have a recorded location clause; also

---

[118] M. Biddle, 'Winchester and King Alfred', public lecture at the Winchester Discovery Centre, 4 March 2008; B. Kjølbye-Biddle and M. Biddle, *The Anglo-Saxon Minsters of Winchester*, Winchester Studies 4.i (Oxford, forthcoming). For Henry de Blois, see N. Riall, *Henry of Blois*, Hampshire Papers 5 (Winchester, 1994), pp. 3–7.

[119] T. Gale, J. Langdon and N. Leishman, 'Piety and Political Accommodation in Norman England: The Case of the South-West', *HSJ* 18 (2007), pp. 12–17, at pp. 114–16. For the significance of Leofric, see F. Barlow, 'Leofric and His Times', in *Leofric of Exeter: Essays in Commemoration of the Foundation of Exeter Cathedral Library in AD 1072*, ed. F. Barlow, K. M. Dexter, A. M. Erskine, and L. J. Lloyd (Exeter, 1972), pp. 1–16.

[120] For Æthelred on Rochester, see ASC 986. Other cases of ravaging as punishment (though not of lands which were explicitly recorded as episcopal) were of Thetford during the reign of Eadred (ASC D 952) and Thanet in the reign of Edgar (ASC DEF 969).

[121] ASC CDE 999.

[122] Lavelle, *Royal Estates in Anglo-Saxon Wessex*, pp. 56–7. S 436 ('AD 937', recorded in WM, GP, ch. 250, pp. 600–1), records an attempt to blind Athelstan in Winchester. While this charter is of dubious provenance, the incidental detail is interesting, as Athelstan did not seem to enjoy good relations with the bishopric of Winchester until after Beornstan's death in 934. (I am grateful to Charles Insley for discussion of this point.) For background, see B. Yorke, 'Æthelwold and the Politics of the Tenth Century', in *Bishop Æthelwold: His Career and Influence*, ed. B. Yorke (Woodbridge, 1988), pp. 65–88, at pp. 72–3.

[123] See above, pp. 194–8.

[124] Benedict Coffin, *pers. comm.*

[125] Lavelle, *Royal Estates in Anglo-Saxon Wessex*, pp. 48–59, 69–76. A key work on the evidence of places associated with royal activities is P. H. Sawyer, 'The Royal *Tun* in Pre-Conquest England', in *Ideal and Reality in Frankish and Anglo-Saxon Society*, ed. P. Wormald, D. Bullough, and R. Collins (Oxford, 1983), pp. 273–99; for the circumstances of the making of royal legislation, see Wormald, *Making of English Law*, pp. 430–49.

the assembly politics of Anglo-Saxon England are complicated, not least because the Anglo-Saxon great and good recorded as the witnesses of charters may have been a selection of those who were at the associated assemblies.[126] Nonetheless, it is interesting that urban sites appear, often more than once, in a list of assemblies recorded in charters which more usually includes royal manors and rather remote fields.[127]

A number of other factors relate to towns, which are placed in the table under the heading of 'other'. Amongst these, the gild statutes are a seam of evidence which has not been particularly deeply tapped in the study of Anglo-Saxon England. While Ann Williams has considered their implications for thegnly piety,[128] the gild statutes are also relevant as they may indicate the presence of communities of thegns (or those considering themselves as being of thegnly rank), in Cambridge, and perhaps in Exeter and the small town of Bedwyn in Wiltshire. The statutes were seen by F. W. Maitland as evidence of the emergence of systems of interaction for 'the most professionally warlike' men in newly established urban communities.[129] Maitland may have overstated his case in order to counter what he viewed as his contemporaries' notions of the defence of towns by 'the civic militia',[130] but the association of such statutes with newly established urban communities should not be ignored. For example, evidence of a hall of the *cniht*-gild of Winchester is provided by *Winton Domesday*.[131] The fact that there are statutes associated with such a places as Woodbury in Devon and Abbotsbury in Dorset is a reminder that thegnly communities also existed outside towns, but given the '-bury' element of the place-names, one might also note their aspirations.[132] Robin Fleming has highlighted notions of 'urban communities' having something to defend, and this could be an important element as a coherent self-identity.[133]

---

[126] Insley, 'Assemblies and Charters in Late Anglo-Saxon England', pp. 51–2. For discussion of the circumstances of the production of charters recording assemblies, see S. D. Keynes, 'Charters and Writs', in *Blackwell Encyclopedia of Anglo-Saxon England*, ed. Lapidge *et al.*, pp. 99–100.

[127] Sawyer, 'Royal *Tun* in Pre-Conquest England'.

[128] A. Williams, 'Thegnly Piety and Ecclesiastical Patronage in the Late Old English Kingdom', *ANS* 24 (2002 for 2001), pp. 1–24, at pp. 22–3.

[129] Maitland, *Domesday Book and Beyond*, p. 191, and Oman, *History of the Art of War: Middle Ages*, p. 111. However, forthcoming work by Duncan Probert questions whether those named in the Exeter gild were of thegnly status.

[130] Maitland, *Domesday Book and Beyond*, p. 190.

[131] F. Barlow, M. Biddle, O. von Feilitzen, and D. J. Keene, *Winchester in the Early Middle Ages: An Edition and Discussion of the Winton Domesday*, ed. M. Biddle, Winchester Studies 1 (Oxford, 1976), no. 10 (pp. 34–5).

[132] *Diplomatarium Anglicum Aevi Saxonici*, ed. Thorpe, pp. 605–10. The historical development of planned towns under private lordship in the high middle ages, such as Alresford (Hants), is a relevant issue here (see M. Beresford, 'Six New Towns of the Bishop of Winchester', *Medieval Archaeology* 3 [1959], pp. 187–215): perhaps Abbotsbury and Woodbury were intended as precursors of such developments.

[133] R. Fleming, 'Rural Elites and Urban Communities in Late-Saxon England', *Past and Present* 141 (1993), pp. 3–37. See also S. Reynolds, *Kingdoms and Communities in Western Europe, 900–1300* (Oxford, 1984), pp. 158–68, and, for a discussion of the link between pre-Conquest knights' gilds and borough communities, Richardson and Sayles, *Governance of*

Winton Domesday also provides evidence of instances of watch-duty (*uuata*).[134] While that survey – distinct from Domesday Book itself – dates from the reign of Henry I, it uses records from the mid eleventh century, and is unique in the level of detail for an English urban community of this period. Although we should be wary of drawing generalizations from such a unique record, it is reasonable to suppose that similar defensive duties were required of citizens elsewhere in England, perhaps indicating why some towns were able to defend themselves in the later Anglo-Saxon period.[135]

Under this final category of 'other', we may also note housecarls from Domesday Book, who, although the evidence is inconsistent, often seem to be associated with royal towns or at least royal interests in certain towns. This suggests that if rulers used a military elite on whom they could rely, some towns were seen as important places by some rulers. Such evidence is reasonably clear for boroughs in Dorset (including Shaftesbury, where Cnut died in 1035),[136] and Berkshire, where the entry for the borough of Wallingford referred to 15 acres 'in which the *huscarles* stayed'.[137] The table is used to note where guard duty recorded in Domesday Book specifically refers to a town; although the Kentish cases noted here are not specifically related to the status of 'housecarls', the connection with royal bodyguards of some description is not unlikely.[138] Of the lands recorded in Domesday Book as holdings of housecarls, a number were in the hinterland of London, some – perhaps providing a parallel with Wallingford's position on the Thames – near to the strategic crossing of the Thames at Staines (see Fig. 6.5).[139] If housecarls are considered a later manifestation of a type of warrior who had given service to the king before 1016, perhaps these lands had been used for *their* endowment before

---

Mediaeval England, pp. 56–7. Cf. the constitutional reading by J. Tait, *The Medieval English Borough: Studies on its Origins and Constitutional History*, Publications of the University of Manchester Historical Series 70 (Manchester, 1936), pp. 15–66.

[134] For example, High Street properties where this was recorded were *Winchester in the Early Middle Ages*, ed. Biddle, nos. 69, 71, 76, 78, 79 (pp. 45–6; editorial comments on p. 15).

[135] Abels, *Lordship and Military Obligation in Anglo-Saxon England*, p. 178, comments on the self-defence of the citizens of Exeter in the eleventh century.

[136] These were Dorchester, Bridport, Wareham and Shaftesbury: DB Dorset B1–4 (fol. 75a). Cnut's death is recorded in ASC 1035.

[137] DB Berks B 1 (fol. 56b). For reservations regarding the status of housecarls, see Hooper, 'Housecarls in England in the Eleventh Century', and the discussion above, pp. 107–10.

[138] Recorded for Canterbury and Sandwich: DB Kent D 22 and D 24 (fol. 1b).

[139] Housecarls' estates recorded in Domesday Book are noted in Fig. 6.5. Lands in counties around London are as follows: in Middlesex, lands were Hanworth (DB Midx. 7:2 [fol. 129a]), Ickenham (7:8 [fol. 129b]), Bedfont (8:3 [fol. 129b]), Stanwell (11:1 [fol. 130a]), and Laleham (17:1 [fol. 130c]); in Hertfordshire, Shenley (15:2 [fol. 136c]), Westmill (22:2 [fol. 138b]), Bengeo (27:1 and 34:15 [fols. 138d and 140c]), and Willian (34:7 [fol. 140b]); in Buckinghamshire, Wavendon (DB Bucks. 12:36 [fol. 146d]), Shenley (13:2 [fol. 146d], Edgcott (14:35 [fol. 147d]), Stone (18:1 [fol. 149b]), Wolverton (43:11 [fol. 152a–b]), Hanslope (46:1 [fol. 152b]), Quainton (49:1 [fol. 152c]), Lavendon (53:4 [fol. 152d]). Of these lands, Bedfont and Willian were held by housecarls of Earls Harold and Leofwine respectively. See ASC CDE 1009 and, in referring to the drowning of many of Swein's men who did not use a bridge to cross the Thames, ASC CDE 1013 for the importance of Staines.

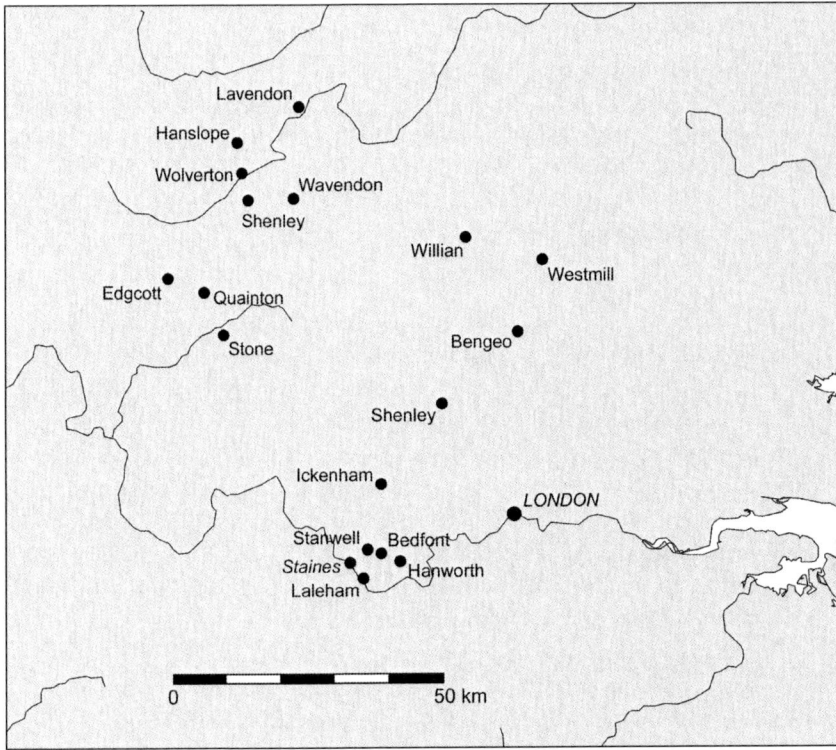

Fig. 6.5 Lands held by housecarls in 1066 in shires around London
(N.B. Staines is marked for information)

Cnut's conquest. This may help to explain the strong defence of London during
the later part of Æthelred's reign.

Table 6.2 shows the occasions on which Viking attacks and Norman seizures
of towns took place, as well as sieges and such other events as the 1002 massacre
of Danes in Oxford[140] and a Viking army's encampment in Canterbury in 1011.[141]
This evidence is tabulated alongside the classification of towns according to their
relative significance, indicated by a 'score' accumulating those factors in Table 6.1
which show the relative importance of towns, alongside their relative sizes (small,
medium, large). This is, admittedly, a simplistic methodology which throws up
some anomalous results (such as those for London and Durham)[142] and, perhaps
unsurprisingly, shows that large towns tended to be comparatively significant and
were often associated with significant events. Nevertheless, the table shows that
large towns were not the only important places in the later Viking Age.

[140] S 909 (AD 1004).

[141] ASC CDE 1011.

[142] This is calculated by assigning 1 point for each of the factors in Table 6.1. The size of towns
is estimated through the evidence in Domesday Book, along with the indications of size
and the relative importance of its mint estimated by Hill, *Atlas of Anglo-Saxon England*,
pp. 130, 143.

Table 6.2 Attacks on English towns and their relative sizes

Town	Shire	Size	Score	Raid/ destruct.	Siege	Sub- mission	Battle (inc. nearby)	Other event
Bath	Som.	med.	4			1013?		1013
Bedford	Beds.	med.	2	1010?				
Berkhampstead	Herts.	small	1			1066		
Cambridge	Cambs.	med.	3	1010				
Canterbury	Kent	large	5		1011	1009 1066		1012
Cricklade	Wilts.	med.	3					1016
Durham	Durham	med.	1		1006			
Exeter	Devon	large	5	1001 1003	1068	1068	1001	
Hereford	Herefords.	med.	3		1055		1055	
Ipswich	Suffolk	med.	2	991				
London	Middx.	large	4	982? 994	1016	1013 1016 1066	1066	
Lydford	Devon	small	3	997				
Maldon	Essex	small	2				991	
Northampton	Northants.	med.	3	1010				
Norwich	Norfolk	large	2	1004				
Oxford	Oxon.	med.	4	1009		1013		1002
Reading	Berks.	small	2	1006				
Rochester	Kent	small	3		999			
Sandwich	Kent	small	3	991?				1014
Southampton	Hants.	med.	4	980				994
Thetford	Norfolk	small	2	1004 1010				
Wallingford	Berks.	large	4	1006				
Watchet	Som.	small	2	988 997			988?	
Wilton	Wilts.	med.	5	1003				
Winchester	Hants.	large	6			1013 1066		1006
York	Yorks.	large	4			1066	1066	

Three observations may thus be made regarding Anglo-Saxon urban defences in the light of events which took place at them. The first is that not all attacks on towns were successful. Second, not all towns are known to have been attacked. Third, there does seem to be some significance in the surrender of towns – and the surrender *at* towns – to the adversaries of the English.

The first observation, that not all attacks were successful, should be taken into consideration when examining the record of the Vikings' activities in Wessex. Whether or not this was due to the defences of towns or the exigencies of the Vikings' campaigns is debatable, but the rebuilding of fortifications in southern England does provide some suggestion that urban fortifications could be of some use.[143] It is striking that many of the 'emergency burh' sites were not particularly well served with supplies of fresh water, thus limiting their abilities to withstand a long siege.[144] But in at least South Cadbury's case that did not prevent the site's continued use for a short period after Cnut's conquest, even if the building work started there during Æthelred's reign was never completed.[145] In the light of this observation, it may be noted that the prolonged sieges which were attempted by Viking forces, at Exeter, Canterbury, Rochester and London, were all at sites which were accessible by sea or by river estuaries, highlighting the importance of lines of communication for the besiegers.[146] The details of the London siege of 1016, recorded in some detail in the Anglo-Saxon Chronicle, the *Encomium Emmae*[147] and, to a lesser extent, in the *Chronicon* of Thietmar of Merseburg,[148] attest to this, suggesting that a strategy had not changed significantly since the Viking siege of Paris in 885–6. Although hardly esturine, the breadth and depth of the Seine so far upriver had allowed the Vikings to travel a considerable distance inland with a large fleet, but it highlighted the importance of protecting riverine routes.[149] The reference to a fleet coming *through* London Bridge in 1052 suggests that London had a role in the defence of the river.[150]

Not all towns were taken through sheer force, however. Treachery and trickery, as Jim Bradbury observed, could be useful tools for the besiegers of a city.[151] Whether or not defences functioned in a conventional military fashion, as a physical defensive barrier against an aggressor, the net result was the same: the city fell. But, in a perverse fashion, this reveals the effectiveness of the defences of the

---

[143] See above, p. 216.

[144] For example, Old Sarum: D. Renn, *Old Sarum*, English Heritage Guidebook (London, 1994), p. 6; *VCH Wilts.*, vol. 6, ed. E. Crittall (Oxford, 1962), p. 60.

[145] Alcock, *Cadbury Castle*, p. 169.

[146] Exeter and Canterbury were taken as a result of what the ASC implies and, in the case of Canterbury, asserts were cases of treachery (ASC CDE 1003 and 1011 respectively) but besieging forces are also likely to have been present (see below).

[147] ASC CDE 1016; *Encomium Emmae*, II.7, pp. 22–5 (for translations, see below, pp. 260–2).

[148] *Thietmari Merseburgensis episcopi Chronicon*, ed. Holzmann, VII.40, pp. 446–7; trans. *EHD* 1, p. 348.

[149] Gillmor, 'War on the Rivers'.

[150] ASC CD 1052. See below, p. 297.

[151] Bradbury, *Medieval Siege*, p. 57. See also Harari, *Special Operations in the Age of Chivalry 1100–1550*, esp. pp. 10–17.

place. This was the case for Exeter in 1003 and Canterbury in 1011.[152] It is pertinent to note here the close connection of the early eleventh-century Normans to the Danes who were then raiding the English kingdom: the story of the ancestor of the Normans, a certain Hasting, who, through his cunning, managed to sack the Italian town of Luna, was one of the fundamental aspects of the self-definition of the Normans. According to Dudo of St Quentin's *Deeds of the Norman Dukes*, Hasting pretended to convert to Christianity in order to gain ingress through the conveyance of his 'body' into the town for Christian burial. This had obvious echoes of the *Aeneid*'s account of the Trojan Horse[153] and is usually considered for its relationship to Dudo's sense of *Normannitas* – a story of a wild pagan Viking who comes good in the end. While it can be safely filed under the category of literary ethnogenesis,[154] the story's wider significance may be more apparent if we recognize that across the Channel, the people who were selling English slaves in Norman ports were engaging in the same sort of activity as that attributed to Hasting.[155] We may not know the details of the low cunning and treachery recorded in the Anglo-Saxon Chronicle but we can be certain that on both sides of the Channel the Danes were perceived as capable of it.

Smaller and (probably) medium-sized towns which were attacked are worth considering at this point. As can be seen from Table 6.2 and Fig. 6.6, these were Cambridge, Durham, Hereford, Ipswich, Lydford, Maldon, Northampton, Oxford, Reading, Rochester, Southampton, Thetford, Watchet, and Wilton, and possibly also Bedford and Sandwich. The Anglo-Saxon Chronicle is quite emphatic that many of them were burnt or completely destroyed during the reign of Æthelred II, a reason why so many commentators have been unimpressed by his reign. The sort of formula which Martin Biddle applies to the ninth-century narrative cannot be employed here: there is no distinction in reference to Vikings entering a town which allows the identification of a wall or guarded gate, as Biddle contends it is possible to do for the ninth-century evidence.[156] Therefore we cannot assess whether the towns were casualties in melees during Æthelred's reign, or were simply named as geographical identifiers with towns as bystanders in events which ranged across the landscape of the English kingdom.

---

[152] ASC CDE 1003 and 1011.

[153] *De moribus et actis primorum Normanniae Ducum*, ed. Lair, I.6–7; trans. Christiansen in *Dudo of St Quentin: History of the Normans*, pp. 19–20; Virgil, *Aeneid*, II, lines 13–297, in *Virgil: Eclogues, Georgics, Aeneid*, trans. H. R. Fairclough, 2 vols (London, 1916), vol. 1, pp. 294–15.

[154] L. Shopkow, *History and Community: Norman Historical Writing in the Eleventh and Twelfth Centuries* (Washington D. C., 1998), pp. 68–71; E. Albu, *The Normans in their Histories*, pp. 15–16.

[155] For the Luna episode as well as the account of the sacking of the Breton town of Nantes by a stratagem of pretending to be merchants, a story which Simon Coupland suggests had developed by the eleventh century from a more straightforward account of effecting an entrance through battery: S. Coupland, 'The Vikings and the Continent in Myth and History', *History* 188 (2003), pp. 186–203, at pp. 192–4, 197–8.

[156] Kjølbye-Biddle and Biddle, *Anglo-Saxon Minsters of Winchester*. This idea was flagged in Biddle's lecture, 'Winchester and King Alfred'.

Fig. 6.6 Attacks on English towns during the later tenth and eleventh centuries to 1066

However, the survival of the smaller burhs of Maldon (Essex) and Lydford (Devon), as well as, perhaps, Watchet (Somerset), in attacks which took place in the 980s and 990s provides some context for the significance of defensible small towns. While the Anglo-Saxon Chronicle records the ravaging of Watchet in 988, the reference to the successful resistance of the Devonshiremen at this time in the *Vita Oswaldi*, a detail picked up by John of Worcester, may show that the burh had functioned effectively.[157] An extended Viking raid into Devon in 997, mostly along the line of the River Tavy, was cut short by Lydford, just as, presumably, this burh

[157] ASC CDE 988. Byrhtferth, *Vita Oswaldi*, in *The Historians of the Church of York and its Archbishops*, vol. i, ed. J. Raine, RS 71 (London, 1879), p. 455; trans. *EHD* 1, p. 916. JW vol. i, s.a. 988, p. 437. See E. John, 'War and Society in the Tenth Century: The Maldon Campaign', *TRHS* 5th series 27 (1977), pp. 173–95, at pp. 184–5.

was meant to do. Although it was an obvious limitation that Lydford's main water supply seems to have been on the edge of the town, by the ramparts, with the defensible location of Lydford's promontory and – significantly – its inland location it was presumably not required to survive a long siege.[158] Considering the size of the Viking force in 997, as opposed to the larger armies which rampaged across Wessex and Mercia in the 1010s, perhaps allows us to see Lydford operating in the way the burhs of Alfred's Wessex had been designed. Its role was against a raiding army probably of moderate size.[159] Similarly, judging by their success in the 890s, it might be argued that Alfred's burhs faced much smaller forces in the 890s than the kingdom had faced in the 870s; such apparent differences in the level of threat faced by fortifications draw attention to acceptable limitations of the system.

Maldon is also an interesting case study. While the battle of Maldon was a famous defeat for the English and the social and military implications are addressed elsewhere in this volume, it is worth considering the context: there was a burh nearby which was an immediate source of protection. It is interesting to see that an English army chose to fight a Viking force outside the walls of the burh rather than waiting inside.[160] As Philip Sabin has pointed out from his work on warfare in the ancient world, venturing out from the safety of fortifications gave the initiative to good-quality troops.[161] The burh of Maldon was evidently functioning properly as a place to muster the troops and from where a force might launch a counter-attack. Indeed, it was used in this fashion in 917.[162] The burh was not recorded by the Anglo-Saxon Chronicle as being destroyed by the Vikings in 991, where the Chronicler would, one might assume, quite happily have recorded this if it had occurred. (By contrast, with his heroic and classical allusions the *Maldon* poet would presumably have had no such qualms about its exclusion.)[163] Byrhtnoth's defeat is remembered as disastrous, but the *Vita Oswaldi*, written not long after by Byrhtferth of Ramsey, refers to the Vikings being barely able to man their ships on their return journey.[164] While Byrhtferth may have exaggerated, and the occurrence of a similar reference to the small number of ships with which the defeated Vikings were allowed to return home after Stamford Bridge suggests

[158] ASC CDE 997. Information about the water supply is from notes provided by P. Addyman on 'Saxon Lydford', at the conference *Vikings '97: An Exploration of the Viking and Saxon World of Tenth-Century Devon and Cornwall*, Tavistock, 11–13 April 1997, and associated field excursion. S. Timms, 'The Royal Town of Lydford', *Devon Archaeology* 3 (1985), pp. 19–23, at p. 20, provides a brief but logical assessment of the role of Lydford in 997.

[159] For the context of Lydford and Anglo-Saxon policies in the south-west, see D. Gore, 'British, Saxons and Vikings in the South West', *Scandinavia and Europe, 800–1350: Contact, Conflict, and Coexistence*, ed. J. Adams and K. Holman, Medieval Texts and Cultures of Northern Europe 4 (Turnhout, 2004), pp. 35–41.

[160] 'Battle of Maldon', ed. Scragg, lines 291–2, pp. 30–1, refer to a certain Offa's death alongside his lord as an alternative to riding back to the *burh*, a term which Scragg translates as 'dwelling', but may equally have been a reference to Maldon itself.

[161] Sabin, *Lost Battles*, p. 55.

[162] See ASC A 917.

[163] For discussion of the influences on the Maldon poet, see below, ch. 7, p. 273.

[164] Byrhtferth, *Vita Oswaldi*, p. 456; trans. *EHD 1*, p. 917.

that it may have been a topos,[165] the *Vita Oswaldi's* relative contemporaneity is apparent in many of its details.[166] Given that the Vikings who engaged Byrht-noth at Maldon thus evidently did not excessively outnumber their opponents, the English decision to fight outside the town in pitched battle appears to have been effective. The topic of pitched battle is considered in chapter 7 but it is worth noting that defending a fortified town from within its walls may not have been the first tactical choice, even if this might make more sense to a historian looking back upon the purely military context of an action.[167] If organized violence was, in part, concerned with honour and reputation, the choice to fight outside the walls of a city may have made greater sense to an early medieval commander on occasions where the outcome had to be decisive. Thus the *Old English Orosius* relates the defence of Rome against Hannibal as taking place *outside* the city walls: 'But the consuls would not consider themselves so cowardly [*swa earge*], as the women had earlier censured them, that they did not dare defend themselves outside the *byrig*; but they arranged [*trymedon*] themselves outside the gates against Hannibal'.[168] The explicit link between a display of bravery and the defence of the city is shown by the fact that the women of Rome had stated their intention to defend the walls of the city with rocks; the consuls' reaction to this was to assert their masculin-ity as the defenders of the city by making their stand *outside* the city.[169] A similar point had been noted by Asser in his account of the Vikings' success from the stronghold (*arx*) at Reading:[170]

> When [King Æthelred I and Alfred's forces] had reached the gate of the fortifi-cation [*ad portam arcis*], by hewing and cutting to the ground whichever of the pagans they had found outside the fortification, the pagans fought energetically; in the manner of wolves, breaking forth from the gates, they joined battle with all their strength.

Although we may assume that a force had the potential to fight better when there was no place of safety to escape to, we may also note that the fact that a walled or palisaded fortification could still be used as a second line of defence by its inhab-itants and a place of refuge should the battle outside the burh be lost. Perhaps this in itself could have been a motivating factor for a force who chose to fight outside it.

---

[165] ASC D 1066.

[166] See the discussion of Byrhtferth's account of the death of Edward the Martyr in B. Yorke, 'Edward, King and Martyr: A Saxon Murder Mystery', in *Studies in the Early History of Shaftesbury Abbey*, ed. L. Keen (Dorchester, 1999), pp. 99–116, at pp. 101–2.

[167] Although Maldon was defended in a siege in 917 (ASC A *sub anno*), this seems to have been because of the small size of the force within the walls of the town. For Maldon, see *VCH Essex*, vol. I, pp. 287–8.

[168] *OE Orosius*, IV.10.

[169] Cf. the original text of Orosius, which does not make such explicit reference to cowardice: Orosius, *Libri VII*, IV.17, an issue considered by R. P. Abels, '"Cowardice" and Duty in Anglo-Saxon England', *JMMH* 4 (2006), pp. 29–45, at p. 35.

[170] Asser, ch. 36. See also the *Fragmentary Annals of Ireland*, ed. Radner, pp. 170–1, cited above, p. 231.

If small, fortified towns could be dangerous places, the second issue raised above may be addressed: not all towns appear to have been attacked. What does the Anglo-Saxon Chronicle reveal about a Viking strategy of avoiding burghal centres? Are Viking activities in the reign of Æthelred II comparable with those during the later years of Alfred's reign? It is striking that large areas of central England were not really affected by Vikings in the campaigns of Swein Forkbeard and his son Cnut; though an infamous Anglo-Saxon Chronicle entry lists the areas 'overrun' by Thorkell the Tall's Vikings in 1011,[171] Viking attacks are not recorded for many towns in the former kingdom of Wessex. This may have been because the strategic interests of Swein Forkbeard and Thorkell's Vikings during the final decade of Æthelred's reign were different from those of the Great Army of the ninth century.[172] For example, Dorset presumably had little strategic value to a conquering army by the later tenth or eleventh century, in contrast to its greater importance in the ninth century,[173] even if the prominent burh of Wareham may have been impressive in the later period.[174] Wareham retained a mint and at some point the walls were rebuilt; it was quite accessible by river and therefore was arguably vulnerable but, presumably in terms of strategic priorities, the risks associated with trying to seize the fortification outweighed the benefits. The same might be said of Shaftesbury, a defensible site some distance inland, even if it was presumably tempting as the site of a well-endowed nunnery with connections to the royal saint, Edward the

---

[171] ASC CDE 1011. These were: '(i) East Anglia, and (ii) Essex, and (iii) Middlesex, and (iv) Oxfordshire, and (v) Cambridgeshire, and (vi) Hertfordshire, and (vii) Buckinghamshire, and (viii) Bedfordshire, and (ix) half Huntingdonshire, and (x) much of Northamptonshire, and to the south of the Thames all Kent, and Sussex, and Hastings [district], and Surrey, and Berkshire, and Hampshire, and much of Wiltshire.'

[172] For Viking strategies from 1006–16, see generally Howard, *Swein Forkbeard's Invasions*, pp. 72–141.

[173] Dorset's use by Cnut could be a result of this comparative survival in the early eleventh century. For Cnut's use of Dorset after 1016, see S. Keynes, 'Wulfsige, Monk of Glastonbury, Abbot of Westminster (*c.* 990–3), and Bishop of Sherborne (*c.* 993–1002)', in *St Wulfsige and Sherborne: Essays to Celebrate the Millennium of the Benedictine Abbey 998–1998*, ed. K. Barker, D. A. Hinton and A. Hunt, Bournemouth University School of Conservation Sciences Occasional Paper 8 (Oxford, 2005), pp. 53–97, at pp. 73–4, although we should note his caveat that the reasons for this 'may not yet be fully understood' (p. 73). Katherine Barker's essay in the same volume, 'Bishop Wulfsige's Lifetime: Viking Campaigns Recorded in the Anglo-Saxon Chronicle for Southern England', pp. 124–32, draws attention to the difficulties of Viking movement in Dorset, although not to the defences of fortifications in the shire.

[174] Royal Commission on Historical Monuments, 'Wareham West Walls', *Medieval Archaeology* 3 (1959), pp. 120–38; L. Keen, 'The Towns of Dorset', in *Anglo-Saxon Towns*, ed. Haslam, pp. 203–47, at p. 232. For the rebuilding of the defences at Christchurch (Hants, now Dorset), including a facing ironstone wall 'within the pre-Conquest period, or soon afterwards' (which, if the latter, would be commensurate with the comparatively good quality stonebuilding at South Cadbury: Alcock, *Cadbury Castle, Somerset*, pp. 44–50), see D. H. Hill, 'Sites X1 and X2 Pound Lane', in K. S. Jarvis, *Excavations in Christchurch 1969–1980*, Dorset Natural History and Archaeological Society Monograph Series 5 (Dorchester, 1983), pp. 22–7, at pp. 25–7. I am grateful to Damien Bates for drawing this to my attention.

Martyr.[175] Similarly, Bristol,[176] Hastings and Chichester are notable omissions from the roster of Viking attacks, notwithstanding the reference to the Vikings' depredations upon the Hastings district in the Anglo-Saxon Chronicle's entry for 1011. That does not mean that such towns were not attacked by raiding parties or affected by the campaigns of the early eleventh century, but it would have been surprising if a force of any size had attempted to seize these sites without the fact being noted by a chronicler who, though having limited knowledge of events in Wessex,[177] seemed to revel in recording the details of destruction to Æthelred's state

The Chronicler's sense of geography is largely conditioned by a knowledge of towns, which are often used to name locations.[178] If the surroundings of an area were identified by the name of a central place, as the Wilton *pagus* (not necessarily the same as the shire of Wiltshire) was identified by Asser,[179] then by reference to a town a writer may have indicated events in an area. This may be demonstrated in the rare case where two different versions of the Chronicle survive. In the usually more garrulous C version of the Anglo-Saxon Chronicle, somewhat removed geographically and chronologically from the events of 1001, the Vikings' activities are recorded as including an attack upon Exeter, referred to as a *byrig*.[180] By comparison, the Winchester-based writer of the A manuscript, despite writing many miles away from the events in Devon, records the devastation wreaked against the estates around Exeter but says nothing about an attack on Exeter itself. Table 6.3 shows a breakdown of the two sources, allowing a consideration of how the burh of Exeter was viewed.

---

[175] A threat to the Shaftesbury community is implied by the intention to move the relics of St Edward to Bradford-on-Avon (Wilts.), recorded in S 899 (AD 1001), a charter which refers to Bradford as an 'impenitrable refuge' (*impenitrabile … confugium*). However, as the charter's editor, Susan Kelly, points out, Shaftesbury was far more defensible and an alternative suggestion is that the reference was 'a smokescreen', taking the opportunity to extend the community's landed interests: S. E. Kelly (ed.), *Charters of Shaftesbury Abbey*, Anglo-Saxon Charters 5 (Oxford, 1995), pp. 119–20. It may also be stated, as David Hinton has pointed out to me, *pers. comm.*, beyond the intention stated in the charter there is no evidence that the move of the relics to Bradford took place. For the location of Bradford, see Haslam, 'Towns of Wiltshire', pp. 90–4. For similar contemporary cases, see E. Cambridge, 'Why did the Community of St Cuthbert Settle at Chester-le-Street?', in *St Cuthbert, His Cult and His Community to AD 1200*, ed. G. Bonner, D. Rollason and C. Stancliffe (Woodbridge, 1989), pp. 367–86, and F. Lifshitz, 'The Migration of Neustrian Relics in the Viking Age: The Myth of Voluntary Exodus, the Reality of Coercion and Theft', *EME* 4 (1995), pp. 175–92.

[176] For Bristol, see D. Sivier, *Anglo-Saxon and Norman Bristol* (Stroud, 2002), pp. 13–37. Bristol was an unlikely centre of Scandinavian settlement *per se*, as used to be believed. Sivier suggests *c.* 1000 for the town's emergence so while its strategic value may not have been high, the possibility of its importance should be acknowledged.

[177] Yorke, *Wessex in the Early Middle Ages*, pp. 138–9.

[178] For a discussion of the memory of locations of battles, see below, pp. 293–314.

[179] Asser, ch. 42; Lavelle, *Royal Estates in Anglo-Saxon Wessex*, p. 67.

[180] For the C Chronicler in Æthelred's reign, see C. Clark, 'The Narrative Mode of the *Anglo-Saxon Chronicle* Before the Conquest', in *England Before the Conquest*, ed. P. Clemoes and K. Hughes (Cambridge, 1971), pp. 224–30, at pp. 224–30, and Keynes, 'Declining Reputation of King Æthelred the Unready', pp. 230–3.

Table 6.3 Viking activities around Exeter

A MS	C (D, E) MS
Here in this year there was great unrest [unfrið] in the land of the English because of a sciphere; and nearly everywhere they ravaged and burnt, such that they took themselves inland in one journey until they came to Æthelingadene [Dean, Sussex]; and there came there against them [forces from] Hampshire and they fought against them; and there was slain Æthelweard the king's high-reeve, and Leofric of Whitchurch and Leofwine the king's high-reeve, and Wulfhere, the bishop's thegn, and Godwine of Worthy, Bishop Ælfsige's son, and eighty-one men in all; and there were far more of the Danes killed, though they held control of the place of slaughter.	
And then they went west from there until they came to Devon; and to them there came Pallig with the ships which he could gather, because he was shaken from [i.e. deserted] King Æthelred against all the pledges which he had given him. And also the king had gifted to him well, in estates [hama] and in gold and silver. And they burnt Teignton and also many other good estates which we cannot name, and afterwards peace was made with them.	Here [i.e. in this year] the here came to the mouth of the Exe and then went inland to the byrig, and there they were fighting resolutely, but they were very strongly withstood. Then they went across the land and did everything as they were wont to, slew and burnt.
Then they went from there to the mouth of the Exe, such that they took themselves inland in one journey until they came to Pinhoe; and there was against them Kola the king's high-reeve, and Eadsige, the king's reeve, with what army [fyrd] they might gather, but they were put to flight there, and there were many slain, and the Danes held control of the place of slaughter.	Then there was summoned there an immense army [fyrd] of the people of Devon and of the people of Somerset, and they came together at Pinhoe; and as soon as they came together, the people turned way and they [i.e. the Danes] made great slaughter there,
And afterwards, in the morning they burnt the estate at Pinhoe and at Clyst, and also many good estates which we cannot name, and then went back east until they reached the Isle of Wight.	and then rode over the land – and ever was their next venture [sið, i.e. raid] worse than the last. And with them they brought much plunder [herehuð] to their ships, and from there went to the Isle of Wight.

Table 6.3 *continued*

A MS	C (D, E) MS
And afterwards, in the morning they burnt the estate at Waltham and many other villages [*cotlifa*].	And there they went about just as they wished, and nothing withstood them, nor dared a *scyphere* at sea nor a *landfyrd* go against them, no matter how far inland they went. It was in every way a dire time, for they never abandoned their evil-doings.
And soon afterwards terms were made with them and they accepted peace.	(1002 entry) Here in this year the king and his *witan* determined that tribute be paid to the fleet and peace [*frið*] made with them as long as they should cease their evil-doings. Then the king sent Ealdorman Leofsige to the fleet, and he then, by the order of the king and his councillors, arranged a truce [*gryð*] with them, and that they should receive provisions and tribute.

In the C version of the Chronicle (followed by the D and E manuscripts), the arrival at the mouth of the Exe has been conflated with all the attacks on Teignton and the surrounding estates. The A Chronicler seems to have the attacking force keeping clear of the immediate vicinity of Exeter itself, while the C version, again perhaps conflating events, records the Vikings meeting resistance at 'the *byrig*', i.e. Exeter (see Fig. 6.7). Of course, it is likely, with references to Vikings harrying across and subduing entire shires which occur in later entries of the Chronicle, that at least the hinterlands of towns, if not towns themselves, were affected by warfare. Nonetheless, the A Chronicler's lack of reference to a direct assault on Exeter is perhaps revealing, suggesting that the Vikings were keeping further from the city than the C Chronicle would have us believe when relating that they were 'very strongly withstood'.

While not wishing to overplay the significance of English defences against the Vikings during the reign of Æthelred or, indeed, during the campaigns of the Norman Conquest half a century later, it should be acknowledged that the very presence of defensible towns meant that they had to figure in the invaders' strategic planning. Towns could be and were razed to the ground, but it took time and energy, as well as exposing the attacking force to a risk. The larger the town, the greater that risk.

The third and final issue raised above may be addressed. If the defeats of the English kingdom appear to have been a catalogue of surrenders, some consideration may be given to the surrenders themselves. They may shed light on the importance of urban fortifications and provide a contrast with private fortifications. I have commented elsewhere on the importance of hostages in signifying submission in an early medieval urban context,[181] and Jinty Nelson has discussed

[181] Lavelle, 'Use and Abuse of Hostages', pp. 274, 279–84.

Fig. 6.7   Locations of Viking activities around Exeter in 1001

the meaning of the submission of the English to William in 1066,[182] but the fact
that there is some correlation between the records of assemblies, and submission
is worthy of note. This suggests a relationship between the assembly politics of
the Anglo-Saxon state and the significance of submission.

It is interesting that when a town surrendered in the 1010s and 1060s, there
is also some evidence that it had been used as a location for an assembly. There
may have been a difference between a town used as a site for a surrender of the
surrounding area and its surrender in its own right. Naturally, large towns were
important. London predominates in these accounts,[183] but other large and not-
so-large towns are also evident: during the 1010s, Canterbury, Winchester, and
Oxford; in the 1060s, Exeter, Winchester again, and York. Bath, in 1013, and
Berkhampstead (Herts.), in 1066, saw the surrender of people who were not the
towns' inhabitants. (Indeed, the Anglo-Saxon Chronicle is somewhat ambiguous

---

[182] J. L. Nelson, 'The Rites of the Conqueror', *ANS* 4 (1982 for 1981), pp. 117–32, 210–21, at
pp. 117–18.

[183] For the suggestion that Cnut's treatment of London was deliberately hostile in view of its
resistance during the reign of Æthelred, see D. Hill, 'An Urban Policy for Cnut?', in *Reign
of Cnut*, ed. Rumble, pp. 101–5.

Fig. 6.8 Urban assemblies and sites of surrender (marked in bold)
N.B. there is no recorded occasion of an assembly at Berkhampstead.

as to whether the surrender in 1013 took place *in* or *outside* Bath.)[184] The surrender
of Archbishop Stigand and the English nobles at Berkhampstead in 1066 may be
explained as strategic exigency as Duke William of Normandy encircled London,
but otherwise there is clarity to these civic submissions.[185] Often backed up by
the surrender of hostages (in the case of York in 1066, the sons of the leading

[184] The latter is perhaps more likely if Ealdorman Æthelmær had, until then, been in
retirement, voluntary or otherwise, at the monastery of Eynsham (Oxon.), to the east of
Bath: C. A. Jones, *Ælfric's Letter to the Monks of Eynsham*, Cambridge Studies in Anglo-
Saxon England 24 (Cambridge, 1998), pp. 13–15. However, it must be noted that the
Prosopography of Anglo-Saxon England Database, <www.pase.ac.uk> [accessed 24 August
2009] reserves judgement on whether these were the same Æthelmærs, noting them as
'Æthelmær 27' and '22' respectively.

[185] For the spatial significance of peacemaking, see P. Dalton, 'Sites and Occasions of
Peacemaking in England and Normandy, *c.* 900–*c.* 1150', *HSJ* 16 (2006 for 2005), pp. 12–26
(discussed in ch. 8, below).

citizens)[186] they highlight a notion that the early English state was made up of political communities as much as or more than a single community.[187] Urban communities had some real political power, perhaps best demonstrated by Exeter's bid to negotiate its rights in the winter of 1067–8, recorded in the *Historia ecclesiastica* of Orderic Vitalis.[188]

> Exeter fought first to claim liberty, but fell down defeated by the most powerful troops who were attacking it. This city is rich and ancient, built in a plain, painstakingly fortified, about two miles distant from the sea shore where it stands apart from Ireland and Brittany by the shortest distance. The citizens held it in great force, full of fury, young and old, threatening the deaths of every man of Gaul. Without doubt they ceaselessly called for allies from neighbouring districts [*pagi*], they detained foreign merchants who were skilled in war, and they put in place or restored battlements and towers [*pinnae ac turres*] as they judged necessary. With envoys they also urged other cities to unite in the same way. And they prepared themselves with all effort against the foreign king, with whom they had previously conducted no business. Truly, when the king found out this fact he gave orders to the foremost citizens to swear fidelity to him. But they responded to him, saying, 'Neither will we make an oath to the king nor will we permit him entry into the city, but we will render him tribute according to the original custom.' On his part the king responded to them, saying 'It is not my will to have subjects by such a condition.' Then he advanced to their territory [*ad fines*] with an army [*exercitus*] and, for the first time, on this expedition [*in ea expeditione*] he summoned [*educere*] Englishmen. Thereupon the elders learnt that the king was approaching with an army, they set out so as to meet [him], begged for peace, declared the opening of the gates to him, promised that they were about to perform the orders he wished, and they took there as many hostages as he demanded. Returning to the citizens, who were afraid of punishment for so much guilt, the hostile preparations which they had begun were nevertheless undertaken, and for many reasons they incited each other to fight. Hearing of this, the king, who had paused four miles from the city, was full of anger and surprise.
>
> Thus firstly, the king speedily advanced with five hundred knights [*equites*] so that he might see the place and the fortifications [*moenia*] and find out what the

---

[186] ASC D; Snorri Sturluson (perhaps making a logical deduction) notes the significance of their being known to Tostig: *Harald's Saga Sigurðarsonar*, ch. 86, in *Heimskringla*, ed. B. S. Kristjánsdóttir (Reykjavik, 1991), p. 680; trans. *Heimskringla*, ed. Hollander, p. 651. See Lavelle, 'Use and Abuse of Hostages', pp. 282–3.

[187] See reference to the witness list of the will of Æthelwyrd (S 1506 [AD 941×58, perhaps 958]), which records in its witness list the 'three brotherhoods of the townspeople [lit. 'in-borough-dwellers']' (ða III *geferscipas Innanburwara*) and 'out-townspeople' (?suburbanites = *utanburhwara*). The interactions of political communities in late Anglo-Saxon England are explored in Stafford, 'Reign of Æthelred II'; see also Fleming, 'Rural Elites and Urban Communities in Late-Saxon England' and, for a wider view on political identities, A. Woolf, 'Community, Identity and Kingship in Early England', in *Social Identity in Early Medieval Britain*, ed. W. O. Frazer and A. Tyrrell, Studies in Early Britain (London, 2000), pp. 91–109.

[188] OV, vol. 2, pp. 210–14.

enemy might do. The gates were held fast, and a large force [*densae turbae*] stood in the towers [*in propugnaculis*] and along all the circuit of the walls [*per totum muri ambitum*]. And then, by the king's command, the army [*exercitus*] was moved to the city, and near the gates one of the hostages was deprived of his eyes. But the stubbornness of the furious populace was neither bowed by fear nor by compassion for the remaining hostages but was sharpened by all determination to defend themselves and their homes. The king, however, strongly surrounded the city in a siege, attacked with warlike ferocity, and for many days he resolutely worked to dislodge the citizens from above and to undermine the walls from below. At length the citizens were driven to take wise counsel by the remarkable resolution of the enemy and they came down to appeal for pardon. And the flower of youth and the elder men with the clergy bearing sacred books and ornaments of this kind went out to the king. Forthwith, as they humbly prostrated themselves, the moderate prince calmly had mercy; in granting clemency to the people he forgave their guilt as if he were ignorant of the fact that they had violently resisted him and that they had crudely and insolently abused some knights [*milites*] whom he had sent from Normandy, and whom a storm had driven into their harbour. The men of Exeter rejoiced and gave thanks to God that after so much anger and terrible threats they were reconciled to the foreign king better than they had hoped. The king refrained from seizing their goods and he protected the gates of the city with a strong and trusty watch [*custodia*] so that common soldiers [*gregarii milites*] could not suddenly enter and violently plunder the wealth of the citizens.

Exeter's position in the siege Orderic describes is debatable. J. O. Prestwich argued for a league with Harold's sons in Ireland, given the later attack and request for aid from Dublin and Denmark,[189] whereas E. A. Freeman and Francis Palgrave, followed over a century later by Gale, Langdon and Leishman, suggested that the city was part of a south-western league of towns.[190] The argument in favour of the latter is that despite a defiant fart apparently made from the ramparts of the city during the siege,[191] William did not punish the citizens of Exeter. Exeter's liability to taxation, recorded in Domesday Book, seems to have been

[189] Prestwich, *Place of War in English History*, pp. 28–30.

[190] Freeman, *History of the Norman* Conquest, vol. 4, pp. 146–8; Freeman acknowledged the observations made on this issue by Francis Palgrave, in *The History of Normandy and of England*, 4 vols (London, 1851–64), vol. 3, pp. 419, and 426–9, and *The Rise and Progress of the English Commonwealth: Anglo-Saxon Period*, 2 vols (London, 1832), vol. 1, p. 645; Gale, Langdon and Leishman, 'Piety and Political Accommodation in Norman England', pp. 114–15. Freeman's laudatory views of Exeter are apparent in his *English Towns and Districts* (London, 1883), pp. 74–5. For criticisms of these views, see J. H. Round, *Feudal England: Historical Studies on the Eleventh and Twelfth Centuries* (London, 1895; reset edn, 1964), pp. 331–46, and, for a historiographical commentary on Freeman's views of urban freedoms, Burrow, *Liberal Descent*, pp. 175–88.

[191] This is recorded by WM, GR III.248, p. 462–3, although, given that WM records that William gained access because part of the walls 'collapsed of its own accord' (*ultro decidens*), the reliability of this record of the Exeter rebel's exuberant gesture may be (reluctantly) questioned. For a similarly crude gesture against William during the siege of Alençon in Normandy and a violent ducal response, see *Gesta Normannorum Ducum*, ed. Van Houts, OMT, 2 vols (Oxford, 1992–5), vol. 2, p. 124–5.

comparatively lenient, recorded as being levied only when also paid by London, York and Winchester, suggesting that Exeter's position was a strong one at the end of the eleventh century.[192] (York may have retained liberties under similar circumstances of conquest, a century earlier during the reign of Eadred, through the Northumbrians' expulsion of the Viking ruler Erik Bloodaxe.)[193] The danger of circularity of argument must be acknowledged here, but a large city was a strategic target that had a good chance of withstanding a siege. Therefore it was worth negotiating with the community's leading inhabitants: how seriously this issue was taken is highlighted by the *Carmen de Hastingae proelio*, which, though for the most part a dynamic narrative of war and preparations for war, spends seventy-two lines relating the details of London's chief man and the city's negotiations with the Conqueror in the wake of the Battle of Hastings.[194] That very negotiation demonstrated that those inhabitants had some sense of *de facto* authority; the very events created a sense of authority within a city.[195] Finally, it is perhaps significant that within 150 years of the creation of burhs as sites intended to augment royal power, they had become places which demonstrated how royal power was exercised through negotiation.[196]

Naturally, London is the most significant case here, and is a case for which details survive. Especially pertinent are the details of the events in 1016, at the time of the death of King Æthelred, who used London as his base while the armies of Cnut ravaged his kingdom, and during the takeover of King Edmund. London lent legitimacy to Edmund's succession, but there were practical issues to take account of. The Chronicle entry for that year arguably showed that the repairs to the city walls by the Rogation Days (7–9 May for 1016), as prescribed by Athelstan in the 920s, were in force and intended to counter the beginning of a military campaign:[197]

> Then it happened that King Æthelred died before the ships came. He ended his days on St George's day, and he had held his kingdom with great toil and hardships while his life lasted. And then after his death all the *witan* who were in London

[192] DB Dev C 4 (fol. 100a). This is noted by Chibnall in *OV*, vol. 2, p. 212n. Freeman, *History of the Norman Conquest*, vol. 4, pp. 146–7, considered such rights to have been long-standing rather than gained by negotiation in 1068.

[193] ASC D 954.

[194] *Carmen de Hastingae proelio*, lines 681–752, pp. 40–5. The negotiations regarding the surrender of Winchester, the other major city taken in the 1066 campaign, are related in lines 627–34, pp. 36–9.

[195] Although mostly focusing on the post-Conquest period, O. Creighton and R. Higham, *Medieval Town Walls: An Archaeology and Social History of Urban Defence* (Stroud, 2005), esp. pp. 165–219, provides a useful consideration of the role of defences in defining urban community identities. See p. 244, above, for evidence of urban defensive duties in Winchester.

[196] For a discussion of negotiation, see below, ch. 8. Haslam, 'Late Saxon Burhs', notes the manner in which 'hilltop fortresses of King Æthelred represented a new development in a tendency towards royal aggrandisement and power', indicating an attempt to wrest power from existing urban elites.

[197] *II Athelstan*, ch. 13: *Gesetze*, vol. 1, p. 156; trans. *EHD* 1, p. 419. The passage here is from ASC C 1016.

and the citizens [*burhwaru*] chose Edmund as king, and he sternly guarded his kingdom while his time lasted. Then the ships came to Greenwich at the Rogation Days, and within a little while went to London; and then dug a great ditch on the south side and dragged their ships to the west side of the bridge, and then afterwards dyked [*bedicodon*] the *burh* outside so that no one could get in or out, and often skilfully attacked the *burh*, but they sternly withstood them. Then before that King Edmund had gone out, and rode then into Wessex and all the people submitted to him; ...

Later in the Anglo-Saxon Chronicle's 1016 entry, the record of the surrender of the city *after* the pact made between Cnut and Edmund reveals the significance of civic independence. Recording that the the 'Londonders made a truce [*griðode*] with the *here* and bought themselves peace [*him frið gebohton*]', the Chronicle entry indicates that such a truce could be made on a local basis. The *Encomium Emmae* provides more details, highlighting the differences of opinions within the city of London, an issue which had perhaps been alluded to in Orderic's later description of Exeter.[198]

Urged on by this example [of Thorkell's successes], a certain Eric, *dux* and *princeps* of the province which is called Norway (for he was among King Cnut's officials, already long subjected to him, was a man energetic in war, and deserving of all honour), receiving leave, departed with his men and, seizing plunder, ravaged part of the country, attacking villages, destroyed [them], conquered the enemies who came to him, and captured many of them; and at length he returned to his allies [*ad socios*], victorious with the spoils. When he returned, the king, showing mercy to the country, forbade it to be plundered further, but ordered the city of London, the chief city of the land [*metropolis terrae*] to be held by a siege. For into it had fled the chief men and part of the army, and – for it is most populous – many common people. And because infantry and mounted troops [*pedites equitesque*] could not accomplish this, for it is surrounded on all sides by a river which is after a certain fashion not unequal to the sea, he made it be restrained with towered ships ['turritibus pup[p]ibus'] and held it with a most strong circumvallation [*uallatio*].

And therefore God, who wishes the more to save all men than to lose them, observing these people to be troubled with such danger, leading from the body that prince who was commanding the city within [i.e. King Æthelred], brought him to eternal rest, so that at his death free access might be open to Cnut, and with peace having been made between the people on either side, there might be, for a short time, an opportunity to draw breath. And this was done. For the citizens [*ciues*], with their prince honourably buried and having entered upon sound counsel, elected to send messengers and to deliver their agreement to the king, namely that he might give to them a pledge of friendship, and peacefully receive the city. This was done as soon as it seemed pleasing enough to Cnut, a treaty was confirmed [*faedus firmatum est*], a day having been arranged for his entry.

But part of the garrison [*pars interioris exercitus*] rejected the decision of the

[198] *Encomium Emmae*, II.7, pp. 22–5.

citizens and that night, the day before the king made his entry, secretly left the city with the son of the dead prince; in order that it be attempted again, with an innumerable force assembled, that they might, with luck, be able to keep the invading king from their own territory. And they did not rest until which time they assembled nearly all the English who were as yet more inclined to them than to Cnut. Cnut, however, entered the city and sat on the throne of the kingdom. But nevertheless, as yet, he did not believe the Londoners to be true to him; and consequently he ordered to be restored the equipment of the ships [*nauium stipendia* = or payments to crews?][199] that summer; if, indeed, by chance the army of his enemies were to besiege the city he would be handed over by enemies within to those without and perish. Taking heed of this, as a prudent man, he withdrew again for the moment, and, the ships having been boarded and the city left, he travelled to the island called Sheppey with his men, where, overwintering, he awaited the outcome of the matter in peace.

The Encomiast's attribution of resistance to Cnut to the 'garrison' (*pars interioris exercitus*) of the city may be a deliberate simplification of the arguments leading to the city's decision. Many of those in the army based in the city (probably not a garrison *per se*) who continued to resist Cnut were killed in subsequent events, while the record of the desire to make peace with the Danish invader cannot be unrelated to the fact that many citizens of London needed to deal with Cnut and his successors in the years after 1016. It may also help to explain why London is recorded separately as making geld payment to Cnut in 1018.[200] Furthermore, John of Worcester's record of Cnut's assembly in London by Cnut following the death of his rival Edmund highlights the later importance of the city to the Danish dynasty.[201]

Summary and observations

Throughout the Viking Age, fortifications appear to have functioned both as places which saw off Viking attacks and, importantly, as locations to be avoided by attacking forces. Although historians have long acknowledged this as a relevant issue for the study of the later part of the reign of Alfred the Great, there is less recognition of the significance of fortifications for the reign of Æthelred II, when parts of Wessex appear to have been safer than others, at least during the earlier part of Æthelred's reign. Gareth Williams has identified a tentative emergence of a burghal system in Lincolnshire during the reign of Æthelred II,[202] as well as the investment in southern English 'emergency burhs'.

Although larger towns attracted Viking attacks and were often the points

---

[199] Cf. Campbell's comment in *Encomium Emmae*, p. 23n, who suggests it would be 'absurd' for Cnut to be discharging his crews 'while Eadmund was still in the field'; however, a payment to crews does not necessarily mean that they were discharged from their obligations.

[200] ASC CDE 1018. See Hill, 'An Urban Policy for Cnut?'.

[201] JW vol. 2, s.a. 1016, pp. 492–5.

[202] Williams, 'Civil Defence or Royal Powerbase?'.

where the English kingdom stood or fell, such towns could be successful. Bishops could have been a factor in this success as central figures in urban defences, although of course not every town had a bishop. The potential independence of towns, backed up in part by their potential self-reliance and defence meant that that very civic independence played a role in their defensive capacity.

However, these issues do not necessarily mean 'policy' in the second Viking Age. The Alfredian defences of the West Saxon kingdom appear to have had a more successful system of defence, and presumably it was the system itself which had been neglected by the end of the tenth century, even if individual units of defence appear to have had some success.

A supplementary question may be raised as to why power in the English kingdom did not become 'cellularized' through the use of private fortifications during the depredations caused by the events of the Second Viking Age, as happened in the domains of post-Carolingian western Francia. Private fortifications – in effect, castles – did emerge in England during the Viking Age,[203] but they are unlikely to have been central to the defences of the Anglo-Saxon kingdom in the way that, for example, the castles along the frontiers of Normandy became important to the defence of that duchy during the early eleventh century.[204] This issue may go some way to explaining the survival of the English state before and after 1066: the continuity of the role of urban fortifications is a significant factor in the continuity of the English state in the ninth to eleventh centuries.

---

[203] See Williams, 'Bell-house and a Burh-geat', and Renn, 'Burhgeat and Gonfanon'. For an archaeological consideration of a specific case, see G. Beresford, *Goltho: The Development of an Early Medieval Manor, c. 850–1150*, Archaeological Report no. 4 (London, 1987), pp. 29–84. For arguments against the existence of 'castles' in pre-Conquest England, see R. A. Brown, 'An Historian's Approach to the Origins of the Castle in England', *Archaeological Journal* 126 (1970 for 1969), pp. 131–48.

[204] For a general discussion of the eleventh-century frontier of Normandy, see Bates, *Normandy Before 1066*, pp. 63–4. For a specific case study, see J. A. Green, 'Lords of the Norman Vexin', in *War and Government in the Middle Ages: Essays in Honour of J. O. Prestwich*, ed. J. C. Holt and J. Gillingham (Woodbridge, 1984), pp. 47–61. For reservations on the functions of castles in defining a frontier, see R. C. Smail, *Crusading Warfare, 1097–1193*, Cambridge Studies in Medieval Life and Thought, 2nd series 3 (Cambridge, 1956; 2nd edn, 1994), pp. 204–14.

✦ 7 ✦

Fields of Slaughter: Battles and Battlefields

Tʜɪs chapter is concerned with places of battle on land and at sea as well as the conduct and perception of battles themselves. Although often seen as central to warfare and attracting a commensurate level of attention,[1] battles are rare in warfare; the Anglo-Saxon period is no exception. Furthermore, what one party perceived as a battle, another may have seen as a skirmish. Without knowing the sizes of armies it is difficult to determine where a hostile encounter was perceived as a battle. Notwithstanding the momentousness of the battles of 1066, the consequences of actions were often alluded to by historical sources a few years after the event, such as the Anglo-Saxon Chronicle's reference to the making of peace after the Battle of Edington or the 'first' payment of geld to the Vikings after the Battle of Maldon,[2] which suggests at least a retrospective awareness of the importance of such events. To this end, the Anglo-Saxon Chronicle's judgement of Alfred's first year of rule, 871, is revealing.[3] Even if the author's purpose was to highlight Alfred's capability as a ruler (and once more it should be noted that the Chronicler was writing in the early 890s)[4] it provides an interesting interpretation on the notion of battles as landmark events: the term *folc gefeoht* used by the Chronicler denoted battles which had required the participation of the king with all of the army units of his ealdormen, who, in turn, had called out their thegns and followers.[5] Dorothy Whitelock's translation of *folc gefeoht* as 'general engagements' should be treated with caution here, as is made clear by Asser's straightforward Latin rendering of the term as 'battles' (*proeliis*) – notwithstanding his reduction of the Chronicle's count of nine battles to eight.[6] Although we cannot assume that the 871 entry can be applied to interpretations of battles across the Anglo-Saxon period, as, for one matter, the events at Maldon in 991, fought by an ealdorman, were recorded as a battle,[7] the 871 entry's interpretation is nonetheless useful. The distinction was not necessarily between the size of the armies, but on who participated in the combat.

---

[1] For a recent nuanced reappraisal, see Y. N. Harari, 'The Concept of "Decisive Battles" in World History', *Journal of World History* 18 (2007), pp. 251–66.

[2] ASC 878; CDE 991.

[3] ASC 871.

[4] Bateley, 'The Compilation of the Anglo-Saxon Chronicle'.

[5] For the participation of kings and other lords in warfare, see Abels, *Lordship and Military Obligation in Anglo-Saxon England*, pp. 146–84, and discussion in ch. 3, above.

[6] EHD 1, p. 193; Asser, ch. 42.

[7] ASC A 991 records that Olaf Tryggvasson's forces 'held control of the place of slaughter' (*wælstowe geweald ahtan*), a topos associated with the record of a battle (see below, p. 299). An edition and translation of the poem is 'Battle of Maldon', ed. Scragg, pp. 15–36.

Then succeeded Alfred, son of Æthelwulf, his [i.e. Æthelred's] brother, to the kingdom of the West Saxons. And then a month after King Alfred fought with a small band [*wiþ … lytle werede*] against all the *here* at Wilton and put it to flight far on into the day; and the Danes held held control of the place of slaughter. And in that year were 9 battles [*folc gefeoht*] fought against the *here* in the kingdom south of the Thames, beside those which the king's brother Alfred and single ealdormen and king's thegns often rode on, which were not counted. And that year were slain nine [Danish] earls and one king. And that year the West Saxons made peace with the army.

This passage seems to stand apart from the other accounts in the 871 entry, perhaps having been compiled from a different record from those used by the rest of that particular annal. It highlights how the evidence for pre-Conquest battles can thus be said to be at once extensive and obscure. The events of the battle of Ashdown in 871 are recorded in detail by Asser[8] but the 871 Chronicle entry also shows that the details can be laconic, leaving the historian with nothing to go on other than the record of the victors or the vanquished, and occasionally some indication of the timescale (as provided by the Chronicle's reference to the battle at Wilton). The comparison of Æthelweard's account of Wilton, as Whitelock notes, must be used to inform us that Alfred may not have been present at the battle, as he was attending his brother's funeral, presumably at Wimborne.[9]

Although the Old English literature of the period relates extensively to battles, it is often circumlocutious, with kennings and metaphors such as a 'sword-play' or 'spear-storm' being used to refer to the concept of a 'battle'. When it comes to consideration of just what happened when armies met on the battlefield in the early middle ages, primary sources, as Guy Halsall has observed, are typically 'laconic' or full of poetic clichés.[10] This observation is no less applicable to the study of Anglo-Saxon warfare. Many historical interpretations have been influenced by the stereotyped descriptions of poetry, and we are all too often faced with historical imaginings which bring out those notions of slaughter and staunch defence, the idea of the lord's death being followed by the resistance of his followers and heroic but ultimately futile deaths.[11] While such interpretations are useful, a focus on the experience of 'the Anglo-Saxon warrior' as a figure of literature serves to isolate the English experience from that of the rest of Continental Europe.[12]

There should be more to our picture of late Anglo-Saxon warfare. This chapter therefore considers the comparative approaches taken to the psychology of warfare, addressing human behaviour on the battlefield, the limits and interpretations

---

[8] Asser, chs 37–9 (below, pp. 276–7).

[9] *EHD* 1, p. 193, n. 11. Whitelock points out that Æthelweard does not note the name of the battle but highlights the small size of the Anglo-Saxon force. See above, p. 187 for consideration of the strategic implications of this.

[10] Halsall, *Warfare and Society in the Barbarian West, 450–900*, p. 180. See also the apposite comments on Norse poetic accounts of battle in L. Lönnroth, 'The Vikings in History and Legend', in *The Oxford Illustrated History of the Vikings*, ed. P. H. Sawyer (Oxford, 1997), pp. 225–49, at p. 226, cited by Halsall.

[11] For example, Stephenson, *Late Anglo-Saxon Army*, pp. 119–30.

[12] See here the otherwise very useful Pollington, *English Warrior from Earliest Times till 1066*.

of the source material, considerations of tactics, the evidence for naval battles, and the memory of the battlefields themselves.

Courage, cowardice and motivation

In recent years, comparative work, including that by archaeologists, has moved the study of ancient and medieval warfare forward in a manner in which it is possible to think of the experience of the battlefield. Such methods share common ground with approaches to early medieval warfare through anthropological comparisons discussed in chapter 1. The combat experience of participants on the battlefield is also relevant. Such consideration was driven forward by John Keegan's classic study, *The Face of Battle*, which, although not focused on the Anglo-Saxon period (it begins with the Battle of Agincourt), is an important study of the individual and group psychology of combat experience.[13] Barry Molloy's collection, *The Cutting Edge* (2007), contains a useful recent example of such a perspective; the chapter by Molloy and Dave Grossman, effectively a pre-modern perspective on Grossman's work on the psychology of violence,[14] highlights the significance of training, as well as the likelihood that, given the same physiological and psychological stresses, a combat group fighting with 'traditional' weapons would have faced different individual responses:[15]

> This reluctance by the majority of the male population to kill others at close range is very much contrary to machismo's view of the 'ideal' male. Part of the reason for poor understanding of this element of our species is that combat, like sex, is laden with a baggage of expectations and myth. A belief that most soldiers will not kill the enemy in close combat is contrary to what we want to believe about ourselves, and it is contrary to what thousands of years of military history and culture have told us. If for thousands of years the vast majority of soldiers secretly and privately were less than enthused about killing their fellow man on the battlefield, the professional soldiers and their chroniclers would be the last to let us know the inadequacies of their particular charges. One would find it oddly out of context if Thucydides were to explain away the failures of the Sicilian expedition by the reticence of fellow Athenians to actually kill the enemy!

The influence of classical sources upon those of the Middle Ages is a subject for later discussion, but it can hardly go without comment that the Anglo-Saxon Chronicle C manuscript entry for 1003 highlights this very point. The passage is quoted here in full as it highlights an important issue related to leadership and apparent bravery:

> Here [i.e. in this year] Exeter was destroyed because of the French *ceorl* Hugh, whom the queen had appointed as her reeve, and the *here* then did away with the

---

[13] J. Keegan, *The Face of Battle: A Study of Agincourt, Waterloo and the Somme* (Harmondsworth, 1976). See also I. W. Miller, *The Mystery of Courage* (Cambridge, MA, 2000).

[14] Grossman, *On Killing*.

[15] Molloy and Grossman, 'Why Can't Johnny Kill?', p. 197.

burh completely and there seized much plunder. And in that same year the army went inland into Wiltshire. Then was gathered a great army [*fyrd*] from Wiltshire and from Hampshire, and they were going very resolutely against the enemy. Then Ealdorman Ælfric [of eastern Wessex] was to lead the army, but he then drew forth his old tricks. As soon as they were so near that either army looked on the other, he feigned himself sick, and began to force himself to vomit, and declared that he was ill, and thus betrayed the people whom he should have led. As it is said: 'When the leader [*heretoga*] gives way, then all the army [*here*] will be much hindered'. When Swein saw that they were irresolute, and they they all scattered, he led his *here* into Wilton, and they harried and burnt the borough, and he took himself then to Salisbury, and from there went back to the sea, where he knew his wave-stallions were.

The saying quoted by the Chronicler has parallels with a contemporary homily of Ælfric of Eynsham, and may have earlier origins,[16] suggesting that it was apposite to the audience of the Chronicle. If tactics on the battlefield were limited, even allowing for the use of mounted troops, and conduct on the battlefield consisted, as Peter Foote and David Wilson aptly remarked, 'largely of bashing hell out of the opposing side',[17] then morale, leadership and motivation could win a battle. Philippe Contamine's chapter 'Towards a History of Courage' in his *War in the Middle Ages* was an important opening salvo in a historical debate.[18] This was followed up by Richard Abels in his examination of the links between cowardice and duty in Anglo-Saxon England; he suggests that Anglo-Saxon notions of cowardice were different from modern and Aristotelian notions of cowardice: 'the Anglo-Saxons did not credit inner fear with the motive power to override a soldier's rational will, as Aristotle and modern conceptions of cowardice do.' The results of cowardice may have been the same but, as Abels argues, for the Anglo-Saxons 'it was a matter of choice'.[19] As with Abels's other work, one may question how far such notions of behaviour were idealistic, governed by expectations established in literary texts. However, if they were not not prescriptive, texts certainly represented modes of behaviour by which the inhabitants of that society wished to be identified, and through which they wished to conduct their lives. Thus, although Abels is characteristically modest in the article's lack of citations to his own *Lordship and Military Obligation*, the behaviour of warriors appears to have been determined by the bonds of lordship.[20] Articles by Stephen Morillo and Steven Isaac in the same volume of the journal, although not focused on Anglo-Saxon England, also highlight the cultures of bravery and cowardice on the medieval

[16] See T. Hill, '"When the Leader is Brave …": An Old English Proverb and its Vernacular Context', *Anglia: Zeitschrift für englische Philologie* 119.2 (2001), pp. 232–6. See also Abels, '"Cowardice" and Duty in Anglo-Saxon England', pp. 46–7.

[17] P. G. Foote and D. M. Wilson, *The Viking Achievement* (London, 1970), p. 285, quoted by Halsall, *Warfare and Society in the Barbarian West*, p. 194.

[18] Contamine, *War in the Middle Ages*, pp. 250–9.

[19] Abels, '"Cowardice" and Duty in Anglo-Saxon England', p. 49.

[20] Abels, *Lordship and Military Obligation in Anglo-Saxon England*. See above, ch. 3, for discussion of this.

battlefield. In the case of Morillo, the emphasis of the 'expectation' of cowardice is on understanding one's enemy, hence individual displays of prowess before a battle.[21] Similarly, with a twelfth-century case study, Isaac highlights the significance of knowing the limits of one's own troops and, indeed, oneself.[22]

The classic Old English poem, *The Battle of Maldon*, provides a literary case study of the significance of leadership, both in its ideal form and in terms of the inversion of its expression through the cowardice of those who were mistaken for the East Saxon ealdorman when they fled.[23] Abels highlights John of Worcester's 'possibly apocryphal' story of the traitor Eadric *Streona*'s display of the decapitated head of a look-a-like of King Edmund Ironside during the battle of Sherston, in order to provoke a rout from the English side.[24] Leadership was expressed through the bonds of lordship, but leadership was also demonstrated through the knowledge of one's own troops. This would have been relevant for the choice of the right moment to strike or to hold, perhaps indicated by the Maldon poet's emphasis on Byrhtnoth's rejoinder to his troops to stand firm before the battle:[25] this did not imply that the English warriors did not know how to wield their weapons, but rather that the poet emphasized the English ealdorman's leadership.[26] John of Salisbury's record of the right of the men of Kent to strike the first blow in battle is relevant here: writing in an excursus about leadership and skill in war, he used the case of Kentish bellicosity as a virtue which was effectively exploited by Cnut.[27] To this end, the 'leader' model proposed by Philip Sabin with regard to ancient warfare may be applied to generals in the pre-Conquest period. Sabin defines 'leaders' as leading by example. By contrast, his definition of 'commanders' as leaders who moved around the battlefield, taking a more strategic overview, may be more applicable to the battles of mobility characteristic of the ancient world.[28]

---

[21] Morillo, 'Expecting Cowardice', p. 69.

[22] S. Isaac, 'Cowardice and Fear Management: The 1173–74 Conflict as a Case Study', *JMMH* 4 (2006), pp. 50–64.

[23] 'Battle of Maldon', ed. Scragg, lines 185–200, 237–43, pp. 26–9.

[24] Abels, 'English Tactics, Strategy and Military Organization in the Late Tenth Century', p. 151, referring to JW vol. 2, s.a. 1016, pp. 486–9. Abels, n. 43, notes that, although the ASC does not record the story, it is mentioned in HH VI.13, pp. 358–9 (a source which uses the ASC).

[25] 'Battle of Maldon', ed. Scragg, lines 17–21, pp. 18–19.

[26] On the possibility of this as a classical topos, see below, p. 273. Critiques of Byrhtnoth's leadership are provided by Gordon, *Battle of Maldon*, pp. 1, 5; A. D. Mills, 'Byrhtnoth's Mistake in Generalship', *Neuphilologische Mitteilungen*, 67 (1966), pp. 14–27; J. R. R. Tolkien, 'The Homecoming of Beorhtnoth Beorhthelm's Son', *Essays and Studies of the English Association*, new ser. 6 (1953), pp. 1–18. An early defence of Byrhtnoth's reputation was provided by W. A. Samouce, 'General Byrhtnoth', *Journal of English and Germanic Philology* 62 (1963), pp. 129–35.

[27] *Ioannis Saresberiensis episcopi Carnotensis policratici*, ed. Webb, vol. 2, pp. 47–8; trans. Nederman, *Policratus: Of the Frivolities of Courtiers and the Footprints of Philosophers*, p. 118. The historical value of the account is compromised, however, by the fact that he refers to defeats of the Danes and Norse by Cnut 'of the English' (*Anglorum*). See above, p. 106.

[28] Sabin, *Lost Battles*, p. 69.

Medieval or classical sources?

With the strengths and limitations of the account of the Battle of Maldon poem highlighted, we may ask how far the medieval sources mirrored the reality of their own day or showed off the author's knowledge of classical sources. This is a debate which is highlighted by Richard Abels and Stephen Morillo, who discuss Abels's experience of writing on John of Worcester's account of the Battle of Sherston in 1016. As Abels has pointed out, John of Worcester's account of the battle is, at first sight, a 'treasure trove' for the study of the tactics of the battlefield, but it is probably more useful as a study of how medieval historians were influenced by the details of classical authors:

> When [Edmund Ironside] arranged the army [*exercitus*] according to the location [*pro loco*] and his forces [*copiae*], he drew the best into the front line [*in primam aciem*], he arranged the remainder of the army in reserve, and calling each man by name, exhorted and requested that they remember that they fought for country, children, wives and for homes, and with these rousing words he fired the soldiers' hearts; thereafter he ordered the trumpeters [*tubicines*] to sound and the *cohortes* to gradually advance [*paulatim incedere*]. The enemy army did the same. When they had come to where they could join battle they rushed forward with great cla-mour and with hostile standards [*cum infestis signis*]. The battle was borne with lances and swords [*lanceis et gladiis*], with all their might it was fought. Meanwhile King Edmund Ironside took a position [*instabat*] in fierce hand-to-hand fighting in the front rank [*in prima acie*]; he perceived of everything. He himself fought hard, he often struck the enemy; he performed at the same time the duties of a tough soldier and a good general.[29]

Abels's comments on John of Worcester's accounts of Edmund Ironside's bat-tles at Sherston and *Assandun*[30] warrant reproduction at length. They highlight both the experiences of the military historian in dealing with such a source and the approaches necessary. As a personal account (despite the use of the third person, as he wrote with Stephen Morillo in a co-authored article), it is a salutary tale relating to the process of writing his contribution to the invaluable volume edited by Donald Scragg on the Battle of Maldon:[31]

> In comparison with the vague accounts in the Anglo-Saxon Chronicle of these and other battles, John's narratives are a treasure trove of detail about prepara-tions for battle and deployment of troops, derived, Abels then believed, from either a lost recension of the Chronicle or some other near contemporary

---

[29] JW vol. 2, s.a. 1016, p. 486. An alternative translation, from JW vol. 2, p. 487, is cited by Abels and Morillo, 'A Lying Legacy?', p. 1.

[30] JW vol. 2, s.a. 1016, p. 490.

[31] Abels and Morillo, 'A Lying Legacy?', pp. 2–4. The article in question is Abels, 'English Tactics, Strategy and Military Organization in the Late Tenth Century'. A response to Abels and Morillo's article is made in Bernard Bachrach, '"A Lying Legacy" Revisited: The Abels-Morillo Defense of Discontinuity', *JMMH* 5 (2007), pp. 153–93.

source.[32] Edmund's approach to battle, as presented by John, was strikingly similar to that of the ancient Romans, and the resemblance was made even clearer by
John's use of classical phrases such as *copiis instruit* and words like *cohortes*. After
writing a draft of the article, Abels discovered why. John had lifted his accounts,
almost word for word (though in highly edited form), from, respectively, Sallust's
Catiline and his *Jugurthine War*.[33] Chagrined, Abels removed his extended analyses
of Sherston and Ashingdon, added a discussion of 'military organization' to fill out
the article, and hoped his readers would not notice how little there was in it on
battlefield tactics.[34] Before he did this, however, he asked our friend and colleague
Professor Bernard S. Bachrach for advice. Bachrach did not see a real problem.
That John had selected these particular passages from Sallust was to him highly
significant, for John undoubtedly had chosen them because he deemed them to be
accurate characterizations of what had actually occurred in Edmund's battles.

Abels did not agree then nor do we agree now. Rather, we think that all that
John *knew* about these battles came from his main source, the Anglo-Saxon Chronicle, and that he added the details from Sallust to spruce up the narrative and to
demonstrate his own erudition. To be sure, John's compression and editing of the
Sallust texts may be significant. Among the details that he chose not to include
in his narrative of the battle of Sherston are Catiline's decision to drive away his
horses so that his men would have to stand and fight, descriptions of topography
and terrain clearly inappropriate for Sherston, and references to centurions and
subordinate commanders on the wings. John also changed Sallust's *'pila omittunt,
gladius res geritur'* [*they left aside their javelins and fought with their swords*] to *'lanceis
et gladiis pugna geritur'* [*lances and swords were carried for battle*]. Similarly, in his
account of the battle of Ashingdon, John edited out Sallust's description of how
the Roman commander Metellus deployed his slingers (*funditores*) and archers
(*sagittarios*) between the companies of infantry, and placed his cavalry on the wings.
These omissions may reflects John's awareness of differences between armies of his
day, the first decades of the twelfth century, and those described by Sallust. (In this
respect, John's decision to change Sallust's description of soldiers throwing javelins

---

[32] C. R. Hart argues that the Worcester Chronicle up to the year 1016 was compiled
between that year and *c.* 1020 by the monk Byrhtferth of Ramsey, to whom he attributed
the composition of the later annals, including these battle descriptions. C. R. Hart, 'The
Early Section of the Worcester Chronicle', *Journal of Medieval History* 9 (1983), pp. 251–315.
More cautiously, Michael Lapidge, noting the resemblance between the language of the
Worcester Chronicle and Byrhtferth's *Life of St. Oswald*, has suggested that a lost version
of the Anglo-Saxon Chronicle underlies the entries for 958 through 992, and that this
chronicle could possibly have been composed at Ramsey, perhaps even by Byrhtferth. M.
Lapidge, 'Byrhtferth and Oswald', in *St. Oswald of Worcester: Life and Influence*, ed. N. P.
Brooks and C. Cubitt, SEHB: The Makers of England 2 (London, 1996), pp. 64–83, at
p. 76. See also A. P. Smyth, *The Medieval Life of King Alfred the Great* (Basingstoke, and
New York, 2002), pp. 69–71. Cf. P. McGurk, 'Introduction' to JW vol. 2, pp. lxxix–lxxxi,
which rebuts Hart's case.

[33] R. R. Darlington and P. McGurk, 'The "Chronicon ex Chronicis" of "Florence" of
Worcester and Its Use of Sources', *ANS* 5 (1983 for 1982), pp. 185–96, at p. 193, n. 37; Hart,
'Early Section of the Worcester Chronicle', pp. 303–4.

[34] Abels, 'English Tactics, Strategy and Military Organization in the Late Tenth Century'.
John of Worcester's accounts of Sherston and Ashingdon are discussed on p. 153, n. 17.

[*pila*] to soldiers thrusting with lances [*lanceae*] is suggestive.) Or John may have simply wished to condense the narratives. In either case, John probably used Sallust's *Catiline* and *Jurgurtha* not because Edmund Ironside actually commanded and fought like a first century BC Roman general but to demonstrate his familiarity with a classical authority then in vogue.[35] Bachrach's interpretation is indeed possible, but strikes us as inherently less likely.[36] It is less likely unless, of course, one begins, as does Bachrach, with the assumption that 'the picture of medieval history which is emerging today' is that of 'continuity between the ancient and medieval periods.'[37] Bachrach's thesis is founded, in part, upon his careful study and intimate knowledge of the literary and documentary sources that survive from the early and central Middle Ages and, in part, upon his complete rejection of the old historical paradigm of Rome's 'Fall' and the West's descent into 'the Dark Ages'. Early medieval texts, as he takes pains to point out, abound with classical allusions and often employ technical Roman military and administrative terminology in describing events. Bachrach contends, moreover, that the preservation, transmission, and popularity (as measured by numbers of manuscripts) throughout the early Middle Ages of Roman military handbooks, notably Vegetius's *De re militari* and Frontinus's *Strategemata*, attests to the Roman foundations that underlay military organization in the West between the fourth and twelfth centuries. [...] But how much of this apparent continuity is real and how much is the consequence of the classicizing tendencies of medieval chroniclers? All historians when assessing sources face the problem of representation versus reality. For military historians of the Middle Ages, this problem takes the special form of classicizing sources versus the realities of early medieval warfare. ...

35 The growing popularity of Sallust is suggested by the rise in the number of copies of extant manuscripts of his work between the tenth and twelfth centuries: four in the tenth, thirty-three in the eleventh, and fifty-eight in the twelfth. L. D. Reynolds (ed.), *Texts and Transmission: A Survey of the Latin Classics* (Oxford, 1983), pp. xxvi-xxvii.

36 Some obvious questions suggest themselves regarding Bachrach's interpretation that John used Sallust because the description fit what he knew of the battle. Why Sallust? Did John search through any number of classical sources until he found an appropriately parallel battle? What other descriptions did he have available? Given that John edited the accounts in Sallust in ways already noted, why did he not borrow shorter phrases and descriptions from several sources, surely a technique more likely to produce and accurate description than wholesale appropriation of a single battle-piece from a single source? All medieval chroniclers' heads were full of classical words and short phrases, many of which regularly found their way into descriptions of warfare – see for example the discussion of Orderic Vitalis below [i.e. *OV*, vol. 6, p. 472, cited in Abels and Morillo, 'A Lying Legacy?'], pp. 10–11 and nn. 18–20. But when they had clear and abundant information about a battle, either from witnessing it or from other eyewitnesses, they had no trouble creating original descriptions in which classical words and phrases provided some of the bricks of the structure, so to speak, rather than the entire architecture. See, for example, William of Poitiers' description of the Hastings campaign and battle, which positively invited borrowings from Caesar, but whose account of Hastings is clearly his own [WP II.1–27, pp. 100–45]; see further discussion below [i.e. in Abels and Morillo, 'A Lying Legacy?'], pp. 5–6 and nn. 15–16.

37 B. S. Bachrach, 'Medieval Military Historiography', in *Companion to Historiography*, ed. M. Bentley (London, 1997), pp. 192–208, at p. 194. On Charlemagne's study of Roman military tactics and strategy, see B. S. Bachrach, *Early Carolingian Warfare: Prelude to Empire*, Middle Ages (Philadelphia, PA, 2001), p. 162.

Bachrach's theory of continuity presupposes the continuity of drilling and social organization from the Roman period and is a theory which requires a maximal reading of the continuity of state military organization. While late nineteenth- and early twentieth-century views of military organization in battle, such as those of Charles Oman, are somewhat reductionist, assuming the disorganization of units as near rabble,[38] a belief in the ability to manœuvre in the face of the enemy assumes professional standards of organization. Stephenson's argument of direct continuity from the Greek hoplite and the ancient battlefields of Marathon (490 BC) and Thermopylae (480 BC) goes even further than that of Bachrach. He takes an extreme view of the continuity of the infantry warfare, going as far as to note that Anglo-Saxon warriors were aware of their hoplite predecessors, and emphasizing the infantry element of warfare at the expense of the use of horses (somewhat paradoxically, as Stephenson addresses horses in a nuanced fashion elsewhere in the book).[39] Stephenson takes the argument a stage further than the standard discussion of the influence *on* medieval sources: to suggest that behaviour was such because of the influence of the past. This is arguably unduly deterministic. Arguments for continuity of behaviour throughout the Roman period, into the 'sub-Roman' period and into the late Anglo-Saxon period should be tempered by the fact that in England many of the classical and classically styled sources of the tenth, eleventh and twelfth centuries had stemmed, in large part, from Carolingian influence, in the reuse and even revival of these sources on the Continent.[40]

How far should the utility of sources be questioned, then, if medieval authors were happy to borrow, plagiarize and use classical exemplars as they saw fit? Might we see, for example, in Asser's verbose description of the Battle of Ashdown (below), the wholesale reuse of a classical source which is otherwise unknown to us? While such reductionism may not be implausible, where the events were known, terms and phrases from classical sources could be woven into the narrative.[41] Such sources might have been self-consciously clever and, as Abels and Morillo point out, they should not lead us to assume continuity of classical modes of warfare,[42] but this should not lead us to dismiss all early medieval narrative accounts of warfare.

Another issue is the points of difference in the 'altered reality', such as where John of Worcester replaces the javelins and swords of ancient warfare related by Sallust with lances and swords in his description of the Battle of Sherston. Such a change of detail suggest that an author such as John of Worcester was conscious of the implications of adapting a source text, although it perhaps indicates more

---

[38] For example, Oman, *A History of the Art of War: Middle Ages*, pp. 71–2, on the early Anglo-Saxons.

[39] Stephenson, *Late Anglo-Saxon Army*, pp. 28–31.

[40] See generally J. Backhouse, D. H. Turner, and L. Webster (eds), *The Golden Age of Anglo-Saxon Art, 966–1066* (London, 1984), pp. 143–69.

[41] Abels and Morillo, 'A Lying Legacy?', p. 3, n. 8.

[42] Abels and Morillo, 'A Lying Legacy?', pp. 11–12. See also Halsall, *Warfare and Society in the Barbarian West*, pp. 177–8.

about the author's education and literary aspirations than it necessarily reflects on what was known of actual battles which may have occurred a century or more before the time of writing. John of Worcester's Sherston, discussed above by Abels and Morillo, reflects twelfth-century realities. A similar case is the eleventh-century *Encomium Emmae*'s reference to Suetonius' phrase 'prelium pedestre' in the account of *Assandun* (1016), which, Halsall notes, omits Suetonius' 'ac equestre'.[43] Concerned with demonstrating that the sources do not have to have shown the English armies as infantry-only armies, Halsall writes that '[i]n the previous chapter the Danish army has disembarked from its ships, so the Encomiast may have adapted Suetonius' phrase to mean that this was a hard-fought land battle', rather than necessarily an infantry battle.[44] While, as we have seen in chapter 3, Halsall's comments on the English use of horses in battle are logical,[45] the Encomiast's omission may have had another purpose: it would surely have been a distracting detail for the Encomiast to include reference to the battle being fought on horseback if the Danes had just disembarked from ships.

Abels and Morillo, following C. R. Hart, have even drawn attention to the similarity of that staple of Old English literature, *The Battle of Maldon*, to Sallust's description of the drawing up of an army on a battlefield, from ordering that the horses be driven away to instructing the troops on how to hold their shields.[46] Abels and Morillo note that the motif of a leader instructing his troops before a battle can be seen in William of Malmesbury's description of Henry I instructing his English troops how to defend themselves before an abortive battle against his brother Robert Curthose in 1101.[47] Even if these were not necessarily conscious echoes of classical sources (and Eric John has commented on the limited quality of the Maldon poet's Old English vocabulary),[48] the motifs of warfare are instructive. As we have seen, sending horses away in order to make a stand on foot was symbolic of resistance and defiance, a tactic used by ninth-century Frankish warriors and twelfth-century Norman rebels as much as by a later Anglo-Saxon army.[49]

---

[43] *Encomium Emmae* II.10, p. 26, cited in Halsall, *Warfare and Society in the Barbarian West*, p. 182, and compared with Suetonius, *Lives of the Twelve Caesars. Domitian*, ch. 4, in *Suetonius*, ed. and trans. J. C. Rolfe, Loeb Classical Library (London, 1914), pp. 344–5.

[44] Halsall, *Warfare and Society in the Barbarian West*, p. 182.

[45] Above, pp. 129–36. See also below, pp. 283–5.

[46] 'Battle of Maldon', ed. Scragg, lines 2–3; 17–21, pp. 18–19, compared with Sallust, *The War with Catiline*, ch. 59, in *Sallust*, ed. and trans. J. C. Rolfe, Loeb Classical Library 116 (London, 1920), pp. 122–3; Abels and Morillo, 'A Lying Legacy?', p. 5; Hart, *The Danelaw*, pp. 542–3.

[47] Abels and Morillo, 'A Lying Legacy?', p. 5, n. 13, discussing WM, *GR*, V.395, pp. 716–17.

[48] John, *Reassessing Anglo-Saxon England*, p. 143 and n. 7.

[49] For discussion of this, see above, p. 130.

Fighting techniques and battlefield tactics

As discussed above, our images of Anglo-Saxon warfare are very much affected by the notions of battle being a heroic slog, as depicted in the literary sources. The effect of 'racial' readings of English tactics, such as those proffered at the end of the nineteenth century by Sir Charles Oman, had a profound effect upon historiography.[50] Although few historians would now ascribe English tactics to 'Teutonic blood', drawing direct connections between Tacitus's *Germania* and the 'real' Battle of Maldon, the notion that the Anglo-Saxons fought differently from their Continental neighbours has continued to resonate through the study of the period.

This is especially apparent with the view of the concept of an Anglo-Saxon 'shield-wall', which is common currency in views of the period,[51] perhaps spurred on by the notions of the sequence of events described in the *Battle of Maldon* poem.[52]

> Then the slaughter-wolves advanced, for they paid no heed to the water,
> the Viking band, west over the Blackwater
> over the bright water they carried their shields,
> *lithsmen* bore their linden [shields] to land.
> There facing foes, they stood ready,
> Byrhtnoth with his men; he commanded
> that company to form the war-hedge [*wihaga*] with their shields and hold
> firmly against the fiends. There was fighting nigh,
> glory in the battle. The time had arrived
> when the fated men should fall there.
> There the clamour was raised, ravens circled,
> the eagle was eager for carrion, there was uproar in the land.
> They released then from their hands the file-hard spears,
> grimly ground spears flew;
> Bows were busy, shield received spear.
> Bitter was the onslaught, men fell,
> On either side, warriors lay dead.

The ritual activity of a battle may have played into the expectations of behaviour of the early medieval elites. The Maldon poet's reference to spears or javelins being thrown and arrows shot before the two sides came into hand-to-hand combat may have been as much about ritualized expectations as about a tactical decision.[53] A dividing line between the expectations of behaviour and the

---

[50] Oman, *History of the Art of War: Middle Ages*, p. 149.

[51] The 'shieldwall' (note the lack of hyphen) appears to be almost formalized in its treatment in modern writing: see e.g. R. Underwood, *Anglo-Saxon Weapons and Warfare* (Stroud, 1999), p. 90.

[52] 'Battle of Maldon', ed. Scragg, lines 96–112, p. 22.

[53] For the throwing of a spear as an indication of the start of a battle, see ASC C 1055. Manley, 'Archer and Army in the Late Saxon Period', pp. 223–35, deals with the apparent limits of archery in battle, an activity which is only explicitly indicated by a lone archer alongside an English 'shield-wall' on the Bayeux Tapestry (see Fig. 7.1) and with a single named archer,

Fig. 7.1 An Anglo-Saxon 'shield-wall' depicted in the Bayeux Tapestry

practical aspects of combat should not be too clearly drawn. If the throwing of spears was expected – perhaps by both sides – then it made good military sense to do so as much for the fulfilment of social expectations as in order to kill the enemy.

However, it is with the press of the two 'shield-walls' that most attention lies, with a focus on the use of spears by the warriors involved as swords were presumably difficult to wield in such a situation (see the images of the Bayeux Tapestry, Fig. 7.1) Again, Halsall's study of early medieval warfare has drawn attention to how authors of the early middle ages used particular terminology, including 'shield-wall', to refer to the press of bodies in an engagement rather than specific tactical formations.[54] Asser's description of the Battle of Ashdown (871), a source which Halsall has highlighted as one of the more extensive descriptions of an Anglo-Saxon battle,[55] can be read as an engagement of 'shield-walls', but Simon Keynes and Michael Lapidge's translation of Asser's use of the classical term *testudo* in the standard edition of translated Alfredian sources could mislead.[56] To read *testudo* as 'shield-wall' implies that a 'shield-wall' was itself a specific term for a formation of troops rather than a literary device.[57] Presumably the term refers to groups in close-order formation,[58] ready for battle, and should be read as such in the following account:

a hostage named Æscferth, in 'Battle of Maldon', ed. Scragg, lines 265–72, pp. 28–9. For discussion of Æscferth's status, see Lavelle, 'Use and Abuse of Hostages', *EME* 14 (2006), pp. 269–96, at pp. 285–6.

[54] Halsall, *Warfare and Society in the Barbarian West*, pp. 194–5.

[55] Asser, chs 37–9; Halsall, *Warfare and Society in the Barbarian West*, pp. 177–9.

[56] Keynes and Lapidge, *Alfred the Great*, p. 79.

[57] See e.g. the reference in the poem on the Battle of *Brunanburh*, ASC ABCD 937.

[58] This is the reading taken by Halsall, *Warfare and Society in the Barbarian West*, p. 183.

37. From the anguish and shame [i.e. of the defeat at Reading] the Christians were shaken. Once more, after four days, they went forth to battle in full strength and full of determination against the aforesaid army in a place, which is called *Æsces-dun*, which is translated in Latin as 'Hill of the Ash-Tree'. But the pagans, dividing themselves [*se... dividentes*] into two bands [*turmae*] arranged equally sized *testudines* – for they then had two kings and many earls [*comites*] – assigning the central part [*mediam partem*] of the army [*exercitus*] to the two kings and the other to all the earls. When the Christians discerned this, likewise dividing themselves into two bands in the same way, also they quickly made *testudines*. But Alfred arrived at the place of the battle more quickly and more readily with his men, just as we heard from those truthful witnesses who saw it. For doubtless his brother, King Æthelred, was as yet in his tent hearing mass, having been at prayer, and strongly declaring that he would not depart thence alive before the priest had finished mass and not to desert service of God for man. And he did thus. Thereby the faith of the Christian king was of great value to the lord, just as will be revealed more clearly by the following.

38. Because the Christians had decided that King Æthelred with his forces [*copiae*] would engage in battle against the two pagan kings, truly, Alfred, his brother, with his troops [*cohortes*] would know to be obliged to seize the fortunes of war against all the earls [*duces*] of the pagans. Thus, with both parties firmly arranged in this manner, while the king would be delayed a while in prayer, the pagans, having made ready, could have arrived at the battlefield [*locus certaminis*] sooner. Alfred, at that time 'heir apparent' [*secondarius*], might not have been able to hold the enemy battle line [*acies*] for long without either withdrawing from the battle [*bello retrorsum recederet*] or attacking the enemy forces [*contra hostiles ... prorumperet*] before the arrival of his brother on the battlefield; at last, drawing up the Christian forces against the enemy army as they had previously arranged – although the king still had not arrived there – courageously, in the manner of a wild boar, trusting in divine counsel and sustained by divine help, with them having closed ranks in proper order as a *testudo*, he advanced [*movet*] his forces [*vexilla*] immediately against the enemy.

39. But at this point it has to be made clear to those who do not know, that this was an uneven battlefield for those fighting. For the pagans had seized the higher position and the Christians deployed [*dirigebant*] their battle line from a lower position. There was also in the same place a single thorn-tree, short in height, which we have seen with our own eyes, around which the hostile battle lines consequently met each other violently, with great clamour from everyone: those pursuing wrong, and those who were about to fight for life, loved ones, and country. When, thereafter, both sides had been spiritedly and exceedingly ferociously fighting for some time, the pagans, by divine judgment being unable to bear the force of the Christians for long, with the largest part of their forces having been struck down, took shameful flight. In that place one of the two kings of the pagans and five earls were struck down and died, and many thousands of the pagan side in the same place, and across all of the broad field of Ashdown, they were scattered every-

where; far and wide they ran and were cut down. Thus King Bæsecg fell, and Earl
Sidroc the Old and Earl Sidroc the Younger, and Earl Fræna, and Earl Harald, and
all of the army of the pagans was driven to flight until the night and then until the
following day, until they arrived at the fortification [*arx*] whence they had come.
The Christians pursued them until night, while cutting them down wherever they
may be.

Halsall has commented at some length on the significance of this passage,
remarking on the similarities of Asser's witness testimony to that of the Carolingian chronicler Nithard's extensive record of the 842 Battle of Fontenoy (dép.
Yonne),[59] what Halsall had refers to as the 'autopsy' of battlefield records: Nithard
was able to give the impression that, as Halsall paraphrases it, 'I know because
I was there.'[60] While Asser was not at the battle, his account surely stems from
a greater knowledge of warfare than the 'mothers' meeting' that G. P. Baker lik-
ened him to in 1931.[61] Asser, like Nithard, works hard to display his knowledge
of the battlefield, but his writing has a ring of authenticity, showing his connection with the memories of the veterans of the battle at Alfred's court.[62] The question of the memory of a battlefield will be addressed later in this chapter but
the problem, as Halsall observes, is the lack of detail provided by the sources
beyond informing us that the battle lasted for some time: Asser provides no sense
of how the armies engaged with one another what sort of weapons they used
or how the individual units were organized, beyond comments on the division
of the West Saxons' and Vikings' forces into smaller units upon reaching the
battlefield.[63]

Nonetheless, Asser's comments on division may be useful. The principles of
lordship for what Abels termed 'A' and 'B' thegns may be applied to battlefields,
related to different groups of warriors.[64] Even if 871 was not yet the heyday of
the type of military organization Abels describes, the fact that Asser records two
groups of warriors, those of King Æthelred and those of the then ætheling Alfred,

[59] Halsall, *Warfare and Society in the Barbarian West*, pp. 1–2, 178–80, citing *Nithardi
Historiarum Libri IIII*, ed. Pertz, rev. Müller, II.10, p. 27; *Carolingian Chronicles*, trans.
Scholz and Rogers, pp. 153–4. For Nithard, see above, p. 3.

[60] Halsall, *Warfare and Society in the Barbarian West*, p. 1.

[61] G. P. Baker, *The Fighting Kings of Wessex: A Gallery of Portraits* (London, 1931), p. 134. I am
grateful to Matt Russé for this reference.

[62] See Halsall, *Warfare and Society in the Barbarian West*, p. 179, although he does not go as
far as to refer to veterans at court (see above, pp. 14–15, for discussion of the influence of
earlier generations of warriors). I am grateful to Barbara Yorke for this suggestion. Lt-Col.
H. Burne, in attempting to locate the battlefield, suggested that Asser must have seen the
thorn-tree that he describes while riding along the Ridgeway on business, because 'men
were not likely to do "battlefield tours" in those primitive days': Burne, 'Battle of Ashdown',
p. 82. It will be seen from discussion of the memory of battles and battlefields, below, that,
while there are unlikely to have been 'battlefield tours' *per se*, geography and the creation
of memory were issues which were very much interlinked, and Asser's knowledge of the
site is unlikely to have been incidental.

[63] Halsall, *Warfare and Society in the Barbarian West*, pp. 179–80.

[64] Abels, *Lordship and Military Obligation in Anglo-Saxon England*, pp. 116–31. See above,
pp. 102–5.

suggests that the army was composed of those who owed their obligation directly to the king and those who owed it to a lord (Alfred), who, in turn, served his brother, the king. It is possible that the organization of the Vikings, as Anglo-Saxon participants in the battle observed it, was interpreted in a similar manner.[65] Furthermore, Asser records Alfred's move to attack the Vikings before his brother (and royal lord), implying that Alfred anticipated what *might* have happened if the Vikings had been allowed to deploy before his forces attacked.[66] Perhaps such an action by a subordinate of the then king had needed justifying to Alfred and Æthelred's contemporaries, even if it was no longer a point of contention when Asser wrote. If the Maldon poet's record of the events of the battle of Maldon in 991 is read as an accurate account of the battle, insofar as Byrhtnoth's 'hearthtroop' fell with him, the lack of different identifiable contingents[67] may be explained by the possibility that this was a comparatively small army, a 'B' part of the 'national' army. Although accounts of the Battle of Hastings likewise make a good deal of the importance of the close followers of King Harold, the likelihood that Harold's brothers, Gyrth and Leofwine, are shown by the Bayeux Tapestry to have died elsewhere on the battlefield suggests that that army was again made up of different contingents.[68] (See Fig. 7.2.)

Commenting on the parallels between the records of Fontenoy and Ashdown, Halsall makes the acute observation that historians' interpretations of the battlefield are often tempered by their own assumptions: in the case of Fontenoy, by the assumption that the battle was fought by units of mounted warriors; in the case of Ashdown, that it was fought by clashing 'shield-walls' of infantry.[69] If some battles were not over quickly, as may have been the case with Ashdown, it may be surmised that contingents could break off or latecomers might join in the fray.[70] Bringing in another Carolingian comparison, perhaps this casts some light on why shield-sellers were among the troublesome merchants so close to the battlefield in Charles the Bald's baggage train at Andernach.[71] Along with watching from a safe distance, violence was not the only means of

---

[65] Asser, ch. 37.

[66] Asser, ch. 38.

[67] Presumably Ælfwine, who makes much of his Mercian ancestry ('Battle of Maldon', ed. Scragg, lines 209–29, pp. 26–7), was one of Byrhtnoth's commended men. For the possibility of the loss of his family's Mercian estates (a likely reason for commending himself to Byrhtnoth), see M. A. L. Locherbie-Cameron, 'The Men Named in the Poem', in Battle of Maldon, ed. Scragg, pp. 238–49, at pp. 241–2.

[68] It is of course possible that, with respect to the deaths of Harold and his brothers, the Tapestry, as elsewhere in its narrative, does not abide by linear temporal rules and may have split up a relatively short sequence of events by other depictions of the battle for dramatic or other reasons. HH VI.30, pp. 394–5, records the simultaneous demise of Harold and his brothers, and WM, GR, III.241, pp. 452–5, records Harold standing by his standard with his brothers. For discussion of this, see Lawson, Battle of Hastings, pp. 227–30.

[69] Halsall, Warfare and Society in the Barbarian West, p. 180. For nineteenth-century views of Anglo-Saxons, see above, pp. 47–52.

[70] Cf. S. Morillo, 'Hastings: An Unusual Battle', HSJ 2 (1990), pp. 95–104.

[71] AB 876, cited in Leyser, 'Early Medieval Warfare', p. 107.

Fig. 7.2 Gyrth, brother of Harold, at the Battle of Hastings with his brother Leofwine (not in frame) depicted in the Bayeux Tapestry

participating in a battle: notwithstanding the dangers, there could hardly be a more opportune time to sell a few shields, even substandard shields, at inflated prices.[72]

Ian Stephenson posits a novel interpretation of Asser's account of Ashdown, noting that with an uphill attack, columns – effectively a 'pig's head' formation – would have been an appropriate means of manœuvre.[73] In Viking studies, such a formation, following the thirteenth-century Danish account of Saxo Grammaticus is normally interpreted as an array of warriors in a triangular fashion, with a pair of warriors leading.[74] Stephenson's reading is of a 'pig's head' or 'swine's head' formation marked by a formation shape akin to a triangle terminated by a flat 'snout', as with a wild boar, with a more practical mutually supported group of warriors in the vanguard rather than a single man. With this in mind, it is interesting that Asser refers to Alfred's arrival 'like a wild boar'.[75] Perhaps Asser alluded to Alfred's place in the van of that formation; this would have helped Asser's case in putting forward Alfred's right to rule, a key aim of these particular

---

[72] For a prohibition against using sheepskin to cover shields, see *II Athelstan*, ch. 15: *Gesetze*, vol. I, pp. 158–9; trans. *EHD* 1, p. 420.

[73] Stephenson, *Late Anglo-Saxon Army*, p. 35.

[74] Underwood, *Anglo-Saxon Weapons and Warfare*, pp. 131–3; Griffith, *Viking Art of War*, pp. 189–90 (although Griffith holds reservations on the viability of such formations); *Saxonis Gesta Danorum*, vol. I, p. 31; Saxo Grammaticus, *History of the Danes, Books I–IX*, vol. I, p. 31, and for commentary, vol. 2, p. 36. Fisher and Davidson suggest that this followed a late Roman formation described by Vegetius: *Epitoma Rei Militaris*, ed. Reeve, III.19, p. 103; trans. Milner, *Vegetius: Epitome of Military Science*, p. 97.

[75] Asser, ch. 38.

passages.[76] Stephenson's comparisons of early medieval modes of fighting with those of the classical world have been addressed above, but it is pertinent here to raise the question of how far an early medieval army may have been trained or even drilled, an issue which allows us to address whether such complex formations would have been possible in the face of a well-motivated enemy.[77] Arguing for the link between state organization of military systems and effective infantry, Morillo makes the point that the Anglo-Saxons had 'an infantry tradition', although he does not go so far as to make direct comparisons with effectively drilled Roman and later medieval forces.[78] The question of training and organization is a contentious one, dealt with by Hilda Ellis Davison[79] and Nicholas Hooper.[80] Although, as many combat veterans will observe, training is no substitute for real combat experience,[81] hunting and the killing of animals played an important role in group cohesion at different levels of society.

Ælfric *Bata*, writing around the turn of the first millennium, records the duties of a king's huntsman[82] and while we can hardly expect a whole army to have been made up of warriors trained in the hunt, violence against animals, which seems to have been enacted both in a quasi-ritualized and a casual fashion throughout society, was presumably effective practice for war.[83] In a homily for Lent, Ælfric *Bata*'s teacher, Ælfric of Eynsham, refers to the death of a man who drank without the bishop's blessing during Lent and who, taking part in boar-baiting immediately afterwards, was run through by the boar.[84] Ælfric's disapproval is not at the boar-baiting nor, indeed, at doing so whilst under the influence of alcohol, but at the act of drinking in Lent without the bishop's blessing.

A similarly little-cited anecdote used by Ælfric of Eynsham in the same homily shows the relationship between violence against animals (and by animals upon humans) and fighting practices:

> There was a certain foolish man with Bishop Ælfstan [of Ramsbury] in Wiltshire, in his household: this man would not go to the ashes on the Wednesday, as other men did, who attended at mass. Then his companions begged that he would go to the mass-priest, and receive the sacred mysteries which they had received. He said

[76] Cf. Keynes and Lapidge, *Alfred the Great*, p. 242, n. 70, citing Williams, *Armes Prydein*, p. xxix, n. 2, for the observation that the term may be influenced by Welsh poetic vocabulary to describe Alfred's bravery as a warrior.

[77] Morillo, 'Expecting Cowardice', p. 69.

[78] Morillo, '"Age of Cavalry" Revisited'. See also Morillo's paper, 'The Sword of Justice: War and State Formation in Comparative Perspective', *JMMH* 4 (2006), pp. 1–17.

[79] Davison, 'Training of Warriors', , pp. 11–24.

[80] Hooper, 'Anglo-Saxons at War', pp. 196–7.

[81] See generally Grossman, *On Killing*. See above, ch. 2, for discussion of the significance of participation in 'small wars' in the late Anglo-Saxon period.

[82] *Ælfric's Colloquy*, ed. G. N. Garmonsway, Methuen's Old English Library (London, 1939; 2nd edn, 1947), pp. 23–5. See Lavelle, *Royal Estates in Anglo-Saxon Wessex*, p. 74.

[83] A reading of this ritualization of violence is developed in B. Ehrenreich, *Blood Rites: Origins and History of the Passions of War* (London, 1997).

[84] Ælfric of Eynsham, 'Sermon for Ash Wednesday', in *Aelfric's Lives of Saints*, ed. Skeat, , vol. I, pp. 260–83, at pp. 266–7.

'I will not.' They still begged him. He said that he would not, and spoke strangely in his talk, and said that he would enjoy his wife at the forbidden time. Then they left him so.

It befell that the heretic was riding in that week about some errand, when hounds attacked him very fiercely, and he defended himself until his spear-shaft stood up before him, and the horse carried him forward so that the spear went right through him, and he fell dying. He was then buried, and there lay upon him many loads of earth within seven nights, because he had refused those few ashes.[85]

The story raises a number of issues, not least being that a bishop might have such an apparently belligerent man within his household (hired). The man is not named, but the story – or at least the sense that Ælfric might use such an episode to appeal to a contemporary audience – has an air of authenticity. While the trials, tribulations and beliefs of a messenger, a 'riding man' (radman: the pun on his description as an ungerad – unwise, foolish – man is surely intentional) may be beyond the remit of this volume,[86] it is worth commenting that an attack made by hounds is described in a matter-of-fact way. This reminds the modern reader that travel was a dangerous business; it was as well to travel armed and to ensure that the correct religious strictures had been observed before doing so. On the latter point, the parallel with the battlefield need hardly be stressed,[87] but here the relevance of the rider's ability to engage the hounds with his spear is pertinent to the issue of training. Of course, for 'ability' one might read 'inability', with parallels to readings of the unfortunate events at Hereford in 1055,[88] but the accidental, self-inflicted death of the unfortunate man was attributed to his lack of religious morals, not a lack of training with a spear on horseback. After all, Alfred's law-code's provision for cases of accidental spearing suggests that such mishaps were not uncommon, especially as the carrying of a spear was the mark of a freeman's status.[89] While of course we cannot extrapolate thegnly fighting practices from one sorry salutary tale, a case may be made that the episode indicates adaptability on the battlefield, fighting from horseback where necessary.

It is therefore relevant here to revisit a theme raised in chapter 3, on the use of horses on the pre-Conquest battlefield. As discussed, a number of scholars on this subject are emphatic: the Anglo-Saxons rode to battle but, with 'a lack of specific cavalry tactics' they did not ride into battle.[90] Modern historians who suggest this have much historiographical weight behind them, and indeed,

[85] Ælfric, 'Sermon for Ash Wednesday', pp. 264–5 (translation adapted from Skeat).

[86] Gillingham, 'Thegns and Knights', pp. 139–41, makes the sensible observation that messenger duties should not be thought of as minor duties. For radmen, see also Williams, World Before Domesday, pp. 79–80.

[87] On this issue, see Halsall, Warfare and Society in the Barbarian West, pp. 6–7.

[88] ASC C 1055; see below, pp. 284–5.

[89] Alfred, chs 36–36.2: Gesetze, vol. 1, pp. 68–9; trans. EHD 1, p. 414.

[90] Above, pp. 129–39. Quotation from Hooper, 'Anglo-Saxons at War', p. 200. See also M. Strickland, 'Military Technology and Conquest', ANS 19 (1997 for 1996), pp. 353–82. Strickland's thoughts on this issue, and his agreement with Hooper are emphasized in his introduction to his collection Anglo-Norman Warfare, p. xxi and n. 51.

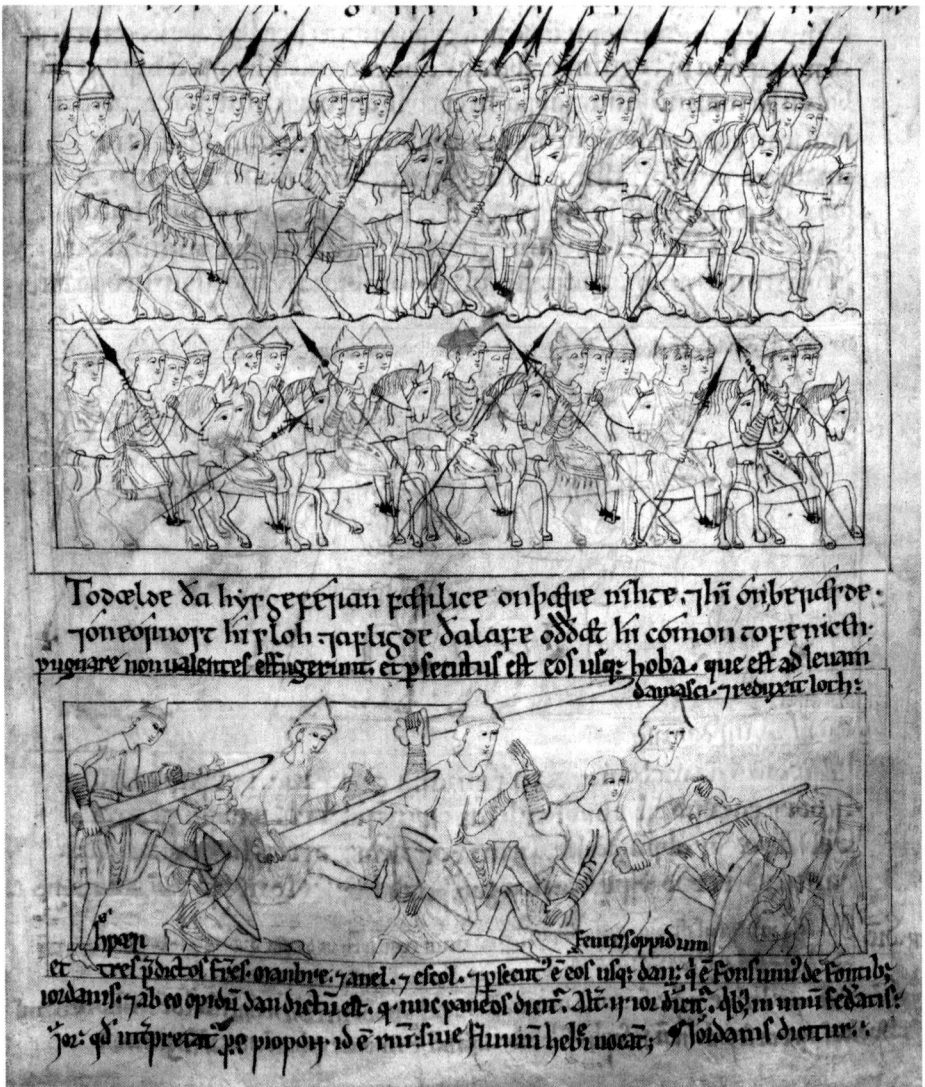

Fig. 7.3 Eleventh-century depiction of Abraham's army in pursuit of Lot's captors, followed by a battle on foot, illustrated in the *Old English Hexateuch*

contemporary sources such as the *Old English Hexateuch* indicate such practices (Fig. 7.3),[91] but, as we have seen, there is evidence that Anglo-Saxons saw horses as weapons to be used in battle. As well as the examples cited by J. H. Clapham,[92] Old English versions of earlier Latin sources, Ælfric's version of the *Maccabees* and the *Old English Orosius*, make extensive references to mounted

[91] BL Cotton MS Claudius B.IV, fol. 24r. See also 'Battle of Maldon', ed. Scragg, lines 1–4, pp. 18–19.

[92] Clapham, 'Horsing of the Danes'. See above, p. 135.

armies and the record of horses within armies.[93] Given that their authors were willing to adapt the text to suit their audience, it is perhaps indicative of a pre-Conquest expectation that horses could be used in battle that they retained these references.

Perhaps revealing in this respect are English views of Continental warfare in British Library Harley MS 603, the early eleventh-century Canterbury version of the Utrecht Psalter.[94] While one artist's depiction of an attacking army on horseback to illustrate Psalm 17 is, like other illustrations, a copy of its Carolingian exemplar,[95] it is interesting that, as Jennie Kiff noted, another artist added new illustrations for a depiction of Psalm 134, which was surprisingly different from the walled city depicted on the exemplar.[96] The two groups of warriors, both depicted as unarmoured, with a combination of kite-shaped and round shields, are evidently in combat on horseback. The spears are depicted as being launched overarm by some riders, with some spears in flight, others embedded in shields and some horses are depicted as having fallen (Fig. 7.4). Kiff frames the illustration in the context of the depiction of a new type of warfare to an eleventh-century audience,[97] but an alternative interpretation, given the context of Psalm 134 as an image of the triumph of Israel, is that the triumphal imagery associated with the use of horses in battle is more fitting, perhaps visualized in the manner of the mounted West Saxon troops (*eorodcistum*) who pursued their foes at the Battle of *Brunanburh*.[98] Although the angels depicted on the manuscript illustration as attacking from overhead with double-headed axes obviously did not constitute 'normal' warfare (even if pious warriors presumably hoped for such divine intervention), the illustration of mounted combat shows an expectation of early medieval warfare which was entirely plausible to an English audience.

However, flexibility should be assumed in relating literary and artistic ideals into conduct on the battlefield. As Halsall usefully argues, we should not assume that warriors fought as *either* cavalry *or* foot.[99] They were adaptable as the

---

93 Ælfric of Eynsham, 'The Maccabees', in S. D. Lee, *Ælfric's Homilies on Judith, Esther, and The Maccabees* <users.ox.ac.uk/~stuart/kings/main.htm>, p. 26 (accessed 1 Sept 2009). OE *Orosius*, III.9, III.10, IV.1, IV.6, IV.8, V.7. However, references to elephants in OE *Orosius*, IV.1, IV.6, V.7, should be a necessary rejoinder against assuming that its author *always* translated modes of ancient warfare into an Anglo-Saxon context!

94 Utrecht University Library MS 32. See K. van der Horst, D. Samson and F. Anskersmit, *The Utrecht Psalter: Digital Facsimile of Ms. 32 of Utrecht University Library* <http://psalter.library.uu.nl/> (accessed 13 June 2009).

95 BL Harley MS 603, fol. 9r; Utrecht Psalter, fol. 15v. Kiff, 'Images of War', pp. 183–4 (Harley 603 is reproduced by Kiff on p. 183).

96 BL Harley MS 603, fol. 69r; Utrecht Psalter, fol. 66r; Kiff, 'Images of War', pp. 184–6. For a recent periodization of the hands at work in Harley 603, see W. Noel, *The Harley Psalter*, Cambridge Studies in Palaeography and Codicology 4 (Cambridge, 1995), pp. 121–40, who dates Psalm 134's artist, 'hand F', to 'the second decade of the eleventh century' (p. 139).

97 Kiff, 'Images of War', p. 186. Kiff (pp. 181–2) draws contrasts with other depictions of warfare in Carolingian manuscripts, which pay more attention to the use of cavalry.

98 ASC ABCD 937. For triumphal images of mounted warriors, see above, pp. 131–4. If the illustration is interpreted as dating from after 1066, one would hardly expect the Norman 'way' of warfare to have been used to depict the victory of God's chosen people.

99 Halsall, *Warfare and Society in the Barbarian West*, pp. 180–8.

ALLELVIA
AUOATENO   ·C·XXXIIII·
men dni. laudate   Qui producit uentof de   dne memoriale tuum
ferui dnm   thefaurif fuif. qui per   infeculum feculi
                   cuffit primo genita   Quia iudicabit dnf popu

Fig. 7.4 Mounted warriors depicted in the Harley Psalter

circumstances suited and, indeed, the term 'cavalry' itself is unhelpful, as it presupposes anachronistically fixed modes of fighting for 'types' of troops which did not
exist in the early middle ages.[100] The same Old English proverb which recorded
that a 'nobleman shall be on horseback' and a 'troop shall ride closely together' also
stated that a foot-soldier – meaning a soldier on foot rather than a soldier of specific status – 'shall stand firm'.[101] Thus, as Richard Glover argued, the often-cited
Anglo-Saxon Chronicle C manuscript's entry for 1055,[102] which relates the defeat
of an English force in the Welsh March near Hereford, is not evidence of the lack
of martial equestrian skills of the English but an ill-chosen spot to use mounted
troops against a mobile force:

> And they [King Gruffudd and Earl Ælfgar] gathered then a great army [*mycle
> fyrde*] with the Irishmen and with the Welsh, and Earl Ralph [of Hereford] gath-
> ered a great army against them at Hereford town, and they sought them there. But
> before any spear was thrown, the English people first fled because they were on
> horseback [*forðan þe hig wæran on horsan*], and many were slain there – about four
> or five hundred men – and they [killed] none in return.

The account of the Anglo-Saxons' defeat at Hereford because they were
ordered to fight on horseback, 'contrary to custom [*contra morem*]', as John of
Worcester adds,[103] is often taken as evidence for an Anglo-Saxon inability to fight

---

[100] Halsall, *Warfare and Society in the Barbarian West*, pp. 181–2, makes a case for avoiding
fixed notions of military organization when using the terms 'cavalry' and 'infantry'. Cf.
Morillo, '"Age of Cavalry" Revisited', p. 47.

[101] 'Maxims I', lines 62–3, in *Anglo-Saxon Poetic Records, No. 3: The Exeter Book*, ed. Krapp
and Dobbie, p. 159; an alternative translation is in Bradley, *Anglo-Saxon Poetry*, p. 347.

[102] ASC C 1055. Gover, 'English Warfare in 1066'.

[103] JW vol. 2, s.a. 1055, p. 576–7.

from horseback, with the Norman Earl Ralph having taken a rash decision.[104] However, it should be said that the most contemporary account, that of the Anglo-Saxon Chronicle, does not record that the mounted combat was against the Anglo-Saxons' custom. The D manuscript does not mention the use of horses and mentions a short struggle before the English fled. Only the account of John of Worcester provides information on the English 'custom', and also relates that Ralph with his French and Normans were the first to flee. Although John is often useful as a historian of the late pre-Conquest period, the account he gives is based on twelfth-century views of the eleventh-century English, and the distinction he makes between French and Normans seems unlikely to have come from a pre-Conquest English source.[105] After all, it is much more likely that a Norman earl might make an inappropriate decision about deploying his forces than that he should persuade or force his English warriors to remain – untrained – on horseback on the battlefield. It was also unlikely to have been those on horseback who were amongst the majority of those recorded as killed but, given the context of a battle fought by English forces gathered from western Mercia against forces which included a rebellious Mercian earl, the premature flight of part of that army is not entirely unlikely.

There are more famous accounts of English defeat, at Maldon and Hastings.[106] The records of the Battles of Maldon and Hastings are influential in the historiography as they are the only sizeable accounts of Anglo-Saxon battles. The accounts of Ashdown and *Brunanburh* are not particularly revealing of the modes of fighting themselves, although the references in the *Brunanburh* poem to the troops of mounted warriors (*eorodcistum*) are often overlooked.[107] The sources for the former two battles are emphatic that the English fought on foot. However, as Halsall points out, there may be significance in the circumstances of determined defence during these battles.[108] *The Battle of Maldon*'s account had to confirm to heroic literary expectations, regardless of whether it was accurate,[109] and William of Poitiers' record of an 'combat of an unusual kind' (*insoliti generis pugna*) at Hastings, refers to the resistance encountered by the Norman side;[110] while not necessarily being a battle which was culturally different,[111] the circumstances of the aftermath and the effects of the battle which resounded in the decades after the Norman Conquest were enough for William of Poitiers to emphasize the extent of the resistance which they faced and the chivalric equestrian skills of the

---

[104] See e.g. Strickland, 'Military Technology and Conquest', p. 360.

[105] See above, pp. 111, 137–9.

[106] 'Battle of Maldon', ed. Scragg. For the most recent review of the primary sources for the Battle of Hastings, see Lawson, *Battle of Hastings*, pp. 47–123.

[107] Halsall, *Warfare and Society in the Barbarian West*, p. 184, is an exception here. Halsall cites the reference to a mounted troop in *Maxims* I in this context (see above, p. 134).

[108] Halsall, *Warfare and Society in the Barbarian West*, pp. 181–3.

[109] For a sceptical account, see N. F. Blake, 'The Genesis of the Battle of Maldon', *ASE* 7 (1978), pp. 119–29.

[110] WP II.21, pp. 132–3.

[111] Cf. Morillo, 'Hastings, An Unusual Battle'.

Normans. Indeed, in the earliest of the accounts of the Battle of Hastings, the *Carmen de Hastingae proelio*, probably written from a northern French rather than Norman perspective, less is made of the Normans' use of cavalry and indeed, the English resistance on foot. Perhaps this indicates that it was only in hindsight that these issues became so significant.[112]

Naval battles

While, as we have seen, the term 'navy' may be as inappropriate as 'army' in references to early medieval warfare,[113] it is acceptable to refer to 'naval battles'. Along with evidence for the construction and crewing of ships, there are indications that the organization of 'ship armies' was concerned with seaborne battles as well as with the transport of land forces. In a short but important book, Susan Rose has addressed the significance of warfare at sea in the Middle Ages. Though not commenting on Anglo-Saxon naval warfare, she argues that a lack of direct references to sea battles in the source material does not mean that naval warfare did not happen.[114]

However, a discussion of naval warfare does not necessarily mean that battles were always fought in the open sea. From what we know of the only account of an Anglo-Saxon naval battle in the Anglo-Saxon Chronicle for 896, the subject of discussion below, battles could take place in and/or by coastal waters, subject to tides and shallow waters. For this reason, small numbers of vessels may have been involved in naval battles in English waters. We do not know whether large pitched battles took place in the manner which has been suggested for later Viking Age Scandinavia, in which ships were tied together to make stable fighting platforms.[115] However, as Viking rulers who fought such pitched sea battles in Scandinavian waters[116] operated under different conditions from Viking fleets in western European waters, whose mobility often depended on avoiding direct combat as much as possible, such actions seem unlikely to have been common. There are laconic references to battles 'at sea' during the 880s (and perhaps Æthelweard's reference to the stowing of – presumably not all – rowing gear before battle in 885 was born from practical knowledge)[117] but it seems unlikely that they were large-scale battles.[118]

Although narrative sources do not memorialize naval battles, perhaps because,

[112] Above, pp. 137–9. A useful rejoinder on the seductive image of cavalry warfare is Bennett, 'Myth of the Military Supremacy of Knightly Cavalry'.

[113] See above, ch. 4.

[114] S. Rose, *Medieval Naval Warfare, 1000–1500*, War and Society (London, 2002), pp. 1–4.

[115] J. Jesch, *Ships and Men in the Late Viking Age: The Vocabulary of Runic Inscriptions and Skaldic Verse* (Woodbridge, 2001), p. 210.

[116] Jesch, *Ships and Men*, pp. 203–15.

[117] Æthelweard, *Chronicon*, p. 45.

[118] ASC 882 refers to what seems to be a small encounter, though Asser, ch. 64, refers to a naval battle. The encounter in 885 (ASC 885; Asser, ch. 67) seems to have been on a larger scale, though with sixteen Viking ships recorded in the ASC, this was hardly a titanic clash. For details, see Table 4.1 above.

unlike on land, they could not be associated with a single specific location, the notion of a 'naval battle' itself is nonetheless not incompatible with the source material. Domesday Book's rare reference to an Englishman's loss of land in Essex after his participation in a 'naval battle' at an unknown time indicates that such events may have been more common than we might expect.[119]

Hundred of ONGAR

Æthelric held KELVEDON [Hatch] TRE as a manor; 2 hides.

Now St Peter's [Westminster holds it]. ... This above-mentioned Æthelric went away to a naval battle [in nauale p[roe]liu[m]] against King William and when he returned he fell ill; then he gave to St Peter's this manor but only one man from the County knows this. And up to now St Peter's has held this manor in this way and they have had neither a writ nor a servant of the King [famulu[m] reg[is]] on [his] behalf after the King came to this land.

The reference in the extract to *King* William and the *Tempore Regis Edwardi* dating of Æthelric's holding suggest that it is not impossible that events recorded in the entry occurred after 1066. However, there is some ambiguity to the entry, as, as noted in chapter 3, the Domesday agents were not particularly interested in the details that a military historian might like to see. A grant made in the immediate aftermath of the Hastings campaign, alluded to by the reference to the lack of a royal writ or servant as witness, shows that we should not rule out the possibility that Æthelric had participated in a naval operation related to William's invasion.[120]

As we have seen, the 896 entry of the Anglo-Saxon Chronicle shows the details of the construction of Alfred's new ships. The entry also records a naval battle somewhere along the English Channel coast between the Solent and Devon. A 1942 article by Francis Peabody Magoun on this subject is included below as a useful reading of and commentary on the events.[121] Although the events of the 896 chronicle are well known, Magoun's article is a neglected source which merits republication, as he made sense of a somewhat opaque Chronicle entry. The fluid nature of the coastal battles of the Viking Age, and the need for warriors to confront each other on land rather than at sea can be seen from Magoun's article and my own diagram which has been devised from his interpretation (Fig. 7.5). Magoun's interpretation was presumably influenced by his First World War experiences as a pilot – indeed an ace – in the Royal Flying Corps.[122] He shows an ability to understand the individual elements in the battle as well as their contribution to the overall course of events, a skill which would have been needed to survive aerial battles. In this respect, it is interesting that he is less concerned with such

[119] DB Essex 6:9 (fols 14v–15r).

[120] See generally Williams, *English and the Norman Conquest*, pp. 71–97.

[121] F. P. Magoun, 'King Alfred's Naval and Beach Battle with the Danes in 896', *Modern Language Review* 37 (1942), pp. 409–14.

[122] J. J. Hudson, 'Lt Francis Peabody Magoun Jr: An American Ace in the RFC', *Cross and Cockade International: The First World War Aviation Historical Society Quarterly Journal* 34:1 (2003), pp. 28–9.

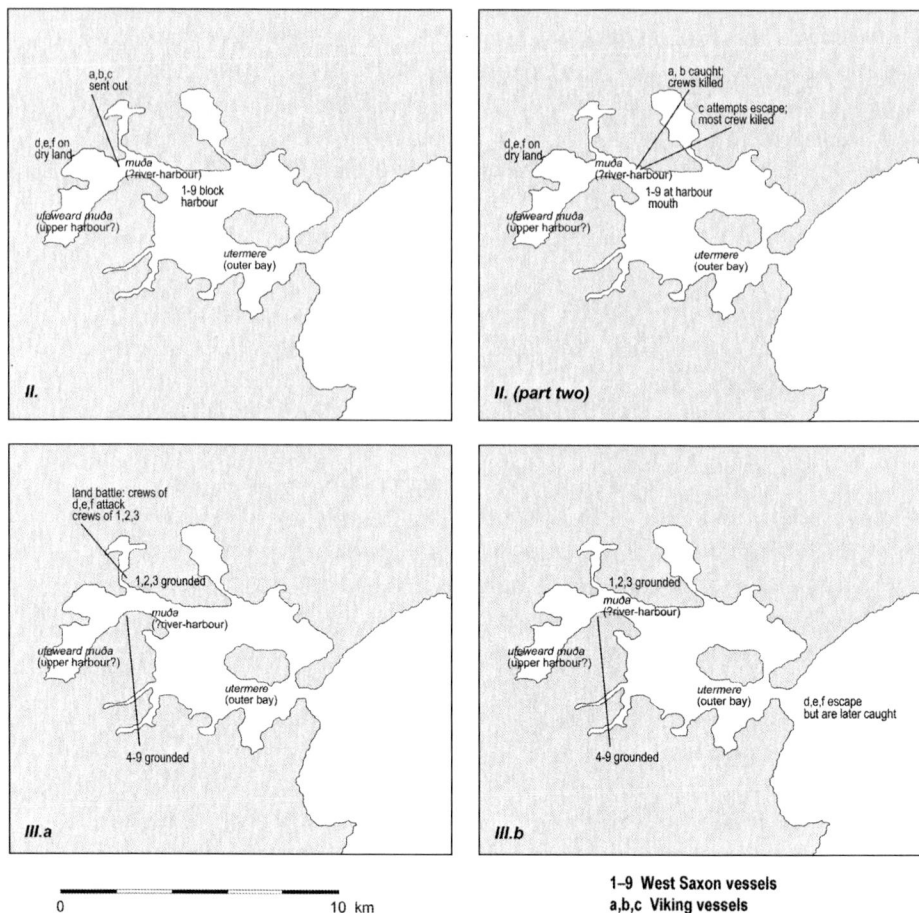

Fig. 7.5 The possible course of actions recorded in the Anglo-Saxon Chronicle entry for 896 applied to Poole Harbour, on the English Channel coast. The sequence of events follows that suggested by F. P. Magoun. (N.B. The modern coastline is unmodified.)

details as the draught and relative manœuvrability of individual ships and calculations of tides to explain some of the events than with the evident fact that Alfred's crews would have been unfamiliar with their new vessels.[123]

Given that the Chronicle's entries for the 890s are unusually detailed, we might reasonably expect other such actions to have been a regular occurrence, even if the record of sixty-two deaths and the departure (Old English *faran*) of the vessels at the king's command indicates that this was significant and can realistically be described as a battle.[124] Although Magoun was circumspect about the location

---

[123] This view may be compared with that of G. P. Krapp, 'Anglo-Saxon Chronicle, 897', *Modern Language Notes* 19 (1904), pp. 232–4. Contrary to Magoun's reading of Krapp's article, Krapp *did* attempt to calculate the tides around the Isle of Wight but (p. 234) confesses 'a complete failure in an attempt to work [them] out'.

[124] However, see above, p. 147, for the notion that this is not described as a *scipfyrd*. For the West Saxon use of a *sciphere* see ASC 875.

of the 896 battle, my diagram ascribes the actions to Poole Harbour.[125] However, it should be said that both the location and the movements have been estimated. While Christchurch Harbour could be another suggested theatre for these events, as it matches the criterion for a location between Devon and the Isle of Wight,[126] Poole Harbour is and was larger: the fast movement and pursuit which took place in 896, along with the record of the tide ebbing by 'furlongs', suggest a large body of water (which is especially pertinent as it was used by a Viking fleet in the 870s).[127] To propose a title for the events as 'the Battle of Poole Harbour' is probably an overstatement, not least because, as we shall see below, the memorialization of battles seems to have been quite specific in the late Anglo-Saxon period. (The results of this particular battle were, after all, somewhat embarrassing to the West Saxons.) The anonymity of the location of the events in the Chronicle is also instructive, as, notwithstanding that this was apparently the first outing of Alfred's 'new ships', such actions could take place in many locations in Alfred's kingdom. Nevertheless, it is useful to suggest a location for the events, even if it is entirely putative.

---

[125] Here I have followed D. Howarth, *Sovereign of the Seas: The Story of British Sea Power* (London, 1974), p. 30.

[126] For a reading of the battle taking place off the Isle of Wight, see Krapp, 'Anglo-Saxon Chronicle, 897'.

[127] Speeds of approximately 5 knots (using 4.5-knot and 5.4-knot 'average' and 'sprint' speeds recorded for *Helge Ask*, the reconstruction of 'Skuldelev 5', a small warship) would have been appropriate for the sequence of actions and response. Speeds read from O. Crumlin-Pedersen, 'Problems of Reconstruction and the Estimation of Performance', in *The Earliest Ships: The Evolution of Boats into Ships*, ed. R. Gardiner and A. E. Christiansen, Conway's History of the Ship (London, 1996), pp. 110–19, at p. 119; trial data from the reconstruction of the eleventh-century Skuldelev 2/4 reconstruction, 'Sea Stallion' (a vessel which may have been of comparable length, albeit probably not handling, to the Alfredian ships) has not yet been fully published (see P. Nygaard, 'Sea Trials with the Sea Stallion from Glendalough', *Viking Ship Museum* website <http://vikingeskibsmuseet.dk/index.php?id=624&L=1> [accessed 4 Sept. 2009]). Extensive discussion of the performance of Mediterranean oared vessels is in papers in R. Gardiner (ed.), *The Age of the Galley: Mediterranean Oared Vessels Since Pre-Classical Times*, Conway's History of the Ship (London, 1995). For the use of Poole Harbour by Vikings, see ASC 875 and 876. Peddie, *Alfred the Good Soldier*, pp. 103–5, logically posits the use of Brownsea Island in 875–6, though there is no direct evidence for its use beside analogy with Viking practice elsewhere (e.g. ASC 894, ABCD 914).

. . . .

King Alfred's Naval and Beach Battle with the Danes in 896

F. P. MAGOUN

Under the year 897 (for 896)[128] there occurs in most versions of the Old English Annals[129] a circumstantially described naval and beach battle between a Danish squadron of six and an English squadron of nine vessels under the command of Alfred the Great. This is the first naval engagement in English history of which an account worthy of the name has come down,[130] and hence must be reckoned as one of the most interesting passages in the *Annals*.[131] Almost crudely obvious recognition of its importance is its inclusion in many Old English readers.[132]

The language of the passage is in a sense straightforward enough, but the manœuvres and adventures of the fifteen vessels are not always by any means easy to follow, partly on account of the complication of the operations, more so perhaps on account of the annalist's relative indifference – not uncharacteristic of Old English vernacular writers in general – to unambiguous identification of his pronouns with their antecedents.[133]

---

[128] On the dislocation of dates between 892 and 926 see Smith (ed. cit., next note), p. 41, note on the annal for 892.

[129] In versions A, B, C, D, but not in E or F (Latin or English). For parallel texts of all versions, see B. Thorpe, *The Anglo-Saxon Chronicle, According to the Several Original Authorities*, RS 23, 2 vols (London, 1861), vol. I, pp. 176–9. For the A-text (Parker MS), see Plummer-Earle, vol. I, pp. 90–1, and notes in vol. 2, pp. 111–12; cf. also the short edition of the same (ann. 787–1001, Oxford, 1889, and later printings), pp. 42–3; also for a part of A, A. H. Smith, *The Parker Chronicle (832–900)*, Methuen's Old English Library (London, 1935), pp. 50–2, lines 24–51 (notes at the foot of page). For the C-text, see H. A. Rositzke, *The C-Text of the Old-English Chronicles*, Beiträge zur Englischen Philologie 34 (Bochum-Langendreer, 1940), pp. 40–1. For the D-text, see E. Classen and F. E. Harmer, *An Anglo-Saxon Chronicle from British Museum, Cotton MS. Tiberius B. IV* (Manchester, 1926), pp. 38–9. Attention is called to three modern translations of the passage in question: R. W. Chambers, *England before the Norman Conquest* (London, 1926), p. 215; M. Hoffmann-Hirtz, *Une Chronique anglo-saxonne traduite d'après le Manuscrit 173 de Corpus Christi College, Cambridge* (Strasbourg, 1933), pp. 99–101 (notes at foot of page); and T. Dahl, *Den oldengelske krønike i udvalg: oversat med indledning og noter* (Copenhagen, 1936), pp. 22–3.

[130] Reports of clashes between Danish and English naval units (to the death of Alfred) occur in the A-text under ann. 875, 882, 885. Not in A or F (see Thorpe, *Anglo-Saxon Chronicle*, vol. I, pp. 122–3), but perhaps genuine, is the entry under 851, also perhaps that in Asser ch. 50, on which see C. Plummer, *The Life and Times of Alfred the Great* [Oxford, 1902], p. 101, n. 3).

[131] Rather lightly relegated to a footnote as a 'petty fight' by C. Oman, *England Before the Norman Conquest*, 5th edn (London, 1923), p. 490, n. 2.

[132] E.g., J. W. Bright, *An Anglo-Saxon Reader*, rev. ed. J. R. Hulbert (New York, 1935), pp. 23–5; G. T. Flom, *Introductory Old English Grammar and Reader* (Boston, MA, 2nd edn, 1930), pp. 196–7 (notes, p. 327); F. Kluge, *Angelsächsisches Lesebuch* (Halle, 4th edn, 1915), p. 47, lines 424–48; G. P. Krapp and A. G. Kennedy, *An Anglo-Saxon Reader* (New York, 1929), p. 23 (notes, pp. 178–9); H. Sweet, *An Anglo-Saxon Reader*, rev. edn, C. T. Onions (Oxford, 9th edn, 1925), pp. 41–2, lines 184–211 (notes, p. 211); M. H. Turk, *An Anglo-Saxon Reader* (New York, 2nd edn, 1930), pp. 71–2 (notes, pp. 258–9); A. J. Wyatt, *An Anglo-Saxon Reader* (Cambridge, 1919), pp. 9–10, lines 308–35 (notes, p. 206).

[133] Not dissimilar difficulties arise in the great annal of 755 (for 757) on Cynewulf, Cyneheard and Osric, on which see my paper in *Anglia* 41 (1933), pp. 361–76.

The purpose of the present paper is to set forth the pertinent part of the annal for 896 in such a way as to make as clear as possible the details of the engagement. First comes the text itself,[134] then a commentary on the several actions, finally a translation. Throughout, the individual ships are identified: the six Danish ships by the letters *a–f*, the nine English by the numerals 1–9.

TEXT/ TRANSLATION

[*Note: although Magoun's original intention seems to have been to work through the commentary in order to set out a translation at the end of the article, for the modern reader's convenience his translation has been placed alongside the text in this reprint edition*]

§I

Þa æt sumum cirre þæses ilcan geares comon þær sex scipu (*a–f*) to Wiht ⁊ þær mycel yfel gedydon, ægðer ge on Defenum ge welhwær be ðem særiman.

[Then at a certain time of this same year (896) there came there six (Danish) vessels (*a–f*) to the Isle of Wight and did a great deal of damage there, also in Devonshire and pretty nearly everywhere along the south coast.]

§II

Þa het se cyng faran mid nigonum to þara niwena scipa (1–9), ⁊ forforon him þone muðan foran on utermere. Þa foron hie mid þrim scipum (*a, b, c*) ut ongen hie, ⁊ þreo (*d, e, f*) stodon æt ufeweardum þæm muðan on drygum; wæron þa men uppe on londe of agane.

Þa gefengon hie þara þreora scipa tu (*a, b*) æt ðæm muðan uteweardum ⁊ þa men ofslogon ⁊ þæt an (*c*) oðwand: on þæm (*c*) wæron eac þa men ofslægene buton fifum; þa comon for ðy on weg, ðe ðara oþerra scipu (1–9?) asseton.

[Then the king (Alfred) ordered (his men) to put out with nine of the new ships (1–9), and they blocked off to them (the Danes) the harbour entrance from in front in the outer bay. Then they (the Danes) came out against them (the English) with three ships (*a, b, c*). And three (Danish ships, *d, e, f*) were in the upper part of the harbour on dry land; the crews had gone off (their ships) ashore.

Then they (the English) captured two (*a, b*) of the three (Danish) ships (*a, b, c*) at the outside of the harbour entrance and massacred the crews. And one (Danish ship, *c*) made its escape, and on that, too, the men were killed except for five; those (five) got away because the ships (1–9?) of the others (the English) were grounded.]

---

[134] According to the Parker MS (A-text), kindly checked by Miss Husbands. Punctuation, paragraphing and the addition of italic letters and numerals to identify the ships are mine.

••

§IIIa

Þa wurdon eac swiðe uneðelice aseten: þreo (1, 2, 3) asseton on ða healfe þæs deopes ðe ða Deniscan scipu (*d, e, f*) aseten wæron, ꝺ þa oðru (4–9?) eall on oþre healfe, þæt hira ne mehte nan to oðrum.

[These (English ships) were, furthermore, very disadvantageously grounded: three (1, 2, 3) were grounded on that side of the harbour channel on which the Danish ships (*d, e, f*) were beached, and the others (4–9?) on just the other side (of the channel), so that none of those (English crews) could (cross over) to the (assistance of the three) others (1, 2, 3).]

§IIIb

Ac ða þæt wæter wæs ahebbad fela furlanga from þæm scipum (*d, e, f;* 1, 2, 3), þa eodan ða Deniscan from þæm þrim scipum (*d, e, f*) to þæm oðrum þrim (1, 2, 3) þe on hira healfe beebbade wæron, ꝺ hie þa þær gefuhton.

Þær wearð ofslsegen: Lucumon, cynges gerefa, ꝺ Wulfheard Friesa ꝺ Æbbe Friesa ꝺ Æðelhere Friesa ꝺ Æðelfreð, cynges geneat, ꝺ ealra monna, Fresiscra ꝺ Engliscra, lxii, ꝺ þara Deniscena cxx.

Þa com þæm Deniscum scipum (*d, e, f*) þeh ær flod to, ær þa Cristnan mehten hira (1, 2, 3) ut ascufan, ꝺ hie (*d, e, f*) for ðy ut oðreowon.

[But when the tide had ebbed out many furlongs from those Danish (*d, e, f*) and English (1, 2, 3) ships, then the Danes went from those three ships (*d, e, f*) to the other three (1, 2, 3) that were grounded by the ebbing tide on their side. And then they fought a battle there.

There was slain there: Lucumon, king's reeve, also Wulfheard a Frisian, and Æbbe a Frisian, and Æthelhere a Frisian,[135] and Æthelfreth, king's geneat, and of Frisians and Englishmen 62 and of the Danes 120.

Then, however, the flood tide reached the Danish ships (*d, e, f*) before the Christian (crews of the English ships 1, 2, 3) were able to launch theirs and, consequently, they (Danish ships *d, e, f*) escaped by rowing away.]

§IV

Þa wæron hie (*d, e, f*) to þæm gesargode, þæt hie ne mehton Suð-Seaxna lond utan berowan, ac hira þær tu (*d, e*) sæ on lond wearp. ꝺ þa men mon lædde to Winteceastre to þæm cynge, ꝺ he hie ðær ahon het. ꝺ þa men comon on East-Engle þe on þæm anum scipe (*f*) wæron, swiðe forwundode.

[Then they (the Danish crews) were so wounded that they could not row out around Sussex (Selsey Bill?), but there the Channel current cast two (*d, e*) ashore, and then the crews were conducted to Winchester to the king (Alfred), and he

---

[135] On these Frisian personal names, see T. Forssner, *Continental-Germanic Personal Names in England in Old and Middle English Times* (Uppsala, 1916), s.vv.

ordered them to be hung there. And those men who were in that one (Danish) vessel (*f*) reached East Anglia very severely wounded.]

COMMENTARY
§I Preliminary: viking raids on the south coast

The setting of the events to come is briefly stated and is, in terms of the history of the times, a commonplace: raids along the south coast[136] by Danish vikings, who, up to this time at any rate, had not been effectively stopped. But in the year 896 Alfred had built a new fleet, whose vessels were designed to embody, and improve on, the best of various types.[137] It was with a squadron of nine vessels (1–9) of this newly constructed fleet, apparently partly under Frisian command (see b below), that on the present occasion the king ventured to engage a squadron of six Danish vessels (*a–f*). From what ensues it would appear that the English were still far from skilful in handling their new ships, which were larger than those to which they were accustomed.

§II Alfred traps six Danish ships in a harbour.

At a given moment a Danish squadron of six vessels (*a–f*) is trapped by the English in an unidentified river mouth or harbour. Of its location no indication is given beyond the general statement made in §I that raids had been going on between the Isle of Wight and Devonshire.[138] The general lay of the land is,

---

[136] For good working maps of the area, see J. Bartholomew, *The Survey Gazetteer of the British Isles*, 8th edn (Edinburgh, 1932), maps nos. 32–5.

[137] The construction of this fleet is described in the paragraph immediately preceding the sections here under discussion. On this see J. Spelman, *The Life of Alfred the Great* (Oxford, 1707), pp. 150–2, §§75–9; J. A. Giles, *The Life and Times of Alfred the Great* (London, 1848), pp. 277 ff., pp. 364–6, for an analysis of the battles; Plummer-Earle, vol. 1, p. 111, under 'unwealtran', and C. Plummer, *Life and Times of Alfred the Great*, pp. 118–20; A. F. Major, *Early Wars of Wessex: Being Studies from England's School of Arms in the West* (Cambridge, 1913), p. 128; Hodgkin, *History of the Anglo-Saxons*, vol. 2, pp. 583–5, also p. 669 for a passing reference to the battles of 896; also Hoffmann-Hirtz, *Une Chronique anglo-saxonne*, p. 99, n. 3. From the interesting point of view, not always taken into account, of Danish colonial expansion this episode is discussed by J. Steenstrup, *Normannerne*, 4 vols (Copenhagen, 1876–82), vol. 1, p. 268; vol. 2, p. 84; J. Jónsson, *Vikingasaga um Herferðir Víkinga frá Norðurlöndum* (Reykjavík, 1915), p. 107; and T. D. Kendrick, *A History of the Vikings* (London and New York, 1930), p. 245.

[138] The general vicinity of Wight is suggested but really nothing more. The waters of the Solent Channel are suggested by Major, *Early Wars of Wessex*, p. 128. Krapp and Kennedy, *Anglo-Saxon Reader*, p. 179 (based on Krapp, 'Anglo-Saxon Chronicle, 897') likewise argue for this region, specifically for the meeting point of the Solent and Spithead, and hint at the mouth of the Hamble (Hants), emptying into the lower part of the Southampton Water. For an especially good map (1 inch to 1 mile) of these channels, see Kökeritz, *Place-Names of the Isle of Wight*, at very end; also Bartholomew, *Survey Gazetteer of the British Isles*, map no. 33. Wyatt, *Anglo-Saxon Reader*, p. 206, note to line 312, urges Poole Harbour (Dorset), some 25 miles west of Wight. Smith, *Parker Chronicle*, p. 50, n. 28, notes both suggestions but without comment. I do not believe that this harbour can be identified, but see further §III *b* below.

however, suggested: there is an *utermere* or 'bay',[139] a *muða* or 'river (?)-harbour',[140] and an *ufeweard muða* or 'upper harbour'.[141] Such a scene is not difficult to imagine. It is reported that the Danes had beached a unit of three of their vessels (*d, e, f*) up in the harbour and presumably at or very near the high-water mark, and that their crews had gone ashore, most likely to raid on the neighbourhood. Three others (*a, b, c*) were evidently free to cover the three beached ships of their fellows and were thus in a position to meet the challenge of the English. Alfred orders his squadron of nine new ships (1–9) to proceed against the Danes and, as a first step, to block from the outside in the bay or inlet the entrance to the harbour in which the Danes were. The Danish unit (*a, b, c*) that was mobile up in the harbour now came out (*foron ut*) against the English and engaged them, either a little distance outside of (*ut*) or perhaps, though in my opinion less likely, at or just inside the inlet of the harbour,[142] where two (*a, b*) are captured and the crews massacred. One (*c*) escapes and is heard of no more.[143] It probably cannot be settled how many, if any, of the nine English vessels became detached from the squadron in this naval battle, whether, for example, any English ships pursued the Danish vessel (*c*) that made good its escape, and so forth. The matter is, perhaps, of no great importance, and precise information on this point would at best only let us know how large an English unit was meant by 'the (inactive) others' (*þa oðru*), mentioned in §IIIa below.

§III The battle on the harbour beach

(a) *The disposition of the English and Danish ships*. The narrative now turns to the situation up in the harbour (*se ufewearda muða*) where the Danes, as noted in

---

[139] *Utermere*, m., of unique occurrence, does not, I believe, mean 'outer sea', 'open sea' as Bosworth-Toller, s.v., define it. In prose writings *mere* means 'pool', fresh or salt, and here may well mean 'bay' or '(conspicuous) inlet' as possibly in the place-name Mersea (Essex); see P. H. Reaney, *The Place-Names of Essex*, English Place-Name Society 12 (1935), pp. 319–20, but cf. F. P. Magoun, 'Territorial, Place-, and River-Names in the Old-English Chronicle, A-text (Parker MS.)', *Harvard Studies and Notes in Philology and Literature* 18 (1935), pp. 69–111, at p. 90. The normal word for the 'sea' or 'open sea' would be *sæ* which in the Annals, however, ordinarily refers to the Channel; see also n. 148, below.

[140] *Muða*, m., of course, ordinarily means 'river-mouth', 'estuary', but not always. A striking case to the contrary is in the name Portsmouth (Hants) where the element *muða* means merely the 'mouth' or 'entrance' to the port itself; see E. Ekwall, *The Concise Oxford Dictionary of English Place-Names*, 2nd edn (Oxford, 1940), p. 354, under 'Portsdown'. *Muða* is also used once at least in the sense of 'strait' (Bosworth-Toller, s.v.: *ofer þone muðan* = Lat. *trans fretum*, cf. Matthew, VIII.18, 28). The point of all this is that a *river* mouth is not necessarily to be sought for as the site of the engagement of 896.

[141] *se ufewearda muða* is the upper part of the *muða* discussed in the preceding note. It is marked, as we are told, by a channel (*deop*), apparently navigable at all stages of the tide. This part of the harbour would also appear to have contained spits, bars, shoals, or the like, and, furthermore, to have been of some extent, spacious enough to permit, let us say, the manœuvring, however unsuccessfully, of a number of good-sized boats.

[142] It would help if one could be sure whether *foron ut* meant 'were going, were on the way out' or 'went, got out'. I do not feel competent to decide on this important refinement of O. E. verbal aspect.

[143] Not to be confused with *f*, whose escape is discussed in §IV below.

§II above, had beached three of their vessels (*d, e, f*). Farther from the harbour entrance, but on the same side, three English ships (1, 2, 3) had in the course of their manœuvres run aground, presumably on a bar or shoals near the shore, and, since the tide was ebbing, remained fast. Other English ships (4–9, or fewer?) were grounded on the opposite shore, or at any rate on the opposite side of the harbour channel (*deop*), and remain isolated during the ensuing action. The circumstances under which the English ships had effected their entry into the harbour and run aground so disadvantageously (*uneðelice*) are not detailed: perhaps after the naval battle reported in §II, perhaps during it, perhaps even before.[144] In the latter instance the open conflict must have been something of a general melee, in the course of which all nine of the English ships sooner or later grounded and the Danish ship (*c*) made its escape.

(*b*) *The beach battle.* This most elaborately narrated section deals exclusively with a beach battle between the crews of the three beached Danish ships (*d, e, f*) and the crews of the three English vessels (1, 2, 3) which had run aground, evidently farther up the harbour, though on the same side. At the beginning the English and Danish crews, though on the same side of the harbour, cannot get at one another since the ebbing tide still separates them. The crews of the Danish unit (*d, e, f*) which had been ashore (see §II) have in the meanwhile returned to their ships. Finally land emerges between the Danish and English units, perhaps a long sand-spit; the Danes assume the offensive and, making their way along this bar or the like, engage the English.

Among others, three important Frisians,[145] presumably fighting for the English, are slain; the annalist reports the ultimate loss of 62 English and Frisians, 120 Danes.

Meanwhile the tide has turned and flood, according to the annalist, reaches the Danish unit first. This made possible the launching of the Danish vessels (*d, e, f*), which, as pointed out above, must have been beached at or near the high-water mark and nearer the harbour inlet than the English unit (1, 2, 3)[146] was grounded. All three Danish ships are, accordingly, able to escape, though, as is clear here and

---

[144] See p. 293 above.

[145] On the Frisians as an important sea-faring people in Alfred's time, see Plummer, *Life and Times of Alfred the Great*, pp. 119–20; Hodgkin, *History of the Anglo-Saxons*, vol. 2, p. 585; Forssner, *Continental-Germanic Personal Names in England*, pp. xlv ff., esp. p. xlvi. On the Frisians as mariners and traders earlier still, see F. Kauffmann, *Deutsche Altertumskunde*, 2 vols (Munich, 1913–23), vol. 2, pp. 171 ff.

[146] I see no good reason to start reckoning with complicated tides in the Solent or marked differences in the draught of the English and Danish to account for the floating of the Danish ships before the English (as does Krapp, 'Anglo-Saxon Chronicle, 897', p. 234). We know nothing of the conditions under which the English ships (however many) went up into the harbour or of the harbour topography, the position of bars, shoals, and the like. But it requires no great effort to imagine that the English, in manœuvring their new and unaccustomedly large vessels, and quite possibly ignorant of the harbour waters, went aground in thoroughly disadvantageous positions – *swiðe uneðelice*, says the annalist.

from §IV, not without having suffered heavy losses of men in the course of the battle on the beach.

§IV. The aftermath

The sequel is briefly told and deals only with the fate of the crews of the Danish unit which had been engaged up in the harbour (IIIb above). All three (d, e, f) get out of the harbour, but in their attempt to reach some undesignated point in East Anglia two ships (d, e) with weakened and reduced crews are unable to row out around Sussex (Suð-Seaxna lond utan berowan),[147] and are driven by currents (sæ)[148] somewhere on to the Sussex coast, perhaps, as very tentatively suggested above [here p. 147], while trying to round Selsey Bill. At whatever point they were driven ashore, they were apprehended, taken to Winchester (Hants), and, at Alfred's command, hung. The single surviving Danish vessel (f) reached an East Anglian destination.

From the 896 example we can see that ships could be manœuvred in battle tactics which were intended to force enemy vessels to disembark under unfavourable conditions. The Alfredian vessels evidently had the potential to be used as fighting platforms[149] but using a ship in this way is effective only if the enemy vessels can be caught. Forced disembarcation did not require physical contact with the enemy and had the potential advantage of being supported by land forces. Even if no landfyrd came to the aid of the crews of Alfred's vessels in 896, the

---

[147] In this remark about 'rowing out around Sussex' may lie a reference to local topography and it may not at all impossibly refer to the prominent headland of Selsey Bill; see Bartholomew, *Survey Gazetteer of the British Isles*, map no. 34, and A. Mawer and F. M. Stenton, *The Place-Names of Sussex*, English Place-Name Society 6–7 (Cambridge, 1926), part I, pp. 82–4, with map at end of volume. Off Selsey Bill in West Sussex lies an extensive series of banks, the Owers, in the past almost certainly far more conspicuous than to-day (perhaps *Cymenes ora* of the Annals under ann. 477); see R. G. Collingwood and J. N. L. Myres, *Roman Britain and the English Settlements*, Oxford History of England 1 (Oxford, 2nd edn, 1937), p. 367, n. 2. East of Selsey Bill and the Owers the Sussex coast runs pretty straight for nearly fifty miles and offers nothing in particular that would oblige mariners to row 'out around' or navigate especially far offshore. On the possible hazards attendant on rowing around Selsey Bill I am most grateful to Rear-Admiral H. Pott, R. N., for the following comment (5 February 1942): '... there are very strong currents off Selsey Bill, especially, of course, at the spring-tide periods. These currents would certainly make the rounding of the cape hazardous to a vessel propelled by oars, and more particularly so in the case of strong easterly or south-easterly winds.' It may be further observed that, if the Danish vessels d and e were swept ashore anywhere near Selsey Bill, it would not take long or be out of the way to conduct the captured crews to Winchester. Once one starts thinking about Selsey Bill, it is perhaps tempting to imagine that the escaping ship (f) might have come out of the waters of nearby Portsmouth or Chichester harbours, but this is no doubt going far too far in the way of local identification!

[148] On *sæ* meaning the Channel see p. 411, n. 2 above, and F. P. Magoun, review of Rositzke, *C-Text of the Old-English Chronicles*, Speculum 16 (1941), pp. 505–6, at p. 506.

[149] See O. Crumlin-Pedersen, 'Large and Small Warships of the North', in *Military Aspects of Scandinavian Society in a European Perspective*, AD 1–1300, ed. Jørgensen and Clausen, pp. 184–94; Rodger, *Safeguard of the Sea*, pp. 15–17.

threat seems to have been enough to force the Viking crews onto the back foot. These were tactics which were presumably simpler than co-ordinating the boarding of a number of vessels.

Although it was not strictly an Anglo-Scandinavian encounter, the Anglo-Saxon Chronicle records similar tactics to those of 896, in a potential 'battle of the Thames' in 1052:[150]

> When he [Godwine] had arranged all his expedition [*fare*], there came the tide, and they then brought up their anchors, they kept to the south bank through the bridge. And the land force [*landfyrd*] came from above and arrayed [*trymedon*] themselves along the shore, and then they manœuvred [*hwemdon*] with the ships [C MS adds: 'against the north bank'], as though they intended to encircle [*abutan betrymman*] the king's ships. The king [Edward] likewise had a great land force [*landfyrd*] on his side besides his sailors [*scypmannum*] …

Given that the CD Chronicler is normally hostile to the Godwine family, the record of the organization of the flotilla may be taken seriously. The verb that the Chronicler uses to refer to the manœuvre of Godwine's ships, *hwemdon*, provides a sense of encirclement, cornering the enemy with an unbroken line of ships. Ælfric uses the noun *hwem*, 'corner', in one of his homilies, referring to a corner of a city wall faced by an attacking army, so the Chronicler's use of the word in this context has a military significance.[151] The process of the manœuvres suggests that vessels must have used some means of communication to signal to one another in order to move in formation and probably in co-ordination with the land force (presumably some of those who took part in the action were crews who were experienced in defending the English coast in the 1040s).[152] Their manœuvres were evidently successful, having moved up the Thames 'through' London Bridge. Whether or not they really intended to move to a state of open hostility or were deliberately posturing, the peacemaking that resulted, presumably backed up by the effects of the campaigns across the south coast, was decided in the Godwine family's favour, perhaps because the king had been faced down. This was not a proto-Whig Godwine acting in favour of English democracy, in the manner that E. A. Freeman heralded it in the 1870s,[153] but if it was the predecessor of anything it was the recognition that naval power, deftly used, could be a useful weapon and indicator of power: a kind of proto-gunboat diplomacy.

---

[150] ASC CD 1052. For the campaigns relating to this episode, see above, pp. 202–7.

[151] Ælfric, 'Dominica XII Post Pentecosten', in *Ælfric's Catholic Homilies: The Second Series: Text*, ed. M. Godden, EETS supplementary series 5 (Oxford, 1979), pp. 249–54, at p. 251; see Bosworth-Toller, p. 573.

[152] ASC CD 1045.

[153] Freeman, *History of the Norman Conquest*, vol. 2, pp. 326–7 (below, pp. 323–4).

Locating and remembering battlefields

A battle can often be as much a construction of succeeding generations as it is the achievement of the generation who fought it. The remembrance of the site of the battle is an important part of this, indicating the relationship between space and memory. Such a relationship constructed, as Pierre Nora's famous phrase has it, a *lieu de memoire* – a realm or place of memory.[154] It may hardly be a coincidence that amongst the best-known late Anglo-Saxon battles, Edington, Maldon, Fulford, Stamford Bridge, and, of course, Hastings, there is a general consensus as to the location of the area in which the battle took place, even if during this period it can be difficult to pinpoint exactly what happened where.[155] Other locations of battles have been lost, and attempts to locate them are debated according to the perceived significance of the battle and whether the contemporary source material allows the site to be narrowed down to a region such as the Berkshire Downs, in the case of Ashdown (871)[156] or East Anglia in the case of the Holme (902).[157]

Nonetheless, knowing the precise location of a battlefield is not the only criterion for its remembrance, as, while skirmishes and small battles such as those in 1001, at Pinhoe (Devon) and Æthelingadene (Sussex) can be located with tolerable accuracy they are not necessarily well remembered beyond the immediate communities of local historians and the academics who choose to take an interest in them.[158] In the case of *Brunanburh* the very attempts to recover the memory of a battlefield augment our sense of the importance of the site. The battlefield of *Brunanburh* is one of the most controversial of the sites from our period, as the source material is enigmatic but varied, with references in a number of early

---

[154] See P. Nora, 'Between Memory and History: *Les Lieux de Mémoire*', *Representations* 26 (1989), pp. 7–24, which discusses ideas in his project *Les Lieux de mémoires*, 6 vols (Paris, 1984–92). Nora's conception of the creation of *lieux de mémoire* suggests that this was a modern phenomenon, but many of their characteristics are arguably present in the early middle ages. I am grateful to Chris Aldous for drawing this work to my attention.

[155] For an example of an attempt to assess positions at Edington based on 'Inherent Military Probability', see A. H. Burne, *More Battlefields of England* (London, 1952), pp. 34–40. Maldon, Stamford Bridge and Hastings are on the English Heritage *Register of Historic Battlefields*, with extensive reports published online at <http://www.english-heritage. org.uk/server/show/nav.001002004000d002> (accessed 5 Sept. 2009). Although it is not the object of this discussion to enter into current debates regarding the heritage and preservation of battlefields, the short discussion provided in C. Jones, *The Forgotten Battle of 1066: Fulford* (Stroud, 2006), pp. 248–9, and discussion at greater length on the author's website <www.battleoffulford.org.uk> (accessed 11 Sept. 2009) indicate the controversies and importance invested in the preservation of battlefields. It is perhaps revealing of these debates that the English Heritage *Register* includes only discussion of the Fulford site in connection with the report on Stamford Bridge. For comments on archaeological interpretations and the challenges of medieval battlefield archaeology, see generally G. Foard, 'English Battlefields, 991–1685: A Review of Problems and Potentials', in *Fields of Conflict: Battlefield Archaeology from the Roman Empire to the Korean War*, ed. D. D. Scott, L. E. Babits, C. M. Haecker, 2 vols (Westport, CT, 2007), vol. I, pp. 133–59.

[156] Although for an interpretation of the evidence, see Burne, 'Battle of Ashdown'.

[157] Hart, *The Danelaw*, pp. 511–15.

[158] O. J. Reichel, 'The Vicar of Pinhoe and the Danish Raid of 1001 AD, the Story of the Raid', *Devon and Cornwall Notes and Queries* 11 (1921), pp. 185–9; B. Dickins, 'The Day of the Battle of Æthelingadene (ASC 1001 A)', *Leeds Studies in English* 6 (1937), pp. 25–7.

medieval chronicles and annals, including – crucially – a seventy-three-line Old English poem in the Anglo-Saxon Chronicle.[159] Arguably not yet a *lieu de memoire*, the range of scholarly interpretations on the subject is not unlike the liveliness of the debates on the battle of Edington during the nineteenth century. Onomastic studies have been an important element of the studies of *Brunanburh*, often attributing the battle to the area of the Wirral,[160] but the ambiguity of references in the source material along with the importance of the context of the battle in the history of the British Isles has meant that it has also been interpreted as being in Yorkshire and the Scottish lowlands.[161]

In referring to places of battles, the Anglo-Saxon Chronicle often uses a formula, referring to an army, usually Vikings, having 'held control of the place of slaughter' (*wælstowe geweald ahtan*).[162] It is perhaps revealing in these cases that the battlefield was seen as a place that could be controlled, and maybe helps to explain why sea battles are not remembered, but it does not necessarily mean that Anglo-Saxon victories were any less significant – as we have already seen, an action did not have to be large in order to qualify as a 'battle' – rather that to an English audience Viking armies contested control of the landscape, whereas victorious Anglo-Saxon armies were reasserting the *status quo*. Either way, the sites of battles were often important. In a useful article, Philip Morgan highlighted how battlefields were 'what might be termed accidental landscapes'.[163] Battlefields were constructs: created by both the actions of military forces, by the memories

[159] These included Æthelweard's *Chronicon*, John of Worcester, Geffrei Gaimar, a 'Pictish Chronicle', *Annales Cambriae*, and the *Annals of Clonmacnoise*. The different names given to the battlefield by the sources are discussed in *The Battle of Brunanburh*, ed. A. Campbell, Methuen's Old English Library (London, 1938), pp. 57–80, with a list of sites at p. 60, and P. Cavill, 'The Site of the Battle of *Brunanburh*: Manuscripts and Maps, Grammar and Geography', in *A Commodity of Good Names: Essays in Honour of Margaret Gelling*, ed. O. J. Padel and D. N. Parsons (Donnington, 2008), pp. 303–19, at pp. 303–9.

[160] For recent discussion, see, in addition to Cavill, 'Site of the Battle of *Brunanburh*', P. Cavill, S. Harding, and J. Jesch, 'Revisiting *Dingesmere*', *Journal of the English Place-Name Society* 36 (2004), pp. 25–38, for the a localization of the *Dinges mere*, referred to in the poem. Some other interpretations of the Wirral are J. M. Dodgson, 'The Background of Brunanburh', *Saga Book of the Viking Society for Northern Research* 14 (1957), pp. 303–16; N. J. Higham, 'The Context of Brunanburh', in *Names, Places and People: An Onomastic Miscellany in Memory of John McNeal Dodgson*, ed. A. R. Rumble and A. D. Mills (Stamford, 1997), pp. 144–56; and S. Harding, *Viking Mersey: Scandinavian Wirral, West Lancashire and Chester* (Birkenhead, 2002), pp. 153–73.

[161] For Yorkshire, see Burne, *More Battlefields of England*, pp. 44–60; Wood, 'Brunanburh Revisited'; and, in a work which shows the manner in which the search for *Brunanburh* can capture the imagination, M. Wood, *In Search of England: Journeys into the English Past* (London, 1999), pp. 203–21. For the most recent reading of Burnswark, Dumfriesshire, see K. Halloran, 'The Brunanburh Campaign: A Reappraisal', *Scottish Historical Review*, 84 (2005), pp. 133–48. For a review of suggested locations, see Hill, *Age of Athelstan*, pp. 135–53, who favours the eastern side of the Pennines. I am grateful to Charles Insley for discussion on the site of *Brunanburh* and the value of the historical context.

[162] ASC 836 (Carhampton), 840 (Portland), 860 (location uncertain – a West Saxon victory near Winchester?), 871 (Reading, *Meretun*, Wilton), ?843 (Carhampton), 903 ('Holme'), A 991 (Maldon), A 1001 (*Æthelingadene* and Pinhoe).

[163] P. Morgan, 'The Naming of Battlefields in the Middle Ages', in *War and Society in Medieval and Early Modern Britain*, ed. D. Dunn (Liverpool, 2000), pp. 34–52, at p. 35.

of the participants and the local populace. Morgan posited three stages to the establishment of a battlefield, the first being the notion that a battle would have no name at all; secondly, a period of fluidity with regard to its naming; finally, only when the battle had been recognized as important would it gain an 'official' name.[164] Although Morgan refers to the memorialization of the battles of Stamford Bridge and Hastings and the controversies over the location of *Brunanburh* and *Assandun*, pre-Conquest battles are not a focus of his article.[165] However, this methodology can be applied to the early medieval period. The memory of battles that were important to the new West Saxon dynasty seem to have become established in their own day; it seems more likely, though, to be true of those battles that took place in the core territory of the West Saxon dynasty during the ninth century rather than those in their newly conquered territory in the tenth.[166]

Thus *Brunanburh*, although central to the reputation of Athelstan and the West Saxon royal family as quasi-imperial conquerors of the island of Britain,[167] was not remembered as a physical battle site because it could not be commemorated by the West Saxon dynasty. Its importance was noted more for the reputation of Athelstan's brother, King Edmund. The poem, as Simon Walker observed, made use of 'vigorous archaism' in referring to a sense of staunch West Saxon resistance more relevant to the ninth century,[168] during a time when Edmund was clawing back territory from northern rulers.[169] Parallels with the ninth-century situation of the West Saxons, between Athelstan with Æthelred I and Edmund with Alfred, are possible but should not be pressed too far, as Asser's account of Ashdown is not directly comparable with the *Brunanburh* poem. However, a case may be made, as Alaric Trousdale has recently done, for assigning Edmund a central role to the achievements of the tenth-century English state.[170] If Edmund's hold over the *re*-conquered Danelaw (in this context it is realistic to refer to a

---

[164] Morgan, 'Naming of Battlefields', pp. 42–8.

[165] Morgan, 'Naming of Battlefields', pp. 36, 46–8.

[166] Note the royal control of the estate at Edington, bequeathed by King Alfred in S 1507 (amongst other estates, including Alfred's birthplace at Wantage) to his wife. Edington seems to have been an estate of familial importance a century later: see below, p. 302; the foundation of a monastery at Athelney (Somerset), recorded in Asser, chs 92–4, suggests that although it was not a battlefield *per se*, a significance could be invested in the memory of Alfred's wars against the Vikings. Estates on the Berkshire Downs, the location of Ashdown, appear to have been granted in the tenth century to Abingdon, a monastery with royal connections. For Abingdon's endowment in this area, see S. D. Kelly (ed.), *Charters of Abingdon Abbey Part 1*, Anglo-Saxon Charters 7 (Oxford, 2000), pp. clvi–clxii. For the importance of the family control of particular manors, see Lavelle, *Royal Estates in Anglo-Saxon Wessex*, pp. 91–101.

[167] See S. Foot, 'Where English Becomes British: Rethinking Contexts for *Brunanburh*', in *Myth, Rulership, Church and Charters*, ed. Barrow and Wareham, pp. 127–44.

[168] Walker, 'A Context for "Brunanburh"?', p. 37.

[169] ASC ABCD 942 and ASC 944.

[170] Trousdale, 'An Investigation of the Anglo-Saxon Political Situation during the Reign of King Edmund'. A useful overview of Edmund's achievement is provided by A. Williams, 'Edmund I (920/21–946)', *ODNB* <www.oxforddnb.com/view/article/8501> (accessed 8 Sept. 2009).

'reconquest') was tenuous, due to a resurgent York dynasty in the years after Athel-stan's death in 939,[171] a secure memorialization of the *Brunanburh* battlefield may not have been possible, or indeed necessary, whether the battle had been in the Wirral or near Leeds, let alone in Dumfriesshire. The poem, in the new entries of the official dynastic chronicle, sufficed to secure Edmund's place alongside his brother, while a diverging memory of the battle, of questionable accuracy, devel-oped in the Icelandic saga tradition. It was recorded in the early thirteenth-cen-tury saga of Egil Skallagrimsson.[172]

> After this they sent messengers to king Olaf,[173] giving this as their errand, that King Athelstan would hazel a field for him [i.e. challenge him to battle] and offerred battle [*orustustað*] on Vinheath by Vin Forest; And he wanted them to stop harrying his land; but of the two he should rule England who should conquer in the battle [*orusta*]. He proposed a week hence for the meeting [i.e. battle], and whoever came first should wait a week for the other. It was then the custom, that as soon as a king had enhazelled a field, it was shameful to harry before the battle was ended. King Olaf did accordingly; he halted his army [*her*] and harried not, but waited till the appointed day, when he moved his army to Vin-heath.
>
> A town [*borg*] stood north of the heath. King Olaf set himself there in the town, and there had the greatest part of his force, because there was a wide district around which seemed to him the better for the bringing in of such provisions as the army needed. But he sent men of his own up to the heath where the battle-field was appointed; these were to take camping-ground, and make all ready there before the army came. But when the men came to the place where the field was enhazelled, there were all the hazel-poles set up to mark the place where the battle should be. The place had to be chosen carefully, it had to be level, where a large army might be set in array [*fylkja*]. And such was this; for in the place where the battle was to be, there the heath was level, with a river flowing on one side, on the other a large wood.
>
> But where the distance between the wood and the river was least (and this was a very long way), there King Athelstan's men had pitched tents, and their tents stood all between wood and river. They had so pitched that in every third tent there were no men, and few in the others.

[171] For the York dynasty, see A. P. Smyth, *Scandinavian York and Dublin: The History and Archaeology of Two Related Viking Kingdoms*, 2 vols (Dublin, 1975–9), vol. 2, pp. 89–125.

[172] *Egils Saga: Skalla-Grímssonar*; Sigurður Nordal gaf út, Íslenzk Fornrit 2 (Reykjavik, 1933), ch. 52, pp. 131–3. The translation used here is adapted from that of W. C. Green, *The Story of Egil Skallagrimsson: Being an Icelandic Family History of the Ninth and Tenth Centuries* (London, 1893), though B. Scudder's translation in O. Thorsson (ed.), *The Sagas of Icelanders* (New York and London, 2000), pp. 1–184, is an alternative (there the battle is dealt with on pp. 81–92). For the literary topos of this episode, see I. McDougall, 'Discretion and Deceit: A Re-examination of a Military Stratagem in "Egils Saga"', in *The Middle Ages in the North-West: Papers Presented at an International Conference Sponsored Jointly by the Centres of Medieval Studies of the Universities of Liverpool and Toronto*, ed. T. Scott and P. Starkey (Oxford, 1995), pp. 109–42.

[173] ?Óláfr Sigtryggsson, King of Dublin and York: referred to here as King of Scotland (perhaps a conflation, as both Olaf and Constantine of Scotland are referred to in the ASC's account of *Brunanburh*).

Yet when King Olaf's men came to them, they had then a crowd before all the tents, and the others could not get to go inside. Athelstan's men said that their tents were all full, so full that their troops [lið] had not nearly enough room. But the front line of tents stood so high that it could not be seen over them whether they stood many or few in depth. They imagined a vast host would be there.

King Olaf's men pitched north of the hazel-poles, toward where the ground sloped a little. From day to day Athelstan's men said that the king would come, or had come, to the town that lay south of the heath. Meanwhile forces flocked to them both day and night.

By contrast, *Ethandun* (Edington) was remembered as the location of an important royal estate associated with the continuity of the West Saxon dynasty, an estate which had been significant in the reign of Æthelwulf.[174] L. S. Dutton attempted to ascribe the location of 'Egbert's Stone', recorded in the Anglo-Saxon Chronicle, to Shaftesbury and thus the foundation of Shaftesbury Abbey as a memorialization of Alfred's victory to parallel the foundation at Athelney (Somerset); as Simon Keynes has observed, this identification was probably misdirected,[175] but all the same there was arguably a real sense of the importance of *Ethandun*.

Although the long-ranging historical debates on the location of *Ethandun* will be addressed below as a case study of antiquarians' interests in locating a particular battlefield, it should be said here that the Edington near Westbury in Wiltshire is the most likely candidate. Michael Wood has drawn attention to a charter which records 'the vill which is called *Eðandun*' (*uilla que dicitur Eðandun*) as the location of an assembly during the reign of Eadwig, recorded in a charter in which Eadwig invoked 'the gift of divine grace and the example of the lineage of my ancestors' (*Diuina gratia largiente et originali prosapia antecessorum meorum*) in 957, using a formula which was unique in the surviving corpus of Anglo-Saxon charters.[176] *Ethandun* was presumably a place to invoke.

Although not directly a 'royal' battle, Maldon arguably lies between the two: a memorialization in a poem which evokes the physical activity of the battle[177] and

---

[174] S. D. Keynes, 'The West Saxon Charters of King Æthelwulf and his Sons', *EHR* 109 (1994), pp. 1109–49, at p. 1133, citing S 290 (AD 841 [for 840]).

[175] L. S. Dutton, 'King Alfred at Shaftesbury: The Location of Egbert's Stone', *Proceedings of Dorset Natural History and Archaeological Society* 109 (1987), pp. 141–2; S. D. Keynes, 'King Alfred the Great and Shaftesbury Abbey', in *The Early History of Shaftesbury Abbey*, ed. L. Keen (Dorchester, 1999), pp. 17–72, at pp. 60–1.

[176] S 646 (AD 957). Michael Wood noted the wording of this charter in his opening address to the *Alfred the Great: Wealth, Wisdom and Warfare* exhibition, Winchester Discovery Centre, 1 February 2008. I am grateful to him for subsequent discussion on this.

[177] H. Philips, 'The Order of Words and Patterns of Opposition in the *Battle of Maldon*', *Neophilogus* 81 (1997), pp. 117–28. See also A. D. Jorgensen, 'Power, Poetry and Violence: The Battle of Maldon', in *Aspects of Power and Authority in the Middle Ages*, ed. B. Bolton and C. Meek, International Medieval Research 14 (Turnhout, 2007), pp. 235–49.

the specific geography of the site of the battle.[178] The memory of the battle lay in both the battlefield referred to in the poem and Byrhtnoth's association with the monastery of Ely, where he was remembered with the aid of donations of landed and portable wealth, including, through his widow, a tapestry embroidered with his deeds.[179]

For the early Anglo-Saxon period Bede provides us with little indication of monasteries established for the expiation of sins committed through participation in specific battles, beyond the monastery founded at Gilling (Yorks.) for the murder of King Oswine after an abortive battle.[180] It is not unlikely that successful campaigns of seventh-century Christian rulers against pagans were followed by the establishment of monasteries associated with the memory of the victories in battle, perhaps benefiting from the wealth attained in those victories. Notwithstanding Bede's account of the establishment of a church at the site of King Oswald of Northumbria's victory at *Heavenfield* (634), which took place after Oswald's death and has more to do with Bede's interests in the miracles associated with the cross established there,[181] a link between Christian military conquest and monastic foundation is also indicated by the records of Cædwalla's conquest of the Isle of Wight (686) and Oswiu's victory against the Mercian king Penda at *Winwæd* (655).[182] Such references are rare, however, and any links between specific victories and foundations are ambiguous.[183] Given that the seventh-century writings of Archbishop Theodore include details of penances necessary for homicide, including ten years' penance for those who killed 'in a public war with the king' (*in publico bello cum rege*),[184] perhaps the association of monasteries with specific victories, even Christian victories, was becoming less favourable in early Christian England. Furthermore, in view of the relatively short durations of dynasties during this period, we may wonder whether some minster churches founded in

---

[178] J. M. Dodgson, 'The Site of the Battle of Maldon', in *Battle of Maldon*, ed. Scragg, pp. 170–9. Dodgson (p. 171), responded to an assertion made by J. B. Bessinger, '*Maldon* and *the Óláfsdrápa*: An Historical Caveat', in *Studies in Old English Literature in Honor of Arthur G. Brodeur*, ed. S. B. Greenfield (Eugene, OR, 1963), pp. 23–35, at p. 27, that only 'bare literary topography' was required in heroic literature.

[179] *Liber Eliensis*, ed. Blake, II.62–3, pp. 133–6; trans. Fairweather, *Liber Eliensis*, pp. 160–3. See Hart, *The Danelaw*, pp. 131–5; A. Kennedy, 'Byrhtnoth's Obits and Twelfth-Century Accounts of the Battle of Maldon'; and M. Budny, 'The Byrhtnoth Tapestry or Embroidery', in *Battle of Maldon*, ed. Scragg, pp. 59–78 and pp. 263–78.

[180] Bede, *HE* III.14, pp. 256–7.

[181] Bede, *HE* III.2, pp. 214–19.

[182] For Wight, see Bede, *HE* IV.15–16, pp. 380–5, and, by implication, Stephen of Ripon, *Vita Wilfridi*, ch. 42, in *Life of Bishop Wilfrid by Eddius Stephanus*, ed. and trans. Colgrave, pp. 84–5. For *Winwæd*, see Bede, *HE* III.24, pp. 288–93.

[183] Yorke, *Kings and Kingdoms of Early Anglo-Saxon England*, p. 174, notes the manner in which monasteries founded in conquered territories were 'part of the consolidation process through which subjected areas were brought to identify themselves with the main kingdom and its royal house.' I gratefully acknowledge Professor Yorke's discussion on the limits of this early evidence.

[184] *Liber poenitentialis Theodori archiepiscopi Cantuariensis ecclesiae*, §§3 and 21, in *Ancient Laws and Institutes of England*, ed. B. Thorpe, 2 vols (London, 1840), vol. I, pp. 278–9, 287–9 (quotation at p. 288).

order to celebrate a suddenly redundant victory would have done well to quietly forget it within a generation or so.

Beyond the foundation of Athelney following Alfred's victorious campaign – although even here Asser does not say explicitly that it was a result of Alfred's victory[185] – there is little indication of monasteries associated with battles or even campaigns in the later Anglo-Saxon period. If battles were fought in and around royal estates, perhaps it may not have made good sense in terms of family strate-gies to give away too much land in those sites.[186] Thus Cnut and William the Con-queror's foundations associated with *Assandun* and Battle (Sussex), although at one level playing an important penitential and ostensibly conciliatory role, served to secure the memory of victories attained by conquering dynasties, albeit per-haps only for a generation in the case of Cnut's foundation.[187] In the light of the establishment of early Anglo-Saxon minster churches in conquered territory, we should not forget that in memorializing their victories, Cnut and William gave away land which had not been theirs for long.[188]

Notwithstanding the actions of conquerors, there were other ways in which a battlefield might be remembered. Asser reported the sight of a thorn-tree at the site of the battle of Ashdown. Thorns were a type of tree associated with assembly places,[189] and the implications of the control of the territory may have been apparent to Asser's audience, though one cannot help but suspect that Asser drew attention a tree which had Christian connotations rather than to 'the arche-typal sacred tree of northern paganism',[190] after which the battlefield was named.[191] (Certainly the 'ash' place-name was important to the author of the *Historia Sancto Cuthberto*, who conflated Ashdown and *Ethandun* by confusing it with the 1016

---

[185] Asser, ch. 92.

[186] For the retention of the interests of the royal family in particular lands, see Lavelle, *Royal Estates in Anglo-Saxon Wessex*, pp. 97–101, and, for the relationship between royal estates and battles, pp. 59–68, an issue also discussed in my paper, 'Geographies of Power in the Anglo-Saxon Chronicle'.

[187] For *Assandun* (often associated – though not securely – with Ashingdon, Essex), ASC CDEF 1020. See W. Rodwell, 'The Battle of *Assandun* and its Memorial Church: A Reappraisal', in *The Battle of Maldon: Fiction and Fact*, ed. J. Cooper (London, 1993), pp. 127–58. Rodwell (p. 155) comments on the church's apparent lack of longevity, though does not associate this with the changes of dynasty in the eleventh century. The penance and triumphalism of Battle Abbey piety is dealt with in E. Searle, 'The Abbey of the Conquerors: Defensive Enfeoffment and Economic Development in Anglo-Norman England', *ANS* 2 (1980 for 1979), pp. 154–64, 197–8.

[188] For a reading of land disposition strategies in the eleventh century, see generally Fleming, *Kings and Lords in Conquest England*.

[189] Hooke, *Landscape of Anglo-Saxon England*, p. 23.

[190] J. Blair, *The Church in Anglo-Saxon Society* (Oxford, 2005), p. 477. Blair cites, amongst other evidence, a reference in a set of Somerset charter bounds to an 'ash-tree which the ignorant call sacred'. S 311 (AD 854).

[191] Asser certainly had form: Richard Abels draws attention to the manner in which Asser elsewhere (ch. 49) changed a reference to Alfred's receipt of Viking oaths on a pagan holy ring recorded in ASC 876, to the use of Christian relics. Abels, 'King Alfred's Peace-Making Strategies with the Vikings', pp. 27–8.

Fig. 7.6 The end of the Battle of Hastings, depicted in the Bayeux Tapestry. The border shows images of the fate of the battle-dead, which link with the main narrative of the deaths of the English warriors.

battle of *Assandun*.)[192] Jennie Kiff has noted the importance of the artistic remembrance of the slain could play a part in the memory of a battle, following literary and artistic conventions.[193] (See Fig. 7.6.) Writing in a different tradition from Old English battle literature, though perhaps not entirely unaware of it, Orderic Vitalis famously recorded the memory of a pile of whitening bones at the site of the Battle of Stamford Bridge, a powerful topographical memorialization, which differed from Orderic's exemplar text of William of Poitiers, and evokes the inclusion of others' memories in his narrative.[194]

> The field of battle obviously shows itself to travellers, where a great heap of the bones of the dead lie to this day, and bears witness to the destruction of many of both peoples.

Accounts of the dead after the battle of Hastings vary, as John Gillingham has noted. The differing accounts of the burial of the slain represent, according

[192] *Historia de Sancto Cuthberto: A History of Saint Cuthbert and a Record of his Patrimony*, ed. and trans. T. Johnson South, Anglo-Saxon Texts 3 (Cambridge, 2002), pp. 54–5. See Simpson, 'The King Alfred/St Cuthbert Episode in the *Historia de sancto Cuthberto*'.

[193] J. [Kiff] Hooper, 'The "Rows of the Battle-Swan": The Aftermath of Battle in Anglo-Saxon Art', in *Armies, Chivalry and Warfare in Medieval Britain and France: Proceedings of the 1995 Harlaxton Symposium*, Harlaxton Medieval Studies new series 7 (Stamford, 1998), pp. 81–99. For a Continental parallel, see references to the dead of the victorious side draped with linen and other corpses (by implication, those of the defeated side) stripped naked, in Angelbert's poem on the Battle of Fontenoy (841), in *Poetry of the Carolingian Renaissance*, ed. and trans. P. Godman, Duckworth Classical, Medieval and Renaissance Editions (London, 1985), pp. 264–5.

[194] *OV*, vol. 2, p. 168 (there is no equivalent account of Stamford Bridge in WP, a source which Orderic often followed closely). See Morgan, 'Naming of Battlefields', p. 36.

to Gillingham, 'a confrontation of views about the good old ways of making war [i.e. leaving the enemy dead unburied] and the newly fashionable chivalry'.[195] Gillingham places William of Poitiers and, following him, Wace, in the chivalrous school, noting William of Poitiers' reference to a willingness to allow the English to bury their dead after the battle.[196] In contrast, the earlier *Carmen*, written immediately after the battle, makes more of the significance of leaving the dead 'to be eaten by worms and wolves, by birds and dogs'.[197] Gillingham's emphasis on the changes in values during the eleventh century, which were arguably not fully established until the twelfth century, is useful, highlighting as it does the 'foreign' reception of the last of the great Anglo-Saxon battlefields. Nonetheless, William of Jumièges, Wace and the *Carmen's* accounts of William spending the night on the battlefield amongst the dead (William of Poitiers does not comment on this, Gillingham notes)[198] may give us an insight into the rituals of memorialization.[199] William of Poitiers's report that Harold could be identified only by *signi* on his body is not incompatible with the notion that his body lay neglected for a period after the battle: if the *signi* ('marks') were a rare medieval reference to tattooed marks, it should be noted that, notwithstanding Harold's probable dismemberment, tattoos are often a significant distinguishing feature on a body in the early stages of decomposition.[200]

Battlefield locations were not consciously forgotten, but in subsequent centuries they could be transposed. Polydore Vergil, one of the key Tudor historians of the middle ages, seems to have misread Old English placenames, referring to

[195] J. Gillingham, '"Holding to the Rules of War (*Bellica Iura Tenentes*)": Right Conduct Before, During and After Battle in North-Western Europe in the Eleventh Century ', *ANS* 29 (2007 for 2006), pp. 1–15, at p. 14.

[196] Gillingham, 'Holding to the Rules of War', pp. 1–7; WP II.26, pp. 142–3; Wace, III.8881–8966.

[197] Gillingham, 'Holding to the Rules of War', p. 1. *Carmen de Hastingae proelio*, lines 567–72, pp. 34–5.

[198] Gillingham, 'Holding to the Rules of War', p. 2.

[199] See generally C. Lee, *Feasting the Dead: Food and Drink in Anglo-Saxon Burial Rituals*, Anglo-Saxon Studies 9 (Woodbridge, 2007). Also *Encomium Emmae*, II.11, p. 29, an account of the aftermath of *Assandun*, which refers to the victors spending the night on the battlefield, then stripping the enemy dead, leaving the corpses to be devoured.

[200] WP II.25, pp. 140–1. A source written not long after 1177, *The Waltham Chronicle: An Account of the Discovery of Our Holy Cross at Montacute and its Conveyance to Waltham*, ed. and trans. L. Watkiss and M. Chibnall, OMT (Oxford, 1994), pp. 50–7, records the identification of Harold's body by his mistress, Edith Swan-Neck, who had been summoned to the battlefield because she 'knew the secret marks on the king's body better than others did, for she had been admitted to a better intimacy of his person. Thus they would be assured by her knowledge of his secret marks [*secretiora in eo signo*] when they could not be sure from his external appearance' because 'the body of a man when dead and drained of blood does not usually have the same appearances when alive' (pp. 54–5). See S. M. Black and T. J. U. Thompson, 'Body Modifications', in *Forensic Human Identification: An Introduction*, ed. T. J. U. Thompson and S. M. Black (Boca Raton, FL, 2007), pp. 379–99, at pp. 383–4, who note a period when a tattoo comes clearer at early stages of a decomposing body before obscuring in advanced decomposition. For the dismemberment of Harold's body, Gillingham, 'Holding to the Rules of War', pp. 10–12.

the battle taking place at 'Abingdon' (*Abyndoniam*) instead of Edington.[201] This is understandable, given Alfred's association with Wantage and the Berkshire Downs, and Polydore Vergil's interest in securing historical events to specific places.[202] As an Italian reader of English, he might well have misread the 'crossed d' of the Old English character *eth* (ð) and, understanding that A, Æ, and E could be homophonous, might easily interpret *Æðandune* as *Abyndoniam*, given that early place-name forms for Abingdon included *Æbbandune*.[203] Polydore Vergil also has Æthelwold's rebellious force, who crossed the River Thames at Cricklade (Wilts.) in 902, sacking Basingstoke (Hants) rather than, as the Anglo-Saxon Chronicle records, Braydon (Wilts.), presumably the result of another early onomastic interpretation.[204]

Many medieval battle sites have proved notoriously elusive in modern study. The detailed studies of the dead from the Battle of Towton (Yorks.) (1471) and, in a Swedish example, from the early twentieth-century excavation of mass graves from Visby, Gotland (1361), serve to highlight what we wish we could know from so many other medieval confrontations.[205] However, this is understandable, given the precarious nature of evidence (much of which was organic) from before an age when weapons firing large quantities of solid shot left their mark on the archaeological record.[206]

[201] Polydore Vergil, *Anglica Historia* (1555 version), ed. D. F. Sutton, The Philological Museum <www.philological.bham.ac.uk/polverg/> (accessed 10 Sept. 2009), V.7.

[202] On Polydore Vergil's work, see M. McKisack, *Medieval History in the Tudor Age* (Oxford, 1971), pp. 98–103.

[203] For Abingdon and Edington's early forms, see Ekwall, *Concise Oxford Dictionary of English Place-Names*, 4th edn (1960), pp. 1 and 160 respectively.

[204] Polydore Vergil, *Anglica Historia*, VI.3. Cf. ASC s.a. 903. However a battle at Andover (Hants) between Cnut and King Edmund in 1016 is recorded in *Anglica Historia* VII.9, for which no immediate onomastic exemplar is apparent to this author. Given Polydore Vergil's form, it may be wise to be sceptical as to whether this is evidence of a lost source; cf. the Hampshire survey of historic sites, *Hampshire Treasures Survey*, vol. 8: *Test Valley North* (Winchester, 1983), p. 225 (available online at <www.hants.gov.uk/hampshiretreasures/vol08/page225.html> [accessed 10 Sept. 2009]), which suggests the Iron Age fort of Bury Hill, Upper Clatford, near Andover as a camp for Cnut's forces in 1016, based on an idea originally suggested by R. C. Hoare, *The Ancient History of South [and North] Wiltshire*, 2 vols (London, 1812–21), vol. 1, p. 18, but refuted by J. Hawkes, 'Excavations at Balkesbury, 1939', *PHFCAS* 14 (1940), pp. 338–45.

[205] V. Fiorato, A. Boylston, C. Knüsel (eds), *Blood Red Roses: The Archaeology of a Mass Grave from the Battle of Towton, AD 1461* (Oxford, 2000), which also reviews evidence from other medieval battles; B. Thordeman, P. Nörlund and B. E. Ingelmark, *Armour from the Battle of Wisby, 1361*, 2 vols (Stockholm, 1939–40).

[206] See the reading of the hasty burials at Bran Ditch, Cambridgeshire, in A. Gray, 'The Massacre at the Bran Ditch, AD 1010', *Proceedings of the Cambridgeshire Antiquarian Society* 31 (1931), pp. 77–87, a burial which is noted in Reynolds, *Anglo-Saxon Deviant Burial Customs*, pp. 106–8, to have been from very different circumstances. Reynolds (pp. 40–4) provides a discussion of burials of likely victims of battles, though it is often difficult to identify any with specific battlefields, and it may be more appropriate to refer to them as victims of combat rather than of battles *per se*. The tentative archaeological evidence for a mass burial at Riccall (Yorks.), the Norwegian landing site of 1066, is reviewed in Lawson, *Battle of Hastings*, p. 40. Reynolds, *Anglo-Saxon Deviant Burial Customs*, pp. 42–3, discusses the burial of eight individuals who had suffered weapon injuries from Fishergate, York.

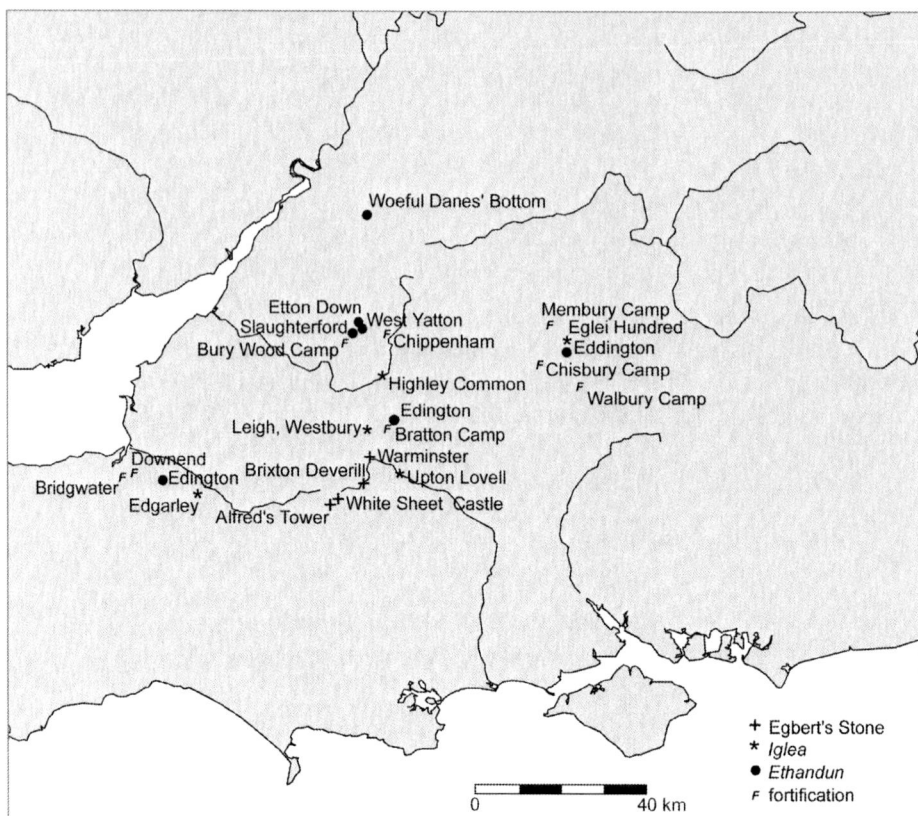

Fig. 7.7 The suggested locations for events in the *Ethandun* campaign, 878

Even if battlefields themselves often escape us, we can at least consider how the general area of a battle can be located. The discussion of the location of the battlefield site of Edington was contentious amongst late eighteenth-, nineteenth-, and early twentienth-century antiquarians, whose disputes arose because they associated the location of the battlefield site with the importance of a national event. *Ethandun* is a significant case study to employ in the historiography of Anglo-Saxon battlefields because the campaigns leading to that particular battle gave (and, to an extent, still give) students of the subject a range of debatable interpretations. The antiquarian significance of Alfred the Great can hardly be underestimated, and one might expect that the authors were somewhat partisan

These may be associated with victims of the nearby battles of Fulford and/or Stamford Bridge, though they hardly compare with the mass graves of Visby and Towton, and may have been the result of other acts of violence. The fifty-one decapitated skulls with randomly deposited bodies – all identified as male – found on the site of building of the Weymouth relief road in Dorset, recently carbon-dated to between 890 and 1030, is more promising because of the scale of the mass burial, though at the time of writing these comments are provisional.'Weymouth Relief Road Burial Pit Update', *Oxford Archaeology: Exploring the Human Journey* website, 13 July 2009 <http://thehumanjourney.net/index.php?option=com_content&task=view&id=502&Itemid=40> (accessed 18 Sept. 2009).

in their opinions and, not infrequently, into flights of wishful thinking. Nonetheless, the opinions held had a bearing on the scholarly interpretations of Alfred's reacquisition of his kingdom. Although he failed to reach a conclusion as to his preferred location for the battle, R. C. Alexander, writing in 1859, is instructive in highlighting how the scientific analysis of the significance of place-names was developing at a local level, which had an impact on the wider study of the subject:

> Many again look upon [onomastic] enquiries of this kind as mere literary curiosities, but conducted judiciously they throw the most unexpected and interesting light upon the history of a people's civilization, its ancient manners and modes of thought, and not unfrequently upon historical events, and in this point of view deserve the full attention of the local antiquary. I greatly regret that I cannot prove the latter assertion by more decisive testimony upon this question of Æthandun, but imperfect as this paper is, it may stimulate those who are better qualified than myself to investigate this and other points of county history by the same method, and follow them up to more satisfactory conclusions. I trust that I shall not have occupied these pages of the Magazine quite uselessly, if I have only shown how little reliance is to be placed upon the mere chiming of names with each other without analysis of the intrinsic meaning of them.[207]

Early antiquarian interpretations of the site, those of Richard Gough's additions to his translation of William Camden's *Britannia* in the late eighteenth century, and Richard Colt Hoare in the early nineteenth, had read Edington in Wiltshire as the location of the battle, as indeed have most modern historians.[208] The original basis for their identification may have been the analogy of the hillside carving of the white horse at nearby Bratton Camp with the traditional association of the site of the Battle of Ashdown with the Vale of the White Horse in the Berkshire Downs (now in Oxon.).[209] It is interesting that opinion on the

---

[207] R. C. Alexander, 'Edington or Yatton the Ethandun of Alfred's Victory?', *Wiltshire Archaeological and Natural History Magazine* 5 (1859), pp. 193–207, at pp. 206–7.

[208] W. Camden, *Britannia: Or, A Chorographical Description of the Flourishing Kingdoms of England, Scotland, and Ireland, and the Islands Adjacent; From the Earliest Antiquity*, trans., with additions by R. Gough, 3 vols (London, 1789), vol. 1, pp. 100–1; Hoare, *Ancient History of Wiltshire*, vol. 1, pp. 59–65. For discussion of these, and other authors on the subject, see Peddie, *Alfred the Good Soldier*, pp. 121–34, although Peddie mistakenly attributes Gough's additions to *Britannia* as Camden's identification. A twentieth-century academic commentator on *Ethandun* as Edington near Westbury is Hodgkin, *History of the Anglo-Saxons*, vol. 2, pp. 567–70.

[209] See Gough's comments in Camden, *Britannia*, vol. 1, p. 101. For the tradition of the association of the design of the Uffington White Horse with the battle of Ashdown (albeit presented in the form of fiction), see T. Hughes, *The Scouring of the White Horse: Or, The Long Vacation Ramble of a London Clerk* (London, 1859). G. K. Chesterton's poem, *The Ballad of the White Horse* (London, 1911), alludes to a greater antiquity, recently confirmed by archaeological investigation, referring to the notion that 'the White Horse knew England / When there was none to know'. For work on the Uffington horse, see D. Miles, *Uffington White Horse and its Landscape: Investigations at White Horse Hill, Uffington, 1989–95 and Tower Hill, Ashbury, 1993–4*, Thames Valley Landscapes Monograph 18 (Oxford, 2003). It should be stressed that the association of King Alfred's Ashdown victory with the Uffington horse can only be traced back to the eighteenth century, though this should not undermine our understanding of its influence on contemporary historiography.

location of the battle has effectively turned full circle since Edington near West-bury was proposed in the late eighteenth century, although the location of the battle site is now secured for different reasons from those which were originally proposed. Such identification can be seen as accurate in the light of the correla-tion of the *Ethandun* place name with the Domesday toponym and that of the tenth-century charter mentioned above. However, as can be seen from the sum-mary of a range of both amateur and professional scholarship (Table 7.1), largely during the nineteenth century, a wide range of opinions were held, which placed the putative location of the battle at Slaughterford (Wilts.),[210] Yatton (Wilts.),[211] Edington (Somerset),[212] Eddington (Berks.),[213] and near Minchampton (Glos.),[214] as well as the now generally accepted site of Edington near Westbury (Wilts.).[215] A number of different methodologies were used by the authors for locating sites, most often on the basis of place-names. Although the phrase 'inherent military probability' does not appear in the range of articles examined, making assump-tions about the movement of armies was a methodology that was employed, which at least kept the range of suggested locations for the events within a limited geographical area of Somerset, Wiltshire, Berkshire, and, on one occasion, Gloucestershire. It is perhaps inevitable that with the homophones in English place-names, there will be a range of opinions on the location of an important event.

[210] J. Whitaker, *The Life of Saint Neot, the Oldest of all the Brothers to King Alfred*, ed. J. Stockdale (London, 1809), pp. 268–9.

[211] Thurnham, 'On the Barrow at Lanhill near Chippenham'; G. Poulett Scrope, 'The Battle of Ethandun', *Wiltshire Archaeological and Natural History Magazine* 4 (1858), pp. 298–308.

[212] W. Clifford, 'An Inquiry Concerning the Real Site of the Battle of Aethan-dune', *Proceedings of the Somersetshire Archaeological and Natural History Society* 21 (1875), pp. 1–27; W. H. P. Greswell, 'The Sequel to the Battle of Edington, AD 878', *Proceedings of the Somersetshire Archaeological and Natural History Society* 53 (1907), pp. 174–8.

[213] D. Lysons, *Magna Britannia: Being a Concise Topographical Account of the Several Counties of Great Britain*, vol. 1, 3 parts (London, 1813), part 2: Berkshire, p. 162; J. E. Jackson, The Sheriff's Turn, Co. Wilts, AD 1439', *Wiltshire Archaeological and Natural History Magazine* 13 (1871), pp. 105–18; W. Money, 'The Battle of Ethandune', *The Antiquary* 27 (1893), pp. 146–8.

[214] J. M. M[offat], 'Battle of Ethandun', in *The Graphic and Historical Illustrator: An Original Miscellany of Literary, Antiquarian, and Topographical Information*, ed. E. W. Brayley (London, 1834), pp. 106–10.

[215] As well as Gough's additions to Camden, *Britannia*, vol. 1, pp. 100–1, and Hoare, *Ancient History of Wiltshire*, vol. 1, pp. 59–65, this view can be seen in Pauli, *Life of Alfred the Great*, p. 107n. Mistakenly believing that Camden had been the originator of the attribution of *Ethandun* to Edington near Westbury, Thurnham complained in 'One the Barrow at Lanhill', pp. 73–4, that '[t]hese views are now so generally received as to be incorporated, not only in popular histories, but also, very improperly, in most of the modern editions of the ancient chronicles.' However, Thurnham's complaint of authorial follow-my-leader was unfair: the anonymously authored account of the Third Quarterly Meeting of the Somersetshire Archaeological and Natural History Society, in *Proceedings of the Somersetshire Archaeological and Natural History Society* 1 (1850), pp. 34–7, reports a lecture by J. A. Giles, in which it was noted that a standard raised at the site of Alfred's Tower (near Stourton, Wilts.), would not have been visible to Danes encamped between Westbury and Edington. For a local historian's support of Edington near Westbury, see G. Matcham, 'The Battle of Ethandun', *Wiltshire Archaeological and Natural History Magazine* 4 (1858), pp. 175–88.

Table 7.1 Antiquarians' suggested locations for the events in the *Ethandun* campaign, 878

Authors	Date of publication	Egbert's Stone	Iglea	Ethandun	Fortification	Others
R. Gough; R. C. Hoare	1789 (Gough); 1812–21 (Hoare)			Edington (Wilts.)	Bratton Camp, nr Edington (Wilts.)	
J. Whitaker	1809		Highley Common, nr Melksham (Wilts.)	Slaughterford, nr Yatton (Wilts.)	Bury Wood Camp, nr Colerne (Wilts.)	
D. Lysons	1813 (Berks.)	Brixton Deverill (Wilts.)	Eglei hundred (Berks.)	Eddington/ Hedington, nr Hungerford (Berks.)	?	
J. M. Moffat	1834		Highley Common, nr Melksham (Wilts.)	'Woeful Danes' Bottom', nr Minchinhampton (Glos.)		
J. A. Giles, reported at meeting	1850	'Alfred's Tower', nr Stourton (Wilts.)		Bratton Camp/ Edington (Wilts.)		
R. Pauli	1852	Brixton Deverill (Wilts.)	Leigh, Westbury (Wilts.)	Edington (Wilts.)	Chippenham (Wilts.)	
J. Thurnham	1857	Brixton Deverill (Wilts.)	Highley Common, nr Melksham (Wilts.)	West Yatton (Wilts.)		

Table 71 continued

Authors	Date of publication	Egbert's Stone	Iglea	Ethandun	Fortification	Others
G. Matcham	1858	Brixton Deverill (Wilts.)		Edington (Wilts.)	Bratton Camp, nr Edington (Wilts.)	
G. Poulett Scrope	1858	Brixton Deverill (Wilts.)	Highley Common, nr Melksham (Wilts.)	Etton Down, Yatton (Wilts.)	Bury Wood Camp (Wilts.)	
R. C. Alexander	1859 (Wilts.)	Brixton Deverill (Wilts.)	Island in the R. Wyle (Upton Lovell, Wilts.)	None suggested (doubts on Edington and Yatton [Wilts.])		
J. E. Jackson	1871	Stone north-west of Warminster (Wilts.)	Eglei hundred (Berks.)	Eddington, nr Hungerford (Berks.)		
W. Clifford	1875	White Sheet Castle, near Kingston Deverill (Wilts.)	Edgarley, nr Glastonbury (Som.)	Edington (Som.)	Bridgwater (Som.)	Cynuit as Cannington (Som.)
W. Money	1893	Brixton Deverill (Wilts.)	Eglei hundred (Berks.)	Eddington, near Hungerford (Berks.)	Walbury Camp, Chisbury Camp, or Membury Camp (Berks.)	
W. H. P. Greswell	1907	n/a	n/a	Assumes Edington (Som.)	Downend, Puriton Manor (Som.)	Cynuit as Combwich (Som.)

As a former resident of the Somerset village of Edington, where for a time a 'King Alfred School' was to be found, I have a sympathy for the desire for a nationally important event to have taken place in one's back yard. With the cries of the neatherd's wife resounding through the historical imagination as Alfred burned the cakes just over the Polden Hills at Athelney,[216] an Edington resident could hardly help but feel that 'it happened here'.

A characteristic of the *Ethandun* battle is the fact that, as we have seen in chapter 5,[217] the Anglo-Saxon Chronicle is particularly forthcoming on the details leading up to and after the battle; the battle is seen as part of a campaign, and so the events can be used to locate the area where it was fought, even if the battlefield itself remains elusive.[218] The place to which the Vikings retreated, where the West Saxons besieged them, has some bearing on the nature of the battle and exercised many commentators, who seem to have plumbed their local knowledge for likely candidates in support of their preferred sites. Bratton Camp, an imposing Iron Age hillfort, was favoured by many because of its proximity to Edington near Westbury,[219] but was also questioned as a site because it may have been difficult for a retreating army to access.[220] Fewer scholars proposed Chippenham, which was further from Edington than Bratton Camp: Pauli's biography of Alfred 'supposed' Chippenham but gave no reason for this, while John Thurnham followed his suggestion before moving on to write of Bury Wood Camp, Colerne, near his preferred candidate for *Ethandun*, West Yatton (Wilts.).[221] One Somerset partisan, the Reverend W. H. P. Greswell, even suggested Downend, near Bridgwater for the Vikings' fortification, on the premise that 'Somerset archæologists generally assume [the battle] to have been fought on the Poldens [i.e. in Somerset]', though he presented very little evidence in support of his suggestion.[222]

Domesday Book has Edington in Somerset as *Eduuinetone*, which had a completely different origin for its spelling from the *Ethandun* of the Anglo-Saxon Chronicle.[223] *Ethandun* was much closer matched to the Wiltshire vill's

---

[216] For the resonance of this episode, see D. Horspool, *Why Alfred Burnt the Cakes: A King and His Eleven-Hundred-Year Afterlife* (London, 2006) and J. Parker, '*England's Darling*': *The Victorian Cult of Alfred the Great* (Manchester, 2007). The account is in *Annals of St Neots*, ed. Dumville and Lapidge, pp. 125–6; trans. Keynes and Lapidge, *Alfred the Great*, pp. 197–8. Indicating the esteem in which Alfred was held in Somerset, this famous account was apparent in a rendering of the episode in Somerset dialect, spoken to me by an elderly Edington (Som.) resident *c*. 1994 (which, to my regret, I failed to record).

[217] Above, pp. 179–80.

[218] For the geography of the campaign, see above, pp. 180, n. 14.

[219] E.g. Matcham, 'Battle of Ethandun', pp. 178–81.

[220] Thurnham, 'On the Barrow at Lanhill near Chippenham', p. 76.

[221] Pauli, *Life of Alfred the Great*, p. 107; Thurnham, 'On the Barrow at Lanhill near Chippenham', pp. 77–9.

[222] Greswell, 'Sequel to the Battle of Edington', p. 174. The 'Somerset archæologists' (*sic*.) he cited was a single author's article: Clifford, 'Inquiry Concerning the Real Site of the Battle of Aethan-dune', whose suggestion of Bridgwater as the Danes' fortification (p. 25), seems to have been based on even more limited evidence.

[223] DB Som. 8:5 (fol. 90a). This is likely to have been a place-name associated with a privately held manor established in the later Anglo-Saxon period. See generally M. Costen, 'The

place-name of *Edendone*, effectively a trump card in the argument, whose full significance does not seem to have been recognized by any of the figures discussed here.[224] The reasoning is provided by a case of elementary onomastics, but the ongoing discussion of the location in various publications through the nineteenth century reveals the contentiousness of the subject. As a defining event in English history, its study had potential repercussions beyond purely local interests.

Summary

This chapter has addressed a range of issues associated with the conduct of one of the rarest and yet most significant aspects of Anglo-Saxon warfare. The effects of battle upon groups and individuals have been noted, as have the effects of the responses of groups and individuals themselves upon the conduct of battles. The difficulties of sources are specifically relevant to battles, as the use of descriptions of battles in classical sources is one of the key issues associated with records of early medieval battles. Nonetheless, fighting techniques and tactics on the battlefield can be read, if the limitations of sources are acknowledged, and sources which do not focus on the battlefield can reveal something about conduct upon it. The Anglo-Saxons are seen to have been flexible in their use of a range of weaponry, including horses – certainly more flexible than is usually acknowledged – and the appearance of ships in what may be referred to as naval battles gives another dimension to their warfare.

However, the inherently retrospective element of battles is perhaps of the greatest significance. In the chronicles of the new English kingdom, battles formed links between the local and national entities, both during the immediate aftermath and in the eyes of succeeding generations. Participation in battles was something to be recorded for its own sake, and battles were recognized as having historical consequences in their own right. Battles may not have been frequent events, but, associated with 'places of memory', they became significant for participants and for the generations to come.

Late Saxon Landscape: The Evidence From Charters and Placenames', in *Aspects of the Mediæval Landscape of Somerset: Contributions to the Landscape History of the County*, ed. M. Aston (Taunton, 1988), pp. 33–47.

[224] DB Wilts. 15:1 (fol. 68b); 68:1 (fol. 74c). Although cf. Thurnham, 'On the Barrow at Lanhill near Chippenham', p. 76, who mentions the place-name but is evidently unconvinced by it. Alexander, 'Edington or Yatton?' has a philological focus but does not bring this to bear on the Domesday place-name.

✦ 8 ✦

After the Battle:
Peacemaking and Peace Agreements

Even if running the risk of perpetuating the notion that war and peace are diametric opposites, it is logical that the final chapter should be a discussion of peacemaking.[1] In recent years, definitions of peace in the early middle ages have shifted from seeing it in 'negative' terms, visible only through the absence of hostility amongst secular elites, to viewing agreements between certain groups of people, with spatial and chronological specificity. This chapter will consider that peace could actually hold a multi-layered significance as an effective political tool in Anglo-Saxon England. It could range from a 'natural' cessation of hostility to the imposition of peace as submission to a dominant force: as with warfare, peace could be a continuation of politics by other means. As we have seen, violence sustained and justified the existence of a small but significant section of early medieval society. Warfare was a message in itself, a projection of power which used its own set of codes of behaviour. The vested interests of military elites lay in states of warfare, threats of war and its discriminate use on an intensive scale. It is almost counter-intuitive to consider that this picture of almost perpetual warfare can be reconciled with a universal concept of 'peace', especially in a Christian context. If good kingship and warcraft were the total defeat of the enemy, the receipt of tribute and even the reduction of their populace to slavery, habits which we have seen in discussion of the English prosecution of warfare against their neighbours in chapter 2, was peace therefore a compromise?

For such warrior elites, the concept of warfare was integral to their set of social values, placing the warrior within a defined hierarchy.[2] Warfare brought out leadership and developed and maintained group identity and aristocratic cohesion, as well as a steady turnover of aristocrats, who led short, violent lives. But in our enthusiasm for applying societal interpretations of warfare as a way of life, we must not forget that warfare was more than a destructive social activity for misguided aristocratic males: it was also political, and understood as such, many centuries before the Prussian military writer Carl von Clausewitz deemed

---

[1] With the additions of primary source extracts and updated discussion, this chapter is adapted from my paper 'Towards a Political Contextualization of Peacemaking and Peace Agreements in Anglo-Saxon England', in *Peace and Negotiation: Strategies for Coexistence in the Middle Ages and the Renaissance*, ed. D. Wolfthal, Arizona Studies in the Middle Ages and the Renaissance 4 (Turnhout, 2000), pp. 39–55. I wish to record my grateful thanks to Brepols for allowing me to do this.

[2] Abels, *Lordship and Military Obligation in Anglo-Saxon England*, pp. 36–7, 179–86.

it so.[3] Although, as we have seen, Karl Leyser had reservations on the subject,[4] politics could still be concerned with the art of the possible: certain groups in Anglo-Saxon society acted in order to fulfill an agenda of gaining power and maintaining their hold on it. It was therefore in the interests of few of the male secular nobility to stop warfare altogether, but, within this political agenda, it was equally in their interests that certain limitations could be imposed: to make the ritual, the fragile diplomacy and the symbolism of war, peace and submission count for something more than merely *violence* and *non-violence*. This area of studies is not unexplored. For example, Richard Abels has suggested that such strategies were an important element of early medieval peacemaking,[5] while Paul Kershaw argues for the use of peace as part of a construction of royal power in the early medieval west.[6] Nonetheless, the details of Anglo-Saxon peace-making are not as well known as those of the use of violence in warfare. This chapter will deal with the use of peacemaking by and associated with the warrior classes in later Anglo-Saxon society and their rationale for the politics of peacemaking.

Although there are numerous examples of active peacemaking and peace agreements in pre-Viking England,[7] the later Anglo-Saxon period presents us with the most evidence for the practice of peacemaking. Asser's *Life of King Alfred* seems to record the largest number (proportionately, for the size of the work) of peace agreements, with records of fourteen occasions of peace-agreements and submission during the ninth century.[8] In the Anglo-Saxon Chronicle, there are nine pre-Conquest occurrences of peace as agreements from the ninth century onwards,[9] but submission was evidently the clearest, most desirable form of 'peace', including that guaranteed by hostage-giving. This occurred, or was at least implied, more often than agreement on equal terms in the Chronicle.[10]

Politically distinct from the philosophical concept of peace, the Anglo-Saxon construct of peace – *frið* – was limited by time and space, often to a defined group of people. It was actively pursued in some cases and was not only a 'natural' cessation of hostilities. J. M. Wallace-Hadrill's interpretation of peace in the early medieval Germanic world was essentially a 'negative' one: it was only the temporary absence of hostility that defined a state of peace, resting on the knowledge that the

---

[3] Clausewitz, *On War*, trans. Howard and Paret, pp. 75–99.

[4] Leyser, 'Early Medieval Warfare', p. 108. See above, p. 9.

[5] Abels, 'King Alfred's Peace-Making Strategies with the Vikings'.

[6] P. J. E. Kershaw, '*Rex Pacificus*: Studies in Royal Peacemaking and the Image of the Peace-Making King in the Early Medieval West' (PhD thesis, Univ. of London, 1998); to be revised and published as *Peaceful Like Solomon: the Image and Practice of the Peacemaking King in the Early Medieval West* (Oxford, forthcoming). For the Carolingian use of hostages in a similar context, see also A. J. Kosto, 'Hostages in the Carolingian World (714–840)', *EME* 11 (2002), pp. 123–47.

[7] Bede, *HE*, III.1, pp. 212–5; III.24, pp. 290–1; IV.21, pp. 400–1; V.23, pp. 560–1.

[8] Asser, chs 7, 20, 27, 30, 43, 44, 45, 46, 49, 56, 72, 80, 81, 83.

[9] ASC 867, 868, 871, ABCD 906, CDE 994, D 1048, E 1049, CD 1052, C 1055.

[10] ASC 830, 865, 876, 877, 878, 886, ABCD 893, A 915, A 918, MR 918, D 927, 945, 948, CDE 1006, CDE 1009, CDE 1011, CDE 1012, CDE 1013, CDE 1015, CDE 1016, DE 1063.

world at large, and especially the world just beyond one's own experience, is naturally hostile'.[11] By contrast, studying Scandinavian agreements, Niels Lund argued
that an empathetic medieval interpretation of *frið* 'as a positive concept implying
some set of agreed terms will lead to a much improved understanding of texts
and situations',[12] something which was arguably important for the Anglo-Saxons
as for their Viking opponents. (Although Lund does not state it, the Old English
frið was synonymous with the Old Norse *friðr*.)[13] Though the early medieval world
at large may have remained a hostile place, the premise of Lund's suggestion is
important.

After outlining instances of peace and peacemaking within the narrative sources,
this chapter will concentrate on the political realities of the Anglo-Saxon concept of
peace: the systems available and used for composition; the differences and similarities between truce and peace, including the differing contexts of peace as a defined
agreement; the negotiation process, especially within mutually understood codes of
conduct, which could lead to peace agreement; and the 'strategic dimension' that was
intrinsic to peace. The chapter concludes with a discussion of the three extant documented treaties, from the ninth and tenth centuries. Beyond the establishment of
bounds of peace in these agreements, there were further political agendas which can
be seen in Anglo-Saxons' strategies with both Vikings and Celts.

Questions of authority and responsibility in early medieval warfare inevitably
apply to peacemaking. Adam Kosto has drawn attention to how Charlemagne had
to make separate peace with numerous 'semi-independent political subdivisions' of
Continental Saxons, taking hostages from each group,[14] and similar circumstances
might be noted in terms of dealings with Vikings. 'Hosts' could consist of different
groups owing different allegiances, both permanent and temporary, to minor lords
who then owed their allegiances to the host's leader(s). This may have been the case
for the 'great army' (*micel here*) of the Vikings. Of course, as we have seen, to think
of the Vikings as an 'army' in any modern sense would be misleading: *micel here*
was a term imposed by the ninth-century author of the Anglo-Saxon Chronicle in
order to refer to an amalgam of Scandinavian (and perhaps Anglo-Scandinavian)
warbands in the ninth century.[15] Early medieval warfare varied considerably in scale,
and thus there may similarly have been a range of means to bring about its cessation. At one end of the scale, disputes between small groups of nobles could entail

[11] Wallace-Hadrill, 'War and Peace in the Early Middle Ages', p. 23.

[12] Lund, 'Peace and Non-Peace in the Viking Age', p. 256. The linguistic misapprehension
that *frið* was a less specific term than *grið* was dispelled in Fell, 'Unfrið: An Approach to a
Definition'. However, cf. W. Davies, '"Protected Space" in Britain and Ireland in the Middle
Ages', in *Scotland in Dark Age Britain: The Proceedings of a Day Conference held on 18 February
1995*, ed. B. A. E. Crawford, St John's House Papers 6 (St Andrews, 1996), pp. 1–19, at p. 10.

[13] Bosworth-Toller, p. 338; R. Cleasby and G. Vigfusson, *An Icelandic–English Dictionary*
(Oxford, 1874), p. 173.

[14] Kosto, 'Hostages in the Carolingian World', p. 124.

[15] Abels, 'Alfred the Great, the *Micel Hæðen Here* and the Viking Threat'; see also Abels,
Lordship and Military Obligation in Anglo-Saxon England, pp. 11–37, 58–96. For the first
revisionist observations of the possible complexities of Viking allegiances, see Sawyer, *Age
of the Vikings*, esp. pp. 120–47.

sequences of sporadic outbursts of violence characteristic of events discussed in chapter 1,[16] while, at the other extreme, there were comparatively large battles and associated campaigns fought between many hundreds, even thousands, of men. Narrative sources could refer to either in the same way, without necessarily indicating the numbers concerned. It is logical to presume that the numbers of belligerents in 'large-scale' warfare gradually increased proportionately with the size of political units and as the resources that could be obtained from them increased.[17] By the eleventh century, as we have seen, more resources were certainly needed for warfare: the historical sources bear out the scale of the 1066 campaigns and money was spent on 'professional' forces, which included mercenary elements.[18] It does not necessarily follow that peace agreements could have been easier to reach in small-scale warfare; a feud could continue indefinitely until (if at all) it was settled,[19] while large armies were difficult to keep together for long. The fragmentation of Harold's forces in September 1066 and Æthelred II's difficulties (or rather his generals' difficulties) in confronting the Vikings on the battlefield in the late tenth and early eleventh centuries show this dramatically. With a large army, peace could very quickly have become a practical necessity.

Opportunities for negotiation

Conditions existed within which peace negotiation could take place, showing that peace was ingrained as a political option. Examples exist from the pre-Viking 'Heptarchy'. An attempt upon the life of Edwin, king of the Northumbrians, described in Bede's *Historia ecclesiastica* shows the importance of negotiation within diplomatic channels between the West Saxons and Northumbrians.[20] Though it is not stated that the assassin masqueraded as a messenger for peace negotiation, it is an important indication of diplomacy that he was allowed to come so close to the king – close enough to stab him. This was face-to-face negotiation by proxy; both king and messenger expected to meet unarmed in mutual trust – the bodyguard,

---

[16] See G. Halsall, 'Reflections on Early Medieval Violence: The Example of the 'Blood Feud', *Memoria y Civilización* 2 (1999), pp. 7–29, in which a view of noble violence is offered that differs somewhat from that of the institutionalism of 'feud' presented by J. M. Wallace-Hadrill, 'The Bloodfeud of the Franks', in his *The Long-Haired Kings* (Toronto, 1982), pp. 121–47. Various interpretations have been offered regarding the conduct and motives of 'feud', though a consensus seems to exist that the violence involved was often (albeit not invariably) on a small scale. P. R. Hyams, *Rancor and Reconciliation in Medieval England* (Ithaca, NY, 2003), pp. 71–110, deals with the continuation of small-scale feuds and the limits of royal authority in preventing them, thus showing that 'West Saxon kings were also tacitly approving and reshaping legitimate violence' (p. 98).

[17] See Brooks, 'Development of Military Obligations in Eighth- and Ninth-Century England'.

[18] See, e.g., ASC C 1066 and, for the preparations of the Norman invading force, see WP II.1 and II.2, pp. 100–5; resources necessary for maintenance and transportation are considered in some detail by B. S. Bachrach, 'Some Observations on the Military Administration of the Norman Conquest', *ANS* 8 (1986 for 1985), pp. 1–26.

[19] R. Fletcher, *Bloodfeud: Murder and Revenge in Anglo-Saxon England* (London, 2002).

[20] Bede, *HE*, II.9, pp. 164–5.

Lilla, who saved Edwin's life, apparently had no shield: he could only put his body between the assassin's blade and the king. Whether the event actually took place like this is immaterial; here, the important matter is Bede's familiarity with a set of normative values – enough to recognize a transgression of a code of conduct, which was well deserving of Bede's righteous indignation.

The presence of a third party, an intermediary, could help the process of peacemaking itself, allowing the exchange of messages, even bringing leaders together, but again there was political manipulation of this process by all parties working in their own interests. Before the arrival of large Viking forces in the English kingdoms, the clergy had been the most obvious intermediary and peacemakers. As a theoretically neutral supra-political organization that was (again, *theoretically*) respected by the nobility, the Church's position could be advantageous. However, in a fragmented political situation that relied upon the patronage of local magnates, with subsequent clashes of ecclesiastical and secular loyalties, it could also be problematic. The blurring of secular boundaries of Church and states presented obvious difficulties. This is most clearly shown in the letter from Wealdhere, Bishop of London, to Brihtwold, Archbishop of Canterbury, requesting authority on a conflict between the West Saxon and East Saxon kings in 704 or 705; Wealdhere reflects that he was *expected* to 'reconcile them, and become as it were a hostage of peace [*obses pacis*]'.[21] The latter concern is especially interesting, as hostages were really to be given by the political groups themselves; its vernacular equivalent, *friðgisl*, seems to be a term used in a legal context to refer to a hostage used to ensure smooth communications between two communities.[22] Wealdhere relates the difficulties involved: were it not for a decree regarding the ordination of bishops given by the archbishop, which meant that 'we ought to have no intercourse with [the West Saxons] if they did not hasten to fulfil your decree', then Wealdhere's role would have been more tenable. Somewhat removed from the uncomplicated picture of unbiased peacemaker, Wealdhere's position was politically motivated, evidently compromised by the political geography of episcopal sees and his own subordination to archiepiscopal authority.[23]

This pattern of ecclesiastical involvement in political interests may be seen to have continued into the Viking period. The rapid conversion of Viking polities shows the significance of turning pagan sea-kings into Christian Anglo-Saxon rulers who could be dealt with on even terms. That churchmen were involved in negotiating with newly converted groups of Vikings is indicated by the successful dealings of the abbot of Carlisle with Vikings in northern Northumbria, depicted

[21] The letter's authenticity is discussed and verified, with a facsimile, in P. Chaplais, 'The Letter from Bishop Wealdhere of London to Archbishop Brihtwold of Canterbury: The Earliest Original "Letter Close" Extant in the West', in *Medieval Scribes, Manuscripts and Libraries: Essays Presented to N. R. Ker*, ed. M. B. Parkes and A. G. Watson (London, 1978), pp. 3–25; trans. *EHD 1*, pp. 792–3.

[22] Lavelle, 'Use and Abuse of Hostages', p. 292, discussing the *Ordinance of the Dunsæte*, ch. 9: *Gesetze*, vol. 1, pp. 378; trans. F. Noble, *Offa's Dyke Reviewed*, ed. M. Gelling, BAR British Series 114 (Oxford, 1983), p. 109.

[23] N. P. Brooks, *The Early History of the Church of Canterbury: Christ Church from 597 to 1066*, SEHB (Leicester, 1984), p. 80.

in the *Historia de Sancto Cuthberto*,[24] and the remarkable survival of archbishops of York through the tenth century.[25] However, the fate of Archbishop Ælfheah, captured by a Viking army in Canterbury in 1012 and executed in London in 1013 (albeit after negotiations for his ransom), shows that negotiating with Vikings held very real dangers for a prominent churchman.[26]

As part of the negotiation processes, codes were probably recognized on and around the battlefield, which imposed necessary limitations upon the prosecution of violence and allowed negotiation to take place. The raising of a shield may have signified non-hostility, the visual equivalent of the modern white flag of truce, perhaps with the symbolic submission of the person to the enemy's mercy. This may at least have been a Scandinavian code of truce (shown on the Bayeux Tapestry at a point where the Norman fleet needed to recognize one another as mutually friendly: see Fig. 8.1). Although there appear to be no written records of this from Anglo-Saxon England, an example in the *Annals of Fulda* seems to illustrate the custom's parameters. Frankish nobles entered a Viking fortress on the banks of the Meuse, at *Asselt*, an unidentified site, after an exchange of hostages in 882.[27]

> The Northmen took this [i.e. the exchange of hostages] as a good sign; and so that peace established on their part would not be doubted, they hung a shield in a lofty position according to their custom [*iuxta morem suum*] and opened the gates of the fortification [*munitio*]. Our men, however, lacking knowledge of their cunning, entered the same fortification, some, in fact, for the purpose of trading, others, truly, for considering the strength of the place. But the Northmen, turning to their usual cunning, pulled down the shield of peace [*clipeum pacis*], closed the gates, and all of our men found inside were either killed or kept to be ransomed, bound in chains of iron.

Once the Franks were inside, the Vikings lowered the fortress gates, capturing their visitors, but as a significant ignominy they first followed the convention of taking down the shield in order to show termination of the peace. However, the apparent treachery seen by the Frankish annalist may be tempered by the possibility that he had misunderstood a code of peace that was specific to one culture. After all, the Vikings had raised the shield 'according to their custom' [*iuxta morem suum*] and, by the standards of this, one of their own cultural norms, the peace had not been 'treacherously' broken: it had merely begun and ended with the raising and lowering of the shield.

A paper by Paul Dalton has emphasized the importance of rivers or islands in

[24] *Historia de Sancto Cuthberto*, ed. and trans. Johnson South, pp. 52–3.

[25] For the liminal position of archbishops of York, see D. Whitelock, 'The Dealings of the Kings of England with Northumbria in the Tenth and Eleventh Centuries', in *The Anglo-Saxons: Studies in Some Aspects of their History and Culture Presented to Bruce Dickins*, ed. P. Clemoes (London, 1959), pp. 70–88.

[26] ASC CDE 1012, 1013.

[27] AF 882.

Fig. 8.1 Norman vessels with shields raised, depicted in the Bayeux Tapestry

rivers for negotiations.[28] For example, as we saw in chapter 2, the meeting of Edgar with other British rulers on the River Dee may have been – as Julia Barrow has argued – less a ceremony demonstrating Edgar's status over the other rulers than a triumphal gloss on a peaceful meeting between (relative) equals.[29] But there are other examples, the best known being the island of Alney near Deerhurst (Glos.), where Cnut and Edmund Ironside were able to meet to discuss the partition of the English kingdom.[30]

Dalton argues that rivers may have been less important for the liminal representation of an area between boundaries, than for the very logical purpose of saving face for two bellicose parties, who could argue that a river represented an obstacle that could not be overcome or physically prevented the threat of violence 'from spilling over into actual violence', thus justifying the making of peace.[31] However, given the occasions when battles took place at river crossing-points during the early middle ages, as Guy Halsall has observed,[32] we might note that peacemaking at such sites was an inevitable corollary of the manner in which they were treated in warfare. We should not forget that, given the *expectations* of the conduct of violence expressed in the *Battle of Maldon*, two sides could also

---

[28] Dalton, 'Sites and Occasions of Peacemaking in England and Normandy', pp. 12–26.

[29] Barrow, 'Chester's Earliest Regatta?', discussing JW vol. 2, s.a. 973, pp. 422–5. See above, pp. 20–1.

[30] ASC CDE 1016. Dalton, 'Sites and Occasions of Peacemaking in England and Normandy', p. 14. Amongst his pre-Conquest English examples, Dalton (pp. 14–15) also cites Eamont Bridge (ASC D 927), Southwark in 1051 (*Vita Ædwardi Regis*, ed. Barlow, pp. 34–5) and 1052 (ASC C 1052), and the banks of the River Severn in 1056 (Walter Map, *De Nugis Curialium: Courtiers' Trifles*, ed. and trans. M. R. James, C. N. L. Brooke and R. A. B. Mynors, OMT (Oxford, 1983), II.23, pp. 192–5).

[31] Dalton, 'Sites and Occasions of Peacemaking in England and Normandy', pp. 16–18.

[32] Halsall, 'Anthropology and the Study of Pre-Conquest Warfare and Society', pp. 165–6.

negotiate across a river in order to fight as well as to step back from the brink of battle.[33]

Nonetheless, whatever river sites symbolized to early medieval participants in peacemaking, their importance, as outlined by Dalton, is striking. It is unlikely that the choice of river sites was not solely determined by the presence of high-status settlements close by. Although the Anglo-Saxon Chronicle D manuscript documents the presence of Deerhurst near Alney, the author nonetheless records that the meeting was at Alney rather than Deerhurst. Indeed, Alfred's triumphal baptism of Guthrum at Aller in 878 does not stretch the definition of a river site. It is striking that the ninth-century geography meant that it was an island, and the Chronicler is again careful to report Aller, rather than nearby Athelney or Wedmore, as the site of the occasion.[34] The records of these sites show that the geography of a peacemaking site, like the sites of battles, was often consciously determined as best as the circumstances allowed.

Strategic peace: the use and abuse of peace?

The agreement of peace could often be used strategically, perhaps as a means of temporary recovery during campaigns or for political alliance. The Vikings' ninth-century agreements can be seen in the context of examples of such opportunistic peace, certainly when agreements allowed them to winter in peace. In the Anglo-Saxon Chronicle entry for 868, the Vikings made winter quarters in Nottingham, but, after a siege, there 'occurred no serious battle there and the Mercians made peace with the enemy.'[35] Presumably here fighting was in no one's interest during winter. It is unlikely that the writer of the Chronicle was so naïve as to have been unaware of the strategic dimensions of the Vikings' peace agreements with the West Saxons before the victory at Edington in 878, or even of Viking strategies on the Continent. The Anglo-Saxon Chronicle gives accounts of 'broken' peace and implied treachery, but there also seems to have been an acceptance that peace could be agreed to in the short term, towards short-term ends and for at least one group's benefit, rather like the modern cease-fire. If a pause in the state of war suited neither group, then it simply would not happen.

Forces could quickly lose their impetus and exhaust themselves, especially in the preliminary stages of a battle. The macho boasts made before a battle might, while boosting the warriors' fighting spirit, demoralize the enemy to the extent that they would sue for peace: a period of standoff which could lead to truce or surrender as easily as, or even *more* easily than it could lead to the battle itself.[36]

---

[33] 'The Battle of Maldon', ed. and trans. D. Scragg, lines 84–95, in *The Battle of Maldon, AD 991*, ed. D. Scragg (Oxford, 1991), pp. 15–36, at pp. 20–3.

[34] ASC 878.

[35] ASC 869.

[36] For the mid eleventh century, see Gillingham, 'William the Bastard at War', pp. 141–58. Prestwich, *Place of War in English History*, pp. 23–4, provides a list of twelve 'battles not fought' between 1101 and 1197. Cf. Morillo, 'Expecting Cowardice: Medieval Battle Tactics Reconsidered', p. 71, who considers the tactical implications of delays before a battle.

In that most macho of the works of the period, the *Battle of Maldon*, the device of the Viking messenger's call for tribute not only adds to the tension leading to the battle but also emphasizes how tribute was a possible option.[37] The East Saxon ealdorman Byrhtnoth is not shown as yielding to temptation so easily, but the poem indicates that paying for peace was not entirely dishonorable; it could be a sensible decision, not just in humanitarian terms, but also militarily. The payment of monetary tribute, as *geld*, was not an innovation under King Æthelred (even if it became an institution during his reign), nor was it even necessitated first by the Vikings. Paying tribute was an accepted way of creating short-term peace. Importantly, it worked.[38]

However, peace might be made between belligerents, whether royal or noble, simply because they paused to consider the slaughter of battle. Though the ecclesiastical sources' interpretations might be influential here, backing down from hostility could be a sound manœuvre. The 1051–2 crisis between King Edward the Confessor and Godwine, Earl of Wessex, was defused because 'it was hateful to almost all of them that they should fight with their own kinsmen, because there was little else which was anything great except English men on either side [*healfe*]; and also they did not wish that this land through this were more open to foreign people because they destroyed each other themselves.'[39] This was an example of the existence of a state of peace, enforced by the exchange of hostages, in order for two sides to come to a formal agreement.[40] Edward Freeman's triumphant nineteenth-century account attributed the agreement made in 1052 and recorded by the Anglo-Saxon Chronicle to the defence of the Anglo-Saxons' state of democracy by his proto-Whig hero, Earl Godwine, and the level of popular support which he had:[41]

> And a memorable and happy day it was. Events were so thickly crowded into its short hours, events which, even after so many ages, may well make every English heart swell with pride. It is something indeed to feel ourselves of the blood and speech of the actors of that day and of its morrow. The tide for which the fleet had waited came soon after the Earls had received the promise of support from the burghers of London. The anchors were weighed; the fleet sailed on with all confidence. The bridge was passed without hindrance, and the Earls found themselves, as they had found themselves a year before, face to face with the armies of their sovereign. But men's minds had indeed changed since the Witan of England had passed a decree of outlawry against Godwine and his house. Besides his fleet,

---

[37] 'Battle of Maldon', ed. Scragg, lines 25–41, pp. 18–19; see also D. M. Metcalf, 'Large Danegelds in Relation to War and Kingship: Their Implications for Monetary History, and Some Numismatic Evidence', in *Weapons and Warfare in Anglo-Saxon England*, ed. Hawkes, pp. 179–89, at p. 183.

[38] Abels, 'King Alfred's Peace-Making Strategies with the Vikings', p. 25, citing Reuter, 'Plunder and Tribute in the Carolingian Empire'. See also Halsall, 'Playing by Whose Rules?', pp. 2–12.

[39] ASC CD 1052. See above, pp. 44–5.

[40] See K. E. Cutler, 'Godwinist Hostages: The Case for 1051', *Annuale Mediaevale* 12 (1971), pp. 70–7.

[41] Freeman, *History of the Norman Conquest*, vol. 2, pp. 326–7.

Godwine now found himself at the head of a land force which might seem to have sprung out of the earth at his bidding. The King's troops lined the north bank of the Thames, but its southern bank was lined, at least as thickly, with men who had come together, like their brethren of the southern coasts, ready to live and die with the great Earl. The whole force of the neighbourhood, instead of obeying the King's summons, had come unsummoned to the support of Godwine, and stood ready in battle array awaiting his orders. And different indeed was the spirit of the two hosts. The Earl's men were eager for action; it needed all his eloquence, all his authority, to keep them back from jeopardising or disgracing his cause by too hasty an attack on their sovereign or their countrymen.

After a discussion of the king's side, Freeman continues the eulogy of his hero's actions:

But it was not with axe and javelin that that day's victory was to be won. The mighty voice, the speaking look and gesture, of that old man eloquent could again sway assemblies of Englishmen at his will. His irresistable tongue now pleaded with all earnestness against and hasty act of violence or disloyalty. His own con-science was clear from any lack of faithfulness; he would willingly die rather than do, or allow to be done on his behalf, any act of wrong or irreverence towards his Lord the King. The appeal was successful in every way. The eagerness of his own men was checked, and time was given for wiser counsels to resume their sway on the other side.[42]

Freeman's attributions of motives to the earl and his family seem like wishful thinking. What appears to have operated in 1052 was a sense of group solidarity, perhaps not unrelated to what Ann Williams has argued was the ability of the later Anglo-Saxon nobility to recognize and treat with one another.[43] A desire to prevent slaughter was applauded by the Church, but evidently this was more than wishful thinking and, if the context of the campaign and near-battle considered in chapters 5 and 7 are taken into account, the threat of force was not far beneath the surface.[44]

Truce, peace and peace treaties

Even though it may not always have been consciously distinguished by the bel-ligerents, some differentiation may still be made between truce and peace. While the Anglo-Saxon Chronicle records that King Alfred made peace (*frið nam*) with the Vikings at Wareham in 876,[45] Æthelweard, in his late tenth-century account of the same event, relates that Alfred made a *pactum*, backed up by money payment, with the Vikings at Wareham.[46] It may be possible to attribute Æthelweard's addition of

---

[42] Freeman, *History of the Norman Conquest*, vol. 2, pp. 328–9.

[43] Williams, *World Before Domesday*, esp. pp. 39–61.

[44] See pp. 202–7 and 297, above.

[45] ASC 876.

[46] Æthelweard, *Chronicon*, p. 41.

this treaty of some sort to his late tenth-century perception, by surmising that the nature of peacemaking changed over the course of a century. Asser specifies that Alfred 'firmly made a treaty [*foedus*] with the Vikings, the condition being that they should leave him.'[47] In this sense, there does not appear to have been a distinction of the treaty being a written one: the active component was that it was a formal agreement – as Abels has it, a contract of employment.[48] As with the Chronicle's reference to the Old English *frið*, Asser's terminology is necessarily ambiguous here – certainly he does not refer to a state of *pax*. This may have been a recognition (albeit one with hindsight) that the peace was not going to last. One important tool by which the limits of peacemaking were circumvented was the use of hostages. I have discussed the use of hostages in more detail elsewhere, and the range of ways in which they were employed was wide ranging. As Paul Kershaw and Adam Kosto observe, they were important as a symbolic indicator of prestige for late Anglo-Saxon rulers who wished to project their sense of overlordship[49] but it should also be noted that their potency lay in being a very practical tool with cross-cultural peacemaking, backed up by the not inconsequential threat of bodily violence or mutilation.[50]

The Anglo-Saxon Chronicle illustrates the transitory nature of Anglo-Saxon *frið*. It was specific to a certain context (and crucially, one might argue, expected to be so) but in the meantime, to contemporaries, it projected control: Alfred had made the peace.[51] Interestingly, in his twelfth-century account of the same events, Henry of Huntingdon translated the *frið* into a more specific sense of a truce (*induciæ*),[52] while the *Historia Regum* attributed to Simeon of Durham, again recorded in the twelfth century, related that the Vikings 'tore up' the treaty (*foedere dirupto*).[53] The latter may have been a powerful metaphor, but these accounts appear to make their own sense of the events by putting them in a twelfth-century context: there may be a concern for emphasizing the chronological limits of the peace in a manner that does not seem to appear in the Anglo-Saxon sources.

There are only three surviving documents from the Anglo-Saxon period which resemble what we might refer to as a peace treaty. However, these documents fit more properly into a tradition of Anglo-Saxon royal legislation:[54] the treaty made between Alfred and Guthrum at some point in the 880s,[55] the document known as II *Æthelred*,[56] concerning an agreement of peace between Scandinavians and

---

[47] Asser, ch. 49.

[48] Latham and Howlett, *Dictionary of Medieval Latin from British Sources*, vol. 1, fasc. 4, p. 971; Abels, 'Paying the Danegeld', pp. 173–92; see also Abels, 'Household Men, Mercenaries and Vikings'.

[49] Kershaw, *Peaceful like Solomon*; Kosto, 'Hostages in the Carolingian World'.

[50] Lavelle, 'Use and Abuse of Hostages', pp. 286–96.

[51] This was emphasized by C. E. Fell in her review of F. D. Logan, *The Vikings in History* (London, 1983), in *Slavonic and East European Review* 62 (1984), pp. 592–4, at p. 593.

[52] HH V.6, pp. 284–5.

[53] *Historia Regum*, s.a. 876, in *Symeonis Monachi Opera Omnia*, ed. Arnold, vol. 2, p. 111.

[54] Wormald, *Making of English Law*, pp. 285–6, 381–2, 321, 326.

[55] *Gesetze*, vol. 1, pp. 126–9; trans. *EHD* 1, pp. 416–17.

[56] *Gesetze*, vol. 1, pp. 220–5; trans. *EHD* 1, pp. 437–9.

English in the 990s, and the tenth-century *Ordinance of the Dunsæte*,[57] establishing frontier conditions under which contact could be made between English and Welsh. In two of these documents, the Alfred–Guthrum treaty and *Dunsæte*, priority is given to territorial jurisdiction, establishing boundaries between peoples, and all documents establish conditions under which trade and/or contact could have taken place. Such documents demonstrate that the peace was more complex than a simple statement of the cessation of hostilities. These recorded agreements cover only a very small fraction of the occasions that peace was agreed in Anglo-Saxon England, but as evidence of attempting to lay down conditions of contact between two potentially hostile groups, they most certainly should not be ignored.

Despite highly convoluted language, the prologue to the Alfred–Guthrum treaty is essentially a legitimization of territory for *both* sides. While the treaty legitimized the Danes' position in East Anglia, Alfred presided over Mercian territory and needed to augment his own legitimacy:

> This is the peace [*frið*] which King Alfred and King Guthrum and the *witan* of all the English race [*Angelcynn*] and all the people which is in East Anglia have all declared and confirmed with oaths, for themselves and for their subjects, both born and unborn, who care for God's mercy or ours.

> 1. First about our boundaries [*landgemæra*]: up the Thames, and then up the Lea, and along the Lea to its source, then straight to Bedford, then up the Ouse to Watling Street.

> 2. This is next, if a man is slain, we all permit [to be] equally dear [both] Englishman and Dane, at 8 half-marks of pure gold, except the *ceorl* who sits on [i.e. occupies] tributary land [*gafol-land*], and their [the Danes'] freedmen [*liesengum*]; these are also equally dear, both at 200 shillings.

> 3. And if a king's thegn is accused of manslaughter, if he dare clear himself, he shall do it with [the oaths of] 12 king's thegns; if a man is accused who is less powerful than a king's thegn, he shall clear himself with 12 of his equals and with one king's thegn – and likewise in every suit which is more than four mancuses – and if he dare not, he shall pay three-fold payment, according to how it is valued.

> 4. And that each man is to know his warrantor for [the purchase of] men and for horses and for oxen.

> 5. And we all declared on the day when the oaths were sworn, that no slaves nor freemen might go into the *here* without leave, none more than theirs to us. But if should happen that by necessity any of them wishes to have commerce with us, or we with them – with cattle or with goods – it is to be allowed on the condition that hostages are given as a pledge of peace [*friðe to wedde*] and as evidence that it is known that one has a clean back [i.e. that no fraud is intended].

The treaty used the dispositive language of royal law-making, implying the

---

[57] *Gesetze*, vol. 1, pp. 374–9; trans. Noble, *Offa's Dyke Reviewed*, pp. 104–9.

establishment of a *universal* peace, through God's grace and second to this, that of the king. It was the use within a lay context of religious sanction for a political peace: King Alfred was projected as the royal Christian lawmaker.[58] The Alfred–Guthrum treaty allowed both populations, the 'English' and those living in East Anglia, to be at peace in terms of feuds, as it laid out the 'blood money' values of men according to their status – the *wergild* – in clauses 2 and 3 (although the word itself is not specifically used). Here the agreement is essentially technical, treating warfare as an extended and interrelated series of feuds.[59] *Wergild* values on both sides of the treaty's border meant the integration of the Danes, at least to an extent, into Anglo-Saxon laws: private conflict became a civil matter that could be defused rather than one used as an excuse for escalation. Also, by bringing Vikings into the *wergild* system, Alfred theoretically addressed one problem: that the Vikings' seaborne attacks had frustrated Anglo-Saxon reprisal raids, which were, as Guy Halsall has suggested, one of the 'norms' of Anglo-Saxon warfare.[60] Thereby, Alfred cut a vicious circle. However, the fact that Danelaw Vikings who had agreed to the peace treaty gave aid and shelter to those involved in the Scandinavian assaults during the 890s was technically not an infringement of the treaty. The politics of such peacemaking were intricate: we cannot know of the many ways in which the bounds of law might be stretched. A century later, II *Æthelred* addressed such a problem, stating that those giving harbour to enemies within their territories would be treated as enemies themselves.[61]

R. H. C. Davis, while emphasizing the geography of the frontier laid out in the Alfred–Guthrum treaty, stressed the limited length of time in which the boundaries stood and that a collapse of the frontier in the late 880s was met with by silence in the Anglo-Saxon Chronicle.[62] D. N. Dumville refuted this, as well as Sir Frank Stenton's earlier theory that the treaty was intended to impose united 'English' kingship over all Anglo-Saxons (including those in the Danelaw),[63] advancing instead that it was an acknowledgement or even legitimization of Danish control over East Anglia and part of Mercia made soon after the battle of Edington, with the payoff for Alfred of control of other Mercian and East Saxon territory.[64] However, Abels has reasserted the 'traditional' interpretation of treaty's

[58] See Wormald, *Making of English Law*, p. 286. It must be noted Guthrum is not referred to by his baptismal name of 'Æthelstan' in the Alfred–Guthrum treaty.

[59] An interesting example of this is portrayed by Bede, *HE*, IV.22, pp. 402–5: the Mercian nobleman who had captured the Northumbrian warrior, Imma after the late seventh-century battle of the River Trent tells him 'you ought to die because all my brothers and kinsmen were killed in the battle.'

[60] Halsall, 'Playing by Whose Rules?', pp. 6–7.

[61] II *Æthelred*, ch. 1.2: *Gesetze*, vol. 1, p. 222; trans. *EHD* 1, p. 438 (see below, p. 330).

[62] R. H. C. Davis, 'Notes and Documents: Alfred and Guthrum's Frontier', *EHR* 97 (1982), pp. 803–10, at pp. 803–5; this followed on from his earlier theories in 'Alfred the Great: Propaganda and Truth'.

[63] Stenton, *Anglo-Saxon England*, 3rd edn, pp. 261–2.

[64] Dumville, *Wessex and England from Alfred to Edgar*, p. 23. However, Simon Keynes has argued for friendly relations between Wessex and Mercia in the later ninth century: 'King Alfred and the Mercians', pp. 1–45.

boundaries, associating them with the political creation of a 'buffer state' under Guthrum, as Alfred was concerned with *other* Vikings in the early 880s.[65] It can be inferred that while military strength lay temporarily with Alfred and Wessex, the treaty was not a way of the West Saxons forcing Vikings to submission, but an acknowledgement of their strategic position. Simon Keynes's discussion of the Alfred–Guthrum treaty's clauses is useful here, considering that the final clause deliberately separated the territories, *limiting*, rather than allowing trade.[66] Perhaps, as Keynes suggests, Viking raiders would try to pass themselves off as traders, but the two were probably reasonably synonymous.[67] As Abels suggests, regarding the treaty in the context of Guthrum's baptism as a remodelled Christian king, the West Saxons' intention in the Alfred–Guthrum treaty may have been to establish these Vikings as a kingdom with which they could deal as an entity, rather than separate groups.[68]

We can speculate on whether an earlier written treaty had existed immediately following the West Saxon victory in 878, however. As the use of the written word backed by religious sanction was a major political element of the Christian world into which Guthrum was allowed in 878, it did not matter whether he could actually understand the words themselves, but it did matter that the written word was invoked. As with the renegotiation of the conditions of a charter, the Alfred–Guthrum treaty in the form in which we have it may represent the treaty in its final form, having necessitated the destruction of earlier copies after a politically inspired revision.[69] In the same milieu, it is interesting that Æthelweard describes the Vikings defeated in 893 as specifically requesting 'conditions set out by treaty [*faderis*]'.[70] The Vikings are described with little respect, and one might imagine their wish to be allowed into the Christian world, in which the written word counted for something tangible. It may not be unrelated that Æthelweard added that '[d]eed and word together were completed at the same time.'[71]

II Æthelred may date from 994, when, as the Anglo-Saxon Chronicle C MS

---

[65] Abels, *Alfred the Great*, pp. 163–4. See also Abels, 'Alfred the Great, the *Micel Hæðen Here* and the Viking Threat'.

[66] Keynes and Lapidge, *Alfred the Great*, p. 313. Cf. the creation of a frontier by Charlemagne with the Slavs and Avars in his *Capitulare missorum in Theodonis villa datum secundum, generale* (AD 806), §7, in *Capitularia regum francorum* 1, ed. A. Boretius, MGH Leges 2 (Hanover, 1883), pp. 122–6; discussed by J. L. Nelson, 'Charlemagne in History', in the Graduate School for Medieval Studies day conference, *Legendary Rulers*, University of Reading, 24 June 2009.

[67] See L. Hedeager, 'Warrior Economy and Trading Economy in Viking-Age Scandinavia', *Journal of European Archaeology* 2 (1994), pp. 130–48.

[68] Abels, 'King Alfred's Peace-Making Strategies with the Vikings', p. 31.

[69] In the surviving copy of his will, King Alfred states that he had burnt the earlier versions: Keynes and Lapidge, *Alfred the Great*, p. 177. See P. J. E. Kershaw, 'The Alfred–Guthrum Treaty: Scripting Accommodation and Interaction in Viking-Age England', in *Cultures in Contact*, ed. Hadley and Richards, pp. 43–59, on the meaning of the treaty.

[70] Æthelweard, *Chronicon*, p. 49.

[71] Æthelweard, *Chronicon*, pp. 49–50.

entry for 994 records, tribute (*gafol*)of 16,000 pounds was paid to Olaf Tryggvason and Swegn Forkbeard.[72]

> Then the king and his *witan* decided to send to them and promise them tribute and provisions, if then they ceased their harrying. And they then undertook that, and all the *here* came then to Southampton and there took winter quarters; and they were fed from throughout all the kingdom of the West Saxons, and they were paid 16,000 pounds in money.
>
> Then the king sent after King Olaf Bishop Ælfheah [of Winchester] and Ealdorman Æthelweard, and meanwhile hostages were granted [*gislude*] to the ships. And they then led Olaf with much ceremony to the king at Andover, and King Æthelred stood sponsor to him at confirmation, and royally gave [gifts] to him. And then Olaf promised – just as he also fulfilled it – that he never would come back to England in hostility [*in unfriðe*].

There is no specific mention of the making of the treaty itself in any of the chronicles, however. This could indicate that such documents were not uncommon in Anglo-Saxon and Anglo-Scandinavian peacemaking (at this stage, at least). The 'world-peace' (*woroldfrið*) which is established does not set out specific geographical boundaries, but is instead concerned with having bought the allegiance of a particular force (*here*) specified in the prologue and first clause. In this respect it is interesting that the term *mal*, 'agreement', in *friðmal* and *formæl*, is likely to have been a borrowing from Old Norse,[73] perhaps indicating that it was an agreement which the Vikings subject to it were also intended to understand, or had even played a part in framing.

> These are the peace agreement [*friðmal*] and the stipulations which King Æthelred and all his *witan* have made with the *here* which Olaf and Jostein and Guthmund, Steita's son were with.

> 1. That first a world-peace [*worold-frið*] be established [*stande*] between King Æthelred with all his people and all the *here* which the king gave the tribute to, after the [?]preliminary agreement [*formæl*] which Archbishop Sigeric, Ealdorman Æthelweard and Ealdorman Ælfric made, when they asked of the king that they might purchase peace for that district [*læppa*] which, under the king, they had control [*hand*] over.

---

[72] ASC CDE 994. This was first suggested in E. V. Gordon, 'The Date of Æthelred's Treaty with the Vikings: Olaf Tryggvason and the Battle of Maldon', *Modern Language Review* 32 (1937), pp. 24–32, and later in Lund, 'Peace and Non-Peace in the Viking Age', p. 265. See T. M. Anderson, 'The Viking Policy of Ethelred the Unready' and P. Sawyer, 'Ethelred II, Olaf Tryggvason, and the Conversion of Norway', in *Anglo-Scandinavian England: Norse-English Relations in the Period Before the Conquest*, ed. J. D. Niles and M. Amodio, Old English Colloquium Series 4 (London, 1989), pp. 1–11, 17–24. See generally P. Sawyer, 'English Influence on the Development of the Norwegian Kingdom', in *Anglo-Saxons: Studies Presented to Cyril Roy Hart*, ed. S. D. Keynes and A. P. Smyth (Dublin, 2006), pp. 224–9.

[73] Bosworth-Toller, p. 666; Cleasby and Vigfusson, *Icelandic–English Dictionary*, pp. 415–16.

1.1. And if any ship-force [*sciphere*] harry in England, that we shall have the help of all of them; and we must supply them with food while they are with us.

1.2. And any of the regions which keeps peace [*friðige*] with any of those who harry England is to be an outlaw with us and with all the *here*.

2. And any merchant ship which comes into an estuary is to have peace, even if it is an unfriendly ship [*unfriðscyp*, i.e. is not subject to the treaty], so long as it is not driven [ashore].[74]

2.1. And even if it be driven [ashore], and it flees to any *friðbyrig* [i.e. a burh subject to the peace], and the men escape into the *burh*, then the men and what they bring with them are to have peace.

3. And each of the [king's] own *friðmen* is to have peace both on land and on water, both within the estuary and outside.

3.1. If King Æthelred's *friðman* comes into an unfriendly district [*unfriðland*], and the *here* comes thereto, his ship and all his goods are to have peace.

3.2. If he has drawn his ship ashore or built a cabin or pitched a tent, then he is to have peace, and all his goods.

3.3. If he bear his goods into a house in commerce with goods of unfriendly men [*unfriðmen*] he is to suffer [the loss of] his goods, and have himself peace and life, if he declares himself.

3.4. If the *friðman* flees or fights, and will not declare himself, he shall lie uncompensated, if he is slain.

4. If a man is robbed of his goods, and he knows of which ship, the steersman shall give [back] the goods, or go with four others and deny [the charge] – and he shall be himself the fifth – [proving] that he took it legally, as it was earlier agreed.

5. If an Englishman slay a Dane, freeman [slaying] free, he shall pay for him with 25 pounds, or the one who did the deed [*handdæda*] is to be given [up]. And the Dane is to do likewise to the Englishman, if he slay him.

5. If an Englishman slay a Danish slave, he shall pay for him with one pound, and the Dane likewise for an Englishman, if he slay him.

5.2. If eight men are slain, then it is the breach of the peace [*friðbrec*], within a *byrig* or outside. For less than eight men the full wergild is to be paid.

6. If the breach of the peace is made within a *byrig*, the citizens [*burhwaru*] are to go themselves and to take the slayers, alive or dead – [or] their nearest kinsmen – head for head. If they will not, the ealdorman shall go; if he will not, the king shall go; if he will not, that ealdormanry shall lie outside the peace [*on unfriðe*].

---

[74] This suggestion for *undrifen bið* follows *EHD* 1, p. 438; also possible is the alternative translation of 'provided it is not pursued', in Robertson, *Laws of the Kings of England*, p. 57.

6.1. Regarding all the slaughter and all of the harrying and regarding all the harm which was done before the peace was established, all of them shall be dismissed, and no one shall ask for either vengeance or compensation.

6.2 And that neither they nor we shall receive the other's slave, or other's thief, or other's foe.

7. And if a man of our country [*landesman*] is charged that he stole cattle or slew a man, and one ship-man [*scieðman*] and one man of this country shall make the charge, then he is then worthy of no denial.

7.1. And if their men slay eight of ours, then they shall be outlawed both by them and by us, and are to be worthy of no compensation.

7.2. Twenty-two thousand pounds of gold and silver were paid to the *here* from England for this peace.

Felix Liebermann, followed by Dorothy Whitelock, saw this as primarily an agreement outlining trade conditions,[75] but, by contrast, Lund considers the treaty to have been one with which Æthelred tried to keep the foreign warriors who had taken his service under 'as peaceful conditions as possible', though accepting that he had few means of enforcing the agreement.[76] In both senses, however, it was a code of law that recognized the political *status quo*, and was essentially a political document. In contrast to the Alfred–Guthrum treaty's invocation of divine grace, II *Æthelred* has no such prologue and uses entirely secular language. Here, conversion does not seem to have been a prerequisite for written peace between Christians and Vikings. This certainly does not imply that the religious preamble had become an anachronistic relic in the composition of a political treaty over the course of a century, however, but it may imply that it was significant when it was used. By this time, the evidentiary document had emerged in Anglo-Saxon diplomatic, in the form of the writ, and II *Æthelred* could be seen in a similar milieu. The document is not the peace itself, but, as the prologue puts it, it records the 'the peace agreement and the stipulations' (*ða friðmal 7 ða forword*), a somewhat more tempered reality than stating 'this is the peace' (*ðis is ðæt frið*) in the manner of the Alfred–Guthrum treaty's prologue. Whitelock has suggested that the term 'world-peace' (*woroldfrið*) used in II *Æthelred* (ch. 1) may have specifically set this treaty out as a wholly secular document.[77] As a recognition of political reality at the end of the tenth century, this was a far cry from the concept of 'world peace' as envisaged in the twentieth century.

II *Æthelred* attempts to create a *tabula rasa* regarding *wergild*, with its statement that all 'slaughter and harrying' committed before the establishment of the peace 'are to be dismissed, and no one is to avenge it or ask for compensation' (ch. 6.1). While that might be considered a somewhat vain hope, this emphasizes

---

[75] *Gesetze*, vol. 3, pp. 149–50; *EHD 1*, p. 437.

[76] Lund, 'Peace and Non-Peace in the Viking Age', p. 268. See also Abels, 'Household Men, Mercenaries and Vikings', pp. 155–6.

[77] *EHD 1*, p. 437.

the document as a political act of peacemaking: in a sense, the king became the personification of justice and took responsibility for it himself.[78]

By contrast, however, the *Dunsæte* agreement might be seen as quite realistic regarding Anglo-Welsh relations, for example in clause 5 considering cross-border *wergild* to have been to be worth only half of what it would otherwise be. Some illustrative extracts warrant reproduction here:[79]

> 5. If a Welshman slays an Englishman, he need not pay over to his side more than half the wergild; no more than an Englishman for a Welshman on the other side, whether he be thegn-born or *ceorl*-born; half the the *wergild* falls away.

> 6. Neither is a Welshman to cross over into English land, nor an Englishman into Welsh without the appointed men from that land [*landmen*], who shall meet him at the bank and bring him back there again without deceit.

> 6.1. If the *landman* be an accessory to any deceit, then he is guilty of the punishment, unless he clear himself of that witnessing

> 6.2. So also, let all who be an accessory or involved, when a foreign man harms a native, clear himself of the involvement, according to the value of the property: and that must be [with a] select oath; and he who accuses him must begin his case with a preliminary oath.

> ...

> 9. Formerly the *Wentsæte* were subject to the *Dunsæte*; but more correctly they are subject to the West Saxons; and they shall send tribute and hostages there.

> 9.1. The *Dunsæte* also need, if the king grant to them, that they be allowed hostages for peace [*friðgislas*].

As may be seen from these clauses, *Dunsæte* might, like *II Æthelred*, be a realistic appreciation of an inability to impose justice upon a group over whom jurisdiction was necessarily limited. *Dunsæte* is also concerned with the establishment of conditions under which cattle raiders could be pursued.[80] These conditions are strict, and are actually given more attention than *wergild*. They are arguably given more priority, being dealt with in the first of the clauses of the lawcode with some detailed subclauses (chs 1, 1.1, and 1.2). The attention to cattle-raiding shows some attempt to limit friction from what was probably a constant problem and to establish the boundaries between war, peace and trade.

Dunsæte is somewhat different from *II Æthelred*, as the West Saxons were probably the dominant force: during the ninth and tenth centuries they often compelled Welsh/British submission, such as with Athelstan's peace at Eamont

---

[78] For similar settlements made between the Danes and continental Saxons, see *AF* 873, discussed in Abels, 'Paying the Danegeld', pp. 185–6. I am grateful to Richard Abels for this reference.

[79] *Gesetze*, vol. I, pp. 376–9.

[80] This is suggested by Noble, *Offa's Dyke Reviewed*, pp. 85–6; see also Davies, *Wales in the Early Middle Ages*, pp. 39, 135–6.

in 926, which may have been the historical context of this agreement.[81] However, *Dunsæte* does not seem to have been the result of a major battle (at least none are recorded) and it simply sets itself as an agreement (*ge{ræ}dnes*), perhaps reflecting the status of a regional, 'West Saxon', rather than 'Anglo-Saxon' or 'English' concern.[82] *Dunsæte* is not peace defined as an absence of war, but as political agreement. Clearly, however, it is concerned with the conduct of two groups of people across a jurisdictional boundary.

For a document produced under conditions of domination and submission, *Dunsæte* might at first appear to have been almost even-handed, concerned with the *wergilds* of both English and Welsh in clause 5, respecting each other's territory in clause 6 and allowing the people of the Dunsæte 'hostages for peace' (*friðgislas*) from the *Wentsæte* (probably the people of Gwent) in the final clause (ch. 9.1), 'if the [West Saxon] king grant to them' (*gif heom se cyning an*). Nevertheless, the document's apparent magnanimous equality from a West Saxon dictation may conversely show that while a peace agreement could be well-contrived, in practice the more powerful group held dominance: clause 9.1 indicates that the West Saxons seem to have taken the lion's share of domination over the *Wentsæte*.

In all these agreements, however, there was a common element. By regulating contact and defining specific boundaries, the leaders were actually defining themselves and their jurisdictional territory. Peace had a political agenda beyond the words of the treaty itself.

Summary

Throughout the whole Anglo-Saxon period there may have been normative codes of conduct which were relatively acceptable, applicable, and transgressed only rarely. The fact that the subject of peace is considered in one of the shorter chapters of this volume should not be allowed to overshadow its importance in this period; it is more a reflection of the limits of the scholarship on the issue than the limits of the issue itself. Peace and agreement, negotiation and declarations of fidelity were ritual activities: the nature of political peace could be as complex as the philosophical concepts of peace, and it was defined with similar complexity by those involved. The reality of peace agreement in this period reflects this. Just as Anglo-Saxon warfare worked as a ritualized concept, and could be of a differing scale, then the settlement of warfare, the 'art of peacemaking', was a practice that followed a set of political rituals. Peace could be imposed, as overlordship, or

---

[81] ASC D 927. However, this is questioned in Davies, *Wales in the Early Middle Ages*, p. 205. A paper by Alex Woolf, '"Anglo-Saxon, Norse, and Celtic": The Ordinance Concerning the Dunsaete' delivered at the International Medieval Congress, University of Leeds, 16 July 2009, made a good case for a mid-eleventh-century context on the basis of the interests of the earldom of Wessex in south Wales during this period.

[82] Wormald, in *Making of English Law*, p. 382, considers it to have been 'most like a (very) local example of the sort of initiative so strongly encouraged by Æthelstan's government and its successors.' This notion has been explored by M. Fordham, 'Peacekeeping and Order on the Anglo-Welsh Frontier in the Early Tenth Century', *Midland History* 32 (2007), pp. 1–18. See also Lavelle, 'Use and Abuse of Hostages', pp. 291–2.

settled on an equal basis. The implications of overlordship in peacemaking meant that codes of submission developed which could be used to portray peace as an 'imperial' concept, including hostage-exchange and the use of the written treaty. Such quasi-propaganda was augmented by a use of Christian imagery within peacemaking, especially if this entailed the baptism of a heathen leader.[83] At a more fundamental level, there were necessary limitations on Anglo-Saxon (as well as Anglo-Scandinavian and perhaps Anglo-Celtic) warfare, that were politically exploited, but nonetheless allowed social and political survival.

It has been necessary to refer to warfare as often as peace in this chapter, but I hope that, by doing so, some movement has been made towards a political con-textualization of Anglo-Saxon peacemaking and peace agreements. In contrast to Wallace-Hadrill's interpretation outlined at the beginning of this chapter, Anglo-Saxon peacemaking was certainly more than simply the creation of an absence of war. Contemporaries recognized that political peace could be as complex and hold as many implications as the philosophical peace of the Christian West: peace carried its own connotations and also had rational aims which could be strategic in their scope. Anglo-Saxon elites, especially kings, made active use of such peace within a political context.

---

[83] For this issue, see J. H. Lynch, *Christianizing Kinship: Ritual Sponsorship in Anglo-Saxon England* (Ithaca, NY, 1998).

✦ 9 ✦

Conclusions

THE death of the Anglo-Saxon kingdom on the battlefield of Hastings on
14 October 1066 is thought, with some justification, to have been the nadir
of the English state and, famously, of its military system. However, catastrophic
though the defeat may have been for many of the warriors who responded to the
royal summons at this low moment or even for those who responded at the times
of the defeats of the Æthelredian state by the armies of Thorkell the Tall and
Swein Forkeard, it can hardly be said that the military system did not function.
The vastly less auspicious circumstances of 1094 stand in sharp contrast to those
of 1066 and 1013–16. In 1094 the royal minister Ranulf Flambard summoned the
fyrd, and, pocketing ten shillings of the money brought by each warrior, promptly
dismissed them to use it to pay for mercenaries.[1] Mercenaries were, of course, very
flexible in the way they could be employed, with the added bonus that, as they
were to be both contracted and were to serve on the Continent, transport was not
needed to take them across the English Channel.[2]

It is unlikely that the force summoned in 1094, if indeed it can be called a force,
was composed purely and simply of warriors of 'English' descent. Moreover, it is
of no use arguing that such warriors were simply not of good enough quality to
fight for William II. English warriors had fought for William I in Maine in 1073,
in an 'English and French force [here]', in which the English participation (singled
out for damage to the county), led to Maine's surrender to William.[3] A generation
after 1066, 'English' was a term that could be used to describe those from Franco-
Norman families who were settled in England as much as those who were of pre-
Conquest English descent. It is likely that the warriors of 1094 were those holders
of lands (presumably, though not certainly, of multiples of five hides), from whom
a canny administrator could assert an obligation to provide military service in the
form of monetary payments. After all, notwithstanding David Roffe's controversial argument that Flambard provided the brains behind the writing of Domesday
Book,[4] the Domesday account was very clear about the monetary contribution
which groups of five hides of land could provide. This, more than a record of aristocratic obligation before 1066, had been an evident purpose of the 1086 survey;
thus the levying of taxes was allowed without the need to admit that it was taking
place. It is is open to debate whether or not all twenty-thousand of the warriors

---

[1] ASC 1094 and JW vol. 3, s.a. 1094, pp. 72–3. Above, p. 60.

[2] For a consideration of the policy of hiring mercenaries and its consequences, see J. R.
Maddicott, 'Responses to the Threat of Invasion, 1085', *EHR* 122 (2007), pp. 986–97.

[3] ASC DE 1073.

[4] Roffe, *Domesday: The Inquest and the Book*, pp. 246–8.

reached the sea *en masse*, paid up and went home, as asserted by the Anglo-Saxon Chronicle, followed by John of Worcester, but it seems likely that, as with the king's right to administer vacant bishoprics, another Flambardian abuse, the system was being used as a very profitable *Milchcow*. Had the Chronicler reread the earlier, Æthelredian entries of the Anglo-Saxon Chronicle, he would have been aware that the ten-thousand pounds raised by the 1094 levy once had the buying power for the (temporary) services of a substantial Viking force.[5]

However, the 1094 entry of the Chronicle shows the limits of a system which, while it may have been effective while the English kingdom was limited to the coastal bounds of Britain with occasional jaunts to Ireland, Normandy, and Scandinavia so long as rich pickings were promised, could not be employed to shuffle resources from one part of the Anglo-Norman realm to another. We have seen how military obligations were reassessed during the ninth century, probably under Alfred, and the systems we see at the eve of the Norman Conquest seem to have been relatively effective so long as defences could be organized within England itself. However, insofar as the resources – including military resources – of the English kingdom were a reason for the success of the Norman Conquest, the military systems of the kingdom could be said to have been a victim of that success. It may appear perverse to follow the argument that the Norman Conquest was a war of dynastic succession, but in its initial phases it was just that,[6] undertaken in a similar way to that in which the Angevin realm of Henry II was the successor to the Anglo-Norman state. If the control of the English kingdom gave the Norman ducal dynasty the heavyweight punch it desired after 1066, then, to take the point to its logical conclusion, it may be said that the Anglo-Norman realm was the last stage in the Carolingianesque development of the Anglo-Saxon kingdom as envisaged by Alfred the Great and his successors. However, as happened with the Carolingians, the snowball stopped rolling.[7] The military system available to the Anglo-Norman realm had its limits.

But to project the administrative abuse of 1094 and even the defeat of 1066 onto the military systems available for the pre-Conquest English kingdom is to undermine the achievements of the state as it stood before 1066. The West Saxon kingdom under Alfred could be organized to meet a tangible threat, using systems which had existed since before the Viking Age but modifying those systems as circumstances required. Whether the burghal system, for example, was quite as well organized as a maximal reading of the Burghal Hidage would suggest is debatable, of course, but a working system of fortifications certainly existed in parts of ninth- and early tenth-century England, whose effectiveness could be said to have

---

[5] ASC CDE 994, notwithstanding discussion of the validity of these figures (above, p. 144, n. 14).

[6] I am grateful to Matt Bennett for raising this issue for me. This notion is alluded to in M. Bennett, *Campaigns of the Norman Conquest*, Essential Histories (Oxford, 2001); see also the questions on the subject raised by D. Matthew, *Britain and the Continent, 1000–1300: The Impact of the Norman Conquest*, Britain and Europe (London, 2005), pp. 26–36.

[7] The metaphor was used by Mary Garrison on *In Our Time: The Carolingian Renaissance*, BBC Radio 4, broadcast 30 March 2006.

echoed down to the later Anglo-Saxon period. Similarly, an early English state of the tenth century can be seen to have been aggressive against its neighbours in the manner in which the pre-Viking kingdoms used warfare against their neighbours as a means of enhancing aristocratic prestige and cohesion. The West Saxon and subsequently English kingdoms' wars against their neighbours may not have been on the scale of the wars of plunder of the Carolingian empire, made famous in Tim Reuter's classic study,[8] but the intention was certainly there. To this end, the potential for the projection of defence *and* aggression through naval power is certainly noteworthy. Attention was paid to the fighting of battles, too. They may not always have arisen from 'battle-seeking strategies' *per se*, but the later Anglo-Saxon sources highlight the significance of military victories in battle, and there is an evident recognition that battles could be decisive. Finally, the making of peace was a significant tool for the later Anglo-Saxons, and a recognition that peace could be made, where necessary, for strategic ends, and a realistic recognition of its limits shows a sophisticated understanding of political thought.

Æthelweard, the tenth-century ealdorman introduced at the beginning of this volume and brought in to illustrate points in a number of chapters, thus stands as a figure who was able to look back across the Anglo-Saxons' defeats and successes in the early Viking Age and the tenth-century conquest of England by his West Saxon forebears. If, while writing his *Chronicon*, he did not anticipate what would become disasters in Æthelred II's reign, he was to experience some of them. While the possible unease which Æthelweard may have felt in the 970s and early 980s, which I have highlighted in chapter 1, may be overplayed, he was certainly a high-ranking figure who understood the tensions and the dynamics with which warfare in the Viking Age operated.

This high rank is important. We cannot know the thoughts, trials and tribulations of the high reeves, who ranked lower than ealdormen but in whose hands Anglo-Saxon defence often seemed to devolve in the later Viking Age; nor can we get down to the individual soldier's experience in the manner of the 'new' military history. But in some ways it would be inappropriate to believe that addressing such experiences would democratize our picture of late Anglo-Saxon warfare. 'Ordinary' people were participants in warfare, it must be said. This is apparent by the manner in which campaigns could range across the countryside, which show us the everyday dangers of the Viking Age (although those dangers could be exaggerated);[9] the ordinary participation in warfare presumably also included that of townspeople and those who lived around towns who may have found themselves perched on a parapet throwing stones at snarling Vikings below or, if the *Fragmentary Annals* are to be believed, boiling beer or collecting beehives to throw down, or those with obligations on an estate may have found themselves trailing far from home, driving carts with the range of supplies necessary

---

[8] Reuter, 'Plunder and Tribute in the Carolingian Empire'.

[9] I owe to Tim Reuter the observations, made at a seminar held by the former Wessex Medieval Centre, that the progress of a campaign could easily bypass areas of population, and that in a north-west European economy crops destroyed could be grown again the following year without having to re-establish entire agrarian infrastructures.

for warfare, an experience of battle of sorts. But the sharp end of warfare was an aristocratic experience. Thus it is appropriate to cite an ealdorman as representative of this experience. While, as Stephen Baxter has observed, we do not even know if Æthelweard proved a good military leader[10] (and, in all fairness, there is nothing in his *Chronicon* which suggests that he thought of himself as such), an ealdorman still stood not only as a loyal retainer of the king, but also as a man who commanded his own retinue. Ealdormen thus had responsibilities in, and interests in, the successful prosecution of large-scale campaigns and – with some notable exceptions[11] – in victory in pitched battle. The late Anglo-Saxon state was also about the detail of the organization for war and the organization of defences. While we should acknowledge that the system had limitations and that the personal politics of the agencies of the state brought those limitations into sharp relief, especially but not only during the reign of Æthelred II, it was the intricacies of that system at work, the details of its operation, which show us the interplay between late Anglo-Saxon society, politics and the prosecution of warfare during the Viking Age. The Anglo-Saxon state made war, but although the kingdom was seized in a battle, the state was not destroyed by war. Viking Age warfare made the English state.

[10] Baxter, *Earls of Mercia*, pp. 84–5.
[11] E.g. ASC CDE 1003.

A chronology of key events and military campaigns from the ninth to eleventh centuries

For the sake of simplicity regnal dates of only the West Saxon and, subsequently, English dynasty have been given here. For details of other kings and kingdoms, see S. Keynes, 'Rulers of the English, *c*. 450–1066', in *The Blackwell Encyclopaedia of Anglo-Saxon England*, ed M. Lapidge *et al.* (Oxford, 1999), pp. 500–20. Most of the events referred to here are recorded in the Anglo-Saxon Chronicle; for more events concerning Anglo-Welsh relations recorded in the *Annales Cambriae*, see above, pp. 26–9.

c. 789	First recorded Viking raid in Wessex, at Portland (Dors.)
793	Viking raid on Northumbrian monastery of Lindisfarne
802–39	Reign of King Egbert
825	Battle of *Ellendun* (Wroughton, Wilts.) between Egbert and Beornwulf, King of Mercians; West Saxon victory and emergence of West Saxon domination of southern England
829	Declaration of Egbert as *Bretwalda* ('ruler of Britain'); temporary West Saxon dominance over Mercian and Northumbrian kingdoms
835	Viking raid on Sheppey (Kent)
836	Battle at Carhampton (Devon); Viking victory
838	West Saxon defeat of combined Viking and Cornish force at Hingston Down (Cornwall)
839–58	Reign of King Æthelwulf (of eastern Wessex only after trip to Rome in 855–6)
840	West Saxon victory at Southampton against Vikings; defeat of men of Dorset at Portland, resulting in the death of Ealdorman Æthelhelm
841	Death of Ealdorman Hereberht of Kent at the hands of Vikings at Romney Marsh
842	'Great slaughter' at London and Rochester (Kent)
855–60	Reign of King Æthelbald over western Wessex
858–60	Reign of King Æthelbert over eastern Wessex (having ruled during Æthelwulf's absence, 855–6)
860–6	Reign of King Æthelbert over all Wessex
866–71	Reign of King Æthelred I
868	West Saxon and Mercian siege of Viking forces at Nottingham; peace made

871	'Year of Nine Battles' between West Saxons and Vikings, including Viking victory at Reading (Berks.) and West Saxon victory at Ashdown (on Berkshire Downs, location unknown)
871–99	Reign of King Alfred 'the Great'
874–5	Viking force overwinters at Repton (Derbys.), holding Mercian kingdom
876	Peace treaty made with Viking force at Wareham (Dors.), lasting until their departure by night for Exeter (Devon); Vikings in Northumbria 'share out' the kingdom between themselves
878	Viking force dispossesses Alfred of Wessex by seizing Chippenham (Wilts.); Alfred gathers armies at *Ethandun* (Edington, Wilts.); following West Saxon victory and siege of defeated force, the leader Guthrum and his chief men are converted to Christianity under Alfred
880–5	Settlement of Vikings in East Anglia; activities of another Viking force in Francia
885	Arrival of Viking force from Francia in Rochester (Kent); West Saxon relief force compels some Vikings to retreat to Continent and others to make peace; Alfred sends (?punitive) naval force into East Anglia, which, after initial success, is defeated
886	Alfred occupies London, entrusting it to Ealdorman Æthelred of Mercia
892	Viking force storms unfinished fortress in *Andredesweald* (Kent, location unknown); Viking fleets build fortresses at Milton and Appledore (Kent)
893	Alfred leads force against the two Viking armies, intercepting one at Farnham (Surrey); West Saxon siege of the force called off due to the limits of service; West Saxons seize a Viking fortress at Benfleet (Essex) and relieve a siege of Exeter (Devon); Vikings besieged by West Saxon, Mercian and Welsh forces at Buttington (now in Powys) and, later, Chester
894	Vikings go to Mersea (Essex) from Chester via Wales and Northumbria; Vikings from Exeter ravage Sussex but are defeated
895	Campaigns against Viking fortress on River Lea; Vikings encamp at Bridgnorth (Salop.)
896	Viking force divides between East Anglia, Northumbria and Francia; West Saxon coast suffers piratical attacks; newly built West Saxon vessels see mixed results in combat
899–924	Reign of King Edward 'the Elder' over 'Kingdom of the Anglo-Saxons'
899/900	Seizure of Wimborne (Dors.) and *Twinham* (now Christchurch, Dors.) by Æthelwold, ætheling, cousin of King Edward, who goes to Northumbria, receiving submission, after Edward responds by taking Badbury Rings
902	Æthelwold receives submission of Essex
903	East Anglian force with Æthelwold harries across Mercia; Edward responds by harrying across East Anglia; Kentish force meets Æthelwold's army at 'the Holme', where Æthelwold, amongst others, is killed
906	Edward makes peace with East Angles and Northumbrians at Tiddingford (Beds.)
909	West Saxon and Mercian force ravages Northumbria for five weeks

910	West Saxon and Mercian force defeats a raiding Northumbrian force at Tettenhall (Staffs.); Viking army from Brittany arrives in River Severn; burh built by Æthelflæd at *Bremesbyrig*
911	Death of Æthelred, ealdorman (or 'lord') of the Mercians
912	Burhs built at Hertford (Herts.), Witham (Essex), *Sceregeat*, and Bridgnorth (Salop.)
913	Raids from east midlands against Hook Norton (Oxon.) and Luton (Beds.)
914	Raiding force arrives in Severn from Brittany, ravaging in Wales and borders; Vikings besieged until they leave for Ireland via Dyfed; burhs built at Buckingham; Edward receives submission from men of Bedford and Northampton
915	Æthelflæd builds burhs at Chirbury (Salop.), *Weardbyrig*, and Runcorn (Ches.)
916	Edward builds burh at Maldon (Essex); Æthelflæd sends a force into Wales, which destroys *Brecananmere*, on Llangorse Lake, Brecon
917	Edward builds burhs at Towcester (Northants) and *Wigingamere*; Viking force from Northampton, Leicester 'and north of these places' (ASC) attacks Towcester and ravages part of Bucks. and Oxon.; another Viking force builds fortress at Tempsford (Beds.), ravaging as far as Bedford; Tempsford later stormed by an Anglo-Saxon force; yet another Viking force, from East Anglia and Mercia besieges *Wigingamere* with limited success; Anglo-Saxon force seizes burh at Colchester (Essex), later repairing it; Viking force besieges Maldon without success; Anglo-Saxon forces seize and restore burh at Huntingdon; Edward receives submission from various Viking forces in eastern England
918	Edward builds burh at Stamford (Lincs.) to force submission of the inhabitants of the existing burh; Æthelflæd receives submission of inhabitants of Leicester and negotiates control of York but dies soon after in Tamworth (Staffs.); occupying Tamworth, Edward receives submission of Æthelflæd's Mercian subjects and Welsh rulers; capturing and repairing the burh at Nottingham, Edward receives submission of remaining Mercians
919	Edward builds burh at Thelwall (Ches.) and seizes Manchester; Ælfwyn, daughter (and probable successor) of Æthelred and Æthelflæd, 'deprived of all authority in Mercia and taken into Wessex' (ASC MR)
920	Edward builds second burh at Nottingham, as well as burh at Bakewell (Derbys.), receiving submission of (or coming to agreement with) northern rulers
921	Edward builds burh at *Cledemutha*
924–39	Reign of King Athelstan over kingdom of the English
926	Marriage of Athelstan's sister to Sihtric of Northumbria
927	Death of Sihtric; Guthfrith Sihtricson driven from York by Athelstan, who takes the Northumbrian kingdom; peace agreement between Athelstan and other rulers of Britain at Eamont (near Penrith, Cumbria)
934	Athelstan ravages Scotland with land and naval force

937	Battle of *Brunanburh* between Anglo-Saxon forces and combined Celtic-Norse force, resulting in Anglo-Saxon victory
939–46	Reign of King Edmund
940	Northumbrians break peace agreement, choosing a Hiberno-Norse ruler, Olaf Guthfrithson, who seizes Mercian territory in east midlands but dies in 941, on a raid in Lothian
942	Edmund retakes Mercian territory from Olaf Sihtricson, ruler of York
943	Edmund makes peace with Olaf, standing sponsor at his baptism
944	Edmund takes Northumbria, driving Kings Ragnall and Olaf from York
945	Edmund ravages the kingdom of Strathclyde, granting it to Malcolm, King of Scots
946	Edmund stabbed to death at Pucklechurch (Glos.) while protecting his steward
946–55	Reign of King Eadred
947	Eadred receives Northumbrian submission at Tanshelf (Yorks.)
948	Northumbrian acceptance of Erik Bloodaxe as king results in a ravaging expedition by Eadred in which the minster at Ripon (Yorks.) is burnt by the English; Northumbrians defeat English army at Castleford (Yorks.); Eadred's threats force Northumbrians to desert Erik and pay compensation
949	Olaf Sihtricson takes Northumbrian kingship
952	Imprisonment of Archbishop Wulfstan of York by Eadred; Eadred orders slaughter of the inhabitants of the burh of Thetford (Norfolk) in response to the killing of the Abbot of ?St Augustine's Canterbury; Olaf driven from Northumbria; Erik Bloodaxe accepted as king again
954	Erik Bloodaxe driven from Northumbria; Eadred succeeds to the kingdom
955–9	Reign of King Eadwig
957	Edgar succeeds to Mercia and Northumbria; Eadwig continues as ruler of Wessex
959–75	Reign of King Edgar over entire English kingdom
964	Secular clergy expelled from Old Minster Winchester and other monasteries
969	Edgar orders ravaging of Isle of Thanet in response to robbing of York merchants
973	Recrowning of Edgar at Bath (Som.); meeting with other British kings at Chester
975–8	Reign of King Edward 'the Martyr'
978	Murder of Edward at Corfe (Dors.); succession of Æthelred
978–1016	Reign of King Æthelred II, 'the Unready'
980	Vikings attack Southampton, Thanet and Cheshire
981	Vikings raid St Petroc's Monastery, Padstow (Cornwall); coastal raids on Devon and Cornwall
982	Viking raid on Portland (Dors.)
986	Lands of Rochester diocese laid waste by Æthelred

988	Battle against Vikings at Watchet (Som.)
991	Viking fleet active along Kent coast, landing at Maldon (Essex), via Ipswich (Suffolk); death of Ealdorman Byrhtnoth of Essex in battle at Maldon; peace made and 10,000 pounds payment to Vikings recorded in ASC
992	Attempt to muster a navy from London; Ælfric, ealdorman of Hants., betrays plan
993	Bamburgh attacked (probably by Vikings); Viking fleet ravages in Lindsey and Northumbria, from the Humber mouth
994	Attack on London; ravaging on coast and Essex, Kent, Sussex, Hants.; Vikings winter in Southampton; 16,000 pounds' tribute recorded; probable date of peace treaty *II Æthelred*, agreed with Norwegian Viking leader Olaf Tryggvason
997	Viking force ravages around Watchet (Som.), as well as in Cornwall, Wales, and Devon; Viking attack on burh at Lydford and Tavistock Abbey (Devon)
998	Ravaging in Dorset; Vikings encamp on Isle of Wight, receiving supplies from Hants. and Sussex
999	Vikings defeat Kentish army at Rochester and ravage west Kent
1000	Viking force in Normandy; Æthelred ravages Cumbria, Strathclyde, and Isle of Man, and perhaps also sends force to attack Cotentin region of Normandy
1001	Ravaging by Vikings 'almost everywhere' (ASC); Hants. force defeated at *Æthelingadene* (East and West Dean, Sussex); Vikings ravage around Exeter (Devon), burning nearby manors and fighting an English force at Pinhoe; Vikings encamp on Isle of Wight, burning manors, probably in Hants.
1002	24,000 pounds tribute recorded; massacre of Danes in England ordered by King Æthelred on St Brice's Day (13 Nov.)
1003	Exeter stormed and destroyed by Vikings; Vikings under Swein Forkbeard, King of Denmark, attack Wilton (Wilts.) after Ealdorman Ælfric fails to lead English army
1004	Vikings attack and burn Norwich; peace agreement fails and Thetford (Norfolk) is burnt by Vikings
1006	Vikings attack and burn Sandwich (Kent) after political upheaval in English kingdom; Vikings encamp on Isle of Wight, ravaging in Hants. and Berks., and burning Wallingford (now in Oxon.), before issuing a challenge at Scutchamer Knob (now Oxon.), which results in English defeat on River Kennet; peace and tribute arranged by Æthelred; Uhtred of Bamburgh victorious against Scots at Durham
1007	36,000 pounds tribute recorded
1008	Military reorganization in England ordered by Æthelred
1009	English fleet brought together at Sandwich; Wulfnoth *Cild* accused of crimes and so ravages south coast; storm destroys English ships sent in pursuit; people of eastern Kent sue for peace with Thorkell the Tall ('3,000 pounds') but Vikings ravage in Sussex, Hants. and Berks. from Isle of Wight; unsuccessful English attempt to intercept Vikings; Vikings winter on Thames

1010   Unsuccessful attack on London by Vikings; burning Oxford; Vikings repair ships in Kent during spring; unsuccessful resistance at *Ringmere* (prob. in Norfolk) by the men of Cambs. results in Viking ravaging in East Anglia, burning Thetford and Cambridge; burning in Bucks., Oxon., Northants., and Wilts.

1011   Peace agreed in return for tribute and provisions for Vikings; Thorkell's army besiege and ransack Canterbury, taking captive Archbishop Ælfheah and others

1012   Martyrdom of Ælfheah by Vikings; peace and tribute at '48,000 pounds'; Thorkell takes service with Æthelred

1013   Swein returns to England, with his son, Cnut; Swein acclaimed king at Gainsborough (Lincs.), receiving submission from Northumbria and much of rest of England; Swein fails to capture London; submission of western nobles at Bath (Som.), followed by submission of London; exile of the royal family; Thorkell demands tribute and provisions at Greenwich, but ravages anyway

1014   Death of Swein; acclamation of King Cnut amongst Danes; return of Æthelred, who ravages Lindsey where Cnut was staying; English hostages mutilated by Cnut; 21,000 pounds recorded as payment to Thorkell's army at Greenwich

1015   Edmund (later 'Ironside') ætheling rebels against his father, receiving the submission of the Five Boroughs (Lincoln, Nottingham, Derby, Leicester, Stamford); Cnut ravages in Dorset, Wilts. and Som. while Æthelred lies ill; Ealdorman Eadric of Mercia allies with Cnut

1016 (Apr.–Nov.) Reign of King Edmund 'Ironside'

1016   Cnut enters Mercia, ravaging and burning; Edmund and Earl Uhtred ravage in north-west England; Cnut ravages much of eastern England into Northumbria to York; Earl Uhtred submits to Cnut and is murdered; death of Æthelred 23 April; succeeded by Edmund; battles at Penselwood (Som.) and Sherston (Wilts.); Edmund relieves London and defeats Vikings at Brentford (Essex); Vikings attack London again and ravage Mercia, returning to Kent; Vikings set out to Mercia but are intercepted at *Assandun* (Essex, location unknown), where Cnut is victorious and many English nobles killed; peace agreement between Cnut and Edmund at Alney by Deerhurst (Glos.); payment to Danes and separation of kingdom between Wessex and Mercia agreed; London buys peace from Cnut; King Edmund dies 30 Nov.

1016–35 Reign of King Cnut 'the Great'

1018   Payment of '72,000 pounds' recorded; Northumbrian force defeated by Scots at Carham on the River Tweed *c.* 1018, resulting in Scottish control of Lothian

1023   Relics of St Ælfheah transferred from London to Canterbury

1026   Battle at 'Holy River' (location unknown) in Scandinavia; Cnut's Anglo-Danish force defeated by Swedes

1027   Expedition to Scotland by Cnut, who receives submission

1028   Cnut conquers Norway with large fleet which includes English thegns

1030   King Olaf of Norway returns; is defeated at Stiklestad (in Trondelag, Norway)

1035	Death of Cnut; succession dispute between his sons; Harold 'Harefoot' chosen as regent north of the Thames; Wessex controlled by Emma-Ælfgifu, Harthacnut's mother
1036	Alfred and Edward, sons of Æthelred II, come from Normandy to Wessex; Alfred captured and blinded by Earl Godwine of Wessex, resulting in Alfred's death
1037–40	Reign of King Harold I, 'Harefoot'
1039	Rise to Welsh dominance of Gruffudd ap Llywellyn King of Gwynedd; Edwin, brother of Earl Leofric of Mercia, killed by Welsh
1040–42	Reign of King Harthacnut
1040	High tax imposed on English kingdom, probably to pay for a fleet
1041	Harthacnut's housecarls ravage Worcs.
1042–66	Reign of King Edward 'the Confessor'
1045	Fleet gathered by Edward at Sandwich (Kent) against the threat of Magnus of Norway
1046	Swein Godwineson allies with Gruffudd, in expedition into Wales; Swein kidnaps abbess of Leominster (Herefords.)
1047	Swein of Denmark requests help from an English fleet against Magnus of Norway
1048	Viking fleet successfully raids Sandwich but is driven from the Isle of Thanet, before ravaging Essex and selling plunder in Flanders
1049	English fleet sent to Sandwich, in response to a request from the German king and Roman Emperor Henry III for aid against the count of Flanders; Osgot Clapa, an exiled nobleman, attacks the Naze (Essex)
1051	Abolition of payments of *heregeld*; Earl Godwine's refusal to punish the townspeople of Dover for the killing of Count Eustace of Boulogne results in the exile of the earl and his family
1052	Godwine and Harold launch raids on the southern coast of England, while Gruffudd ravages Herefords.; confrontation on the Thames results in the reconciliation of the king and his earls
1053	Many English watchmen (*weardmen*) killed by Welsh at Westbury (?-on-Severn, Glos.)
1054	Earl Siward of Northumbria launches an expedition into Scotland, winning battle with King Macbeth
1055	At Hereford, Welsh and Irish force headed by King Gruffudd and Earl Ælfgar, then outlawed earl of East Anglia, routs English force led by Earl Ralph of Hereford; Earl Harold of Wessex leads a force in retaliation, (re-)fortifying Hereford
1056	Bishop Leofgar of Hereford killed while campaigning against Gruffudd
1057	Arrival in England and death of Edward, the exiled son of King Edmund Ironside
1058	Earl Ælfgar banished but returns allied with Gruffudd; Viking raid, probably on northern England, from Norway

1063   Earl Harold burns Rhuddlan (Clwyd), residence of Gruffudd; later sails fleet around Wales to receive submission; Gruffudd killed by his own men

1065   Caradoc ap Gruffudd launches raid against Earl Harold's residence at Porteskewitt (Gwent).; Northumbrians depose Earl Tostig; Morcar, brother of Earl Edwin of Mercia, appointed earl of Northumbria; Northumbrians ravage Northampton, where a royal council had been held

1066 (Jan.–Oct.) Reign of King Harold II

1066   Death of King Edward and accession of Earl Harold; invasions of English kingdom by Norwegian force led by King Harold 'Hardrada' of Norway and Norman-French force led by Duke William 'the Bastard' of Normandy; battles of Gate Fulford and Stamford Bridge (both Yorks.) between English and Norwegian armies; death at Stamford Bridge of King Harold 'Hardrada' and Tostig Godwineson, former earl of Northumbria; battle of Hastings, between Norman-French and English armies; death of King Harold of England; Normans campaign in southern England in autumn 1066 until surrender of English magnates supporting young ætheling Edgar (grandson of King Edmund Ironside) at Berkhampstead (Herts.); acclamation of Duke William as King of England on Christmas Day

1067   Eadric 'the Wild' raids Herefords.; Eustace of Boulogne launches unsuccessful attempt on Dover while William absent in Normandy

1068   Exeter rebels against William, who successfully besieges city, taking it by negotiation after meeting strong resistance; Earl Edwin of Mercia and his brother Morcar (no longer earl of Northumbria) rebel, seeking Welsh support against William; William launches punitive campaign in northern England after ætheling Edgar is supported in York; expedition's passage through midlands leads to Edwin and Morcar's surrender

1069   Rebellions against William in south-west, west midlands, and Northumbria; Robert de Commines, earl of Northumbria, killed at Durham; Northumbrians, allied with a Danish fleet, storm castle at York; city burnt by Normans; William ravages Northumbria as punishment during the winter of 1069–70 (the 'Harrying of the North')

1070   William crosses Pennines in winter to attack rebels in Chester; Fenland rebellion of Hereward 'the Wake' in alliance with Swein of Denmark; Ely used as base by rebels; Peterborough sacked by Danes, who depart soon after

1071   Earl Edwin of Mercia, fleeing, perhaps to join rebellion, killed by his own men; Morcar joins rebellion at Ely, which surrenders after a siege by William

1072   William goes to Scotland with land force and fleet, receiving submission of Malcolm, King of Scots, at Abernethy (Perthshire)

1073   English warriors participate in William's conquest of Maine

1075   Unsuccessful rebellion by Ralph, Earl of Norfolk, Roger, Earl of Hereford, and Waltheof, Earl of Huntingdon; castle garrisons resist rebels and William returns from Normandy; Danish fleet, sent for by rebels, does not fight William but sacks York

1076   William campaigns unsuccessfully in Brittany

1079   Battle fought by William against his son Robert at Gerberoy (dép. Oise);
        ravaging of Northumbria to River Tyne by Malcolm of Scotland

1080   Northumbrians kill the bishop of Durham

1081   Expedition into Wales by William

1085   Threat of Danish invasion by King Cnut of Denmark, leading to the billeting
        of mercenaries across the English kingdom; decision made by William for a
        survey of English kingdom (leading to Domesday Book)

1087   Death of William after campaigning in France; succession of William II 'Rufus'
        (1087–1100)

Select Bibliography

Primary sources

Aelfric's Lives of Saints, Being a Set of Sermons on Saints' Days Formerly Observed by the English Church, ed. W. W. Skeat, EETS original series 76, 82, 2 vols (London, 1881–1900)

'Alfred's Anglo-Saxon Version of Orosius', trans. B. Thorpe, in R. Pauli, *The Life of Alfred the Great*, ed. B. Thorpe (London, 1857), pp. 238–528

Alfred the Great: Asser's Life of King Alfred and Other Contemporary Sources, ed. and trans. S. D. Keynes and M. Lapidge (Harmondsworth, 1983)

Anglo-Saxon Charters, ed. A. J. Robertson (Cambridge, 1939)

Anglo-Saxon Charters: An Annotated List and Bibliography, ed. P. H. Sawyer, Royal Historical Society Guides and Handbooks 8 (London, 1968)

The Anglo-Saxon Chronicles, ed. and trans. M. J. Swanton (London, 1996)

The Anglo-Saxon Poetic Records. A Collective Edition, No. 3. The Exeter Book, ed. G. Krapp and E. Dobbie (New York, 1936)

Anglo-Saxon Poetry: An Anthology of Old English Poems, ed. and trans. S. A. J. Bradley, Everyman's Library (London, 1982)

Anglo-Saxon Wills, ed. D. Whitelock (Cambridge, 1930)

Anglo-Saxon Writs, ed. and trans. F. Harmer (Manchester, 1952)

Annales Bertiani, ed. G. Waitz, MGH Scriptores Rerum Germanicarum 5 (Hanover, 1883)

Annales Cambriae, ed. J. Williams ab Ithel, RS 20 (London, 1860)

Annales Fuldenses, ed. F. Kurze, MGH Scriptores Rerum Germanicarum 7 (Hanover, 1891)

The Annals of St Bertin, ed. and trans. J. L. Nelson, Manchester Medieval Sources Ninth-Century Histories 1 (Manchester, 1991)

The Annals of Fulda, ed. and trans. T. Reuter, Ninth-Century Histories 2 (Manchester, 1992)

The Annals of St Neots with Vita Prima Sancti Neoti, ed. D. N. Dumville and M. Lapidge, Anglo-Saxon Chronicle: A Collaborative Edition 17 (Cambridge, 1985)

Armes Prydein: The Prophecy of Britain, from the Book of Taliesin, ed. I. Williams and trans. R. Bromwich, Mediaeval and Modern Welsh 6 (Dublin, 1972)

The Battle of Maldon, ed. E. V. Gordon, Metheun's Old English Library (London, 1937; 2nd edn, 1949)

'The Battle of Maldon', ed. and trans. D. Scragg, in *The Battle of Maldon AD 991*, ed. D. Scragg (Oxford, 1991), pp. 15–36

Bede, *Historia ecclesiastica gentis Anglorum: Bede's Ecclesiastical History of the English People*, ed. and trans. B. Colgrave and R. A. B. Mynors, OMT (Oxford, 1969)

The Carmen de Hastingae proelio of Guy, Bishop of Amiens, ed. and trans. F. Barlow, OMT (Oxford, 1999)

Carolingian Chronicles: Royal Frankish Annals and Nithard's Histories, trans. B. W. Scholz, with B. Rogers (Ann Arbor, 1970)

A Choice of Anglo-Saxon Verse, ed. and trans. R. Hamer (London, 1970)

The Chronicle of John of Worcester: Volume II: The Annals from 450–1066, ed. and trans. R. R. Darlington and P. McGurk, OMT (Oxford, 1995)

Chronicon Æthelweardi: The Chronicle of Æthelweard, ed. A. Campbell, Medieval Texts (London, 1962)

De moribus et actis primorum Normanniae Ducum, ed. J. Lair (Caen, 1865)

Diplomatarium Anglicum Aevi Saxonici, ed. B. Thorpe (London, 1865)

Domesday Book [various county volumes], general ed. J. Morris, History from the Sources (Chichester, 1975–86)

Dudo of St Quentin: History of the Normans, trans. E. Christiansen (Woodbridge, 1998)

Egils Saga: Skalla-Grímssonar; Sigurdur Nordal gaf út, Íslenzk Fornrit 2 (Reykjavik, 1933)

Encomium Emmae Reginae, ed. A. Campbell, Camden 3rd series 72 (London, 1949)

English Historical Documents, volume 1, c. 550–1042, ed. D. Whitelock (London, 1955; 2nd edn, 1979)

Fragmentary Annals of Ireland, ed. and trans. J. N. Radner (Dublin 1978)

Geiffrei Gaimar, *L'Estoire des Engleis*, ed. A. Bell, Anglo-Norman Texts 14–16 (Oxford, 1960)

Gerald of Wales, *Itinerarium Kambriae et description Kambriae*, ed. J. F. Dimock (London, 1868)

The Gesta Guillelmi of William of Poitiers, ed. and trans. R. H. C. Davis and M. Chibnall, OMT (Oxford, 1998)

Gildas, *The Ruin of Britain and Other Works*, ed. and trans. M. Winterbottom, History from the Sources (Chichester, 1978)

Henry of Huntingdon, *Historia Anglorum: The History of the English People*, ed. and trans. Diana Greenway, OMT (Oxford, 1996)

Historia de Sancto Cuthberto: A History of Saint Cuthbert and a Record of his Patrimony, ed. and trans. T. Johnson South, Anglo-Saxon Texts 3 (Cambridge, 2002)

History of the Norman People: Wace's Roman de Rou, ed. and trans. G. S. Burgess with E. M. C van Houts (Woodbridge, 2004)

The Homilies of Wulfstan, ed. D. Bethurum (Oxford, 1957; corrected edn, 1971)

Ioannis Saresberiensis episcopi Carnotensis policratici, sive, de nugis curialium et vestigiis philosophorum libri VIII, ed. C. C. J. Webb (Oxford, 2 vols, 1909)

John of Salisbury, *Policratus: Of the Frivolities of Courtiers and the Footprints of Philosophers*, ed. and trans. C. J. Nederman, Cambridge Texts in the History of Political Thought (Cambridge, 1990)

King Alfred's Old English Version of Boethius De Consolatione Philosophiae, ed. W. J. Sedgefield (Oxford, 1899),

Liber Eliensis, ed. E. O. Blake, Camden 3rd series 92 (London, 1962)

Liber Eliensis: A History of the Isle of Ely from the Seventh Century to the Twelfth, trans. J. Fairweather (Woodbridge, 2005)

The Life of Bishop Wilfrid by Eddius Stephanus, ed. and trans. B. Colgrave (Cambridge, 1927)

Nithardi Historiarum Libri IIII, ed. G. H. Pertz, revised by E. Müller, MGH Scriptores rerum Germanicarum 44 (Hannover, 1907)

The Old English Exodus: Text, Translation and Commentary, ed. and trans. J. R. R. Tolkien and J. Turville-Petre (Oxford, 1981)

The Old English Orosius, ed. J. Bately, EETS supplementary series 6 (London, 1980)

The Old English Version of Bede's Ecclesiastical History of the English People, ed. and trans. T. Miller, EETS 95, 96, 2 parts (Oxford, 1890–1)

Orderici Vitalis Historia Æcclesiastica / The Ecclesiastical History of Orderic Vitalis, ed. and trans. M. Chibnall (Oxford, 6 vols., 1968–80)

Pauli Orosii Historiarum adversum Paganos libri VII, ed. C. F. W. Zangemeister (Leipzig, 1889)

Paulus Orosius. The Seven Books of Histories against the Pagans, trans. R. J. Deferrari, Fathers of the Church. A New Translation 50 (Washington DC, 1964)

Le Roman de Rou de Wace, ed. A. J. Holden, Société des anciens textes français (Paris, 3 vols, 1970–3)

Saxo Grammaticus, *The History of the Danes, Books I–IX*, transl. P. Fisher and ed. H. E. Davidson (Cambridge, 2 vols, 1979)

Saxonis Gesta Danorum, vol. 1, ed. J. Olrik and H. Ræder (Copenhagen, 1931)

Select English Historical Documents of the Ninth and Tenth Centuries, ed. F. E. Harmer (Cambridge, 1914)

The Story of Egil Skallagrimsson: Being an Icelandic Family History of the Ninth and Tenth Centuries, ed. W. C. Green (London, 1893)

Symeonis Monachi Opera Omnia, ed. T. Arnold, RS 75 (London, 2 vols, 1882–5)

'Textual Appendix: *Translatio Sancti Ælfegi Cantuariensis archiepiscopi et martiris (BHL 2519)*: Osbern's account of the translation of St Ælfheah's relics from London to Canterbury, 8–11 June 1023', ed. and trans. A. R. Rumble and R. Morris, in *The Reign of Cnut: King of England, Denmark and Norway*, ed. A. R. Rumble, SEHB (London, 1994), pp. 283–15

Vegetius, *Epitoma Rei Militaris*, ed. M. D. Reeve, Scriptorum classicorum bibliotheca Oxoniensis (Oxford, 2004)

Vegetius: Epitome of Military Science, trans. N. P. Milner, Translated Texts for Historians vol. 16 (Liverpool, 1993) *Vita Ædwardi Regis: The Life of King Edward who Rests at Westminster*, ed. F. Barlow, OMT (Oxford, 2nd edn, 1992)

William of Malmesbury, *Gesta Regum Anglorum: The History of the English Kings, Volume 1*, ed. R. M. Thomson, M. Winterbottom and R. A. B. Mynors, OMT (Oxford, 1998)

—— *Gesta Pontificum Anglorum, The History of the English Bishops: Volume I*, ed. M. Winterbottom and R. M. Thomson, OMT (Oxford, 2007)

Winchester in the Early Middle Ages: An Edition and Discussion of the Winton Domesday, ed. M. Biddle, Winchester Studies 1 (Oxford, 1976)

Secondary sources

Abels, R. P., *Lordship and Military Obligation in Anglo-Saxon England* (London, 1988)

——'English Tactics, Strategy and Military Organization in the Late Tenth Century', in *The Battle of Maldon* AD 991, ed. D. Scragg (Oxford, 1991), pp. 143–55

——'King Alfred's Peace-Making Strategies with the Vikings', *HSJ* 3 (1992), pp. 23–34

——'English Logistics and Military Administration, 871–1066: The Impact of the Viking Wars', in *Military Aspects of Scandinavian Society in a European Perspective, AD 1–1300*, ed. A. N. Jørgensen and B. L. Clausen, PNM Studies in Archaeology and History 2 (Copenhagen, 1997), pp. 257–65

——'From Alfred to Harold II: The Military Failure of the Late Anglo-Saxon State', in *The Normans and their Adversaries: Essays in Memory of C. Warren Hollister*, ed. R. P. Abels and B. S. Bachrach, Warfare in History (Woodbridge, 2001), pp. 15–30

——'Alfred the Great, the *Micel Hæðen Here* and the Viking Threat', in *Alfred the Great: Papers from the Eleventh-Centenary Conferences*, ed. T. Reuter, Studies in Early Medieval Britain (Aldershot, 2003), pp. 265–79

——'"Cowardice" and Duty in Anglo-Saxon England', *JMMH* 4 (2006), pp. 29–45

——'Paying the Danegeld: Anglo-Saxon Peacemaking with Vikings', in *War and Peace in Ancient and Medieval History*, ed. P. DeSouza and J. France (Cambridge, 2008), pp. 173–92

——'Household Men, Mercenaries and Vikings in Anglo-Saxon England', in *Mercenaries and Paid Men: The Mercenary Identity in the Middle Ages: Proceedings of a Conference held at University of Wales, Swansea, 7th–9th July 2005*, ed. J. France, History of Warfare 47 (Leiden, 2008), pp. 143–66

—— and S. Morillo, 'A Lying Legacy? A Preliminary Discussion of Images of Antiquity and Altered Reality in Medieval Military History', *JMMH* 3 (2005), pp. 1–13

Bachrach, B. S., 'Anthropologists and Early Medieval History: Some Problems', *Cithara* 34 (1994), pp. 3–10

—— and R. Aris, 'Military Technology and Garrison Organization: Some Observations on Anglo-Saxon Military Thinking in Light of the Burghal Hidage', *Technology and Culture* 31 (1990), pp. 1–17

Banton, L. N., 'Ealdormen and Earls in England from the Reign of King Alfred to the Reign of King Æthelred II' (DPhil thesis, Oxford University, 1981)

Barlow, F., *Edward the Confessor*, English Monarchs (London, 1970)

Barrow, J., 'Chester's Earliest Regatta? Edgar's Dee-Rowing Revisited', *EME* 10 (2001), pp. 81-93

—— and A. Wareham (eds), *Myth, Rulership, Church and Charters: Essays in Honour of Nicholas Brooks* (Aldershot, 2008)

Bateley, J., 'The Compilation of the Anglo-Saxon Chronicle, 60 BC to AD 890: Vocabulary as Evidence', *Proceedings of the British Academy* 64 (1978), pp. 93-129

Baxter, S., *The Earls of Mercia: Lordship and Power in Late Anglo-Saxon England*, Oxford Historical Monographs (Oxford, 2007)

Bennett, M., 'The Myth of the Military Supremacy of Knightly Cavalry', in *Armies, Chivalry and Warfare in Medieval Britain and France*, ed. M. Strickland, Harlaxton Medieval Studies New Series 7 (Stamford, 1998), pp. 304-16

Biddle, M., 'Towns', in *The Archaeology of Anglo-Saxon England*, ed. D. M. Wilson (London, 1976), pp. 99–150

——'*Object and Economy in Medieval Winchester: Artefacts from Medieval Winchester*, Winchester Studies 7.2 (Oxford, 1990)

Bosworth, J., and T. Toller, *An Anglo-Saxon Dictionary* (Oxford, 1898)

Bradbury, J., *The Medieval Siege* (Woodbridge, 1992)

Brooks, N. P., 'The Development of Military Obligations in Eighth- and Ninth-Century England', in *England Before the Norman Conquest: Essays Presented to Dorothy Whitelock*, ed. P. Clemoes and K. Hughes (Cambridge, 1971), pp. 69–84

——'Arms, Status and Warfare in Late-Saxon England', in *Ethelred the Unready: Papers from the Millenary Conference*, ed. D. H. Hill, BAR British Series 59 (Oxford, 1978), pp. 85–90

——'England in the Ninth Century: The Crucible of Defeat', *TRHS* 5th series 29 (1979), pp. 1–20

——'Weapons and Armour', in *The Battle of Maldon AD 991*, ed. D. Scragg (Oxford, 1991), pp. 208–19

——'The Administrative Background to the Burghal Hidage', in *The Defence of Wessex: The Burghal Hidage and Anglo-Saxon Fortifications*, ed. D. Hill and A. R. Rumble (Manchester, 1996), pp. 128–50

—— review of G. Halsall, *Warfare and Society in the Barbarian West, c.450-900*, Warfare and History series (London, 2003), *EHR* 120 (2005), pp. 424-6

Brown, R. A., 'The Status of the Norman Knight', in *War and Government in the Middle Ages: Essays in Honour of J. O. Prestwich*, ed. J. C. Holt and J. Gillingham (Woodbridge, 1984), pp. 18–32

Burne, H., 'The Battle of Ashdown', *Transactions of the Newbury and District Field Club* 10 (1953), pp. 71-85

Campbell, J., 'What is not known about the Reign of Edward the Elder', in *Edward the Elder, 899–924*, ed. N. J. Higham and D. H. Hill (London, 2001), pp. 12–24

Cavill, P., 'The Site of the Battle of *Brunanburh*: Manuscripts and Maps, Grammar and Geography', in *A Commodity of Good Names: Essays in Honour of Margaret Gelling*, ed. O. J. Padel and D. N. Parsons (Donnington, 2008), pp. 303–19

Chadwick, H. M., *Studies on Anglo-Saxon Institutions* (Cambridge, 1905)

Clapham, J. H., 'The Horsing of the Danes', *EHR* 25 (1910), pp. 287–93

Contamine, P., *War in the Middle Ages*, trans. M. Jones (Oxford, 1984)

Cooper, A., *Bridges, Law and Power in Medieval England, 700–1400* (Woodbridge, 2006)

Cooper, J. (ed.), *The Battle of Maldon: Fiction and Fact* (London, 1993)

Cross, J. E., 'The Ethic of War in Old English', in *England Before the Conquest: Studies in Primary Sources Presented to Dorothy Whitelock*, ed. P. Clemoes and K. Hughes (Cambridge, 1971), pp. 269–82

Crumlin-Pedersen, O., 'Large and Small Warships of the North', in *Military Aspects of Scandinavian Society in a European Perspective, AD 1–1300*, ed. A. Nørgård Jørgensen and B. L. Clausen, PNM Studies in Archaeology and History 2 (Copenhagen, 1997), pp. 184–94

Dalton, P., 'Sites and Occasions of Peacemaking in England and Normandy, c. 900-c. 1150', *HSJ* 16 (2006 for 2005), pp. 12–26

Davidson, H. E., 'The Training of Warriors', *Weapons and Warfare in Anglo-Saxon England*, ed. S. C. Hawkes, Oxford University Committee for Archaeology Monograph 21 (Oxford, 1989), pp. 11-24

Davies, W., *Wales in the Early Middle Ages*, SEHB (Leicester, 1982)

Davis, R. H. C.,'Alfred the Great: Propaganda and Truth', *History* 56 (1971), pp. 169–82

——'Did the Anglo-Saxons have Warhorses?', in *Weapons and Warfare in Anglo-Saxon England*, ed. S. C. Hawkes, Oxford University Committee for Archaeology Monograph 21 (Oxford, 1989), pp. 141–4

—— *The Medieval Warhorse: Origin, Development and Redevelopment* (London, 1989)

DeVries, K.,'Harold Godwinson in Wales: Military Legitimacy in Late Anglo-Saxon England', in *The Normans and their Adversaries at War*, ed. R. P. Abels and B. S. Bachrach, Warfare in History (Boydell, 2001), pp. 65–85

Dickinson, T., and H. Härke, *Early Anglo-Saxon Shields*, Society of Antiquaries Archaeologia 110 (London, 1992)

Dodgson, J. M.,'The Site of the Battle of Maldon', in *The Battle of Maldon* AD 991, ed. D. Scragg (Oxford, 1991), pp. 170–9

——'Appendix I: OE *Weal-stilling*', in *The Defence of Wessex: The Burghal Hidage and Anglo-Saxon Fortifications*, ed. D. Hill and A. R. Rumble (Manchester, 1996), pp. 176–7

English Heritage, *Register of Historic Battlefields* [online database], <http://www.english-heritage.org.uk/server/show/nav.00100200400d002>

Fell, C. E.,'Unfrið: An Approach to a Definition', *Saga Book of the Viking Society for Northern Research* 21 (1982-83), pp. 85-100

Fleming, R.,'Monastic Lands and England's Defence in the Viking Age', *EHR* 100 (1985), pp. 247–65

—— *Kings and Lords in Conquest England*, Cambridge Studies in Medieval Life and Thought 4th series 15 (Cambridge, 1991)

——'Rural Elites and Urban Communties in Late-Saxon England', *Past and Present* 141 (1993), pp. 3–37

Foard, G.,'English Battlefields, 991–1685: A Review of Problems and Potentials', in *Fields of Conflict: Battlefield Archaeology from the Roman Empire to the Korean War*, ed. D. D. Scott, L. E. Babits, C. M. Haecker, 2 vols (Westport, CT, 2007), vol. I, pp. 133–59

Fordham, M.,'Peacekeeping and Order on the Anglo-Welsh Frontier in the Early Tenth Century', *Midland History* 32 (2007), pp. 1–18

Freeman, E. A., *The History of the Norman Conquest of England, its Causes and its Results* (Oxford, 6 vols, 1867–79)

Gifford, E., and J. Gifford,'Alfred's New Longships', in *Alfred the Great: Papers from the Eleventh-Centenary Conferences*, ed. T. Reuter, Studies in Early Medieval Britain (Aldershot, 2003)

Gillingham, J.,'Richard I and the Science of War in the Middle Ages', in *War and Government in the Middle Ages*, ed. J. Gillingham and J. C. Holt (Woodbridge, 1984), pp. 78–91

——'William the Bastard at War', in *Studies in Medieval History Presented to R. Allen Brown*, ed. C. Harper-Bill, C. Holdsworth and J. Nelson (Woodbridge, 1989), pp. 141–58

——'Thegns and Knights in Eleventh-Century England: Who was then the Gentleman?', *TRHS* 6th series 5 (1995), pp. 129–33

——'"Holding to the Rules of War (*Bellica Iura Tenentes*)": Right Conduct Before, During and After Battle in North-Western Europe in the Eleventh Century', *ANS* 29 (2007 for 2006), pp. 1–15

Glover, R., 'English Warfare in 1066', *EHR* 67 (1952), pp. 1–18

Graham-Campbell, J., R. Hall, J. Jesch, and D. N. Parsons (eds), *Vikings and the Danelaw: Select Papers of the Thirteenth Viking Congress* (Oxford, 2001)

Green, J. R., *The Conquest of England* (London, 1883)

Grierson, P., 'Weights and Measures', in *Domesday Book Studies*, ed. A. Williams and R. W. H. Erskine (London, 1986), pp. 80-5

Griffith, P., *The Viking Art of War* (London, 1996)

Grossman, D., *On Killing: The Psychological Cost of Learning to Kill in War and Society* (Boston, MA, 1995)

Hadley, D. M., and J. D. Richards (eds), *Cultures in Contact: Scandinavian Settlement in England in the Ninth and Tenth Centuries*, SEMA 2 (Turnhout, 2000)

Halsall, G. R., 'Anthropology and the Study of Pre-Conquest Warfare and Society: The Ritual War in Anglo-Saxon England', in *Weapons and Warfare in Anglo-Saxon England*, ed. S. C. Hawkes, Oxford University Committee for Archaeology Monograph 21 (Oxford, 1989), pp. 155–77

——'Playing by Whose Rules? A Further Look at Viking Atrocity in the Ninth Century', *Medieval History* 2:2 (1992), pp. 2–12

—— *Warfare and Society in the Barbarian West, c. 450–900*, Warfare and History (London, 2003)

Hare, K. G., 'Apparitions and War in Anglo-Saxon England', in *The Circle of War in the Middle Ages: Essays on Medieval Military and Naval History*, ed. D. J. Kagay and L. J. A. Villalon, Warfare in History (Woodbridge, 1999), pp. 75–86

Harper-Bill, C., C. Holdsworth, and J. L. Nelson (eds), *Studies in Medieval History presented to R. Allen Brown* (Woodbridge, 1989)

Harrison, D., *The Bridges of Medieval England*, Oxford Historical Monographs (Oxford, 2004)

Haslam, J. (ed.), *Anglo-Saxon Towns in Southern England* (Chichester, 1984)

——'King Alfred and the Vikings: Strategies and Tactics 876–886 AD', *ASSAH* 13 (2006), pp. 122–54

Hassall, M., and D. Hill, 'Pont de l'Arche: Frankish Influence on the West Saxon Burh?', *Archaeological Journal* 127 (1970), pp. 188–95

Hill, D. H., 'The Burghal Hidage: The Establishment of a Text', *Medieval Archaeology* 13 (1969), pp. 84–92

—— *Atlas of Anglo-Saxon England* (Oxford, 1984)

——'The Calculation and Purpose of the Burghal Hidage', in *The Defence of Wessex: The Burghal Hidage and Anglo-Saxon Fortifications*, ed. D. Hill and A. R. Rumble (Manchester, 1996), pp. 92–7

—— and A. R. Rumble (eds), *The Defence of Wessex: The Burghal Hidage and Anglo-Saxon Fortifications* (Manchester, 1996)

——— and S. Sharp, 'An Anglo-Saxon Beacon System', in *Names, Places and People: An Onomastic Miscellany in Memory of John McNeal Dodgson*, ed. A. R. Rumble and A. D. Mills (Stamford, 1997), pp. 157–65

Hill, P., *The Age of Athelstan: Britain's Forgotten History* (Stroud, 2004)

Hinton, D. A., 'The Fortifications and their Shires', in *The Defence of Wessex: The Burghal Hidage and Anglo-Saxon Fortifications*, ed. D. H. Hill and A. R. Rumble (Manchester, 1996), pp. 151-9

Hodgkin, R. H., *A History of the Anglo-Saxons*, 2 vols (Oxford, 1935)

Hollister, C. W., *Anglo-Saxon Military Institutions on the Eve of the Norman Conquest* (Oxford, 1962)

Hooper, N., 'The Housecarls in England in the Eleventh Century', *ANS* 7 (1985 for 1984), pp. 161–76

——— 'The Anglo-Saxons at War', in *Weapons and Warfare in Anglo-Saxon England*, ed. S. C. Hawkes, Oxford University Committee for Archaeology Monograph 21 (Oxford, 1989), pp. 191–202

——— 'Some Observations on the Navy in Late Anglo-Saxon England', in *Studies in Medieval History presented to R. Allen Brown*, ed. C. Harper-Bill, C. Holdsworth, and J. L. Nelson (Woodbridge, 1989), pp. 203–13

Howard, I., *Swein Forkbeard's Invasions and the Danish Conquest of England, 991–1017*, Warfare in History (Woodbridge, 2003)

Insley, C., 'Athelstan, Charters and the English in Cornwall' in *Changing Charters: Charters and Charter Scholarship in Britain and Ireland*, ed. J. Green and M. T. Flanagan (Basingstoke, 2005), pp. 15-31

Jayakumar, S., 'Some Reflections on the "Foreign Policies" of Edgar "the Peaceable"', *HSJ* 10 (2002 for 2001), pp. 17–37

Jesch, J., *Ships and Men in the Late Viking Age: The Vocabulary of Runic Inscriptions and Skaldic Verse* (Woodbridge, 2001)

John, E., *Land Tenure in Early England: A Discussion of Some Problems*, Studies in Early English History 1 (Leicester, 1960)

——— *Orbis Britanniae and Other Studies*, Studies in Early English History 4 (Leicester, 1966)

Jørgensen, A. N., and B. L. Clausen (eds), *Military Aspects of Scandinavian Society in a European Perspective, AD 1–1300*, PNM Studies in Archaeology and History 2 (Copenhagen, 1997)

Keefer, S. L. 'Hwær Cwom Mearh? The Horse in Anglo-Saxon England', *Journal of Medieval History* 23 (1996), pp. 115–34

Keynes, S. D., 'The Declining Reputation of King Æthelred the Unready', in *Ethelred the Unready: Papers from the Millenary Conference*, ed. D. H. Hill, BAR British Series 59 (Oxford, 1978), pp. 227-53

——— *The Diplomas of King Æthelred 'The Unready', 978–1016: A Study in Their Use as Historical Evidence*, Cambridge Studies in Medieval Life and Thought, 3rd series 13 (Cambridge, 1980)

——— 'A Tale of Two Kings: Alfred the Great and Æthelred the Unready', *TRHS*, 5th series, 36 (1986), pp. 195-217

——'King Alfred and the Mercians', in *Kings, Currency and Alliances: History and Coinage of Southern England in the Ninth Century*, ed. M. A. S. Blackburn and D. N. Dumville, Studies in Anglo-Saxon History 9 (Woodbridge, 1998), pp. 1-46

Kiff, J., 'Images of War: Illustrations of Warfare in Early Eleventh-Century England', *ANS* 7 (1984), pp. 177–94

King's College London and University of Cambridge, *Prosopography of Anglo-Saxon England* <www.pase.ac.uk>

Lavelle, R., 'Towards a Political Contextualization of Peacemaking and Peace Agreements in Anglo-Saxon England', in *Peace and Negotiation: Strategies for Coexistence in the Middle Ages and the Renaissance*, ed. D. Wolfthal, Arizona Studies in the Middle Ages and the Renaissance 4 (Turnhout, 2000), pp. 39–55

—— 'The Use and Abuse of Hostages in Later Anglo-Saxon England', *Early Medieval Europe* 14 (2006), pp. 269–96

—— *Royal Estates in Anglo-Saxon Wessex: Land, Politics and Family Strategies*, BAR British Series 439 (Oxford, 2007)

—— *Aethelred II: King of the English* (Stroud, 2002; rev. edn, 2008)

——'The Politics of Rebellion: The Ætheling Æthelwold and West Saxon Royal Succession, 899–902', in *Challenging the Boundaries of Medieval History: The Legacy of Timothy Reuter*, ed. P. Skinner, SEMA 22 (Turnhout, 2009), pp. 51–80

——'Geographies of Power in the Anglo-Saxon Chronicle: The Royal Estates of Wessex', in *Reading the Anglo-Saxon Chronicle: Language, Literature, History*, ed. A. D. Jorgensen, SEMA 23 (Turnhout, 2010), pp. 187–219

Lawson, M. K., 'Danegeld and Heregeld Once More', *EHR* 105 (1990), pp. 951–61

—— *Cnut: The Danes in England in the Early Eleventh Century*, The Medieval World (London, 1991)

——'Observations on a Scene in the Bayeux Tapestry, the Battle of Hastings and the Military System of the Late Anglo-Saxon State', in *The Medieval State: Essays Presented to James Campbell*, ed. J. R. Maddicott and D. M. Palliser (London, 2000), pp. 73–91

—— *The Battle of Hastings 1066*, Battles and Campaigns (Stroud, 2002; reset edn, 2007)

Leyser, K., 'Early Medieval Warfare', in *The Battle of Maldon: Fiction and Fact*, ed. J. Cooper (London, 1993), pp. 87–108

Loyn, H. R., *The Governance of Anglo-Saxon England, 500–1087*, The Governance of England 1 (London, 1984)

Lund, N., 'Peace and Non-Peace in the Viking Age: Ottar in Biarmaland, the Rus in Byzantium, and Danes and Norwegians in England', in *Proceedings of the Tenth Viking Conference: Larkollen, Norway, 1985*, ed. J. E. Knirk (Oslo, 1987), pp. 255–69

Magoun, F. P., 'King Alfred's Naval and Beach Battle with the Danes in 896', *Modern Language Review* 37 (1942), pp. 409–14

Maitland, F. W., *Domesday Book and Beyond: Three Essays in the Early History of England* (Cambridge, 1897)

Manley, J. M., 'The Archer and the Army in the Late Saxon Period', *ASSAH* 4 (1985), pp. 223–35

Molloy, B. P. C., and D. Grossman, 'Why Can't Johnny Kill? The Psychology and Physiology of Interpersonal Combat', in *The Cutting Edge: Studies in Ancient and Medieval Combat*, ed. B. Molloy (Stroud, 2007), pp. 188–202

Morgan, P., 'The Naming of Battlefields in the Middle Ages', in *War and Society in Medieval and Early Modern Britain*, ed. D. Dunn (Liverpool, 2000), pp. 34–52

Morillo, S., *Warfare under the Anglo-Norman Kings, 1066–1135* (Woodbridge, 1996)

——'The "Age of Cavalry" Revisited', in *The Circle of War in the Middle Ages: Essays on Medieval Military and Naval History*, ed. D. J. Kagay and L. J. A. Villalon, Warfare in History (Woodbridge, 1999), pp. 45–58

——'Battle Seeking: The Contexts and Limits of Vegetian Strategy', *JMMH* 1 (2002), pp. 21–41

——'Expecting Cowardice: Medieval Battle Tactics Reconsidered', *JMMH* 4 (2006), pp. 65–73

Morini, C., 'OE *Hring*: Anglo-Saxon or Viking Armour?', *ASSAH* 13 (2005), pp. 155–72

Nicholson, H. J., *Medieval Warfare: Theory and Practice of War in Europe, 300–1500* (Basingstoke, 2004)

Noble, F., *Offa's Dyke Reviewed*, ed. M. Gelling, BAR British Series 114 (Oxford, 1983)

Oman, C., *A History of the Art of War: The Middle Ages from the Fourth to the Fourteenth Century* (Oxford, 1898)

Pauli, R., *König Aelfred* (Berlin, 1851) [translated by 'A. P.' as *Life of Alfred the Great*, ed. B. Thorpe (London, 1853)]

Peddie, J., *Alfred the Good Soldier: His Life and Campaigns* (Bath, 1989)

Pollington, S. *The English Warrior from Earliest Times till 1066* (Hockwold-cum-Wilton, 1996; 2nd edn, 2001)

Poole, R., *Viking Poems on War and Peace: A Study in Skaldic Narrative*, Toronto Medieval Texts and Translations 8 (London, 1991)

Pullen-Appleby, J., *English Sea Power, c. 871 to 1100* (Hockwold-cum-Wilton, 2005)

Prestwich, J. O., *The Place of War in English History, 1066–1214*, ed. M. Prestwich [from the Ford Lectures, 1983], Warfare in History (Woodbridge, 2004)

Reuter, T., 'Plunder and Tribute in the Carolingian Empire', *TRHS* 5th series 35 (1985), pp. 75–94

——(ed.), *Alfred the Great: Papers from the Eleventh-Centenary Conferences*, Studies in Early Medieval Britain (Aldershot, 2003)

Reynolds, A. J., *Anglo-Saxon Deviant Burial Customs*, Medieval History and Archaeology (Oxford, 2009)

Richardson, H. G., and G. O. Sayles, *The Governance of Mediaeval England from the Conquest to Magna Carta*, Edinburgh University Publications. History, Philosophy and Economics 16 (Edinburgh, 1963)

Rodger, N. A. M., 'Cnut's Geld and the Size of Danish Ships' *EHR* 110 (1995), pp. 392–403

——*Safeguard of the Sea: A Naval History of Britain*, vol. 1: 660–1649 (London, 1997)

Roffe, D., *Domesday: The Inquest and the Book* (Oxford, 2000)

Round, J. H., *Feudal England: Historical Studies on the Eleventh and Twelfth Centuries* (London, 1895; reset edn, 1964)

Rumble, A. R. (ed.), *The Reign of Cnut: King of England, Denmark and Norway*, SEHB (London, 1993)

——'Appendix II: OE *Waru*', in *The Defence of Wessex: The Burghal Hidage and Anglo-Saxon Fortifications*, ed. D. Hill and A. R. Rumble (Manchester, 1996), pp. 178–81

Sabin, P., *Lost Battles: Reconstructing the Great Clashes of the Ancient World* (London, 2007)

Sawyer, P. H., 'The Density of the Danish settlement in England', *University of Birmingham Historical Journal* 6 (1958), pp. 1-17

—— *The Age of the Vikings* (London, 1962; 2nd edn, 1971)

Scragg, D. (ed.), *The Battle of Maldon* AD 991(Oxford, 1991)

Simpson, L., 'The King Alfred/ St Cuthbert Episode in the *Historia de sancto Cuthberto*: Its Significance for Mid-Tenth-Century English History', in *St Cuthbert, His Cult and His Community to AD 1200*, ed. G. Bonner, D. Rollason and C. Stancliffe (Woodbridge, 1989), pp. 397-411

Stafford, P., *Unification and Conquest: A Political and Social History of England in the Tenth and Eleventh Centuries* (London, 1989)

Stenton, F. M., 'The Road System of Medieval England', *Economic History Review* 7 (1936), pp. 1–21

—— *Anglo-Saxon England*, Oxford History of England 2 (Oxford, 1943; 3rd edn, 1971)

Stephenson, I. P., *The Late Anglo-Saxon Army* (Stroud, 2007)

Stevenson, W. H., 'Trinoda Necessitas', *EHR* 29 (1914), pp. 689–703

Strickland, M., 'Introduction', in *Anglo-Norman Warfare: Studies in Late Anglo-Saxon and Anglo-Norman Military Organization and Warfare*, ed. M. Strickland (Woodbridge, 1992), pp. ix-xxiii

Taylor, P., 'The Endowment and Military Obligations of the See of London: A Reassessment of Three Sources', *ANS* 14 (1992 for 1991), pp. 287-312

Thurnham, J., 'On the Barrow at Lanhill near Chippenham, with Remarks on the Site of, and on the Events Connected with the Battles of Cynuit and Ethandun, A.D. 878', *Wiltshire Archaeological and Natural History Magazine* 3 (1857), pp. 67-86

Trousdale, A. 'An Investigation of the Anglo-Saxon Political Situation during the Reign of King Edmund, 939-46 AD' (PhD thesis, Edinburgh University, 2007)

Tsurushima, H., 'The Eleventh Century in England through Fish-Eyes: Salmon, Herring, Oysters, and 1066', *ANS* 29 (2007 for 2006), pp. 193–213

Tyler, E. M., '"The Eyes of the Beholders Were Dazzled": Treasure and Artifice in *Encomium Emmae Reginae*', *EME* 8 (1999), pp. 247–70

Vinogradoff, P., *English Society in the Eleventh Century: Essays in English Mediaeval History* (Oxford, 1908)

Wainwright, F. T., 'Æthelflæd, Lady of the Mercians', in *The Anglo-Saxons: Studies in Some Aspects of their History and Culture Presented to Bruce Dickins*, ed. P. Clemoes (London, 1959), pp. 53–69

Wallace-Hadrill, 'War and Peace in the Early Middle Ages', in J. M. Wallace-Hadrill, *Early Medieval History* (Oxford, 1975), pp. 19–38

Walker, S., 'A Context for "Brunanburh"?', in *Warriors and Churchmen in the High Middle Ages: Essays Presented to Karl Leyser*, ed. T. Reuter (London, 1992), pp. 21–39

Williams, Alan, *The Knight and the Blast Furnace: A History of the Metallurgy of Armour in the Middle Ages & the Early Modern Period*, History of Warfare 12 (Leiden, 2003)

Williams, Ann, 'A Bell-house and a Burh-geat: Lordly Residences in England before the Norman Conquest', in *Medieval Knighthood, 4: Papers From the Fifth Strawberry Hill Conference, 1990*, ed. C. Harper-Bill and R. Harvey (Woodbridge, 1992), pp. 221–40

—— *Æthelred the Unready: The Ill-Counselled King* (London, 2003)

—— *The World Before Domesday: The English Aristocracy, 900–1066* (London, 2008)

Williams, G., 'Military Institutions and Royal Power', in *Mercia: An Anglo-Saxon Kingdom in Europe* ed. M. P. Brown and C. Farr, SEHB (London, 2001), pp. 295–309

Wood, M., 'Brunanburh Revisited', *Saga Book of the Viking Society for Northern Research* 20 (1980), pp. 200–17

Wormald, P., 'The Ninth Century', in *The Anglo-Saxons*, ed. J. Campbell (London, 1982), pp. 132–59

—— *The Making of English Law: King Alfred to the Twelfth Century, Volume 1: Legislation and its Limits* (Oxford, 1999)

Yorke, B., *Kings and Kingdoms of Early Anglo-Saxon England* (London, 1989)

—— *Wessex in the Early Middle Ages*, SEHB (London, 1995)

Index

Æthelingadene (East and West Dean, Sussex), 254, 298

Alençon, siege of, 259n

Abbo of St-Germain, 228

abbots, 183

Abbotsbury (Dorset), 39, 243

Abels, Richard, 7, 8, 29, 32, 43, 48, 55, 58, 62, 63, 64, 69, 91, 92–100, 101–5, 109–10, 112–13, 114, 115, 177, 200, 216, 236, 267, 269–73, 277, 304n, 316, 327–8

Abingdon (Berks., now Oxon.), 300n, 307

Abraham, 191, 193, 282

Adelbero of Laon, 10n, 97

Ælfgar, Earl, 163, 284, 285

Ælfgar, will of, 116

Ælfgifu, will of, 117

Ælfheah, Bishop of Winchester, 329

Ælfheah, ealdorman of central Wessex, 117

Ælfheah, St, Archbishop of Canterbury, 107, 194–7, 242, 320

Ælfhelm, will of, 118, 121, 162

Ælfric *Bata*: *Colloquy* of, 280

Ælfric of Eynsham, 3n, 12, 95, 97n, 98, 100, 267

homilies of, 280–1, 282, 297

Maccabees, 282–3

Ælfric, Archbishop of Canterbury, 119, 148, 162

Ælfric, Ealdorman of eastern Wessex, 267, 329

Ælfstan, Bishop of Ramsbury, 280

Ælfswith, will of, 117

Ælfthryth, Queen, 117

Ælfweard, Abbot of Evesham, 72

Ælfwine, warrior at Maldon, 278n

Ælfwold, Bishop of Crediton, 119, 121, 148, 149, 162

Aeneias the Tactician, 233

Æscferth, Northumbrian hostage, 274n

Æthelberht, King of Kent, 54, 71

Æthelflæd, 'Lady of the Mercians', 13, 22, 26, 63, 93, 182, 215, 216, 229, 230, 232

Æthelflæd, will of, 118

Æthelflæd, widow of Ealdorman Byrhtnoth, 303

Æthelgifu, will of, 118

Æthelhelm, ealdorman of Dorset, 4

Æthelhelm, ealdorman of Wilts., 5 and 5n, 95

Æthelmær, ealdorman of Hants., will of, 117

Æthelmær, ealdorman of south-western provinces, 164, 257n

Æthelnoth, Archbishop of Canterbury, 194

Æthelnoth, ealdorman of Som., 5, 95

Æthelred I, King of the West Saxons, 50, 187, 198–9, 251, 265, 276, 277–8, 300

Æthelred II 'the Unready', King of the English, 21, 25, 30, 32, 105, 109, 110, 119, 162–3, 180, 241, 242, 247

as ætheling, 117

charters of, 172–3, 222, 225

exile to Normandy, 154

and fleets, 150, 153, 163, 175, 202

laws of, *see* laws and legal codes

and London, 113, 200, 260

organization of defences under, 216, 225, 236, 260n, 262, 318, 323, 335, 336, 338

and Vikings, 166, 245, 247, 248, 249–51, 252–7, 260–1, 328–32

Æthelred, ealdorman of Mercia, 5, 24, 45, 63, 93, 95, 182, 215, 230, 232, 241n

Æthelred, King of Northumbria, 152

Æthelric of Bocking, will of, 118

Æthelric, bishop of Sherborne, 158, 161, 164–5

Æthelweard, ealdorman of the south-western provinces, 189, 219, 337–8

Chronicle of, 2–6, 198, 213, 265, 286, 324–5, 328

military practice in, 110, 165–70, 171, 286

governance, 100, 172, 329

Æthelwold, ætheling, 95–6, 207, 230, 235n

Æthelwold, will of, 117

Æthelwold, St, bishop of Winchester, 173

Æthelwulf, ealdorman of Berks., 5, 199
Æthelwyrd, will of, 258n
Agincourt, Battle of, 48n, 134, 134n, 266
Al-Andalus, 42
Alcuin of York, Deacon, 9, 43, 152
Aldred, provost of Chester-le-Street,
    193–4
Alexander, R. C., 309, 314n
Alfred 'the Great', King of the West
    Saxons, 26, 53, 99, 215, 262, 308–9, 313,
    193
  as ætheling, 213, 276, 277–8, 279–80,
    300
  as author, 10–11, 12
  charters of, 174–5
  court and household of, 95n, 110, 152,
    193, 277n
  laws of, see laws and legal codes
  military organization under, 139, 150,
    152, 175, 209, 212–14, 225, 250, 263,
    336
  ships of, 141, 141n, 145–8, 288–97
  and towns, 235, 262; see also Burghal
    Hidage
  and Vikings, 251, 252, 264–5, 275–9,
    324–8
  as war-leader, 10, 24, 48, 49, 50, 59,
    92–9, 152, 166–7, 187, 188, 190, 198–9,
    207–8, 251, 264–5, 276, 277–8, 279
  will of, 12n, 123n, 328n
Aller (Som.), 322
Alney near Deerhurst (Glos.), 321, 322
Alresford (Hants.), 243n
Álvarez Borge, Ignacio, 64
Amazons, depiction of, 92
Andernach, Battle of, 60n, 198, 278
Andover (Hants.), 307n, 329
Andredesweald (Weald, Kent and Sussex),
    19, 187, 188, 214, 234n
Angelbert, Frankish poet, 305n
Anglo-Saxon Chronicle, 4, 19, 26, 59, 91,
    94, 112, 113, 134, 139, 146, 148–51, 166–9,
    170, 186, 187,189, 190, 196, 202–6, 213,
    218, 228–9, 230, 232, 233, 247, 248, 249,
    250, 252–5, 256–7, 260–1, 264, 265–7,
    270n, 284–5, 286, 287–97, 299, 301, 313,
    314, 316, 322, 324, 325, 327, 336
Anglo-Saxons, identity of, see English
Annales Cambriae ('Annals of Wales'),
    25–9, 232, 299n
Annals of Fulda, 320
Annals of St Bertin, 169n

anthropology, role in early medieval
    studies, 16–17, 43, 266
Apocalypse, 32
Appledore (Kent), 168, 188
Aris, Rutherford, 210, 226
aristocracy
  relationship with warfare, 17, 63–4, 98,
    139–40, 315; see also thegns
  and social status, 121–8, 145, 191
Aristotle, 267
Armes Prydein ('Prophecy of Britain',
    poem), 22, 25
arms and armour
  armour, 40, 67, 112–14, 115–21 passim,
    121–2, 136, 162, 240
  bequests of, 86, 96n, 113, 115–28, 162
  costs, 67, 112–13
  missile weapons, 64,188, 270–1, 272, 274
  production, 65, 129
  rudimentary, 49, 50, 52, 111, 226, 231, 251,
    337
  shields, 60n, 62, 115–21 passim, 128,
    274–5, 278, 283, 284, 320
  spears, 40, 54n, 115–21 passim, 128,
    274–5, 281, 283, 284, 284
  status, 111, 116, 121–3, 128, 129
  swords, 23, 41, 42, 54, 65, 67, 85, 97n,
    115–21 passim, 270, 272, 273
armies and land forces, xvi, 130, 134
  cohesion, 178, 186–7, 199, 202
  personnel, 47, 48, 63, 66, 68–91, 96–7,
    98
  organization, 50, 53, 54, 59–60, 92–3,
    94–7, 99–106, 149–51, 152–63, 159,
    171, 197, 208, 219, 258, 335–6
  logistical support, 60–3, 97, 99, 183, 186
Arques, siege of, 138n
Ashdown, Battle of, 15, 265, 272, 275–9,
    285, 298, 300, 300n, 304–5, 309
Ashingdon (Essex), 304n; see also
    Assandun, Battle of
Assandun, Battle of, 269–71, 273, 300,
    304–5
assassination, 27, 318–19
Asselt, unidentified fortification, 229, 320
assemblies, 2, 2n, 32–4, 52, 94, 99–101, 151,
    179–80, 182–5, 237, 242–3, 256–8, 262,
    304
Asser: Life of King Alfred, 24, 110, 110n,
    146n, 167–9, 170, 193, 213, 253, 264, 265,
    272, 275–80, 300, 304, 316, 324

Athelney (Som.), 48, 110, 179, 234n, 300n, 302, 304, 313, 322

Athelstan, ætheling, 119, 121, 129n

Athelstan, King of the English, 27, 220, 237, 242, 260, 300–2, 332
  charters of, 182–5, 192–3, 221
  and fleets, 148, 150, 166, 175, 202
  laws of, see laws and legal codes
  as war-leader, 10, 22, 62–3, 94, 99, 182–6, 192–3, 300–2

Athelstan, sub-king of Kent, 152n

Avars, 328n

Aylesbury (Bucks.), 117, 161

Bachrach, Bernard S., 16–17, 192n, 210, 226, 235n, 270–2, 318n

Badbury Rings, hillfort (Dors.), 188, 230, 234n

baggage trains, 31n, 60n, 191, 198, 278

Baker, G. P., 277

Baldersby (Yorks.), sculpture at, 131, 133

Banton, Nicholas, 115, 129n

Barker, Katherine, 164, 252n

Barlow, Frank, 138n

Barrow, Julia, 20, 321

Barthélemy, Dominique, 130n

Basingstoke (Hants.), 307

Bassett, Steve, 215n

Bath (Som.), 39, 256–7

Battle Abbey (Sussex), 303

Battle of Maldon (poem), 1, 7, 15, 55, 73, 75, 83, 113, 250, 267, 273, 278, 285, 302–3, 323

battlefields
  archaeology of, 298n, 307
  arrangement of armies upon, 106, 269, 276–9, 285, 301–2
  geography and topography of, 270, 276, 303, 321
  memories of, 277, 298–314

battles
  decisiveness, 337
  definitions of, 264–5
  memories and representations of, 7, 7n, 265, 277n, 314, see also under battlefields
  scale/duration of, 278, 318

Baudri of Bourgueil: Adelae Comitissae, 111n

Baxter, Stephen 3, 5, 26, 29, 45, 338

Bayeux Tapestry, 52, 135, 137–8, 138, 139, 234, 274n, 275, 278, 279, 305, 320, 321

Beacon Hill, Burghclere (Hants.), 222

beacons, 174, 190, 217–25

Beaduheard, Dorset reeve, 4, 171, 174

Bede: Historia Ecclesiastica, 61, 150, 303, 318–19; see also Old English Bede

Bedfont (Middx), 244n

Bedford (Beds.), 161, 248, 326

Bedfordshire, 252n

Bedwyn (Wilts.), gild statutes of, 243

Beer (Devon), 172

bees and beehives, as weapons, 232, 233

Bembridge (Isle of Wight), 224

Bennett, Matthew, 336n

Beorhtwulf, ealdorman of Essex, 175

Beorn Estrithsson, 155

Beowulf, 21n, 171–2, 218, 219

Berkhampstead (Herts.), 256

Berkshire, 87, 218, 224, 252n, 310
  Domesday customs of, 56, 60, 62, 67, 72, 73–4, 76, 77, 78, 82, 86–7, 99, 105, 162, 244

Berkshire Downs, 298, 300n, 307, 309

Bessinger, J. B., 303n

Bible, Old Testament, 146, 199, 283
  Exodus, 199; see also Old English Exodus
  Psalms, 283

Biddle, Martin, 111, 226, 235, 242, 248

Binns, Alan, 142

bishops and bishoprics, 237–42, 280, 336
  defensive responsibilities of, 158–9, 164–5, 241–2, 263

Bisson, Thomas, 109n

Blackwater, River, 274

Blair, John, 304n

Blake, N. F., 285n

Boars, 279, 280

Bocking (Essex), 118

Boethius: Consolation of Philosophy, Old English translation of, 10–11, 97–8

Boniface, St, Anglo-Saxon missionary, 9

Bookland, 66, 92, 93, 101, 103, 104, 171; see also land and charters and writs

Bosworth, Joseph, 221

Boulogne, 168, 214, 219

Bradbury, Jim, 236, 247

Bradford-on-Avon (Wilts.), 253n

Bran Ditch (Cambs.), 307n

Bratton Camp (Wilts.), 229n, 309, 313

Braydon (Wilts.), 307

Brecan Mere (Llangorse, Powys), 22

bridges and bridge-work, 66, 70, 71, 73, 79, 81, 89, 93, 171, 195, 199–200, 217, 219

Bridgnorth (Salop.), 198, 234

Bridgwater (Som.), 313

Brihtric, leader of fleet, 150, 157

Brihtric, will of, 117

Brihtwold, Archbishop of Canterbury, 319

Bristol, 163, 252

Britons, *see* Wales and Welsh

Brittany, 139, 258

Bromley (Kent), 221, 222, 224

Brompton (Yorks.), sculpture at, 131

Brooks, Nicholas, 42, 43, 59, 60, 92, 93, 113–14, 116, 121–2, 159n, 209n, 211–12, 217n, 229n

Brown, R. A., 56, 152, 263n

Brownsea Island (Dors.), 289

Bruges, 203, 204

Brunanburh, battle of, 4, 15, 26, 198, 283, 285, 298–9, 300–2

memory of and possible location, 300

poem on, 134, 299, 300

Buckinghamshire, 160, 161, 252n

bullion, 121n

Burbage (Wilts.), early crossbow find at, 111n

Burghal Hidage, administrative document, 7, 7n, 59–60, 65, 81, 112n, 139, 147, 209–12, 214, 215, 226, 233, 234, 235, 237–41, 336

Burghclere (Hants.), 221, 222

Burley (Hants.), 224

Burne, Lt-Col. H., 277n

Burnswark (Dumfriesshire), 299n, 301

Burpham (Sussex), 147n

Bury Hill, hillfort (Hants.), 307n

Bury St Edmunds (Suffolk), 81, 122n

Bury Wood Camp (Wilts.), 313

butsecarls, 57, 84, 151, 155–6, 157, 205

Butser (Hants.), 224

Buttington (Montgomerys., now Powys), 95, 229n, 234n

Byrhtferth of Ramsey, 250, 270n

Byrhtnoth, East Saxon ealdorman, 73, 75, 83, 146, 250, 251, 268, 274, 278, 303, 323

Byzantium, English service in, 108n

Cædwalla, King of the *Gewisse*, 303

Caligula, Roman emperor, 219

Cambridge, 248

Cambridgeshire, 58, 252n

Camden, William, 309, 310n

campaigns, 93, 96, 97, 99, 114, 136, 158, 176–200 *passim*, 297, 337

Campbell, Alistair, 166, 299n

Campbell, James, 44, 106, 107, 142, 182

Canfield Castle (Essex), 206

Canterbury, 151, 202, 244, 245, 247–8, 256, 320

Carhampton (Som.), 167

Carlisle, abbot of, 320

Carlyle, Thomas, 55

Carmen de Hastingae proelio, 138, 138n, 260, 286, 306

Carolingians, Frankish dynasty

conquests by, 9, 336, 337

rulership, 21, 99

influence on England, 182, 272

carrying service, 62, 89

Carthage and Carthaginians, 187

carts, 61, 183, 192, 192n, 193, 195, 208, 215, 337

carucates, *see* land, assessment of

Castile, 64

castles and castle-building, 92, 233n, 236–7, 255, 262

Catiline, Roman politician, 270–1

cattle, 175, 204, 326, 331, 332

cavalry, 89, 134, 137, 220, 270, 281, 283–4, 286; *see also* horses

Cenwulf, King of Mercia, 54

Ceolmund, ealdorman of Kent, 181

ceorls, 131, 326, 332

in historiographical traditions, 47, 48, 51, 69, 98, 99n, 137

military services of, 53–5, 62, 73, 83, 85, 90, 92, 98, 214

wealth of, 55, 85

Chadwick, H. M., 25, 55, 68, 69, 85, 88, 135

Chamberlain, King's, 82–3

Chaplais, Pierre, 171, 319n

Charlemagne, Frankish ruler, 146, 198, 219, 220, 271n, 317, 328; *see also* Carolingians

Charles the Bald, Frankish ruler, 60n, 94, 137, 198, 200, 212, 218–19; *see also* Carolingians charters/writs

Anglo-Saxon, 2, 22n, 69, 70–3, 103, 165,
171–4, 192–3, 214–15, 215n, 219, 225,
242–3, 287, 302, 328, 331

citations of individual charters, S 59:
70; S 141: 84; S 186: 229; S 201: 54;
S 206: 181; S 208: 181; S 211: 181;
S 212: 181; S 214: 181; S 223: 214–15;
S 272: 183; S 273: 183; S 290: 174;
S 291: 181; S 294: 181; S 294b: 181;
S 311: 304; S 315: 181; S 316: 181;
S 327: 181; S 328: 71; S 344: 181;
S 347: 174–5; S 350: 214; S 397: 46;
S 405: 71; S 407: 22, 182–5, 192–3;
S 425: 22, 182–5, 192–3; S 436: 242;
S 548: 46; S 599: 80; S 646: 71, 302;
S 731: 148; S 832: 171–2, 174–5; S 836:
172; S 837: 172; S 842: 172; S 869:
172; S 872: 172; S 877: 172; S 895:
172; S 896: 174; S 899: 253; S 909:
245; S 910: 172, 173; S 911: 172, 173;
S 912: 173; S 914: 172; S 915: 173;
S 918: 173; S 938: 172, 173; S 939: 118;
S 944: 172; S 951: 171; S 956: 173;
S 985: 82; S 1004: 39; S 1063: 39;
S 1064: 39; S 1104: 39; S 1129: 103;
S 1143: 103; S 1144: 103; S 1196: 181;
S 1186a: 71; S 1202: 181; S 1203: 181;
S 1264: 229; S 1309: 89; S 1326: 89;
S 1332: 89; S 1383: 148; S 1394: 82;
S 1406: 80, 82; S 1409: 72, 80, 82;
S 1423: 72; S 1454: 34; S 1458a: 148;
S 1483: 116; S 1485: 117; S 1486: 117;
S 1487: 106, 118, 122; S 1488: 119, 122,
148; S 1490: 86, 122; S 1492: 119, 120,
148; S 1493: 114; S 1494: 118; S 1497:
118; S 1498: 89, 117, 122; S 1500: 114;
S 1501: 114, 118; S 1502: 115; S 1503:
67, 119, 129; S 1503a: 115; S 1506: 115;
S 1507: 12; S 1508: 115, 181; S 1509:
115; S 1510: 115, 121; S 1511: 117; S 1513:
115; S 1514: 115; S 1517: 120, 122;
S 1518: 115; S 1519: 120, 122; S 1522:
115; S 1526: 116; S 1531: 89, 120;
S 1532: 115, 120; S 1533: 115; S 1534:
118; S 1535: 122; S 1536: 118; S 1537:
120, 122, 128

witness lists, 2, 3n, 22n, 173, 181n,
182–5, 243, 258n

bounds, 174n, 175, 187, 211, 221–2

Anglo-Norman, 161, 287

Frankish, 191n

Cheshire, 230

Domesday customs relating to, 73, 77

Chester, 229, 234

defences, 215–16, 230–3

Domesday customs of, 29, 73, 77, 103n,
215–16, 233

Edgar's Dee-rowing at, 20, 28

Chester-le-Street (Co. Durham),
bishopric of, 183

Chester-le-Street (Co. Durham),
sculpture at, 131, 132

Chesterton, G. K., 309n

Chibnall, Marjorie, 260n

Chichester (Sussex), 253

Chichester Harbour, 296n

Chippenham (Wilts.), 199, 229, 229n,
234n, 235, 313

chivalry, 111, 138, 138n

Christ Church Canterbury, 118, 121n, 196

Christchurch (Hants.; now Dors.), 207,
241n, 252n

Christchurch Harbour, 289

Christianity

conversion to, 8–9, 38, 319, 331, 334

influence on historical sources, 43

mass, 215, 276, 280–1

miracles, 194, 303

papal prohibition, 229n

and peacemaking, 315, 319–20, 328

penance, 303, 304n

minsters and monasticism, 21, 91–2, 109,
152, 225, 302–4

saints and sanctity, 11, 173, 194–7, 303

and social organization, 10–12, 34, 63,
97–8

Cinque Ports, 156

Cissbury (Sussex), 216

civil war, see rebellion and civil war

Clapham, J. H., 282

Clausewitz, Carl von, 9, 315–16

clothing, 110n, 154

cnihts, see knights and knighthood

Cnut, King of England and Denmark, 9,
28, 104n, 106, 107, 109, 116, 162, 194, 195,
196, 242, 245, 247, 261–2, 307n, 321

death of, 155, 244

grants and endowments, 173, 303; see
also charters and writs

laws of, see under laws and lawmaking

and fleets, 154, 175

and Scandinavia, 137, 153

as war-leader, 144, 189, 252, 260, 268

coastal topography, 174, 175, 286, 293–5,
296n

coins and mints, 216, 237–41, 245n, 252
'combined operations', 200, 202, 208, 297;
   see also ships and boats
Contamine, Philippe, 15–16, 267
Cooling (Kent), 95
Cooper, Alan, 217n
Corduan, Isle of, 219
Cornwall, Bishopric of, 183
Cornwall and Cornish, 23, 25, 106, 168,
   171–2, 174, 175, 203
cottars, 220, 222
Coupland, Simon, 248n
courage and cowardice, 15–16, 34, 251, 252,
   266–8, 276, 322–3
Crayford (Kent), 196
Crediton, bishop and bishopric of, 119, 148,
   149, 162, 221
Creighton, Oliver, 260n
Creodantreow, Battle of, 183n
Cricklade (Wilts.), 307
Crondall (Hants.), 224
Cross, J. E., 12
crossbows, 111, 226
Crowle (Lincs.), sculpture at, 131
Crowle (Worcs.), 216, 224
Crusades
   Second, 170n
   Third, 177
Crux Easton (Hants.), 222
Cuckhamsley Barrow, see Scutchamer
   Knob
Cyfeiliog, Bishop ?of Archenfield, 23
Cyneheard, ætheling, 19, 290n
Cynewulf, King of West Saxons, 14, 19,
   290n

Dalton, Paul, 320–2
Danelaw, 212, 216
   assessments of land, 57, 62
   identities in, 131–3
   legal distinctiveness of, 70
   organization of, 100
   political interests in, 46, 183, 230, 300–1
   see also Northumbria
Darby, H. C., 241
Dartmouth (Devon), 170n
Davidson, Hilda Ellis, 279n, 280
Davies, Wendy, 333n
Davis, R. H. C., 135–6, 137, 327
De Obsessio Dunelmi, 30–1, 217

dead, treatment of, 30–1, 31n, 305–6
Dee, River, 20, 321
Deerhurst (Glos.), 103n, 321, 322
Denewulf, Bishop of Winchester, 80
Denmark, 39, 160, 259
Derby, 14
Derbyshire, Domesday assessments in, 57
Devon, 167, 234n, 287, 291, 293
   fyrd of, 104n, 106, 203, 249, 254
   Viking activities in, 24, 253–5
Devries, Kelly, 22
Dibberworth (Dors.), 164
disease, 15, 175, 178, 186
Dodgson, J. M., 303n
Dodwell, C. R., 145
Domesday Book, 96, 108, 244
   customs in, 50, 56, 67, 73, 76–7, 81, 84,
     103, 104, 139, 156, 159, 237–41, 244,
     259–60
   evidence of landholdings 59, 60, 74, 77,
     85, 86–7, 147, 152, 287, 313–14; see
     also lands, assessments of
   parage tenure, 78, 82, 86–7
Dorcester (Dors.), 167, 244n
Dorset, 174, 244, 252
Dover (Kent), 156, 186n, 205, 219–20
Dream of the Rood, poem, 227
drinking, 151, 280; see also feasting
Droitwich (Worcs.), 215
Dromon, 166, 169
Dublin, 232, 259
Dudo of St Quentin, 138n, 248
Dumville, D. N., 327
Dungeness (Kent), 156, 203, 205
Dunkirk, retreat from, 198
Dunnere, ceorl at Battle of Maldon, 55,
   73, 83
Dunstan, St, Archbishop, 173
Durham, 30–1, 217, 241n, 245, 248
Durham Ritual, 193
Durnford (Wilts.), 86–7
Dutton, L. S., 302
Dutton, Paul, 146n
Duxford, Cambs., 116
Dyer, Christopher, 241n

Eadgifu, Queen, 95
Eadred, King of the English, 109, 221, 260
Eadric Streona, Ealdorman of Mercia, 116,
   150, 154n, 268

Eadric, steersman, 102, 159, 160

Eadwig, King of the English, 71, 302

ealdormen and earls, 115, 122, 129, 183
    duties of, 2–4, 165, 166–70, 241, 264,
        265, 338

Ealdred, Bishop of Worcester, 72, 80

Ealhhere, Ealdorman, 152n

Eamont Bridge (Cumberland), 321n,
    332–3

East Anglia, 46, 58, 86n, 106, 143, 153,
    252n, 293, 296, 298, 326, 327

Ecgfrith, King of Northumbrians, 199n

Eddington (Berks.), 310

Edgar, ætheling, 157

Edgar 'the Peaceable', King of the English,
    15, 28, 30, 105n, 110, 146, 321
    charters of, 159, 221
    and fleets, 150, 153, 158, 163, 171, 175
    as overlord, 15, 20, 25, 158n

Edington, Battle of, 93, 145, 179–82, 199,
    212, 235, 264, 298, 299, 300n, 302,
    304–5, 307, 308–14, 322, 327

Edington (Som.), 310, 313–14

Edington (Wilts.), 300n, 302, 310, 313

Edith Swan-Neck, mistress of Harold
    Godwineson, 306n

Edmund I, King of the English, 22n, 116,
    146, 221, 300–1

Edmund Ironside, King of the English,
    45, 48, 119, 189, 260–2, 268, 269–71,
    307n, 321

Edward I, 98

Edward the Confessor, King of the
    English, 22, 83, 104n, 154, 203, 205,
    241, 323
    and fleets, 157, 158, 163, 202, 297
    lands and rights, 102–3, 156–7

Edward the Elder, King of the Anglo-
    Saxons, 212, 221
    as ætheling, 97, 188, 214
    as war-leader, 10, 22, 46, 63, 94, 95, 99,
        106, 182, 188, 216, 229–30

Edward the Martyr, King, 172, 173, 219,
    251n, 252–3

Edwin, Earl of Mercia, 156

Edwin, King of Northumbrians, 12, 318

Egbert, King of Wessex, 183n

Egbert's Stone, 179, 180n, 302

Egil Skallagrimson, saga of, 301

Einhard: Vita Karoli Magni, 146

Elene, 135

Ellendun (Wroughton, Wilts.), Battle of,
    183n

Ely (Cambs.), 157, 303

embassies, 189, 261

Emma, Queen, 109n, 155, 195, 266

Encomium Emmae, 108n, 144–5, 247,
    261–2, 273, 306n

English
    identities of, xvi, 10, 19, 32, 44, 45–6,
        130, 139, 327
    in historiography, 111, 134
    relations with neighbouring polities,
        see Cornwall and Cornish; Franks;
        Scotland and Scots; Wales and
        Welsh

English Channel, 147n, 153, 174, 189, 248,
    287, 292, 335

Eorpeburnan, unidentified fortress, 214

Eric, earl in Norway, 261

Erik Bloodaxe, King of York, 260

Essex and East Saxons, 118, 234n, 252, 319,
    327
    warriors of, 73, 75, 203

Estates, control and use of, 179, 180, 189,
    210; see also tun, royal

Eustace, Count of Boulogne, 235

Evesham (Worcs.), church of, 72, 102

Ewyas Harold (Herefs.), 206

Exe, River, 254

Exeter, 67, 161, 167, 241n, 247–8, 253–5,
    256, 261, 266–7
    gild statutes, 243
    rebellion and siege of, 1067–8, 242,
        258–60

Exeter Book, 131, 134

exile and outlawry, 156, 160, 202, 331

Eye (Suffolk), 241n

Farley Mount (Hants.), 222, 224

'Farm of one night', 180n; see also feorm

Farnham (Surrey), Battle of, 15

feasting and eating, 99, 193, 241, 306; see
    also feorm

Fell, Christine, 317n

feorm, 101n, 110, 178–80, 191

Fern, Chris, 131n

feud and retribution, 43, 318, 327

feudal service and feudalism, 51, 64, 68,
    241–2

Finberg, H. P. R., 225

Fisher, Peter, 279n

fishing, 163

Five Boroughs, poem on recapture of, 232

fleets, see navy and naval forces

Fleming, Robin, 109, 173, 243

flooding, 199

Florence of Worcester, see John of Worcester

Folkestone (Kent), 156, 205

Fontenoy, Battle of, 191n, 277, 278, 305n

Foot, Sarah, 43

Foote, Peter, 267

Fordham, Michael, 333n

Forte, Angelo, 43

fortifications, 320
   building and maintenance of, 14, 60, 62, 66, 70, 71, 77–8, 79, 89, 103, 171, 209, 213, 219, 252n, 258, 261
   defence of, 59, 92, 92–3, 187–8, 199, 213–14, 217, 226, 244, 336
   as refuges, 225, 250–1, 277, 313
   relationship with army organization, 60, 92–3, 94–5, 250
   size of, 233, 236, 247–51
   strategic placement of, 146, 147, 210, 217, 233, 236
   temporary and battlefield, 42, 52, 233–5
   see also Burghal Hidage; castles

Fragmentary Annals of Ireland, 230–3, 337

France, 167, 186, 200, 202, 212, 258, 263

France, John, 91

Frank, Roberta, 40, 41

Franks
   economic activity, 9
   politics of, 44, 99, 316n
   military service, 67, 68
   and Vikings, 34, 137, 146, 229, 320
   warfare of, 18, 43, 49, 61, 67, 91, 111, 130, 136, 200, 212–13, 273, 278–9, 305n

Freeman, E. A., 50, 52, 91, 92, 98, 114n, 234n, 259, 260n, 297

Frisians, 152, 153n, 292, 293, 295

Frontinus: Strategemata, 271

Fulford, Battle of, 298, 308n

fyrd, terminology of, xvi, 139, 146–7; see also armies and land forces

Gaels, see Scotland and Scots

Gainford (Co. Durham), sculpture at, 131

Gale, Tara, 259

Garmonsway, G. N., 148

Garrison, Mary, 336n

geburs, 98

Geibig, Alfred, 128

Geffrei Gaimar: Estoire des Engleis, 166, 180–1, 182, 198–9

geld, payments and receipt of, 35–8, 100, 144, 145–6, 154, 262, 264, 323; see also taxation

George, Archbishop of Ravenna, 191n

Gerald of Wales: Description of Wales, 22–3, 114n

gesith, 54, 75, 82; see also thegn

gestures, see rituals, customs, codes of conduct

Gifford, Edwin and Joyce, 143, 147

Gildas, sixth-century British author, 4n, 169n

gilds, 107, 237–40, 241, 243

Giles, J. A., 310n

Gilling (Yorks.), minster founded at, 303

Gillingham (Dorset), 180n

Gillingham, John, 64, 130, 177, 178–9, 189, 190, 235n, 281n, 305–6

Gillmor, Carol, 151

Gloucestershire, 108, 310

Glover, Richard, 135, 284

Goda, Kentish thegn, 95

Godwine, Earl of Wessex, 154, 155, 156, 163, 202–5, 323–4
   family of, 44, 45, 202–7, 297, 324
   as war-leader, 157, 206n, 297

Gokstad ship, 142, 143, 144

Gosforth (Cumberland), sculpture at, 131, 132

Gough, Richard, 309

Graham-Campbell, James, 131

Gransden, Antonia, 182n

Grateley (Hants.), 59n, 62, 237

grave goods, 12, 128

Graveney boat, 142, 143, 158

Greece, Ancient, 51, 266, 272

Green, J. R., 49–51, 52, 55, 63, 91, 98, 107

Greenwich (Kent), 154, 261

Gresswell, Rev. W. H. P., 313

Griffith, Paddy, 279n

Grossman, Dave, 16n, 199, 266

Gruffudd ap Llywelyn, King of Gwynedd, 22, 28, 29, 206n, 284

Guthrum, Viking leader, 322, 325, 326; see also Alfred-Guthrum under laws and legal codes

Gwent, people of (*Wentsæte*), 332, 333
Gwynnedd, Welsh kingdom, 27, 28, 202
Gyrth Godwineson, 278

Hadley, Dawn, 131
Hakon the Good, King of Norway, 220
Halloran, Kevin, 299n
Halsall, Guy, 15, 16–17, 26, 32, 43, 92–3,
    114, 129–30, 134, 135, 265, 273, 275, 277,
    283, 285n, 318n, 321, 327
Hamble, River, 293n
Hampshire, 64, 182n, 218, 222, 252n
    military organization in, 179, 222, 254,
    266
Hannibal, 251
Harari, Yuval Noah, 194n
Hare, Kent, 11
Harold Godwineson, Earl and King, 318
    and Battle of Hastings, 29, 52, 106,
        107–8, 189, 191, 278, 306
    and Battle of Stamford Bridge, 39
    campaign in Brittany, 138
    campaigns in Wales, 22–3, 114n, 163,
        202, 206, 207
    household men of, 138, 244n
    role in rebellion, 44, 202–7
    as war leader, 58, 106, 155, 158, 162, 183,
        186, 206–7
Harold Harefoot, 154, 155
Harrison, David, 187n
Hart, C. R., 270n, 273
Hart (Co. Durham), sculpture at, 131
Harthacnut, King of England and
    Denmark, 107, 108, 154, 155, 162, 195
Hasting, Norman ancestor, 248
Hastings (Sussex), 156, 157, 253
    district of, 203, 252n
Hastings, campaign and Battle of, 29, 49,
    75, 106, 107, 108, 111, 111n, 138, 189, 191,
    218, 260, 271n, 285–6, 287, 298, 300,
    335
    preparations for, 318
    fortifications in, 52, 234–5
    deaths in, 87, 278
Hawkes, Jacquetta, 307n
Haywood, John, 142
Heavenfield, Battle of, 303
Hedeby ship, 143, 169
Hemming's Cartulary, 102, 103, 159
Henry de Blois, Bishop of Winchester,
    242

Henry I, King of England, 157, 244, 273
Henry II, King of England, 336
Henry III, Emperor, 153
Henry of Huntingdon: *Historia
    Anglorum*, 268n, 278n, 325
Hereford, 28, 206, 248, 281, 284
herepaths, see roads and routeways
Hereward 'the Wake', 80
heriots, 56, 62, 85–6, 114–28, 137, 148
heroic traditions and ideals, literary, 7, 83,
    84n, 188, 265, 273, 285, 305
herring fleets, 163
Hertfordshire, 252n
hides, see land, assessment of
Higham, Nicholas, 151
Higham, Robert, 260n
Highclere (Hants.), 221, 222, 224
Hill, David, 174, 200n, 211, 216, 217–25
Hill, John, 188, 299n
Hill, Paul, 114n
Hincmar, Archbishop of Rheims, 212
Hinton, David, 121n, 211–12, 253n
Historia de Sancto Cuthberto, 304–5, 320
Historia Regum, 325
Hoare, R. C., 307n
Hoare, Sir Richard Colt, 309
Hodgkin, R. H., 309n
Holcombe Rogus (Devon), 164
Hollings, M., 72
Hollister, C. W., 51, 68–91, 92, 101, 107,
    140, 152, 156, 157n, 161, 162
Holme, Battle of the, 106, 298
Hooke, Della, 174
Hooper, Nicholas, 69, 107–8, 109, 141,
    151–63, 164, 280, 281
Hoplites, Greek, 272
horses and riding, 5n, 67–8, 96, 137, 140,
    189, 196, 199, 200, 206, 229n, 265, 271,
    273, 281, 309, 314
    breeding, 96n, 118, 121, 130n, 136, 137
    differences between English and
        Norman, 130n, 135–6
    equipment of, 131
    political significance of riding, 186, 189,
        261
    depictions in sculptures, 131–4
    use as transport, 67, 94, 95, 96, 183, 189,
        191–2, 192n, 208
    use in war, 129–39, 231, 278, 281–6
    in wills, 86, 96n, 114–21, 136n

hostages, 19, 20, 180, 205, 255, 258, 259, 316n, 319, 320, 323, 325, 326, 329, 332, 334

hounds, 281

housecarls, 39, 106, 107–10, 140, 155, 194–5, 196, 237–40, 244

households, royal and noble, 106, 109, 110, 119, 121, 138, 281–2, 318–19

Hugh the Great: *Dux Francorum*, 148, 220

Hugh, French reeve of Exeter, 266

Hughes, Thomas, 309n

Humber, River, 159

hundred and hundredal organization, 57, 66, 68, 99–101 102, 103, 159, 160–1, 180n

hunting, 280

Huntingdonshire, 252n

Hyams, Paul, 318n

Hyland, Ann, 136

Hythe (Kent), 156, 205

Hywel Dda ('the Good'), King of Deheubarth, 230

Iley Oak (Wilts.), 179, 180n

Imma, captured Northumbrian thegn, 61, 327n

infantry and foot-soldiers, 134, 137, 138n, 273, 283, 284, 286

Ingimund, Viking leader, 230, 232

Insley, Charles, 23, 172

Ipswich (Suffolk), 248

Ireland, 168, 202, 203, 204, 231, 232, 258, 336

  historical sources from, 230–3

  Vikings and, 229n, 231

  warfare of, 43, 284

Irish Sea region, 21, 153, 200

Isaac, Stevn, 267–8

Isle of Man, 9, 202

Isidore of Seville, 12

Jayakumar, Shashi, 110, 163

John of Oxenedes, attr. author of St Benet at Holme chronicle, 160

John of Salisbury: *Polycratus*, 106, 114n, 268

John of Worcester: *Chronicle*, 20, 139, 154, 249, 262, 268, 269–71, 272–3, 284–5, 336

John, Eric, 55, 63, 68, 69, 92, 98, 99–100, 139, 159n, 273

Jolliffe, J. E. A., 77

Jomsburg, Vikings of, 107

Jones, C., 298

Judith, Countess, 160

Julius Caesar, 271n

Just War, concept of, 12

Keefer, Sarah Larratt, 136

Keegan, John, 16n, 266

Kelly, Susan, 253n

Kelvedon Hatch (Essex), 287

Kemble, J. M., 50, 64

Kennedy, A. G., 293n

Kennet, River, valley of, 224

Kent and inhabitants, 167, 168, 196, 214, 234n, 252n

  assessments of land, 58, 62, 214

  bequest to, 119, 148

  maritime customs of, 143, 152, 153, 156

  warriors, 54, 106, 203, 268

Kershaw, Paul, 316, 325, 328n

Keverne Beacon (Cornwall), 174n, 175

Keynes, Simon, xvi, 3, 214, 275, 302, 327n, 328

Kiff, Jennie, 283, 305

Kings Worthy (Hants.), 242

kingship and rulership, 24, 25, 217, 232, 260, 288, 327

  manifested through royal presence in war, 22, 106, 178–83, 202, 315

  overlordship, 142, 334

  see also Carolingians; Ottonians

Kingsteignton (Devon), 254–5

Knightlow (Warwicks.), 161

knights and knighthood, 56, 64–5, 67, 74, 81, 99, 259

  pre-Conquest cniht, 88–9, 90, 119, 120, 121, 135, 243

Kökeritz, Helge, 218

Kosto, Adam, 316n, 317, 325

Krapp, G. P., 288n, 293n

Lambarde, William, 219

Lancashire, land assessment in, 58

land

  assessment of, 54, 56, 57, 58, 59, 62,63, 66–7, 68, 71, 72, 73, 74, 77, 80n, 86, 87, 90, 112, 113n, 148–9, 156, 157, 158–9, 161, 162, 164–5, 210–12, 214, 335

land, *continued*
  holding of, 47, 55–6, 66–7, 71, 123, 128, 155; *see also under* Domesday Book
  læn ('leased') land, 72, 80, 89, 102n, 105, 159
landscape
  control of, 34, 186, 304
  as evidence, 222–5
  movement through, 77, 186–7, 187n, 197, 207
Langdon, John, 259
Langlands, Alex, 187n
Lapidge, Michael, 270n, 275
Larson, L. M., 107, 109
Latin vocabulary, 166, 225
Latouche, Robert, 220
laws and legal codes, 242, 326–7
  English
    Ine, 41, 54, 79, 85, 105n, 114n
    Alfred, 4n, 88, 98, 111, 236n, 281
    Alfred-Guthrum, 96, 325, 326–8, 331
    II Athelstan ('Grately code'), 59n, 62–3, 96n, 137, 183, 237, 260n, 279n
    VI Athelstan, 96n
    Hundred Ordinance, 100
    III Edgar, 105n
    II Æthelred, 241n, 325–6, 327, 328–32
    V Æthelred, 104n, 157n
    VI Æthelred, 104n, 105n, 157n
    II Cnut, 70, 86, 104n, 105n, 115, 122, 137, 137n
    Geðyncðu, 55, 59, 84
    Norðleoda laga, 55, 59, 85, 104n
    Rectitudines Singularum Personarum, 79, 84, 104, 171, 220
    Dunsæte, 96n, 326, 332–3
    imagined, 77
    Leges Henrici Primi, 88, 104n, 159
  Carolingian Frankish
    Capitularia concerning military service, 67
    Capitulare 'de villis', 61
    Capitulare missorum in Theodonis villa datum secundum, Generale, 328n
    Edictum Pistense, 137, 212
  Lombard
    Ahistulf, 97
  Roman
    Theodosian Code, 137, 212
Lawson, M. K., 234

Lea, River, 97, 145, 234n, 326
leadership, 4, 15, 39, 134, 145, 179, 180, 266–7, 268, 273, 315, 333, 338
Leckhamstead (Berks.), 221, 224
Leeds, 301
Leicester, Domesday customs of, 57, 161
Leishman, Natalie, 259
Leland, John, 219–20
Leofric, Bishop of Exeter, 242
Leofwine Godwineson, Earl, 244n, 278
Lewes (Sussex), 147n
Leyser, Karl, 9, 191, 198, 316
Liðsmannaflokkr, Skaldic poem, 40–1
Liège, 241n
Liebermann, Felix, 331
Lincolnshire, 57, 78, 89, 216, 262
Lindisfarne, 43, 152
lithsmen, 154–5, 156, 157; *see also* ships; crews
Little, A. G., 58, 84
Lizard Peninsula (Cornwall), 174, 174
Lockwood, Jeffrey, 233
Lodden, River, 199
logistics, 60–3, 97, 99, 112, 145–65 *passim*, 177, 178, 191–3
Lombards, military service of, 67, 68
London, 48, 97, 150, 155, 161, 194–5, 196, 197, 206, 242, 245, 247, 257, 260, 323
  military role of, 5n, 41, 95, 106, 113, 157, 158, 162, 200, 204, 205, 228, 234, 245, 260–1
  political importance of, 256, 260–2
  Bridge, 200, 247, 261, 297, 323
  maritime customs, 152, 155
  bishopric, *see* St Paul's
Longphoirt, 229n
lordship, 14, 121
  ideals of, 19, 83, 267
  link with military organization, 101, 105, 140, 268; *see also* leadership
Lothar, Frankish emperor, 218
Louis d'Outremer, King of France, 148, 220
Louis the Pious, Frankish Emperor, 219
Luna, legendary Viking raid on, 248
Lund, Niels, 317, 331
Luttwak, Edward, 210
Lydford (Devon), 172, 248, 249–50
Lympne, River, 168, 214

Mack, Kathryn, 109

Magoun, F. P., 287, 290–6

Magyars, 198

Maine, County of, 335

Maitland, F. W., 56, 58, 212, 243

Major, A. F., 293n

Maldon, Battle of, 75, 83–4, 113, 145, 234n, 250, 264, 269, 278, 285, 298, 302–3; see also Battle of Maldon, poem

Maldon (Essex), town of, 161, 234n, 248, 249, 250–1

Malmesbury (Wilts.), Domesday customs of, 57, 67, 84, 156

Manley, J. M., 274n

manuscripts

British Library

Cotton Claudius B.IV (Old English Hexateuch), 191, 192n, 193, 282

Harley MS 603 (Harley Psalter), 226, 283

Utrecht University Library MS 32 (Utrecht Psalter), 283

writing of, 193–4

Marathon, Battle of, 272

maritime guard, 171–5, 219, 222, 225

Marlborough (Wilts.), 241n

masculinity and war, 12, 13, 16, 131, 251

Maslow, A. H., 178

Matilda, abbess of Essen, 2

Matthew, Donald, 336n

Maxims, Old English, 131, 134, 284, 285n

Maxwell, Sir Herbert, 134n

McGurk, Patrick, 270n

McLeod, Shane, 229n

memorial stones, 23; see also rune-stones

mercenaries and stipendiaries

inclusion in armies, 73, 83, 105, 318

use in fleets, 153–7, 163

payment for, 61, 107, 335

see also Vikings

Mercia and Mercians, 30, 63, 86n, 182, 202, 322, 327

relations with Wessex, 24–5, 30, 45, 46n, 232, 326

relations with Welsh, 28, 284–5

warriors of, 30, 61, 157, 198, 229, 284–5

organization, 63, 71, 91, 93, 100–1, 210, 212, 214–16, 215n

Viking activities in, 250, 322

Mersea (Essex), 168, 294

Metellus, Roman commander, 270

Meulan, 218

Meuse, River, 320

Middlesex, 72, 73, 252

millenarianism, 196

'military probability', 7, 310

Milton Regis (Kent), 188

Minchampton (Glos.), 310

Molloy, Barry, 16n, 266

Morale, 191, 198, 267

Morcar, Earl, 156

Morgan, Philip, 299–300

Morillo, Stephen, 49, 190, 267–8, 269–73, 322

Morini, Carla, 113, 116

Murray, K. M. E., 156

names, personal, 4, 5, 29, 181, 183

Nantes, 248n

naval battles, 152, 286–97, 314

navy and naval forces, 1, 145, 146, 149–51, 157–9, 162–3, 166, 175, 222, 297, 337

as terms, xvi, 141, 286

in historiography, 141

logistical support of, 149–50

post-conquest use, 157

Naze, The (Essex), 206

Nelson, Jinty, 255–6, 328n

Neston (Cheshire), sculpture at, 131, 133

Newnham Murren (Oxon.), 221, 224

Nicholson, Helen, 13

Niles, John, 5

Nithard, and Histories of the Sons of Louis the Pious, 3, 218–19, 277

Noel, William, 283n

Nora, Pierre, 298

Norfolk, 160

Norman Conquest, perceptions of impact, 29, 138–9, 336

Normandy, duchy of, and Normans, 9, 154, 158, 202, 336

frontier, 263

identities, 130, 138–9, 248

resources of duchy, 151, 161

strategies and tactics of, 189, 255, 263, 273, 282

North Sea and region, 9, 38, 142, 189

Northampton, 95, 248

Northamptonshire, 62n, 252n

Northumbria and Northumbrians, 46, 159, 186, 260
  campaigns in, 148, 182–4
  relations with other kingdoms, 24, 30, 318
  warriors of, 30, 31, 61
Norway and Norwegians, 153, 220, 230–2, 261
Nottingham, 45, 81, 182–5, 193, 234n, 322
Nottinghamshire, Domesday assessments in, 57
Numidians, 187

Oakley (Dorset), 193
oaths, making and breaking, 111, 231, 258, 304n, 326, 332
Oda, Archbishop of Canterbury, 71
Odda, Earl, 203
O'Donovan, Mary, 164n, 165, 172
Odstock (Wilts.), 221, 224
Offa, warrior at Battle of Maldon, 250n
Offa, King of Mercia, 71, 72, 73, 93
offensive and defensive warfare, distinctions, 91
Olaf Haraldsson, 154
Olaf Sigtryggsson, King of Dublin and York, 301–2
Olaf Tryggvasson, Viking leader and King of Norway, 264n, 329
Old English Bede, 61
Old English Exodus, 135, 189n
Old English Orosius, 92, 94n, 187–8, 251, 282–3
Old Sarum (Wilts.), 216
Oman, Sir Charles, 272, 274, 290n
Oram, Richard, 43
Orc, Dorset housecarl, 39
Orderic Vitalis: Historia Ecclesiastica, 130, 234, 258–9, 261, 271n, 305
Osbern of Canterbury, hagiographer, 194, 196–7
Ostrogoths, 130
Oswald, St, Bishop of Worcester, 80, 173
Oswald, King of Northumbrians, 303
Oswaldslow, 102, 103, 148, 159
Oswine, King of Deira, 303
Oswiu, King of Northumbrians, 303
Otar the Black, Skald, 154n
Otto the Great, German emperor, 21
Ottonians, German dynasty, 9, 18, 21
Ouse, River, 326

Owers, banks off Sussex coast, 296n
Oxford, 245, 248, 256
Oxfordshire, 76, 77, 224, 252

pagans and paganism, 8–9, 31,34, 42, 43, 110n, 229n, 248, 303, 304, 319
Page, R. I., 42, 145
Palgrave, Francis, 259
Pallig, Viking leader, 153–4, 254
Pamplona, 198
Paris, 218, 228, 228n, 247
Parrett, River, 234n
Pauli, Reinhold, 48, 181, 313
peace
  negotiation for, 165, 318–19, 320–2
  peace agreements, 324–33
  peacemaking, 205, 255, 257n, 260, 261, 265, 297, 315–22, 323–4, 337
    locations of, 320–2
  terminology of, 316–17, 325, 329
peasants, use in warfare, 91–2, 96–8, 102n, 139, 337; see also ceorls
Peddie, John, 289, 309n
Pederson, Frederik, 43
Pelteret, David, 235n
Penda, King of Mercians, 303
Penselwood, area in Wessex, 180n
Pershore (Worcs.), church of, 102, 103, 160
Peterborough Abbey (Cambs.), estates of, 80, 89–90
Pevensey (Sussex), 156, 204, 205, 241n
Picts, see Scotland and Scots
Pinhoe (Devon), Battle of, 172, 254, 298
pipe rolls, 160–1
place-names, 224, 294n, 306–7, 309, 310, 313–14
Plummer, Charles, 94n
Plumstead (Kent), 195, 196
Plympton Priory (Devon), 172
Polden Hills (Som.), 313
'police' actions, relationship with warfare, 95–6, 100, 151, 200
Pollington, Stephen, 226, 227
Polydore Vergil, and Anglica Historia, 306–7
Pont de l'Arche (dép. Eure), 200n
Poole Harbour, 288–9, 288
Poole, Russell, 40, 41
population, estimates of, 60, 65
Porlock (Som.), 204

Portland (Dors.), 4, 32, 169, 171, 174–5, 204, 206

Portsdown (Hants.), 224

Portsmouth Harbour, 296n

Praetorian Guard, 107

Pratt, David, 10

prestige, importance of, 106, 137, 178–9, 180, 182, 198, 207–8, 325, 337; *see also* leadership

Prestwich, J. O., 170, 259, 322n

Probert, Duncan, 243n

Pullen-Appleby, John, 141, 202

Pyrenees, 198

queens, 13, 14n

radcnihts and 'riding men', 88, 90, 281

Radner, Joan, 232

Ralph de Mantes, Earl of Hereford, 203, 284–5

Ramsey (Hunts., now Cambs.), church of, 118, 162, 270n

Ranulf Flambard, minister of King William II, 60, 335, 336

ravaging/harrying and foraging, 107, 109, 157, 178–9, 186, 191, 202, 204, 242, 249, 255, 301, 329, 331

Reading (Berks.), 118, 198, 218, 248, 251, 276

rebellion and civil war, 19–20, 34, 44, 45, 130, 188, 196, 202–7, 230, 242, 258–9, 273, 285, 307

reeves, 95, 103n, 174, 241n, 337

regiones (units of early kingdoms), 101

Repton (Derbys.), 229n
  stone sculpture from, 128

Reuter, Tim, 91, 109n, 337

Reynolds, Andrew, 307n

Rhuddlan (Clwyd), 206n, 216n, 241n

Rhyd-y-Groes (Powys), 28

Riccall (Yorks.), 307

Richard I, 'the Lionheart', King of England, 74

Richardson, H. G., 135, 136

Richer of St-Remi: *Historiae*, 220, 225

riddles, Old English, 226–7

rituals, customs, codes of conduct, 280, 319, 320, 327, 333–4
  in warfare, 16, 32, 43, 130, 231, 251, 259, 273, 274

rivers, 93, 169, 186, 199, 252, 320–2

roads and routeways, 172–3, 186, 187 and 187n, 196–7, 199, 200, 217, 277n

Robert Curthose, Duke of Normandy, 157

Robertson, A. J., 129n

Rochester (Kent), 73, 109, 196, 221, 234n, 242, 247

Rodger, N. A. M., 141, 144, 145–6, 200

Rodwell, Warwick, 304n

Roffe, David, 335

Rogers, Clifford, 190

Rome and *Romanitas*, 10, 21, 134n, 150n, 181, 210, 213, 226, 241, 251, 270–2, 280
  funerary sculptures, 128
  graffiti, 181

Romney (Kent), 156, 203, 205

Roncesvalles, Battle of, 198

Rose, Susan, 286

Round, J. H., 56, 57, 58, 63, 68, 259n

Royal Flying Corps, 287

Rumble, Alexander, 60, 113n, 196

Runciman, W. G., 55

rune-stones, Scandinavian, 34–9, 108–9

Rye (Sussex), 241n

Sabin, Philip, 233, 250, 268

sagas, Norse, 40, 201

St Alban's, thirteenth-century chronicle of, 153

St Augustine's, Canterbury, 196

St Benet at Holme (Norfolk), 160

St Brice's Day Massacre, 110, 245

St Cloud, 218

St Davids, 28

St Keverne (Cornwall), 219

St Paul's, London, church and bishopric of, 108, 160, 164, 194–5, 196, 241n, 242

Salisbury, Bishop of, 159; *see also* Sherborne

Salisbury (Wilts.), 216, 267

Sallust, 270–1, 272, 273

Samouce, W. A., 268n

Sandford (Devon), 221, 224

Sandwich (Kent), 149, 151, 156, 157, 158, 163, 203, 204, 205, 244, 248

Sawyer, Peter, 41, 42, 43, 170

Saxo Grammaticus: *Gesta Danorum*, 108n, 279

Saxons (Continental), 317

Sayers, William, 166
Sayles, G. O., 135, 136
Scharer, Anton, 146n
Scipio (Publius Cornelius Scipio Africanus Major), 187–8
Scotland and Scots (incl. Gaels and Picts), 199n, 230n, 299
  in English campaigns, 22, 30, 114, 148, 153, 182–3, 198, 200, 202
  treatment by English, 30–1, 217
scouts and reconnaissance, use of, 187–91, 258–9
Scragg, Don, 250n, 269
Scutchamer Knob (Berks., now Oxon.), 32–4, 33, 222, 224
Seaton (*Fleet*) (Devon), 172
Seine, River, 94, 200n, 247
Selsey Bill, 292, 296
seneschals, 83
sergeants, 67, 88, 109
service, limits of, 162
Seven Sleepers of Ephesus, legend of, 31, 217
Severn, River, 23, 95, 165, 203, 321n
Shaftesbury (Dors.), 211, 244, 252–3, 302
Sharp, Sheila, 174, 217–25
Sheppey, Isle of, 205, 262
Sherborne, bishopric of, 148, 158, 159, 164–5, 225
sheriffs, 77, 102, 103, 105, 159
Sherston (Wilts.), Battle of, 268, 269–71
'shield-wall', *see* strategies and tactics
ships, 20, 43, 119, 144–5, 145n, 150, 156, 161, 162, 166, 176, 195, 203, 206, 247, 273, 286
  'Alfredian', 143, 143, 145–7, 288–96
  in campaigns, 186, 200–7, 208
  crews, 102, 112, 113, 144, 147, 149–50, 162, 164, 176, 250–1, 262, 286, 291–6, 297
  design and technology, 119n, 142–5, 146, 166, 261, 289n
  Frisian, 142
  as gifts/bequests, 119, 145n, 148, 162
  observation of, 169–70
  provision, 112–13, 148–51, 151n, 158, 163–5, 262
  Scandinavian, 141, 142–4, 158, 286, 287–97
  terminology, 166–70
ship-scot, 158, 161, 164
ship-sokes, 148, 159–60, 163

shires, 112n, 165
  landholdings in, 112
  organization of forces of, 91, 95, 107, 163
Shoebury Ness (Essex), 299n, 234
Shropshire, 45
sieges and siege warfare, 190, 226–33, 250, 258–60, 261, 297
Sigeric, Archbishop of Canterbury, 118, 329
signalling, 297; *see also* beacons
Simeon of Durham (attr.): *Historia Regum*, 325
Siward, Earl of Northumbria, 202
Siwate (Sighvatr), Lincolnshire landholder, 78, 82
Skaldic poetry, 34, 40–1, 154n
Skaney, 167
Slaughterford (Wilts.), 310
slaves and slavery, 13n, 54, 87, 96n, 98, 187n, 235, 244, 326, 330, 331
Slavs, 328n
'Smerdown' (Isle of Wight), 224
Smyth, Alfred, 146
Snorri Sturluson: *Heimskringla*, 135, 258n
Sockburn (Co. Durham), sculpture at, 131, 133
sokemen, 81, 88, 89–90
Solent, 224, 287, 293n, 295n
Solomon, Biblical king, 146
Somerset, 93, 180, 310
  fyrd of, 104n, 179, 203, 254
South Cadbury (Som.), 216, 247
Southampton, 147n, 211, 248, 329
Southampton Water, 293n
Southwark, 195, 196, 321n
Spurell, F. C. J., 229n
Stafford, Pauline, 13n, 32n, 44n, 109n, 151n, 258n
Staffordshire, 45
Staffordshire Hoard, 117n
Staines (Surrey), 244
Stallers, 137
Stamford (Lincs.), 161, 229
Stamford Bridge (Yorks.), Battle of, 39n, 135, 250, 298, 307n
  memory of, 300, 305
states, 44, 111
  military systems of, 8, 58, 107, 113–14, 139, 151, 200, 222–5, 263, 280, 335–6; *see also* armies and land forces

states, *continued*
  political institutions and
    administration, 10, 58, 217, 256, 258
  relationship with warfare, 9, 47, 99, 111,
    207, 208, 337–8
  Roman continuity of, 272
steersmen, 102, 154, 159, 160, 330
Stenton, Sir Frank, 53–4, 55, 61, 62, 68,
  69, 73, 74, 75–7, 79, 81–3, 102n, 199,
  218, 327
Stephenson, Ian, 134–5, 272, 279, 280
stewards, 83
Stigand, Archbishop of Canterbury, 115,
  120, 122, 205
Stoodley, Nick, 12
Stour, River, 158n, 168, 205
strategies and tactics, 17, 93, 134n, 177,
  180n, 190, 236, 250–1, 255, 257, 276,
  278, 279, 281, 287, 296–7, 314, 334
  ruses de guerre, 138n, 231, 232, 320
Strickland, Matthew, 281n
Suetonius: *Lives of the Twelve Caesars*, 273
surrender and submission, 190, 247,
  255–62, 322
Surrey, 203, 224, 252n
Sussex, 203, 292, 296
  maritime customs, 156
Sutton Hoo (Suffolk), 128
  ship from, 142, 143, 144
Sutton Poyntz (Dors.), 174
Swanage (Dors.), 167
Swanton, Michael, 25, 113
Sweden, 35–8, 153
Swein Estrithson, King of Denmark, 153
Swein Forkbeard, King of Denmark, 28,
  118, 149, 153, 244n, 252, 267
Swein Godwineson, Earl, 155
Swithun, Bishop of Winchester, 242

Tacitus: *Germania*, 83, 114n, 131, 134, 267,
  269, 270–1
Taillefer, Norman juggler, 138
tanks, 213
tattoos, 306
Taunton (Som.), hundred of, 160
Tavy, River, 249
taxation, 2, 150 and 150n, 155, 161, 259–60,
  335–6; *see also* geld
Tees, River, 112, 149
tents, 191, 191n, 193, 193, 194, 276, 301–2
Tettenhall (Staffs.), 198

Thames, River, 40, 41, 145, 158n, 195, 167,
  224, 244, 252n, 265, 297, 307, 323–4,
  326
Thanet, Isle of (Kent), 158n, 178n, 242n
thegns, 54, 55–6, 63, 82, 115, 183, 332
  obligations of, 73–87, 96, 171, 220
  distinctions between, 96, 101–6, 107, 122,
    122n, 277
  royal, 109, 122, 265, 326
Theobald, count of Blois-Chartres, 138n
Theodore, Archbishop of Canterbury, 303
Theodred, Bishop of London, 116
Thermopylae, Battle of, 272
Thetford (Norfolk), 59, 109
Thietmar of Merseberg, 113, 247
Thorkell the Tall, Viking leader, 40–1,
  149, 151, 154, 252, 261, 335
Thorney, Islet of (prob. near Iver, Bucks.),
  97, 98, 99, 199
Thucydides: *History of the Peloponnesian
  War*, 266
Thurnham, John, 310n, 313, 314n
Thurstan, will of, 120
Tidenham (Glos.), estate survey, 62
tithings, 100, 101
Toller, Thomas, 221
Toot Hill, Nursling (Hants.), 224
Tostig Godwineson, Earl, 45, 114n, 155,
  156, 160, 163, 202, 206, 258n
Towcester (Northants.), 229
towns
  communities in, 243, 258–62, 263, 330,
    337
  organization, 81, 209, 212n, 235, 243,
    244; *see also* fortifications
  roles and definitions of, 237–62
  sizes of, 245, 245n
Towton (Yorks.), Battle of, 307
trade and traders, 4n, 9, 326, 328, 330, 331,
  332
training, 16n, 266, 272, 280, 285
travel, 195, 202, 206, 305
  dangers of, 281
  speed of, 187n, 191–3, 197
treachery, 247, 248, 320, 322
trees, 227, 276, 277n, 304
Trent, River, 81
Trent, River, Battle of the, 61, 327n
tribute, payments of, 21, 25, 255, 258, 323,
  329, 332

Trinoda Necessitas ('common burdens'), 51, 56, 66, 70–3, 79, 81, 84, 92, 93, 104, 171
Trojan Horse, 248
Troston (Suffolk), 118, 121
Trousdale, Alaric, 300
Tsurushima, Hirokazu, 163–4
tuns, royal, 174, 180, 230
Twyford (Berks.), 199
Tyler, Elizabeth, 145n

Uffington White Horse (Berks., now Oxon.), 309n
Uhtred, Earl of Bamburgh, 30–1, 45
Ulf, will of, 120, 121
Ulfcetel, East Anglian nobleman, 40, 119n, 173n
University College London, 217
Uppland, Sweden, 8

Vegetius: *De Re Militari*, 1, 1n, 190, 226n, 271, 279n
Vierck, H., 131
Vikings, 32, 34, 108–9, 111, 163, 172, 230
  fleets of, 42, 153, 166–70, 286
  identities and allegiances of, 108–9 and 108n, 232, 242, 317, 319–20, 327–8, 329–31
  as mercenaries/stipendiaries, 15, 20, 22n, 110, 153–7, 329–31, 336
  mobility of, 93, 146, 199, 210, 327
  organization of forces, 43, 50, 250, 317
  'otherness', 32, 33, 42, 113, 228
  strategies and tactics of, 179, 187, 189–90, 199, 202, 206, 229–30, 247, 251, 255, 276, 279, 288, 299, 322
Vinogradoff, Paul, 65–8, 88, 134
Virgil: *Aeneid*, 248
Visby (Gotland, Sweden), Battle of, 307
Vita Ædwardi Regis, 114n, 145n
Vita Oswaldi, 249, 250–1, 270

Wærferth, Bishop of Worcester, 214–15
Wace: *Roman de Rou*, 49, 50, 106, 111, 138, 306
Wainwright, F. T., 13, 182n, 216, 232n
Wales and Welsh
  in Anglo-Saxon law, 85
  as auxiliaries in English service, 22, 25
  physical geography, 186

relations with English, 20, 21, 19–30, 114, 136, 163, 182, 200, 202, 284, 321, 332–3
  rulers and political geography 24–5, 216, 230
Walker, Simon, 300
Wallace-Hadrill, J. M., 316, 318n, 334
Wallingford (Berks., now Oxon.), 200n, 244, 307
wapentakes, 66, 100n; *see also* hundreds and hundredal organization
Wareham (Dors.), 216, 229n, 252, 324
Warminster (Wilts.), 180n
Warwick, 57, 77, 161, 147n
Warwickshire, 160–1
watch duty, 244; *see also* beacons
Watchet (Som.), 216, 248, 249
water, drinking, supplies of, 151n, 231–2, 247, 250
Wealdhere, Bishop of London, 319
weather, 186, 191, 204, 222
Wedmore (Som.), 322
wergild, 82, 326, 327, 330–2, 333
Wessex and West Saxons, 10, 182, 229, 232, 234n, 252, 261, 283, 318, 319, 329, 332, 333, 337
  geography, 158n, 167, 168, 180, 181n, 186n, 210, 300
  overlordship, 24–5, 45–6, 63
  organization/equipment of forces, 59–60, 92–8, 114, 134, 139, 147, 157, 198, 209–13, 235
  Viking activities in, 4, 32, 174, 179, 186, 198, 199, 210, 229, 247, 250, 252–5, 255–7, 262, 287–97
Westminster, church of, 102, 160, 287
Weymouth Relief Road (Dors.), excavations on, 307n
Whistley (Berks.), 199
Whitelock, Dorothy, 62, 129n, 171, 264, 265, 331
Wight, Isle of, 147, 158, 204, 206, 218, 222, 254, 289, 291, 293, 303
Wileman, Julie, 114n
William II 'Rufus', King, 60, 335
William of Jumièges: *Gesta Normannorum ducum*, 306
William of Malmesbury: *Gesta Pontificum/Gesta Regum Anglorum*, 20, 101, 189, 234n, 259n, 273, 278n
William of Poitiers: *Gesta Guillelmi*, 138, 234n, 271n, 285, 305, 306

William, Duke of Normandy and King
  of England, 138, 157, 161, 162, 258–60,
  287, 303, 335
  in Battle of Hastings, 29, 52, 235
  submission to, 255–6, 257, 258–60, 335
Williams, Alan, 112–13
Williams, Ann, 21n, 110n, 112n, 130, 146,
  243, 300n, 324
Williams, Gareth, 91, 216, 262
Willibrord, Anglo-Saxon missionary, 9
wills and will-making, 62, 89, 113, 114–28,
  129, 136n, 148, 162
Wilson, David, 39, 234n, 267
Wilton (Wilts.), church of, 86, 187, 248,
  253, 265, 267
Wiltshire, 119, 148, 180, 224, 252, 253, 310
  fyrd of, 106, 179, 266
Wimborne (Dors.), 188, 230, 235n
Winchester (Hants.), 111, 155, 212n, 222,
  226, 243, 253, 256, 260, 292–3, 296
  assemblies in, 182–5, 193, 242
  bishopric of/Old Minster, 119, 160, 183,
    221, 242
  charters from/archives in, 113n, 121n, 173
  defences of, 198, 244
Winterbottom, Michael, 169n
Winton Domesday, 243, 244
Winwæd, Battle of, 303
Wirral, The, 299, 301
witan, 50, 215, 255, 260, 323, 329; *see also*
  assemblies

women, 122n
  as landholders, 114–15
  roles in warfare, 13, 13n, 251
Wood, Michael, 182, 198, 302
Woodbury (Devon) gild statutes, 243
Woodyates (Dors.), 193
Woolf, Alex, 258n, 333n
Worcester, 214–15
  bishop/bishopric of, 89, 102, 159, 183,
    214–15
Worcestershire, 76, 77, 101, 103–5, 107, 148,
  159
Wormald, Patrick, 34, 42, 98, 146, 333n
Wulfhere, Ealdorman of Wiltshire, 182n
Wulfnoth *cild*, Sussex nobleman, 45, 150,
  151, 206n
Wulfric Spot, will of, 118
Wulfsige, will of, 120, 128
Wulfstan, Archbishop, 96, 97n, 98, 187n
Wyke Regis (Dors.), 173

Yatton (Wilts.), 310, 313
York, 6, 31, 256, 257–8, 260, 307n
  Kingdom of, 301; *see also* Northumbria
    and Northumbrians
  archbishops and archbishopric of, 320
Yorke, Barbara, 142, 233–4, 236, 303n
Yorkshire, 57, 58, 299
young warriors, 15–16, 55, 63–4
Yser, River, 203

WARFARE IN HISTORY

The Battle of Hastings: Sources and Interpretations,
edited and introduced by Stephen Morillo

Infantry Warfare in the Early Fourteenth Century:
Discipline, Tactics, and Technology, *Kelly DeVries*

The Art of Warfare in Western Europe during the Middle Ages,
from the Eighth Century to 1340 (second edition), *J. F. Verbruggen*

Knights and Peasants: The Hundred Years War
in the French Countryside, *Nicholas Wright*

Society at War: The Experience of England and France
during the Hundred Years War, *edited by Christopher Allmand*

The Circle of War in the Middle Ages: Essays on Medieval Military and
Naval History, *edited by Donald J. Kagay and L. J. Andrew Villalon*

The Anglo-Scots Wars, 1513–1550: A Military History, *Gervase Phillips*

The Norwegian Invasion of England in 1066, *Kelly DeVries*

The Wars of Edward III: Sources and Interpretations, *edited by Clifford J. Rogers*

The Battle of Agincourt: Sources and Interpretations, *Anne Curry*

War Cruel and Sharp: English Strategy under Edward III, 1327–1360, *Clifford J. Rogers*

The Normans and their Adversaries at War: Essays in Memory of
C. Warren Hollister, *edited by Richard P. Abels and Bernard S. Bachrach*

The Battle of the Golden Spurs (Courtrai, 11 July 1302): A Contribution to the
History of Flanders' War of Liberation, 1297–1305, *J. F. Verbruggen*

War at Sea in the Middle Ages and the Renaissance,
edited by John B. Hattendorf and Richard W. Unger

Swein Forkbeard's Invasions and the Danish
Conquest of England, 991–1017, *Ian Howard*

Religion and the Conduct of War, *c.* 300–1215, *David S. Bachrach*

Warfare in Medieval Brabant, 1356–1406, *Sergio Boffa*

Renaissance Military Memoirs:
War, History and Identity, 1450–1600, *Yuval Noah Harari*

The Place of War in English History, 1066–1214,
J. O. Prestwich, edited by Michael Prestwich

War and the Soldier in the Fourteenth Century, *Adrian R. Bell*

German War Planning, 1891–1914: Sources and Interpretations, *Terence Zuber*

The Battle of Crécy, 1346, *Andrew Ayton and Sir Philip Preston*

The Battle of Yorktown, 1781: A Reassessment, *John D. Grainger*

Special Operations in the Age of Chivalry, 1100–1550, *Yuval Noah Harari*

Women, Crusading and the Holy Land in Historical Narrative, *Natasha R. Hodgson*

The English Aristocracy at War: From the Welsh Wars of
Edward I to the Battle of Bannockburn, *David Simpkin*

The Calais Garrison: War and Military Service
in England, 1436–1558, *David Grummitt*

Renaissance France at War: Armies,
Culture and Society, *c.* 1480–1560, *David Potter*

Bloodied Banners: Martial Display on the
Medieval Battlefield, *Robert W. Jones*

Alfred's Wars: Sources and Interpretations of
Anglo-Saxon Warfare in the Viking Age, *Ryan Lavelle*

The Dutch Army and the Military Revolutions, 1588–1688, *Olaf van Nimwegen*

In the Steps of the Black Prince: The Road to Poitiers, 1355–1356, *Peter Hoskins*

Norman Naval Operations in the Mediterranean, *Charles D. Stanton*

Shipping the Medieval Military: English Maritime Logistics
in the Fourteenth Century, *Craig L. Lambert*

Edward III and the War at Sea:
The English Navy, 1327–1377, *Graham Cushway*

The Soldier Experience in the Fourteenth Century,
edited by Adrian R. Bell and Anne Curry

Warfare in Tenth-Century Germany, *David S. Bachrach*